AA

BED AND BREAKFAST IN EUROPE 1990

Produced by the Publishing Division of The Automobile Association

Gazetteer compiled by the AA's Research Unit, Information Control, and generated by the AA's Establishment Database.

Additional research: Gerry Crawshaw and Sarah Anderson

Maps prepared by the Cartographic Department of the Automobile Association

Cover Design: The Paul Hampson Partnership

Head of Advertisement Sales: Christopher Heard
Tel 0256 20123
Advertisement Production: Karen Weeks
Tel 0256 20123

Typeset, printed and bound in Great Britain by William Clowes Ltd, Beccles and London

A CIP catalogue record for this book is available from the British Library.

Published by The Automobile Association, Fanum House, Basingstoke, Hampshire RG21 2EA

ISBN 0 7495 0029 8

CONTENTS

INTRODUCTION

'Bed and Breakfast' has become synonymous for the independent traveller with good-value accommodation in Britain, and anyone who has travelled on the Continent will know that there are just as many bargains to be had, from the auberges in Alsace to the Zimmer in Zurich, providing you know where to find them, and how to get there.

Whether you go by car, train or plane, tour Europe for a month or visit a city for the weekend, if you are travelling on a budget **'Bed and Breakfast in Europe'** can guide you to hundreds of places which offer good-value accommodation, with some prices starting from £9 (approximately $13) per person per night.

A relaxed holiday can depend on knowing that you will have somewhere clean and comfortable to sleep.

If you are touring by car or train this may mean finding different accommodation every two or three days, and in the high season this can sometimes prove difficult.

It is important, therefore, that from the moment you arrive at your next destination you can find your way around as quickly as possible.

Our 'insider information' will help you to orientate yourself in an unfamiliar city, whether you arrive at the airport, railway station or by car. We give you tips on using the local transport and the addresses of good value places to eat and sleep: AA-classified hotels, pensions, inns and farmhouses in 19 countries throughout Europe. And if you cannot find accommodation there, we tell you where you can find further information, on the spot.

Once your accommodation is booked you can start to get to know your surroundings, and enjoy the sights, and we give you tips on those too.

The AA publishes a European Phrasebook which contains useful everyday vocabulary, plus an illustrated car components guide to help you when dealing with garages in the event of a breakdown. The languages covered are French, German, Spanish, Portuguese, Italian, Dutch, Danish, Swedish and Serbo-Croat. The book is available at all AA Centres and from European Motoring Clubs affiliated to the AIT.

PREPARATIONS

Planning your holiday can be almost as much fun as actually going, and often the more organised a holiday before you go, the more rewarding – and relaxing – it will be.

Planning does not necessarily mean drawing up a rigid itinerary, but rather identifying the essential elements you want in a holiday – particularly important if you intend to tour several countries. Time and/or budget will impose some restrictions on your route but you may also encounter less predictable reasons to change your plans as you travel – the weather, recommendations from fellow travellers met en route, a city you particularly like, or even one you dislike.

Make the most of **maps and guides before** you go as well as while you are travelling. Of the wide range available, a good complement to this book would be any of the more detailed country and city guides in the Baedecker or AA Essentials series.

Other valuable sources of information are the National Tourist Boards, all of whom have offices in London and other capital cities. Their addresses can be found in the respective Country Introductions. Unless you can visit in person it is advisable to write rather than telephone, being as specific as possible and enclosing a stamped, self-addressed envelope.

As well as where to travel, it is also worth considering **when,** for although late summer might be preferable climatically, some cities become unbearably overcrowded and the price of any available accommodation will rise accordingly. Unless your plans are totally flexible it might be advisable to book ahead at least your first few nights' 'bed and breakfast'.

PRACTICALITIES

HEALTH

If you must take certain medicines you

should make sure that you have a supply sufficient to last your trip, as they may be difficult to get abroad.

If you suffer from certain diseases (diabetes for example) you should carry a letter from your doctor giving treatment details, which should preferably be translated into the languages of the countries you intend to visit.

Travellers who must carry drugs, syringes etc. for legitimate health reasons may encounter difficulties with Customs. Again a letter explaining treatment details and a statement for Customs should be translated into the relevant languages, as should details of any dietary requirements which may be useful in hotels and restaurants.

The National Health Service is available in the United Kingdom only and medical expenses incurred overseas cannot generally be reimbursed by the UK Government. There are reciprocal health agreements with most of the countries in this guide, but this cover is not always comprehensive. For example the cost of medical care needed as the result of a road accident is not covered in the Republic of Ireland. Full costs of medical care must be paid in Andorra, Liechtenstein, Monaco, San Marino and Switzerland.

If you are touring between countries, therefore, it is strongly advisable to take out comprehensive, adequate personal insurance cover before leaving the UK, such as that offered under the AA's **5-Star Service,** personal insurance section.

Urgently needed medical treatment in the event of an accident or unforeseen illness can be obtained by most visitors, free of charge or at reduced cost, from the health-care schemes of those countries with whom the UK has health-care arrangements. Details are in the Department of Health (DH) leaflet **SA40 'The Travellers' Guide to Health – Before You Go'.** Free copies are available from local social security offices of the Department of Social Security or from its Health Publications Unit, No 2 Site, Manchester Road, Heywood, Lancs. OL10 2PZ. In some countries you can obtain urgently needed treatment by showing your UK passport or NHS Medical Card, but in most countries a certificate of entitlement (E111) is necessary. A form to obtain this certificate is included in the DH leaflet **SA40.** You should allow at least a month for the form to be processed although in an emergency the E111 can be obtained over the counter of the local DH office (residents of the Republic of Ireland should apply to their Regional Health Board for the E111). The DH guide **SA40** also gives advice about health precautions and international vaccination requirements.

Further information about health care and how to deal with an emergency abroad is given in the DH leaflet **SA41 'The Travellers' Guide to Health – While You're Away'.** A free copy is available by ringing 0800 555 777 or from Health Publications Unit, No 2 Site, Manchester Road, Heywood, Lancs. OL10 2PZ.

Travellers from the United States should check whether their insurance policy covers them for overseas travel, and may want to amend it accordingly. A useful leaflet called **Health Information for International Travel** is published by the Superintendent of Documents, US Government Printing Office, Washington, DC 20402-9325.

Embassies or consulates in Europe should be able to give information about hospitals or practices where you can receive medical assistance from an English-speaking doctor.

For minor treatment, however, a simple First Aid Kit is essential. Depending on the climate of the countries you plan to visit it should include aspirin, plasters, insect repellent, antiseptic cream, and diarrhoea tablets. If you wear spectacles or contact lenses, take a copy of your prescription.

PASSPORTS AND VISAS

You must hold, or be named on, a current passport valid for all the countries through which you intend to travel. The UK, Channel Islands, Republic of Ireland and Isle of Man form a common travel area and citizens of these countries may travel within this area without a passport.

You should carry your passport at all times, as well as a photocopy clearly showing the number, date and place of issue, kept separate from your passport.

There are various types of British passports: a standard passport is valid for ten years and can be issued to British Citizens, British Dependent Territories Citizens, British Nationals (Overseas), British Subjects and British Protected Persons. A related passport may cover the holder and children under 16, although children may be issued with a separate passport valid for five years. Application forms for a standard UK passport may be obtained from a main Post Office or from one of passport offices at Belfast, Douglas (Isle of Man), Glasgow, Liverpool, London, Newport (Gwent), Peterborough, St Helier (Jersey) and St Peter Port (Guernsey). Allow from one to three months for the application to be processed, and include the appropriate fees.

British Visitor's Passports are issued to British Nationals over the age of 8 and are valid for one year only for travel in Western Europe and West Berlin, but not for overland travel through the German Democratic Republic to West Berlin. Full information and application forms may be obtained from Post Offices in Great Britain or Passport Offices in the Channel Islands, Isle of Man and Northern Ireland, but NOT from Passport Offices in Great Britain. Applications at a Post Office must be submitted **in person** where the passport will be issued immediately. Take two passport-type photographs, NHS Card or Birth Certificate and the current fee.

Irish citizens resident in the Dublin Metropolitan area or in Northern Ireland should apply to the Passport Office, Dublin, and if resident elsewhere to the nearest Garda Station. Irish citizens resident in Britain should apply to the Irish Embassy in London.

US passports are valid for travel without a visa for up to three months in Austria, Belgium, West Germany, Greece, Ireland, Italy, Luxembourg, Morocco, Netherlands, Spain and Switzerland, and for 60 days in Portugal. US citizens may travel within Scandinavia (Denmark, Finland, Sweden and Norway) for a total of three months without a visa. Visas are requred, however, for travel in France and should be obtained in advance from French Consulates.

Useful publications include **Your Trip Abroad** available from the Passport Office, Department of State, Washington, DC 20520 and **Foreign Visa Requirements** from the Superintendent of Documents, US Government Printing Office, Washington, DC 20402.

If you lose your passport or it is stolen, notify your nearest consulate or embassy, and the local police, immediately. You will need to be able to establish your identity and citizenship to have it replaced.

INTERNATIONAL STUDENT AND YOUTH DISCOUNTS

Students and travellers under 26 years of age are entitled to discounts on museum admission and local transport etc. on presentation of an identification card which you should purchase before travelling. To obtain an **International Student Identification Card (ISIC)** you will need a certificate from your college or school as proof of your student status, a passport-sized photograph and proof of your date of birth and nationality; cards can be issued from your local Student Travel Office. Cards issued in the US provide insurance against illness or accident for travel outside the US.

Similar benefits can be obtained by travellers under 26 who are not students if they hold a Federation of International Youth Travel Organisations Card which can be bought from any Student Travel Office.

INTERNATIONAL YOUTH HOSTEL FEDERATION

Most Youth Hostels require you to be a member of the Federation in order to stay there and while membership can sometimes be purchased at the hostel, if you intend to stay in several, it is easier to buy a membership card before you start your holiday. Contact the British Youth Hostel Association (YHA) at Trevelyan House, 8 St Stephen's Hill, St Albans, Herts, AL1 2DY (tel (0727) 55215), and American Youth Hostels, Inc. (AYH) at PO Box 37613,

Washington, DC 20013-7613 (tel (202) 783-6161).

CURRENCY, CHEQUES AND CREDIT CARDS

However you carry your 'money' keep it safe, preferably in a money-belt, or pouch inside your shirt. It is advisable to use a combination of cash, traveller's cheque, Eurocheque and credit card rather than relying on just one and do not carry them in the same place. Travellers cheques should if possible come from a major bank or agency so that they are easily recognisable abroad and are more flexible in smaller denominations. If you know which countries you will be visiting before setting off it is a good idea to have a small amount of currency for each – if not, remember that most major railway stations and airports have a bureau de change, though exchange rates might be less favourable than banks. The major credit/charge cards are accepted throughout Europe, and their use is subject to the conditions of the issuing company who will provide further information. Establishments will display symbols of the cards they accept. Eurocheques are useful for cashing personal cheques up to £75 with no commission payable, although you do have to pay your bank an annual fixed fee for the service.

Don't forget . . . . . .

- Carry shampoo and travel detergent in screw-top plastic bottles and a small washing kit with towel, soap etc. for night-time train or ferry travel.
- A knife for cutting bread and spreading soft cheese or pâté is essential for picnic lunches.

GETTING THERE

BY TRAIN

Train travel is especially popular with under 26s, who qualify for the Inter Rail and Eurail Youth passes, allowing unlimited, free train travel for a month (or two months with Eurail) throughout Europe. Further details, costs and conditions can be obtained from all British Rail Stations for Inter Rail, or travel agents in the United States for Eurail. Inter Rail is only available to residents of 6 months or more of a participating European country, while Eurail is available to anyone outside Europe or North Africa.

These are ideal for those who wish to do a 'grand tour of Europe' or even travel extensively within one group of countries, but there are alternatives which may suit your particular holiday better. A BIJ ticket (Billet International de Jeunesse) – also for those under 26 – sold by Eurotrain (kiosk at Victoria Railway Station or details through major travel agents) offers fixed routes to various destinations, along which you may stop as many times as you wish.

If you only wish to tour within one country however you should consider a pass exclusively for that country. The advantage of these are flexibility of routes, but remember that added to the cost of the pass will be travel to that country. These are available to independent travellers of any age.

Some countries also offer youth passes such as the French Carte Jeune and Carré Jeune. Further details are available from British Rail Travel Centres or individual Tourist Offices.

One of the greatest advantages of international train travel for those on a grand tour on a budget is that the train can provide overnight accommodation, and delivers you to your next destination, if not bright, at least early. If you want to guarantee a good night's sleep then reserve a couchette – six to a compartment and no sex segregation – but many trains have 'pull-down seats' so that the whole compartment becomes a large 'bed'.

If you are travelling with friends, board the train as early as possible, find a compartment, close the door and draw the curtains and settle down to sleep. Make sure that your carriage actually goes to your final destination, as many trains split and regroup en-route, and that the compartment has not been reserved by anyone else for your part of the journey.

If you will be crossing an international frontier the guard should collect your ticket and passport before departure to prevent waking you in the night.

Always keep valuables with you when you sleep, and a small padlock can be useful to secure your luggage.

Eating on trains can be expensive, so bring food and drink – especially bottled mineral water – with you.

To plan your route most effectively it is essential to carry a comprehensive International Timetable, such as the Thomas Cook Continental Timetable (from Thomas Cook travel agents) or the Eurail timetable. As they are frequently updated, check that you have a current one, although older issues can be useful for planning routes before you leave.

BY BUS

Long-distance bus and coach journeys can be particularly economical if you plan to travel from one major city to another.

Hoverspeed operates City Sprint services from London to Paris, Brussels and Amsterdam, while National Express operate to 250 places in Ireland and on the Continent. Details from any National Express agent or by telephone (021-456 1122).

BY CAR

Travelling by car is perhaps the most independent way to see Europe. Whether you take your own car across the Channel or hire one on the other side, this ABC of Motoring covers many of the points to remember.

The **AA European Phrasebook** includes a complete illustrated car components guide, with the names of parts translated into nine European languages, should you need a garage to repair or replace anything.

EUROPEAN ABC OF MOTORING

Motoring laws in Europe are just as wide and complicated as those in the UK and USA, but they should cause little difficulty to a good motorist. You should, however, take more care and extend greater courtesy than you would normally do at home, and bear in mind the essentials of good motoring – avoiding any behaviour likely to obstruct traffic, to endanger persons or cause damage to property. It is also important to remember that tourists are subject to the laws of the country in which they are travelling.

Road signs are mainly international and should be familiar to British motorists but in every country there are a few exceptions. You should particularly watch for signs indicating crossings and speed limits. Probably the most unusual aspect of motoring abroad to the British motorist is the universal and firm rule of giving priority to traffic coming from the right (except in the Republic of Ireland) and unless this rule is varied by signs it must be strictly observed.

As well as a **current passport** (except for Republic of Ireland, see *Passports* page 5) a tourist temporarily importing a motor vehicle should always carry a valid full national driving licence, even when an international Driving Permit (IDP) is held, the registration document of the car and evidence of insurance. The proper international distinguishing sign should be affixed to the rear of the vehicle. The appropriate papers must be carried at all times and secured against loss. The practice of spot checks on foreign cars is widespread and, to avoid inconvenience or a police fine, ensure that your papers are in order and that the international distinguishing sign is of the approved standard design.

Make sure that you have clear all-round vision. See that your seat belts are securely mounted and not damaged, and remember that in most European countries their use is compulsory. If you are carrying skis, remember that their tips should point to the rear. You must be sure that your vehicle complies with the regulations concerning dimensions for all the countries you intend to pass through. This is particularly necessary if you are towing a trailer of any sort. If you are planning to tow a caravan, you will find advice and information in the AA guide **Camping and Caravanning in Europe.**

We know as well as anyone how expensive mechanical repairs and replacement parts can be abroad. While not all breakdowns are avoidable, a vast number of those we deal with occur because the vehicle has not been prepared properly before the start of the journey. A holiday abroad involves many miles of hard driving over roads completely new to you, perhaps without the facilities you have come to take for granted in this country. Therefore you should give serious thought to the business of preparing your vehicle for a holiday abroad.

We recommend that your car undergoes a major service by a franchised dealer shortly before your holiday or tour abroad. In addition, it is advisable to carry out your own general check for any audible or visible defects. It is not practicable to provide a complete list of points to look for but the ABC contains information under the following headings:

> Automatic gearboxes; Automatic transmission fluid; Brakes; Cold weather touring; Direction indicators; Electrical; Engine and mechanical; Lights; Spares; Tyres; Warm climate touring.

These, used in conjunction with the manufacturer's handbook, should ensure that no obvious faults are missed. However, as a precaution, obtain a list of service agencies for your make of vehicle from your dealer and carry this with you on your journey. If it is necessary to take your vehicle to a garage for repairs, always ask for an estimate before authorising the repair as some European garages make extremely high charges for repairing tourists' cars. **It cannot be emphasised too strongly that disputes with garages on the Continent must be settled on the spot.** It has been the AA's experience that subsequent negotiations can seldom be brought to a satisfactory conclusion.

A

Accidents International regulations are similar to those in the UK; the following recommendations are usually advisable.

If you are involved in an accident you **must** stop. A warning triangle should be placed on the road at a suitable distance to warn following traffic of the obstruction. The use of hazard warning lights in no way affects the regulations governing the use of warning triangles. See also *Breakdowns* below. Medical assistance should be obtained for persons injured in the accident. If the accident necessitates calling the police, leave the vehicle in the position in which it comes to rest; should it seriously obstruct other traffic, mark the position of the vehicle on the road and if possible get the details confirmed by independent witnesses before moving it.

The accident must be reported to the police if it is required by law, if the accident has caused death or bodily injury, or if an unoccupied vehicle or property has been damaged and there is no one present to represent the interests of the party suffering damage. Notify your insurance company by letter if possible, within 24 hours of the accident: see the conditions of your policy. If a third party is injured, the insurance company or bureau, whose address is given on the back of your Green Card or frontier insurance certificate, should be notified; the company or bureau will deal with any claim for compensation to the injured party.

Make sure that all essential particulars are noted, especially details concerning third parties, and cooperate with police or other officials taking on-the-spot notes by supplying your name, address or other personal details as required. It is also a good idea to take photographs of the scene, endeavouring to get good shots of other vehicles involved, their registration plates and any background which might help later enquiries. This record may be useful when completing the insurance company's accident form.

If you are not involved in the accident but feel your assistance as a witness or in any other useful capacity would be helpful, then stop and park your car carefully well away from the scene. If all the help necessary is at the scene, then do not stop out of curiosity or park your car at the site.

Automatic gearboxes When towing a caravan, the fluid in an automatic gearbox becomes hotter and thinner, so there is more slip and more heat generated in the gearbox. Many manufacturers recommend the fitting of a gearbox oil cooler. Check with the manufacturer as to what is suitable for your car.

Automatic transmission fluid Automatic transmission fluid is not always readily available, especially in some of the more remote areas of Western Europe and tourists are advised to carry an emergency supply with them.

Boats All boats taken abroad should be registered in the UK, except for very small craft to be used close inshore in France*. You must take the original Certificate of Registry with you, not a photocopy. Registration may be carried out through the Royal Yachting Association at a current fee of £10.00. A Helmsman's Overseas Certificate of Competence is required for Germany (Federal Repubic of), Italy (in some parts), Netherlands (if using a speedboat), Portugal, Spain and Yugoslavia. All applications to the Royal Yachting Association, RYA House, Romsey Road, Eastleigh, Hampshire SO5 4YA tel (0703) 629962. See also **Carnet de passages** page 11, **Identification plate** page 13 and **Insurance** page 13.

* In France, very small craft are exempt from registration and the dividing line falls approximately between a Laser dinghy (which should be registered) and a Topper (which need not). The precise details are available from the RYA.

Brakes Car brakes must always be in peak condition. Check both the level in the brake fluid reservoir and the thickness of the brake lining/pad material. The brake fluid should be completely changed in accordance with the manufacturer's instructions, or at intervals of not more than 18 months or 18,000 miles. However, it is advisable to change the brake fluid, regardless of the foregoing, prior to departing on a Continental holiday particularly if the journey includes travelling through a hilly or mountainous area.

Breakdowns If your car breaks down, endeavour to move it to the side of the road or to a position where it will obstruct the traffic flow as little as possible. Place a warning triangle at the appropriate distance on the road behind the obstruction.

Bear in mind road conditions and, if near or on a bend, the triangle should be placed where it is clearly visible to following traffic. If the car is fitted with hazard warning lights these may be switched on but they will only warn on the straight and will have no effect at bends or rises in the road. If the fault is electrical, the lights may not operate and it is for these reasons that they cannot take the place of a triangle. Having first taken these precautions, seek assistance if you cannot deal with the fault yourself.

Motorists are advised to take out **AA 5-Star Service,** the overseas motoring emergency service, which includes breakdown and accident benefits, and personal travel insurance. It offers total security and peace of mind to all motorists travelling in Europe. Cover may be purchased by any motorist although a small additional premium must be paid by non-members of the AA. Details and brochures may be obtained from AA Centres, or by telephoning 021-550 7648.

Note Members who have not purchased AA 5-Star Service prior to departure and who subsequently require assistance may request spare parts or vehicle recovery, but in this case the AA will require a deposit to cover estimated costs and a service fee prior to providing the service. All expenses must be reimbursed to the AA in addition to the service fee.

Caravan and luggage trailers Take a list of contents, especially if any valuable or unusual equipment is being carried, as this may be required at a frontier. A towed vehicle should be readily identifiable by a plate in an accessible position showing the name of the maker of the vehicle and production or serial number.

Carnet de passages en douane The *Carnet de passages en douane*, for which a charge is made, is a valuable document issued by the AA to its members or as part of the AA 5-Star Service – further information may be obtained from most AA Centres. Generally it is not required for motor vehicles temporarily imported by *bona fide* visitors into Western European countries. However, it is necessary in some countries for a boat or trailer, enabling them to be temporarily imported without the need to deposit customs duty with the local authorities. Of the countries dealt with in this Guide a *Carnet* is required:

in **Belgium** – for all trailers not accompanied by the towing vehicle;

in **Luxembourg** – for all boats unless entering and leaving by water.

If you are issued with a *Carnet de passages en douane* you must ensure that it is returned to the AA correctly discharged in order to avoid inconvenience and expense, possibly including payment of customs charges, at a later date. See also under *Boats* page 10 and *Identification plate* page 13.

Claims against third parties The law and levels of damages in foreign countries are generally different from our own. It is important to remember this when considering making a claim against another motorist arising out of an accident abroad. Certain types of claims invariably present difficulties, the most common probably being that relating to the recovery of car hiring charges. Rarely are they recoverable in full and in some countries they may be drastically reduced or not recoverable at all. General damages for pain and suffering are not recoverable in certain countries, but even in those countries where they are recoverable, the levels of damages are, in most cases, lower than our own.

The negotiation of claims against foreign insurers is extremely protracted and translation of all documents slows down the process. A delay of three months between sending a letter and receiving a reply is not uncommon.

If you have taken out the AA's 5-Star Service cover, this includes a discretionary service in respect of certain matters arising abroad requiring legal assistance including the pursuit of uninsured loss claims against third parties arising out of a road accident. In this event, members should seek guidance and/or assistance from the AA.

Cold-weather touring If you are planning a winter tour, make sure that you fit a high-temperature (winter) thermostat and make sure that the strength of your anti-freeze mixture is correct for the low temperatures likely to be encountered. If you are likely to be passing through snow-bound regions, it is important to remember that for many resorts and passes the authorities insist on wheel chains, or spiked or studded tyres. However, as wheel chains and spiked or studded tyres can damage the road surface if it is free of snow or ice, there are definite periods when these may be used and in certain countries the use of spiked or studded tyres is illegal. If wheel chains or spiked or studded tyres are compulsory, this is usually signposted.

Note The above comments do not apply where extreme winter conditions prevail. It is doubtful whether the cost of preparing a car, normally used in the UK, would be justified for a short period. However, the **AA's Technical Services Department** will be pleased to advise on specific enquiries.

Crash or safety helmets All countries in this guide (except Belgium where they are strongly recommended) require visiting motorcycles and their passengers to wear crash, or safety helmets.

Dimension and weight restrictions For an ordinary private car, a height limit of 4 metres and a width limit of 2.50 metres is generally imposed. Apart from a laden weight limit imposed on commercial vehicles, every vehicle, private or commercial, has an individual weight limit. For the manner in which private cars are affected, see *Overloading* page 16. If your route involve using one of the major road tunnels through a mountainous area, there may be additional restrictions. If you have any doubts, consult the AA.

Direction indicators All direction indicators should be working at between 60–120 flashes per minute. Most standard car-flasher units will be overloaded by the extra lamps of a caravan or trailer and a special heavy duty unit or a relay device should be fitted.

Drinking and driving There is only one safe rule – **if you drink, don't drive.** The laws are strict and penalties severe.

Driving licence You should carry your national driving licence with you when motoring abroad. If an International Driving Permit (IDP) is necessary (*see page* 14) it is strongly recommended that you still carry your national driving licence. In most of the countries covered by this guide you can drive a temporarily imported car without formality for up to three months with a valid full licence (not provisional) issued in the United Kingdom or Republic of Ireland, but you must be 18 or over, unless driving in Denmark, German Federal Republic (West Germany), Luxembourg, Norway and Portugal* where you can drive at 17. In Greece a UK licence holder can drive at 17, but Republic of Ireland licence holders should obtain an IDP. In Italy** your licence must be accompanied by a translation which can be supplied by the AA. If you should wish to drive a hired or borrowed car in the country you are visiting, make local enquiries. The minimum age at which visitors may ride motorcycles varies according to the cylinder capacity of the machine. Therefore, persons under 21 intending to travel by motorcycle are recommended to make appropriate enquiries either through the AA or the relevant national tourist office. If your licence is due to expire before your anticipated return, it should be renewed in good time prior to your departure. The Driver and Vehicle Licensing Centre (in Northern Ireland, the Licensing Authority) will accept an application two months before the expiry of your old licence. In the Republic of Ireland licensing authorities will accept an application one month before the expiry of your old licence.

* Visiting UK or Republic of Ireland motorists may drive at 17 but, as the official minimum age for Portuguese driving licence holders is 18, local officials in some areas may not be conversant with the regulations.

** If you hold a pink EC type UK or Republic of Ireland driving licence this translation is not required. The respective licensing authorities cannot exchange a licence purely to facilitate continental travel.

'E' Card This card may be displayed on the windscreen of your vehicle to assist the traffic flow across certain frontiers within the European Community. Full conditions of use are given on the card which may be obtained from AA Centres.

Electrical (vehicle) Check that all electrical connections are sound and that the wiring is in good condition. Should any problems arise with the charging system, it is essential to obtain the services of a qualified auto-electrician.

Engine and mechanical Consult your vehicle handbook for servicing intervals. Unless the engine oil has been changed recently, drain and refill with fresh oil and fit a new filter. Deal with any significant leaks by tightening up loose nuts and bolts and renewing faulty joints and seals.

Brands and grades of *engine oil* familiar to the British motorist are usually available in Western Europe but may be difficult to find in remote country areas. When available they will be much more expensive than in the UK and generally packed in 1 litre cans. Motorists can usually assess the normal consumption of their car and are strongly advised to carry with them what oil they are likely to require for their trip.

If you suspect that there is anything wrong with the engine, however insignificant it may seem, it should be dealt with straight away. Even if everything seems in order, don't neglect such commonsense precautions as checking valve clearances, sparking plugs and contact breaker points where fitted, and making sure that the distributor cap is sound. The fan belt should be checked for fraying and slackness. If any of the items mentioned previously are showing signs of wear, you should replace them.

Any obvious mechanical defects should be attended to at once. Look particularly for play in steering connections and wheel bearings and, where applicable, ensure that they are adequately greased. A car that has covered a high mileage will have absorbed a certain amount of dirt into the fuel system and, as breakdowns are often caused by dirt, it is essential that all filters (fuel and air) should be cleaned or renewed. However, owners should think twice about towing a caravan with a car that has already given appreciable service. Hard driving on motorways and in mountainous country puts an extra strain on ageing parts, and repairs to items such as a burnt-out clutch can be very expensive.

The cooling system should be checked for leaks and the correct proportion of anti-freeze and any perished hoses or suspect parts replaced.

Fire extinguisher It is a wise precaution (compulsory in Greece) to equip your vehicle with a fire extinguisher when motoring abroad. A fire extinguisher may be purchased from the AA.

First-aid kit It is a wise precaution (compulsory in Austria, Greece and Yugoslavia) to equip your vehicle with a first-aid kit when motoring abroad. A first-aid kit may be purchased from the AA.

Green Cards (See *Insurance* next column)

Identification plate If a boat, caravan or trailer is taken abroad it must have a unique chassis number for identification purposes. If your boat, caravan or trailer does not have a number, an *identification plate* may be purchased from the AA. Boats registered on the Small Ships Register (see **Boats** page 10) are issued with a unique number which must be permanently displayed.

Insurance Motor insurance is compulsory by law in all the countries covered in this guide and you are strongly advised to ensure that you are adequately covered for all countries in which you will travel. Temporary policies may be obtained at all frontiers except the Repubic of Ireland, but this is a most expensive way of effecting cover. It is best to seek the advice of your insurer regarding the extent of cover and full terms of your existing policy. Some insurers may not be willing to offer cover in the countries that you intend to visit and it may be necessary to seek a new, special policy for the trip from another insurer. Should you have any difficulty, AA Insurance Services will be pleased to help you.

Note Extra insurance, in the form of a *Bail Bond*, is strongly recommended when visiting Spain. Third party insurance is compulsory for craft used on Swiss lakes; it is also compulsory in Italian waters for craft with engines of more than 3hp, and an Italian translation of the insurance certificate should be carried. Third party insurance is recommended elsewhere for all boats used abroad (see also *Boats* page 10). It is compulsory for trailers temporarily imported into Austria.

An international motor insurance certificate or Green Card is recognised in most countries as evidence that you are covered to the minimum extent demanded by law. Compulsory in Andorra and Yugoslavia, the AA strongly advises its use elsewhere. It will be issued by your own insurer upon payment of the additional premium for extension of your UK policy cover to apply in those countries you intend visiting. It will name all the countries for which it is valid and should be specially endorsed for a caravan or trailer if one is to be towed. The document will not be accepted until you have signed it. Green Cards are internationally recognised by police and other authorities and may save a great deal of inconvenience in the event of an accident.

In accordance with a European Community Directive, the production and inspection of Green Cards at the frontiers of European Community countries is no longer a legal requirement and the principle has been accepted by other European countries who are not members of the EEC. However, the fact that Green Cards will not be inspected does not remove the necessity of having insurance cover as required by law in the countries concerned.

Finally, make sure you are covered against damage in transit (*eg* on ferry or motorail). Most comprehensive motor insurance policies provide adequate cover for transit between ports in the UK, but need to be extended to give this cover if travelling outside the UK. You are advised to check this aspect with your insurer before setting off on your journey.

International Distinguishing Sign An International Distinguishing Sign (nationality plate) of the approved pattern (oval with black letters on a white background) and size (GB at least 6.9in by 4.5in) must be displayed on a vertical or near vertical surface at the rear of your vehicle (and caravan or trailer if you are towing one). These distinguishing signs signify the country of registration of the vehicle. On the Continent checks are made to ensure that a vehicle's nationality plate is in order. Fines are imposed for failing to display a nationality plate, or for not displaying the correct nationality plate. See *Police fines* page 18.

International Driving Permit An International Driving Permit (IDP) is an internationally recognised document which enables the holder to drive for a limited period in countries where their national licence is not recognised. The permit is compulsory in **Austria** and **Greece** for the holder of a red three-year Republic of Ireland driving licence: recommended if pink EC type Republic of Ireland licence is held. It is compulsory in **Spain** for the holder of a green UK or red three-year Republic of Ireland driving licence, unless the licence is accompanied by an official Spanish translation stamped by a Spanish Consulate. The IDP is not compulsory in Spain for the holder of a pink EC type UK or Republic of Ireland driving licence but, as local difficulties may arise over its acceptance, an IDP is recommended. The respective licensing authorities cannot however exchange a licence purely to facilitate Continental travel.

The permit, for which a statutory charge is made, is issued by the AA to an applicant who holds a valid British driving licence and who is over 18 years old. It has a validity of 12 months, cannot be renewed and application forms are available from any AA Centre. Residents of the Republic of Ireland, Channel Islands and the Isle of Man should apply to their local AA Centre for the relevant application form. The permit cannot be issued to the holder of a foreign licence, who must apply to the appropriate authority in the country where the driving licence was issued.

Level crossings Practically all level crossings are indicated by international signs. Most guarded ones are of the lifting barrier type, sometimes with bells or flashing lights to give warning of an approaching train.

Lights For driving abroad (except in the Republic of Ireland) headlights should be altered so that the dipped beam does not dazzle oncoming drivers. The alteration can be made by fitting headlamp converters (PVC mask sheets) or beam deflectors (clip-on lenses) which may be purchased from your nearest AA Centre.

It is important to remember to remove the headlamp converters or beam deflectors as soon as you return to the UK.

In France a regulation requires all locally

registered vehicles to be equipped with headlights which show a yellow beam and, in the interests of safety and courtesy, visiting motorists are advised to comply. If you are able to use beam deflectors to alter your headlights for driving abroad, you can purchase deflectors with yellow lens. However, with headlamp converters it is necessary to coat the outer surface of the headlamp glass with yellow plastic paint which is removable with a solvent. Yellow headlamp paint can be purchased from the AA.

Dipped headlights should also be used in conditions of fog, snowfall, heavy rain and when passing through a tunnel irrespective of its length and lighting. In some countries police will wait at the end of a tunnel checking this requirement. Headlight flashing is used only as a warning of approach or a passing signal at night. In other circumstances it is accepted as a sign of irritation and should be used with caution lest it be misunderstood.

In Norway and Sweden the use of dipped headlights during the day is compulsory for all motor vehicles including motorcycles. Generally motorcyclists visiting Europe should always use dipped headlights during the day as it is a compulsory requirement or recommendation in many countries.

It is a wise precaution (compulsory in Spain and Yugoslavia and recommended in France, Italy and Norway) to equip your vehicle with a set of replacement bulbs when motoring abroad. An AA Emergency Auto Bulb Kit suitable for most makes of car can be purchased from your nearest AA Centre. Alternatively a Spares Kit or Motoring Emergency Pack, both of which contain spare bulbs, may be hired from the AA.

Note Remember to have the lights set to compensate for the load being carried.

Liquified Petroleum Gas/LPG The availability of this gas in Europe makes a carefully-planned tour with a converted vehicle limited but feasible. The gas is retailed by several companies in Europe who will supply information as to where their product may be purchased. A motorist regularly purchasing the fuel in the UK could possibly obtain lists of European addresses from his retailer.

When booking a ferry crossing it is advisable to point out to the booking agent/ferry company that the vehicle runs on a dual-fuel system.

M

Minibus A minibus constructed and equipped to carry 10 or more persons (including the driver*) and used outside the UK is subject to the regulations governing international bus and coach journeys. This will generally mean that the vehicle must be fitted with a tachograph and documentation in the form of a Driver's Certificate, Model Control Document and waybill obtained. For vehicles registered in Great Britain (England, Scotland and Wales) contact the authorities as follows:

i for Driver's Certificate and details of approved tachograph installers, apply to the local Traffic Area Office of the Department of Transport;

ii for Model Control Document and waybill, apply to the Bus and Coach Council, Sardinia House, 52 Lincoln's Inn Fields, London WC2A 3LZ tel 01(071 from 6 May)-831 7546.

For vehicles registered in Northern Ireland contact the Department of the Environment for Northern Ireland, Road Transport Department, Upper Galwally, Belfast BT8 4FY tel (0232) 649044.

For vehicles registered in the Republic of Ireland contact the Department of Labour, Mespil Road, Dublin 4 for details about tachographs and the Government Publications Sales Office, Molesworth Street, Dublin 2 for information about documentation.

When contacting any of the above authorities, do so well in advance of your departure.

* A minibus driver must be at least 21 years of age and hold a full driving licence valid for group 'A' or, if automatic transmission, group 'B'.

Mirrors When driving abroad on the right it is essential, as when driving on the left in the UK and Repubic of Ireland, to have clear all-round vision. Ideally external rear view mirrors should be fitted to both sides of your vehicle, but certainly on the left to allow for driving on the right.

Motorway tax The Swiss authorities levy an annual tax of 30 Swiss Francs for use of their motorway network. The tax is levied on all vehicles using Swiss motorways (including motorcycles, trailers and caravans) not exceeding 3.5 tonnes (unladen) registered in Switzerland or abroad. An adhesive disc, known locally as a *vignette*, must be displayed as evidence of payment. Motorists may purchase the discs from AA Centres or at the Swiss frontier.

Vehicles over 3.5 tonnes (unladen) are taxed on all roads in Switzerland; a licence for one day, 10 days, one month and one year periods can be obtained. There are no discs and the tax must be paid at the Swiss frontier.

O

Octane ratings (See Petrol page 17)

Oil (See Engine and mechanical page 12)

Overloading This can create safety risks, and in most countries committing such an offence can involve on-the-spot fines (see *Police fines* page 18). It would also be a great inconvenience if your car were stopped because of overloading – you would not be allowed to proceed until the load had been reduced.

The maximum loaded weight, and its distribution between front and rear axles, is decided by the vehicle manufacturer and if your owner's handbook does not give these facts, you should seek the direct advice of the manufacturer. There is a public weighbridge in all districts and when the car is fully loaded (not forgetting the passengers, of course) use this to check that the vehicle is within the limits.

When loading a vehicle, care should be taken that lights, reflectors, or number plates are not masked and that the driver's view is in no way impaired. All luggage loaded on a roof rack must be tightly secured and should not upset the stability of the vehicle. Any projections beyond the front, rear, or sides of a vehicle must be clearly marked where their projection might not be noticed by other drivers.

Overtaking When overtaking on roads with two lanes or more in each direction, always signal your intention in good time. After the manoeuvre, signal and return to the inside lane. Do **not** remain in any other lane. Failure to comply with this regulation, particularly in France, will incur an on-the-spot fine (see *Police fines* page 18).

Always overtake on the left (on the right in the Republic of Ireland) and use your horn as a warning to the driver of the vehicle being overtaken (except in areas where the use of the horn is prohibited). Do not overtake whilst being overtaken or when a vehicle behind is preparing to overtake. Do not overtake at level crossings, at intersections, the crest of a hill or at pedestrian crossings. When being overtaken keep well to the right (left in the Republic of Ireland) and reduce speed if necessary – never increase speed.

Parking Parking is a problem everywhere in Europe and the police are extremely strict with offenders. Heavy fines are inflicted as well as the towing away of unaccompanied offending cars. This can cause inconvenience and heavy charges are imposed for the recovery of impounded vehicles. In Athens, number plates may be removed and confiscated from illegaly parked vehicles. You should acquaint yourself with local parking regulations and endeavour to understand all relative signs. As a rule, always park on the right-hand side of the road (left-hand side in the Republic of Ireland) or at an authorised place. As far as possible, park off the main carriageway but not on cycle tracks or tram tracks.

Passengers For passenger-carrying vehicles constructed and equipped to carry 10 or more persons (including the driver) there are special regulations (see *Minibus* page 15). As a general rule it is recommended that children do not travel in a vehicle as front-seat passengers. However, the following countries have restrictions on the ages of front-seat passengers. In Austria*, Germany* (West), Netherlands*, Norway, Portugal, Republic of Ireland*, Switzerland* and Yugoslavia it is illegal for a child under 12 (in Andorra, Greece and Italy** under 10, Sweden*** 7 or under) to travel in a vehicle as a front seat passenger. In Belgium it is illegal for a child under 12 (France and Luxembourg under 10) to travel in a vehicle as a front seat passenger when rear seating is available.

* In Austria, Germany (West), Portugal and Republic of Ireland except for children using special seats or safety belts suitable for children, in Netherlands except for children under 4 sitting in a special baby seat and children over 4 using a safety belt which does not cross the chest of the child.
** In Italy from 26 April 1990 all children between 4 and 10 seated in the front or rear must use a restraint system.
*** In Sweden except for children seated in special child restraints or special seats which enable them to use the normal seat belts.

Petrol In Western Europe, and indeed throughout the world, grades of petrol compare favourably with those in the UK. International brands are usually available on main tourist and international routes, but in the more remote districts named brands may not be so readily available. The minimum amount of petrol which may be purchased is usually five litres (just over one gallon). It is advisable to keep the petrol tank topped up, particularly in remote areas or if wishing to make an early start when garages may be closed, but when doing this use a lockable filler cap as a security measure. Some garages may close between 12.00 and 15.00hrs for lunch. Generally, petrol is readily available and in most of the countries featured in this guide you will find that petrol stations on motorways provide a 24 hour service.

In the UK the motorist uses either leaded or unleaded fuel as recommended by the vehicle manufacturer, and this is related to the minimum octane requirement. For unleaded this usually will be the single grade *Premium* of 95 octane, but for leaded the recommendation may be 90 octane–2 star, 93 octane–3 star or 97 octane–4 star.

Overseas both unleaded and leaded petrol is graded as **Normal** and **Super** and the local definitions are generally recognisable. You should be careful to use the recommended type of fuel, particularly if your car has a catalytic converter, and the octane grade should be the same or higher. If your car is designed only for leaded petrol and you accidentally use unleaded, it will not do any harm, but ensure that the next fill is of the correct type and grade. A *low lead* petrol is being sold in Denmark, Norway and Sweden, but we suggest this is only used if you know that your car is suitable for unleaded petrol. Any queries regarding the suitability of a vehicle for the different fuels should be directed to the vehicle manufacturer or his agent. A leaflet containing further information on *Unleaded Petrol in Europe* is available through AA Centres.

Petrol prices at filling stations on motorways will be higher than elsewhere, whilst at self-service pumps it will be slightly cheaper. Although petrol prices are not quoted in this guide, the current position can be checked with the AA. At the time of going to press, petrol price concessions in the form of petrol coupons are available for Italy and Yugoslavia. A package of Italian petrol coupons and motorway toll vouchers may be purchased from the AA. The package is available to personal callers only and a passport and vehicle registration document must be produced at the time of application; fuller information may be obtained from any AA Centre. Yugoslav petrol coupons can only be purchased at the frontier with a freely convertible currency.

The petrol contained in a vehicle tank may be imported duty-free; the use of a lockable filler cap to secure the tank is always a wise precaution. In some countries an additional quantity may be imported duty-free in cans whilst others forbid the carrying of petrol in cans in a vehicle (Greece and Italy) or impose duty (Sweden and Yugoslavia). If you intend carrying a reserve supply of petrol in a can remember that, on sea and air ferries and European car-sleeper trains, operators insist that spare cans must be empty.

Note A roof rack laden with luggage increases petrol consumption; this should be taken into consideration by the motorist when calculating mileage per gallon.

Police Fines Some countries impose on-the-spot fines for minor traffic offences which vary in amount according to the offence committed and the country concerned. Other countries (*eg* France) impose an immediate deposit and subsequently levy a fine which may be the same as or greater or lesser than this sum. Fines are either paid in cash to the police or at a local post office against a ticket issued by the police. They must usually be paid in the currency of the country concerned, and can vary in amount from £3–£690 (approximate amounts). The reason for the fines is to penalise and at the same time keep minor motoring offences out of the courts. Disputing the fine usually leads to a court appearance and delays and additional expense.

If the fine is not paid then legal proceedings will usually follow. Some countries immobilise a vehicle until the fine is paid and may sell it to pay the penalty imposed.

Once paid, a fine cannot be recovered, but a receipt should always be obtained as proof of payment. Should AA members require assistance in any motoring matter involving local police, they should apply to the legal department of the relevant national motoring organisation.

Pollution Tourists should be aware that pollution of the sea water at European coastal resorts, including the Mediterranean, may still represent a severe health hazard, although the general situation has improved in recent years. A number of countries publish detailed information on the quality of their bathing beaches, including maps, which are obtainable from national authorities. Furthermore, in many, though not all, popular resorts where the water quality may present dangers, signs (generally small) are erected which forbid bathing. These signs would read as follows:

French	
No bathing	Bathing prohibited
Défense de se baigner	*Il est défendu de se baigner*
Italian	
No bathing	Bathing Prohibited
Vietato bagnàrsi	*È vietato bagnàrsi*
Spanish	
No bathing	Bathing prohibited
Prohibido bañarse	*Se prohibe bañarse*

Priority including roundabouts The general rule is to give way to traffic entering a junction from the right (except in the Republic of Ireland), but this is sometimes varied at roundabouts (see below). This is one aspect of European driving which may cause British drivers the most confusion because their whole training and experience makes it unnatural. Road signs indicate priority or loss of priority and tourists are well advised to make sure that they understand such signs.

Great care should be taken at intersections and tourists should never rely on receiving the right of way, particularly in small towns and villages where local traffic, often slow moving, such as farm tractors, etc, will assume right of way regardless of oncoming traffic. Always give way to public service and military vehicles. Blind or disabled people, funerals and marching columns must always be allowed right of way. Vehicles such as buses and coaches carrying large numbers of passengers will expect and should be allowed priority.

Generally priority at roundabouts is given to vehicles entering the roundabout unless signposted to the contrary. This is a complete reversal of the United Kingdom and Republic of Ireland rule and particular care should be exercised when manoeuvring while circulating in an anti-clockwise direction on a roundabout. It is advisable to keep to the outside lane on a roundabout, if possible, to make your exit easier. However, be watchful in France for changed priority when negotiating roundabouts. At roundabouts with signs bearing the words *"Vous n'avez pas la priorité"* or *"Cédez le passage"*, traffic on the roundabout has priority; where no such sign exists, traffic entering the roundabout still has priority.

Registration document You must carry the original vehicle registration document with you. If for any reason your registration document has to be sent to the licensing authorities you should bear in mind that, as processing can take some time, the document may not be available in time for your departure. Under these circumstances a *certificate of registration (V379)* will normally be issued to cover the vehicle for international circulation purposes. It can be obtained free of charge from your nearest Vehicle Registration Office upon production of proof of identity (*eg* driving licence) and proof of ownership (*eg* bill of sale).

If you plan to use a borrowed, hired or leased vehicle you should be aware that:

i for a borrowed vehicle the registration document must be accompanied by a letter of authority to use the vehicle from the registered keeper (for Yugoslavia this letter must be countersigned by the AA, for Portugal a special certificate is required and this is available FREE from the AA);

ii for a UK registered hired or leased vehicle the registration document will normally be retained by the hiring company. Under these circumstances a *Hired/Leased Vehicle Certificate (VE103A)* issued by the AA should be used in its place (for Portugal the certificate should be accompanied by an officially authenticated photocopy of the registration document).

Road signs Most road signs throughout Europe are internationally agreed and the majority will be familiar to the British motorist. Watch for road markings – do not cross a solid white or yellow line marked on the road centre.

Rule of the road In all countries in this Guide except Ireland, drive on the right and overtake on the left; in Ireland drive on the left and overtake on the right.

Seat belts All countries in this Guide require visitors to wear seat belts. If your car is fitted with belts, then in the interest of safety, wear them; otherwise you may run the risk of a police fine.

Spares (See also *Lights* page 14) The problem of what spares to carry is a difficult one; it depends on the vehicle and how long you are likely to be away. However, you should consider hiring an AA Spares Kit for your car and full information about this service is available from any AA Centre. AA Emergency Windscreens are also available for hire. In addition to the items contained in the spares kit, the following would also prove useful:

a pair of windscreen wiper blades
a length of electrical cable
an inner tube of the correct type
a roll of insulating or adhesive tape
a torch
a fire extinguisher
a tow rope

Remember that when ordering spare parts for dispatch abroad you must be able to identify them as clearly as possible and by the manufacturer's part numbers if known. When ordering spares, always quote the engine and chassis numbers of your car.

Speed limits It is important to observe speed limits at all times. Offenders may be fined and driving licences confiscated on the spot, thus causing great inconvenience and possible expense. Speed limits are included in the introduction which precedes the gazetteer for each country. These may be varied by road signs and, where these are displayed, the lower limit should be accepted. At certain times limits may also be temporarily varied and information will be available at the frontier. It can be an offence to travel without good reason at so slow a speed as to obstruct traffic flow.

Temporary importation A motor vehicle, caravan, boat, or any other type of trailer is subject to strict control on entering a country and attracts Customs Duty and a variety of taxes, but much depends upon the circumstances and the period of the import and also upon the status of the importer. People entering a country in which they have no residence, with a private vehicle for holiday or recreational purposes and intending to export the vehicle within short periods, enjoy special privileges and the normal formalities are reduced to an absolute minimum in the interests of tourism. Importers of any type of commercial vehicle or one to be used to support commercial enterprises do not have the same tolerance.

People entering a country with a motor vehicle for a period of generally more than six months (see also *Visas* page 21) or to take up residence, employment, or with the intention of disposing of the vehicle should seek advice concerning their position well in advance of their departure. Any AA Centre will be pleased to help.

A temporarily imported vehicle should not:

i be left in the country after the importer has left;
ii be put at the disposal of a resident of the country;
iii be retained in the country longer than the permitted period;
iv be lent, sold, hired, given away, exchanged or otherwise disposed of.

A *bona fide* tourist will generally be allowed to import anything considered in use or in keeping with his or her status, but such articles, where not consumable, must be exported when the importer leaves the country. In the case of some portable items of high value, *eg* a portable television set, the Customs may make a note in the importer's passport and in their own interest they should ensure the entry is cancelled when exporting the item.

Traffic lights In principal cities and towns traffic lights operate in a way similar to those in the United Kingdom, although they are sometimes suspended overhead. The density of the light may be so poor that lights could be missed – especially those overhead. There is usually only one set on the right-hand side of the road some distance before the road junction, and if you stop too close to the corner, the lights will not be visible. Watch out for 'filter' lights which will enable you to turn right at a junction against the main lights. If you wish to go straight ahead, do not enter a lane leading to 'filter' lights or you may obstruct traffic wishing to turn right.

Trams Trams take priority over other vehicles. Always give way to passengers boarding and alighting. Never position a vehicle so that it impedes the free passage of a tram. Trams must be overtaken on the right except in one-way streets.

Tyres Inspect your tyres carefully; if you think they are likely to be more than three-quarters worn before you get back, it is better to replace them before you start out. Expert advice should be sought if you notice uneven wear, scuffed treads or damaged walls, on whether the tyres are suitable for further use. In some European countries, drivers can be fined if tyres are badly worn. The regulations in the UK governing tyres call for a minimum tread depth of 1mm over 75% of the width of the tyre all around the circumference, with the original tread pattern clearly visible on the remainder. European regulations are tougher, a minimum tread depth of 1mm or 1.6mm over the whole width of the tyre around the circumference.

When checking tyre pressures, remember that if the car is heavily loaded, then the recommended pressures may have to be raised. This should also be done for high-speed driving. Check the recommendations in your handbook but remember pressures can only be checked accurately when the tyres are cold and don't forget to make the same check on the spare tyre.

Vehicle excise licence When taking a vehicle out of the UK for a temporary visit (eg holiday or business trip) you must remember that the vehicle excise licence (tax disc) needs to be valid on your return. Therefore, if your tax disc is due to expire whilst you are abroad, you may apply by post before you leave to The Post Office for a tax disc up to 42 days in advance of the expiry date of your present disc. You should explain why you want the tax disc in advance and ask for it to be posted to you before you leave, or to an address you will be staying at abroad. However, your application form must always be completed with your UK address.

To find out which post office in your area offers this service, you should contact your local Post Office Customer Services Unit on the number listed in your local telephone directory.

Visas A visa is not normally required by United Kingdom and Republic of Ireland passport holders when visiting Western European countries for periods of three months or less (Portugal 60* days). However, if you hold a passport of any other nationality, a UK passport not issued in this country, or are in any doubt at all about your position, you should check with the embassies or consulates of all the countries you intend to visit.

* Visitors wishing to stay in Portugal for more than 60 days must apply in person for an extension to the Servio de Estrangeiros (Foreigners Registration Service), 1200 Lisboa, Av Antonio Augusto de Aguiar 20 tel 7141027/7141179. Applications must be made before expiry of the authorised period of stay. The cost is *ESC* 1,500.

Warm climate touring In hot weather and at high altitudes, excessive heat in the engine compartment can cause carburation problems. It is advisable, if you are towing a caravan, to consult the manufacturers about the limitations of the cooling system and the operating temperature of the gearbox fluid if automatic transmission is fitted (see *Automatic gearboxes* page 10).

Warning triangles/Hazard warning lights A warning triangle is required in most European countries – **two** are required in Spain for vehicles with more than nine seats and those weighing more than 3,500kg and in Yugoslavia for vehicles towing trailers. They are not required for two-wheeled vehicles.

A warning triangle should be used when a vehicle has stopped for any reason – not only breakdowns. It should be placed on the road behind the stopped vehicle to warn traffic approaching from the rear of an obstruction ahead. The triangle should be placed in such a position as to be clearly visible up to 100m (110yds) by day and by night, about 2 feet from the edge of the road but not in such a position as to present a danger to oncoming traffic. It should be set about 30m (33yds) behind the obstruction but this distance should be increased up to 100m (110yds) on motorways. An AA Warning Triangle, which complies with the latest International and European standards, can be purchased from the AA. Alternatively a warning triangle forms part of the Motoring Emergency Pack which may be hired from the AA.

Although four flashing indicators are allowed in the countries covered by this guide, they in no way affect the regulations governing the use of warning triangles. Generally, hazard warning lights should not be used in place of a triangle although they may complement it in use. (See also *Breakdowns* page 10).

OVERSEAS ROUTES SERVICE

INDIVIDUALLY PREPARED ROUTES TO YOUR OWN REQUIREMENTS

The AA's Overseas Routes Unit has a comprehensive and unique database of road and route information built into the very latest computerised equipment.

The database includes all relevant information needed for an enjoyable trouble-free route including distance in miles and kilometres for estimating journey times.

The route also includes route numbers, road signs to follow, motorway services, landmarks, road and town descriptions, frontier opening times etc.

Overseas Routes can supply you with any route you may require: – scenic routes – direct routes – by-way routes – fast routes – coach routes – caravan routes – motorway routes – non-motorway routes – touring routes – special interest routes – etc.

You may believe you know the best route – we can confirm if you are correct or tell you if we believe you are wrong and we will probably save you time and money by doing so!

Can we help you further? If we can, please contact any AA Centre for an Overseas Route Application form. Alternatively, telephone Overseas Routes on Basingstoke (0256) 493748/493907 or complete the application form below and we will send you full details of the Overseas Routes Service and the prices charged.

Send the form below to:
Overseas Routes,
The Automobile Association,
Fanum House, Basingstoke, RG21 2EA.

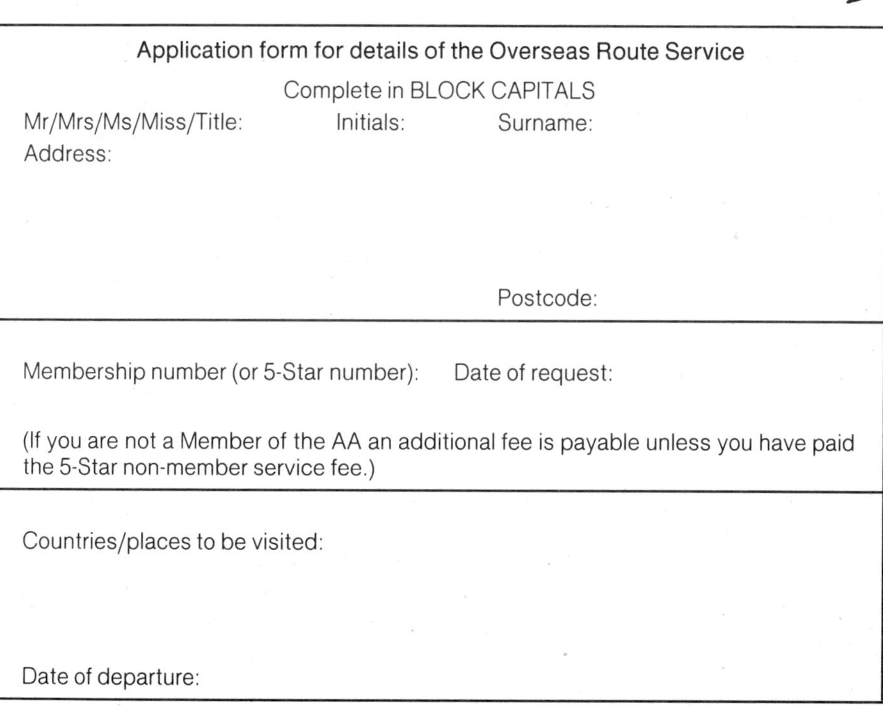

Application form for details of the Overseas Route Service

Complete in BLOCK CAPITALS

Mr/Mrs/Ms/Miss/Title: Initials: Surname:

Address:

Postcode:

Membership number (or 5-Star number): Date of request:

(If you are not a Member of the AA an additional fee is payable unless you have paid the 5-Star non-member service fee.)

Countries/places to be visited:

Date of departure:

MEASUREMENT CONVERSIONS

Capacity			Temperature	
litres	gallons or litres	gallons	Centigrade	Fahrenheit
4.546	1	0.22	−20	− 4
9.092	2	0.44	−10	+14
13.64	3	0.66	− 5	+23
18.18	4	0.88	0	+32
22.73	5	1.10	+ 5	+41
27.28	6	1.32	+10	+50
31.82	7	1.54	+15	+59
36.37	8	1.76	+20	+68
40.91	9	1.98	+25	+77
45.46	10	2.2	+30	+86
90.92	20	4.4	+35	+95
136.38	30	6.6	+36.9*	+98.4*
181.84	40	8.8	+40	+104
227.30	50	11.0	+45	+113
272.76	60	13.2	+50	+122
318.22	70	15.4	+60	+140
363.68	80	17.6	+80	+176
409.14	90	19.8	+100**	+212**
454.60	100	22.0		
909.20	200	44.0		

*Normal body temperature
**Boiling point (of water)

MEASUREMENT CONVERSIONS

Pressure

lb per sq in	kg per sq cm (bar)
18	1.266
20	1.406
22	1.547
24	1.687
26	1.828
28	1.969
30	2.109
32	2.250
34	2.390
36	2.531
38	2.672
40	2.812
42	2.953
44	3.093
46	3.234
48	3.375
50	3.515

Weight

kb	lb or kg	lb
0.454	1	2.205
0.907	2	4.409
1.361	3	6.614
1.814	4	8.818
2.268	5	11.02
2.722	6	13.23
3.175	7	15.43
3.629	8	17.64
4.082	9	19.84
4.536	10	22.05
9.072	20	44.09
13.61	30	66.14
18.14	40	88.18
22.68	50	110.23
27.22	60	132.28
36.29	80	176.37
45.36	100	220.46

Fuel: miles/kilometres/gallons/litres

miles per gallon	miles per litre	km per litre
10	2.2	3.5
15	3.3	5.3
20	4.4	7.1
25	5.5	8.8
30	6.6	10.6
35	7.7	12.4
40	8.8	14.2
45	9.9	15.9
50	11.0	17.7
55	12.1	19.5
60	13.2	21.3
65	14.3	23.0
70	15.4	24.8

Fuel: pence/gallons/litres

pence per gallon	pence per litre
160	35.2
165	36.3
170	37.4
175	38.5
180	39.6
190	41.8
200	44.0
210	46.2
220	48.4
230	50.6
240	52.8
250	55.0
260	57.2

Length: miles/kilometres

km	miles or km	miles	km	miles or km	miles
1.609	1	0.621	48.28	30	18.64
3.219	2	1.243	64.37	40	24.85
4.828	3	1.864	80.47	50	31.07
6.437	4	2.485	96.56	60	37.28
8.047	5	3.107	112.65	70	43.50
9.656	6	3.728	128.75	80	49.71
11.27	7	4.350	144.84	90	55.92
12.87	8	4.971	160.93	100	62.14
14.48	9	5.592	402.34	250	155.34
16.09	10	6.214	804.67	500	310.68
32.19	20	12.43	1,609.34	1,000	621.37

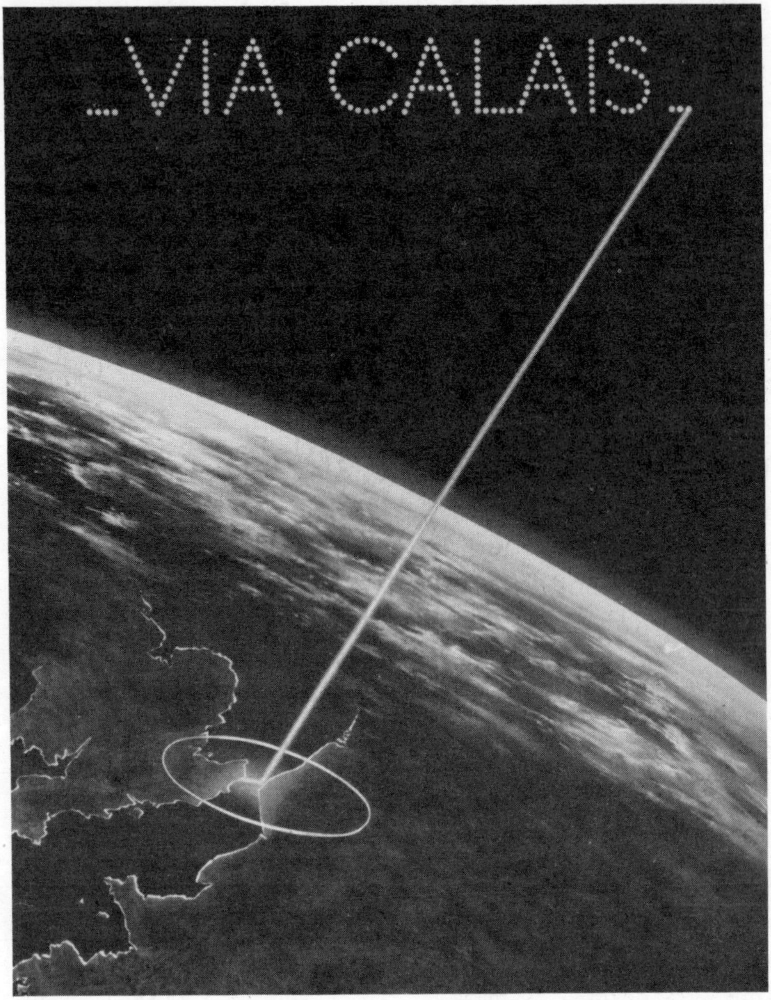

The countries, the towns and the establishments in them, are listed in alphabetical order. The town is followed by the name of the region or province in which it is located. If you have difficulty in locating any of these establishments, you are advised to seek assistance from the local tourist information office who should also be able to suggest other accommodation, should you have no luck at our recommendations. The different names for 'Bed and Breakfast' accommodation appear in each country introduction section.

ACCOMMODATION

The number of rooms has been shown to indicate the size of the establishment; where this information is not available the number of beds are given. Accommodation in an annexe may be of a different standard from rooms in the main building; it is advisable to check the exact nature of the accommodation at the time of reservation. We have endeavoured to select establishments which open all year but opening dates (*eg* 15 May–30 Oct) are shown where applicable. Where no dates are shown, according to our information, the establishment is open all year.

The gazetteer lists four main types of establishment, all selected on the basis that, within their respective countries, they offer accommodation of a cheaper nature. They are represented as follows:

1 **AA-classified hotels** are graded by stars. The AA classification system used in Europe is similar to that used in this country, although the variations in traditions and customs of hotel-keeping abroad often make identical grading difficult.

The stars indicate the type of hotel rather than the degree of merit; meals, service and hours of service should be in keeping with the classification. The requirements for classification as a one-star hotel are included in those for a two-star hotel.

- * **Hotels simply furnished but clean and well kept; all bedrooms with hot and cold running water; adequate bath and lavatory facilities.**
- ** **Hotels offering a higher standard of accommodation; adequate bath and lavatory facilities on all floors and some private bathrooms and/or showers.**
- *** **Well-appointed hotels with a large number of bedrooms with private bathrooms/showers.**

Four and **five-star** hotels, due to the nature of their accommodation and services, are in a higher price category and therefore not represented in this Guide.

2 **Inexpensive, unclassified hotels and motels** are indicated by the abbreviations **H** and **M** respectively. They are selected from information supplied by official local or national tourist offices and are not specifically recommended by the AA. They should provide bed and breakfast and many of them offer full or demi-pension terms.

3 ◆ This symbol indicates **guesthouses, pensions, inns, boarding houses and restaurants** providing overnight accommodation. Types of accommodation specific to a particular country are described in the country introductions. They are selected from the same source as category **2** and are not specifically recommended by the AA.

4 **Farmhouses** offering holiday accommodation are indicated by the abbreviation **FH**. Selected from the same source as category **2**, they are not specifically recommended by the AA. They offer simple, inexpensive accommodation in rural surroundings.

Whilst every effort is made to exclude from our gazetteer establishments which are felt to be unsatisfactory, it shoud be borne in mind that it is not possible for the AA to inspect large numbers of widely spread establishments overseas. It is therefore of great importance that **you should exercise your right to inspect accommodation which you are offered before making any kind of payment.** It is virtually impossible to obtain a refund once money has changed hands, especially as only limited English (or none at all) is likely to be spoken at many of the smaller establishments featured in the Guide, and particularly those away from the main tourist areas. With this in mind, it is a good idea to provide yourself with a basic phrase-book before setting out on your journey although the Useful Words and Phrases at the end of the book should help in most situations.

LOCATION MAPS

The location maps are at the beginning of each country section except those for Luxembourg, Portugal and Sweden where they are incorporated in the Belgian, Spanish and Norwegian maps respectively. These maps are intended to assist the reader who wishes to stay in a certain area by showing only those towns for which there is an entry in the gazetteer. Thus someone wishing to stay in the Innsbruck area will be able to select suitable towns by looking at the map. The location maps in this book use the symbols on page 29 to indicate adjoining countries.

It must be emphasised that these maps are not intended to be used to find your way around the country and we recommend readers to buy the **AA Big Road Atlas Europe**.

PARKING

A charge is often made for parking spaces whether under cover or in the open. Before leaving your car in a street overnight, you are advised to ascertain the local regulations. Wherever you leave your car it is essential that all valuables are removed and that the vehicle is locked. Remember also to unload the roof-rack if you are carrying one.

PRICES

Gazetteer entries have generally been selected on the basis that they offer accommodation at nightly rates of no more than £19 per person ($29 per person, taking the US dollar exchange rate at $1.61=£1) at some time during the year. The prices have been banded as follows: **A** from £9 to £14 per person per night ($13 to $23) and **B** from £14 to £19 per person per night ($23 to $29). You are advised to check before booking as accommodation terms may change, without warning, for a variety of reasons. Each country introduction gives the price bands in local currency followed by the exchange rate with both sterling and US dollars, at the time of going to press.

RESERVATIONS

It may be advisable, especially during July and August, to telephone ahead to reserve the next night's accommodation before setting out. On arrival at your destination, it is the custom in Europe to inspect the room(s) offered and to ask the price before accepting it/them. No embarrassment is caused by this practice and, in your own interest, you are urged to adopt it.

EXAMPLE OF GAZETTEER ENTRY

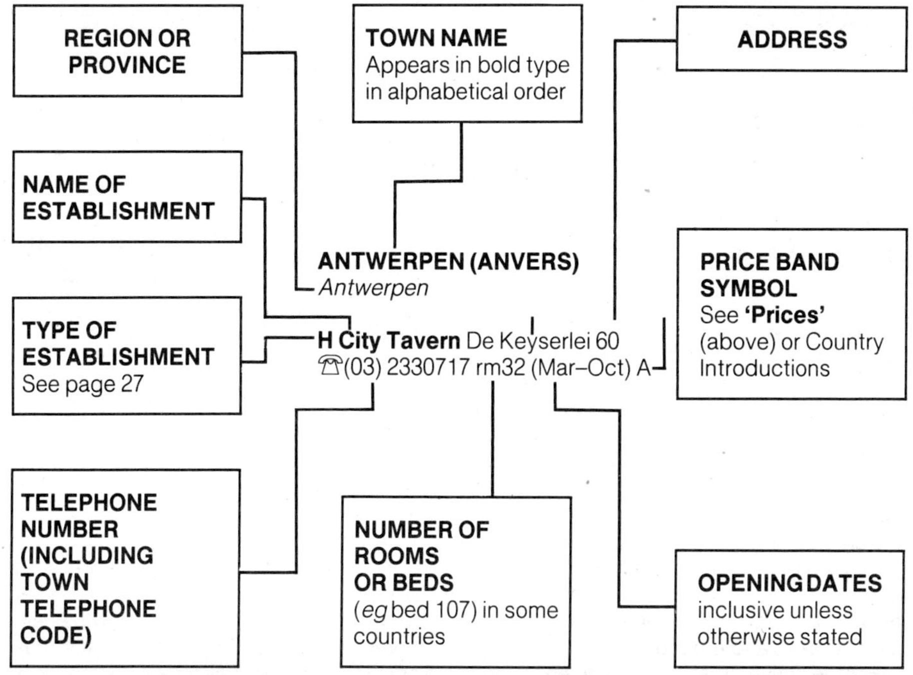

SYMBOLS USED FOR COUNTRY IDENTIFICATION

All location maps in this book use the following symbols to indicate adjoining countries.

AL	Albania	SF	Finland	I	Italy	RO	Romania
AND	Andorra	F	France	FL	Liechtenstein	E	Spain
A	Austria	D	Germany (Fed. Republic of)	L	Luxembourg	S	Sweden
B	Belgium	DDR	Germany (DDR)	NL	Netherlands	CH	Switzerland
BG	Bulgaria	GR	Greece	N	Norway	TR	Turkey
CS	Czechoslovakia	H	Hungary	PL	Poland	SU	USSR
DK	Denmark	IRL	Ireland (Rep. of)	P	Portugal	YU	Yugoslavia

AUSTRIA

FACTS & FIGURES

Capital: Wien (Vienna)
Language: German
IDD code: 43 To call the UK, dial 0044
Currency: Schilling (Aus 1.00=100 Groschen)
Local time: GMT+1 (Summer GMT+2)
Emergency Services: Police 133; Fire 122; Ambulance 144

Business hours
Banks:
0800–1230, 1330–1500 Mon, Wed and Fri
0800–1230, 1330–1730 Thur
Shops: 0800–1800 Mon–Fri
0800–1200 Sat

Average daily temperatures:
Vienna °C

Jan −1	Jul 20
Mar 3	Sep 16
May 15	Nov 5

Tourist Information:
Austrian National Tourist Office
UK 30 St George Street
London W1R 0AI
Tel 01-629 0461

USA 500 Fifth Avenue,
Suite 2009-2022
New York, NY, 10110
Tel (212) 944 6880

Whether you are seeking peace and relaxation with little to disturb your tranquillity, fun and activity, or a rewarding time exploring exquisite and fascinating cities and towns, Austria cannot fail to delight. You can take to the meadows and mountains, either alone or with a guide, following beautiful trails which reveal the splendour of the unspoiled countryside. Or you can scale great mountains by chairlift or mountain railway and be rewarded with magnificent panoramas of peaks and a land full of forests, lakes and meadows.

For the active, Austria offers an enormous range of sports facilities and amenities throughout the year. In winter, skiers head for Austria's slopes and are pampered in some of the world's finest winter holiday resorts, while summer visitors can enjoy wind-surfing, golf, tennis, sailing, water-skiing, para-sailing, cycling, horse-riding, hang-gliding, walking and hiking, swimming, fishing, canoeing and rafting.

Then there are the cities – Vienna, the cultural showcase of Europe, where old-world charm is blended with imperial splendour; Salzburg, stunningly located at the foot of the snow-capped Austrian Tyrol; and Innsbruck, which preserves its delightful medieval core.

HOW TO GET THERE

BY CAR

The most direct approach from Calais, Oostende or Zeebrugge is the German Autobahn network, via Karlsruhe and Stuttgart for Innsbruck or the Tirol, or eastwards via Nürnberg and München (Munich) for Salzburg and Central Austria. The distance to Salzburg is about 700 miles (1127 Km) and usually requires at least one overnight stop. Wien (Vienna) is a further 200 miles (322 Km) east. Travelling via the Netherlands, join the German Autobahn system near Arnhem. From Dieppe, Le Havre, Caen or Cherbourg, Austria can be reached via Northern France to Strasbourg and Stuttgart, or via Basel and Northern Switzerland (all vehicles using Swiss motorways must display a 'vignette' disk which costs S.Fr 30 available at the frontier). Car sleeper services operate during the summer from Brussels and 's-Hertogenbosch (Netherlands) to Salzburg and Villach.

For details of the AA's Overseas Routes Service consult the Contents page.

SPEED LIMITS

These limits may be varied by signs, in which case the lower limit must be observed: in built-up areas (between placename signs) 31 mph (50 kph); outside built-up areas, 62 mph (100 kph) and on motorways 80 mph (130 kph).

LIMITED PARKING ZONES

'Blue zones' with a maximum parking time of three hours are clearly marked. Parking clocks can be obtained free of charge in tobacconists' shops (Tabak-Trafik). In major towns and cities there is a charge for parking vouchers which can be obtained in banks, petrol stations and Tabak-Trafik.

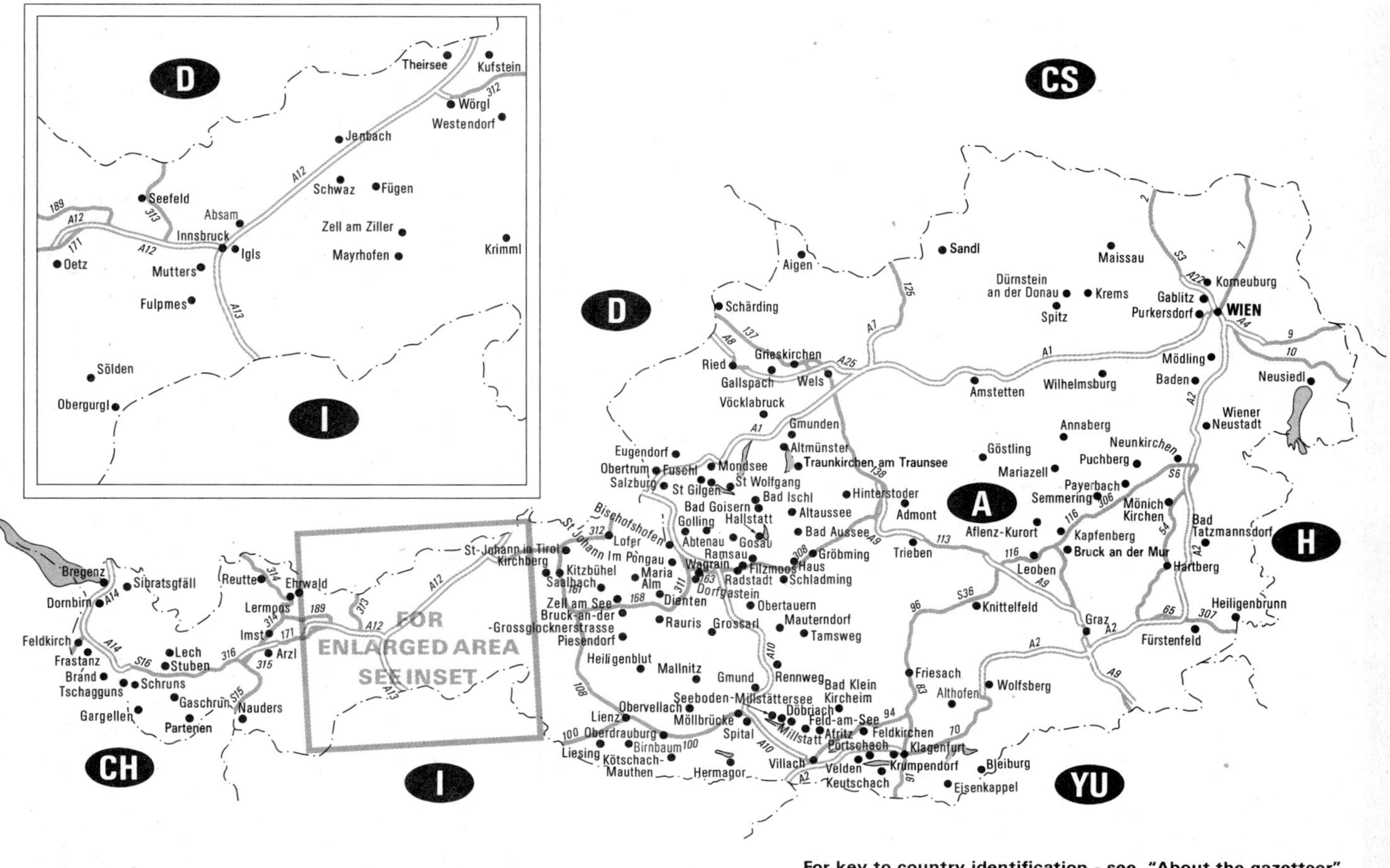

For key to country identification - see "About the gazetteer"

BY TRAIN

If you do not have an Inter Rail or Eurail pass, national and regional tickets can be purchased for rail travel within Austria. The Bundes-Netzkarte entitles you to travel on all the trains of the Austrian Federal Railways (ÖBB), including the Schafberg and Schneeberg Railways, and the ÖBB ships on the Wolfgangsee. Most private railways offer a 50 per cent reduction.

The Regional-Netzkarten give a choice of 18 different regions in any one of which you may travel from 4 to 10 days.

The Rabbitcard entitles you to travel for 4 out of 10 days on all the Austrian Federal Railways, including the ÖBB Ships on the Wolfgangsee.

All tickets can be purchased from larger railway stations and travel agencies.

BY BICYCLE

Bicycles can be hired from many ÖBB railway stations from April to October. The price is AS 70 per day, with a 50% reduction if you arrive by train. You will need a passport or identity card.

BY BUS

Yellow Austrian Post-buses and orange Bahn-buses can be very useful for travelling in mountainous areas not served by trains; most cities also have excellent bus and tram services. Tickets can be bought from Tabak-Trafik shops, ticket machines or on board.

ACCOMMODATION

The gazetteer which follows includes a wide range of hotels, guesthouses, farmhouses and inns.

The majority of these offer accommodation for less than AS 437 per person per night at some time of the year. The price bands are:

A 207–322
B 322–437

taking a rate of exchange at

AS 23=£1
AS 14=US $1

It is possible, however, that prices may change during the currency of this book, particularly in the high season and at winter holiday resorts.

Other details of accommodation can be obtained from local tourist offices ('Verkehrsvereine'). In smaller towns look out for Gasthäuser, Zimmer Frei and Privat Zimmer which should offer reasonably priced accommodation.

Abbreviations: g gasse HNr House Number pl platz str strasse

ABSAM *Tirol*

◆ **Bogner** ☎ (05223) 7987 bed50 Dec-Oct **B**

ABTENAU *Salzburg*

◆ **Gutjahr** (n.rest) ☎ (06243) 2434 bed36 Closed Nov **A**

H Lammertalerhof ☎ (06243) 2313 bed57 Closed Nov **B**

ADMONT *Steiermark*

★★**Post** ☎ (03613) 2416 bed55 May-Oct **A**

H Zur Traube ☎ (03613) 2440 bed30 **A**

AFLENZ-KURORT *Steiermark*

H Aflenzerhof ☎ (03861) 2245 bed65 **A**

H Hubertushof ☎ (03861) 31310 bed41 Closed Nov **A**

◆ **Rosenpension** (n.rest) ☎ (03861) 2333 bed20 **A**

◆ **Troiss Gertrude** (n.rest) ☎ (03861) 2223 bed15 Closed Nov **A**

AFRITZ *Kärnten*

◆ **Almrausch** ☎ (04247) 2084 bed40 Dec-Mar & May-Sep **B**

◆ **Glinzner** ☎ (04247) 2133 bed13 **A**

H Laerchenhof ☎ (04247) 2134 bed39 Dec-Mar & May-Sep **A**

AIGEN IM MÜHLKREIS
Oberösterreich

◆ **Haagerhof** ☎ (07281) 388 bed50 Closed Nov **A**

ALTAUSSEE *Steiermark*

◆ **Kohlbacherhof** ☎ (06152) 71651 bed50 **B**

H Landhaus Elizabethpark (n.rest) ☎ (06152) 71205 bed19 May-Sep **B**

◆ **Zum Hirschen** ☎ (06152) 71347 bed35 Closed Oct & Nov **B**

ALTHOFEN *Kärnten*

H Prechtlhof ☎ (04262) 2614 bed45 **A**

ALTMÜNSTER *Oberösterreich*

H Alpenhotel am See ☎ (07612) 8377 bed78 **B**

◆ **Huemerhof** ☎ (07612) 8395 bed35 Closed Nov-Mar **A**

◆ **Schlipfinger** (n.rest) ☎ (07612) 88134 bed10 **A**

AMSTETTEN *Niederösterreich*

H Gürtler Rathausstr 13 ☎ (07472) 2765 bed60 **A**

◆ **Kiermaier** Waidhofnerstr 31 ☎ (07472) 2490 bed60 **A**

◆ **Ybbstalhof** ☎ (07472) 2362 bed32 **A**

ANNABERG *Niederösterreich*

◆ **Touristen** ☎ (02728) 8243 bed90 **A**

ARZL IM PITZTAL *Tirol*

★★**Post** ☎ (05412) 3111 bed100 Dec-Mar & May-Oct **A**

AUSSEE, BAD *Steiermark*

◆ **Blaue Traube** ☎ (06152) 2363 bed21 **A**

★**Stadt Wien** ☎ (06152) 2068 bed24 Closed Nov, Feb & Mar **A**

H Wasnerin ☎ (06152) 2108 bed58 Closed Nov **A**

BADEach name preceded by 'Bad' is listed under the name that follows it.

BADEN BEI WIEN *Niederösterreich*

H Baden (n.rest) Schuetzeng 36 ☎ (02252) 87131 bed30 **B**

◆ **Elfi** Karlsg 11 ☎ (02252) 48145 bed14 **A**

H Frauenhof Josefspl 4 ☎ (02252) 80666 bed45 **A**

H Haus Rainerring (n.rest) Rainerring 17 ☎ (02252) 48291 bed23 **A**

H Inge (n.rest) Weilburgstr 24-26 ☎ (02252) 43171 bed30 Mar-Oct **A**

◆ **Kahrer** Radetzkystr 43 ☎ (02252) 41103 bed35 Mar-Nov **A**

◆ **Maria** Elizabethstr 11 ☎ (02252) 87937 bed33 Mar-Nov **A**

H Rauch (n.rest) Pelzgasse 3 U 3 A ☎ (02252) 44561 bed53 **B**

BIRNBAUM *Kärnten*

◆ **Post** ☎ (04719) 224 bed30 **A**

BISCHOFSHOFEN *Salzburg*

◆ **Alte Post** ☎ (06462) 2646 bed30 **A**

BLEIBURG *Kärnten*

H Breznik ☎ (04235) 2026 bed54 Nov-Sep **A**

◆ **Linde** ☎ (04235) 2105 bed54 Closed Apr, Oct & Nov **A**

At **ST MICHAEL**(4Km SW)

◆ **Kraut** ☎ (04235) 3134 bed32 Closed Oct & Nov **A**

BRAND *Vorarlberg*

FH Galaverda ☎ (05559) 263 rm7 **A**

◆ **Sonne** ☎ (05559) 243 bed20 Dec-Mar & Jun-Sep **A**

BRAND-LAABEN *Niederösterreich*

H Steinberger Werner ☎ (02774) 8363 bed106 Closed Jan **A**

◆ **Stöhr** ☎ (02774) 8378 bed24 Closed Nov **A**

BREGENZ *Vorarlberg*

H Berghof Fluh ☎ (05574) 24213 bed22 **B**

◆ **Gomania** ☎ (05574) 22766 bed33 Dec-Oct **B**

H Kinz (n.rest) ☎ (05574) 22092 bed78 **B**

BRUCK AN DER GROSSGLOCKNERSTRASSE *Salzburg*

◆ **Hoellern** ☎ (06545) 240 bed82 Dec-Sep **B**

★★**Lukashansl** ☎ (06545) 458 bed150 **B**

◆ **Woferlgut** ☎ (06545) 303 bed36 **A**

DIENTEN AM HOCHKÖNIG *Salzburg*

◆ **Salzburgerhof** ☎ (06461) 217 bed72 Closed Nov **B**

DÖBRIACH *Kärnten*

◆ **Brunner Anton** ☎ (04246) 7723 bed37 **A**

◆ **Haus Kärnten** ☎ (04246) 7122 bed33 **A**

H Zur Post ☎ (04246) 7713 bed70 **B**

DORFGASTEIN *Salzburg*

◆ **Christina** ☎ (06433) 252 bed15 **A**

H Kirchenwirt ☎ (06433) 251 bed55 Closed Apr, Oct & Nov **B**

◆ **Steindlwirt** ☎ (06433) 219 bed52 Closed Nov **B**

DORNBIRN *Vorarlberg*

◆ **Hirschen** (n.rest) ☎ (05572) 66363 bed74 **B**

◆ **Katharinenhof** (n.rest) ☎ (05572) 62577 bed26 **B**

◆ **Sonne** ☎ (05572) 62212 bed32 **A**

DÜRNSTEIN *Niederösterreich*

◆ **Sänger Blondel** ☎ (02711) 253 bed32 Mar-Nov **B**

H Weinhof (n.rest) ☎ (02711) 271 bed32 Mar-Nov **B**

EHRWALD *Tirol*

◆ **Alpenhotel** ☎ (05673) 2254 bed50 Dec-Mar & May-Oct **B**

◆ **Daniela** (n.rest) ☎ (05673) 2279 bed33 Dec-Mar & May-Sep **A**

◆ **Ehrwalderhof** ☎ (05673) 2364 bed56 **B**

EISENKAPPEL *Kärnten*

H Kurhotel Schlosspark ☎ (04238) 455 bed85 Closed Nov **B**

H Obir ☎ (04238) 381 bed100 **A**

EUGENDORF *Salzburg*

◆ **Holznerwirt** ☎ (06212) 8205 bed59 **B**

◆ **Santner** ☎ (06212) 82140 bed19 **A**

FELD AM SEE *Kärnten*

◆ **Seeblick** ☎ (04246) 2673 bed38 Dec-Sep **B**

H Strand ☎ (04246) 2452 bed46 **B**

FELDKIRCH *Vorarlberg*

★★**Alpenrose** (n.rest) Rosengasse 6 ☎ (05522) 22175 bed40 **B**

H Büchel ☎ (05522) 23306 bed83 **B**

◆ **Hochhaus** (n.rest) ☎ (05522) 22479 bed30 **A**

◆ **Loewen** ☎ (05522) 22183 bed96 **B**

H Loewen Central ☎ (05522) 22070 bed120 **B**

H Montfort ☎ (05522) 22189 bed50 **B**

◆ **Post** (n.rest) ☎ (05522) 22820 bed30 **A**

H Schäfle ☎ (05522) 22203 bed20 **A**

FELDKIRCHEN *Kärnten*

◆ **Berghof** ☎ (04276) 636 bed65 May-Sep **A**

◆ **Brandstätter** ☎ (04276) 2145 bed65 **A**

H **Bresitz** (n.rest) ☎ (04276) 2710 bed25 **A**

◆ **Fischinger** ☎ (04276) 3446 bed29 Apr-Oct & Dec **A**

◆ **Fruehstueckspension** ☎ (04276) 2632 bed52 **A**

H **Germann** ☎ (04276) 2287 bed57 **A**

◆ **Jost Renelde Katharina** ☎ (04276) 337 bed35 May-Sep **A**

FILZMOOS *Salzburg*

◆ **Edelweiss** (n.rest) ☎ (06453) 231 bed21 Dec-Oct **A**

◆ **Rottenau** (n.rest) ☎ (06453) 256 bed25 Closed May & Nov **A**

FRASTANZ *Vorarlberg*

★★**Stern** ☎ (05522) 51517 bed121 Closed Nov **B**

FRIESACH *Kärnten*

◆ **Lustigen Baur** ☎ (04268) 2232 bed13 **A**

FÜGEN *Tirol*

◆ **Annemaria** ☎ (05288) 2432 bed42 Jan-Mar & May-Sep **A**

◆ **Edelweiss** ☎ (05288) 2964 bed260 Closed Nov **A**

H **Sonne** ☎ (05288) 2266 bed80 **B**

FULPMES *Tirol*

H **Atzinger** (n.rest) ☎ (05225) 3135 rm60 **B**

◆ **Landhaus Heck** (n.rest) ☎ (05225) 2710 bed16 Dec-Apr & Jun-Oct **B**

FÜRSTENFELD *Steiermark*

◆ **Froehlick Maria Rosa** ☎ (03382) 2322 bed26 **A**

★★**Hitzl** ☎ (03382) 2144 bed60 Feb-Dec **B**

FUSCHL AM SEE *Salzburg*

★★**Seehotel Schlick** ☎ (06226) 237 bed83 **B**

H **Sporthotel Leitner** ☎ (06226) 208 bed84 **B**

GABLITZ *Niederösterreich*

H **Rosner Elisabeth** ☎ (02331) 3330 bed60 **A**

◆ **Stadlmaier** bed59 Mar-Dec **A**

GALLSPACH *Oberösterreich*

H **Austria** ☎ (07248) 2479 bed34 **B**

H **Gallspacher Hof** ☎ (07248) 2519 bed76 Dec-Jan & Mar-Oct **B**

H **Linzerhof** ☎ (07248) 2631 bed45 **A**

◆ **Wienerhof** ☎ (07248) 2614 bed33 Dec-Oct **A**

GARGELLEN *Vorarlberg*

H **Marmotta** ☎ (05557) 6301 bed25 Closed May & Nov **B**

GASCHURN *Vorarlberg*

FH **Jagerheim** ☎ (05558) 8507 bed5 **A**

GMÜND *Kärnten*

◆ **Kohlmayr** ☎ (04732) 2149 bed48 **A**

◆ **Pension** ☎ (04732) 2745 bed35 Dec-Jan & Apr-Oct **A**

GMUNDEN *Oberösterreich*

◆ **Grünberg** ☎ (07612) 3653 bed38 **A**

H **Magerl** ☎ (07612) 3675 bed70 **B**

H **Moosberg** ☎ (07612) 3654 bed42 **A**

GOISERN, BAD *Oberösterreich*

◆ **Agathawirt** ☎ (06135) 8342 bed78 Closed Nov **B**

◆ **Alpengasthof** ☎ (06135) 7241 bed79 Dec-Oct **A**

◆ **Heller** ☎ (06135) 8388 bed32 **A**

◆ **Predigtstuhl** bed28 Dec-Mar & May-Oct **A**

GOLLING *Salzburg*

★**Goldener Stern** ☎ (06244) 2200 bed79 **A**

◆ **Hauslwirt** ☎ (06244) 229 bed65 **A**

◆ **St-Nikolaus** ☎ (06244) 493 bed30 Dec-Jan & Apr-Oct **A**

◆ **Torrenerhof** ☎ (06244) 380 bed130 Jan-Oct **A**

GOSAU *Oberösterreich*

◆ **Koller** ☎ (06136) 207 bed40 **B**

H **Sommerhof** ☎ (06136) 258 bed65 Closed Nov **B**

GÖSTLING AN DER YBBS *Niederösterreich*

H **Ensmann** ☎ (07484) 7235 bed43 Closed May **B**

H **Waldesruh** ☎ (07484) 2275 bed91 Closed Nov **A**

GRAZ *Steiermark*

◆ **Goigner** Kaerntnerstr 324 ☎ (0316) 285451 bed40 **A**

◆ **Iris** ☎ (0316) 32081 bed16 **B**

◆ **Raben** Idlhofg 3 ☎ (0316) 912686 bed100 **B**

◆ **Schmidbaur** (n.rest) Kaerntnerstr 451 ☎ (0316) 283436 bed24 **B**

GRIESKIRCHEN *Oberösterreich*

H **Lugmayr** ☎ (07248) 8252 bed20 **B**

GRÖBMING *Steiermark*

◆ **Alpenpension Sperling** ☎ (03685) 2634 bed25 Closed Oct & Nov **A**

◆ **Landhaus Tirol** ☎ (03685) 2910 bed21 Closed Nov **A**

◆ **Reisslerhof** ☎ (03685) 2364 bed50 **A**

H **Spanberger** ☎ (03685) 2106 bed35 **B**

GROSSARL *Salzburg*

◆ **Alpenhof** ☎ (06414) 317 bed40 **A**

◆ **Gaestehaus** ☎ (06414) 312 bed30 **B**

H **Grossarlerhof** ☎ (06414) 219 bed50 **B**

◆ **Rattersberg** ☎ (06414) 333 bed30 Jan-Sep **A**

HALLSTATT *Oberösterreich*

◆ **Gruener** ☎ (06134) 263 bed60 May-Oct **B**

HARTBERG *Steiermark*

H **Alten Gericht** ☎ (03332) 3356 bed32 **A**

◆ **Sonnenhof** ☎ (03332) 2842 bed68 **A**

HAUS *Steiermark*

◆ **Becker** ☎ (03686) 2686 bed30 Dec-Apr & Jun-Oct **B**

◆ **Stenitzer Isabella** ☎ (03686) 2202 bed62 Closed May, Oct & Nov **A**

HEILIGENBLUT *Kärnten*

◆ **Ambrosi** (n.rest) ☎ (04824) 2218 bed17 Closed Nov **A**

◆ **Heiserhof** ☎ (04824) 2276 bed28 Closed May, Oct & Nov **A**

H **Sonnenhof** ☎ (04824) 2084 bed50 Closed May, Oct & Nov **A**

◆ **Tauerngold** ☎ (04824) 2045 bed10 Jan-Sep **A**

◆ **Trojerhof** ☎ (04824) 2241 bed32 Dec-Apr & Jun-Sep **A**

HEILIGENBRUNN *Burgenland*

◆ **Schwabenhof** ☎ (03324) 333 bed41 **A**

HERMAGOR *Kärnten*

FH Mathei Guggenberg 10 ☏ (04282) 2289 bed26 **A**

FH Schleibach Kameritsch 1 ☏ (04282) 280 bed40 **A**

FH Unter-Gerald ☏ (04282) 284 bed44 **A**

HINTERSTODER *Oberösterreich*

◆ **Hubertus** ☏ (07564) 5502 bed26 Nov-Sep **A**

◆ **Poppengut** ☏ (07564) 5268 bed45 **A**

IGLS *Tirol*

H Tirolerhof (n.rest) ☏ (05222) 77194 bed75 **B**

◆ **Tyrol** (n.rest) ☏ (05222) 77184 bed26 **B**

IMST *Tirol*

H Stern ☏ (05412) 3342 bed60 Closed Nov **B**

INNSBRUCK *Tirol*

Innsbruck, a well preserved ancient city in the heart of the Austrian Tirol, is set against a majestic backdrop of Alps.

A good place to begin a tour is the *Goldenes Dachl* (Golden Roof) where the Olympic Museum features videotapes of the Innsbruck Winter Olympics. Other notable attractions include the Imperial Palace (*Hofburg*); *Hofkirche*, the Imperial Church which was built as a mausoleum for Maximilian; and the Tyrolean Folk Art Museum (*Tiroler Volkskunstmuseum*) which displays costumes, rustic furniture and farmhouse rooms decorated in various styles. Also worth visiting is the Ferdinandeum, which exhibits Austria's largest collections of Gothic art, together with 19th- and 20th-century paintings.

When shopping for souvenirs look out for Tyrolean hats, Loden cloth and wood carvings.

EATING OUT Hearty, unpretentious food tends to be the order of the day in Innsbruck. Most establishments prepare delicious soups, such as *bohnensuppe*, bean soup often served with chunks of sausage or bacon; and a chicken or beef soup with dumplings and bacon known as *knodelsuppe*. Another local speciality is *Tyrolean geröstl*, beef or pork sauteed with potatoes, chives and other herbs. The *Schwarzer Adler*, in Kaiserjagerstrasse, is one of the most atmospheric restaurants in Innsbruck, and serves specialities such as dumplings and pot roasts. Another long-standing favourite with residents and visitors is the charming *Ottoburg*, in Herzog-Friedrich-Strasse, while for inexpensive food in a lively, convivial atmosphere, the wine tavern *Goethstube*, in the same street as *Ottoburg*, is highly recommended.

The area around the Herzog-Friedrich-Str is a pedestrian precinct and only open to vehicular traffic at certain times of the day.

◆ **Bierwirt** Bichlweg 2 ☏ (05222) 42143 bed70 **A**

◆ **Dollinger** Hallerstr 7 ☏ (05222) 37351 bed71 **A**

H Heimgartl ☏ (05222) 37650 bed25 **B**

◆ **Linde** Hungerburgweg 30 ☏ (05222) 37103 bed15 **B**

◆ **Roessl in der Au** ☏ (05222) 86846 bed250 Jul-Sep **A**

◆ **Serles** Salurner Str 18 ☏ (05222) 589171 bed23 Closed Nov **B**

H Weisses ☏ (05222) 21890 bed68 **B**

ISCHL, BAD *Oberösterreich*

◆ **Goldener Ochs** ☏ (06132) 35290 bed58 **B**

◆ **Zur Stadt Salzburg** ☏ (06132) 3564 bed45 **B**

JENBACH *Tirol*

◆ **Esterhammer** ☏ (05244) 2212 **A**

◆ **Herzoglicher Alpenhof** ☏ (05244) 207 bed56 Closed Apr & Nov **A**

KAPFENBERG *Steiermark*

H Boehlerstern ☏ (03862) 22559 bed50 **A**

H Steirerhof ☏ (03862) 23448 bed34 **B**

KEUTSCHACH *Kärnten*

◆ **Brueckler** bed56 Apr-Sep **A**

◆ **Gabriel Florian** ☏ (04273) 2441 bed63 May-Sep **B**

KIRCHBERG IN TIROL *Tirol*

◆ **Eva** ☏ (05357) 2353 bed44 **A**

◆ **Jagdhaus Fremdenheim** ☏ (05357) 2371 bed37 Closed Oct & Nov **A**

◆ **Kirchenwirt** ☏ (05357) 2852 bed60 Dec-Mar & Jun-Sep **B**

KITZBÜHEL *Tirol*

◆ **Eggerwirt** ☏ (05356) 2455 bed37 **B**

◆ **Foidl** ☏ (05356) 2189 bed35 Closed May, Oct & Nov **B**

KLAGENFURT *Kärnten*

H Aragia Völkermarkterstr 100 ☏ (04222) 31222 bed98 **B**

H Blumenstöckl (n.rest) Oktoberstr 11 ☏ (0463) 57793 bed27 **B**

H Europark Villacherstr 222 ☏ (0463) 21137 bed60 **B**

◆ **Geyer** Priesterhausgasse 5 ☏ (04222) 57886 bed43 **A**

H Loewenkeller Voelkermarkterstr 10 ☏ (0463) 512994 bed25 **A**

KLEINKIRCHHEIM, BAD *Kärnten*

◆ **Alpenblick** ☏ (04240) 241 bed28 Dec-Apr & Jun-Oct **A**

H Felsenhof ☏ (04240) 681 bed60 Closed Nov **B**

◆ **Fortin** (n.rest) ☏ (04240) 623 bed14 **A**

◆ **Gitzl** ☏ (04240) 642 bed30 Closed Nov **A**

◆ **Hinteregger** ☏ (04240) 477 bed26 Nov-Sep **B**

◆ **Kaiserburg** ☏ (04240) 365 bed40 Jan-Mar & May-Oct **B**

◆ **Sonnblick** ☏ (04240) 331 bed38 Closed Nov **B**

KNITTELFELD *Steiermark*

◆ **Enzingerhof** ☏ (03512) 22809 bed20 Mar-Nov **A**

◆ **Neumann** ☏ (03512) 2289 bed13 **B**

KORNEUBURG *Niederösterreich*

H Jagdhaus Stockerauerstr 31A ☏ (02262) 2322 bed100 **A**

KÖTSCHACH-MAUTHEN *Kärnten*

H Berghof ☏ (04715) 245 bed32 Dec-Oct **A**

◆ **Gailberghoehe** ☏ (04715) 368 bed40 **A**

H Gesundheits ☏ (04715) 259 bed90 Dec-Oct **B**

◆ **Kellerwand** ☏ (04715) 269 bed20 **B**

KREMS *Niederösterreich*

◆ **Anger** ☏ (02732) 2205 bed25 **A**

◆ **Jell** Schiesstattgasse 1 ☎ (02732) 3952 bed14 Closed Apr-Nov **A**

◆ **Unter den Linden** Schillerstr 5 ☎ (02732) 2115 bed70 **A**

◆ **Wienerbruecke** ☎ (02732) 2143 bed24 **A**

KRIMML *Salzburg*

★★**Klockerhaus** ☎ (06564) 208 bed90 **A**

◆ **Krimmlerfaelle** ☎ (06564) 203 bed170 **A**

◆ **Post** ☎ (06564) 358 bed85 **A**

KRUMPENDORF *Kärnten*

◆ **Feuchter** ☎ (04229) 2204 bed32 **A**

◆ **Koch** (n.rest) ☎ (04229) 2324 bed28 Jun-Sep **B**

H Mozarthof ☎ (04229) 2453 bed43 Apr-Nov **A**

H Rosenheim ☎ (04229) 2250 bed52 May-Oct **B**

KUFSTEIN *Tirol*

H Auracher-Löchl ☎ (05372) 2138 bed58 **A**

◆ **Goldener Löwe** ☎ (05372) 2181 bed67 **A**

◆ **Pfandl** ☎ (05372) 2460 bed30 **A**

◆ **Tirolerhof** ☎ (05372) 2331 bed22 **A**

LECH AM ARLBERG *Vorarlberg*

H Alexandra ☎ (05583) 2848 bed33 Closed May, Oct & Nov **A**

◆ **Arabell** ☎ (05583) 2181 bed37 Dec-Apr & Jul-Aug **A**

◆ **Aurora** ☎ (05583) 2354 bed46 Dec-Apr & Jul-Sep **A**

◆ **Braunarl** ☎ (05583) 3664 bed36 Dec-Apr & Jun-Sep **A**

◆ **Haldenhof** ☎ (05583) 2444 bed39 Dec-Apr & Jul-Sep **A**

◆ **Kilian** ☎ (05583) 2430 bed24 Dec-Apr & Jul-Sep **A**

FH Lavendal ☎ (05583) 2657 bed16 **A**

◆ **Stuelzis** ☎ (05583) 2471 bed30 Dec-Apr & Jul-Aug **A**

LEOBEN *Steiermark*

H Kindler (n.rest) ☎ (03842) 43202 bed61 **B**

LERMOOS *Tirol*

★★★**Drei Mohren** ☎ (05673) 2362 bed103 Dec-Mar & May-Oct **B**

H Hubertushof ☎ (05673) 2161 bed55 Closed Nov **B**

H Pechtl Theresia Regina ☎ (05673) 2898 bed30 Jan-Mar & May-Sep **B**

H Tyrol ☎ (05673) 2217 bed89 Dec-Sep **B**

LEUTASCH *Tirol*

◆ **Gaube** ☎ (05214) 6402 bed28 Dec-Mar & Jun-Sep **A**

◆ **Kreith** ☎ (05214) 6680 bed40 Closed Nov **B**

LIENZ *Tirol*

★★**Glocknerhof** ☎ (04852) 2167 bed35 Dec-Mar & Jun-Oct **A**

◆ **Goldener Fisch** ☎ (04852) 2132 bed74 Closed Nov **A**

◆ **Haiderhof** ☎ (04852) 2440 bed50 Closed Nov **B**

H Tyrol ☎ (04852) 3482 bed100 **A**

LIESING *Kärnten*

FH Lahnerhof Obergail 8 ☎ (04716) 239 bed21 **A**

LOFER *Salzburg*

H Braeu ☎ (06588) 2070 bed58 **B**

H Dax ☎ (06588) 389 bed36 **A**

◆ **Egger** ☎ (06588) 205 bed35 Closed Nov **A**

◆ **Eva-Maria** ☎ (06588) 232 bed19 Closed Nov **A**

★**Linter** ☎ (06588) 240 bed46 Dec-Mar & May-Oct **A**

◆ **Salzburgerhof** ☎ (06588) 333 bed24 Closed Nov **A**

◆ **Tannenhof** (n.rest) ☎ (06588) 332 bed32 **A**

MAISSAU *Niederösterreich*

H Manhartsberg ☎ (02958) 334 bed22 **A**

MALLNITZ *Kärnten*

H Alber ☎ (04784) 525 bed90 Dec-Sep **B**

◆ **Gatterer Johannes** ☎ (04784) 228 bed43 Dec-Apr & Jun-Sep **A**

◆ **Koenigshof** ☎ (04784) 210 bed46 Closed May, Oct & Nov **A**

H Oswald ☎ (04784) 223 bed68 **A**

◆ **Romatenblick** ☎ (04784) 266 bed31 Jan-Sep **A**

H Sonnenhof ☎ (04784) 260 bed36 Closed Oct & Nov **A**

MARIA ALM *Salzburg*

◆ **Almerwirt** ☎ (06584) 7714 bed74 Closed Nov **B**

◆ **Dreimaederlhaus** (n.rest) ☎ (06584) 409 bed26 Dec-Apr & Jun-Oct **A**

◆ **Lohningerhof** ☎ (06584) 355 bed52 Closed Nov **A**

◆ **Niederreiter** (n.rest) ☎ (06584) 254 bed70 Closed Nov **A**

MARIAZELL *Steiermark*

H Drei Hufeisen ☎ (03882) 2456 bed71 Closed Nov **A**

H Feichtegger ☎ (03882) 2416 bed98 Dec-Mar & May-Oct **B**

H Goldene Krone ☎ (03882) 2583 bed45 Closed Nov **A**

◆ **Goldenen Ochsen** ☎ (03882) 2407 bed22 Closed Mar & Nov **A**

H Goldenes Kreuz ☎ (03882) 2309 bed60 **A**

H Grazerhof ☎ (03882) 2263 bed31 **A**

H Gruener Kranz ☎ (03882) 2456 bed65 **A**

H Schwarzer Adler ☎ (03882) 2863 bed65 **B**

H 3 Hasen ☎ (03882) 2410 bed110 Closed Nov **B**

MAUTERNDORF *Salzburg*

◆ **Neuwirt** ☎ (06472) 7268 bed65 **B**

H Post ☎ (06472) 7316 bed40 Closed Nov **A**

MAYRHOFEN *Tirol*

◆ **Laendenhof** ☎ (05285) 3451 bed17 Dec-Oct **A**

H Maria-Theresia ☎ (05285) 2433 bed54 Closed Nov **B**

H Rose ☎ (05285) 2229 bed60 Closed Nov **A**

◆ **Waldheim** ☎ (05285) 2211 bed23 **A**

MILLSTATT *Kärnten*

◆ **Gertraud** (n.rest) ☎ (04766) 3250 bed34 May-Oct **A**

◆ **Haering** ☎ (04766) 2554 bed28 May-Sep **B**

◆ **Matzelsdorferhof** ☎ (04766) 2650 bed24 Dec-Oct **A**

H Nikolasch ☎ (04766) 2041 bed50 Dec-Jan & Apr-Oct **B**

◆ **Schretter** ☎ (04766) 3176 bed19 Closed Nov-Dec **A**

◆ **Villa Madl** ☎ (04766) 2501 bed30 **A**

MÖDLING *Niederösterreich*

H Babenbergerhof Babenbergergasse 6 ☎ (02236) 22246 bed94 **B**

MÖLLBRÜCKE *Kärnten*

◆ **Winkler** ☎ (04769) 2424 bed52 **A**

MONDSEE *Oberösterreich*

★★★**Mondsee** ☎ (06232) 2154 bed55 Apr-Oct **B**

◆ **Schlossl** ☎ (06232) 2390 bed43 Mar-Dec **A**

◆ **Schwarzes Roessl** ☎ (06232) 2235 bed45 **A**

H Seehotel Lackner ☎ (06232) 2359 bed32 **B**

H Stabauer ☎ (06232) 2285 bed30 Mar-Oct **A**

MÖNICHKIRCHEN *Niederösterreich*

H Lang Margit ☎ (02649) 257 bed16 **B**

H Lift Pension ☎ (02649) 232 bed40 Dec-Oct **A**

H Reidinger ☎ (02649) 242 bed65 Closed Nov **A**

MUTTERS *Tirol*

H Altenburg ☎ (05222) 27053 bed70 Dec-Mar & May-Sep **A**

★★**Mutterhof** ☎ (05222) 27491 bed50 Dec-Mar & May-Oct **B**

H Seppl ☎ (05222) 23114 bed50 Closed Nov **B**

NAUDERS *Tirol*

◆ **Dreilaenderblick** ☎ (05473) 262 bed42 Jan-Oct **A**

◆ **Kristall** ☎ (05473) 233 bed52 Closed Oct & Nov **A**

H Schwarzer Alder ☎ (05473) 254 bed60 Closed Nov **B**

NEUNKIRCHEN *Niederösterreich*

H Goldenen Löwen Triesterstr 10 ☎ (02635) 2426 bed47 **B**

NEUSIEDL AM SEE *Burgenland*

H Leiner ☎ (02167) 24890 bed33 Closed Nov **A**

H Wende ☎ (02167) 8111 bed200 **B**

OBERDRAUBURG *Kärnten*

◆ **Pontiller** ☎ (04710) 244 bed68 **A**

◆ **Post** ☎ (04710) 257 bed80 **A**

◆ **Stoecklmühl** ☎ (04710) 205 bed40 Dec-Jan & Apr-Oct **A**

OBERGURGL *Tirol*

H Tirol ☎ (05256) 217 bed42 **A**

OBERTAUERN *Salzburg*

H Berghotel ☎ (06456) 209 bed34 Dec-Apr & Jul-Sep **B**

H Tauernpasshoehe (n.rest) ☎ (06456) 215 bed53 Dec-Apr **B**

H Winter ☎ (06456) 391 bed40 Dec-Apr & Jul-Aug **B**

OBERTRUM *Salzburg*

◆ **Neumayr** ☎ (06219) 302 bed55 **A**

OBERVELLACH *Kärnten*

H Alpenhof ☎ (04782) 2246 bed115 Dec-Mar & May-Oct **A**

OETZ *Tirol*

★★**Alpenhotel** ☎ (05252) 6232 bed87 Dec-Oct **B**

H Seerose ☎ (05252) 6220 bed46 Closed Nov **A**

PAYERBACH *Niederösterreich*

H Alpenhof Kreuzberg ☎ (02666) 2911 bed28 **A**

H Payerbacherhof ☎ (02666) 2430 bed60 **A**

PIESENDORF *Salzburg*

◆ **Kapeller** ☎ (06549) 212 bed12 **A**

◆ **Neuwirt** ☎ (06549) 224 bed30 **A**

◆ **Piesendorf** ☎ (06549) 7226 bed32 **A**

◆ **Schett** ☎ (06549) 251 bed45 Dec-Oct **A**

PÖRTSCHACH *Kärnten*

H Ambassador ☎ (04272) 2526 bed160 **A**

◆ **Angelina** ☎ (04272) 2543 bed36 May-Sep **B**

H Glocknerhof ☎ (04272) 3314 bed90 Mar-Oct **A**

◆ **Haus Diana** ☎ (04272) 2604 bed33 Apr-Oct **A**

H Miralago ☎ (04272) 2430 bed30 May-Sep **B**

H Wallerwirt ☎ (04272) 2316 bed100 May-Sep **A**

FH Wirth ☎ (04272) 6214 bed50 **A**

PUCHBERG A SCHNEEBERG *Niederösterreich*

◆ **Bruckerhof** ☎ (02636) 2315 bed40 Closed Nov **A**

H Puchbergerhof ☎ (02636) 2278 bed38 Closed Nov **A**

◆ **Schmirl** ☎ (02636) 2277 bed27 Closed Nov **A**

◆ **Triebl** ☎ (02636) 2268 bed22 **A**

PURKERSDORF *Niederösterreich*

H Feuchtl (n.rest) Bergg 11 ☎ (02231) 3533 bed20 Apr-Oct **A**

H Friedl Weiner Strasse 46 ☎ (02231) 3489 bed90 **B**

H Moder Deutschwaldstr 10 ☎ (02231) 3387 bed80 **B**

◆ **Reiger Franz** ☎ (02231) 3107 bed128 Closed Feb **A**

RADSTADT *Salzburg*

H Diana ☎ (06452) 7333 bed43 **A**

H Post ☎ (06452) 306 bed47 Closed Nov **A**

◆ **Seitenalm** ☎ (06452) 490 bed55 Closed May & Nov-Dec **A**

◆ **Stegerbraeu** ☎ (06452) 313 bed76 **A**

RAMSAU AM DACHSTEIN *Steiermark*

H Almfrieden ☎ (03687) 81021 bed89 Closed May & Nov **B**

◆ **Alpenperle** ☎ (03687) 81877 bed22 Dec-Mar & May-Oct **A**

◆ **Erlbacher** ☎ (03687) 81153 bed50 Jan-Apr & Jul-Oct **A**

H Feistererhof ☎ (03687) 81980 bed65 **B**

◆ **Hermann** ☎ (03687) 81615 bed20 Closed Nov **A**

◆ **Kielhuberhof** ☎ (03687) 81750 bed68 **A**

H Post ☎ (03687) 81708 bed160 Closed Nov **B**

◆ **Sonnenhügel** ☎ (03687) 81437 bed19 Jan-Mar & Jun-Sep **A**

◆ **Stierer** ☎ (03687) 81751 bed40 **A**

◆ **Stocker** ☎ (03687) 81780 bed40 **B**

H Tuerlwandhuetle ☎ (03687) 81230 bed56 Closed Nov **A**

RAURIS *Salzburg*

◆ **Braeu** ☎ (06544) 6206 bed70 Closed Nov **A**

◆ **Platzwirt** ☎ (06544) 6333 bed38 Closed Nov **A**

RENNWEG *Kärnten*

◆ **Katschtalerhof** ☎ (04734) 210 bed40 **B**

◆ **Post** ☎ (04734) 204 bed21 **A**

REUTTE *Tirol*

◆ **Ammerwald** ☎ (05672) 8131 bed200 **B**

H Goldener Hirsch ☎ (05672) 2508 bed90 Closed Nov **A**

◆ **Goldene Rose** ☎ (05672) 2411 bed38 Closed Nov **A**

◆ **Krone** ☎ (05672) 2354 bed58 Nov-Mar & May-Sep **A**

H Maxmilian ☎ (05672) 2585 bed68 Dec-Mar & May-Oct **B**

◆ **Mohren** ☎ (05672) 2345 bed54 Closed Oct **B**

RIED IM INNKREIS *Oberösterreich*

H Kaiser ☎ (07752) 2488 bed70 **A**

M Ried ☎ (07752) 3144 bed42 **B**

SAALBACH *Salzburg*

◆ **Barbarahof** ☎ (06541) 7132 bed54 Closed Nov **A**

H Haider ☎ (06541) 228 bed80 Dec-Apr & Jun-Oct **B**

◆ **Helvetia** ☎ (06541) 202 bed32 Jan-Sep **A**

H Peter ☎ (06541) 236 bed40 **A**

◆ **Rupertihof** (n.rest) ☎ (06541) 7176 bed28 Dec-Apr & Jun-Sep **A**

◆ **Schattberg** (n.rest) ☎ (06541) 7602 bed55 Jan-Apr & Jun-Sep **B**

H Seidl-Alm ☎ (06541) 7229 bed100 Dec-Apr & Jul-Sep **A**

◆ **Siegmundshof** (n.rest) ☎ (06541) 572 bed60 Dec-Apr & Jun-Sep **B**

◆ **Unterwirt** ☎ (06541) 274 bed90 Dec-Sep **B**

ST GILGEN *Salzburg*

◆ **Aberseehof** ☎ (06227) 2882 bed50 **A**

◆ **Bachler** ☎ (06227) 571 bed35 Apr-Oct **A**

H Frisch ☎ (06227) 511 bed60 Closed Nov **A**

◆ **Seehang** ☎ (06227) 2385 bed38 Closed Mar & Nov **A**

◆ **Tirol** ☎ (06227) 317 bed24 **A**

H Zum Goldenen ☎ (06227) 223 bed31 Closed Nov **A**

ST JOHANN IM PONGAU *Salzburg*

◆ **Silbergasser** ☎ (06412) 421 bed421 Closed Apr & Nov **B**

ST JOHANN IN TIROL *Tirol*

◆ **Flora** ☎ (05352) 2980 bed28 **A**

H Granada (n.rest) ☎ (05352) 2830 bed32 Closed Nov **A**

ST MICHAEL See **BLEIBURG**

ST WOLFGANG *Oberösterreich*

H Belvedere ☎ (06138) 2302 bed34 **A**

◆ **Wiesser Bar** ☎ (06138) 2303 bed37 Dec-Jan & May-Oct **A**

SALZBURG *Salzburg*

This city of quaint streets, graceful mansions, busy squares and peaceful churches reclines on the banks of the River Salzburg, protected by a lofty 900-year-old fortress.

As befits the birthplace of Wolfgang Amadeus Mozart, Salzburg offers a wide choice of concerts, and hosts international festivals, but music of a different kind brought more recent fame to the city when the *Sound of Music* was filmed on location at the Leopoldskron Palace. Galleries and museums display works by Rembrandt, Titian and Rubens, and the Mirabelle gardens are a delight.

EATING OUT Soups are popular, such as *knodelsuppe* – chicken broth with spicy bacon and garlic dumplings. The meat dishes are hearty and flavoursome. Try *Troler geröstl*, beef sauteed with potatoes and herbs, or the *schnitzels* – veal coated in breadcrumbs. Austrian pastries *küchen* and *torten* are irresistible, including things such as apples, cherries, nuts and chocolate as well as the classic apfelstrudel.

Of Salzburg's many acclaimed restaurants, the *Alt Salzburg*, in Burgerspitalgasse, is one of the best. Also highly recommended is the *Zum Eulenspiegel*, located in an old city house in Hagenauerplatz. For pastries and cakes the *Ratzka*, in Imbergstrasse, is outstanding.

◆ **Eisl** Itzlinger-Hauptstr 13 ☎ (0662) 50105 bed26 **A**

H Goldfasan Stauffeneggstr 2 ☎ (0662) 31436 bed72 **A**

◆ **Helmhof** Kircheng 29 ☎ (0662) 33079 bed31 **A**

◆ **Karl** (n.rest) ☎ (0662) 661934 bed16 Mar-Oct **A**

◆ **Landhaus Wegscheider** Thumeggerstr 4 ☎ (0662) 841764 bed20 **A**

H Lehenerhof (n.rest) Ignaz-Harrer-Strasse 46 ☎ (0662) 32119 bed46 **A**

★★**Traube** (n.rest) Linzer g 2-4 ☎ (0662) 740625 bed82 Jul-Sep **A**

SCHÄRDING *Oberösterreich*

◆ **Gugerbauer** ☎ (07712) 3151 bed76 **A**

H Kreuzberghof ☎ (07712) 2302 bed34 **A**

◆ **Zur Stiege** ☎ (07712) 3070 bed50 **A**

SCHLADMING *Steiermark*

◆ **Barbara** ☎ (03687) 22077 bed33 **A**

◆ **Druschhof** ☎ (03687) 22873 bed50 Dec-Sep **A**

◆ **Planaihof** ☎ (03687) 22152 bed26 Closed May **A**

◆ **Tritscher** ☎ (03687) 22435 bed30 **B**

SCHRUNS *Vorarlberg*

FH Bitschnau Maria ☎ (05556) 32824 bed5 **A**

H Chesa Platina ☎ (05556) 2323 bed40 **B**

H Obwegeser ☎ (05556) 3558 bed28 Dec-Apr & Jun-Oct **B**

H Schäfle ☎ (05556) 2424 bed23 Closed Nov **A**

SCHWAZ *Tirol*

◆ **Goldener Löwe** ☎ (05242) 2373 bed60 **A**

◆ **Goldenes Kreuz** ☎ (05242) 2578 bed60 **A**

H Grafenast ☎ (05242) 3209 bed40 Closed Nov **B**

SEEBODEN *Kärnten*

◆ **Gastein** ☎ (04762) 81306 bed37 Apr-Oct **A**

H Moser bed60 **A**

◆ **Seeblick** ☎ (04762) 81703 bed30 May-Oct **A**

SEEFELD *Tirol*

H Baronet ☎ (05212) 2333 bed27 Closed May & Nov **B**

◆ **Glas** (n.rest) ☎ (05212) 2550 bed50 Dec-Mar & Jun-Sep **B**

H Olympia (n.rest) ☎ (05212) 2334 bed40 Closed Nov **B**

◆ **Tiroler Weinstube** ☎ (05212) 2208 bed70 Closed Apr, Oct & Nov **B**

SEMMERING *Niederösterreich*

H Alpenheim ☎ (02664) 322 bed40 Dec-Oct **B**

H Belvedere ☎ (02664) 270 bed36 Closed Nov **B**

◆ **Daheim** ☎ (02664) 382 bed18 Closed Nov **A**

SIBRATSGFÄLL *Vorarlberg*

◆ **Ifenblick** ☏ (05513) 6432 bed43 Closed Nov **A**

◆ **Marxgut** ☏ (05513) 2213 bed40 Closed Nov **A**

SÖLDEN *Tirol*

H Alpenland ☏ (05254) 2365 bed44 **A**

◆ **Bellevue** ☏ (05254) 2444 bed14 **A**

◆ **Mirabell** ☏ (05254) 2125 bed29 **A**

H Rosengarten ☏ (05254) 2444 bed32 Jun-Apr **B**

SPITTAL AN DER DRAU *Kärnten*

H Alte Post Hauptpl 13 ☏ (04762) 2217 bed83 **A**

H Ertl Bahnhofstr 26 ☏ (04762) 2048 bed86 Closed Nov **B**

◆ **Kleinsasserhof** Kleinsastr 3 ☏ (04762) 2292 bed48 Closed Apr & Nov **A**

SPITZ AN DER DONAU *Niederösterreich*

◆ **Donaublick** ☏ (02713) 2552 bed24 Mar-Oct **A**

H Mariandl ☏ (02713) 311 bed89 Mar-Oct **A**

H Mistelbauer ☏ (02713) 2303 bed55 Apr-Oct **A**

◆ **Neue Welt** ☏ (02713) 2254 bed50 Closed Nov **A**

STUBEN *Vorarlberg*

H Albona ☏ (05582) 712 bed40 Closed Nov **B**

TAMSWEG *Salzburg*

◆ **Weinstüberl** ☏ (06474) 287 bed28 **B**

TATZMANNSDORF, BAD *Burgenland*

H Zum Kastell ☏ (03353) 428 bed58 Mar-Nov **B**

TRIEBEN *Steiermark*

◆ **Draxlerhaus** ☏ (03615) 215 bed46 **A**

◆ **Triebener Hof** ☏ (03615) 2234 bed30 **A**

TSCHAGGUNS *Vorarlberg*

H Cresta ☏ (05556) 2395 bed65 Dec-Mar & May-Sep **B**

FH Gafrina ☏ (05556) 3306 bed14 **A**

H Sonne ☏ (05556) 2333 bed62 Dec-Mar & May-Sep **B**

VELDEN AM WÖRTHERSEE *Kärnten*

H Annotte ☏ (04274) 2087 bed35 **A**

H Kaerntnerhof ☏ (04274) 2681 bed90 Apr-Oct **B**

◆ **Michäela** ☏ (04274) 3254 bed28 Apr-Oct **A**

H Schwarz ☏ (04274) 2120 bed55 **B**

VIENNASee **WIEN**

VILLACH *Kärnten*

◆ **Gretl** Gretlstr 7-9 ☏ (04242) 41881 bed100 May-Sep **A**

◆ **Moser Heinz** 18 Novemberplatz 8 ☏ (04242) 24933 bed62 **A**

H Seestuben Treffnerstr 94 ☏ (04242) 27759 bed50 **A**

VÖCKLABRUCK *Oberösterreich*

H Auerhahn (n.rest) ☏ (07672) 3456 bed110 **B**

WAGRAIN *Salzburg*

H Enzian ☏ (06413) 8502 bed55 Closed Nov **B**

◆ **Grafenwirt** ☏ (06413) 8230 bed30 Dec-Sep **B**

◆ **Schatteur** ☏ (06413) 8227 bed67 Closed Apr, Oct & Nov **B**

WELS *Oberösterreich*

◆ **Bayrischer** Dr-Schauerstr 23 ☏ (07242) 7214 bed77 **A**

WESTENDORF *Tirol*

H Briem ☏ (05334) 6310 bed95 Dec-Mar & May-Sep **A**

◆ **Mesnerwirt** ☏ (05334) 6206 bed74 Closed Apr & Nov **A**

WIEN (VIENNA)

Wien is a city of legends, elegance and grace, of mouth-watering *sachertorte* and delicious coffee. It has fine traditions, beautiful woods and spectacular architecture. Wien has also been called the musical capital of the world, and with good reason. Synonymous with Strauss, Schubert and Mozart, it offers a setting every bit as capital. Along its great boulevards – the Ring – are the grand façades of museums and parliament buildings and the state theatre (*Burgtheatre*).

In addition to the musical mementos littering the city there are concert halls and an opera house (*Staatsoper*) that is known throughout the world. Even the native tongue is spoken with a musical lilt, and there are accordion players in the cafés and concerts in the Stadtpark in summer.

Among Wien's many interesting sights are impressive historic residences, from the Schonbrunn Palace, to the personal homes of Freud, Schubert, Mozart, Strauss and Beethoven; and art galleries such as the Museum of Fine Arts (*Kunsthistorisches Museum*) and the Belvedere. A 'must' is a visit to the famous Spanish Riding School (*Spanische Reitschule*), housed in the Hofburg, the Hapsburgs' winter palace, while a popular outing is a visit to the Vienna Woods where one can take a boat trip on Europe's largest subterranean lake.

St Stephen's Cathedral (*Stephansdom*), the south spire of which rises to 450ft, is the most important Gothic building in Austria.

Wien's finest shops lie between Graben and Karntner-Strasse, and they open on weekdays and Saturday mornings. Viennese specialities include Loden clothing for men and women, petit-point embroidery and Austrian jade. The *Naschmarkt*, near Karlplatz, is the best known of the city markets.

EATING OUT Good restaurants and wine taverns can be found throughout the centre of the city. Bohemian dumplings, Hungarian goulash and Polish stuffed cabbage feature prominently on Viennese menus, along with local specialities such as *wienerschnitzel*, a thin cutlet of veal cooked with a coating of breadcrumbs, and *tafelspitz* (boiled beef). The city is justly famous for its pastries, and you can try the genuine *sachertorte* at the Hotel Sacher.

The Viennese claim – and with some justification – that the best pastries in the world are served at the *Konditorei Oberlaa*, in Neuer Markt; while those looking for atmosphere should seek out the *Glacis-Beisl* restaurant in the Messepalast, complete with delightful, vine-filled garden.

Bezirk I

◆ **Elite** Wipplingerstr 32/33 ☏ (0222) 5332518 bed48 **B**

◆ **Nossek** Graben 17 ☏ (0222) 5337041 bed60 **B**

H Post Fleischmarkt 24 ☏ (0222) 515830 bed180 **A**

Bezirk III

◆ **Stadtpark** Landstr Hauptstr 7 ☎ (0222) 733123 bed33 **A**

Bezirk V

H Sommer Matzleinsdorfer Pl 1 ☎ (0222) 552743 bed65 **B**

Bezirk VI

H Mariahilf Mariahilfer Str 121 ☎ (0222) 5973605 bed120 **A**

Bezirk VII

H Fuerstenhof Neubauguertel 4 ☎ (0222) 933267 bed98 **B**

H Wimberger Neubauguertel 34-36 ☎ (0222) 937636 bed174 **B**

Bezirk VIII

◆ **Andreas** Schloesselg 11 ☎ (0222) 4234880 bed76 **B**

Bezirk IX

◆ **Astra** (n.rest) Alser Str 32 ☎ (0222) 424354 bed40 **A**

◆ **Falstaff** Müllnerg 5 ☎ (0222) 349127 bed29 **A**

Bezirk X

◆ **Transaustria** Angelig 74 ☎ (0222) 625228 bed50 **A**

Bezirk XII

H Cryston Gaudenzdorfer Guertel 63 ☎ (0222) 835682 bed75 **A**

Bezirk XIV

◆ **Kreiner** Haupstr 14 ☎ (0222) 971131 bed26 **A**

Bezirk XXI

H Karolinenhof Jedleseer Str 75 ☎ (0222) 381339 bed95 **A**

Bezirk XXIII

◆ **Aschauer** Kalksburg-Kirchenpl 5 ☎ (0222) 884163 bed18 Closed Oct **A**

WIENER NEUSTADT *Niederösterreich*

H Zentral ☎ (02622) 23169 bed90 **A**

WILHELMSBURG *Niederösterreich*

◆ **Reinberger** ☎ (02746) 2364 bed30 **A**

WOLFSBERG *Kärnten*

◆ **Pfundner** ☎ (04352) 2695 bed20 **A**

WÖRGL *Tirol*

H Inntalerhof bed49 Closed Nov **A**

H Rosenberger Autobahn-Raststaette ☎ (05332) 4375 bed104 **B**

◆ **Schachtner** ☎ (05332) 2286 bed84 **A**

ZELL AM SEE *Salzburg*

◆ **Andrea** (n.rest) ☎ (06542) 3781 bed32 Jun-Sep **A**

◆ **Atlenberger** (n.rest) ☎ (06542) 2449 bed22 **A**

◆ **Bernhofer** ☎ (06542) 7133 bed75 Dec-Sep **B**

◆ **Fischerhof** ☎ (06542) 3138 bed30 Closed Nov **A**

◆ **Heitzmann** (n.rest) ☎ (06542) 2152 bed56 Dec-Apr & Jun-Sep **A**

◆ **Margarette** (n.rest) ☎ (06542) 2724 bed42 Dec-Mar & Jun-Sep **A**

H St Hubertushof ☎ (06542) 3130 bed200 Closed Nov **B**

◆ **Schuetthof** ☎ (06542) 7391 bed160 **B**

H Seehof ☎ (06542) 2666 bed52 Dec-Sep **A**

ZELL AM ZILLER *Tirol*

H Dörflwirt ☎ (05282) 3162 bed55 Closed Nov **B**

◆ **Neuwirt** ☎ (05282) 2209 bed80 Closed Nov **A**

★★★**Tirolerhof** ☎ (05282) 2227 bed81 Closed Nov **B**

Looking across the old quarter of Salzburg to the castle

BELGIUM

FACTS AND FIGURES

Capital: Bruxelles (Brussel, Brussels)
Language: French, Dutch, German
IDD code: 32. To call the UK dial 00 44
Currency: Belgian Franc (BFr1 = 100 centimes)
Local time: GMT + 1 (summer GMT + 2)
Emergency Services: Police 101; Fire 100; Ambulance 100.

Business hours

Banks:
0900–1200, 1400–1600 Mon–Fri
Shops:
0900–1800 Mon–Sat

Average daily temperatures:
Bruxelles °C

Jan 3	Jul 17
Mar 5	Sep 14
May 13	Nov 5

Tourist Information:
Belgian National Tourist Office

UK	Premier House 2 Grayton Road Harrow Middlesex HA1 2XU Tel 01-861 3300
USA	745 Fifth Ave New York, NY 10151 Tel (212) 758-8130

Belgium has more than its fair share of beautiful cities, artistic treasures, magnificent beaches and lovely countryside, yet this little country is often overlooked and ignored by so many.

The Belgians themselves are a jolly lot. They love pageantry, processions and riotous festivals and they have a peculiar weakness for funfairs; you might even come across one in the very centre of the capital. Here, too, you will find some of the most elegant and cosmopolitan shops in the world and some of the finest restaurants. In Brussels, and in Belgium's great art cities like Gent and picturesque Brugge, there are magnificent masterpieces of 15th and 16th-century architecture and of the Flemish school of art.

Belgium has a good selection of beaches and resorts, Oostende is the biggest, and has excellent beaches, a casino and a picturesque port. But Belgium's best-kept secret is the Ardennes, a land of deep forests, dramatic waterfalls, lakes and awe-inspiring grottos like great underground cathedrals. Here you can drive for miles on almost traffic-free roads, or walk on well-signed paths following clear sparkling rivers which twist and turn at the foot of rocky cliffs, or flow placidly through picturesque towns. You will discover magnificent cliff-top castles, charming rustic villages and a rare peace and tranquillity.

HOW TO GET THERE

BY CAR

There are many direct cross-Channel services to Belgium: Dover to Oostende ($3\frac{3}{4}$–4 hrs) or to Zeebrugge from Dover (4–$4\frac{1}{2}$ hrs), Felixstowe ($5\frac{1}{2}$ hrs day, 8–9 hrs night) or Hull (14 hrs). Alternatively, it is possible to use the shorter Channel ferry or hovercraft services that operate from Dover to Calais or Boulogne in France, and drive along the coastal road to Belgium.

For details of the AA's Overseas Routes Service consult the Contents page.

SPEED LIMITS

These limits may be varied by signs, in which case the lower limit must be observed: in built-up areas (between placename signs) 37 mph (60 kph); outside built-up areas 56 mph (90 kph); and on motorways 74 mph (120 kph). (Minimum speed on motorways on straight level stretches is 43 mph (70 kph).

PARKING

Parking discs must be displayed in short-term parking zones – 'blue zones'. A parking disc must also be used if the parking sign has an additional panel showing a parking disc. There are other areas with parking meters where discs are invalid.

BY TRAIN

If you do not have an Inter Rail or Eurail pass, a range of tickets can be purchased for rail travel within Belgium. Un Beau Jour/Een Mooie Dag ticket offer 50% off same-day returns.

The B–Tourrail '5/17' Pass allows five days' travel on all Belgian trains during a 17-day period.

The Benelux Tourrail Pass is a similar permit to the one above for use throughout Belgium, Luxembourg and the Netherlands.

There is also a new TTB (train, tram, bus) pass. All tickets can be purchased from larger railway stations and travel agencies.

BY BICYCLE

Many roads have cycle lanes. Bicycles can be hired from most train stations; you can return a bicycle to any station.

ACCOMMODATION

The gazetteer which follows includes a selection of hotels, and pensions. The majority of these offer accommodation for less than BFr1292 per person per night at some time of the year. Single rooms tend to be more expensive. The price bands are:

A 612–952BFr
B 952–1292BFr

taking a rate of exchange at

68BFr=£1
41BFr=US $1

It is possible, however, that prices may change during the currency of this book, particularly in the high season. Further information can be obtained from local tourist authorities. Standards for amenities and comforts are laid down by law for establishments designated as Hotel, Pension, Hostellerie, Auberge, Gasthof and Motel. They exhibit the distinctive sign issued by the Belgian Tourist Office.

Abbreviations: av avenue bd boulevard pl place, plein r rue rte route str straat, strasse

AALST (ALOST) *Oost-Vlaanderen*

★Borse Van Amsterdam Grote Markt 26 ☎ (053) 211581 rm6 Closed Jul 1-15 **A**

H Gare Stationspl 11 ☎ (053) 213911 rm19 **A**

H Lange Muur Stationspl 13 ☎ (053) 773746 rm8 **A**

AALTER *Oost-Vlaanderen*

H Capitole Stationsstr 95 ☎ (091) 741029 rm34 Closed Jan **A**

ACHEL *Limburg*

H Heidehof (n.rest) Odilialaan 81 ☎ (011) 643709 rm8 **A**

AMEL (AMBLEVE) *Liège*

H Kreusch Auf dem Kamp 179 ☎ (080) 349050 rm11 **A**

ANTWERPEN (ANVERS) *Antwerpen*

Antwerpen is a bustling international seaport, rich in art and culture. Its favourite son, Rubens, lived and worked here, drawing his inspiration from the city, and visitors can still see his house, and his work is displayed in churches and galleries.

For a nautical flavour take a harbour cruise and visit the National Maritime Museum, housed in a 12th-century fortress which was also once a prison. The Cathedral of Our Lady *Onze Leive Vrouwekahedraal* has glorious stained glass windows, as well as Rubens' masterpieces, including the *Descent from the Cross.*

Visitors should be sure to visit the diamond centres for which the city is world-famous. Even if one has no intention of buying, the complex process which transforms dull stones to sparkling gems is facinating.

Antwerpen takes great pride in its zoo, which houses such unusual inmates as tree kangaroos and electric eels. There is also a dolphinarium, aquarium and baby zoo.

Shoppers will enjoy the animals, plants and food on sale at the bird market and the antiques and curiosities on offer at the North Gate of the cathedral. There are also super modern shopping centres and attractive shopping streets such as the Meir and De Keyserlei.

EATING OUT Especially good value are the restaurants in the Suikerrui and the Handschoenmarkt area, near the cathedral. Mussels, eels and rabbit are tasty specialities, as are *Antwerpse handjes* – biscuits and pastries. You can dine in restaurants overlooking the Schelde and enjoy the view as much as the food. Of the city's many fine restaurants, *La Rade*, in Van Dyckaai, and the *Criterium* in De Keyserlei, enjoy outstanding reputations. *Rooden Hoed*, Oude Koornmarkt, near the cathedral, is Antwerpen's most ancient restaurant and specialises in various preparations of eels and mussels.

Belgium produces hundreds of quality beers and lagers, with even small bars usually stocking at least 20 or so. If you fancy something stronger, try *jenever* (Antwerp gin).

H Billard Palace Kon-Astridpl 40 ☎ (03) 2334455 rm49 **A**

H Caribou (n.rest) Gl-Lemanstr 45 ☎ (03) 2370219 rm30 **A**

H Colombus (n.rest) Frankrijklei 4 ☎ (03) 2330390 rm27 **B**

H Dijksterhuis (n.rest) Kon-Astridpl 22 ☎ (03) 2330800 rm15 **A**

H Florida (n.rest) De Keyserlei 59 ☎ (03) 2321443 rm51 **B**

◆ Rubenshof (n.rest) Amerikalei 115-117 ☎ (03) 2370789 rm20 **A**

H Terminus (n.rest) Franklin Rooseveltplaats 9 ☎ (03) 2314795 rm45 **B**

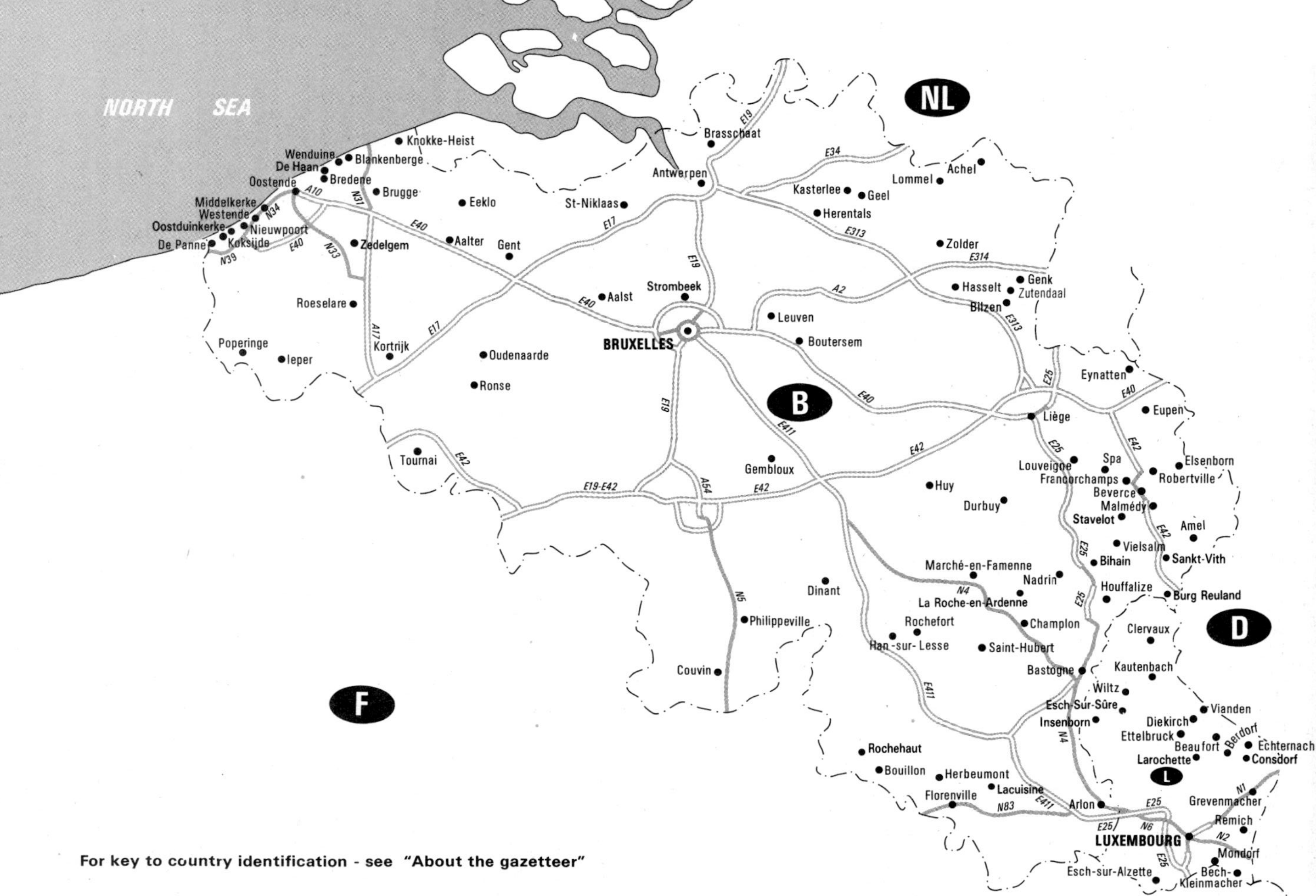

For key to country identification - see "About the gazetteer"

ARLON (AARLEN) *Luxembourg*

H Druides (n.rest) r de Neufchâteau 106-108 ☎ (063) 220489 rm27 **A**

H Ecu de Bourgogne (n.rest) place Leopold 9 ☎ (063) 220222 rm19 Closed Dec 24-25 & Jan 1 **B**

★★**Nord** r des Faubourgs 2 ☎ (063) 220283 rm23 Closed Dec 16-Jan 2 **B**

BASTOGNE *Luxembourg*

H Sud (n.rest) r de Marche 39 ☎ (062) 211114 rm12 **A**

BEVERCE *Liège*

H Tchession r-de Brialmont ☎ (080) 330087 rm16 Closed Apr **B**

BIHAIN *Luxembourg*

H Casseroles Baraque de Fraiture ☎ (080) 418808 rm32 **B**

H Hautes Ardennes rte de Houffalize 41 ☎ (080) 418845 rm7 **A**

H Val d'Hebron r Hebronvat 59 ☎ (080) 418873 rm12 Closed Aug 16-31 **A**

BILZEN *Limburg*

H British Maastrichterstr 20 ☎ (011) 411801 rm20 **A**

BLANKENBERGE *West-Vlaanderen*

◆ **Alfa** (n.rest) Kerkstr 92 ☎ (050) 418172 rm52 **A**

H Berkeley Zeedijk 93 ☎ (050) 411002 rm24 Mar 26-Sep **A**

H Commerce Weststr 64 ☎ (050) 411430 rm27 Mar 26-Oct 14 **A**

◆ **E.T.M Bach** (n.rest) Vissersstr 20 ☎ (050) 419771 rm13 Closed Nov 15-Feb 15 **A**

◆ **Jules Cesar** Vanderstichelenstr 25 ☎ (050) 411427 rm18 Mar 26-Sep 17 **A**

H Louvre Kertstr 147 ☎ (050) 411188 rm13 Closed Jan 15-30 **A**

H Martinique (n.rest) Seb Vernieuwestr 10 ☎ (050) 411158 rm14 May-Sep 14 **A**

H Metro J-De-Troozlaan 42 ☎ (050) 411164 rm49 Mar 26-Sep **A**

H Miramar Zeedijk 169 ☎ (050) 412949 rm34 **A**

H Providence Zeedijk 191 ☎ (050) 411198 rm33 Feb 16-Nov 14 **A**

H Reyns Verwéehelling 4 ☎ (050) 412459 rm20 Apr-Sep **A**

H Richmond Van Maerlanstr 81 ☎ (050) 411538 rm22 May 16-Sep **A**

H Rotessa Conscienzsestr 47 ☎ (050) 418625 rm36 Feb-Nov 2 **A**

H St-Sauveur Langestr 50 ☎ (050) 418585 rm63 **A**

◆ **Thierry** Vanderstichelenstr 11-13 ☎ (050) 418570 rm10 Mar-Sep **A**

H Thonnon De Smet de Nayerlaan 54 ☎ (050) 411538 rm40 May 16-Sep **B**

◆ **Tourist** Weststr 15 ☎ (050) 412581 rm10 Closed Jan **A**

H Trianon Elisabethstr 2 ☎ (050) 411715 rm13 Mar-Sep **A**

BOUILLON *Luxembourg*

H Aux Armes de Bouillon r de la Station 9-15 ☎ (061) 466079 rm72 **A**

H Cerf rte de Florenville ☎ (061) 467011 rm13 Closed Oct 4-15 **A**

H France Faubourg de France 1 ☎ (061) 466068 rm16 **A**

★★**Panorama** r au-dessus de la Ville 25 ☎ (061) 466138 rm45 Mar 16-Nov **A**

★★**Poste** pl St-Arnould 1 ☎ (061) 466506 rm80 **A**

BOUTERSEM *Brabant*

H Corona (n.rest) Leuvensesteenweg 143 ☎ (016) 733218 rm6 **B**

BRASSCHAAT *Antwerp*

H Pendennis Castle Augustijnslei 52 ☎ (03) 6518318 rm25 **A**

BREDENE *West-Vlaanderen*

H Europa Kapellestr 181 ☎ (059) 321193 rm58 Mar-Sep **A**

◆ **Lusthof** Zegelaan 18 ☎ (059) 325959 rm13 **A**

H Meiboom Kapellestr 7 ☎ (059) 321677 rm17 Closed Jan 15-Feb 15 **A**

BRUGGE (BRUGES) *West-Vlaanderen*

Brugge is a picture-postcard town of pretty gabled houses and quiet backwaters crossed by arched bridges and overhung with willows. It has a reputation as the best preserved medieval town in Europe, and it is easy to understand why. Savour this 'Venice of the North', with its distinctive 16th-century merchants' houses, on a pleaceful cruise along the canals and the Lake of Love, or wend your way through the cobbled streets in a horse-drawn carriage. Or simply stroll along quiet lanes and quaysides.

The main square is dominatd by the 225ft belfry, from where the carillon peals out across the town, and which offers a panoramic view of the surroundings.

EATING OUT Brugge has a range of restaurants which cater for all tastes and budgets and which live up to the high reputation of Belgian cuisine. Being so close to the coast, fresh fish and seafood are delicious specialities, and there is plenty to satisy the heartiest appetite.

If money is no object, *De Witte Poorte*, in Jan Van Eyckplein, is highly recommended. It specialises in fresh fish and game in season. The moderately-priced *Oud Brugge* is located in an ancient, vaulted building in Kuiperstraat, while for inexpensive local dishes and Flemish ambience the *Gistelhof*, in West Gistelhof, is justly popular.

◆ **Imperial** (n.rest) Dweerstr 28 ☎ (050) 339014 rm6 **A**

H Koningshof (n.rest) Clarastr 103 ☎ (050) 337250 rm17 **A**

H Lodewijk Van Male Malseweg Steenweg 488 ☎ (050) 355763 rm13 **B**

★**Lybeer** Korte Vuldersstr 31 ☎ (050) 334355 rm22 Mar-Nov 14 **A**

H Rembrandt-Reubens (n.rest) Walplein 38 ☎ (050) 336439 rm12 Mar 16-Sep **A**

H Smedepoort (n.rest) Gistelsteenweg 7 ☎ (050) 387949 rm12 Jul & Aug **A**

H Ter Poel (n.rest) Handboogstr 1 ☎ (050) 316797 rm12 Closed Nov 10-30 **A**

BRUXELLES (BRUSSEL) *Brabant*

Bruxelles is one of the relatively undiscovered capitals of Europe and has a genuinely friendly and cosmopolitan atmosphere. Its international flavour is born partly from playing host to the headquarters of NATO, the EEC and the European Parliament, and partly from its trading heritage at the crossroads of Europe.

This is a bi-lingual city, the natives switching from French to Flemish with nonchalant ease. The best known symbol of its international appeal is the Atomium, built it 1958 for the World Fair and representing an iron molecule magnified 20 billion times.
Much of Bruxelles' charm lies in its old world atmosphere, however, and this is epitomised in the Grand' Place, which ranks among the most beautiful squares in the world, and in the Baroque architecture of the merchants' houses and the Town Hall. The wealth of museums and art galleries includes a Brewery Museum, a Museum of Costume and Lace, the Autoworld Motor Museum and a magnificent collection of paintings by such masters as Rubens and Breugel in the Gallery of Ancient Art.
The city offers the best of both worlds for shopping – the small shops in the narrow streets of the old quarter and department stores in the modern arcades; souvenirs include luxurious confectionary, spicy gingerbread, crystal and Brussels lace.
EATING OUT Among the experts of the gourmet world Bruxelles is held in very high esteem. You will find the highest standards in restaurants of modest appearance, but even at inexpensive places you will find speciality dishes of remarkable value. Seafood, especially mussels, is a great favourite, and the meat dishes are unusual and extremely tasty, particularly Flemish *carbonnade* – beef braised in beer. There are creamy cheeses and syrupy waffles, and it is difficult to resist the chocolates and pralines. There are self-service restaurants in large stores which provide excellent meals at reasonable prices.
Chez Vincent and the restaurants of the Rue des Bouchers, just off the Grand' Place in the centre of the city, have excellent reputations, as do those at Sainte Catherine near the old fish market.

H Armorial (n.rest) bd B-Whitlock 101 ☏ (02) 7345636 rm15 **A**

H France (n.rest) bd Jamar 21, Jamarlaan ☏ (02) 5227935 rm27 **A**

H Gascogne bd A-Max 137 ☏ (02) 2176962 rm18 Closed Aug **A**

◆ **Grande Cloche** (n.rest) pl Rouppe 10 ☏ (02) 5126140 rm45 **A**

◆ **Les Bluets** r Breckmans 124 ☏ (02) 5384428 rm9 **A**

H Madeleine (n.rest) r de la Montagne 22 ☏ (02) 5132971 rm52 **B**

◆ **New Galaxy** (n.rest) r du Progrès 7A ☏ (02) 2194775 rm36 **A**

★★**Noga** (n.rest) r de Beguinage 38 ☏ (02) 2186763 rm19 **A**

◆ **Paris** (n.rest) bd Poincaré 80 ☏ (02) 5238153 rm27 **A**

◆ **Rembrant** (n.rest) r de la Concorde 57 ☏ (02) 5127139 rm10 **A**

H Sabina (n.rest) r du Nord 78 ☏ (02) 2182637 rm22 **A**

◆ **St-Michel** Grand place ☏ (02) 5110956 rm15 **A**

★★**Van Belle** Chaussée de Mons 39 ☏ (02) 5213516 rm137 **B**

H Yser r d'Edingbourg 9-13 ☏ (02) 5117459 rm42 Closed Jul 15-Aug 15 **A**

BURG REULAND *Liège*

H Burghof Wenzelbach 43 ☏ (080) 329801 rm12 **A**

H Dreiländerblick Oouren 29 ☏ (080) 329071 rm15 Closed Jan- Feb 15 **A**

H Paquet Lascheid 43 ☏ (080) 329624 rm14 **A**

H Rittersprung (n.rest) Dorfstrabe 19 ☏ (080) 329135 rm22 Closed Dec-15 Jan **B**

CHAMPLON *Luxembourg*

◆ **Barrière de Champion** Barrière 31 ☏ (084) 455155 rm21 **B**

COUVIN *Namur*

H Forges de Pernelle r de Pernelle 29 ☏ (060) 344802 rm16 Closed Feb 1-28 **A**

H Place Verte r Faubourg St Germain 71 ☏ (060) 344822 rm7 Closed Aug 16-31 **A**

H Sapiniere Pied de la Montagne 7 ☏ (060) 344381 rm8 Closed Jan **A**

DINANT *Namur*

H Belle-Vue (n.rest) rte de Philleville 1-3 ☏ (082) 222924 rm7 **B**

H Citadelle pl R-Astrid 5 ☏ (082) 223543 rm20 Mar-Nov **B**

★★**Couronne** r A-Sax 1 ☏ (082) 222441 rm22 Closed Jan 2-14 & Jun 15-30 **B**

H Routiers r F-d'Esperey ☏ (082) 222709 rm10 **A**

DURBUY *Luxembourg*

H Clos des Recollets (n.rest) ☏ (086) 211271 rm11 **A**

H Falize (n.rest) r A-Eloi 59 ☏ (086) 212666 rm13 **B**

H Prevôt r des Recollectines 71 ☏ (086) 212300 rm9 Closed Feb 15-31 **A**

EEKLO *Oost-Vlaanderen*

★**Rembrandt** Kon-Astridpl 2 ☏ (091) 772570 rm8 Closed Sep **A**

H Zeewende Zeelaan 5 ☏ (091) 773692 rm10 **A**

ELSENBORN *Liège*

H Zum Truschbaum Lagerstr 2 ☏ (080) 446047 rm9 Closed Jun 26-Jul 7 & Aug 28-Sep 28 **A**

EUPEN *Liège*

H Bosten Hassstr 77-81 ☏ (087) 740800 rm29 **B**

★★**Bosten Hotel** Verviersstr 2-4 ☏ (087) 742209 rm11 Closed Dec 24-26 **A**

EYNATTEN *Liège*

◆ **Tychon** Aachenerstr 30 ☏ (087) 851236 rm8 Closed (Dec 23-Jan 2) **A**

FLORENVILLE *Luxembourg*

★★**France** r des G-Cuvelier 26 ☏ (061) 311032 rm30 **B**

FRANCORCHAMPS *Liège*

H Beau Sejour Hockai 435 ☏ (087) 275020 rm27 Closed Jul **A**

H Belle Vue Hockai 455 ☏ (087) 275024 rm11 **B**

◆ **Bruyeres** pl de la Gare 240 ☏ (087) 275038 rm8 **A**

GEEL *Antwerpen*

◆ **Postiljon** Technische Schoolstr 41 ☏ (014) 586478 rm12 **A**

H Sportwarande Markt 91 ☏ (041) 588019 rm9 **A**

GEMBLOUX *Namur*

H Les 3 Clés chaussée de Namur 17 ☏ (081) 611617 rm43 **A**

GENK *Limburg*

◆ **t'Hert** Winterslagstr 11 ☏ (011) 352769 rm8 **A**

◆ **Bij Ford** Sledderlo 82 ☏ (011) 612865 rm14 **A**

◆ **Drive-Inn** Hasseltweg 475 ☏ (011) 229556 rm15 **A**

H Majestic (n.rest) Europalaan 68 ☎ (011) 352006 rm12 **A**

◆ **Uilenspiegel** Socialestr 4 ☎ (011) 380157 rm12 **A**

GENT (GAND) *Oost-Vlaanderen*

The former capital of the Counts of Flanders, Gent has had a fascinating history from which it has emerged as a very beautiful city, with numerous medieval buildings, churches and art galleries. It has as many canals as Brugge, and these all lead in the direction of the picturesque old port area of Graslei. Beside the canals of the Graslei area stand a wealth of beautifully preserved medieval merchants' houses and guildhalls; the Butchers' Hall (*Groot Vleehuis*), the Korenlei and the Fishmongers' Hall are particularly interesting.
The countryside around the town forms a coloured carpet of flowers tended by horticulturists who have made the garden fields of Gent famous.
EATING OUT *Carbonnades flamandes*, a dish of beef cooked in beer, is generally better here than in most other regions of Belgium. Other specialities include *waterzooi*, a delicious fish stew with herbs, leeks and cream – and *gentse hutsepot*, containing all sorts of meats and virtually all the vegetables Flanders produces.

H Benelux (n.rest) Recollettenlei 1 ☎ (091) 250731 rm15 **B**

H Karper Kortrijksesteenweg 2 ☎ (091) 221053 rm15 **A**

◆ **Maldegem** Antwerpsesteenwegh 7 ☎ (091) 282177 rm10 Closed Dec 22-Jan 2 **A**

HAAN, DE *West-Vlaanderen*

H Astel Koninklijke Baan 17 ☎ (059) 234333 rm25 Closed Nov-Dec 20 **A**

H Belle Vue Koninlijk Plein 5 ☎ (059) 233439 rm49 Mar 16-Oct 9 **A**

H Bon Accueil (n.rest) Montaignelaan 2 ☎ (059) 233114 rm20 Mar 26-Nov 4 **A**

H Bristol Leopoldlaan 5 ☎ (059) 233465 rm20 Mar 16-Nov 14 **A**

H Internos Leopoldlaan 12 ☎ (059) 233579 rm17 **A**

H Strand Zeedijk 19 ☎ (059) 233425 rm15 Closed Nov **A**

HAN-SUR-LESSE *Namur*

H Escale r d'Hamptay 54 ☎ (084) 377210 rm7 Closed Jan **A**

H Lesse r des Grottes 1 ☎ (084) 377433 rm7 Closed Jan-Mar **B**

★★**Voyageurs** r des Chasseurs Ardennais 1 ☎ (084) 377237 rm30 Closed Jan-Mar **B**

HASSELT *Limburg*

★**Century** Leopoldplein 1 ☎ (011) 224799 rm17 **A**

H Schoofs Stationspl 7 ☎ (011) 223188 rm14 Closed Jul 15-30 **A**

HEISTSee **KNOKKE-HEIST**

HERBEUMONT *Luxembourg*

H Bravy Grand Place 9 ☎ (061) 411035 rm22 Jan-Mar **B**

H Châtelaine Grand pl 8 ☎ (061) 411422 rm35 Mar 16-Dec **B**

H Renaissance Grand Place 3 ☎ (061) 411083 rm12 Closed Jan-Feb 15 **B**

HERENTALS *Antwerp*

H Golf Lierseweg 321 ☎ (014) 211836 rm12 Closed Jul 7-Aug 1 **B**

H Zalm Grote Markt 21 ☎ (014) 221417 rm11 Closed Aug 1-15 **A**

HOUFFALIZE *Luxembourg*

◆ **Relais** r de Bastogne 12 ☎ (062) 288164 rm9 **A**

HUY (HOEI) *Liège*

H Aige Noir Q-Dautrebande 8 ☎ (085) 212341 rm11 **A**

H Reserve Chaussée de Napoléon 9 ☎ (085) 212403 rm9 **B**

IEPER (YPRES) *West-Vlaanderen*

★**St-Nicolas** G-de Stuerstr 6 ☎ (057) 200622 rm6 Closed Jul 16-Aug 7 **B**

KASTERLEE *Antwerpen*

H Bergenhof Geelsebaan 85 ☎ (014) 556044 rm14 Closed Oct **A**

◆ **Den En Heuvel** Geelsebaan 72 ☎ (014) 556097 rm28 **A**

★★**Dennen** Lichtaartsebaan 79 ☎ (014) 556107 rm12 **A**

H Fauwater Lichtaartsebaan 104 ☎ (014) 556445 rm18 **A**

H Kempenrust Geelsebaan 51-53 ☎ (014) 556009 rm20 **A**

H Sparrenhof Lichaartsebaan 77 ☎ (014) 556161 rm14 Closed Oct **A**

KNOKKE-HEIST *West-Vlaanderen*

H Arcades (n.rest) Elizabetlaan 50 ☎ (050) 601073 rm11 Mar 26-Sep 14 **B**

H Argousiers Josi Nellenslaan 229 ☎ (050) 601468 rm22 Feb 4-Nov 6 **A**

H Britannia Elizabetlaan 85 ☎ (050) 601441 rm35 Closed Nov 15-Dec 19 **B**

H Chatel Tinel Elizabetlaan 83 ☎ (050) 603653 rm27 **A**

H Corner House Hazegrasstr 1 ☎ (050) 607619 rm20 **A**

H Lautrec (n.rest) Duinenstr 3 ☎ (050) 513625 rm8 Closed Nov 10-Dec 12 **A**

◆ **Loris** Elizabetlaan 8 ☎ (050) 601523 rm9 Closed Oct 1-26 **A**

H Pingouins ☎ (050) 513340 rm11 Closed Oct 5-25 **A**

H Prins Boudewijn Lippenslaan 35-37 ☎ (050) 601016 rm28 **A**

◆ **St.Christophe** Antoine Breartstr 10 ☎ (050) 601152 rm17 Closed Nov 13-Dec 15 **A**

H Sint-Yves Zeedijk 204 ☎ (050) 511029 rm17 **A**

H Trianon Zeedijk 499 ☎ (050) 601948 rm43 Closed Mar 26-Sep 19 **A**

KOKSIJDE (COXYDE-SUR-MER) *West-Vlaanderen*

◆ **Astrid** Koninklijke Baan 315 ☎ (058) 512342 rm18 Feb 11-Nov 14 **A**

H Carlton Koninklijke Baan 174 ☎ (058) 511012 rm16 Closed Jan 18-Feb 15 **A**

H Echo de la Mer Koninklijke Baan 105 ☎ (058) 511281 rm14 Closed Nov 15-Dec 15 **A**

◆ **Equateur** Zeelaan 75 ☎ (058) 515603 rm5 **A**

H Inter-Nos Koninklijke Baan 120 ☎ (058) 511313 rm15 Apr-Sep **A**

H Lehouck Koninklijke Baan 122 ☎ (058) 511457 rm27 Mar-Sep **B**

◆ **Normandie** Koninklijke Baan 1 ☎ (058) 511091 rm23 **A**

★★**Royal** (n.rest) Zeedijk 65 ☎ (058) 511300 rm29 Closed Nov 15-Dec 22 **A**

H Vieren Zeedijk 59 ☎ (058) 511349 rm20 Mar 26-Sep **A**

H Zouaves Zeelaan 254 ☎ (058) 511316 rm15 Mar-Jan 14 **A**

KORTRIJK (COURTRAI) *West-Vlaanderen*

H Groeninge Groeningestr 1A ☎ (056) 226000 rm11 **B**

H Jagershof (n.rest) Noordstr 1 ☎ (056) 354093 rm8 Closed Aug 1-15 **A**

H Kapittel (n.rest) Kapittelstr 18 ☎ (056) 219515 rm9 **A**

LACUISINE *Luxembourg*

H Belvedere (n.rest) r des Iles 34 ☎ (061) 311101 rm13 Apr-Sep 14 **A**

H Vallee r du Fond des Naux 7 ☎ (061) 311140 rm12 Closed Feb 1-15 **B**

H Vieux Moulin ☎ (061) 311076 rm16 Closed Feb 1-28 **B**

LEUVEN (LOUVAIN) *Brabant*

H Industrie Martelarenpl 7 ☎ (016) 221349 rm18 **B**

◆ **Jackson's** Brusselestr 110-112 ☎ (016) 202491 rm14 **A**

H Majestic (n.rest) Bondgenotenlaan 110-112 ☎ (016) 224365 rm14 **A**

H Royale (n.rest) Martelarenpl 6 ☎ (016) 221252 rm22 Closed Dec 23-Jan 2 **A**

LIÈGE (LUIK) *Liège*

H Couronne pl des Guillemins 11 ☎ (041) 512168 rm78 **B**

◆ **Darchis** Darchis 18 ☎ (041) 234218 rm18 **A**

H Metropole r des Guillemins 141 ☎ (041) 524293 rm28 **A**

H Midi pl des Guillemins 1 ☎ (041) 522004 **A**

◆ **Nations** r Guillemins 139 ☎ (041) 524434 rm10 **A**

H Univers (n.rest) r des Guillemins 116 ☎ (041) 522650 rm51 **B**

LOMMEL *Limburg*

◆ **Susamie** (n.rest) Kerkhovensteenweg 350 ☎ (011) 341872 rm4 **A**

LOUVEIGNE *Liège*

H Nations r de l'Esplanade 28 ☎ (041) 608105 rm14 **A**

MALMÉDY *Liège*

H Albert pl Albert Ier 40 ☎ (080) 330452 rm7 **B**

H Warche pl de Rome 12 ☎ (080) 330364 rm6 **A**

MARCHE-EN-FAMENNE *Luxembourg*

★**Alfa** (n.rest) rte de Rochefort 11 ☎ (084) 311793 rm21 **A**

MIDDELKERKE *West-Vlaanderen*

H Atlanta (n.rest) Koninginnelaan 46 ☎ (059) 300376 rm20 Mar-Sep **B**

H Kapelle Diksmuidestr 68 ☎ (059) 278434 rm4 Closed Jan 9-Feb 2 **A**

H Leopold Leopoldlaan 87 ☎ (059) 300201 rm13 **A**

H Littoral Zeedijk 79 ☎ (059) 300754 rm10 Closed Nov 20-Dec 23 **A**

H Terminus De Smet Denaeyerstr 42 ☎ (059) 300142 rm8 Mar 19-Sep 15 **A**

MONS (BERGEN) *Hainaut*

H St-Georges (n.rest) r des Clercs 15 ☎ (065) 311629 rm9 **A**

NADRIN *Luxembourg*

◆ **Belvedere** r du Hérou 70 ☎ (084) 444193 rm17 Closed Jan **B**

H Cinq Ourthes r du Hérou 72 ☎ (084) 444131 rm7 Closed Jan **B**

H Hérou (n.rest) r du Hérou 66 ☎ (084) 444131 rm7 Closed Jan **B**

◆ **Ondes** Villa Romaine 21 ☎ (084) 444111 rm12 Mar 16-Jan 14 **B**

NIEUWPOORT *West-Vlaanderen*

H Beau Séjour Albert I-Laan 98 ☎ (058) 233522 rm14 **A**

◆ **Kogge** Albert-I-Laan 167 ☎ (058) 233148 rm11 **A**

H Pacific Albert-I-Laan 97 ☎ (058) 234034 rm8 Closed Nov 14-31 **A**

OOSTDUINKERKE *West-Vlaanderen*

H Flandria Zeedijk 240 ☎ (058) 511783 rm8 Jan 16-Dec 14 **A**

H Gauquie Leopold II-str 251 ☎ (058) 511088 rm75 seasonal **A**

H Hof Ter Duinen Albert-I-laan 141 ☎ (058) 513241 rm18 Closed Jan 2-Feb 4 **A**

H Rayon d'Or Albert-I-laan 177 ☎ (058) 233379 rm9 Closed Jan 8-Feb 5 **A**

H Westland Zeedijk 9 ☎ (058) 513197 rm28 **B**

OOSTENDE (OSTENDE) *West-Vlaanderen*

Oostende is the largest resort on the Belgian coast, offering extensive sandy beaches, an attractive promenade, picturesque yacht harbour and excellent hotels, restaurants and visitor facilities. The five main beaches are free except for the Lido Beach, where the small entrance fee includes the use of deck chairs. The Dolphin's Beach next to the Lido is reserved exclusively for children under 14 and most of the wide promenade is traffic-free. The Olympic-size indoor swimming pool is open all year round, while during July and August there is also an excellent outdoor sea-water pool.

The centre of Oostende has large traffic-free shopping precincts with a range of boutiques and stores to match any major city. The town square is lined with flower-decked pavement cafés where you can sit and listen to the band while enjoying a drink or a celebrated Belgian waffle with fresh strawberries and cream.

EATING OUT The Casino's restaurant, *Périgord*, is one of the most fashionable places to eat.

H André Diksmuidestr 4 ☎ (059) 702207 rm16 Closed Nov 9-Dec 19 **B**

H Ariel Ad-Buylstr 1A ☎ (059) 700837 rm13 Closed Jan 7-Feb 7 **A**

H Clifford Passchijnstr 4 ☎ (059) 703625 rm13 **A**

◆ **Die Prince** Albert I Promenade 41-42 ☎ (059) 706507 rm46 **B**

H Flandria (n.rest) Visserskaai 43 ☎ (059) 805184 rm6 **A**

★**Glenmore** Horfstr 25 ☎ (059) 702022 rm40 Closed Jan-Feb 15 **A**

◆ **Maritime** (n.rest) St-Petrus en Paulusplein 20 ☎ (059) 701457 rm12 **A**

H Polaris Groentemarkt 19 ☎ (059) 501602 rm19 **A**

H Serge Brusselstr 15 ☎ (059) 803434 rm15 **A**

H Touring Visserskaai 4 ☎ (059) 703578 rm15 **A**

H Valldemosa Kapucijnenstr 31 ☎ (059) 706416 rm24 **A**

H Viking Boekarestr 2 ☎ (059) 707661 rm25 **A**

OUDENAARDE (AUDENARDE) *Oost-Vlaanderen*

H Elnik (n.rest) Deinzestr 55 ☎ (055) 313788 rm14 **A**

◆ **Moriaanshoofd** Moriaanshoof 27 ☎ (091) 843787 rm7 **A**

H Zalm Hoogstr 4 ☎ (055) 311314 rm7 Closed Jul 10-31 **B**

PANNE, DE *West-Vlaanderen*

H Ambassadeurs Duinkerlaan 43 ☎ (058) 411612 rm33 Mar 26-Sep **A**

H Artevelde (n.rest) Sloepenlaan 24 ☎ (058) 411051 rm25 Feb 3-Sep **A**

H Botaniek (n.rest) Zeelaan 8 ☎ (058) 415010 rm14 **A**

H Cecil Markplien 14 ☎ (058) 411341 rm18 **A**

H Français Kasteelstr 31 ☎ (058) 411739 rm12 Mar 16-Oct 14 **A**

H Hamburg Zeelaan 61 ☎ (058) 411382 rm8 **A**

H Princes Nieuwpoortlaan 46 ☎ (058) 411091 rm36 Feb-Oct **A**

◆ **Roucoufou** Duinkerkelaan 29 ☎ (059) 411517 rm10 **A**

PHILIPPEVILLE *Namur*

★**Croisée** r de France 45 ☎ (071) 666231 rm15 Closed Jan-Feb 15 **B**

POPERINGE *West-Vlaanderen*

H Kring Burg Bertenpl 7 ☎ (057) 333861 rm7 Closed Feb 1-14 & Aug 8-29 **B**

H Palace Leperstr 34 ☎ (057) 333093 rm11 Closed Apr 11-Mar 26 **B**

ROBERTVILLE *Liège*

H Edelwiess r de Botrange 105 ☎ (080) 446441 rm10 Closed Mar **B**

H Fagna D-Mont Jacques 12 ☎ (080) 446479 rm8 Closed Sep 1-15 **A**

H Frequence r Centrale 32 ☎ (080) 445480 rm9 **A**

H Vieux Hetre Andrifosse 47 ☎ (080) 446445 rm9 **B**

ROCHE-EN-ARDENNE, LA *Luxembourg*

H Bristol r Châmont 3 ☎ (084) 411385 rm6 Closed Nov 20-Dec 20 **A**

H Chalet r du Châlet 61 ☎ (084) 411197 rm17 Apr-Jan 2 **B**

H Herou av de Villez 53 ☎ (084) 411420 rm8 **A**

H Moderne r Chamont 26 ☎ (084) 411124 rm12 Dec 20-Jan 10 **A**

H Villa les Oliivettes chemin de Saret 12 ☎ (084) 411652 rm12 Closed Jan 15-Feb 15 **B**

ROCHEFORT *Namur*

H Central (n.rest) pl Albert 1er 30 ☎ (084) 211044 rm12 Closed Mar 1-15 **A**

★**Fayette** r Jacquet 87 ☎ (084) 214273 rm9 Closed Oct 1-13 **A**

H Limbourg pl Albert 1er 21-23 ☎ (084) 211036 rm6 Closed Feb & Aug 28-Sep 9 **A**

H Trou Maulin rte de Marché 19 ☎ (084) 213240 rm7 Closed Jan 2-Feb 9 & Sep 25-Oct 6 **A**

H Vieux Logis (n.rest) r Jacquet 71 ☎ (084) 211024 rm11 Closed Sep 15-31 **B**

ROCHEHAUT *Luxembourg*

H Falaises (n.rest) r de Nazareth 47 ☎ (061) 466538 rm6 Closed Jan 6-26 **A**

H Naturel des Ardennes r Section Hour 19 ☎ (061) 466516 rm14 Closed Jan-Feb 15 **A**

ROESELARE (ROULERS) *West-Vlaanderen*

H Java Ooststr 18 ☎ (051) 200007 bed15 **A**

RONSE (RENAIX) *Oost-Vlaanderen*

H Alfa Grete Markt 40 ☎ (055) 213846 rm7 **A**

H Auberge St-Sebastien St-Pietersnieuwstr 38 ☎ (055) 213866 rm6 Closed Aug 1-15 **A**

◆ **Savoy** W.Churchillplien 1 ☎ (055) 213756 rm14 **A**

ST-HUBERT *Luxembourg*

H Borquin pl le l'Abbaye 6 ☎ (061) 611456 rm9 Closed Aug 16-Sep 3 **A**

◆ **Luxembourg** pl du Marché 7 ☎ (061) 611093 rm16 **B**

SANKT-VITH *Liège*

H Luxembourg Haupstrabe 71 ☎ (080) 228022 rm7 Closed Jul 1-18 **A**

H Marquet Haupstrabe 41 ☎ (080) 228200 rm8 Closed Nov 15-Dec 15 **A**

H Pip-Margraff Haupstrabe 7 ☎ (080) 228663 rm21 **A**

SINT NIKLAAS (ST-NICOLAS) *Oost-Vlaanderen*

H Spiegel (n.rest) Stationsstr 1 ☎ (03) 7763437 rm26 **A**

SPA *Liège*

H Gai Séjour bd Rener 6 ☎ (087) 773840 rm13 **A**

STAVELOT *Liège*

H Baron r Petit Coo 6 ☎ (080) 684093 rm12 **A**

H Mal Aime r Neuve 12 ☎ (080) 862001 rm10 Closed Sep 14-Oct 2 **A**

H Orange r de Spa 8 ☎ (080) 862005 rm23 Seasonal **A**

STROMBEEK *Brabant*

◆ **Auberge de Strombeek** Temselaan 6 ☎ (02) 4606467 rm13 Closed Jul **A**

◆ **Chateau d'Eau** Romeinsesteenweg 578 ☎ (02) 4601085 rm11 Closed Jul & Aug **A**

◆ **Pere Boudart** Romeinsesteenweg 592 ☎ (02) 4607496 rm22 **A**

TOURNAI *Hainaut*

H Cathedrale pl Saint-Pierre ☎ (069) 215077 rm45 **B**

H Europe Grand Pl 36 ☎ (069) 224067 rm8 Closed Jul **A**

H Tour St-Georges r St-Georges 2 ☎ (069) 225035 rm10 **A**

VIELSALM *Luxembourg*

H Belle Vue r J-Bertholet 5 ☎ (080) 216261 rm14 **A**

H Myrtilles r du V-Marché 1 ☎ (080) 215140 rm18 Closed Jan 15-Feb 15 **A**

WELLIN *Luxembourg*

◆ **The Trees** (n.rest) 1 r des Marronniers ☎ (084) 388461 **A**

WENDUINE *West-Vlaanderen*

★★**Mouettes** Zeedijk Wenduine 7 ☎ (050) 411514 rm30 Mar 25-Sep 25 **A**

◆ **Yvan** Zeedijk 8 ☎ (050) 411453 rm25 Apr-Sep **A**

WESTENDE *West-Vlaanderen*

H Marie-Joseph (n.rest) H-Jasparlaan 150 ☎ (059) 303248 rm15 **B**

H Maritime (n.rest) Distellaan 5 ☎ (059) 300671 rm15 **B**

★★**Rotonde** Zeedijk 300 ☎ (059) 300495 rm15 Apr-Sep **B**

◆ **Westendia** Duinenlaan 35 ☎ (059) 233663 rm10 Closed Nov 15-Dec 25 **A**

ZEDELGEM *West-Vlaanderen*

H Bonne Auberge Torhoutsesteenweg 201 ☎ (050) 209525 rm27 **B**

H Zuidwege Torhoutsesteenweg 126-128 ☎ (050) 201339 rm22 **A**

ZOLDER *Limburg*

H Pergola St-Jobstr 77 ☎ (011) 252350 rm10 **B**

ZUTENDAAL *Limburg*

H Klok Daalstr 9 ☎ (001) 611131 rm8 **A**

The fairytale Castle of Beersel

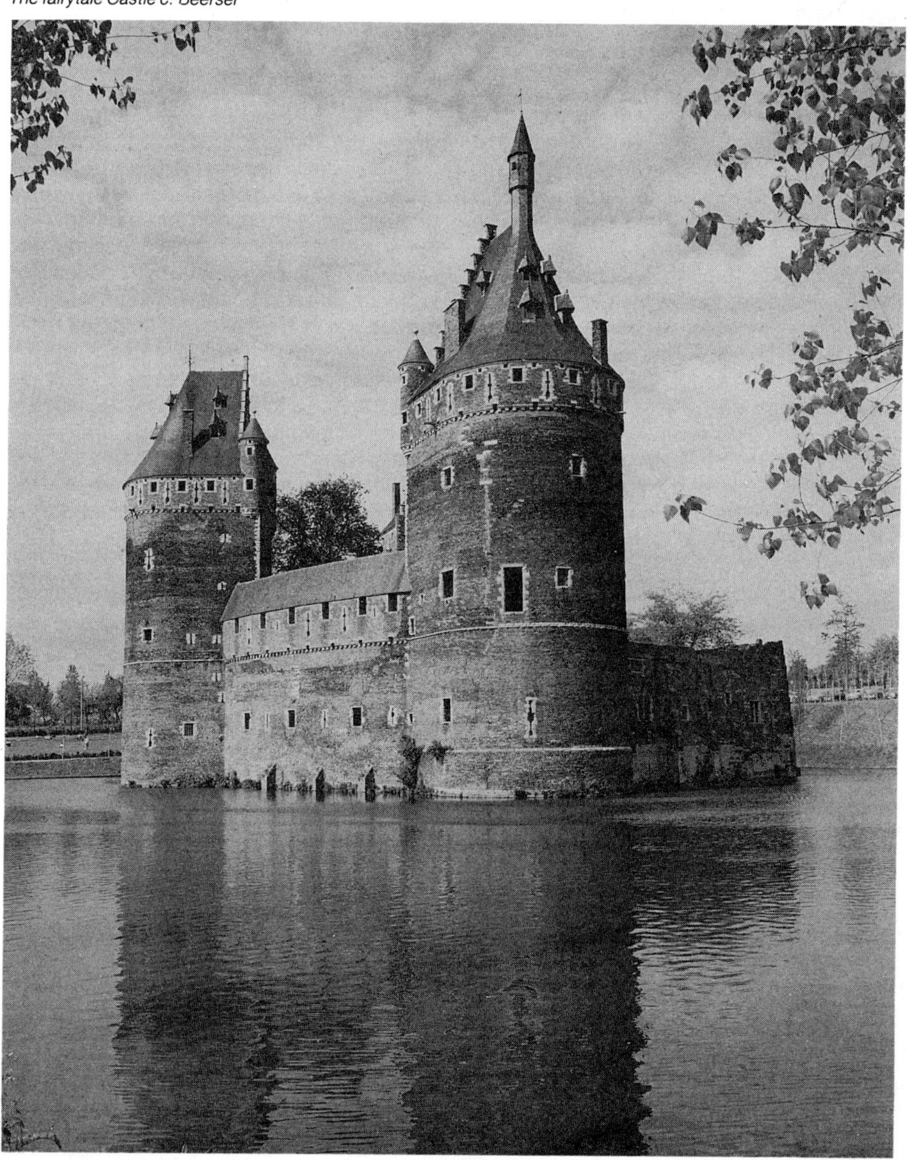

DENMARK

FACTS & FIGURES

Capital: København (Copenhagen)
Language: Danish
IDD code: 45. To call the UK dial 009 44
Currency: Danish krone (DKK1 = 100øre)
Local time: GMT+1 (Summer GMT+2)
Emergency Services: Police, Fire & Ambulance 000

Business hours

Banks:
0900–1600 Mon–Wed & Fri, 0930–1800 Thur
Shops:
0900–1730 Mon–Fri, 0930–1300 Sat

Average daily temperatures:
København °C

Jan 0	Jul 18
Mar 2	Sep 14
May 11	Nov 5

Tourist Information:
The Danish Tourist Board

UK Sceptre House
169/173 Regent Street
London W1R 8PY
Tel 01–734 2637

USA 655 Third Ave
New York, NY 10017
Tel (212) 949–2333

This land of fairytales is also a land that loves children and where everyone seems to live life to the full. Denmark has pretty countryside, a marvellous coastline with vast, sandy beaches ideal for watersports of all kinds, and fun-filled leisure attractions that have wide appeal. Wherever you go in this ancient kingdom, famed for its warmth and hospitality, you will never be more than 30 miles from the sea, and all around will be lovely countryside of forests and heather-clad moors, rolling meadowlands or nature reserves.

Denmark is divided into three distinct regions, and although the country is by no means large, there is considerable water between them. The 'garden island' of Funen in the middle separates mainland Jutland to the west and in the other direction Sjaelland, with Copenhagen its main, but by no means only, target for visitors. Indeed, the undeniable attractions of the capital tend to obscure the rest of Denmark – and quite unfairly. Like most capitals, Copenhagen is not typical of the country, and any balanced visit should include one or more other centres, too.

HOW TO GET THERE

BY CAR

To reach Denmark you can use one of the direct ferry services that operate between Harwich and Esbjerg in western Jutland (15–20 hrs), Newcastle and Esbjerg (summer only, 19–22 hrs) or Newcastle and Hirsthals in northern Jutland (approx 25 hrs); alternatively, you could use one of the short Channel crossings to France or Belgium and drive through the Netherlands and northern Germany to Denmark. The distance from the Channel ports to København (Copenhagen) is about 660 miles and the journey would require one or two overnight stops.

Another possibility is to use the ferry operating between Harwich and Hamburg ($19\frac{1}{2}$–$21\frac{1}{2}$ hrs) and drive the short distance to southern Denmark.

Inter-island travel is made easy by either bridge links or frequent vehicle ferries.

For details of the AA's Overseas Routes Service consult the Contents page.

SPEED LIMITS

Unless indicated by signs the following limits apply: built-up areas (marked by white signs with town silhouettes) 31 mph (50 kph); outside built-up areas 49 mph (80 kph); motorways 62 mph (100 kph).

PARKING

It is advisable to use public car parks. Parking discs (obligatory for short term kerbside parking) are available from petrol stations, post offices, police stations, most tourist offices and some banks.

BY TRAIN

If you do not have an Inter Rail or Eurail pass, you can purchase rail tickets at any station (tickets for buses as well as connecting ferry crossings are also issued at all stations). Generally, there is no price reduc-

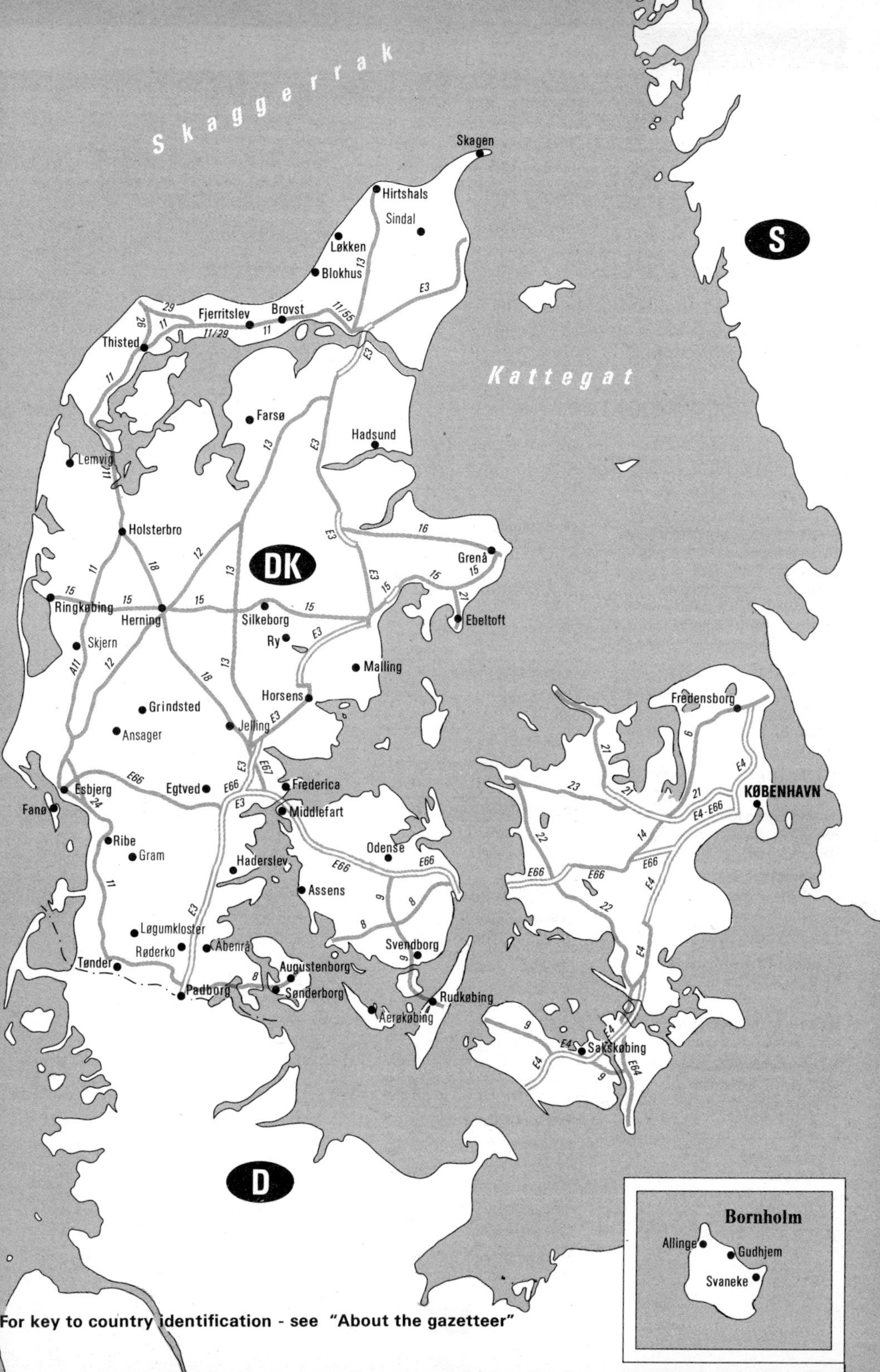

For key to country identification - see "About the gazetteer"

tion for return journeys by train; there are, however, large discounts for groups of 3 or more persons. Nordic Tourist Tickets offer unlimited travel by rail and to a certain extent by sea in Denmark, Norway, Sweden and Finland for 21 days.

BY BICYCLE

Bicycles can be rented from tourist offices (except in København), and a few railway stations in North Zealand.

ACCOMMODATION

The gazetteer contains hotels and pensions which offer accommodation for less than Dkk247 per person per night at some time during the year.

The price bands are:

A 117–182Dkk
B 182–247Dkk

taking a rate of exchange at

13Dkk=£1
8Dkk=US $1

These prices may vary during the currency of this book. The Accommodation Service, Kiosk P, Central Railway Station in København will help you find accommodation in a hotel or private house. Provincial tourist services can also provide information on accommodation in their area.

The Danish alphabet differs from the English one in that the last letters after Z are Æ, Ø, Å; this must be borne in mind when using Danish reference books. Some Danish telephone numbers are likely to change during the currency of this guide.

ÅBENRÅ *Jylland*

◆ **Bovrup** Storegade 14 ☏ (74) 680206 rm7 **A**

H Garni Bøgen Haderslevvej 48 ☏ (74) 624671 rm7 **A**

H Lundsbjerg Kro Flensborgvej 260 ☏ (74) 663595 rm14 Closed Dec 23-Jan 6 **B**

◆ **Tumbøl Kro** Tornhøjvej 21 ☏ (74) 685828 rm6 Closed Dec 20-Jan 1 **B**

AERØKØBING *Aerö*

H Aerøhus Vestergade 38 ☏ (09) 521003 rm35 Closed Dec 25-Jan 19 **B**

H Det Lille Smedegade 33 ☏ (09) 522300 rm6 Apr-Oct **A**

◆ **Dunkaer Kro** Dunkaervej 1 ☏ (09) 521554 rm8 **B**

ALLINGE *Bornholm*

◆ **Holiday** Strandvejen 82 ☏ (03) 980216 rm11 May-Sep **A**

◆ **Lindesdal** Hammersøvej 1 ☏ (03) 981750 rm15 **A**

◆ **Mary** Strandvejen 49 ☏ (03) 980333 rm21 May 12-Sep 17 **A**

◆ **Næsgården** Løsebækgade 20 ☏ (03) 980218 rm5 May 15-Sep 15 **B**

◆ **Sandbogärd** Landemaerket 3 ☏ (03) 980303 rm25 May-Sep **A**

◆ **Sandvig** Strandvej 99 ☏ (03) 980313 rm42 May-Oct 15 **B**

ANSAGER *Jylland*

H Ansager Torvet ☏ (75) 297050 rm5 **A**

ASSENS *Fyn*

◆ **Stubberup** Middelfartvej 113 ☏ (09) 791011 rm10 **B**

AUGUSTENBORG *Jylland*

◆ **Voigt Strand** Graeskobbel 21 ☏ (74) 464115 rm7 May 28-Sep 25 **A**

BLOKHUS *Jylland*

H Karnappen Strandvejen 14 ☏ (98) 249020 rm9 **A**

BROVST *Jylland*

H Brovst Kirkegade 1 ☏ (98) 231008 rm12 **B**

H Skovsgaard Hovedgaden 26 ☏ (98) 231423 rm4 Closed Dec 25-Jan 1 **A**

COPENHAGENSee **KØBENHAVN**

EBELTOFT *Jylland*

H Ebeltoft Adelgade ☏ (86) 341090 rm10 **A**

H Egsmark ☏ (86) 341303 rm6 May 15-Sep 15 **A**

EGTVED *Jylland*

◆ **Aagaard Kro** ☏ (75) 553015 rm5 **A**

H Egtved Dalgade 16 ☏ (75) 551484 rm11 Closed Dec 24-Jan 1 **B**

ESBJERG *Jylland*

◆ **Ølufvad** Ølufvadhovedvej 85 ☏ (75) 169006 rm4 **A**

H Sømandshjemmet Auktionsgade 3 ☏ (75) 120688 rm21 **A**

FANØ *Fanø*

H Kellers Strandvejen 48 ☏ (75) 163088 rm22 Mar 17-Oct 15 **B**

◆ **Tusculum** Kystvejen 13 ☏ (75) 163869 rm9 Mar 30-Sep 12 **B**

FARSØ *Jylland*

◆ **Hvalpsund Færgekro** Sundvej 87 ☏ (98) 638044 rm32 **B**

◆ **Trend Kro** Viborgvej 605 ☏ (98) 678135 rm6 **A**

FJERRITSLEV *Jylland*

◆ **Grønhøjgaard** Hjorthøj ☏ (98) 217010 rm2 Jun-Aug **A**

◆ **Havblik** Slettestrandvej 60 ☏ (98) 217026 rm2 Jun 20-Nov 1 **A**

H Klim Bjerg Klim Strandvej 156 ☏ (98) 225242 rm2 May-Sep 15 **B**

H Sanden Bjerggård Slettestrandvej 88 ☏ (98) 217133 rm2 **B**

FREDENSBORG *Sjælland*

H Country House Holmeskovvej 5 ☏ (04) 280238 rm22 **A**

FREDERICIA *Jylland*

H Snoghøjgård Gl. Færgevej 2 ☏ (75) 942225 rm16 **B**

H Sømandshjemmet Oldenborggade 13 ☏ (75) 920295 rm24 **B**

GRAM *Jylland*

★★Den Gamle Kro Slotsvej 47 ☏ (74) 821620 rm48 Closed Jan 1 **B**

◆ **Gram Slotskro** Slotsvej 52 ☏ (74) 821614 rm14 Mar-Dec **B**

GRENÅ *Jylland*

H Grenå Strand Havneplads 1 ☏ (86) 326814 rm16 **A**

◆ **Sostrup Slot** Hestehavevej 33 ☏ (86) 384111 rm32 **A**

GRINDSTED *Jylland*

H Grand Borgergade 1 ☏ (75) 320255 rm32 **B**

GUDHJEM *Bornholm*

◆ **Elleback** Melstedvej 27 ☏ (03) 985100 rm25 Apr-Oct **B**

◆ **Holkarenden** Malkestein 24 ☏ (03) 985161 rm7 May 15-Sep 20 **A**

H Therns Brøddegade 31 ☏ (03) 985099 rm24 Jun 4-Sep 5 **A**

HADERSLEV *Jylland*

H Harmonien Gåskaergade 19 ☏ (74) 523720 rm28 Closed Dec 24-Jan 1 **B**

HADSUND *Jylland*

H Øster Hurup Kystvejen ☏ (98) 588014 rm13 **A**

HERNING *Jylland*

M Herning Vardevej 9 ☏ (97) 222400 rm92 **B**

HIRTSHALS *Jylland*

H Hirtshals Sømandshjem Havnegade 24 ☏ (98) 941944 rm26 **B**

H Munch's Badehotel Tornby Strand ☏ (98) 977115 rm9 May-Sep **A**

H Strandlyst Tornby Strand ☏ (98) 977076 rm44 May 15-Sep 15 **B**

HOLSTEBRO *Jylland*

◆ **Borbjerg Mølle** Borbjerg Møllevej 3 ☏ (97) 461010 rm16 **B**

H Krabbes Stationsvej 18 ☏ (97) 420622 rm20 **B**

HORSENS *Jylland*

◆ **Søvind Kro** Haldrupvej 5 Søvind ☏ (75) 659055 rm10 **B**

JELLING *Jylland*

◆ **Tøsby** Bredsten Landevej 12 ☏ (75) 881130 rm9 **B**

KØBENHAVN (COPENHAGEN)

The little mermaid, inspired by Hans Christian Andersen's story, is a familiar image of København, a welcoming city of green parks and fairytale castles. The Amalienborg Palace (not open) is the royal residence, and also worth a visit are the Christiansborg Palace, the Stock Exchange and the university. For a spectacular view, climb the spiral ramp up one of the city's landmarks, the Round Tower (*Rundetårn*). You may glimpse that renowned Danish lager being delivered around the city in horse-drawn drays, and the Carlsberg and Tuborg breweries give interesting conducted tours explaining the production process – and offering tastings of the finished product.
The city's many other attractions include a zoo and museums of dolls, toys and puppets. The renowned Tivoli is a fantasy land built on the site of the ancient city walls, where the landscaped gardens are a myriad of lakes, fountains and flowers, lit after nightfall by twinkling fairy lights and fireworks. Here you can ride the switchback, listen to the music from the bandstands, laugh at the puppets and admire the show at the Mime Theatre. And when you have worked up an appetite, there are 22 restaurants from which to choose.
Souvenirs from Denmark are unusual and make interesting presents, expecially silverware, porcelain, pipes, wooden toys and distinctive Scandinavian sweaters.
EATING OUT The fame of the Scandinavian buffet – *det store kolde bord* – has spread worldwide, and here in København is the genuine article. It is a mouthwatering array of cold and hot dishes, usually including fish such as herring, meats, cheeses, vegetables and salads. Also delicious are the desserts, such as *rodgrod* – a red fruit pudding. Open sandwiches *smorrebrod* are wonderful, too, while for substantial and simpler food seek out the basement cafés for the speciality of the day, known as *dagens ret*. Eating out can be expensive, but there are plenty of frokost-restaurants (lunch restaurants) along Stroget, offering light salads and *smorrebrod*, while hotdog stands are practically everywhere. Also look out for restaurants displaying the sign *Dan Menu*, which serve inexpensive two-course meals.
Number one seafood restaurant in København is *Den Gyldne Fortun – Fiskkaelderen*, in Ved Stannden, which specialises in the products of the waters around Denmark and Greenland. The moderately priced *Peder Oxe*, in Graabrode Torv, is charmingly located in the old part of town, with whitewashed walls, wooden floors, and lots of atmosphere.

H West Westend 11 ☏ (01) 242761 rm24 **A**

LEMVIG *Jylland*

H Industrihotellet Vassen 11 ☏ (97) 820200 rm18 **B**

LØGUMKLOSTER *Jylland*

H Central Markedsgade 15 ☏ (74) 743050 rm6 **A**

H Postgården Vestergade 7 ☏ (74) 743824 rm16 **A**

LØKKEN *Jylland*

H Furreby Løkkensvej 910 ☏ (98) 991238 rm28 Closed Jan & Dec **B**

H Løkkenshus Søndergade 21 ☏ (98) 991046 rm16 **A**

MALLING *Jylland*

◆ **Lille Strandgård** Ajstrup Strandvej 95 ☏ (86) 931465 rm10 Closed Dec 24-31 **A**

◆ **Malling Kro** Stationspladsen 2 ☏ (86) 931025 rm11 Closed Dec 23-Jan 9 **B**

MIDDELFART *Fyn*

H Grimmerhus Kongebrovej 42 ☏ (09) 410399 rm20 Closed Dec 15-Jan 15 **B**

ODENSE *Fyn*

H Kahema Dronningensgade 5 ☏ (09) 122821 rm12 Closed Dec 16-Jan 1 **B**

PADBORG *Jylland*

◆ **Frøslev Kro** Vestergade 3 ☏ (74) 673204 rm12 Dec 24-Jan 1 **B**

H Motorvejscafeteriet Lejrvej 11 ☎ (74) 672575 rm6 Mar 15-Dec **B**

RIBE *Jylland*

◆ **Backhaus** Grydergade 12 ☎ (75) 421101 rm4 **B**

◆ **Mandø Kro** Byvej 26 Mandø ☎ (75) 445106 rm5 **A**

RINGKØBING *Jylland*

H Ringkøbing Torvet 18 ☎ (97) 320011 rm16 Closed Dec 24-31 **B**

◆ **Røgind** Herningvej 109 ☎ (97) 343265 rm4 **A**

H Strandkroen Nordsøvej 2 ☎ (97) 339002 rm16 **B**

RØDEKRO *Jylland*

◆ **Hellevad Kro Kløver Es** Brystrupvej 2 ☎ (74) 669140 rm9 Closed Dec 24-Jan 1 **A**

◆ **Hovslunds** Stationsvej 14 ☎ (74) 684164 rm10 **A**

RUDKØBING *Langeland*

H Degnehaven Spodsbjerg 277 ☎ (09) 501092 rm5 **A**

H Spodsbjerg Spodsbjerg 317 ☎ (09) 501064 rm14 **A**

RY *Jylland*

◆ **Galgebakken** Galgebakken 10 ☎ (86) 898025 rm12 **A**

◆ **Gammel Rye Kro** Ryesgade 8 ☎ (86) 898042 rm33 **B**

SAKSKØBING *Lolland*

H Våbensted Krårup Møllevej 6 ☎ (03) 896363 rm20 **A**

SILKEBORG *Jylland*

◆ **Lina Kro** Linåvej 57 ☎ (86) 841443 rm9 **A**

◆ **Svostrup Kro** Svostrup Vej 58-60 ☎ (86) 877004 rm11 **B**

SINDAL *Jylland*

◆ **Mosbjerg Kro** Mosbjergvej 425 ☎ (98) 930055 rm8 **A**

SKAGEN *Jylland*

◆ **Marienlund** Fabriciusvej 8 ☎ (98) 441320 rm12 **B**

H Skagen Sømandshjem Østre Strandvej 2 ☎ (98) 442110 rm36 **B**

H Strandly Skagen Østre Strandvej 35 ☎ (98) 441131 rm19 Closed Dec 24-Jan 8 **B**

SKJERN *Jylland*

H Astrup Højevej 39 ☎ (97) 364015 rm12 **A**

H Bundgårds Borgergade 1 ☎ (97) 366400 rm11 **A**

SØNDERBORG *Jylland*

H Ansgar Nørrebro 2 ☎ (74) 422472 rm38 Closed Dec 21-Jan 1 **B**

◆ **Ballebro Færgeko** Faergevej 5, Blans ☎ (74) 461303 rm8 Closed Dec 24-Jan 9 **B**

H Baltic Høruphav ☎ (74) 445200 rm16 Closed Dec 24-31 **A**

SVANEKE *Isle of Bornholm*

◆ **Solgården** Skolebakken 5 ☎ (03) 996437 rm18 Jun 20-Aug 20 **A**

SVENDBORG *Fyn*

H Ny Vemmenæs Stenoddenvej 39 ☎ (09) 541313 rm7 Apr-Sep **A**

H Royal Toldbodvej 5 ☎ (09) 212113 rm27 **B**

THISTED *Jylland*

★★★**Aalborg** Storegade 29 ☎ (97) 923566 rm32 **B**

TØNDER *Jylland*

H Abild Ribe Landevej 66 ☎ (74) 722292 rm16 **B**

H City Storegade 9 ☎ (74) 722108 rm18 **B**

One of Denmark's most charming towns – Fåborg on the Island of Funen

FRANCE AND MONACO

FACTS & FIGURES
France
Capital: Paris
Language: French
IDD: 33. To call the UK dial 1944
Currency: Franc (Fr1 = 100 centimes)
Local time: GMT+1 (summer GMT+2)
Emergency Services: Police 17, Fire & Ambulance 18

Business hours
Banks:
0900–1200 & 1400–1600 Mon–Fri
Shops:
0900–1830 Mon–Sat (times may vary for food shops)

Average daily temperatures:
Paris °C

Jan 3	Jul 18
Mar 6	Sep 15
May 13	Nov 6

Tourist Information:
French Government Tourist Office
UK 178 Piccadilly
London W1V 0AI
Tel 01–491 7622

USA 610 First Ave
New York, NY 10020
Tel (212) 757–1125

With its endless variety of countryside and coastline, its legendary cuisine and fine wines, and its diverse culture and heritage, France has long been a much-loved holiday destination. Every region of the country is steeped in its own unique character and traditions, offering something to suit all tastes.

There's the romantic and enchanting capital, Paris, with its unique atmosphere, art treasures and historic buildings; the quiet calm of Brittany, with its safe, sandy beaches and lush, green countryside; the cosmopolitan charm and spectacular surfing of Biarritz; the glamour of the French Riviera; the seemingly endless sands of Languedoc-Roussillon in the South of France; the spectacular scenery of the Savoie Alps; and delightful cities, towns and villages throughout the country containing much of interest to the visitor.

There is every possible scenic variation. The Atlantic coast has rugged capes and deserted dunes beloved by surfers; the Channel coast sandy beaches and quiet coves; while in the south the Alps and Pyrenees plunge down to the Mediterranean, creating some of the most dramatic coastal scenery in Europe. Inland there are mountain pastures, deserted plateaux, gentle river valleys and stony hillsides.

MONACO

The tiny Principality of Monaco is an independent, sovereign state very much under the influence of France; its laws are similar to those of the major country. Motoring regulations are the same as in France.

Monaco Government Tourist
and Convention Office
50 Upper Brook Street
London W1Y 1PG
Tel 01–629 4712

HOW TO GET THERE

BY CAR

Motorists can cross the Channel by ferry: Dover to Boulogne (1 hr 40 mins) or to Calais (1¼ to 1½ hrs); Folkestone to Boulogne (1 hr 50 mins); Ramsgate to Dunkerque (Dunkirk) (2¼ hrs); Newhaven to Dieppe (4 hrs); Portsmouth to Le Havre (5¾–7½ hrs) or to Caen (5¾–7 hrs); or to *Cherbourg (4¾–6 hrs) or to St-Malo (9–11 hrs); *Poole to Cherbourg (4½ hrs); Plymouth to Roscoff (6–6½ hrs); Weymouth to Cherbourg (4–6 hrs). There are also fast hovercraft services that operate between Dover and Boulogne (40 mins) or Calais (35 mins). Car-sleeper trains run from Boulogne, Calais and Dieppe to the south of the country.

* Summer service only.

For details of The AA's Overseas Routes Service consult the Contents page.

SPEED LIMITS

Unless otherwise signposted, speed limits are: in built-up areas (indicated by place-name signs) 37 mph (60 kph); outside built up areas on normal roads 56 mph (90 kph); dual carriageways with central reservation

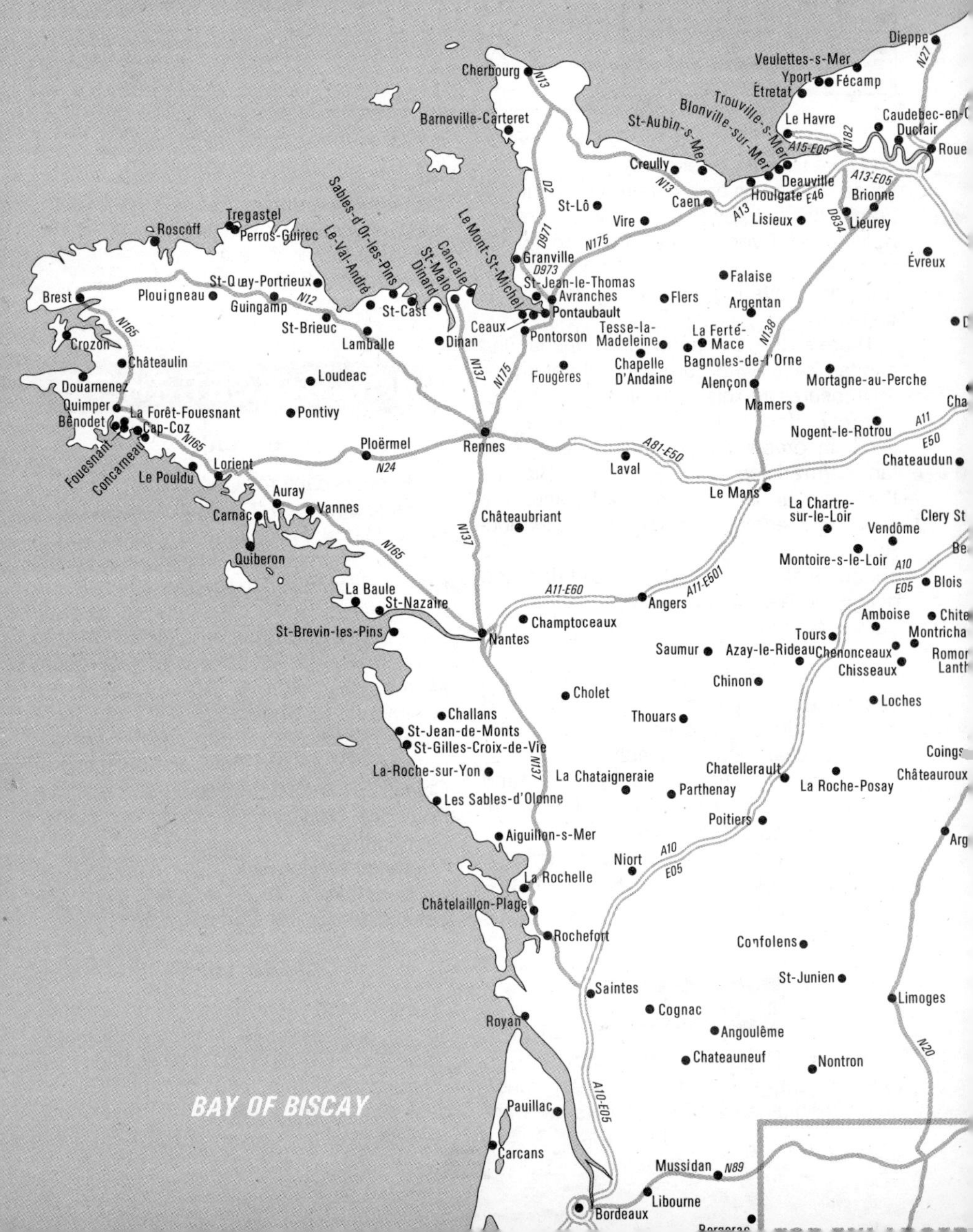

ENGLISH
CHANNEL
BAY OF BISCAY
Dieppe
N27
Veulettes-s-Mer
Yport
Fécamp
Étretat
Trouville-s-Mer
Blonville-sur-Mer
Le Havre
Duclair
St-Aubin-s-Mer
N182
A15-E05
Cherbourg
N13
Barneville-Carteret
Creully
N13
Deauville
Houlgate
E46
A13-E05
Brionne
D2
St-Lô
Caen
A13
Lisieux
D834
Lieurey
Vire
N175
Évreux
Tregastel
Roscoff
Perros-Guirec
Sables-d'Or-les-Pins
Le-Val-André
Le Mont-St-Michel
Cancale
St-Malo
Dinard
D971
Granville
D973
St-Jean-le-Thomas
Avranches
Pontaubault
Falaise
Flers
Argentan
Brest
Plouigneau
St-Quay-Portrieux
Guingamp
N12
St-Cast
St-Brieuc
Lamballe
Ceaux
Dinan
Pontorson
Tesse-la-Madeleine
La Ferté-Mace
N138
Crozon
N165
Châteaulin
N137
N175
Chapelle D'Andaine
Bagnoles-de-l'Orne
Fougères
Douarnenez
Loudeac
Alençon
Mortagne-au-Perche
Quimper
La Forêt-Fouesnant
Bènodet
Cap-Coz
Pontivy
Mamers
Fouesnant
Concarneau
N165
Rennes
Nogent-le-Rotrou
A11
E50
Ploërmel
N24
Lorient
Le Pouldu
A81-E50
Laval
Chateaudun
Auray
Vannes
Le Mans
Carnac
Quiberon
Châteaubriant
La Chartre-sur-le-Loir
Vendôme
N165
N137
Montoire-s-le-Loir
A10
E05
Blois
La Baule
St-Nazaire
A11-E60
Angers
A11-E501
St-Brevin-les-Pins
Champtoceaux
Nantes
Amboise
Tours
Saumur
Azay-le-Rideau
Chenonceaux
Chisseaux
Chinon
Loches
Cholet
Challans
Thouars
St-Jean-de-Monts
St-Gilles-Croix-de-Vie
N137
La-Roche-sur-Yon
La Chataigneraie
Chatellerault
La Roche-Posay
Châteauroux
Parthenay
Les Sables-d'Olonne
Poitiers
Aiguillon-s-Mer
Niort
A10
E05
La Rochelle
Châtelaillon-Plage
Rochefort
Confolens
St-Junien
Saintes
Limoges
Cognac
Royan
Angoulême
Chateauneuf
Nontron
N20
A10-E05
Pauillac
Carcans
Mussidan
N89
Libourne
Bordeaux

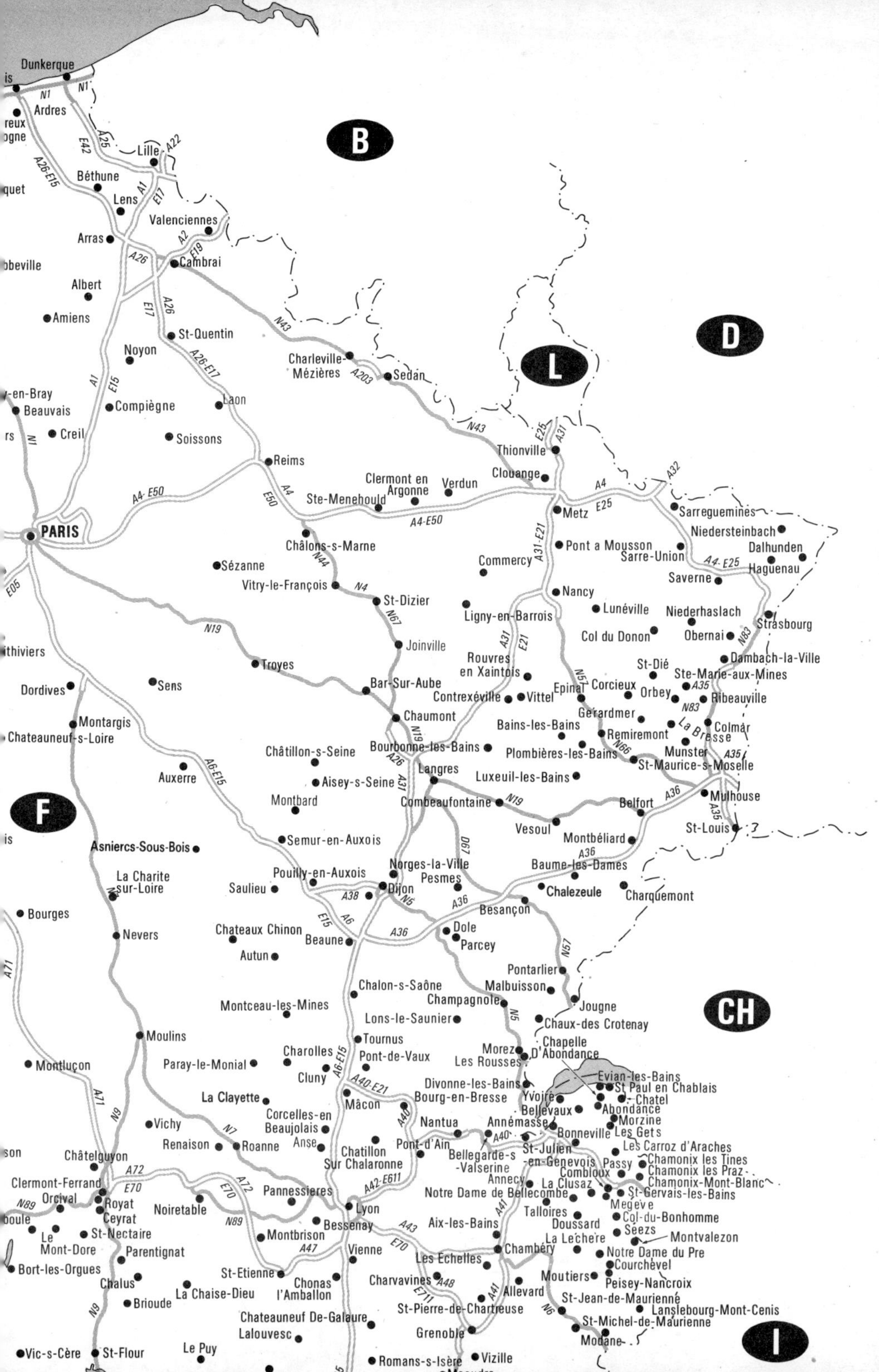

Dunkerque
N1
Ardres
B
Lille
A22
A25
E42
A26-E15
Béthune
Lens
A1
E17
Valenciennes
Arras
A2
E19
A26
Cambrai
Albert
Amiens
E17
A26
St-Quentin
N43
Noyon
A26-E17
Charleville-Mézières
A203
Sedan
D
L
A1
E15
Beauvais
Compiègne
Laon
Creil
N1
Soissons
N43
E25
A31
Thionville
Reims
Clouange
A32
Clermont en Argonne
Verdun
A4-E50
E50
A4
Ste-Menehould
A4-E50
A4
E25
Metz
Sarreguemines
PARIS
Niedersteinbach
Châlons-s-Marne
Pont a Mousson
Dalhunden
Sézanne
N44
Commercy
A31-E21
Sarre-Union
A4-E25
Haguenau
E05
Vitry-le-François
N4
St-Dizier
Nancy
Saverne
N67
Ligny-en-Barrois
Lunéville
Niederhaslach
Strasbourg
N19
Col du Donon
Obernai
N83
Joinville
A31
E21
Rouvres en Xaintois
St-Dié
Dambach-la-Ville
Troyes
Ste-Marie-aux-Mines
Dordives
Sens
Bar-Sur-Aube
N57
Epinal
Corcieux
Orbey
A35
Contrexéville
Vittel
N83
Ribeauville
Montargis
Chaumont
Gerardmer
Bains-les-Bains
La Bresse
Colmar
Chateauneuf-s-Loire
N19
Remiremont
Munster
Châtillon-s-Seine
Bourbonne-les-Bains
Plombières-les-Bains
N66
A35
A26
St-Maurice-s-Moselle
Auxerre
A6-E15
Langres
Luxeuil-les-Bains
Aisey-s-Seine
A31
F
Montbard
Combeaufontaine
N19
Belfort
A36
Mulhouse
Vesoul
A35
St-Louis
Semur-en-Auxois
Montbéliard
D67
Asniercs-Sous-Bois
A36
Norges-la-Ville
Baume-les-Dames
La Charite sur-Loire
Pouilly-en-Auxois
Pesmes
Saulieu
Dijon
Chalezeule
Charquemont
A38
N5
A36
Besançon
Bourges
E15
A6
Chateaux Chinon
A36
Dole
Nevers
Beaune
Parcey
Autun
N57
A71
Pontarlier
Chalon-s-Saône
Malbuisson
Champagnole
Jougne
CH
Montceau-les-Mines
N5
Lons-le-Saunier
Chaux-des Crotenay
Moulins
Tournus
Chapelle D'Abondance
Charolles
Pont-de-Vaux
Morez
Montluçon
Paray-le-Monial
A6-E15
Les Rousses
Cluny
Evian-les-Bains
Divonne-les-Bains
St Paul en Chablais
A40-E21
Chatel
La Clayette
Mâcon
Bourg-en-Bresse
Yvoire
Bellevaux
Abondance
A71
N9
Corcelles-en Beaujolais
A40
Nantua
Annémasse
Morzine
Vichy
N7
Anse
A40
Bonneville
Les Gets
Renaison
Roanne
Chatillon Sur Chalaronne
Pont-d'Ain
Bellegarde-s -Valserine
St-Julien -en-Genevois
Les Carroz d'Araches
Châtelguyon
Passy
Chamonix les Tines
A72
Combloux
Chamonix les Praz
Clermont-Ferrand
E70
A72
A42-E611
Annecy
La Clusaz
Chamonix-Mont-Blanc
Orcival
Royat
Pannessieres
Notre Dame de Bellecombe
St-Gervais-les-Bains
N89
Ceyrat
Noiretable
E70
Lyon
A41
Megeve
N89
Talloires
Col-du-Bonhomme
Le Mont-Dore
St-Nectaire
Bessenay
A43
Aix-les-Bains
Doussard
Seezs
Montbrison
Montvalezon
Parentignat
A47
Vienne
E70
La Lechere
Notre Dame du Pre
Les Echelles
Chambéry
Courchevel
Bort-les-Orgues
St-Etienne
Chonas l'Amballon
Charvavines
A48
Moutiers
Peisey-Nancroix
Chalus
La Chaise-Dieu
E711
A41
Allevard
Brioude
St-Pierre-de-Chartreuse
N6
St-Jean-de-Maurienne
N9
Lanslebourg-Mont-Cenis
Chateauneuf De-Galaure
St-Michel-de-Maurienne
Lalouvesc
Grenoble
Modane
Le Puy
Vic-s-Cère
St-Flour
Romans-s-Isère
Vizille
I

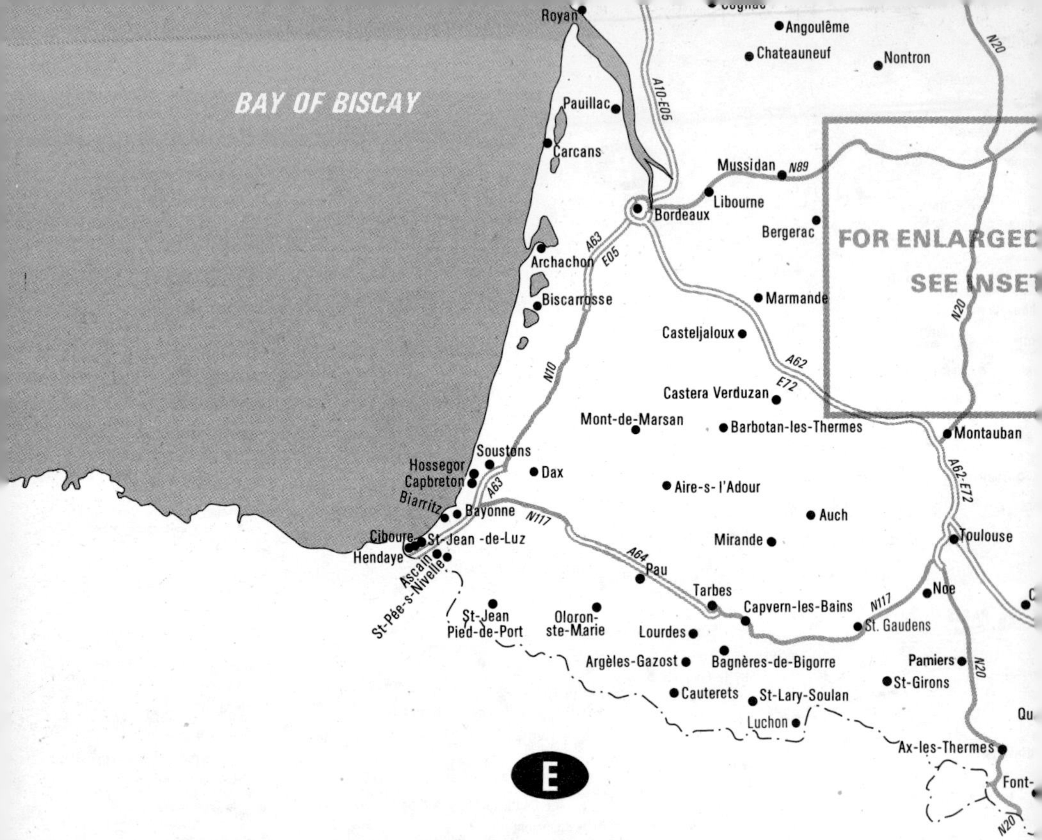

Royan
Angoulême
Chateauneuf
Nontron
N20
BAY OF BISCAY
Pauillac
A10-E05
Carcans
Mussidan
N89
Libourne
Bordeaux
Bergerac
FOR ENLARGED
SEE INSET
A63
E05
Archachon
Biscarrosse
Marmande
N20
Casteljaloux
A62
E72
N10
Castera Verduzan
Mont-de-Marsan
Barbotan-les-Thermes
Montauban
Soustons
Hossegor
Capbreton
Dax
A63
Aire-s- l'Adour
A62-E72
Biarritz
Bayonne
N117
Auch
Ciboure
St-Jean -de-Luz
Toulouse
Hendaye
Mirande
Ascain
St-Pée-s-Nivelle
A64
Pau
Tarbes
Noe
St-Jean
Pied-de-Port
Oloron-
ste-Marie
Capvern-les-Bains
N117
St. Gaudens
Lourdes
Argèles-Gazost
Bagnères-de-Bigorre
Pamiers
N20
St-Girons
Cauterets
St-Lary-Soulan
Luchon
Ax-les-Thermes
Font-
N20
E

Périgueux
N20
N89
Tulle
N89
Brive-la-Gaillarde
Notre-Dame de Sanilhac
Collonges la-Rouge
Argentat
Cressensac
Les Eyzies-de-Tayac
N20
Martel
Carlux
Souillac
Siorac-en-Périgord
Beynac et
Cazenac
Payrac
Rocamadour
St-Céré
Gramat
Gourdon
Figeac
Capdenac-Gare
Villeneuve-
s-Lot
N20
Villefranche
de Rouergue
Agen
Moissac
Caussade
Najac

N85
Chateau-Arnoux
Digne
Brignoles
N97
A57
Toulon

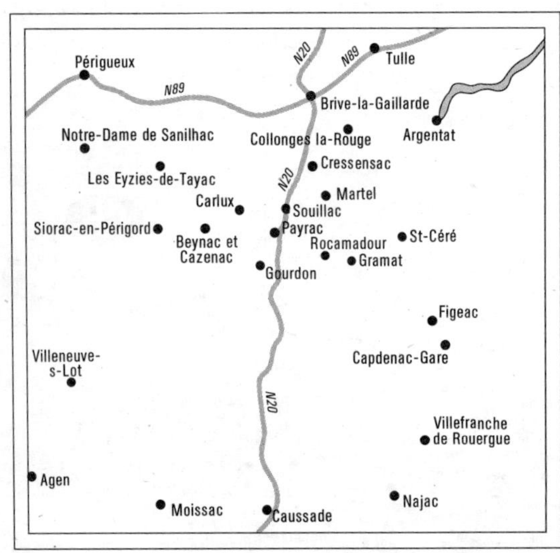

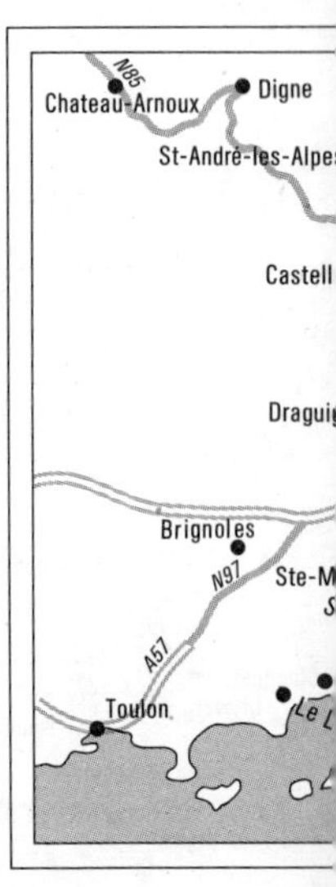

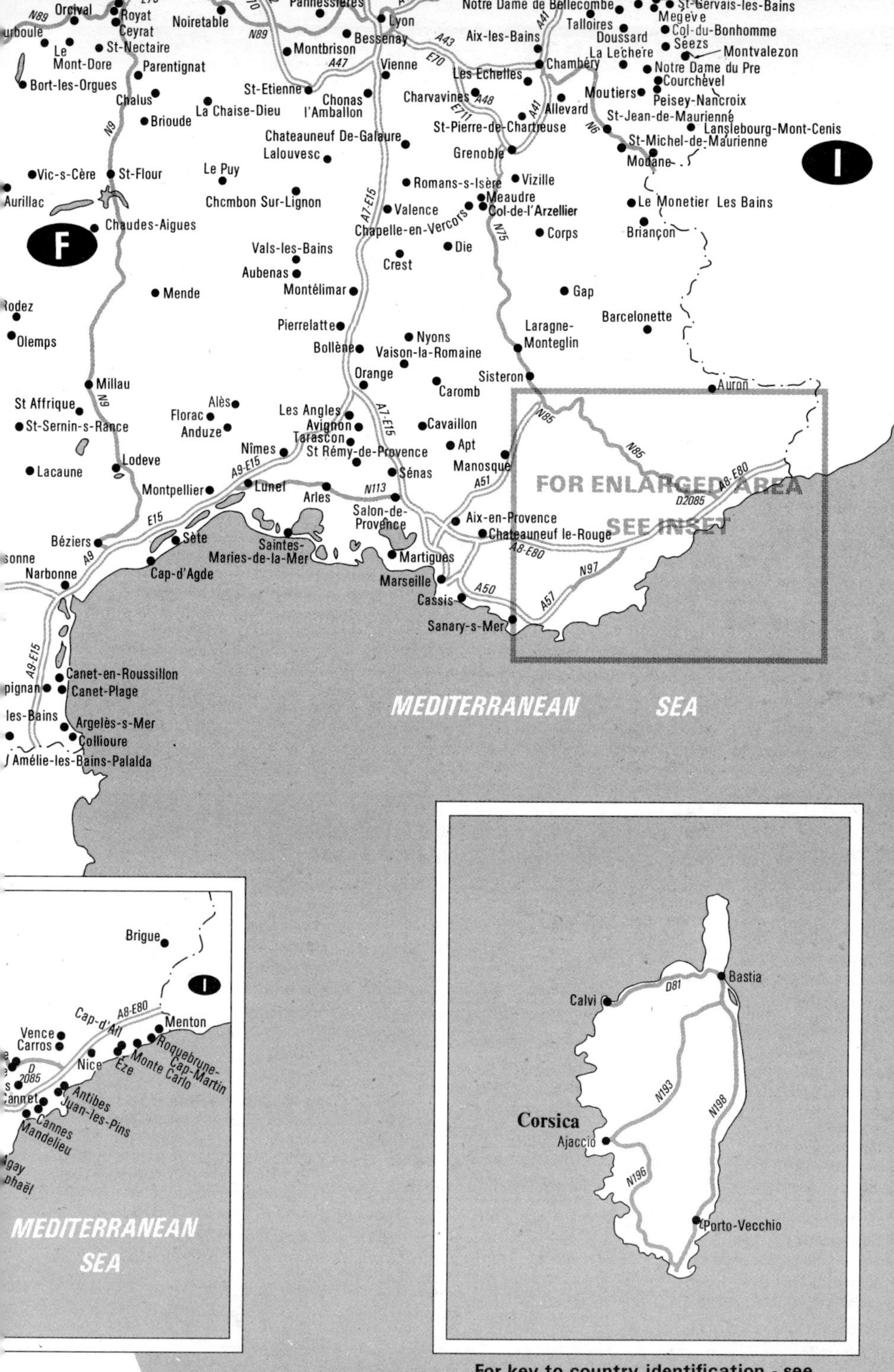

For key to country identification - see "About the gazetteer"

68 mph (110 kph); motorways 80 mph (130 kph). There is a minimum speed of 49 mph (80 kph) in the fast lane of a level stretch of motorway in good visibility. In wet weather, speed limits outside built-up areas are reduced. If you have not held a full driving licence for one year, you are restricted to a top speed of 56 mph (90 kph).

PARKING

There are short-term parking areas known as blue zones in most principal towns – discs must be used in these areas between 0900 and 1230 hrs and 1430 and 1900 hrs every day except Sundays and Public Holidays. Discs, permitting parking for up to one hour are sold at police stations, but at tourist offices they are available free of charge.

BY TRAIN

If you do not have an Inter Rail or Eurail pass, national and regional tickets can be obtained for rail travel within France. Always remember to validate (composter) your ticket by inserting it in the orange machine at the entrance to the platforms. All Eurailpass and France Railpass holders must validate their passes before boarding their first train.

The France Railpass comes in three versions: 4 days of travel within a 15-day period; 9 days within a month; and 16 days within a month. Limited use of transport in Paris is included. The pass must be purchased outside France. Other special tickets apply during specified periods.

ACCOMMODATION

The gazetteer contains details of accommodation for less than 209 Fr per person per night at some time during the year. These are our price bands:

A 99–154 Fr
B 154–209 Fr

taking as an exchange rate: 11 Fr=£1
7 Fr=US $1

Prices may change during the currency of this book. Other details of accommodation may be obtained from local tourist offices (syndicats d'initiative and offices de tourisme).

Abbreviations: Aml Admiral av avenue bd boulevard ch chaussée, chemin Cl Colonel Cmt Commandant espl esplanade fbg faubourg Gl Général Ml, Maréchal pl place Prés Président prom promenade r rue rte route sq square

ABBEVILLE *Somme*

H France 19 pl du Pilori ☎ 22240042 rm77 **B**

ABONDANCE *Haute-Savoie*

H Bel Air Richebourg ☎ 50730171 rm23 (Seasonal) **A**

H Mont-Jorat ☎ 50730108 rm26 (Seasonal) **A**

AGAY *Var*

H Débarquement Le Dramont ☎ 94820251 rm15 Closed Jan **B**

AGEN *Lot-et-Garonne*

H Bordeaux 8 pl Jasmin ☎ 53472566 rm22 **B**

H Jasmin Terminus 40 bd Sylvain ☎ 53663108 rm50 **A**

H Pont Neuf 62 cours du 14 Juillet ☎ 53661567 rm10 **A**

H Regina (n.rest) 139 bd Carnot ☎ 53470797 rm32 **A**

H Royal 129 bd République ☎ 53472884 rm18 **B**

AIGUILLON-SUR-MER *Vendée*

★★Port 2 r Belle Vue ☎ 51564008 rm33 Mar-Oct **B**

AIRE-SUR-L'ADOUR *Landes*

H Commerce 3 bd des Pyrénées ☎ 58716006 rm20 **A**

AISEY-SUR-SEINE *Côte-d'Or*

★★Roy ☎ 80932163 rm10 **B**

AIX-EN-PROVENCE *Bouches-du-Rhône*

H Arquier (n.rest) Roquefavour par Ventabren ☎ 42242045 rm18 **A**

H Caravelle (n.rest) 29 bd du Roi René ☎ 42215305 rm30 **B**

H Cardinal (n.rest) 24 r Cardinale ☎ 42383230 rm21 **B**

H Casino (n.rest) 38 r Leydet ☎ 42260688 rm24 **B**

H Concorde (n.rest) 68 bd du Roi René ☎ 42260395 rm39 **B**

H Pasteur 14 av Pasteur ☎ 42211176 rm20 **A**

★★★Residence Rotonde (n.rest) 15 av des Belges ☎ 42262988 rm42 **B**

AIX-LES-BAINS *Savoie*

H Alexandra Wilson 27 bd Wilson ☎ 79350407 rm17 **A**

H Azur (n.rest) 18 av Victoria ☎ 79350096 rm16 Closed Jan **B**

H Beaulie 29 av Gl-de-Gaulle ☎ 79350102 rm31 Apr-Sep **B**

H Genève 11 r de Genève ☏ 79350194 rm36 (Mar-Nov) **B**

★★**Paix** 11 r Lamartine BP 513 ☏ 79350210 rm70 Mar-Nov **B**

H Palma (n.rest) 19 bis sq Boucher ☏ 79350110 rm16 Apr-Oct **A**

H Paris 9 r Dacquin ☏ 79353660 rm65 Apr-Nov **A**

H Revotel (n.rest) 40 r Genève ☏ 79350337 rm18 **B**

H Soleil-Couchant 130 av St-Simon ☏ 79350583 rm31 May-Oct **A**

H Suisse (n.rest) 16 av Marie de Solms ☏ 79350609 rm39 Apr-Oct **A**

H Thermal 2 r Davat ☏ 79352000 rm76 Mar-Nov **B**

AJACCIO *Corse-du-Sud*
See **CORSE (CORSICA)**

ALBERT *Somme*

★**Basilique** 3-5 r Gambetta ☏ 22750471 rm10 **A**

★**Paix** 43 r V-Hugo ☏ 22750164 rm15 **B**

ALENÇON *Orne*

H Auberge Normande rte de Paris-Valframbert ☏ 33294329 rm10 **A**

H Chapeau Rouge 1 & 3 bd Duchamps ☏ 33262023 rm16 **A**

★★**France** (n.rest) 3 r St-Blaise ☏ 33262636 rm31 **B**

★★★**Grand Cerf** 21 r St-Blaise ☏ 33260051 rm33 **A**

H Grand Saint-Michel 7 r du Temple ☏ 33260477 rm13 Closed Jul **A**

★**Industrie** 20-22 pl du Gl-de-Gaulle ☏ 33271930 rm10 **A**

ALÈS *Gard*

H Orly 10 r d'Avejan ☏ 66524327 rm44 **B**

H Parc 174 rte de Nîmes ☏ 66306233 rm5 **A**

H Riche 42 pl de la Gare ☏ 66860033 rm20 **B**

ALLEVARD *Isère*

H Bains 15 r L-Chataing ☏ 76975178 rm38 **A**

M Parc (n.rest) Parc de l'Etabliss Thermal ☏ 76975422 rm49 May-Sep **B**

AMBOISE *Indre-et-Loire*

H Belle-Vue 12 quai C-Guinot ☏ 47570226 rm30 (Mar-Dec) **B**

★**Breche** 26 r J-Ferry ☏ 47570079 rm15 **B**

★★**Lion d'or** 17 quai C-Guinot ☏ 47570023 rm23 (Apr-Oct) **A**

AMÉLIE-LES-BAINS-PALALDA *Pyrénées-Orientales*

H Castel Emeraude rte Corniche ☏ 68390283 rm31 (Feb-Nov) **B**

H Palmarium 44 av du Vallespir ☏ 68391938 rm63 **B**

AMIENS *Somme*

★★**Paix** (n.rest) 8 r de la République ☏ 22913921 rm26 **A**

ANDUZE *Gard*

H Porte des Cevennes rte de St-Jean-du-Gard ☏ 6661 9944 rm18 (Apr-Oct) **B**

ANGERS *Maine-et-Loire*

★★**Boule D'Or** 27 bd Carnot ☏ 41437656 rm33 **A**

H Continental (n.rest) 12-14 r L-de-Romain ☏ 41886380 rm25 **B**

H Europe (n.rest) 3 r Château-Gontier ☏ 41886745 rm29 **B**

H Gare 5 pl de la Gare ☏ 41884069 rm54 **B**

H Royal (n.rest) 8 bis pl de la Visitation ☏ 41883025 rm40 **A**

H St-Julien (n.rest) 9 pl du Ralliement ☏ 41884162 rm35 **B**

★★**Univers** (n.rest) 2 pl & 16 r de la Gare ☏ 41884358 rm45 **A**

ANGLES, LES *Gard*

◆ **L'Ermitage** av de Verdun ☏ 90254102 rm16 Closed Feb **B**

H Olivier ch de Laurette ☏ 90254222 rm21 **B**

H Petit Manoir av J-Ferry ☏ 90250336 rm40 **B**

ANGOULÊME *Charente*

H Coq d'Or 98 r de Périgueux ☏ 45950245 rm25 **A**

★**Flore** 414 rte de Bordeaux ☏ 45919946 rm40 **A**

H Terminus pl de la Gare ☏ 45923900 rm38 **A**

H Valois (n.rest) 32 r de Pisany Place ☏ 45682240 rm20 **A**

ANNECY *Haute-Savoie*

H Alery (n.rest) 5 av d'Aléry ☏ 50452475 rm20 **B**

H Coin Fleuri (n.rest) 3 r Filaterie ☏ 50452730 rm14 **B**

H Crystal (n.rest) 20 r L-Chaumontel ☏ 50573390 rm22 **B**

H Nouvel (n.rest) 37 r Vaugelas ☏ 50450578 rm50 **B**

H Parmelan 41 av des Romains ☏ 50571489 rm28 (Apr-Sep) **A**

ANNEMASSE *Haute-Savoie*

H Terminus 8 r Dr-Favre ☏ 50372226 rm42 **B**

ANSE *Rhône*

H St-Romain rte de Graves ☏ 74680589 rm25 **B**

ANTIBES *Alpes-Maritimes*

H Belle Epoque 10 av du 24 Août ☏ 93345300 rm10 **B**

H Relais du Postillon 8 r Championnet ☏ 93342077 rm14 **B**

APT *Vaucluse*

★★★**Ventoux** 67 av V-Hugo ☏ 90740758 rm13 Closed Jan **B**

ARCACHON *Gironde*

H Gascogne 79 cours H-de-Thury ☏ 56834252 rm38 **A**

H Pergola 40 cours Lamarque ☏ 56830789 rm22 (Mar-Oct) **B**

ARDRES *Pas-de-Calais*

★**Chaumière** (n.rest) 67 av de Rouville ☏ 21354124 rm12 **A**

★★**Relais** bd C-Senlecq ☏ 21354200 rm11 **B**

ARGELÈS-GAZOST *Hautes-Pyrénées*

H Bon Repos rte du Stade ☏ 62970149 rm20 (Seasonal) **A**

H Cimes 1 pl d'Ourout ☏ 62970010 rm28 **A**

H Gabizos 33 av des Pyrénées ☏ 62970136 rm26 (Feb & May-Oct) **A**

ARGELÈS-SUR-MER *Pyrénées-Orientales*

★**Commerce** 14 rte de Collioure ☏ 68810033 rm40 **A**

H Cottage 21 r A-Rimbaud ☏ 68810733 rm22 (Apr-Oct) **B**

ARGENTAN *Orne*

H France 8 bd Carnot ☎ 33670365 rm13 **A**

★★**Renaissance** 20 av de la 2e D-B ☎ 33361420 rm15 **A**

ARGENTAT *Corrèze*

★★**Gilbert** av J-Vachal ☎ 55280162 rm30 Closed Feb **A**

ARGENTON-SUR-CREUSE *Indre*

H Cheval Noir 27 r Auclert-Descottes ☎ 54240006 rm30 (Mar-Nov) **A**

★★**Manoir De Boisvillers** (n.rest) 11 r Moulin de Bord ☎ 54241388 rm15 **A**

ARLES *Bouches-du-Rhône*

★★**Cloître** (n.rest) 18 r du Cloître ☎ 90962950 rm33 (Mar-Nov) **B**

H Diderot (n.rest) 5 r Diderot ☎ 90961030 rm15 Closed Feb-Mar **A**

★**Mirador** (n.rest) 3 r Voltaire ☎ 90962805 rm15 **B**

★★**Montmajour** 84 rte de Tarasçon ☎ 90939833 rm20 (Mar-Nov) **B**

H Regence (n.rest) 5 r M-Jouveau ☎ 90963985 rm17 (Mar-Nov) **A**

H Saint-Trophime (n.rest) 16 r de la Calade ☎ 90968838 rm22 (Mar-Nov) **A**

H Source pont de Crau ☎ 90961242 rm15 **A**

ARRAS *Pas-de-Calais*

★★**Astoria** 10 pl Foch ☎ 21710814 rm31 **A**

★**Chánzy** 8 r Chánzy ☎ 21710202 rm24 **B**

★★**Commerce** (n.rest) 28 r Gambetta ☎ 21711007 rm40 **A**

★★**Commerce** 10 pl Foch ☎ 21710814 rm31 **A**

★★★**Univers** 3 pl Croix Rouge ☎ 21713401 rm36 **B**

ASCAIN *Pyrénées-Atlantiques*

H Basque ☎ 59540012 rm37 (Apr-Oct) **B**

H Oberena rte des Carrières ☎ 59540306 rm19 Closed Feb **B**

H Pont ☎ 59540040 rm28 **A**

★★**Rhune** ☎ 59540004 rm45 Closed Feb **B**

ASNIERES-SOUS-BOIS *Yonne*

FH Les Oiseaux ☎ 86333344 rm2 mid Apr-Oct **B**

AUBENAS *Ardèche*

H Cevenol (n.rest) 77 bd Gambetta ☎ 75350010 rm45 **B**

H Provence (n.rest) 5 bd de Vernon ☎ 75352843 rm24 **A**

AUBUSSON *Creuse*

★★**France** 6 r des Deportes ☎ 55661022 rm21 **A**

AUCH *Gers*

H D'Artagnan pl Villaret-Joyeuse ☎ 62050049 rm20 **B**

H Robinson (n.rest) rte de Tarbes ☎ 62050283 rm26 **B**

AURAY *Morbihan*

H Branhoc (n.rest) rte du Bono ☎ 97564155 rm28 **B**

AURILLAC *Cantal*

H Terminus (n.rest) 8 r de la Gare ☎ 71480117 rm22 **B**

AURON *Alpes-Maritimes*

H Las Donnas r M-Madeleine ☎ 9320003 rm48 (Seasonal) **B**

AUTUN *Saône-et-Loire*

H St-Louis 6 r de l'Arbalete ☎ 85522103 rm52 (Mar-Nov) **A**

★★**Tête Noire** 1-3 r de l'Arquebuse ☎ 85522539 rm19 Closed Mar **A**

AUXERRE *Yonne*

H Arcade (n.rest) 1 av J-Jaurès ☎ 86483055 rm38 **B**

★★**Cygne** (n.rest) 14 r du 24-Aout ☎ 86522651 rm24 **B**

H Morin 4 av Gambetta ☎ 86469026 rm18 **A**

H Poste 9 r d'Orbandelle ☎ 86521202 rm21 **A**

★★**Seignelay** 2 r du Pont ☎ 865203848 rm23 **A**

AVIGNON *Vaucluse*

★★**Angleterre** (n.rest) 29 bd Raspail ☎ 90863431 rm40 **A**

H Constantin 46 r Carnot ☎ 90863537 rm40 **B**

H Glycines Sortie Autoroute ☎ 90224007 rm27 **B**

H Magnan 63 Portail Magnanen ☎ 90863651 rm31 **B**

AVRANCHES *Manche*

★★**St-Michel** 7 pl Gl-Patton ☎ 33580191 rm22 (Mar-Nov) **B**

AX-LES-THERMES *Ariège*

H Breilh pl du Breilh ☎ 61642429 rm25 Closed Nov **A**

★**Lauzeraie** prom du Couloubret ☎ 61642070 rm25 (May-Nov) **A**

★★**Moderne** 20 av du Dr-Gomma ☎ 61642024 rm22 (Feb-Oct) **A**

H Teich 2 av Turrel ☎ 61642299 rm52 **B**

AZAY-LE-RIDEAU *Indre-et-Loire*

H Beincourt (n.rest) 7 r Balzac ☎ 47452075 rm8 (Feb-Nov) **B**

★★**Grand Monarque** pl de la République ☎ 47454008 rm26 (Mar-Nov) **A**

BAGNÈRES-DE-BIGORRE *Hautes-Pyrénées*

H Commerce 2 pl Fourcade ☎ 62950733 rm23 **A**

BAGNOLES-DE-L'ORNE *Orne*

H Albert 1er av Dr-Poulain ☎ 33378097 rm20 (Mar-Sep) **A**

H Forêt 56 bd P-Chalvet ☎ 33378288 rm24 (Apr-Oct) **A**

H Grand Veneur 6 pl de la République ☎ 33378679 rm23 (Apr-Oct) **A**

H L'Ermitage (n.rest) 24 bd P-Chalvet ☎ 33379622 rm39 (Apr-Oct) **B**

H Normandie 2 r du Dr P-Lemuet ☎ 33308016 rm24 (Apr-Oct) **A**

H Potinière du Lac av de l'Hippodrome ☎ 33378267 rm16 (May-Oct) **B**

BAINS-LES-BAINS *Vosges*

H Ombrees 13 r du Million ☎ 29363185 rm18 (Apr-Sep) **B**

H Parc r du Dr-Mathieu ☎ 29304000 rm26 **A**

BARBOTAN-LES-THERMES *Gers*

H Midi av des Thermes ☎ 62095202 rm34 (Mar-Nov) **A**

H Mousquetaires (n.rest) r de la Tour ☎ 62695209 rm50 Closed Jan **B**

BARCELONNETTE *Alpes-de-Hautes-Provence*

H Alpes (n.rest) 3 pl Manuel ☎ 92810002 rm13 **A**

H Grand 6 pl Manuel ☎ 92810314 rm22 **B**

BARNEVILLE-CARTERET *Manche*

★★**Angleterre** r de Paris ☎ 33538604 rm43 (Etr-Nov) **A**

BAR-SUR-AUBE *Aube*

★**Commerce** 38 r Nationale ☎ 25270876 rm15 Closed Jan **A**

BASTIA *Haute-Corse*

H Napoléon (n.rest) 43 bd Paoli ☎ 95316030 rm13 **B**

BAULE, LA *Loire-Atlantique*

H Lutetia 13 av des Evens ☎ 40651 rm15 **B**

★★**Riviera** (n.rest) 16 av des Lilas ☎ 40602897 rm20 (May-Sep) **B**

BAUME-LES-DAMES *Doubs*

H Central 3 r Courvoisier ☎ 81840964 rm12 **A**

BAYONNE *Pyrénées-Atlantiques*

H Amatcho 27 av Ml-Soult ☎ 59633718 rm36 **B**

H Aux Deux Rivières (n.rest) 21 r Thiers ☎ 59591461 rm66 **B**

H Côte Basque 2 r Maubec ☎ 59551021 rm46 **A**

H Larrequy Auberge du Cheval Blanc 68 r Bourgneuf ☎ 59592933 rm23 **A**

BEAUGENCY *Loiret*

★★**Ecu de Bretagne** pl du Martroi ☎ 38446760 rm23 Closed Feb **A**

H Relais des Templiers (n.rest) 68 r du Pont ☎ 38445378 rm12 **B**

BEAUNE *Côte-d'Or*

◆ **Auberge Bourguignonne** 4 pl Madeleine ☎ 80222353 rm28 (Jul-Dec) **B**

◆ **Bretonnière** 43 fbg Bretonnière ☎ 80221577 rm22 **B**

BEAUVAIS *Oise*

★**Palais** (n.rest) 9 r St-Nicholas ☎ 44451258 rm15 **A**

H Résidence (n.rest) 24 r L-Borel ☎ 44483098 rm23 **A**

BELFORT *Territoire-de-Belfort*

H Capuchins 20 fbg Montbeliard ☎ 84280460 rm35 **B**

H Moder'n 9 av Wilson ☎ 84215945 rm45 **B**

BELLEGARDE-SUR-VALSERINE *Ain*

H Belle Époque 10 pl Gambetta ☎ 50481446 rm10 **B**

H Central Colonne 1 r J-Bertola ☎ 50481045 rm28 **A**

H Sorgia Lancrans ☎ 50481581 rm18 **A**

BELLEVAUX *Haute-Savoie*

H Christania Hirmentaz ☎ 50737077 rm29 (Seasonal) **B**

H Excelsa Hirmentaz ☎ 50737322 rm20 (Seasonal) **A**

H Moineaux ☎ 50737145 rm14 (Seasonal) **B**

H Panoramic ☎ 50737034 rm30 (Seasonal) **B**

H Skieurs ☎ 50737046 rm22 (Seasonal) **A**

BÉNODET *Finistère*

H Bains 11 r de Kerguelen ☎ 98570341 rm30 (Mar-Oct) **A**

★★**Poste** 17 r de l'Église ☎ 98570109 rm37 **B**

BERCK-PLAGE *Pas-de-Calais*

★★**Homard Bleu** 46 pl de l'Entonnoir ☎ 21090465 rm18 **A**

H Marquenterre 31 av F-Tattegrain ☎ 21091213 rm13 **A**

BERGERAC *Dordogne*

★★**Commerce** 36 pl Gambetta ☎ 53273050 rm30 Closed Feb **B**

H Europ (n.rest) 20 r Petit-Sol ☎ 53570654 rm22 **A**

H France (n.rest) 18 pl Gambetta ☎ 53571161 rm20 **B**

H Mounet-Sully (n.rest) rte de Mussidan ☎ 53570421 rm8 (May-Oct) **A**

BESANÇON *Doubs*

H Florel (n.rest) 6 r de la Viotte ☎ 81804108 rm24 **A**

H Foch av Foch ☎ 81803041 rm28 **A**

H Franc-Comtois 24 r Proud'hon ☎ 81832435 rm22 **A**

★**Gambetta** (n.rest) 13 r Gambetta ☎ 81820233 rm26 **A**

★**Granville** (n.rest) 13 r du Gl-Lecourbe ☎ 81813392 rm26 **A**

H Moncey 6 r Moncey ☎ 81812477 rm25 **A**

H Nord (n.rest) 8 r Moncey ☎ 81813456 rm44 **A**

H Paris 33 r des Granges ☎ 81813656 rm60 **A**

H Terrass 38 av Carnot ☎ 81880303 rm38 **A**

BESSENAY *Rhône*

H Auberge de la Brevenne La Brevenne ☎ 74708001 rm7 **A**

BÉTHUNE *Pas-de-Calais*

★★**Vieux Beffroy** 48 Grand-Pl ☎ 21681500 rm67 **A**

BEYNAC-ET-CAZENAC *Dordogne*

★★**Bonnet** ☎ 53295001 rm22 (Apr-Oct) **A**

H Château ☎ 53295013 rm16 **A**

BÉZIERS *Hérault*

H France 36 r Broieldieu ☎ 67284471 rm20 **A**

★★★**Imperator** 28 allée P-Riquet ☎ 67490225 rm45 **B**

H Lux 3 r des Petits-Champs ☎ 67284805 rm22 **A**

H Poetes 80 allée P-Riquet ☎ 67763866 rm14 **A**

H Splendid (n.rest) 24 av du 22 Août 1944 ☎ 67282382 rm26 **A**

H Terminus 76-78 av Gambetta ☎ 67492364 rm40 **A**

BIARRITZ *Pyrénées-Atlantiques*

H Anjou 18 r Gambetta ☎ 59240093 rm30 **A**

H Argi-Eder (n.rest) 13 r Peyroloubilh ☎ 59242253 rm17 **A**

H Atalaye pl de l'Atalaye ☎ 59240676 rm25 (Mar-Oct) **B**

H Auberge du Relais 44 av de la Marne ☎ 59248590 rm14 **A**

★★**Beau Lieu** 3 espl du Port Vieux ☎ 59242359 rm28 (Mar-Oct) **B**

H Beau Soleil (n.rest) 6 r du Port-Vieux ☎ 59242651 rm19 (May-Sep) **A**

H Lorisse (n.rest) 8 av du Ml-Joffre ☎ 59247053 rm10 **B**

H Maitagaria (n.rest) 34 av Carnot ☎ 59242665 rm17 **A**

H Malouthea (n.rest) 3 av du Jardin ☎ 59240600 rm25 **A**

H Monguillot (n.rest) 3 r G-Larre ☎ 59241223 rm15 (Etr-Dec) **A**

★**Palacito** (n.rest) 1 r Gambetta ☎ 59240489 rm26 **B**

H Puerta del Sol (n.rest) 5 r de la Bergerie ☎ 59243418 rm11 (Etr-Oct) **A**

H St-James 15 r Gambetta ☎ 59240636 rm15 (Mar-Oct) **A**

H Washington (n.rest) 34 r Mazagran ☎ 59241080 rm20 (Mar-Nov) **A**

BISCARROSSE *Landes*

H Relais (n.rest) 12 av Ml-Lyautey ☎ 58781046 rm24 **B**

H St-Hubert 44 av P-G-Latecoere ☎ 58780999 rm16 **A**

BLOIS *Loir-et-Cher*

H Anne de Bretagne (n.rest) 21 av J-Laigret ☎ 54780538 rm29 **A**

H Gerbe d'Or 1 r Bourg-Neuf ☎ 54742645 rm26 **A**

H Grand Cerf 40 av Wilson ☎ 54780216 rm11 Closed Feb **A**

H Grand Gare et Terminus 6 et 8 av J-Laigret ☎ 54742457 rm33 **A**

H Renaissance 9 r du Pont-du-Gast ☎ 54780263 rm10 **A**

H Savoie 6-8 r Ducoux ☎ 54743221 rm27 **A**

H Vendôme 10 av de Vendôme ☎ 54741666 rm46 **A**

BLONVILLE-SUR-MER *Calvados*

★**Mer** (n.rest) 93 av de la République ☎ 31879323 rm20 (Mar-Nov) **A**

BOLLÈNE *Vaucluse*

H Lez (n.rest) 16 cours de la République ☎ 90301619 rm17 **B**

BONNEVILLE *Haute-Savoie*

H Avre (n.rest) r du Pont ☎ 50971028 rm16 (Seasonal) **B**

BORDEAUX *Gironde*

Capital of Aquitaine, a region noted for its pleasant climate, beautiful scenery and superb beaches, Bordeaux lies in a sweeping plain beside the wine-producing district of Médoc.

The city – which belonged to the English during the turbulent period from 1154-1453 – retains a wealth of monuments and sites from Roman and medieval times, though much of the present elegance dates from the 18th century.

EATING OUT Aquitaine's cuisine is rich and varied. Among the dishes to look out for are *entrecôte bordelaise*, mushrooms, and all fish and shellfish dishes. Smoked chicken, turkey escalopes, turkey roasts and râgout of wild duck are typical delicacies in and around the city, as are oysters from Arcachon and young eels from the Ardour river near Biarritz. The delicious smoked ham from Bayonne is used in a fish dish made from fresh mountain stream trout, cooked with shredded ham. For dessert, *gâteaux Basque*, a rich moist butter sponge cake flavoured with ground almonds or fruit, is particularly tasty, and stuffed walnuts are another speciality.

Excellent fish dishes can be enjoyed at *Chez Philippe*, in Place du Parlement, and good regional fare at *Tulipa*, in rue Porte de la Monnaie.

H Aquitaine (n.rest) 111 cours d'Albert ☎ 56931960 rm16 **B**

★★**Batonne** (n.rest) 15 cours de l'Intendance ☎ 56480088 rm37 **A**

★★**Bayonne** (n.rest) 15 cours de l'Intendance ☎ 56480088 rm37 **A**

H Buffon 5 r Buffon ☎ 56444225 rm20 **A**

H Centre (n.rest) 8 r du Temple ☎ 56481329 rm15 **A**

H Français (n.rest) 12 r du Temple ☎ 56481035 rm36 **B**

H Madeleine (n.rest) 32 cours Pasteur ☎ 56915155 rm19 **A**

★★★**Normandie** (n.rest) 7 cours du 30 Juillet ☎ 56521680 rm100 **B**

H Presse (n.rest) 6 et 8 r P-Dijeaux ☎ 56485388 rm29 **B**

H Printania 34 r Servandoni ☎ 56965672 rm18 **A**

H Rolland (n.rest) 7 r Rolland ☎ 56481598 rm17 **A**

H Royal Medoc (n.rest) 3 r de Séze ☎ 56817242 rm45 **B**

H St-Martin (n.rest) 2 r St-V-de-Paul ☎ 56915540 rm19 **B**

H Théâtre (n.rest) 10 r de la Maison Daurade ☎ 56790526 rm25 **B**

BORT-LES-ORGUES *Corrèze*

H Central (n.rest) 65 av de la Gare ☎ 55967482 rm25 **B**

BOULOGNE-SUR-MER *Pas-de-Calais*

★★**Alexandre** (n.rest) 93 r Thiers ☎ 21305222 rm20 Closed Jan **A**

★**Londres** (n.rest) 22 pl de France ☎ 21313563 rm20 **A**

★★**Lorraine** (n.rest) 7 pl de Lorraine ☎ 21313478 rm21 **A**

★★**Metropole** (n.rest) 51 r Thiers ☎ 21315430 rm29 **A**

BOURBONNE-LES-BAINS *Haute-Marne*

H Herard 29-31-35 Grand-R ☎ 25901333 rm43 **B**

H Jeanne d'Arc 12 r Aml-Pierre ☎ 25901255 rm37 (Apr-Oct) **B**

H Lauriers Roses 24 pl des Bains ☎ 25900097 rm80 (Apr-Oct) **A**

BOURBOULE, LA *Puy-de-Dôme*

H Aviation r de Metz ☎ 73810977 rm30 (Seasonal) **A**

H Charlet bd L-Choussy ☎ 73810580 rm43 **A**

H Fleurs av Gueneau-de-Mussy ☎ 73810944 rm24 Jan-Sep **A**

H Louvre bd G-Clemenceau B-P ☎ 73810133 rm53 (May-Sep) **A**

H Parc quai Ml-Fayolle ☎ 73810177 rm54 (May-Sep) **A**

H Regina av d'Alsace-Lorraine ☎ 73810922 rm25 (Seasonal) **A**

BOURG-EN-BRESSE *Ain*

H Commerce 1 av P-Sémard ☎ 74213041 rm23 **B**

H France 19 pl Bernard ☎ 74233024 rm53 **A**

★★★**Le Logis de Brou** (n.rest) 132 bd de Brou ☎ 74221155 rm30 **B**

H Les Negociants 9 r C-Robin ☎ 74231324 rm14 **A**

H Mail 46 av du Mail ☎ 74210026 rm9 **A**

H Terminus 19 r A-Baudin ☎ 74210121 rm50 **B**

BOURGES *Cher*

★★**Christina** (n.rest) 5 r de la Halle ☎ 48705650 rm76 **A**

H Cygne 10 pl du Gl-Leclerc ☎ 48705105 rm21 (Seasonal) **A**

H Hostellerie du Grand Argentier 9 r Parerie ☎ 48708431 rm14 Closed Jan **B**

H Olympia (n.rest) 66 av Orléans ☎ 48704984 rm39 **B**

★★St-Jean (n.rest) 23 av M-Dormoy ☎ 48241348 rm24 Closed Feb **A**

H Tilleuls (n.rest) 7 pl de la Pyrotachnie ☎ 48204904 rm21 **A**

BRESSE, LA *Vosges*

H Chalet des Roches (n.rest) 10 r des Noisettes ☎ 29255022 rm28 **A**

BREST *Finistère*

H Bretagne (n.rest) 24 r de l'Harteloire ☎ 98804118 rm21 **A**

H France av A-Reveillere ☎ 98461888 rm40 **A**

H Paix (n.rest) 32 r Algesiras ☎ 98801297 rm25 **B**

H Vauban 17 av Clemenceau ☎ 98460688 rm52 **B**

H Voyageurs av Clemenceau ☎ 98802573 rm39 **A**

BRIANÇON *Hautes-Alpes*

H Edelweiss 32 av de la République ☎ 92210294 rm23 **B**

★★★Montbrison (n.rest) av Gl-de-Gaulle ☎ 92211455 rm44 Closed Nov **A**

H Paris 41 av du Gl-de-Gaulle ☎ 92201530 rm21 **A**

H Relais de Lenlon 43 av de Savoie ☎ 92210298 rm12 **B**

★★★Vauban 13 av Gl-de-Gaulle ☎ 92211211 rm45 **B**

BRIGNOLES *Var*

H Château-Brignoles-en-Provence quartier Tivloi, av de la Liberation ☎ 94690688 rm39 **A**

H Paris 29 av Dréo ☎ 94690100 rm16 **A**

BRIGUE *Alpes-Maritime*

H Mirval 3 r St-Vincent Ferrier ☎ 93046371 rm18 (Apr-Dec) **B**

BRIONNE *Eure*

★Logis de Brionne 1 pl St-Denis ☎ 32457722 rm16 **A**

BRIOUDE *Haute-Loire*

★★Brivas av du Velay ☎ 71501049 rm30 **B**

BRIVE-LA-GAILLARDE *Corrèze*

H Chapon Fin 1 pl de Lattre-de-Tassigny ☎ 55742340 rm30 **B**

H Terminus face de la Gare ☎ 55742114 rm49 **A**

CAEN *Calvados*

H Astrid (n.rest) 39 r de Bernières ☎ 31854867 rm13 **A**

H Au Depart (n.rest) 28 pl de la Gare ☎ 31822398 rm35 **A**

★★Bristol (n.rest) 31 r du 11 Novembre ☎ 31845976 rm25 **A**

★★Château (n.rest) 5 av du 6-Juin ☎ 31861537 rm21 **B**

H France (n.rest) 10 r de la Gare ☎ 31821699 rm47 **B**

H Quatrans (n.rest) 17 r G-Colin ☎ 31862557 rm36 **A**

H Rotonde pl de la Gare ☎ 31822425 rm33 **A**

H Saint-Pierre (n.rest) 40 bd des Allies ☎ 31862820 rm18 **A**

H Savoy (n.rest) 106 r de Falaise ☎ 31822850 rm30 **A**

CALAIS *Pas-de-Calais*

Calais, only 21 miles from Dover, is the nearest French town to England, the largest town of its *département*, an important port and a popular holiday resort. At the north end of the boulevard Jacquard is the Place du Soldat-Inconnu, the Square of the Unknown Soldier, where Rodin's famous statue stands before the *Hôtel de Ville*.

The George V bridge leads to Calais-Nord, largely rebuilt since 1945. The rue Royale runs north and south through this district, the 13th-century *Tour du Guet* standing to its right.

North of the ruined church of Notre-Dame, currently being restored, is the lighthouse (1848), an octagonal tower 167ft high, visible 38 miles away. For shoppers, the Gro supermarket on the Place d'Armes is convenient for car-ferrry users, while the *Maison du Fromage*, across the square, offers a selection of more than 200 cheeses.

EATING OUT One of the best restaurants in town is the comfortable *Le Channel*, in Boulevard de la Résistance. Specialities include *terrine de langoustes*.

H Albert 1er 53 r de la Mer ☎ 21343608 rm14 **B**

★★Bellevue (n.rest) 23-25 pl d'Armes ☎ 21345375 rm54 **A**

★★George V 36 r Royale ☎ 21976800 rm45 **A**

★★Pacific 38 r de Guise ☎ 21345024 rm27 **A**

H Victoria r de Madrid ☎ 21343832 rm15 **A**

CALVI *Haute-Corse*

H Caravelle à la Plage ☎ 95650121 rm20 (Mar-Sep) **B**

H St-Erasme rte de Portol ☎ 95650121 rm31 (Apr-Oct) **B**

CAMBRAI *Nord*

H Commerce 9 r du 11 Novembre ☎ 27813488 rm9 **A**

★France (n.rest) 37 r Lille ☎ 27813932 rm24 Closed Aug **A**

★★Mouton Blanc 33 r d'Alsace-Lorraine ☎ 27813016 rm31 **A**

H Primevère ☎ 64497474 rm42 **B**

M Ulys 67 rte d'Arras ☎ 27838325 rm31 **A**

CANCALE *Ille-et-Vilaine*

H Emeraude quai Thomas ☎ 99896176 rm16 (Mar-Nov) **A**

H Pointe du Grouin ☎ 99896055 rm17 (Etr-Sep) **A**

CANET-EN-ROUSSILLON *Pyrénées-Orientales*

H Inter Les Sables ☎ 68802363 rm41 **B**

H Mes Vacances (n.rest) 2 bd du Roussillon ☎ 68803529 rm20 (Jun-Sep) **B**

CANET-PLAGE *Pyrénées-Orientales*

H Marenda 73 bd Herriot ☎ 68803530 rm32 (Feb-Nov) **A**

CANNES *Alpes-Maritimes*

Cannes is a fashionable resort in the Alpes-Maritimes *département* of France, 13 miles south-west of Nice. Until 1834 it was a small fishing village nestling beneath the ruins of an 11th-century castle at the head of the Golfe de la Napoule, and sheltered from the mistral by the Esterel. That year Lord Brougham, Britain's Lord Chancellor, *en route* to Nice when an outbreak of cholera forced the authorities to freeze all travel, fell in love with Cannes and built a villa here as an annual refuge from the British winter; over the next century the English aristocracy, tsars, kings and princes followed his example, and Cannes became a centre for the international élite. The steep, cobbled streets of le Suquet, the old town, are well worth exploring. The modern resort extends along the littoral behind the Boulevard de la Croisette. Almost all of Cannes' beaches are private, but can be used by visitors for a fee.

EATING OUT The *Mirabelle*, in Rue St-Antoine, in the old part of town, is one of the most popular restaurants in the resort, noted for its imaginative cuisine and regional and national specialities.

H Étrangers (n.rest) 6 pl Pierre ☎ 93388282 rm53 Closed Dec **B**

H Albert (n.rest) 1er 68 av de Grasse ☎ 93392404 rm14 **B**

H Alpes (n.rest) 15 r St-Dizier ☎ 93391290 rm21 **B**

H Ascott (n.rest) 27 r des Serbes ☎ 93991824 rm14 Closed Nov-Dec **B**

H Atlantis (n.rest) 4 r du 24 Août ☎ 93391872 rm38 **A**

H Bivouac 29 r Bivouac Napoléon ☎ 93396217 rm21 Closed Nov & Dec **A**

H Bristol (n.rest) 14 r Hoche ☎ 93391066 rm19 **A**

H Cavendish (n.rest) 11 bd Carnot ☎ 93390695 rm33 **A**

H Couronne d'Or av Beauséjour ☎ 93385369 rm12 **A**

H Delft 20 r J-de-Riouffe ☎ 93393990 rm10 **A**

H Festival (n.rest) 3 r Molière ☎ 93386945 rm17 Closed Dec **A**

H Gabres 62 bd d'Alsace ☎ 93436573 rm24 (Mar-Dec) **B**

H Hippocampe (n.rest) 10 r du Bateguier ☎ 93399742 rm10 **B**

H Lutetia 6 r M-Ange ☎ 93393574 rm8 **A**

H Mistral (n.rest) 13 r des Belges ☎ 93399146 rm12 **B**

H Olympia 7 bis r de Mimont ☎ 93384627 rm25 **A**

H Pullman 9 r J-Daumas ☎ 93386291 rm15 **B**

H Vendôme (n.rest) 37 bd d'Alsace ☎ 93383433 rm19 **B**

CANNET, LE *Alpes-Maritimes*

H Picardy (n.rest) Bretelle de l'Autoroute ☎ 93453535 rm25 **B**

CAPBRETON *Landes*

H Aquitaine 66 av Ml-de-Lattre-de-Tassigy ☎ 58723811 rm24 Closed Jan **B**

H Lou Chaque Dit 69 bd de la Plage ☎ 58720677 rm29 **B**

H Miramar bd du Front de Mer ☎ 58721282 rm44 (May-Sep) **B**

★★Océan 85 av G-Pompidou ☎ 58721022 rm48 (Mar-Oct) **A**

CAP-COZ *Finistère*

H Belle Vue 30 Descente de Belle-Vue ☎ 98560033 rm21 (Mar-Oct) **A**

CAP-D'AGDE *Hérault*

H Palmeria Ile St-Martin ☎ 67260007 rm50 (Apr-Sep) **B**

H Pins (n.rest) r du Labech-Mont-St ☎ 67260011 rm40 **B**

H Voile d'Or ☎ 67263018 rm20 **A**

CAP-D'AIL *Alpes-Maritimes*

★★Miramar 126 av du 3 Septembre ☎ 93780660 rm27 **B**

H Normandy 6 allée des Orangers ☎ 93787777 rm20 **B**

CAPDENAC-GARE *Aveyron*

H Auberge la Diège St-Julien-d'Empare ☎ 65647054 rm15 **A**

CAPVERN-LES-BAINS *Hautes-Pyrénées*

H Paris r de Provence ☎ 62390015 rm50 (Apr-Oct) **A**

CARCANS *Gironde*

H Arcade (n.rest) 5 sq Gambetta ☎ 68723737 rm48 **B**

H Central (n.rest) 27 bd Jean Jaures ☎ 68250384 rm22 **A**

H Lac Maubuisson ☎ 56033003 rm39 (Mar-Oct) **B**

H Logis de Trencavel 286 av Gal Leclerc ☎ 68710953 rm12 **A**

H Residence 25 r Antoine Marty ☎ 68250896 rm25 **A**

CARCASSONNE *Aude*

H Bristol 7 av du Ml-Foch ☎ 68250724 rm70 (Mar-Nov) **A**

H Royal 22 bd J-Jaurès ☎ 68251912 rm27 **A**

CARLUX *Dordogne*

H Cayre et Fils ☎ 53297024 rm21 Closed Oct **A**

CARNAC *Morbihan*

H Celtique av Ker-Mario ☎ 97521149 rm35 (Mar-Nov) **A**

H Marine 4 pl de la Chapelle ☎ 97520733 rm33 Closed Jan **B**

H Tumulus 31 r du Tumulus ☎ 97520821 rm27 (Apr-Oct) **A**

CAROMB *Vaucluse*

H Beffroi Vieux Village ☎ 90624563 rm10 **B**

CARROS *Alpes-Maritimes*

H Lou Castelet Plan-de-Carros ☎ 93291666 rm22 Closed Nov **A**

CARROZ-D'ARÂCHES, LES *Haute-Savoie*

H Croix de Savoie ☎ 50900026 rm19 (seasonal) **B**

CASSIS *Bouches-du-Rhône*

H Grand Jardin 2 r P-Eydin ☎ 42017010 rm26 Closed Jan **B**

CASTELJALOUX *Lot-et-Garonne*

★Cadets de Gascogne pl Gambetta ☎ 53930059 rm14 **A**

CASTELLANE *Alpes-de-Haute-Provence*

H Levant pl M-Sauvaire ☎ 92836005 rm33 (May-Nov) **A**

H Nouvel du Commerce pl de l'Église ☎ 92836100 rm44 (Apr-Oct) **B**

CASTELNAUDARY *Aude*

H France et Notre-Dame 2 r F-Mistral ☎ 68231018 rm26 **A**

★Grand Fourcade 14 r des Carmes ☎ 68230208 rm14 (May-Dec) **A**

CASTERA-VERDUZAN *Gers*

H Tenareze ☎ 62681022 rm22 **A**

★★Thermes Grande Rue ☎ 62681307 rm41 **A**

CASTRES *Tarn*

★★Grand 11 r de la Libération ☎ 63590030 rm40 **A**

CAUDEBEC-EN-CAUX *Seine-Maritime*

★★**Normandie** 19 quai Guilbaud ☏ 35962511 rm16 Closed Feb **A**

CAUSSADE *Tarn-et-Garonne*

★★**Dupont** 25 r des Recollets ☏ 63650500 rm31 Closed Nov **A**

CAUTERETS *Hautes-Pyrénées*

H Etcheona 20 r Richelieu ☏ 62925143 rm35 Closed Oct & Nov **B**

H Ste-Cecile 10 bd Latapie-Flurin ☏ 62925047 rm36 Closed Oct & Nov **A**

CAVAILLON *Vaucluse*

H Parc (n.rest) pl Duclos ☏ 90710779 rm40 **A**

CAVALAIRE-SUR-MER *Var*

H Maya (n.rest) Angle des av Ml-Lyautey ☏ 94643382 rm15 **B**

H Raymond av des Alliès ☏ 94640732 rm35 (Mar-Nov) **B**

CEAUX *Manche*

H Au P'tit Quinquin rte du Mt-St-Michael ☏ 33709720 rm18 (Apr-Sep) **A**

CERET *Pyrénées-Orientales*

H Pyrénées 7 r de la République ☏ 68871102 rm22 (May-Oct) **A**

CEYRAT *Puy-de-Dôme*

H Poste 47 av Wilson ☏ 73613001 rm6 **A**

H Promenade 1 av Wilson ☏ 73614046 rm12 **A**

CHAISE-DIEU, LA *Haute-Loire*

H Echo et Abbaye ☏ 71000045 rm11 (Apr-Nov) **B**

H Lion d'Or Prés de l'Abbaye ☏ 71000158 rm15 (Etr-Nov) **A**

★★**Tremblant** Departementale ☏ 71000185 rm28 (Apr-Nov) **A**

CHALEZEULE *Doubs*

H Trois Iles (n.rest) r du Clos ☏ 81610066 rm16 **B**

CHALLANS *Vendée*

H Antiquite (n.rest) 14 r Gallieni ☏ 51680284 rm12 **B**

H Commerce 17 pl A-Briand ☏ 51680624 rm20 **A**

CHALONS-SUR-MARNE *Marne*

★★**Bristol** (n.rest) 77 av Sémard ☏ 26682463 rm24 **A**

★★**Pasteur** (n.rest) 46 r Pasteur ☏ 26681000 rm28 **A**

H Renard 24 pl de la République ☏ 26680378 rm50 **A**

CHALON-SUR-SAÔNE *Saône-et-Loire*

H Central (n.rest) 19 pl de Beaune ☏ 85483500 rm29 **A**

H Europe (n.rest) 11 r du Port-Villiers ☏ 85487048 rm21 **A**

H Laurentides quai St-Cosme ☏ 85482985 rm29 **A**

★★**St-Jean** (n.rest) 24 q. Gambetta ☏ 85484565 rm25 **A**

CHALUS *Haute-Vienne*

H Carrefour ☏ 55784169 rm10 **A**

H Centre pl de la Fontaine ☏ 55784161 rm9 **A**

CHAMBERY *Savoie*

H Lion d'Or (n.rest) 13 av de la Boisse ☏ 79690496 rm39 **B**

CHAMBON-SUR-LIGNON *Haute-Loire*

H Bois Vialotte rte de la Suchère ☏ 71597403 rm17 (seasonal) **A**

H Central ☏ 71597067 rm25 Closed Oct **A**

CHAMONIX-LES-PRAZ *Haute-Savoie*

H Simond et du Golf 14 r de la Chapelle ☏ 50530608 rm24 (seasonal) **A**

CHAMONIX-LES-TINES *Haute-Savoie*

H Excelsior 251 ch de St-Roch ☏ 50531836 rm43 Closed Oct & Nov **B**

CHAMONIX-MONT-BLANC *Haute-Savoie*

H Bon Coin (n.rest) 80 av Aiguille du Midi ☏ 50531567 rm20 (seasonal) **B**

H Chalet Hotel Beausoleil 60 allée des Peupliers ☏ 50540078 rm16 Closed Oct & Nov **A**

H Eaux Vives (n.rest) 751 rte des Gaillands ☏ 50531629 rm18 (seasonal) **B**

H Étrangers av. M Croz ☏ 50530031 rm45 (seasonal) **A**

H Hermitage et Paccard R. des Cristalliers ☏ 50531387 rm33 (seasonal) **A**

H Relais des Gaillands 964, route des Gaillands ☏ 50531358 rm20 **B**

★★★**Richemond** 228 r Dr-Paccard ☏ 50530885 rm52 (seasonal) **A**

H Roma (n.rest) 289 av Ravanel-le-Rouge ☏ 50530062 rm33 (Seasonal) **A**

CHAMPAGNOLE *Jura*

H Parc 13 r de P-Crétin ☏ 84521320 rm18 **A**

★★★**Ripotot** 54 r du Ml-Foch ☏ 84521545 rm60 (Apr-Oct) **A**

CHAMPTOCEAUX *Maine-et-Loire*

H Côte 2 r du Dr-Giffard ☏ 40835039 rm30 **A**

CHAPELLE-D'ABONDANCE *Haute-Savoie*

H Chabi ☏ 50735014 rm22 (seasonal) **B**

H Rucher ☏ 50735023 rm22 (seasonal) **A**

H Vieux Moulin rte de Chevesnes ☏ 50735252 rm16 (seasonal) **A**

CHAPELLE-D'ANDAINE *Orne*

H Cheval Blanc ☏ 33381188 rm12 **A**

CHAPELLE-EN-VERCORS, LA *Drôme*

H Bellier ☏ 75482003 rm12 (Jun-Sep) **A**

CHARAVINES *Isère*

H Poste Le Bourg ☏ 76066041 rm20 Closed Nov **B**

CHARITÉ-SUR-LOIRE, LA *Nièvre*

H Bon Laboureur quai R-Mollot ☏ 86700199 rm17 **A**

H Grand Monarque 33 quai Clemenceau ☏ 86702173 rm9 Closed Feb **B**

CHARLEVILLE-MÉZIÈRES *Ardennes*

H Pelican 42 av Ml-Leclerc ☏ 24564273 rm20 **B**

H Relais du Square 3 pl Gare ☏ 24333876 rm49 **B**

CHAROLLES *Saône-et-Loire*

★★**Moderne de la Gare** 14 av de la Gare ☏ 85240702 rm18 Closed Jan **B**

CHARQUEMONT *Doubs*

H Poste 6 pl de l'Hôtel-de-Ville ☎ 81440020 rm32 **A**

CHARTRES *Eure-et-Loir*

★Ouest (n.rest) 3 pl Sémard ☎ 37214327 rm26 **A**

★★Poste 3, r du Gal Koenig ☎ 37210427 rm58 **A**

CHARTRE-SUR-LE-LOIR, LA *Sarthe*

★★France 20 pl de la République ☎ 43444016 rm28 **A**

CHÂTAIGNERAIE, LA *Vendée*

H Terrasse 7 r de Beauregard ☎ 51696868 rm14 **A**

CHÂTEAU-ARNOUX *Alpes-de-Haute-Provence*

H Bonne Etape ch du Lac ☎ 92640009 rm18 Closed Jan **A**

H Lac allées des Erables ☎ 92640432 rm17 **A**

H Villard (n.rest) St-Auban ☎ 92641742 rm20 **B**

CHÂTEAUBRIANT *Loire-Atlantique*

★Armor (n.rest) pl.de la Motte ☎ 40811119 rm20 **B**

H Terminus (n.rest) 3, pl. de la Gare ☎ 40281436 rm12 **A**

CHÂTEAUDUN *Eure-et-Loir*

★★Beauce (n.rest) 50 r de Jallans Châteaudun ☎ 37451475 rm22 **A**

H St-Michel 5 r Péan ☎ 37451570 rm18 **A**

CHÂTEAULIN *Finistère*

H Bon Accueil Port-Launay ☎ 98861577 rm59 Closed Jan **A**

CHÂTEAUNEUF *Côte-d'Or*

★★Hostellerie du Château ☎ 80492200 rm14 (May-Nov) **A**

CHÂTEAUNEUF-DE-GALAURE *Drôme*

H Galaure pl de la Poste ☎ 75686222 rm21 **A**

CHÂTEAUNEUF-GRASSE *Alpes-Maritimes*

H Auberge des Santons Pré-du-Lac ☎ 93424097 rm17 (Feb-Oct) **A**

CHÂTEAUNEUF-LE-ROUGE *Bouches-du-Rhône*

H Galinière RN 7 ☎ 42586204 rm21 **A**

CHÂTEAUNEUF-SUR-LOIRE *Loiret*

★Novotel du Loiret 4 pl A-Briand ☎ 38584228 rm20 **A**

CHÂTEAUROUX *Indre*

H Boischaut (n.rest) 135 av de la Châtre ☎ 54222234 rm27 **B**

H Bonnet (n.rest) 14 r du Marché ☎ 54221354 rm20 **A**

H Christina (n.rest) 250 av de la Châtre ☎ 54340177 rm33 **A**

H Continental 17 r du Palais-de-Justice ☎ 54343612 rm26 **A**

H Gare 5 pl de la Gare ☎ 54227780 rm28 **B**

H Mazagran 35 r de la Poste ☎ 54223844 rm7 **B**

H Parc 148 av de Paris ☎ 54343683 rm28 Closed Nov **A**

H St-Hubert 25 r de la Poste ☎ 54340674 rm12 **B**

H Voltaire 42 pl Voltaire ☎ 54341744 rm37 **B**

CHÂTEL *Haute-Savoie*

H Bergerie rte de l'Etringua ☎ 50732231 rm26 (seasonal) **A**

H Castellan la Bechigne ☎ 50732086 rm32 (seasonal) **A**

H Eau Vive l'Essert ☎ 50732114 rm23 (seasonal) **A**

CHÂTELAILLON-PLAGE *Charente-Maritime*

★★Majestic bd de la Libération ☎ 46562053 rm30 **A**

H Orbigny (n.rest) 47 bd de la République ☎ 46562468 rm47 (May-Sep) **A**

H Rivage 36 bd de la Mer ☎ 46562579 rm42 **A**

CHÂTELGUYON *Puy-de-Dôme*

H Bruyères 1 r Chalusset ☎ 73860109 rm28 (Apr-Oct) **A**

H Univers 37 av Baraduc ☎ 73860271 rm40 **A**

CHÂTELLERAULT *Vienne*

★★Croissant 19 av Kennedy ☎ 49210177 rm20 **A**

★★★Grand Moderne 74 bd Blossac ☎ 49213011 rm37 **A**

CHÂTEAU-CHINON *Nièvre*

★★Vieux Morvan 8 pl Gudin ☎ 86850501 rm23 **A**

CHÂTILLON-SUR-CHALARONNE *Ain*

H Chevalier Norbert av C-Desormes ☎ 74550222 rm20 **B**

H Tour pl de la République ☎ 74550512 rm12 Closed Jan **A**

CHÂTILLON-SUR-SEINE *Côte-d'Or*

★★Côte d'Or r C-Ronot ☎ 80911329 rm11 **B**

★★Sylvia (n.rest) 9 av de la Gare ☎ 80910244 rm21 **A**

CHAUDES-AIGUES *Cantal*

H Thermes 21 av Président ☎ 71235118 rm34 (seasonal) **A**

CHAUMONT *Haute-Marne*

H Grand Val rte de Langres ☎ 25039035 rm60 **A**

★★★Mapotel-Terminus-Reine pl de la Gare ☎ 25036666 rm63 **B**

M Val de Villier 29 av Foch ☎ 25035472 rm22 **B**

CHAUX-DES-CROTENAY *Jura*

H Lacs Pt de-la-Chaux ☎ 84515042 rm30 Closed Nov **A**

CHENONCEAUX *Indre-et-Loire*

H Ottoni 7 r Dr-Bretonneau ☎ 47239009 rm27 (Mar-Nov) **A**

★Roy 9 r Dr-Bretonneau ☎ 47239017 rm40 (Feb-Nov) **A**

CHERBOURG *Manche*

The port of Cherbourg, its harbour created by the building of a massive breakwater, is both a naval base and an important terminus of travel. There seems to have been a castle here in early medieval times, and a Count of Cherbourg was with William the Conqueror in 1066. To the west of the Gare Maritime and its jetty is the bathing beach. Next to it is the Place Napoléon, with an equestrian monument to the Emperor, and the Church of the Trinity (1423-1504), a good example of Flamboyant Gothic with a notable south porch. Continuous with the

Place Napoléon is the Place de la République, where the *Hôtel de Ville* houses the Thomas Henry Museum and its interesting collection of paintings. From the *Hôtel de Ville* the Rue de la Paix runs west to the Rue de l'Abbé, which skirts the Parc Emmanuel-Lias, where there are many exotic trees and shrubs, a natural history museum, and a coin collection. EATING OUT *Le Vauban*, on Quai de Caligny, has both a snack bar and a restaurant, the former offering a huge range of reasonably priced *hors d'oeuvres* as well as a *plat du jour* of meat or fish.

★★**Beauséjour** (n.rest) 26 r Grande-Vallée ☎ 33531030 rm27 **A**

★★**Louvre** 2 r H-Dunant ☎ 33530228 rm42 **A**

H Torgistorps (n.rest) 14 pl de la République ☎ 33933232 rm14 **A**

CHINON *Indre-et-Loire*

★**Boule d'Or** 66 quai J-d'Arc ☎ 47930313 rm16 Closed Jan **B**

H Chris Hotel (n.rest) 12 pl J-d'Arc ☎ 47933692 rm24 **B**

H Diderot (n.rest) 4 r de Buffon ☎ 47931887 rm20 **A**

H France (n.rest) 47 pl du Gl-de-Gaulle ☎ 47933391 rm23 (Mar-Dec) **A**

H Gar'Hotel (n.rest) pl de la Gare ☎ 47930086 rm8 **A**

★**Hostellerie Gargantua** 73 r Voltaire ☎ 47930471 rm11 (Mar-Nov) **A**

H Progrès (n.rest) 19 r du Raineau ☎ 47931640 rm13 **A**

CHISSEAUX *Indre-et-Loire*

H Clair Cottage 27 r de l'Europe ☎ 47239069 rm21 **A**

CHITENAY *Loir-et-Cher*

H Auberge du Centre pl de l'Église ☎ 54704211 rm17 **A**

CHOLET *Maine-et-Loire*

H Commerce 194 r Nationale ☎ 41620897 rm15 **A**

H Cormier (n.rest) rte de la Roche-sur-Yon ☎ 41624624 rm14 **A**

H Europe 15 pl de la Gare ☎ 41620097 rm21 **A**

H Le Vieux Chouan (n.rest) 77 av du Ml-Leclerc ☎ 41461099 rm18 **A**

CHONAS-L'AMBALLAN *Isère*

H Domaine de Clairefontaine ☎ 74588152 rm19 Closed Jan **A**

CIBOURE *Pyrénées-Atlantiques*

H Caravelle (n.rest) bd P-Benoit ☎ 59471805 rm20 **A**

CLAYETTE, LA *Saône-et-Loire*

H Poste et du Dauphin 17 r Centrale ☎ 85280245 rm15 **A**

CLERMONT-EN-ARGONNE *Meuse*

H Bellevue ☎ 29874102 rm16 **A**

CLERMONT-FERRAND *Puy-de-Dôme*

H Bordeaux (n.rest) 39 av F-Roosevelt ☎ 73373232 rm32 **B**

H Bristol (n.rest) 6 r St-Rose ☎ 73372565 rm30 **A**

H Confort Hotel (n.rest) 12 r Lamartine ☎ 73930374 rm40 **A**

H Damier 47 bd J-B-Dumas ☎ 73918752 rm22 **A**

H Floride II (n.rest) 30 cours R-Poincaré ☎ 73350020 rm29 **B**

★★★**Gallieni** 51 r Bonnabaud ☎ 73935969 rm80 **B**

H Lyon 16 pl de Jaude ☎ 73933255 rm34 **B**

H Midi 39 av de l'Union-Soviétique ☎ 73924498 rm39 **A**

★★**Minimes** (n.rest) 10 r des Minimes ☎ 73933149 rm27 **A**

★**Ravel** (n.rest) 8 r de Maringues ☎ 73915133 rm16 **A**

H Regina (n.rest) 14 r Bonnabaud ☎ 73934476 rm27 **A**

CLERY-ST-ANDRÉ *Loiret*

H Hostellerie des Bordes 9 r des Bordes ☎ 38457125 rm22 Closed Jan **A**

CLOUANGE *Moselle*

H Europa 19 r Clemenceau ☎ 87670788 rm20 **A**

CLUNY *Saone-et-Loire*

★★**Moderne** Pont de l'Etang ☎ 85590565 rm15 **A**

CLUSAZ, LA *Haute-Savoie*

H Aravis Village (n.rest) ☎ 50024212 rm30 (seasonal) **B**

H Beau Site ☎ 50024047 rm21 (seasonal) **A**

H Bellachat Les Confins ☎ 50024050 rm31 **A**

H Christiania ☎ 50026060 rm30 (seasonal) **A**

H Ferme rte des Aravis-les-Étages ☎ 50025050 rm12 **A**

H Gai Soleil Les Granges ☎ 50024016 rm19 (seasonal) **A**

H Gotty rte des Aravis-les-Étages ☎ 50024328 rm30 (Dec-Etr) **B**

H Montagne ☎ 50026161 rm25 (seasonal) **A**

H Nouvel La Croix ☎ 50024008 rm26 (seasonal) **A**

H Sapins ☎ 50024012 rm27 (seasonal) **A**

COGNAC *Charente*

H Étape 2 av d'Angoulême ☎ 45321615 rm22 **A**

★★**Auberge** 13 r Plumejeau ☎ 45320870 rm24 **A**

H François 1er (n.rest) pl François 1er ☎ 45320718 rm31 **A**

★★**Moderne** (n.rest) 24 r Élysée Mousnier ☎ 45821943 rm40 **B**

H Residence (n.rest) 25 av V-Hugo ☎ 45321609 rm34 **A**

COINGS *Indre*

H Promenade Cere ☎ 54343915 rm16 **A**

COL DE L'ARZELLIER *Isère*

H Deux-Soeurs Château Bernard ☎ 76723768 rm24 **B**

COL DU BONHOMME *Vosges*

H Relais Vosges Alsace ☎ 29503261 rm13 **A**

COL DU DONON *Bas-Rhin*

H Donon ☎ 88972069 rm21 **A**

COLLIOURE *Pyrénées-Orientales*

H Ambielle et Bellevue (n.rest) rte du Port-d'Ayail ☎ 68820874 rm21 (Apr-Sep) **B**

H Bon Port rte de Port-Vendres ☎ 68820608 rm22 (Etr-Sep) **B**

H Frégate 24 quai de l'Amiraute ☎ 68820605 rm24 Closed Dec & Jan **B**

H Templiers 12 quai de l'Amiraute ☎ 68820558 rm50 (Seasonal) **A**

H Triton 1 r J-Bart ☎ 68820652 rm20 **A**

COLLONGES-LA-ROUGE *Corrèze*

H Relais St-Jacques de Compostelle ☎ 55254102 rm12 **A**

COLMAR *Haut-Rhin*

H Arcade Colmar (n.rest) 10 r St-Eloi ☎ 89413014 rm48 **B**

H Beau-Séjour 25 r du Ladhof ☎ 89413716 rm29 **A**

H Colbert (n.rest) 2 r des 3 Epis ☎ 89413105 rm50 **B**

H Majestic 1 r de la Gare ☎ 89414519 rm40 **A**

★★Turenne (n.rest) 10 rte Bâle ☎ 89411226 rm85 **B**

H Ville de Nancy 48 r Vauban ☎ 89412314 rm40 **A**

COMBEAUFONTAINE *Haute-Saône*

★Balcon rte de Paris ☎ 84921113 rm26 **A**

COMBLOUX *Haute-Savoie*

H Aux Ducs de Savoie Le Bouchet ☎ 50586143 rm50 (seasonal) **B**

H Edelweiss ☎ 50586406 rm20 (seasonal) **A**

H Rond-Point des Pistes Le Haut ☎ 50586855 rm29 (seasonal) **B**

COMMERCY *Meuse*

H Paris pl de la Gare ☎ 29910136 rm10 **A**

COMPIÈGNE *Oise*

H Flandre quai de la République ☎ 44832440 rm44 **A**

H France 17 r E-Floquet ☎ 44400274 rm21 **A**

CONCARNEAU *Finistère*

H Halles (n.rest) pl J-Jaurès ☎ 98971141 rm24 **A**

H Modern (n.rest) 5 r du Lin ☎ 98970336 rm19 **A**

CONFOLENS *Charente*

H Emeraude 20 r E-Roux ☎ 45841277 rm18 Closed Jan **A**

CONTREXEVILLE *Vosges*

H Dalia 150 av E-Daudet ☎ 29080440 rm21 (Apr-Oct) **A**

H France av du Roi-Stanislas ☎ 29080413 rm40 **A**

H Lorraine av du Roi-Stanislas ☎ 29080424 rm26 (Apr-Oct) **A**

H Parc 334 av du Shah de Perse ☎ 29080428 rm31 **B**

H Sources (n.rest) 37 r Z-Pacha ☎ 29080448 rm37 (Apr-Sep) **A**

H Souveraine Parc Thermal ☎ 29080959 rm31 (May-Sep) **A**

H Thermes cour d'Honneur ☎ 29081730 rm29 (May-Sep) **A**

CORCELLES-EN-BEAUJOLAIS *Rhône*

H Gailleton Le Bourg ☎ 74664106 rm15 (Mar-Jan) **A**

CORCIEUX *Vosges*

H Conti 2 r d'Alsace ☎ 29506633 rm12 **A**

CORDES *Tarn*

H Hostellerie du Parc rte de Caussade – Les Cabannes ☎ 63560259 rm14 (Mar-Oct) **B**

CORPS *Isère*

H Boustigue ☎ 76300103 rm19 (Seasonal) **B**

H Napoléon pl Napoléon ☎ 76300042 rm22 **A**

★★Poste pl de la Mairie ☎ 76300003 rm19 Closed Dec **B**

CORSE (CORSICA)

AJACCIO *Corse-du-Sud*

H Bella Vista bd Lantivy ☎ 95210797 rm38 **A**

H Imperial 6 bd Albert 1er BP 39 ☎ 95215062 rm58 (Mar-Oct) **B**

H Marengo (n.rest) 2 r Marengo ☎ 95214366 rm18 (Mar-Oct) **B**

PORTO-VECCHIO *Corse-du-Sud*

H Caleche d'Or (n.rest) rte de Bastia ☎ 95701903 rm22 **B**

H Holzer 12 r J-Jaurès ☎ 957005593 rm27 **B**

H Roches Blanches quai Syracuse ☎ 95700696 rm15 (Apr-Oct) **B**

COURCHEVEL *Savoie*

H Avals ☎ 79080378 rm31 (Seasonal) **A**

Isba Quartier des Tovets -, Courchevel 1850 ☎ 79080167 **B**

CREIL *Oise*

★★Climat Zaet de St-Maximin, r H-Bessemer ☎ 44244692 rm42 **B**

H Martinez (n.rest) 9 av J-Uhry ☎ 44550039 rm31 **B**

CRESSENSAC *Lot*

★Chez Gilles ☎ 65377006 rm29 **A**

CREST *Drôme*

H Grand 60 r Hôtel-de-Ville ☎ 75250817 rm20 Closed Jan **A**

CREULLY *Calvados*

FH La Ranconnière (n.rest) ☎ 31222173 rm20 **A**

CROIX-VALMER, LA *Var*

★★Mer quai de la Ricarde ☎ 94795534 rm69 **B**

H Pinède rte de Gigaro ☎ 94543123 rm40 (Apr-Oct) **B**

CROZON *Finistère*

H Mer Le Frêt ☎ 98276165 rm30 (May-Oct) **A**

H Moderne 61 r Alsace-Lorraine ☎ 98270010 rm34 **A**

DALHUNDEN *Bas-Rhin*

H Couronne 24 r du Rhin ☎ 88869716 rm26 **A**

DAMBACH-LA-VILLE *Bas-Rhin*

H Raisin d'Or 28 r Clémenceau ☎ 88924008 rm11 (Feb-Dec) **A**

DAX *Landes*

H Dax Thermal 1 bd Carnot ☎ 58901940 rm128 (Mar-Nov) **B**

H Grand ☎ 58748458 rm138 **B**

H Miradour av E-M-Lacroix ☎ 58749886 rm120 **B**

H Residence de l'Adour bd St-Pierre ☎ 58741811 rm36 (Feb-Nov) **A**

H Tarbelli (n.rest) 5 bd St-Pierre ☎ 58748458 rm40 (Apr-Nov) **B**

H Theodore Denis (n.rest) bd A-Camus ☎ 58900634 rm32 (Mar-Nov) **B**

DEAUVILLE *Calvados*

★★★Altea Port Deauville bd E-Cornuche ☎ 31886262 rm65 **B**

H Brise-Marine (n.rest) 15 r Orliffe ☎ 31882766 rm10 (May-Oct) **A**

H Fresnaye (n.rest) 81 av de la République ☎ 31880971 rm14 **B**

H Marie-Anne (n.rest) 142 av République ☎ 31883532 rm25 **B**

H Nid d'Ete 121 av de la République ☎ 31883667 rm26 **B**

H Patio 178-180 av de la République ☏ 31882507 rm11 (Apr-Dec) **A**

DIE *Drôme*

H St-Dominique (n.rest) 44 r C-Buffardel ☏ 75220308 rm26 Closed Nov & Jan **B**

DIEPPE *Seine-Maritime*

Situated at the mouth of the river Arques on the Channel coast, Dieppe is one of the chief ferry ports in France and a popular seaside resort. At the western end of the town on a cliff-edge is the castle, a picturesque 15th-century building which has now been restored as a museum; among the exhibits are a collection of ivory and examples of Impressionist paintings. The cliff above the castle commands striking panoramic views of land and sea. On the nearby shore, lawns and playgrounds separate the hotels of the broad Boulevard de Verdun from the fine expanse of beach that stretches towards the mouth of the port.

In the town itself are the modern church of Notre-Dame de Bon Secours, and the Church of St James, a fine building of the 13th and 14th centuries, flanked by a square 15th-century tower.

EATING OUT Fish specialities include *sole dieoppoise*, *harengs marinés* (marinated herring), *soupe de poisson* (fish soup) and *marmite dieppoise*, a cream based *bouillabaisse*. *La Marine*, in l'Arcade de la Poissonerie, off la Grande Rue, is noted for its seafood dishes.

★★★Aguado (n.rest) 30 bd de Verdun ☏ 35842700 rm56 **B**

H Arcades 1-3 arcades de la Bourse ☏ 35841412 rm28 **A**

★★Ibis Le Val Druel ☏ 35826530 rm43 **B**

La Presidence bd de Verdun ☏ 35843131 rm89 **B**

H Relais Gambetta 95 av Gambetta ☏ 35841291 rm18 **B**

★★Select (n.rest) 1 r Toustain ☏ 35841466 rm25 **A**

H Univers 10 bd de Verdun ☏ 35841255 rm30 **B**

★★Windsor 18 bd de Verdun ☏ 35841523 rm46 (Dec-Nov) **A**

DIGNE *Alpes-de-Haute-Provence*

H Bourgogne av de Verdun ☏ 92310019 rm20 Closed Dec **A**

H Coin Fleuri 9 bd V-Hugo ☏ 92310451 rm15 (Mar-Oct) **A**

★★Mistre 65 bd Gassendi ☏ 92310016 rm19 (Jan-Nov) **B**

DIJON *Côte-d'Or*

Dijon is an exceptionally rich city of art with numerous fascinating monuments recalling the fact that it was, under the reign of the Dukes of Burgundy, the capital of a state which united Flanders and Bourgogne.

Be sure to visit the *Hôtel Ducal* and the *Palais de Ducs and Palais des Etats* (Palace of the Dukes and Palace of the States of Burgundy) dating from the 14th – 17th centuries; the St Bénigne Cathedral (13th century) with its extremely rare Roman crypt; the Church of Notre-Dame, a masterpiece of Burgundian Gothic; and the Church of St-Michel, a Renaissance jewel. Also well worth visiting are the courthouse, installed in a former headquarters of the Parliament of Burgundy; the many rich private mansions; and the countless well-restored old houses in the pedestrian sector of the city.

Dijon's impressive museums include the *Musée des Beaux-Arts* (Fine Arts Museum), one of the richest in France, the Rude Museum, the Museum of Sacred Art, and the Archaeological Museum.

EATING OUT Widely considered one of the best restaurants in Dijon is the *Jean-Pierre Billoux*, located in a delightfully restored town house in Place Darcy. Good regional cooking can be sampled at *Vinarium*, in Place Bossuet, housed in a 13th-century crypt.

H Allées (n.rest) 27 cours du Gl-de-Gaulle ☏ 80665750 rm37 **A**

★★★Central Ibis 3 pl Grangier ☏ 80304400 rm90 **B**

H Chambellan 92 r Vannerie ☏ 80671267 rm21 **A**

H Ducs (n.rest) 5 r Lamonnoye ☏ 80673131 rm31 **B**

H Gresill 16 av R-Poincaré ☏ 80711056 rm47 **B**

H Inter Hotel du Jura (n.rest) 14 av du Ml-Foch ☏ 80416112 rm75 **B**

H Montchapet (n.rest) 26 r Cellerier ☏ 80353331 rm45 **A**

H Palais 23 r du Palais ☏ 80671626 rm20 **B**

H Paris 9 et 11 av Ml-Foch ☏ 80434188 rm48 **B**

H Poste 5 r du Château ☏ 80305164 rm59 **A**

H Pressoir rte de la Cras ☏ 80414586 rm26 **A**

H Relais Arcade 15 av Albert 1er ☏ 80430112 rm128 **B**

H Relais Bleus Parc de Mirande ☏ 80663240 rm45 **B**

H Saint-Bernard (n.rest) 7 bis, r Courtépée ☏ 80307467 rm19 **A**

H Stade 3 bd Strasbourg ☏ 80653532 rm18 **A**

DINAN *Côtes-du-Nord*

H Alleux rte de Ploubalay ☏ 96851610 rm36 **B**

H Marguerite 29 pl Duguesclin ☏ 96394765 rm19 **A**

DINARD *Ille-et-Vilaine*

★★Bains 38 av George-V ☏ 99461371 rm39 (Mar-Oct) **A**

★★Dunes 5 r Georges Clémenceau ☏ 99461272 rm31 (Mar-Oct) **B**

H Mont-St-Michel 54 bd l'Hôtelier ☏ 99461040 rm27 (Mar-Nov) **B**

H Roche Corneille 4 r G-Clémenceau ☏ 99461447 rm26 (Mar-Oct) **B**

H Tilleuls 36 r de la Gare ☏ 99461806 rm32 (Jan-Nov) **B**

H Vallee 6 av George-V ☏ 99469400 rm26 **A**

DIVONNE-LES-BAINS *Ain*

H Coccinelles (n.rest) rte de Lausanne ☏ 50200696 rm18 **A**

DOLE *Jura*

H Primevère Choisey Zone Commerciale ☏ 84821800 rm30 **A**

DORDIVES *Loiret*

★★César 8 r de la République ☏ 38927320 rm20 **A**

DOUARNENEZ *Finistère*

★★Bretagne (n.rest) 23 r Duguay-Trouin ☏ 98923044 rm27 **A**

DOUSSARD *Haute-Savoie*

H Azur du Lac Brédannaz ☎ 50686749 rm30 (Apr-Oct) **B**

H Port et Lac á Brédannaz ☎ 50686720 rm19 (Feb-Nov) **A**

DRAGUIGNAN *Var*

H Dracenois (n.rest) 14 r du Cros ☎ 94681457 rm14 (Jan-Dec) **A**

H Postillon 27 r G-Gisson ☎ 94680014 rm35 **A**

DREUX *Eure-et-Loir*

★★Auberge Normande 12 pl Metezeau ☎ 37500203 rm16 Closed Jan **B**

H Bec Fin 8 bd Pasteur ☎ 37420413 rm19 **A**

DUCLAIR *Seine-Maritime*

★★Poste 286 quai de la Libération ☎ 35375004 rm20 **A**

DUNKERQUE *Nord*

H Le Xixe Siecle 1 pl de la Gare ☎ 28667928 rm15 **A**

H Metropole 28 r Thiers ☎ 27768418 rm18 **A**

ECHELLES, LES *Savoie*

H Centre r J-J-Rousseau ☎ 79366014 rm15 (Apr-Oct) **A**

ÉPINAL *Vosges*

H Bristol (n.rest) 12 av Gl-de-Gaulle ☎ 29821074 rm46 **A**

H Colombier (n.rest) 104 fbg d'Ambrail ☎ 29355005 rm32 **B**

H Ducs de Lorraine 16 quai Cl-Sorot ☎ 29343520 rm10 **B**

H Moderne (n.rest) 16 r F-Blaudez ☎ 29822104 rm33 **A**

ÉTRETAT *Seine-Maritime*

H Corsaire (n.rest) r du Gl-Leclerc ☎ 35270025 rm12 (Feb-Nov) **A**

EVIAN-LES-BAINS *Haute-Savoie*

H Beaulieu 56 bd J-Jaurès ☎ 50751478 rm35 (Apr-Nov) **A**

H Cygnes av de Grande-Rive ☎ 50750101 rm45 (May-Sep) **A**

★★Materions bd du Royal ☎ 50750416 rm22 (Mar-Oct) **B**

H Moulin a Poivre rte d'Abondance – Neuvecelle ☎ 50752184 rm15 **A**

H Nouvel de France (n.rest) 59 r Nationale ☎ 50750036 rm31 **A**

H Palais (n.rest) 69 r Nationale ☎ 50750046 rm42 (Seasonal) **A**

H Panorama Grande-Rive ☎ 50751450 rm29 (May-Sep) **A**

H Terminus (n.rest) Le Martilay, pl de la Gare ☎ 50751507 rm20 **A**

EVREUX *Eure*

H Biche 9 r Josephine – pl St-Taurin ☎ 32386600 rm42 **A**

H Gambetta (n.rest) 61 bd Gambetta ☎ 32333771 rm32 **A**

★★Orme (n.rest) r des Lombards ☎ 32393412 rm42 **A**

ÉYZIES-DE-TAYAC, LES *Dordogne*

H France-Auberge de Musée r du Moulin ☎ 530698723 rm21 Closed Mar **A**

ÉZE *Alpes-Maritimes*

H Auberge Le Soleil av de la Liberté ☎ 93015146 rm11 **B**

FALAISE *Calvados*

★★Normandie 4 r A-Courbet ☎ 31901826 rm28 **A**

FÉCAMP *Seine-Maritime*

H Angleterre 93-95 r de la Plage ☎ 35280160 rm30 **A**

H Mer (n.rest) 89 bd Albert 1er ☎ 35282464 rm8 Closed Jan **A**

H Poste 4 av Gambetta ☎ 35295511 rm35 **A**

FERTÉ-MACÉ, LA *Orne*

H Auberge d'Andaines La Barbère ☎ 33372028 rm15 **B**

H Auberge du Clouet ☎ 33371822 rm7 **B**

FIGEAC *Lot*

H Hostellerie Champollion 51 allée V-Hugo ☎ 65341016 rm30 (Mar-Jan) **B**

H Pont du Pin 3 allée V-Hugo ☎ 65341260 rm24 **A**

FLERS *Orne*

H Oasis (n.rest) 3 bis r de Paris ☎ 33649580 rm31 **B**

FLORAC *Lozère*

H Central de la Poste ☎ 66450001 rm27 **A**

★★Grand du Parc 47 av J-Monestier ☎ 66450305 rm50 (Mar-Nov) **A**

H Rochefort 106 rte de Mende ☎ 66450257 rm24 (Mar-Nov) **A**

FONT-ROMEU *Pyrénées-Orientales*

H Clair Soleil rte d'Odeillo ☎ 68301365 rm31 (May-Oct) **A**

H Coq Hardi rte de la République ☎ 68301102 rm25 (Seasonal) **B**

H Orée du Bois (n.rest) av E-Brousse ☎ 68300140 rm37 **B**

H Oustalet ☎ 68301174 rm29 Closed (Nov) **A**

★★Pyrénées pl des Pyrénées ☎ 68300149 rm37 Closed Jan **B**

FORÊT-FOUESNANT, LA *Finistère*

★★Baie ☎ 98569715 rm24 **A**

FOUESNANT *Finistère*

★★Pointe à Mousterlin-en-Fouesnant ☎ 98560412 rm67 (May-Sep) **A**

FOUGÈRES *Ille-et-Vilaine*

H Balzac (n.rest) 15 R.N. et r Châteaubriand ☎ 99994246 rm20 **A**

H Grand des Voyageurs 10 pl Gambetta ☎ 99990820 rm36 **A**

FRÉJUS *Var*

H Il Était une Fois r F-Mistral ☎ 94512126 rm20 **A**

GAP *Hautes-Alpes*

★★Mokotel (n.rest) rte de Marseille ☎ 92515782 rm27 **B**

GÉRARDMER *Vosges*

H Bonne Auberge de Martimprey Col de Martimpré ☎ 29631908 rm11 Closed Nov **A**

H Jamagne 2 bd de la Jamagne ☎ 29633686 rm50 (Seasonal) **B**

H Paix Face au Lac ☎ 29633878 rm26 **B**

★★Parc 12 av de la Ville-de-Vichy ☎ 29633243 rm36 (Etr-Sep) **A**

H Romeo 57 bd Kelsch ☎ 29630090 rm17 **A**

H Route Verte 61 bd Jamagne ☎ 29631297 rm35 **A**

★★★**Saut des Cuves** Pont du Saut-des-Cuves ☎ 29633046 rm27 **B**

H Tilleuls les Gouttridos ☎ 29630906 rm38 **A**

H Viry "l'Aubergade" pl des Déportés ☎ 29630241 rm18 **B**

GETS, LES *Haute-Savoie*

H Bel Alpe ☎ 50797411 rm35 (Seasonal) **B**

H Boule de Neige ☎ 50797508 rm22 (Seasonal) **B**

H Regina ☎ 50797476 rm24 (Seasonal) **B**

H Stella (n.rest) BP 4 ☎ 50797087 rm33 (Seasonal) **A**

GISORS *Eure*

H Moderne pl de la Gare ☎ 32552351 rm30 **A**

GOURDON *Lot*

H Bissonnier la Bonne Auberge 51 bd des Marthyrs ☎ 65410248 rm25 **A**

H Château (n.rest) pl St-Pierre ☎ 65410588 rm8 **A**

H Promenade (n.rest) bd Genouilhac ☎ 65410541 rm15 **A**

GOURNAY-EN-BRAY *Seine-Maritime*

H Cygne 20 r Notre-Dame ☎ 35902780 rm30 **A**

GRAMAT *Lot*

H Bourdeaux 17 av du 11 Novembre ☎ 65387010 rm23 **A**

★★**Centre** pl République ☎ 65387337 rm14 **A**

GRANVILLE *Manche*

★★**Bains** 19 r Clémenceau ☎ 33501731 rm56 **A**

H Michelet (n.rest) 5 bis r J-Michelet ☎ 33500655 rm20 **A**

H Simone et Thérèse 520 r du Fourneau, St-Pair-Sur-Mer ☎ 33501127 rm14 (Jun 10-Sep 3) **B**

H Terminus (n.rest) 5 pl de la Gare ☎ 33500205 rm14 **A**

GRASSE *Alpes-Maritimes*

H Bellaudiere rte de Nice ☎ 93360257 rm17 **A**

H Oasis (n.rest) pl de la Buanderie ☎ 93360272 rm13 **B**

GRENOBLE *Isère*

★★**Alpazur** (n.rest) 59 av Alsace-Lorraine ☎ 76464280 rm30 **A**

H Bellevue 1 r de Belgrade ☎ 76466934 rm30 **A**

H Bristol (n.rest) 11 av F-Viallet ☎ 76461118 rm46 **A**

★★**Gallia** (n.rest) 7 bd Ml-Joffre ☎ 76873921 rm36 (Sep-Jun) **A**

H Gambetta 59 bd Gambetta ☎ 76872225 rm46 **A**

H Gloria 12 r A-Bergès ☎ 76461293 rm30 **A**

H Institut (n.rest) 10 r Barbillon ☎ 76463644 rm51 **A**

H Patinoires (n.rest) 12 r M-Chamoux ☎ 76444365 rm35 **B**

H Porte de France (n.rest) 27 quai C-Bernard ☎ 76473973 rm40 **B**

H Splendid (n.rest) 22 r Thiers ☎ 76463312 rm56 **A**

H Stendhal (n.rest) 5 r du Dr-Mazet ☎ 76462144 rm38 **A**

★★★**Terminus** (n.rest) 10 pl de la Gare ☎ 76872433 rm50 **B**

H Touring (n.rest) 26 bd Alsace-Lorraine ☎ 76462432 rm45 **A**

H Trianon 3 r P-Arthand ☎ 76462162 rm38 **A**

GUINGAMP *Cotes-du-Nord*

H Armor (n.rest) 44-46 bd Clemenceau ☎ 96437616 rm23 **A**

H Goeland rte de Conlay ☎ 96210941 rm33 **B**

HAGUENAU *Bas-Rhin*

H Europe Haguenau 15 av du Prof-Leriche ☎ 88935811 rm83 **A**

H Kaiserhof 119 Grand-Rue ☎ 88734343 rm10 **A**

H Motel les Pins (n.rest) rte de Strasbourg ☎ 88936840 rm22 **B**

H National pl de la Gare ☎ 88938570 rm26 **A**

HAVRE, LE *Seine-Maritime*

H Angleterre (n.rest) 1 et 3 r Louis-Philippe ☎ 35424842 rm30 **A**

H Astoria 13 cours de la République ☎ 35250003 rm35 **B**

H Astrid (n.rest) 44 r de Séry ☎ 35422130 rm10 **A**

H Bauza r G-Braque ☎ 35422727 rm26 **A**

H Celtic (n.rest) 106 r Voltaire ☎ 35423977 rm14 **A**

H Du Charolais (n.rest) 134 cours de la République ☎ 35252934 rm15 **A**

H Gambetta (n.rest) 20 r J-Macé ☎ 35422594 rm18 **A**

★★**Monaco** 16 r de Paris ☎ 35422101 rm11 **A**

H Petit Vatel (n.rest) 86 r L-Brindeau ☎ 35417207 rm29 **A**

★★**Richelieu** (n.rest) 132 r de Paris ☎ 35423871 rm20 **A**

H Terminus (n.rest) 23 cours de la République ☎ 35254252 rm44 **A**

HENDAYE *Pyrénées-Atlantiques*

H Lafon bd de la Plage ☎ 59200467 rm60 (May-Oct) **B**

★★★**Liliac** (n.rest) Rond-Point de la Plage ☎ 59200245 rm23 **A**

H Midi (n.rest) 83 bd de Gaulle ☎ 59207048 rm47 (Mar-Oct) **A**

H Sud Americain r d'Othantz ☎ 59207598 rm37 (May-Sep) **A**

HOSSEGOR *Landes*

H Helianthes (n.rest) av de la Côte-d'Argent ☎ 58435219 rm18 (Apr-Oct) **B**

H Huitrières du Lac 1187 av du T-C-F ☎ 58435148 rm9 (Mar-Dec) **B**

HOULGATE *Calvados*

H 1900 17 r des Bains ☎ 31910777 rm18 **A**

JOINVILLE *Haute-Marne*

H Grant Pont 7 r A-Briand ☎ 25943311 rm10 **A**

★**Poste** pl Grève ☎ 25941263 rm11 **A**

★**Soleil d'Or** 9 r des Capucins ☎ 25961566 rm11 (Mar-Jan) **B**

JOUGNE *Doubs*

H Bonjour ☎ 81491045 rm18 (Seasonal) **A**

★**Deux Saisons** ☎ 81490004 rm21 (Seasonal) **A**

JUAN-LES-PINS *Alpes-Maritimes*

★★**Alexandra** r Pauline ☎ 93610136 rm20 (Apr-Oct) **A**

H Castel Mistral 43 r Bricka ☎ 93612104 rm14 (Apr-Oct) **A**

H Central (n.rest) 15 av du Dr-Dautheville ☎ 93610943 rm24 **A**

H Colbert 12 r Bricka ☎ 93612008 rm30 (Mar-Oct) **B**

★★**Cyrano** av L-Gallet ☎ 93610483 rm40 (Apr-Sep) **B**

★★**Emeraude** 11 av Saramartel ☎ 93610967 rm23 (Feb-Nov) **A**

H Marjolaine (n.rest) 15 av Dr-Fabre ☎ 93610660 rm16 **A**

★**Midi** 93 bd Poincaré ☎ 93613516 rm23 (Jan-Oct) **A**

H Pinede av Gallice ☎ 93610395 rm14 (Mar-Nov) **A**

H Regence 2 av de l'Aml-Courbet ☎ 93610939 rm20 (Apr-Oct) **B**

H Savoy 144 bd Wilson ☎ 93611382 rm21 **B**

LAEach name preceded by 'La' is listed under the name that follows it.

LACAUNE *Tarn*

H Central Fusies 2 r de la République ☎ 63370203 rm46 **A**

LALOUVESC *Ardèche*

H Beau Site ☎ 75678214 rm33 (Apr-Sep) **A**

H Relais du Monarque ☎ 75678044 rm20 (May-Oct) **A**

LAMBALLE *Cotes-du-Nord*

★★**Angleterre** 29 bd Jobert ☎ 96310016 rm22 **B**

★★**Tour d'Agent** 2 r du Dr-Lavergne ☎ 96310137 rm30 **A**

LANGRES *Haute-Marne*

★**Cheval Blanc** 4 r de l'Estres ☎ 25870700 rm23 Closed Jan **A**

★★**Grand de l'Europe** 23 r Diderot ☎ 25871088 rm28 (Nov-Sep) **A**

★★**Lion d'Or** rte de Vesoul ☎ 25870330 rm14 Closed Jan **A**

LANSLEBOURG-MONT-CENIS *Savoie*

★★★**Alpazur** Val Cenis ☎ 79059369 rm21 (Seasonal) **B**

★**Relais des Deux Cols** ☎ 79059283 rm30 (Seasonal) **A**

LAON *Aisne*

H Commerce 13 pl de la Gare ☎ 23791038 rm25 **A**

LARAGNE-MONTEGLIN *Hautes-Alpes*

H Chrisma (n.rest) rte de Grenoble ☎ 92650936 rm20 (May-Oct) **B**

H Globe ☎ 92651581 rm10 **A**

LAVAL *Mayenne*

H A La Bonne Auberge 168 r de Bretagne ☎ 43690781 rm15 **A**

H Grand de Paris 22 r de la Paix ☎ 43537620 rm42 **A**

H Imperial (n.rest) 61 av R-Buron ☎ 43535502 rm34 **B**

H Ouest 3 r J-Ferry ☎ 43531171 rm30 **A**

H St-Pierre 95 av R-Buron ☎ 43530610 rm14 **A**

LAVANDOU, LE *Var*

H Beau Site Pramousquier-Plage ☎ 94058008 rm16 (Apr-Sep) **A**

H Galaxie (n.rest) Lotissement Le Belvédère ☎ 94711072 rm45 **A**

★**Petite Bohème** 5 av F-Roosevelt ☎ 94711030 rm19 (May-Oct) **A**

H Ramade 16 r Patron Ravello ☎ 94712040 rm21 (Jan-Jun) **A**

LEEach name preceded by 'Le' is listed under the name that follows it.

LÉCHÈRE, LA *Savoie*

H Darentasia ☎ 79225055 rm45 (Jan-Oct) **A**

H Radiana ☎ 79226161 rm80 (Apr-Oct) **B**

LENS *Pas-de-Calais*

H France 2 pl de la Gare ☎ 21281810 rm23 **A**

H Grand 43 r de la Gare ☎ 21280405 rm20 **A**

LESEach name preceded by 'Les' is listed under the name that follows it.

LIBOURNE *Gironde*

H Gare 43 r de Chanzy ☎ 57510686 rm11 (Dec-Oct) **A**

★★**Loubat** 32 r Chanzy ☎ 57511758 rm25 **B**

LIEUREY *Eure*

H Bras d'Or ☎ 32579107 rm10 **A**

LIGNY-EN-BARROIS *Meuse*

H Nouvel (n.rest) pl de l'Église ☎ 29780122 rm26 **B**

LILLE *Nord*

H Chagnot 24 pl de la Gare ☎ 27062550 rm75 **B**

H Flandre et d'Angleterre 15 pl de la Gare ☎ 20060412 rm48 **B**

H France 10 r Béthune ☎ 20571478 rm32 **A**

H Grand de l'Univers (n.rest) 19 pl des Reignaux ☎ 20069969 rm56 **B**

H Minerva (n.rest) 28 r A-France ☎ 20552511 rm42 **A**

H Monte-Carlo (n.rest) 17 pl des Reignaux ☎ 20060693 rm41 **A**

M Nord 46 r du fbg-d'Arras ☎ 20535340 rm80 **A**

H St-Maurice (n.rest) 8 Parvis St-Maurice ☎ 27062740 rm39 Closed (Aug) **A**

H Strasbourg (n.rest) 7 r J-Roisin ☎ 20570546 rm47 **B**

LIMOGES *Haute-Vienne*

H Belvedere 264 rte de Toulouse ☎ 55305739 rm26 **A**

H De La Paix (n.rest) 25 pl Jourdan ☎ 55343600 rm31 **A**

★★**Ibis Limoges** (n.rest) Zone Industrielle Nord, Beaubrevil ☎ 55375014 rm76 **B**

★★**Jourdan** 1 av du Gl-de-Gaulle ☎ 55774962 rm41 **B**

H Marceau pl Marceau ☎ 55772343 rm28 **A**

H Primevere r F-Bastiat ☎ 55370255 rm30 **B**

H Residence Beaune-les-Mines (N 20) ☎ 55399047 rm20 **B**

LIMOUX *Aude*

H Mauzac (n.rest) av C-Bouche, rte de Carcassonne ☎ 68311277 rm21 **A**

LISIEUX *Calvados*

★**Coupe d'Or** 49 r Pont Mortain ☎ 31311684 rm18 **A**

H Grand de l'Esperance 16 bd Ste-Anne ☎ 31621753 rm100 (May-Oct) **B**

H Mapaotel de la Plage (n.rest) 67 r H-Chéron ☎ 31311744 rm36 **B**

H Maris-stella 56 bis r d'Orbec ☎ 31620105 rm17 **A**

H Regina 14 r de la Gare ☎ 31311543 rm45 (Mar-Nov) **A**

H Terrasse 25 av Ste-Thérèse ☎ 31621765 rm17 (Mar-Nov) **A**

LOCHES *Indre-et-Loire*

H George Sand Sarl 39 r Quintefol ☎ 47593974 rm18 (Jan-Nov) **B**

H Grand de France 6 r Picois ☏ 47590032 rm22 **A**

H Tour Saint-Antoine 2 r des Moulins ☏ 47590106 rm18 **A**

LODÈVE *Hérault*

H Nord 18 bd de la Liberté ☏ 67441008 rm19 **A**

H Paix 11 bd Montalangue ☏ 67440746 rm19 **A**

LONS-LE-SAUNIER *Jura*

H Cheval Rouge 47 r Lecourbe ☏ 84472044 rm19 **A**

H Gambetta (n.rest) 4 bd Gambetta ☏ 84244118 rm24 **A**

H Nouvel (n.rest) 50 r Lecourbe ☏ 84472067 rm26 **A**

H Terminus 37 av A-Briand ☏ 84244183 rm18 **A**

LORIENT *Morbihan*

H Astoria 3 r de Clisson ☏ 97211023 rm40 **A**

H Cleria (n.rest) 27 bd Franchet-d'Esperey ☏ 97210459 rm36 **A**

H Léopol 11 r W-Rousseau ☏ 97212316 rm32 **A**

H Terminus et Gare 5 r Beauvais ☏ 97211462 rm59 **A**

H Victor-Hugo (n.rest) 36 r L-Carnot ☏ 97211624 rm30 **A**

LOUDÉAC *Côtes-du-Nord*

H France 1 r de Cadélac ☏ 96280015 rm40 **A**

★Voyageurs 10 r Cadélac ☏ 96280047 rm29 **A**

LOURDES *Hautes-Pyrénées*

H d'Albert 21 pl du Champ ☏ 62947500 rm27 **A**

H Aquitaine 1 r des Pyrénées ☏ 62942031 rm25 Closed Jan **A**

H Armes de Belgique 22-24 bd de la Grotte ☏ 62940007 rm38 (Mar-Dec) **A**

H Barcelonne er Lavedan 22 pl du Champ-Commun ☏ 62942743 rm23 **A**

H Beausejour (n.rest) 16 av de la Gare ☏ 62943818 rm44 **A**

H Belge et Madrid 60 bd de la Grotte ☏ 62940037 rm57 (Apr-Oct) **B**

H Bon Pasteur 22 av Peyramale ☏ 62947074 rm62 (Etr-Oct) **B**

H Cercles Catholiques 18 bd de la Grotte ☏ 62942530 rm64 (Apr-Oct) **A**

H Commerce et de Navarre 11 r Basse ☏ 62945923 rm38 (Apr-Oct) **A**

H Croix de Malte 5 r des Pyrénées ☏ 62942339 rm70 (Apr-Oct) **A**

H Lutetia 19 av de la Gare ☏ 62942285 rm47 (Feb-Dec) **A**

H Milan 3 bd de la Grotte ☏ 62944113 rm38 (Apr-Oct) **A**

H Monge 49 av A.-Marquis ☏ 62947200 rm38 **A**

H Myosotis av de la R-Astrid ☏ 62940402 rm50 (Apr-Oct) **B**

H Orly (n.rest) 9 bis av Maransin ☏ 62942821 rm15 **A**

H Sainte-Catherine 10 espl du Paradis ☏ 62947470 rm82 (Etr-Oct) **A**

H St-Étienne 61 bd de la Grotte ☏ 62940203 rm44 (Etr-Oct) **B**

H St-Sebastien 63 bd de la Grotte ☏ 62941384 rm76 (Apr-Oct) **B**

H Vallée 28 r des Pyrénées ☏ 62947171 rm60 (Apr-Oct) **A**

H Villa Saint Jean 1 av du Paradis ☏ 62942317 rm80 (Etr-Oct) **A**

LUCHON *Haute-Garonne*

★★Bains 75 allées d'Etingy ☏ 61790058 rm52 (Feb-Oct) **A**

H Beau-Site 11 cours des Quinconces ☏ 61790271 rm24 (May-Oct) **B**

H Bon Accueil 1 pl Joffre ☏ 61790220 rm26 (Dec-Oct) **A**

H d'Etigny 3 av P-Bonnemaison ☏ 61790142 rm58 (Mar-Oct) **B**

H Grand 79 allées d'Etigny ☏ 61793446 rm56 (May-Oct) **A**

LUNEL *Hérault*

H Clausade 456 av Col-Simon ☏ 67710569 rm10 **B**

H Mon Auberge 113 Pont de Lunel ☏ 67714523 rm30 **A**

LUNÉVILLE *Meurthe-et-Moselle*

★★Europe (n.rest) 56 r d'Alsace ☏ 83741234 rm30 **A**

H Pages (n.rest) 8 r Chanzy ☏ 83741142 rm27 **B**

H Voltaire 8 av Voltaire ☏ 83740729 rm10 **A**

LUXEUIL-LES-BAINS *Haute-Saône*

★★Beau Site 18 r des Thermes ☏ 84401467 rm40 **A**

H France 6 r Clémenceau ☏ 84401390 rm22 **A**

LYON *Rhône*

Picturesquely set on the banks of the rivers Saône and Rhône, Lyon lies at the heart of some of France's great vineyards. Her neighbours include Mâcon and St-Etienne, and the names of the surrounding villages read like a wine guide. The cliff-top silhouette of Notre-Dame de Fourvière is the city's most striking symbol, while the medieval Primatale St-Jean Cathédral with its unusual 14th-century astronomical clock is worth visiting.

Lyon's old town, running north of the cathedral along the west bank of the Saône, brims with historic medieval and Renaissance buildings. Focal point is Place Bellecour, one of Europe's lagest squares.

Of the city's museums, the most interesting is the *Musée des Beaux-Arts* (Museum of Fine Arts), which contains sculpture, classical relics and an extensive collection of Old Masters and Impressionists.

EATING OUT Lyon's restaurants have an international reputation for excellence, and are frequently star-rated in top restaurant guides. One of the best in town is the *Léon de Lyon*, which offers a selection of regional specialities such as dumplings and hot sausages, as well as *nouvelle cuisine*. *Orsi*, in Place Kléber, has a menu which provides excellent value.

H Britania (n.rest) 17 r du Prof-Weill ☏ 78528652 rm22 **B**

H Dauphin (n.rest) 9 r V-Hugo ☏ 78371834 rm14 **B**

H Dubost (n.rest) 19 pl Carnot ☏ 78420046 rm56 **A**

★★Globe et Cecil (n.rest) 21 r Gasparin ☏ 78425895 rm65 **A**

H Grand des Terreaux (n.rest) 16 r Lanterne ☎ 78270410 rm50 **A**

H Iris (n.rest) 36 r de l'Arbre Sec ☎ 78399380 rm30 **A**

H Lacassagne (n.rest) 245 av Lacassagne ☎ 78540912 rm40 **A**

H Liberty (n.rest) 3 r J-Larrivé ☎ 78600265 rm18 **A**

H Loire (n.rest) 19 cours de Verdun ☎ 78374429 rm35 **A**

H Lyon-Est 104 rte de Genas ☎ 78546453 rm42 **A**

★★**Moderne** (n.rest) 15 r Dubois ☎ 78422183 rm31 **B**

H Mont Blanc (n.rest) 26 cours de Verdun ☎ 78373536 rm31 **A**

H National (n.rest) 15 cours de Verdun ☎ 78375349 rm29 **A**

H Olympique (n.rest) 62 r Garibaldi ☎ 78894804 rm23 **B**

H Pasteur (n.rest) 17 r Pasteur ☎ 78722808 rm44 **A**

H Piolat et Lutetia 114 bd des Belges ☎ 78244468 rm68 **B**

H Residence 18 r V-Hugo ☎ 78426328 rm65 **B**

H Resthotel Primevere r L-Pradel ☎ 64497474 rm42 **B**

H Richelieu (n.rest) 2 r Lalande ☎ 78247645 rm40 **A**

H Rose des Vins 5 r de la Fromagerie ☎ 78284822 rm11 **A**

H Saint-Pothin (n.rest) 110 r Vendôme ☎ 78520931 rm33 **A**

H Savoies (n.rest) 80 r de la Charité ☎ 78376694 rm46 **A**

H St Pierre des Terreaux (n.rest) 8 r P-Chenavard ☎ 78282461 rm16 **B**

H Terminus-Brotteaux (n.rest) 97 bd des Belges ☎ 78246780 rm20 **A**

H Vaubecour 28 r Vaubecour ☎ 78374491 rm17 **A**

H Vieux Lyon (n.rest) 157 bd Croix-Rousse ☎ 78282985 rm32 **A**

MÂCON *Saône-et-Loire*

★★**Europe et d'Angleterre** (n.rest) 92-109 quai J-Jaurès ☎ 85382794 rm32 (Feb-Nov) **A**

★★**Genève** Direction Gare ☎ 85381810 rm61 **A**

H Nord 313 quai J-Jaurès ☎ 85380868 rm21 **A**

H Promenade 262-266 quai Lamartine ☎ 85381098 rm21 Closed Jan **B**

H Savoie 87 r Rambuteau ☎ 85384222 rm19 **B**

★★**Terminus** 91 r V-Hugo ☎ 85391711 rm48 **B**

H Tour 604 r Vremontoise ☎ 85360270 rm23 **B**

MALBUISSON *Doubs*

★★★**Lac** Grande Rue ☎ 81693480 rm54 **A**

MAMERS *Sarthe*

H Au Bon Laboureur 1 r P-Bert ☎ 43976027 rm10 **A**

MANDELIEU *Alpes-Maritimes*

H Eperon d'Or (n.rest) av de Fréjus ☎ 93495050 rm32 (Dec-Sep) **A**

H Meditérranée 454 av des Vacqueries ☎ 93930093 rm20 **A**

H Pergola pl de la Fontaine ☎ 93499588 rm16 Closed Jan **A**

H Rocamare bd H-Clews ☎ 93499536 rm14 (Jan-Oct) **A**

MANOSQUE *Alpes-de-Haute-Provence*

H François 1 er (n.rest) 18 r Guilhempierre ☎ 92720799 rm25 **A**

H Grand Versailles (n.rest) 17 av J-Giono ☎ 92721210 rm20 **A**

H Peyrache (n.rest) pl Hôtel-de-Ville ☎ 92720743 rm18 **A**

MANS, LE *Sarthe*

H Bon Laboureur 40 r d'Orléans ☎ 43240799 rm15 **A**

H Central 5 et 7 bd R-Levasseur ☎ 43240893 rm37 **B**

★★**Chantecler** 50 r la Pelouse ☎ 43245853 rm36 **B**

H Escale 72 r Chanzy ☎ 43845592 rm47 **A**

H Galaxie (n.rest) 39 bd de la Gare ☎ 43249950 rm47 **A**

★★★**Moderne** 14 r du Bourg-Belé ☎ 43247920 rm32 **B**

H Rennes (n.rest) 43 bd de la Gare ☎ 43248640 rm24 **A**

H Resthotel Primevere Zac ZAC de Gazonfier, av P-Neruda ☎ 43725500 rm42 **B**

MARMANDE *Lot-et-Garonne*

H Capricorne rte d'Agen ☎ 53641614 rm34 **B**

MARSEILLE *Bouches-du-Rhône*

In Marseille, dubbed 'the meeting place of the entire world' by Alexandre Dumas, the French mix with North Africans, gypsies, Indians and sailors from all parts of the world. Centre of the town is the Vieux Port, flanked by two impregnable fortresses and guarded on the surrounding hills by the city's old quarters. Running straight out of the port is Marseille's main artery, La Canebière, a striking contrast to the narrow, dusty streets of the nearby North African quarter.

In the Parc du Pharo stands a castle built by Napoleon III for Empress Eugénie; it offers excellent views of the harbour and city. The 19th-century Basilique de Notre-Dame-de-la-Garde, crowned with a gilded Virgin, and the Ancienne Cathédrale de la Major with its Romanesque altar reliquary from 1122 and a 15th-century altar dedicated to Lazarus are also worth visiting as are the city's many specialised museums.

EATING OUT Marseille is the home of the fish stew cooked with wine, saffron and cayenne pepper, that is known as *bouillabaisse*. The restaurants on Quai de Rive Neuve in the Vieux Port all serve their own versions of this. Mussels, eel and lobster are all widely available. One of the city's longest-established restaurants is *Maurice Brun*, in Quai Rive-Neuve, which serves good regional cuisine.

H Breteuil 25-27 r Breteuil ☎ 91332420 rm39 **B**

H Dieude (n.rest) 21 r Dieudé ☎ 91543236 rm16 **A**

H Duc 19 bd Dugommier ☎ 91907109 rm12 **A**

H Geneve (n.rest) 3 bis r Reine-Elisabeth ☎ 91905142 rm49 **B**

H Le Corbusier 280 bd Michelet ☎ 91771815 rm24 **A**

H Mariette Pacha (n.rest) 5 pl du 4-Septembre ☎ 91523077 rm20 **A**

H Martini (n.rest) 5 bd G-Desplaces ☎ 91641117 rm40 **A**

H Normandie (n.rest) 28 bd d'Athènes ☎ 91622947 rm59 **A**

H Peron 119 Corniche Kennedy ☎ 91310141 rm29 **A**

H Petit Louvre 19 La Canebière ☎ 91901627 rm35 **B**

H Pharo 71 bd du C-Livon ☎ 91310871 rm29 **A**

H Président 12 bd Salvator ☎ 91486729 rm18 **B**

H Rome et Saint-Pierre (n.rest) 7 cours St-Louis ☎ 91541952 rm65 **B**

H Sainte-Anne (n.rest) 23 r Breteuil ☎ 91331321 rm28 **A**

H Velay 18 r Berlioz ☎ 91483137 rm16 **A**

MARTEL *Lot*

★★**Falaises** ☎ 65373359 rm15 (Mar-Nov) **A**

MARTIGUES *Bouches-du-Rhône*

H Lido cours du 4-Septembre ☎ 42070032 rm19 **A**

MEAUDRE *Isère*

H Parc ☎ 7695202 rm20 (Seasonal) **B**

MEGÈVE *Haute-Savoie*

H Gai Soleil 343 r Crêt du Midi B.P. 46 ☎ 50210070 rm19 (Seasonal) **A**

H Sapins rte de Rochebrune ☎ 50210279 rm19 (Seasonal) **A**

MENDE *Lozère*

H France 9 bd L-Arnault ☎ 66650004 rm27 Closed Jan **A**

H Palais (n.rest) pl Urbain V ☎ 66490159 rm21 **A**

H Urbain V 9 bd T-Roussel ☎ 66491449 rm60 **B**

MENTON *Alpes-Maritimes*

★★★**Aiglon** 7 av de la Madone ☎ 93575555 rm31 (Dec-Oct) **B**

H Arcades 41 av F-Faure ☎ 93357062 rm40 (Dec-Oct) **A**

H Claridge (n.rest) 39 av de Verdun ☎ 93357253 rm40 **B**

★★**Londrès** 15 av Carnot ☎ 93357462 rm26 (Jan-Oct) **B**

H Paris-Rome 79 Porte-de-France ☎ 93357345 rm22 Closed Nov **B**

H Pins rte des Ciappes ☎ 93357548 rm17 **B**

H Richelieu (n.rest) 26 r Partouneaux ☎ 93357471 rm32 **A**

H St-Georges (n.rest) 24 bis av Cochrane ☎ 93357609 rm35 **B**

H Stella Bella 850 prom du Soleil ☎ 93357447 rm26 (Jan-Oct) **B**

H Villa – New York av K-Mansfield-Garavan ☎ 93357869 rm14 (Jan-Oct) **B**

METZ *Moselle*

H Bristol (n.rest) 7 r Lafayette ☎ 87667422 rm67 **A**

H Foch (n.rest) 8 av Foch, pl R-Mondon ☎ 87755642 rm42 **A**

H Gare (n.rest) 20 r Gambetta ☎ 87667403 rm40 **A**

H Grand de Metz (n.rest) 3 r des Clercs ☎ 87361633 rm57 **A**

H Metropole (n.rest) 5 pl Gl-de-Gaulle ☎ 87662622 rm80 **A**

H Moderne (n.rest) 1 r Lafayette ☎ 87665733 rm43 **A**

H Novotel Metz Centre Centre St-Jacques, pl des Paraiges ☎ 87373839 rm98 **B**

H Pasteur 18 r Pasteur ☎ 87664096 rm40 **A**

MILLAU *Aveyron*

★★★**International** 1 pl de la Tine ☎ 65602066 rm110 **B**

H Jalabe (n.rest) 18 bis av A-Merle ☎ 65606200 rm23 **B**

MIRANDE *Gers*

H Europ' Maupas 2 av d'Etigny ☎ 62665142 rm22 **A**

MODANE *Savoie*

H Voyageurs 16 pl Sommeiller ☎ 79050139 rm19 **A**

MOISSAC *Tarn-et-Garonne*

★★**Pont Napoléon** 2 allées Montebello ☎ 63040155 rm14 (Seasonal) **A**

H Poste 2-3 pl de Liberté ☎ 63040147 rm18 **B**

MONETIER-LES-BAINS, LE *Hautes-Alpes*

H Alliey Serre Chevalier 1500 ☎ 92244002 rm42 **A**

H Europe 1 r St-E-Serre ☎ 92244003 rm31 (Seasonal) **B**

H Glaciers Col du Lautaret ☎ 92244221 rm40 (Jun-Sep) **A**

MONTARGIS *Loiret*

H Lyon 74 r A-Croquillet ☎ 38853039 rm22 **A**

H Petit Relais 52 av Gl-de-Gaulle ☎ 38980085 rm17 **A**

H Rotisserie de la Tour ☎ 38850116 rm14 **A**

MONTAUBAN *Tarn-et-Garonne*

★★**Midi** 12 r Notre-Dame ☎ 63631723 rm62 **A**

MONTBARD *Côte-d'Or*

H Côte d'Or 26 r Carnot ☎ 80920117 rm17 **B**

★★**Gare** (n.rest) 10 r Ml-Foch ☎ 80920212 rm20 **A**

MONTBÉLIARD *Doubs*

H Balance 40 r de Belfort ☎ 81911854 rm40 **A**

H France 40 r d'Audincourt ☎ 81902148 rm16 **A**

H Grand-Hotel de Mulhouse 13 pl de la Gare ☎ 81944635 rm54 (Sep-Jul) **A**

H Joffre (n.rest) 34 bis av du Ml-Joffre ☎ 81944464 rm44 **B**

MONTBRISON *Loire*

H Lion d'Or 14 quai des Eaux-Minérales ☎ 77583466 rm19 (Sep-Jul) **B**

MONTCEAU-LES-MINES *Saône-et-Loire*

H Primevère av de Ml-Leclerc, rte de Blanzy ☎ 85574949 rm30 **B**

MONT-DE-MARSAN *Landes*

★★★**Richelieu** r Wlerick ☎ 58061020 rm70 **A**

MONT-DORE, LE *Puy-de-Dôme*

H Nouvel 4 r J-Moulin ☎ 73651144 rm65 (Seasonal) **A**

H Parc r Meynadier ☎ 73650292 rm72 (Dec-Oct) **B**

★★**Puy Ferrand** au Pied de Sancy ☎ 73651899 rm42 (Seasonal) **B**

H Sapins 5 av de la Libération ☎ 73650505 rm32 (Seasonal) **A**

MONTÉLIMAR *Drôme*

H Briand ch du Roubion ☎ 75017799 rm18 **B**

H Logis Dauphine Provence (n.rest) 41 av de Gaulle ☎ 75012408 rm24 (Mar-Jan) **A**

H Relais de l'Empereur pl M-Dormoy ☎ 75012900 rm40 **B**

★★**Sphinx** 19 bd Desmarais ☎ 75018664 rm25 **A**

MONTLUCON *Allier*

H Eurotel 2 pl L-Bavay ☎ 70050288 rm36 **A**

H Gare 42 av M-Dormoy ☎ 70054422 rm23 **B**

H Lion d'Or 19 r Barathon ☎ 70050062 rm41 **A**

H Univers 38 av M-Dormoy ☎ 70053347 rm53 **A**

MONTOIRE-SUR-LE-LOIR *Loir-et-Cher*

★★Cheval-Rouge 1 pl Ml-Foch ☎ 54850705 rm17 Closed Feb **A**

MONTPELLIER *Hérault*

H Angleterre 7 r Maguelone ☎ 67585950 rm32 **A**

H Hôtel (n.rest) 6-8 r J-Ferry ☎ 67588875 rm55 **B**

H Mistral 25 r Boussairolles ☎ 67584525 rm18 **A**

H Palais 3 r du Palais ☎ 67604738 rm24 **B**

H Parc 8 r A-Begé ☎ 67411649 rm19 **B**

MONTRICHARD *Loir-et-Cher*

★★Tête-Noire 24 rte de Tours ☎ 54320555 rm38 Closed Jan-Feb **B**

MONT-ST-MICHEL, LE *Manche*

H Mouton Blanc ☎ 33601408 rm26 Closed Dec & Jan **A**

MONTVALEZAN *Savoie*

H Solaret ☎ 79068047 rm30 (Seasonal) **A**

H St-Bernard ☎ 79068048 rm20 (Seasonal) **A**

MOREZ *Jura*

H Poste 1 r du Docteur ☎ 84331103 rm44 **A**

MORTAGNE-AU-PERCHE *Orne*

★Tribunal 4 pl du Palais ☎ 33250177 rm19 **A**

MORZINE *Haute-Savoie*

H Alpen Roc (n.rest) La Piagne ☎ 50791167 rm14 (Seasonal) **A**

H Alpina Les Bois Venant ☎ 50790524 rm18 (Seasonal) **B**

H Aubergade av de Joux Plane ☎ 50790369 rm20 (Seasonal) **A**

H Beau Regard Les Bois Venants ☎ 50791105 rm33 (Seasonal) **A**

H Chamois d'Or ☎ 50791378 rm25 (Dec-Apr) **A**

H Concorde rte des Gets ☎ 50791305 rm27 (Seasonal) **A**

H Laury's rte des Ardoisieres ☎ 50790610 rm18 **B**

H Neige-Roc Les Prodains ☎ 50790321 rm30 (Seasonal) **A**

H Regina Le Nantegue ☎ 50791297 rm35 **A**

H Samoyede pl de la Crusaz ☎ 50790079 rm27 (Seasonal) **B**

H Savoie ☎ 50791331 rm36 (Seasonal) **B**

H Soly Varnay Le Bourg ☎ 50790945 rm19 (Seasonal) **B**

H Voroches (n.rest) La Muraille ☎ 50790851 rm17 **B**

MOULINS *Allier*

★★Chalet Coulandon ☎ 70445008 rm25 (Feb-Nov) **B**

★★Parc 31 av Gl-Leclerc ☎ 70441255 rm28 **B**

★★★Paris 21 r de Paris ☎ 70440058 rm27 **A**

MOUTIERS *Savoie*

★★Ibis Colline de Champoulet ☎ 79242711 rm62 **B**

MULHOUSE *Haut-Rhin*

H Bale 19-21 passage Central ☎ 89461987 rm31 **A**

H Bristol (n.rest) 18 av de Colmar ☎ 89421231 rm55 **B**

H Europe (n.rest) 11 av Ml-Foch ☎ 89451918 rm50 **B**

H Musée (n.rest) 3 r de l'Est ☎ 89454741 rm43 **A**

H Paris 5 passage Hôtel-de-Ville ☎ 89452141 rm20 **B**

H Salvator 29 passage Central ☎ 89452832 rm39 **A**

H Strasbourg 17 av de Colmar ☎ 89454081 rm63 **A**

H Touring 10 r du Moulin ☎ 89453284 rm30 **A**

MUNSTER *Haut-Rhin*

H Cigogne 4 pl du Marché ☎ 89773227 rm10 **A**

H Vosges (n.rest) 58 Grande-Rue ☎ 89773141 rm13 **A**

MUSSIDAN *Dordogne*

H Grand des Voyageurs r de la Libération ☎ 53810012 rm10 **A**

H Midi av de la Gare ☎ 53810177 rm10 **A**

NAJAC *Aveyron*

★★Belle-Rive av Roc du Pont ☎ 65297390 rm40 (Apr-Oct) **B**

NANCY *Meurthe-et-Moselle*

H Albert 1er (n.rest) 3 r Armée-Patton ☎ 83403124 rm100 **B**

H Bon Coin 33 r de Villiers ☎ 83400401 rm24 **A**

H Carnot (n.rest) 2 cours Léopold ☎ 83365958 rm33 **A**

H Cigogne (n.rest) 4 bis r des Ponts ☎ 83328933 rm40 **B**

H Guise (n.rest) 18 r de Guise ☎ 83322468 rm45 **A**

★Poincaré (n.rest) 81 r R-Poincaré ☎ 83402599 rm25 **A**

H Portes d'Or (n.rest) 21 r Stanislas ☎ 83354234 rm20 **A**

H Poste (n.rest) 56 pl Monseigneur-Ruch ☎ 83321152 rm46 **A**

H Stanislas (n.rest) 22 r Ste-Catherine ☎ 83372388 rm16 **B**

NANTES *Loire-Atlantique*

H Chanzy 200 r Gl-Buat ☎ 40748940 rm15 **B**

H Cholet (n.rest) 10 r Gresset ☎ 40733104 rm38 **B**

NANTUA *Ain*

H Lac 15 av de la Gare ☎ 74750012 rm18 **B**

NARBONNE *Aude*

★Lion d'Or 39 av P-Sémard ☎ 68320692 rm21 **B**

NEVERS *Nièvre*

H Relais Bleu (n.rest) 63 bd Dagonneau ☎ 86570741 rm8 **A**

★St-Marie 25 r du Mouësse ☎ 86611002 rm17 (Mar-Jan 20) **A**

NICE *Alpes-Maritimes*
Nice comes nearest to being all things to all visitors, with its beautiful setting, marvellous climate and successful blend of good modern architecture with the narrow streets and alleys of the old town. It provides a good centre from which to tour the Riviera and is within easy reach of the perfume centre at Grasse.
EATING OUT Cooking in this part of France tends to be fairly rich, with plenty of full-flavoured, spicy dishes such as fish soup with garlic, rosemary and saffron (a speciality), and the vegetable stew known as *ratatouille.* Fish in this region is particularly original in its preparation, and red mullet with rosemary and salt cod with garlic

mayonnaise (*aïoli*) are especially delicious.
A pleasant accompaniment to meals is a bottle of one of the vigorous Provençal rosé or fresh red wines, excellent to drink with *banon*, a cheese made from cows', goats' or ewes' milk and wrapped in chestnut leaves. Try the popular local aniseed flavoured *pastis*, a golden-coloured liquid that turns milky when water is added. One of the best places in town for seafood is *l'Ane Rouge*, a family-run restaurant in Quai des Deux-Emmanuels.

H Anges (n.rest) 1 pl Massena ☎ 93821228 rm27 **B**

H Antares (n.rest) 5 av Thiers ☎ 93882287 rm40 **A**

H Avenue (n.rest) 47 bis av J-Medecin ☎ 93884873 rm58 **B**

H Beausoleil 22 r Assalit ☎ 93851854 rm50 **A**

H Bel Azur 5 av Petit Fabron ☎ 93865881 rm19 **A**

H Britannique (n.rest) 49 r de France ☎ 93883038 rm30 **B**

H Camelias 3 r Spitalieri ☎ 93621554 rm32 Closed Nov **B**

H Carlton (n.rest) 26 bd V-Hugo ☎ 93888783 rm29 **B**

H Centre (n.rest) 2 r de Suisse ☎ 93888385 rm20 **A**

H Garden Flower Hotel 56 r St-Philippe ☎ 93441633 rm36 **A**

H Lafayette (n.rest) 32 r l'Hôtel-des-Postes ☎ 93851784 rm18 **B**

H Lepante (n.rest) 6 r Lepante ☎ 93622055 rm26 (Feb-Oct) **B**

H Marina (n.rest) 11 r St-Philippe ☎ 93445404 rm40 Closed Nov **B**

H Midland (n.rest) 41 r Lamartine ☎ 93621443 rm50 **A**

H Normandie (n.rest) 18 r Paganini ☎ 93884883 rm46 **A**

H Ostende (n.rest) 3 r A-Lorraine ☎ 93887248 rm39 **A**

H Parisien (n.rest) 10 r R-Vernier ☎ 93887738 rm22 **A**

H Pavillon de Rivoli 10 r de Rivoli ☎ 93888025 rm24 **A**

H Residence (n.rest) 18 av Durante ☎ 93888945 rm34 **B**

H Verdun (n.rest) 49 r de l'Hôtel-des-Postes ☎ 93622410 rm38 **B**

NIEDERHASLACH *Bas-Rhin*

H Pomme d'Or 36 r Principale ☎ 88509021 rm20 Closed Feb **A**

NIEDERSTEINBACH *Bas-Rhin*

H Cheval Blanc 27 rte de Bitche ☎ 88092531 rm31 Closed Feb **A**

NÎMES *Gard*

Nîmes, like Rome, was built with Roman labour on seven hills, and 2, 000 years later still competes with Arles for the title *la Rome française*. The well-presented Roman arena marks the centre of the city, and a good place to begin a visit is the Jardin de la Fontaine, containing fountains, pools and shady groves as well as the ruins of a Roman temple of Diana.
The most interesting of Nîmes' churches is the Cathédral St-Castor, which has a spacious Romanesque nave and an elaborate façade depicting scenes from the Old Testament. Also of interest is the *Maison Carrée* (Square House), a Roman temple dedicated to the adopted sons of the Emperor Augustus. The temple has a Greek-style portico with fluted Corinthian columns. Inside the building is the *Musée des Antiquités* containing a display of superb Roman mosaics as well as statues of the Venus of Nîmes and Apollo.
EATING OUT Specialities of Nîmes include *brandade de Morue* (puréed fish blended with olive oil and spices) and *herbes de Provence*, a mixture of herbs and olive oil.

H Château (n.rest) 3 pl du Château ☎ 66675747 rm15 **A**

H Maison Carrée (n.rest) 14 r M-Carrée ☎ 66673289 rm20 **A**

H Menant (n.rest) 22 bd A-Courbet ☎ 66672285 rm29 **B**

H Michel (n.rest) 14 bd A-Courbet ☎ 66672623 rm28 **A**

H Milan 17 av Fauchères ☎ 66292990 rm33 **A**

H Nouvel 6 bd Al-Courbet ☎ 66676248 rm17 **A**

H Temple (n.rest) 1 r Ch-Babut ☎ 66675461 rm20 **A**

H Terminus 23 av Fauchères ☎ 66292014 rm34 **B**

NIORT *Deux-Sèvres*

H France (n.rest) 8 r des Cordeliers ☎ 49240134 rm28 **A**

H Paris (n.rest) 96 av de Paris ☎ 49249378 rm47 **A**

NOE *Haute-Garonne*

H Arche de Noe pl de la Bascule ☎ 61874012 rm35 **A**

NOGENT-LE-ROTROU *Eure-et-Loire*

H Chêne Dore 23 r Giroust ☎ 37520080 rm17 **A**

★★Dauphin 39 r Villette-Gate ☎ 37521730 rm26 (Mar-Dec) **B**

NOIRETABLE *Loire*

H Rendez-vous des Chasseurs rte de l'Hermitage ☎ 77247251 rm17 **A**

NONTRON *Dordogne*

H Grand 3 pl A-Agard ☎ 53561122 rm26 (Feb-Dec) **A**

NORGES-LA-VILLE *Côte-d'Or*

H Norges ☎ 80357217 rm34 **A**

NOTRE-DAME-DE-BELLECOMBE *Savoie*

H Bellevue ☎ 79316056 rm22 (Seasonal) **A**

NOTRE-DAME-DE-SANILHAC *Dordogne*

H Chartreuse ☎ 53466021 rm10 **A**

NOTRE-DAME-DU-PRÉ *Savoie*

H Gai-Soleil ☎ 79240995 rm28 (Seasonal) **A**

NOUZERINES *Creuse*

H Bonne Auberge ☎ 55820118 rm8 (Seasonal) **A**

NOYON *Oise*

H Grillon 37-39 r St-Eloi ☎ 44091418 rm34 **A**

H St-Eloi 81 bd Carnot ☎ 44440149 rm31 **B**

NYONS *Drôme*

H Monier av H-Rochier ☎ 75260900 rm20 (Seasonal) **A**

OBERNAI *Bas-Rhin*

★★Hostellerie Duc d'Alsace pl de la Gare ☎ 88955534 rm17 **B**

H Hostellerie La Diligence 23 pl de la Mairie ☎ 88955569 rm26 **B**

H Vosges 5 pl de la Gare ☎ 88954733 rm20 **B**

OLEMPS *Aveyron*

H Peyrières r des Peyrières ☎ 65682052 rm50 **A**

OLORON-SAINTE-MARIE *Pyrénées-Atlantiques*

★★**Bearn** 4 pl G-Clemenceau ☎ 59390099 rm26 **B**

H Relais Aspois ☎ 59390950 rm20 **A**

ORANGE *Vaucluse*

H Glacier (n.rest) 46 cours A-Briand ☎ 90340201 rm29 Closed Jan **A**

H Princes 7 av de l'Arc-de-Triomphe ☎ 90343016 rm52 (Mar-Oct) **B**

ORBEY *Haut-Rhin*

H Bruyères 35 r C-de-Gaulle ☎ 89712036 rm28 (Feb-Oct) **A**

H Croix d'Or de la 13 r de l'Église ☎ 89712051 rm18 **A**

H Pairis r Pairis ☎ 89712015 rm15 **A**

ORCIVAL *Puy-de-Dôme*

H Roche ☎ 73658231 rm9 (Seasonal) **A**

ORLÉANS *Loiret*

H Bec Fin 26 bd A-Briand ☎ 38624355 rm10 **B**

H Central (n.rest) 6 r d'Avignon ☎ 38539300 rm20 **B**

H Grand Hotel d'Orléans 1 r de la Lionne ☎ 38531979 rm28 **B**

H St-Jean (n.rest) 19 r Porte-St-Jean ☎ 38536332 rm27 **A**

H St-Martin 52 bd A-Martin ☎ 38624747 rm21 **A**

PAMIERS *Ariège*

H Paix 4 pl A-Tournier ☎ 61671271 rm15 **A**

PANNESSIÈRES *Jura*

H Monts Jura rte de Champagnole ☎ 84431003 rm9 **A**

PARAY-LE-MONIAL *Saône-et-Loire*

H Grand Hotel de la Basilique 18 r de Visitation ☎ 85811113 rm67 (Mar-Oct) **A**

H Terminus 57 av de la Gare ☎ 85888445 rm22 **A**

H Val d'Or La Beluze ☎ 85810507 rm17 **A**

PARCEY *Jura*

H As de Pique ☎ 84710076 rm15 **A**

PARENTIGNAT *Puy-de-Dôme*

H Tourette ☎ 73550178 rm31 **A**

PARIS

The whole world knows Paris as THE romantic city, a metropolis with a magical atmosphere that has been working its spell on visitors for centuries. Nowhere else is the street life so entertaining, the cafés so animated and the atmosphere so vibrant.

Newcomers to Paris are well advised to take a long, leisurely stroll, soak up the atmosphere, and perhaps take in a famous sight or two; a trip down the Seine on a *bateau mouche* is also rewarding. 'People-watching' on the Champs Elysées, one of the worlds most glamorous thoroughfares, is still high on the list of most visitors' priorities – despite the exorbitant cost of a coffee at a pavement café – whilst art lovers delight in the sheer diversity of the paintings and sculptures in the *Louvre*. The most important thing is not to miss the magic of Paris – to open the senses to this captivating city and then visit the castles, royal cities and forests of the Ile-de-France.

EATING OUT Freshly baked *croissants*, savoury *crêpes*, tasty *patés* or succulent seafood – your only disappointment with French cuisine is likely to be that you just can't eat everything. Eating is practically a national pastime in France, so the variety of food and wine is immense and the quality superb. Make sure you sample not only the main dishes such as *boeuf bourguignon* but also the tasty *hors d'oeuvres*, the delicious desserts and the cheeses – then round off the evening by lingering over coffee and brandy.

The choice of Paris restaurants is so wide, ranging from small side-street bistros and brasseries to well established restaurants with international reputations, that it is impossible to give specific reccomendations. Two famous cafés well worth a visit are: *Le Dôme*, in Montparnasse, where vintage photographs of its bygone clientele adorn the wooden panelling of the dining alcoves – Picasso, Bonnard, Dufy, Gauguin and Modigliani among others, some depicted at work in their studios, gaunt and hungry-looking as artists should look; *La Coupole*, just along the boulevard, is the place to see, and be seen, among the literati and glitterati of the arts and media – and there is still a fair quota of larger-than-life personalities to focus on. Many restaurants serve inexpensive and good quality meals which are excellent value for money. Look out for the *menu du jour* or *menu prix fixe* often chalked up on a blackboard outside. For inexpensive restaurants, the 5th arrondissement, the student quarter, is a good hunting ground, but every quarter has its own restaurants, and provided you steer clear of the main tourist thoroughfares you should do very well.

3rd Arrondissement Bastille, République, Hôtel-de-Ville

H Grand Arts et Metiers 4 r Borda ☎ 48877389 rm35 **B**

H Little Palace 4 r Salomon-de-Caus ☎ 42720815 rm59 **B**

H Moderne (n.rest) ☎ 42771761 rm30 **B**

H Roubaix (n.rest) 6 r Grenéta ☎ 42728991 rm53 **B**

5th Arrondissement Quartier Latin, Luxembourg, Jardin-des-Plantes

H Maxim (n.rest) 28 r Censier ☎ 43311615 rm36 **A**

H St-Jacques (n.rest) 35 r des Écoles ☎ 43268253 rm39 **A**

H Studia (n.rest) 51 bd St-Germain ☎ 43268100 rm35 **A**

6th Arrondissement Quartier Latin, Luxembourg, Jardin-des-Plantes

H Buci Latin 27 r de l'Echaudé ☎ 43290720 rm31 **A**

7th Arrondissement Faubourg-St-Germain, Invalides, École Militaire

H Sevres Vaneau (n.rest) 86 r Vaneau ☎ 45487311 rm42 **A**

8th Arrondissement Champs-Élysées, St-Lazare, Madeleine

H Dore (n.rest) 4 r de la Pepinière ☎ 45227100 rm48 **B**

H Peiffer (n.rest) 6 r de l'Arcade ☎ 42660307 rm41 **A**

H Penthievre (n.rest) 21 r de Penthievre ☎ 43598763 rm20 **A**

H Regence (n.rest) 33 r Léningrad ☎ 43875382 rm29 **A**

9th Arrondissement Opéra, Gare du Nord, Gare de l'Est, Grands Boulevards

H Avenir (n.rest) 39 bd Rochechouart ☎ 48782137 rm43 **B**

H Blanche (n.rest) 69 r Blanche ☎ 48741694 rm53 **A**

H Confort (n.rest) 5 r de Trevise ☎ 42461206 rm45 **A**

H Espagne (n.rest) 9 & 11 Cité Bergère ☎ 47701394 rm43 **B**

H Fenelon (n.rest) 23 r Buffault ☎ 48783218 rm38 **B**

H Georges (n.rest) 53 r Richer ☎ 42462442 rm27 **B**

H Hollande (n.rest) 4 r Cadet ☎ 47705079 rm52 **A**

H Laffitte (n.rest) 38 r Laffitte ☎ 47708420 rm30 **B**

★Laffon (n.rest) 25 r Buffault ☎ 48784991 rm45 **A**

H Legrand Calvados 20 r d'Amsterdam ☎ 48743931 rm25 **A**

H Normandie (n.rest) 4 r d'Amsterdam ☎ 42802018 rm71 **B**

H Regence (n.rest) 3 r Laferrière ☎ 48782996 rm16 **B**

H Royal Navarin (n.rest) 7 r Navarin ☎ 48785173 rm54 **B**

H Trinite (n.rest) 74 r de Provence ☎ 48742907 rm43 **A**

H Turin (n.rest) 6 r V-Massé ☎ 48784526 rm50 **B**

H Victor Massé (n.rest) 6 r V-Massé ☎ 48743753 rm40 **B**

10th Arrondissement Opéra, Gare du Nord, Gare de l'Est, Grands Boulevards

H Albouy (n.rest) 4 r Lucien ☎ 42082009 rm34 **A**

H Apollo (n.rest) 11 r de Dunkerque ☎ 48780498 rm45 **A**

H Cosmotel (n.rest) 17 bd de Strasbourg ☎ 45233255 rm30 **B**

H Deux Gares (n.rest) 162 fbg St-Denis ☎ 46078837 rm30 **B**

H Europe (n.rest) 98 bd Magneta ☎ 46072582 rm36 **B**

H Grand Hotel de Famille 46 r L-Sampaix ☎ 46072387 rm52 **B**

H Liège et Strasbourg (n.rest) 67 bd de Strasbourg ☎ 47701057 rm41 **A**

H Lima (n.rest) 3 r Beaurepaire ☎ 46076958 rm28 **A**

H Little (n.rest) 3 r P-Chausson ☎ 42082157 rm34 **B**

H Londres & Anvers (n.rest) 133 bd Magenta ☎ 42852826 rm73 **B**

H Londres et du Bresil (n.rest) 18 r de la Fidelité ☎ 47707255 rm60 **A**

H Montant Lafayette (n.rest) 164 r Lafayette ☎ 46076933 rm23 **B**

H New (n.rest) 40 r de St-Quentin ☎ 48780483 rm40 **B**

H Nord & Champagne (n.rest) 11 r Chabrol ☎ 47700677 rm43 **B**

H Paradis (n.rest) 9 r de Paradis ☎ 47701828 rm51 **A**

H Paris-Liège (n.rest) 36 r St-Quentin ☎ 42811318 rm36 **A**

H Parisiana (n.rest) 21 r de Chabrol ☎ 47706833 rm61 **A**

H Richmond (n.rest) 15 r de Dunkerque ☎ 48784704 rm45 **A**

H St-Quentin (n.rest) 27 r de St-Quentin ☎ 46076094 rm32 **B**

H Terminus-Est (n.rest) 8 r du Mai 1945 ☎ 42085850 rm201 **B**

H Vielle-France 151 r Lafayette ☎ 45264237 rm50 **A**

11th Arrondissement Bastille, République, Hôtel-de-Ville

H Belfort (n.rest) 37 r Servan ☎ 47006733 rm57 **A**

12th Arrondissement Gare de Lyon, Bois de Vincennes

H Bel Air (n.rest) 6 r de la Voute ☎ 43436606 rm20 **A**

H Chaligny (n.rest) 5 r Chaligny ☎ 43434189 rm43 **A**

H Grand Hotel du Bel Air (n.rest) 102 bd de Picpus ☎ 43453051 rm27 **B**

H Lux (n.rest) 8 av Corbera ☎ 43434284 rm31 **A**

H Lux Hotel Picpus (n.rest) 74 bd de Picpus ☎ 43430846 rm41 **A**

H Modern (n.rest) 98 bis cours de Vincennes ☎ 43431124 rm53 **A**

H Sport (n.rest) 258 av Daumesnil ☎ 43436136 rm43 **B**

13th Arrondissement Bastille, Gare d'Austerlitz, Place d'Italie

H Jacks (n.rest) 19 av S-Pichon ☎ 45851734 rm32 **A**

H Royal (n.rest) 65 bd St-Marcel ☎ 45350248 rm35 **A**

H St-Charles (n.rest) 6 r de l'Esperance ☎ 45895654 rm69 **B**

H Terrasses (n.rest) 74 r de la Glacière ☎ 47077370 rm52 **B**

H Veronese (n.rest) 5 r Veronese ☎ 47072090 rm66 **A**

14th Arrondissement Vaugirard, Gare Montparnasse, Grenelle, Denfert-Rochereau

H Daguerre (n.rest) 94 r Daguerre ☎ 43224354 rm30 **A**

15th Arrondissement Vaugirard, Gare Montparnasse, Grenelle, Denfert-Rochereau

H Ajiel (n.rest) 237 r de la Convention ☎ 48284930 rm68 **B**

H Atlantique (n.rest) 54 r Falguière ☎ 43207070 rm26 **B**

H Ideal (n.rest) 96 av E-Zola ☎ 45790979 rm35 **A**

H Logitel Croix Nivert (n.rest) 62 r de la Croix-Nivert ☎ 45325170 rm30 **B**

★★Pacific (n.rest) 11 r Fondary ☎ 45752049 rm66 **B**

H Royal Lecourbe (n.rest) 268 r Lecourbe ☎ 45580605 rm56 **B**

16th Arrondissement Passy, Auteuil, Bois de Boulogne, Chaillot, Porte Maillot

H Exelmans (n.rest) 73 r Boileau ☎ 42249466 rm53 **B**

17th Arrondissement Clichy, Ternes, Wagram

H Bel (n.rest) 20 r Pouchet ☎ 46273477 rm30 **A**

H Camelia (n.rest) 3 r Darcet ☎ 45225053 rm29 **A**

18th Arrondissement Montmartre, La Villette, Belleville

H André-Gill (n.rest) 4 r A-Gill ☎ 42624848 rm32 **A**

H Bouquet de Montmartre (n.rest) 1 r Durantin ☎ 46068754 rm36 **B**

H Hippodrome (n.rest) 7 r Forest ☎ 43876552 rm15 **A**

H Luxia (n.rest) 8 r Seveste ☎ 46068424 rm48 **B**

H Modern (n.rest) 3 r Forest ☎ 43874761 rm36 **B**

H Prima Lepic (n.rest) 29 r Lepic ☎ 46064464 rm38 **B**

19th Arrondissement Montmartre, La Villette, Belleville

H Parc des Buttes Chaumont (n.rest) 1 pl A-Carrel ☎ 42080837 rm51 **A**

20th Arrondissement Montmartre, La Villette, Belleville

H Super 208 r des Pyrénées ☎ 46369748 rm28 **B**

H Unic (n.rest) r Dupon-de-l'Eure ☎ 43619310 rm35 **B**

PARTHENAY *Deux-Sèvres*

H Commerce 30 bd E-Quintet ☎ 49941155 rm11 **A**

★★**Grand** 85 bd de la Meilleraie ☎ 49640016 rm26 **A**

H Nord 86 av du Gl-de-Gaulle ☎ 49942911 rm13 **A**

H Renotel bd de l'Europe ☎ 49940644 rm26 **B**

H St-Jacques (n.rest) 13 av du 114e RI ☎ 49643333 rm46 **B**

PASSY *Haute-Savoie*

H Centre et Coteau ☎ 50782366 rm35 **A**

H Chamois d'or rte du Plateau d'Assy-Bay ☎ 50588248 rm20 **A**

PAU *Pyrénées-Atlantiques*

H Atlantic (n.rest) 222 av J-Mermoz ☎ 59323824 rm31 **A**

★★**Central** (n.rest) 15 r L-Daran ☎ 59277275 rm28 **A**

H Commerce 9 r du Ml-Joffre ☎ 59272440 rm51 **B**

H Corona 71 av Gl-Leclerc ☎ 59306477 rm20 **A**

H Espagne (n.rest) 38 r L-Barthou ☎ 59277325 rm28 **A**

H Gramont (n.rest) 3 pl Gramont ☎ 59278404 rm32 **B**

★★★**Mapotel-Continental** 2 r du Ml-Foch ☎ 59276931 rm100 **B**

H Montpensier (n.rest) 36 r Montpensier ☎ 59274272 rm22 **A**

H Navarre (n.rest) 9 av Ml-Leclerc ☎ 59302539 rm31 **B**

H Postillon (n.rest) 10 cours Camou ☎ 59324915 rm27 **A**

H Regina (n.rest) 18 r Gassion ☎ 59272919 rm28 **A**

H Trinquet (n.rest) 66 av Didier Daurat ☎ 59627123 rm29 **B**

PAUILLAC *Gironde*

H France et Angleterre quai Albert ☎ 56590120 rm16 **A**

PAYRAC *Lot*

★★**Hostellerie de la Paix** ☎ 65379515 rm50 (Feb-Dec) **B**

PEGOMAS *Alpes-Maritimes*

H Aiglons quartier du Château ☎ 93422819 rm14 **A**

PEISEY-NANCROIX *Savoie*

H Vanoise Plan Peisey ☎ 79079219 rm34 (Dec-Apr) **A**

PÉRIGUEUX *Dordogne*

H Arenes (n.rest) 21 r du Gymnase ☎ 53534985 rm19 **A**

H Bristol (n.rest) 37 r Antonie Gadaud ☎ 53087590 rm28 **B**

★★**Domino** 21 pl Francheville ☎ 53082580 rm37 **A**

PERPIGNAN *Pyrénées-Orientales*

H Athena (n.rest) 1 r Queya ☎ 68343763 rm38 **A**

H Baleares 20 av Gl-Guillaut ☎ 68850493 rm48 **A**

H Christina (n.rest) 50 cours Lassus ☎ 68352461 rm37 **A**

H France 16 quai Sadi-Carnot ☎ 68349281 rm33 **A**

H Helder 4 av du Gl-de-Gaulle ☎ 68343805 rm27 **A**

H Maillol (n.rest) 14 Impasse des Cardeurs ☎ 68511020 rm15 **A**

H Mairie (n.rest) 7 r des Fabriques Couvertes ☎ 68343765 rm17 **B**

H Metropole (n.rest) 3 r des Cardeurs ☎ 68344334 rm25 **A**

H Poste 6 r Fabriques Nabot ☎ 68344253 rm39 **A**

PERROS-GUIREC *Côtes-du-Nord*

H France 14 rue Rouzig ☎ 96232027 rm30 (Feb-Nov) **B**

H Hermitage 20 r des Frères-le-Montreer ☎ 96232122 rm26 (May-Sep) **A**

H Levant 91 r Ernest Renan sur le port ☎ 96232015 rm20 **A**

★★**Morgane** Plage de Trestraou ☎ 96232280 rm32 (Mar-Oct) **A**

H Sternes (n.rest) Rd Pt de Perros Guirec ☎ 96910338 rm20 **B**

PESMES *Haute-Saone*

★★**France** r de la Vanoise ☎ 84312005 rm10 **A**

PIERRELATTE *Drôme*

H Centre pl de l'Église ☎ 75042859 rm25 **A**

★★**Hostellerie Tom II** 5 av Gl-de-Gaulle ☎ 75040035 rm15 **A**

M Pierrelatte (n.rest) 7 lieut dit les Blaches ☎ 75040799 rm22 (Apr-Jan) **A**

PITHIVIERS *Loiret*

H Chaumière 7 av de la République ☎ 38300361 rm12 **A**

★**Relais de la Poste** 10 Mail Ouest ☎ 38304030 rm11 **A**

PLÖERMEL *Morbihan*

★**Commerce-Reberminard** 70 r de a Gare ☎ 97740532 rm21 **A**

PLOMBIÈRES-LES-BAINS *Vosges*

H Alsace 34 r Lietard ☎ 29300222 rm60 (May-Sep) **B**

H Grand Des Bains r Stanislas ☎ 29660008 rm37 (May-Sep) **A**

H Grand Stanislas 2 av Gl-de-Gaulle ☎ 29660216 rm42 (May-Sep) **A**

H Modern av T-Gauthier ☎ 29660402 rm37 **A**

H Touring av L-Francais ☎ 29660173 rm31 (Apr-Oct) **A**

PLOUIGNEAU *Finistère*

H Bruyères (n.rest) R N 12 Sortie Morlaix, vers Plouigneau ☎ 98880868 rm32 **B**

POITIERS *Vienne*

★★**Europe** (n.rest) 39 r Carnot ☎ 49881200 rm50 **A**

★★★**France** 28 r Carnot ☎ 49413201 rm86 **B**

H Modern 153 bd du Grand-Cerf ☎ 49580485 rm24 **A**

H Regina 147 bd du Grand-Cerf ☎ 49582038 rm26 **A**

★★**Relais du Stade** (n.rest) 84 av J-Coeur ☎ 49462512 rm25 **A**

PONT-A-MOUSSON *Meurthe-et-Moselle*

H Providence (n.rest) 41 r V-Hugo ☎ 83811586 rm16 **A**

PONTARLIER *Doubs*

H Commerce 18 r Dr-Grenier ☎ 81390409 rm30 Closed Jan **B**

H Grand de la Poste 55 r de la République ☎ 81391812 rm21 **A**

H Villages 68 r de Salins ☎ 81467178 rm51 **B**

PONTAUBAULT *Manche*

★★★**13 Assiettes** ☎ 33581403 rm36 (Mar 15-Nov 15) **B**

PONT-D'AIN *Ain*

★★**Allies** 1 r B-Savarin ☏ 74390009 rm18 (Seasonal) **B**

PONT-DE-VAUX *Ain*

H Joubert 9 pl Joubert ☏ 85303055 rm16 **B**

H Raisin 2 pl M-Poizat ☏ 85303097 rm7 (Feb-Dec) **B**

PONTIVY *Morbihan*

H Friedland (n.rest) 12 r Friedland ☏ 97252711 rm11 **A**

PONTORSON *Manche*

★★**Montgomery** 13 r Couesnon ☏ 33600009 rm32 (Apr-Oct) **B**

PORTO-VECCHIO *Corse-du-Sud*
See **CORSE (CORSICA)**

POUILLY-EN-AUXOIS *Côte-d'Or*

H Poste pl de la Libération ☏ 80908644 rm7 **A**

POULDU, LE *Finistère*

H Dunes 2 r de Port Castel ☏ 98399088 rm49 (Jun-Sep) **B**

★**Quatre Chemins** Clohars-Carnoët ☏ 98399044 rm38 (Jun-Sep) **B**

PUY, LE *Haute-Loire*

H Bristol et Taverne Lyonnaise 7 av Ml-Foch ☏ 71091338 rm37 **A**

H Cygne 47 bd du Ml-Fayolle ☏ 71093236 rm41 (Feb-Nov) **B**

H Licorn 25 av C-Dupuy ☏ 71024622 rm70 **A**

H Regina 34 bd Ml-Fayolle ☏ 71091471 rm40 **B**

H Val Vert 6 av B-Marcet ☏ 71090930 rm26 **B**

QUIBERON *Morbihan*

H Bellevue r de Tiviec ☏ 97501628 rm44 (Mar-Nov) **B**

H Grand Large 1 bd d'Hoedic ☏ 97501339 rm18 **B**

H Gulf-Stream 17 bd Chanard ☏ 97501696 rm30 (Mar-Oct) **B**

H Mer 8 quai de Houst ☏ 97500905 rm30 (Mar-Nov) **A**

H Navirotel 10 pl du Port Haliguen ☏ 97501652 rm22 (Mar-Dec) **B**

H Neptune 4 quai de Houat ☏ 97500962 rm22 (Feb-Dec) **B**

QUILLAN *Aude*

★**Cartier** 31 bd Ch-de-Gaulle ☏ 68200514 rm30 (Mar-Dec) **A**

H Pierre Lys av de Carcassonne ☏ 68200865 rm18 (Seasonal) **A**

QUIMPER *Finistère*

★★**Gradlon** (n.rest) 30 r de Brest ☏ 98950439 rm25 **A**

H La Tour d'Auvergne 13 r des Reguaires ☏ 98950870 rm45 **A**

★★**Moderne** 21 av de la Gare ☏ 98903171 rm60 **A**

H Transvaal 57 r J-Jaurès ☏ 98900991 rm44 **A**

REIMS *Marne*

H Anvers 2 pl de la République ☏ 26402835 rm28 **B**

H Ardenn (n.rest) 6 r Caqué ☏ 26474238 rm14 **A**

H Cecyl (n.rest) 24 r Buirette ☏ 26475747 rm23 **A**

H Consuls r Général-Sarrail ☏ 26884610 rm23 (Sep-Jul) **A**

H Crystal (n.rest) 86 pl Drouet-d'Erlon ☏ 26884444 rm28 **A**

★★**Europa** (n.rest) 10 bd Joffre ☏ 26403620 rm32 **A**

H Gambetta 11-13 r Gambetta ☏ 26474164 rm14 **B**

★★**Grand du Nord** (n.rest) 75 pl Drouet-d'Erlon ☏ 26473903 rm50 (Jan-Dec) **B**

★★**Grand Continental** (n.rest) 93 pl Drouet-d'Erlon ☏ 26403935 rm60 (Jan-Dec) **A**

H Libergier 20 r Libergier ☏ 26472846 rm17 **A**

★★**Touring** (n.rest) 17 bis bd Gl-Leclerc ☏ 26473815 rm14 **B**

★★**Univers** 41 bd Foch ☏ 26886808 rm41 **A**

H Victoria (n.rest) 1 r Buirette ☏ 26472179 rm28 **A**

★★**Welcome** (n.rest) 29-31 r Buirette ☏ 26473939 rm68 **A**

REMIREMONT *Vosges*

H Cheval de Bronze 59 r Ch-de-Gaulle ☏ 29625224 rm36 **A**

H Poste 67 r Gl-de-Gaulle ☏ 29625567 rm21 **B**

RENAISON *Loire*

H Central pl du 11 Novembre ☏ 77642539 rm10 (Mar-Oct) **A**

RENNES *Ille-et-Vilaine*

H Angelina (n.rest) 1 quai Lamennais ☏ 99792966 rm27 **A**

H Arvor 31 av L-Barthou ☏ 99303647 rm16 (Sep-Jul) **B**

H Astrid (n.rest) 32 av Louis Barthou ☏ 99308238 rm30 **A**

H Bretagne 7 bis pl de Gare ☏ 99314848 rm46 **B**

H Central (n.rest) 6 r Lanjuinais ☏ 99791236 rm43 **B**

H Cheval d'Or pl de la Gare ☏ 99302580 rm42 **A**

H Garden 3 r Duhamel ☏ 99654506 rm22 **A**

H Marechal Joffre (n.rest) 6 r Ml-Joffre ☏ 99793774 rm22 **A**

H Nemours 5 r de Nemours ☏ 99782626 rm26 **B**

H Pingouin (n.rest) 7 pl des Lices ☏ 99791481 rm40 (Sep-Jul) **B**

H Sevigné (n.rest) 47 av Janvier ☏ 99672755 rm48 **B**

H Surcouf 13 pl de Gare ☏ 99305979 rm26 **A**

H Victor Hugo 14 r V-Hugo ☏ 99388533 rm24 **A**

H Voltaire 10 r Guébriant ☏ 99673333 rm32 **A**

RIBEAUVILLE *Haut-Rhin*

H Cheval Blanc 122 Grand Rue ☏ 89736138 rm25 Closed Jan **A**

ROANNE *Loire*

H Artaud 133 av de la Libération-, Le Coteau ☏ 77684644 rm25 **B**

H Central (n.rest) 20 cours de la République ☏ 77716588 rm32 (Seasonal) **A**

★★**France** (n.rest) 19 r Al-Roche ☏ 77712117 rm44 **A**

H Terminus 15 cours de la République ☏ 77717969 rm55 **B**

ROCAMADOUR *Lot*

H Auberge de la Garenne rte de la Lacave ☏ 65336588 rm41 **A**

H Bellevue l'Hospitalet ☏ 65336210 rm20 (Mar-Nov) **A**

H H Panoramic vers Le Château ☏ 65336306 rm13 (Mar-Nov) **A**

★Lion d'Or Porte Figuier ☏ 65336204 rm32 (May-Oct) **A**

★★Sainte-Marie pl des Sehnal ☏ 65336307 rm22 (Apr-Oct) **A**

H Terminus pl de la Carreta ☏ 65336214 rm15 Mar-Oct **A**

ROCHEFORT *Charente-Maritime*

H Caravelle (n.rest) 34 r J-Jaurès ☏ 46990253 rm29 **A**

H France 55 r du Dr-Peltier ☏ 46993400 rm32 Closed Jan **A**

H Paris 27 av Lafayette ☏ 46993311 rm40 **A**

H Roca Fortis 14 r République ☏ 46992632 rm17 **A**

ROCHELLE, LA *Charente-Maritime*

H François (n.rest) 13 r Bazoges ☏ 46412846 rm34 **B**

H Paris (n.rest) 18 r Gargoulleau ☏ 46410359 rm23 **A**

H Savary (n.rest) 2 r Alsace-Lorraine ☏ 46348344 rm32 **A**

H Terminus (n.rest) pl du Cmt-de-la Motte Rouge ☏ 46506969 rm27 **B**

H Tour de Nesles (n.rest) 1 quai L-Durand ☏ 46413072 rm28 **A**

ROCHE-POSAY, LA *Vienne*

H Esplanade cours Pasteur ☏ 49862048 rm25 (Mar-Nov) **A**

ROCHE-SUR-YON, LA *Vendée*

H France 19 av Gambetta ☏ 51370861 rm20 **B**

H Vendee (n.rest) 4 r Malesherbes ☏ 51372867 rm33 **A**

RODEZ *Aveyron*

H Midi-Dauty 1 r Béteille ☏ 65680207 rm34 Closed Jan **A**

H Parc (n.rest) 1 pl d'Armes ☏ 65681122 rm22 **A**

ROMANS-SUR-ISÈRE *Drôme*

H Ors r S-Allende ☏ 75022624 rm24 **A**

★★Terminus (n.rest) 48 av P-Sémard ☏ 75024688 rm32 **B**

H Valence pl Carnot ☏ 75023501 rm18 **A**

ROMORANTIN-LANTHENAY *Loir-et-Cher*

H Orleans 2 pl du Général de Gaulle ☏ 54760165 rm11 **A**

ROQUEBRUNE-CAP-MARTIN *Alpes-Maritime*

★★Westminster 14 av L-Laurens ☏ 93350068 rm31 (Feb-Sep) **A**

ROSCOFF *Finistère*

H Bellevue r J-d'Arc ☏ 98612338 rm20 (Apr-Oct) **A**

H Regina 1 r R-Morvan ☏ 98612355 rm50 (Mar-Oct) **B**

H Triton (n.rest) r du Dr-Bagot ☏ 98612444 rm45 (Feb-Nov) **B**

ROUEN *Seine-Maritime*

H Astrid (n.rest) 121 r J-d'Arc ☏ 35717588 rm40 **B**

H Boieldieu (n.rest) 14 pl Gaillardbois ☏ 35705075 rm17 **A**

H Bordeaux (n.rest) 9 pl de la République ☏ 35719358 rm45 **B**

★★Cardinal (n.rest) 1 pl la Cathédrale ☏ 35702442 rm22 **A**

★★Cathedrale (n.rest) 12 r St-Romain ☏ 35715795 rm24 **A**

★★Europe (n.rest) 87 r aux Ours ☏ 35708330 rm27 **A**

H Gaillardbois (n.rest) 12 pl du Gaillardbois ☏ 35703428 rm22 **A**

★★Grand du Nord (n.rest) 91 r du Gros-Horloge ☏ 35704141 rm62 **B**

H Lisieux (n.rest) 4 r de la Savonnerie ☏ 35718773 rm27 **A**

H Morand (n.rest) 1 r Morand ☏ 35714607 rm17 **A**

★★Normandie (n.rest) 19 & 21 r de Bec ☏ 35715577 rm23 **B**

★★Paris (n.rest) 12 r de la Champmeslé ☏ 35700926 rm23 **A**

★★Quebec (n.rest) 18 & 24 r de Québec ☏ 35700938 rm38 **A**

H Regina 2-4 av de Bretagne ☏ 35730274 rm25 **A**

H Solferino (n.rest) 51 r Thiers ☏ 35711007 rm14 **A**

H Union 13 pl du Gl-de-Gaulle ☏ 35714655 rm16 **A**

★Vieille Tour 42 pl Haute Vieille Tour ☏ 35700327 rm23 **B**

★★Viking (n.rest) 21 quai du Havre ☏ 35703495 rm37 **B**

ROUSSES, LES *Jura*

H Auberge des Piles Les Cressonnières ☏ 84600044 rm20 Closed May **B**

H Noirmont (n.rest) Les Rousses ☏ 84603015 rm7 **A**

ROUVRES-EN-XAINTOIS *Vosges*

H Auberge du Xaintois ☏ 29656343 rm19 **B**

ROYAN *Charente-Maritime*

H Beau Rivage (n.rest) 9 façade de Foncillon ☏ 46387311 rm22 (Feb-Dec) **A**

H France pl de Rénaissance-Front de Mer ☏ 46050229 rm32 **B**

★★Grand de Pontaillac (n.rest) 195 av de Pontaillac ☏ 46390044 rm55 (May-Sep) **A**

H Les Flots Bleus Les Embruns (n.rest) 18 bis, bd Garnier ☏ 46050217 rm24 (Apr-Sep) **A**

H Saintonge (n.rest) 14 r Gambetta ☏ 46057824 rm14 **A**

H Ville (n.rest) 1 bd A-Briand ☏ 46050064 rm20 **A**

ROYAT *Puy-de-Dôme*

H Belle Meunière 25 av de la Vallée ☏ 73358017 rm11 **B**

★★★Metropole 2 et 4 bd Vaquez ☏ 73358018 rm77 (May-Sep) **B**

H Royal St-Mart 6 av de la Gare ☏ 73358001 rm61 (May-Sep) **A**

H Univers 23 av de la Gare ☏ 73358128 rm45 (Apr-Oct) **A**

SABLES-D'OLONNE, LES *Vendée*

H Antoine 60 r Napoléon ☏ 51950836 rm19 (Apr-Sep) **A**

H Arundel 8 bd F-Roosesvelt ☏ 51320377 rm42 (Feb-Oct) **B**

H Atlantic 5 Pde Godet ☏ 51953771 rm30 **B**

H Chêne Vert 5 r de la Bauduère ☏ 51320947 rm33 **A**

H Roches Noires (n.rest) 12 prom Clémenceau ☏ 51320171 rm37 (Apr-Oct) **B**

SABLES-D'OR-LES-PINS *Côtes-du-Nord*

H Abordage ☏ 96415111 rm39 (Apr-Oct) **A**

★★**Ajoncs d'Or** alle des Acacias ☏ 96414212 rm75 (May-Sep) **B**

★★★**Au Bon Accueil** allée des Acacias ☏ 96414219 rm39 (Etr-Sep) **A**

★★**Diane** (n.rest) allée R-Brouard ☏ 96414207 rm50 (Apr-Sep) **A**

H Morgane (n.rest) allé des Acacias ☏ 96414690 rm20 (May-Oct) **A**

ST-AFFRIQUE *Averyron*

★★**Modern** 54 av A-Pezet ☏ 65492044 rm39 **A**

ST-ANDRÉ-LES-ALPES *Alpes-de-Haute-Provence*

H Clair Logis rte de Digne ☏ 92890405 rm12 (Apr-Nov) **A**

H Colombier rte d'Allos la Mure ☏ 92890711 rm24 **B**

H Lac et Fôret rte de Nice ☏ 92890738 rm30 (Feb-Oct) **A**

ST-AUBIN-SUR-MER *Calvados*

H Clos-Normand prom Guynemer ☏ 31973047 rm29 (Mar-Oct) **B**

H Normandie 126 r Pasteur ☏ 31973017 rm27 (Mar-Sep) **A**

★★**St-Aubin** 26 r de Verdun ☏ 31973039 rm26 (Feb-Nov) **B**

ST-BREVIN-LES-PINS *Loire-Atlantique*

H Debarcadere pl de la Marine ☏ 40272053 rm17 (Feb-Nov) **A**

H Petit Triancon 239 av de Mimdin ☏ 40272216 rm18 **A**

ST-BRIEUC *Côtes-du-Nord*

H Duguesclin 2 pl Du Guesclin ☏ 96331158 rm17 **A**

H Pignon Pointu (n.rest) 16 r J-J-Rousseau ☏ 96330239 rm17 **A**

ST-CAST-LE-GUILDO *Côtes-du-Nord*

H Étoile des Mers 32 r du Port ☏ 96418536 rm18 (Mar-Sep) **A**

H Ker Louis r Duguesclin ☏ 96418077 rm28 (Apr-Sep) **A**

H Mielles r Pietonne ☏ 96418095 rm18 (Apr-Sep) **A**

ST-CÉRÉ *Lot*

★★**Coq Arlequin** 1 bd du Dr-Roux ☏ 65380213 rm29 (Mar-Dec) **B**

H France av F-Maynard ☏ 65380216 rm23 **B**

H Parc fbg Lascabanne ☏ 65381729 rm10 **B**

ST-DIE *Vosges*

H France (n.rest) 1 r Dauphine ☏ 29563261 rm11 **A**

H Stanislas 34 r Stanislas ☏ 25565210 rm63 **B**

ST-DIZIER *Haute-Marne*

★★★**Gambetta** 62 r Gambetta ☏ 25565210 rm63 **B**

STE-MARIE-AUX-MINES *Haut-Rhin*

H Grand Hotel Cromer 185 r de Lattre-de-Tassigny ☏ 89587019 rm40 **A**

STE-MAXIME *Var*

H Auberge des Maures r des Frères-Battiglia ☏ 94960192 rm10 **A**

★★★**Beau Site** 5 bd des Cistes St Maxime ☏ 94961963 rm36 (Seasonal) **A**

H Chardon Bleu (n.rest) 20 r de Verdun ☏ 94960208 rm25 **A**

H Croisette (n.rest) ☏ 94961775 rm20 (Mar-Oct) **A**

M Royal Bon Repos (n.rest) r J-Aicard ☏ 94960874 rm23 (Apr-Oct) **A**

H Vièrge Noire (n.rest) La Nartelle ☏ 94963311 rm12 (Etr-Nov) **B**

STE-MENEHOULD *Marne*

H Cheval Rouge 1-3 r Chanzy ☏ 26608104 rm15 **B**

H Poste 54 av V-Hugo ☏ 26608016 rm10 (Mar-Dec) **A**

SAINTES *Charente-Maritime*

H Bosquets rte de Rochefort ☏ 46740447 rm35 **B**

H France r F-Mestraud ☏ 46930116 rm28 (Dec-Oct) **A**

★★**Messageries** (n.rest) r des Messageries ☏ 46936499 rm37 **B**

★★**Terminus** (n.rest) 2 r J-Moulin ☏ 46743503 rm28 **B**

SAINTES-MARIES-DE-LA-MER *Bouches-du-Rhône*

H Galoubet (n.rest) rte de Cacharel ☏ 90978217 rm20 **A**

H Lou Marques (n.rest) ☏ 90478289 rm14 (Apr-oct) **A**

H Mas des Lys Sarl (n.rest) rte d'Arles ☏ 90978235 rm26 (Mar-Dec) **A**

H Palunette rte d'Arles ☏ 90478630 rm12 **B**

H Pont de Gau ☏ 90478153 rm9 (Feb-Dec) **B**

ST-ÉTIENNE *Loire*

H Baladin (n.rest) 12 r de la Ville ☏ 77371797 rm16 **A**

H Carnot (n.rest) 11 bd Jules Janin ☏ 77742716 rm22 **B**

H Central (n.rest) 3 r Blanqui ☏ 77323186 rm25 (Seasonal) **B**

H Cheval Noir (n.rest) 11 r F-Gillet ☏ 77334172 rm46 **B**

H Nord 23 r des 3 Glorieuses ☏ 77742318 rm20 **B**

H Nouvel 35 av D-Rochereau ☏ 77325487 rm28 **A**

★★★**Terminus du Forez** 31 av D-Rochereau ☏ 77324847 rm66 **A**

H Touring-Continental 10 r F-Gillet ☏ 77325843 rm25 **B**

ST-FLOUR *Cantal*

H Massageries 24 av Ch-de-Gaulle ☏ 71601136 rm18 (May-Sep) **A**

★★**St-Jacques** pl de la Liberté ☏ 71600920 rm28 (Jan-Nov) **B**

ST-GAUDENS *Haute-Garonne*

H Esplanade (n.rest) 7 pl Mas-St-Pierre ☏ 61891590 rm12 **A**

H Richelieu (n.rest) 16 bd Gl-de-Gaulle ☏ 61896266 rm26 **A**

ST-GERVAIS-LES-BAINS *Haute-Savoie*

H Beau Soleil 45 Ch-du-Vorasset ☏ 50935076 rm10 (Dec-Sep) **A**

H Belvédère 835 av des Miage ☏ 50934213 rm12 (Dec-Oct) **B**

H Central (n.rest) av de la Gare – Le fayet ☏ 50781599 rm30 **A**

H Couttet pl de l'Église ☏ 50782665 rm22 **B**

H Deux Gares Le Fayet ☏ 50782475 rm28 **A**

H Fleche d'Or Le Bettex ☏ 50931154 rm16 (Seasonal) **A**

H Hostellerie du Nerey 754 av du Mont-d'Arbois ☏ 50934521 rm34 (Dec-Oct) **B**

H Maison Blanche r du Vieux Pont-du-Diable ☏ 50781938 rm14 (Dec-Sep) **B**

H Prarion alt 1860 Voza Prarion ☏ 50934701 rm19 (Seasonal) **B**

H Regina 74 av de Miage ☏ 50935203 rm20 (Seasonal) **B**

★★★Splendid (n.rest) ☏ 50782133 rm20 (Seasonal) **A**

H Val d'Este pl de l'Église ☏ 50936591 rm15 **A**

ST-GILLES-CROIX-DE-VIE *Vendée*

H Lion d'Or 84 r du Calvaire ☏ 51555039 rm55 **A**

H Marina 60 av de la Plage ☏ 51553097 rm40 (Feb-Dec) **B**

ST-GIRONS *Ariège*

★★★Eychenne 8 av P-Laffont ☏ 61662055 rm48 (Feb-Dec) **A**

H Mirouze 19 av Galliéni ☏ 61661277 rm24 **A**

★★★Truite Dorée 28 av de la Résistance ☏ 61661689 rm12 (Jan-Oct) **A**

ST-JEAN-DE-LUZ *Pyrénées-Atlantiques*

H Agur (n.rest) 96 r Gambetta ☏ 59262155 rm21 (Mar-Nov) **B**

H Central et du Commerce (n.rest) bd Cdt-Passicot ☏ 59263199 rm36 **B**

★Continental av de Verdun ☏ 59260123 rm24 **B**

★★★Grand de la Poste (n.rest) 83 r Gambetta ☏ 59260453 rm35 **A**

★★Paris (n.rest) 1 bd Cdt-Passicot ☏ 59260062 rm29 **A**

H Prado (n.rest) pl de la Pergola ☏ 59517273 rm38 **A**

H Trinquet Maitena r du Midi ☏ 59260513 rm13 **B**

ST-JEAN-DE-MAURIENNE *Savoie*

★★St Georges 334 r République ☏ 79640106 rm22 **B**

ST-JEAN-DE-MONTS *Vendée*

H Auberge de la Chaumière Orouet ☏ 51586744 rm29 Closed June **B**

H Espadon 8 av de la Forêt ☏ 51580318 rm50 (Mar-Jan) **A**

★★Plage espl de la Mer ☏ 51580035 rm52 (May-Sep) **A**

H Tante Paulette 32 r Neuve ☏ 51580112 rm41 (Mar-Oct) **A**

ST-JEAN-LE-THOMAS *Manche*

★★Bains ☏ 33488420 rm31 (Apr-Oct) **B**

★★Central 1 pl Ch-de-Gaulle ☏ 59370022 rm14 (Feb-Dec) **A**

ST-JEAN-PIED-DE-PORT *Pyrénées-Atlantiques*

H Etche Ona pl Floquet ☏ 59370114 rm13 **A**

ST-JULIEN-EN-GENEVOIS *Haute-Savoie*

H Relais Bleus ☏ 50493316 rm45 **A**

H Savoie (n.rest) av L-Armand ☏ 50490355 rm20 **B**

ST-JUNIEN *Haute-Vienne*

H Boeuf Rouge 57 bd V-Hugo ☏ 55023184 rm18 **B**

★★Concorde (n.rest) 49 av H-Barbusse ☏ 55021708 rm26 **A**

ST-LARY-SOULAN *Hautes-Pyrénées*

★★Terrasse Fleurie ☏ 62394026 rm28 (Seasonal) **A**

ST-LÔ *Manche*

★Cremaillère pl de la Préfecture ☏ 33571468 rm12 **A**

★★Grand de l'Univers 1 av de Brovère ☏ 33051084 rm24 **A**

H H Voyageurs 5 av Briovère ☏ 33050863 rm15 **B**

★★Marignan pl de la Gare ☏ 33051515 rm18 (Mar-Jan) **A**

★★Terminus 3 av Briovère ☏ 33053860 rm15 **A**

ST-LOUIS *Haut-Rhin*

H Cheval-Blanc 16 r du Ml-Foch ☏ 89697915 rm12 **A**

ST-MALO *Ille-et-Vilaine*

H Ajoncs d'Or (n.rest) 10 r des Forgeurs ☏ 99408503 rm23 **B**

H Beau-Rivage (n.rest) 17 av du Père ☏ 99563019 rm20 (Feb-Dec) **A**

H Bristol-Union (n.rest) 4 pl de la Poissonnerie ☏ 99408336 rm27 (Feb-Nov) **B**

H Brochet (n.rest) 1 Corne de Cerf ☏ 99563000 rm22 (May-Nov) **B**

★★★Central BP 142 ☏ 99408770 rm47 **A**

H Crosieur (n.rest) 2 pl de la Poissonnerie ☏ 99408040 rm14 **A**

H France et Châteaubriand pl Châteaubriand ☏ 99566652 rm85 **A**

H Inter-Hotel 138 bd des Talards ☏ 99820510 rm57 (Apr-Nov) **B**

★Noguette 9 r de la Fosse ☏ 99408357 rm12 **B**

H Porte St-Pierre 2 r du Guet ☏ 99409127 rm25 Closed Dec **A**

H Rochebonne 15 bd Châteaubriand ☏ 99560172 rm39 **B**

H Servannais 4 r Aml-Magon ☏ 99814550 rm46 **A**

H Univers pl Châteaubriand ☏ 99408952 rm70 **B**

H Voyageurs (n.rest) 2 bd des Talards ☏ 99563035 rm18 **A**

ST-MAURICE-SUR-MOSELLE *Vosges*

H Commerce 2 r Alsace ☏ 29251238 rm20 **A**

H Pieds des Ballons 1 rte du Ballon ☏ 29251254 rm22 Closed Nov **B**

H Rouge Gazon r de Rouge Gazon ☏ 29251280 rm22 **B**

ST-MICHEL-DE-MAURIENNE *Savoie*

H Des Alpes 20 r Gl-Ferrié ☏ 79565122 rm22 (Jan-Nov) **A**

★★Savoy 25 r Gl-Ferrié ☏ 79565512 rm18 **A**

ST-NAZAIRE *Loire-Atlantique*

H Berry 1 pl de la Gare ☎ 40224261 rm27 **B**

★★**Dauphin** (n.rest) 33 r J-Jaurès ☎ 40665961 rm20 **A**

ST-NECTAIRE *Puy-de-Dôme*

H Ermitage St-Nectaire-le-Bas ☎ 73885017 rm45 (May-Sep) **A**

H Savoy St-Nectaire-le-Bas ☎ 73885028 rm30 (May-Sep) **A**

ST-PAUL-EN-CHABLAIS *Haute-Savoie*

H Renardière (n.rest) La Beunaz ☎ 50736002 rm20 (Dec-Oct) **A**

ST-PEE-SUR-NIVELLE *Pyrénées-Atlantiques*

H Bide-Kurvizea ☎ 59541142 rm23 Closed Nov **A**

H Bonnet Ibarron ☎ 59541026 rm60 **B**

ST-PIERRE-DE-CHARTREUSE *Isère*

★★**Beau Site** ☎ 76886134 rm34 (Dec-Sep) **A**

H Guiers La Diat ☎ 76886085 rm10 (Seasonal) **B**

H Victoria pl de la Mairie ☎ 76886006 rm9 **A**

ST-QUAY-PORTRIEUX *Côtes-du-Nord*

H Ker Moor ☎ 96705222 rm28 (Mar-Dec) **B**

ST-QUENTIN *Aisne*

H Buffet de la Gare 1 r A-Baudez ☎ 23622433 rm10 **A**

H Carillon 4 pl de la Basilique ☎ 23622897 rm29 **B**

★★**Grill Campanile** ZAC de la Vallée, r ch Naudin ☎ 23092122 rm40 **A**

★★**Paix et Albert** 1er 3 pl du Huit October ☎ 23627762 rm82 **A**

H St-Prix 42 r E-Zola ☎ 23642222 rm31 **A**

ST-RAPHAËL *Var*

H Amandiers 874 bd A-Juin ☎ 94958242 rm10 (Jan-Nov) **A**

H Arènes 31 av Gl-Leclerc ☎ 94950634 rm27 **B**

H Colombette 1351, av de Valescure ☎ 94520178 rm22 (Nov-Oct) **A**

H Cyrnos (n.rest) 840 bd A-Juin ☎ 94951713 rm13 (Apr-Sep) **A**

H Europe Gare Terminus 9 r Aml-Baux ☎ 94953291 rm32 **A**

H Pyramides 77 av P-Doumer ☎ 94950595 rm27 **A**

H Sélect (n.rest) 89 r Boetmann ☎ 94950622 rm20 **A**

H Touring (n.rest) 1 quai Albert-1er ☎ 94950172 rm23 (Dec-Nov) **A**

ST-RÉMY-DE-PROVENCE *Bouches-du-Rhône*

H Arts 30 bd V-Hugo ☎ 90920850 rm9 Closed Feb **B**

H Auberge St-Roumierenco rte de Noues ☎ 90921253 rm10 **A**

H Canto Cigalo ch de Canto Cigalo ☎ 90921428 rm20 (Mar-Oct) **A**

★★**Castelet des Alpilles** 6 pl Mireille ☎ 90920721 rm19 (Mar-Nov) **A**

ST-SERNIN-SUR-RANCE *Aveyron*

★★**Carayon** pl du Fort ☎ 65996026 rm23 **A**

ST-TROPEZ *Var*

H Meditérranée 21 bd L-Blanc ☎ 94970044 rm13 (Mar-Oct) **A**

SALBRIS *Loir-et-Cher*

★**Dauphin** 57 bd de la République ☎ 54970483 rm10 **B**

★★★**Parc** 8 av d'Orléans ☎ 54971853 rm30 **B**

SALON-DE-PROVENCE *Bouches-du-Rhône*

M Domaine de Roquerousse rte d'Avignon ☎ 90595011 rm17 **A**

H Grand d'Angleterre (n.rest) 98 cours Carnot ☎ 90560110 rm26 **A**

H Midi (n.rest) 518 allée de Craponne ☎ 90533467 rm27 **B**

H Sélect (n.rest) 35 r Bailli-du-Suffren ☎ 90570717 rm19 **A**

H Vendôme (n.rest) 34 r Ml-Joffre ☎ 90560196 rm24 **A**

SANARY-SUR-MER *Var*

★★**Tour** 24 quai Gl-de-Gaulle ☎ 94741010 rm28 **B**

SARREGUEMINES *Moselle*

H Grand Terminus (n.rest) 7 av de la Gare ☎ 87985546 rm59 **A**

H Union 28 r Geiger ☎ 87952842 rm22 **B**

SARRE-UNION *Bas-Rhin*

H Cheval Noir 16 r de Phalsbourg ☎ 88001271 rm21 **A**

SAULIEU *Côte-d'Or*

H Côte d'Or 2 r d'Argentine ☎ 80640766 rm24 **B**

★★★**Poste** 1 r Grillot ☎ 80640567 rm48 **A**

SAUMUR *Maine-et-Loire*

H Gare 16 r D-d'Angers ☎ 41673424 rm16 (Apr-Oct) **A**

★★**Londres** 48 r d'Orlans ☎ 41512398 rm28 **B**

★★**Terminus** (n.rest) face de la Gare ☎ 41673101 rm45 **A**

SAVERNE *Bas-Rhin*

★**Chez Jean** 3 r de la Gare ☎ 88911019 rm30 Closed Jan **B**

H Fischer 15 r de la Gare ☎ 88911953 rm18 **B**

SEDAN *Ardennes*

H Univers pl de la Gare ☎ 24270435 rm22 (Sep-July) **A**

SÉEZ *Savoie*

H Belvédere ☎ 79070204 rm28 (Seasonal) **B**

SEMUR-EN-AUXOIS *Côte-d'Or*

★**Côte d'Or** 3 pl Gaveau ☎ 80970313 rm15 **B**

SENAS *Bouches-du-Rhône*

H Terminus RN 7 ☎ 90572008 rm16 (Feb-Dec) **A**

SENS *Yonne*

H Croix-Blanche 9 r V-Guichard ☎ 86640002 rm25 **A**

H René Binet 20 r R-René ☎ 86952150 rm33 **B**

SÈTE *Hérault*

★★★**Grand** 17 quai de Lattre-de-Tassigny ☎ 67747177 rm51 **B**

H Orgue Bleue (n.rest) 10 quai A.-Herber ☎ 67747213 rm30 (Mar-Jan) **A**

SÉZANNE *Marne*

H Relais Champenois et du Lion d'Or 157 r Notre-Dame ☎ 26805803 rm14 **A**

SIORAC-EN-PÉRIGORD *Dordogne*

H Auberge Club de la Petit Reine ☎ 53316042 rm35 (Apr-Oct) **B**

H Escale ☎ 53316023 rm18 (Apr-Oct) **A**

★**Scholly** pl de la Poste ☎ 53316002 rm32 **B**

SISTERON *Alpes-de-Haute-Provence*

H Chênes rte de Gap ☎ 92611508 rm21 Closed Dec **B**

★★★**Grand du Cours** (n.rest) pl de l'Église ☎ 92610451 rm50 (Mar-Nov) **B**

SOISSONS *Aisne*

H Lion Rouge sq St-Martin ☎ 23533152 rm32 **A**

SOUILLAC *Lot*

★★**Ambassadeurs** 7-12 av du Gl-de-Gaulle ☎ 65327836 rm28 (Nov-Sep) **A**

H Grand 1 allée de Verninac ☎ 65327830 rm30 (Apr-Oct) **A**

★**Nouvel** 21 av Gl-de-Gaulle ☎ 65327958 rm29 (Apr-Oct) **A**

H Promenade et des Acacias 12 bd L-Malvy ☎ 65378286 rm48 (Etr-Oct) **B**

★★**Roseraie** 42 av de Toulouse ☎ 65378269 rm26 Apr-Oct **A**

H Vielle Auberge pl de la Minoterie ☎ 65327943 rm20 Closed Feb **A**

SOUSTONS *Landes*

★★**Bergerie** av du Lac ☎ 58411143 rm12 (Apr-Oct) **B**

H Château Bergeron r du Vicomte ☎ 58415814 rm16 (May-Oct) **B**

STRASBOURG *Bas-Rhin*

H Carlton 15 pl de la Gare ☎ 88326239 rm72 **B**

H Eden (n.rest) 16 r Obernai ☎ 88324199 rm28 **A**

H Esplanade (n.rest) 1 bd Leblois ☎ 88613895 rm37 **B**

H Europe (n.rest) 38 r Fosse-des-Tanneurs ☎ 88321788 rm60 **A**

H Hostellerie Louis XIII rte de Colmar ☎ 88343428 rm16 **A**

H Kleber 29 pl Kléber ☎ 88320953 rm32 **A**

H National (n.rest) 13 pl de la Gare ☎ 88323509 rm87 **B**

H Paris (n.rest) 13 r de la Mésange ☎ 88321550 rm78 **B**

H Pax 24-26 r du Faubourg ☎ 88321454 rm119 (seasonal) **A**

H Rhin (n.rest) 7 pl de la Gare ☎ 88323500 rm63 **A**

H Scana (n.rest) 7 r de la Chaîne ☎ 88326660 rm24 **B**

H Tour 18 r de la Tour-Koenigshoffen ☎ 88302277 rm18 **B**

H Union (n.rest) 8 quai Kellermann ☎ 88327041 rm60 **B**

TALLOIRES *Haute-Savoie*

★★**Beau Site** Lac d'Annecy ☎ 50607104 rm38 (May-Oct) **A**

H Charpenterie r A-Theuriet ☎ 50607047 rm20 (Apr-Nov) **B**

★★★**Cottage** ☎ 50607110 rm34 (Mar-Oct) **A**

H Grillons Ancon ☎ 50607031 rm34 **A**

H Villa des Fleurs Route du Port ☎ 50607114 rm7 (Feb-Dec) **A**

★★**Vivier** ☎ 50607054 rm35 (Apr-Oct) **B**

TARASCON *Bouches-du-Rhône*

H Moderne bd Itam ☎ 90910170 rm43 **A**

H Terminus pl du Col-Berrurier ☎ 90911895 rm22 (Mar-Jan) **A**

TARBES *Hautes-Pyrénées*

H Family (n.rest) 64 r V-Hugo ☎ 62930233 rm21 **A**

★**Henri IV** (n.rest) 7 av B-Barère ☎ 62340168 rm24 **A**

H Marne (n.rest) 4 av de la Marne ☎ 62930364 rm26 **A**

H Martinet 13 bd du Martinet ☎ 62379630 rm24 **B**

H Normandie (n.rest) 33 r Massey ☎ 62930847 rm21 **A**

H Terminus 42 av Joffre ☎ 62930033 rm32 **B**

TESSÉ-LA-MADELEINE *Orne*

H Celtic 14-16 r Christople ☎ 33379211 rm16 (Mar-Dec) **B**

H Clos Joli 6 bd Labbe ☎ 33378633 rm33 **A**

THIONVILLE *Moselle*

H Nouvel Parc 10 pl de la République ☎ 82537180 rm42 **B**

THOUARS *Deux-Sèvres*

H Chateau rte de Parthenay ☎ 49661852 rm20 **A**

H Relais (n.rest) à Louzy ☎ 49662945 rm15 **A**

TOULON *Var*

H Continental et Metropole (n.rest) 1 r Racine ☎ 94223626 rm48 **A**

H Regent (n.rest) 3 r A-Guiol ☎ 94926563 rm29 **B**

H Terminus 7 bd de Tesse ☎ 94892354 rm40 **A**

TOULOUSE *Haute-Garonne*

H Bordeaux 4 bd Bonrepos ☎ 61624109 rm31 **B**

H Bristol 15 bd Bonrepos ☎ 61629076 rm16 **B**

H Chez Tony 75 ch de la Glaciere ☎ 61475232 rm24 **A**

H Clocher de Rodez 14 pl J-d'Arc ☎ 61624292 rm46 **B**

H Cosmos 20 r Caffarelli ☎ 61625721 rm21 (Sep-Jul) **B**

H Festival 84 rte de Narbonne ☎ 61524255 rm13 (Sep-Jul) **B**

H François (n.rest) 1er 4 r d'Austerlitz ☎ 61215452 rm20 (Jan-Jul) **A**

H Grand d'Orleans 72 r Bayard ☎ 61629847 rm56 **B**

H Grand Balcon (n.rest) 8 r Romiguières ☎ 61214808 rm54 (Sep-Jul) **A**

H Grand Boulevards (n.rest) 12 r d'Austerlitz ☎ 61216757 rm30 **A**

H Heliot (n.rest) 3 r Héliot ☎ 61624766 rm14 **A**

H Jacobins (n.rest) 52 r Paragaminieres ☎ 61230621 rm26 **A**

H Junior 62 r du Taur ☎ 61216967 rm23 **A**

H Lafayette (n.rest) 5 r Caffarelli ☎ 61627573 rm20 (Sep-Jul) **B**

H Pere Leon 2 pl Esquirol ☎ 61217039 rm41 **B**

H Riquet (n.rest) 92 r Riquet ☎ 61625596 rm74 **A**

H St-Sernin (n.rest) 2 r St-Bernard ☎ 61217308 rm25 **B**

H Star (n.rest) 17 r Baque ☎ 61474515 rm17 **B**

H Touristic (n.rest) 25 pl V-Hugo ☎ 61231455 rm38 **B**

TOUQUET-PARIS-PLAGE, LE *Pas-de-Calais*

★**Chalet** 15 r de la Paix ☎ 21845565 rm18 (Etr-Nov) **B**

★★**Plage** (n.rest) bd de la Mer ☏ 21050322 rm29 (Mar-Nov) **A**

TOURLAVILLE *Manche*

FH St-Jean (n.rest) Prés du Château ☏ 33220086 rm5 **A**

TOURNUS *Saône-et-Loire*

H Clos Mouron ☏ 85512386 rm20 **B**

★**Terrasses** 18 av du 23 Janvier ☏ 85510174 rm12 **A**

TOURS *Indre-et-Loire*

H Akilene 22 r Grand-Marché ☏ 47614604 rm20 **A**

★★**Armor** (n.rest) 26 bis bd Heurteloup ☏ 47052437 rm50 **B**

★**Balzac** (n.rest) 47 r de Scellerie ☏ 47054087 rm12 **A**

H Castel Fleuri 10 r Groison ☏ 47545099 rm10 **B**

★★★**Central** (n.rest) 21 r Berthelot ☏ 47054644 rm42 **A**

★★★**Châteaux de la Loire** (n.rest) 12 r Gambetta ☏ 47051005 rm30 **A**

★**Choiseul** (n.rest) 12 r de la Rotisserie ☏ 47208576 rm16 **B**

★**Colbert** (n.rest) 78 r Colbert ☏ 47666156 rm16 **A**

★★**Cygne** (n.rest) 6 r du Cygne ☏ 47666641 rm20 **A**

H Europe (n.rest) 12 pl Ml-Leclerc ☏ 47054207 rm53 **B**

H Foch (n.rest) 20 r du Ml-Foch ☏ 47611709 rm14 **A**

H Gambetta (n.rest) 7 r Gambetta ☏ 47050835 rm30 **A**

H Italia (n.rest) 19 r-Devilde ☏ 47544301 rm20 **A**

H Moderne 1 et 3 r V-Laloux ☏ 47053281 rm23 **A**

H Musée 2 pl F-Sicard ☏ 47666381 rm15 **A**

H Rosny (n.rest) 19 r B-Pascal ☏ 47052354 **A**

H Trianon (n.rest) 57 av de Grammont ☏ 47053527 rm14 **A**

TRÉGASTEL *Côtes-du-Nord*

H Armoric Hotel Sarl pl du Coz-Pors ☏ 96238816 rm50 (May-Sep) **B**

★★**Beau Séjour** pl du Coz-Pors ☏ 96238802 rm18 (Mar-Sep) **B**

★★**Mer et Plage** ☏ 96238803 rm40 (May-Oct) **A**

TROUVILLE-SUR-MER *Calvados*

H Carmen 24 r Carnot ☏ 31883543 rm16 **A**

H Maison Normande (n.rest) 4 pl Ml-de-Lattre-de-Tassigny ☏ 31881225 rm20 (Feb-Nov) **B**

H Sablettes (n.rest) 15 r P-Besson ☏ 31881066 rm18 (Feb-Dec) **A**

H St-James 16 r de la Plage ☏ 31880523 rm14 **B**

TROYES *Aube*

H Champenois (n.rest) 15 r P-Gauthier ☏ 25761605 rm26 **A**

H Poste 35 av E-Zola ☏ 25730505 rm34 **A**

H Splendid (n.rest) 44 bd Carnot ☏ 25730852 rm16 **A**

H Thiers (n.rest) 59 av du Gl-de-Gaulle ☏ 25734066 rm30 **A**

TULLE *Corrèze*

H Gare 25 av W-Churchill ☏ 55200404 rm15 **A**

★★★**Limouzi** quai de la République ☏ 55264200 rm50 **A**

H Royal (n.rest) 70 av V-Hugo ☏ 55200452 rm14 **A**

H St-Martin 45 quai A-Briand ☏ 55261218 rm24 (Feb-Dec) **A**

USSEL *Corrèze*

H Gravades N89 St-Dezery ☏ 55722153 rm20 **A**

H Midi 24 av Thiers ☏ 55721799 rm18 **A**

VAISON-LA-ROMAINE *Vaucluse*

★★**Beffroi** r de l'Evêche – Haute-Ville ☏ 90360471 rm18 (Mar-Nov) **A**

H Burrhus (n.rest) 2 pl Montfort ☏ 90360011 rm14 Closed Nov **B**

VAL-ANDRÉ, LE *Côtes-du-Nord*

H France 4 r Pasteur ☏ 96722252 rm55 (Mar-Nov) **A**

VALENCE *Drôme*

H "Grand St Jacques" 9 fbg St-Jacques ☏ 75424460 rm32 **A**

H California 174 av M-Faure ☏ 75443605 rm30 (Seasonal) **B**

H Continental (n.rest) 29 av P-Sémard ☏ 75440138 rm30 **A**

H Europe (n.rest) 15 av F-Faure ☏ 75430216 rm26 **A**

H Lyon (n.rest) 23 av P-Sémard ☏ 75414466 rm59 **A**

H Negociants 27 av P-Sémard ☏ 75440186 rm42 **A**

★★**Park** 22 r J-Bouin ☏ 75433706 rm21 **B**

VALENCIENNES *Nord*

H Arcades 19 r St-Jacques ☏ 27301659 rm15 **A**

H Notre-Dame (n.rest) pl Thellier de Poncheville ☏ 27423000 rm40 **A**

H Regent 39 r du Rempart ☏ 27464425 rm18 **A**

VALS-LES-BAINS *Ardèche*

★★**Europe** 88 r J-Jaurès ☏ 75374394 rm35 (Apr-Sep) **A**

H St-Jacques 8 r A-Clément ☏ 75374602 rm28 **B**

H St-Jean 112 bis r J-Jaurès ☏ 75374250 rm32 (Apr-Sep) **A**

H Touring 88 r J-Jaurès ☏ 75374436 rm25 **A**

VANNES *Morbihan*

H Anne de Bretagne (n.rest) 42 r O-de-Clisson ☏ 97542219 rm20 **B**

H Bretagne (n.rest) 34/36 r du Mené ☏ 97472021 rm12 **A**

H Manche Océan (n.rest) 31 r du Lieut-Col-Maury ☏ 97472646 rm42 **B**

H Relais du Golfe (n.rest) 10 pl du Gl-de-Gaulle ☏ 97471474 rm14 **A**

H Richemont 26 av Favel – rte Lincy ☏ 97471295 rm29 **A**

H Roof Presqu'ile de Conleau ☏ 97634747 rm11 **B**

H Verdun (n.rest) 10 av de Verdun ☏ 97472123 rm24 **A**

VENCE *Alpes-Maritimes*

H Victoire pl du Grand Jardin ☏ 93586130 rm15 (Dec-Oct) **A**

VENDÔME *Loir-et-Cher*

H Grand St-Georges 14 r Poterie ☏ 54772542 rm34 **A**

VERDUN *Meuse*

H Bellevue I.R.P. du Mal de Lattre de, Tassigny ☏ 29843941 rm72 (Apr-Oct) **A**

Hostellerie du Coq Hardi 8 av de la Victoire ☏ 29863636 **B**

H Montaulbain (n.rest) 4 r Vieille-Prison ☏ 29860047 rm10 **A**

H Poste 8 av de Douaumont ☎ 29860390 rm23 (Mar-Dec) **A**

VERNET-LES-BAINS *Pyrénées-Orientales*

H Alsina 1 r des Baus ☎ 68055844 rm38 **B**

H Eden 2 prom du Cady ☎ 68055409 rm20 (Apr-Oct) **A**

H Princess r des Lavandières ☎ 68055622 rm42 (Mar-Jan) **A**

VESOUL *Haute-Saône*

H Lion (n.rest) 4 pl de la République ☎ 84765444 rm19 **A**

VEULETTES-SUR-MER *Seine-Maritime*

H Frégates Digue J-Corruble ☎ 35975122 rm16 **A**

VICHY *Allier*

H Carnot 24 bd Carnot ☎ 70983698 rm28 (May-Sep) **B**

H Chambord 84 r de Paris ☎ 70312288 rm35 **B**

H Clememceau (n.rest) 2 r R-Breton ☎ 70988020 rm23 **A**

H Cloche d'Argent 2 r d'Angleterre ☎ 70982288 rm55 (Apr-Oct) **A**

H Colbert 23 r Ml-Foch ☎ 70320600 rm47 (May-Sep) **A**

H Concordia 15 r Roovère ☎ 70982965 rm34 (May-Sep) **A**

H Eaux 101 r du Ml-Lyautey ☎ 70323933 rm51 **A**

H Gallia 10 av P-Doumer ☎ 70318666 rm72 (Apr-Sep) **A**

H Grand Conde 12 r Desbrest ☎ 70312284 rm26 **A**

H Massena 4 sq Albert-1er ☎ 70321476 rm46 (May-Sep) **A**

Monbrun 6 r Prés-Wilson ☎ 70982636 **B**

H Montpensier 48 bd Kennedy ☎ 70321422 rm58 (Apr-Oct) **A**

H Nice-Flore 129 bd des États-Unis ☎ 70982094 rm42 (Apr-Oct) **A**

H Nievre 19 av de Gramont ☎ 70318277 rm19 **A**

H Residence Lafayette (n.rest) 13 r Alquie ☎ 70982348 rm42 (May-Sep) **A**

H Rhone 8 r de Paris ☎ 70982801 rm40 (Mar-Nov) **A**

H Trianon 9 r Desbrest ☎ 70979596 rm24 **A**

H Universel 2 pl de la Gare ☎ 70982234 rm27 **A**

VIC-SUR-CÈRE *Cantal*

★Auberge des Monts à Curebourse ☎ 71475171 rm30 (Feb-Oct) **A**

H Family av E-Duclaux ☎ 71475049 rm39 (Etr-Oct) **A**

VIENNE *Isère*

H Central 3 r Achevêche ☎ 74851838 rm27 **A**

H Poste 47 cours Romestang ☎ 74850204 rm42 **A**

H Residence de la Pyramide (n.rest) 40 quai Riondet ☎ 74531646 rm15 (Dec-oct) **A**

VILLEFRANCHE-DE-ROUERGUE *Aveyron*

H Lagarrigues pl B-Lhez ☎ 65450112 rm20 (Seasonal) **A**

VILLENEUVE-SUR-LOT *Lot-et-Garonne*

★★★Grand du Parc 13 bd de la Marine ☎ 53700168 rm42 **A**

H Platanes (n.rest) 40-42 bd de la Marine ☎ 53401140 rm22 **A**

H Résidence (n.rest) 17 av Carnot ☎ 53401703 rm18 **A**

VIRE *Calvados*

★★Cheval Blanc 2 pl 6-Juin-1944 ☎ 31680021 rm22 **A**

H France 4 r d'Aignaux ☎ 31680035 rm20 (Feb-Nov) **A**

VITRY-LE-FRANÇOIS *Marne*

★Cloche 34 r A-Briand ☎ 26740384 rm24 **A**

VITTEL *Vosges*

H Beausejour 160 av des Tilleuls ☎ 29080934 rm37 (May-Sep) **A**

H Bellevue 503 av Chatillon ☎ 29080798 rm39 (Apr-Sep) **B**

H Castel Fleuri r de Metz et r J-d'Arc ☎ 29080520 rm45 (May-Sep) **A**

H Chalet 6 av G-Clémenceau ☎ 29080721 rm10 **A**

H Continental 80 av Bouloumie ☎ 29080108 rm39 (May-Sep) **A**

H Orée du Bois D18 entrée Hippodrome ☎ 29081351 rm38 **A**

VIZILLE *Isère*

★Parc (n.rest) Restaurant du Parc ☎ 76680301 rm28 **A**

WIMEREUX *Pas-de-Calais*

H Aramis 1 r Romain ☎ 21324015 rm16 **A**

★Centre 78 r Carnot ☎ 21324108 rm25 **B**

YPORT *Seine-Maritime*

H Siréne 3 bd A-Dumont ☎ 35273185 rm10 **A**

YVOIRE *Haute-Savoie*

H Flots Bleus ☎ 50728008 rm8 (May-Sep) **B**

MONACO

The principality of Monaco, which is 350 acres in extent, is an independent enclave within France. It consists of three adjacent towns – Monaco, the capital, la Condamine, along the harbour; and Monte-Carlo along the coast immediately to the north. The headland was known to the Phoenicians, Greeks and Romans, and sailors from Genoa settled here in the 13th century. The Genoese family of Grimaldi made themselves lords of Monaco and established the line which still rules.

Monte-Carlo is famous for its Casino, built in 1878, which has featured in many films and novels. In addition to its gambling tables it has a fine opera house and luxurious grounds. The rest of the town is largely expensive hotels and the villas of the wealthy, plus well-kept sub-tropical gardens.

The harbour of la Condamine is a busy centre of colourful yachts and cabin cruisers. The town is less pretentious and expensive than Monte-Carlo and contains the commercial quarter of the principality.

Monaco, the capital of the principality, occupies a bold and picturesque position on a rock projecting into the sea. Its streets are narrow and shaded. The centre

of the town is the Palace Square, boasting 16 bronze cannons and dominated by the palace itself. The main gate, dating from 1672, bears the family coat-of-arms, while a court of honour contains fine marble staircases and arcades.
There are museums of prehistory and anthropology, and oceanography. The cathedral is a recent Romanesque building (1875-84) but contains reics of an earlier church. The princes of Monaco are buried in the crypt.
EATING OUT One of Monte-Carlo's institutions is the café, brasserie and drugstore of the *Café de Paris*, in Place du Casino. The restaurants *Dominique le Stanc*, in boulevard des Moulins and *Rampoldi* in avenue Spelugues, are both outstanding, the latter specialising in imaginative Italian cuisine.

MONTE CARLO

H Cosmopolite (n.rest) 4 r de la Turbie ☏ 93301695 rm24 **B**

H De l'Etoile 4 r des Oliviers ☏ 93307392 rm11 **A**

H France 6 r de la Turbie ☏ 93302464 rm26 **B**

Le Puy in the Auvergne is famed for its 12th-century cathedral

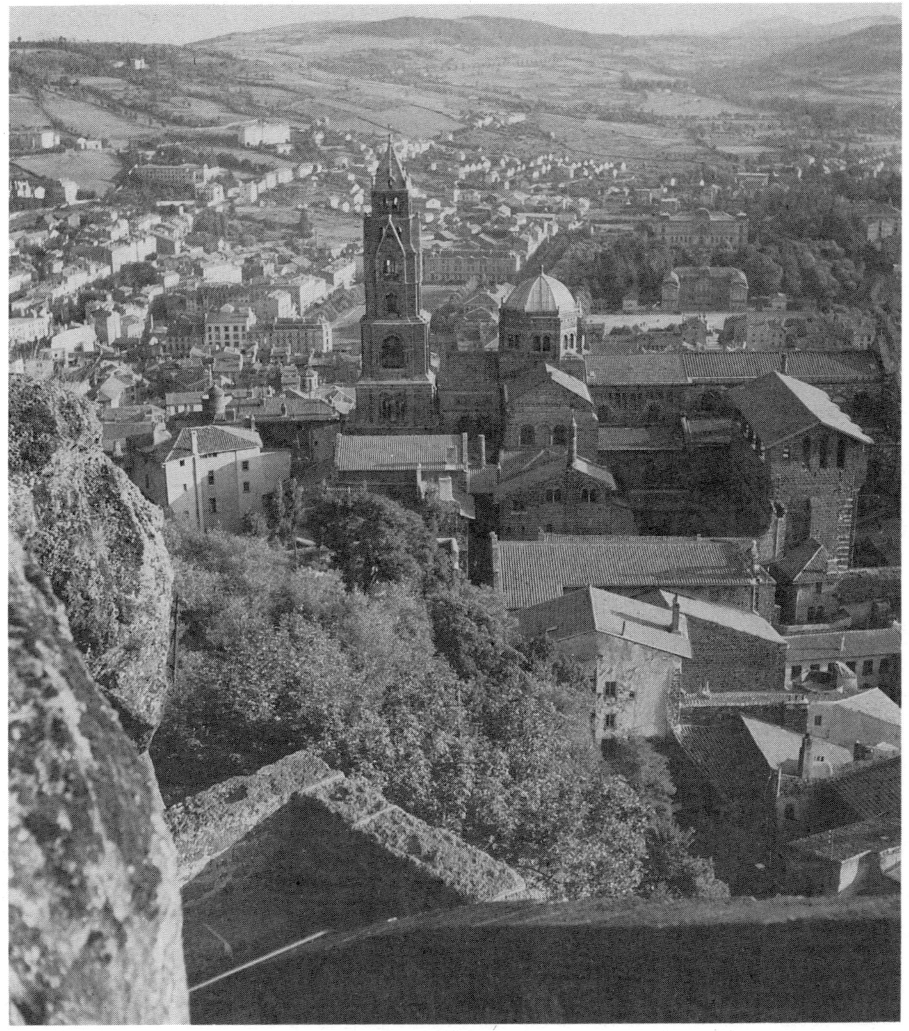

GERMANY (Federal Republic of)

FACTS & FIGURES

Capital: Bonn
Language: German, French, English
IDD code: 49. To call the UK dial 00 44
Currency: Deutsche Mark (DM1 = 100 Pfenninge)
Local time: GMT + 1 (summer GMT + 2)
Emergency services: Police 110; Fire 112; Ambulance 115.

Business hours

Banks: 0830–1300 & 1430–1600 Mon–Fri
Shops: 0900–1800 Mon–Fri, 0900–1300 Sat

Average daily temperatures:
Munich °C

Jan −2	Jul 18
Mar 4	Sep 15
May 13	Nov 3

Tourist Information
German National Tourist Office

UK 65 Curzon Street
London W1Y 7PE
Tel 01–495 3990

USA 747 Third Ave
New York, NY 10017
Tel (212) 308–3300

Germany is a land of mountains and plains, estuaries and inlets, forests and heaths, plus thriving, modern cities and medieval country towns, fairytale castles and colourful traditions. The people are welcoming and encourage visitors to enjoy themselves; the wines, beers and the food are not only good value, but are also hearty and satisfying.

Thanks to the superb German road network, the miles pass swiftly and easily, with motorways linking all the main areas, and delightful country lanes to travel in between. Most things in Germany are reasonably priced, and shopping – particularly in Hamburg and Berlin – is a delight.

Germany is a country of amazing variety, with a constantly changing pattern of scenery from the sea to the mountains, and from the lowlands to the forest-clad Bavarian Alps. Many small towns have preserved the aspect of past centuries, many cities have brought new life into their old town centres. The old Imperial cities in the south have their splendid cathedrals, palaces and town halls, while beyond the towns there are great expanses of open countryside and countless health and holiday resorts.

HOW TO GET THERE

BY CAR

If you use one of the short-crossing Channel ferries, then drive through Belgium, the Federal Republic of Germany is within a comfortable day's drive. The distance from Calais to Köln (Cologne) is just under 260 miles. Alternatively, you might choose to drive down through northern France, particularly if you cross the Channel to Cherbourg, Caen, Dieppe or Le Havre, or if you are heading for southern Germany. The distance from La Havre to Strasbourg is 425 miles.

If you are visiting northern Germany, it might be easier to take a ferry across the North Sea to the Netherlands or from Harwich to Hamburg ($19\frac{1}{2}$–$21\frac{1}{2}$ hrs).

For details of the AA's Overseas Routes Service consult the Contents page.

SPEED LIMITS

Unless otherwise indicated by signs, the speed restrictions are as follows: 50 kph (31 mph) in built-up areas – indicated by placename signs; 100 kph (62 mph) outside built-up areas; motorways (Autobahnen) and dual-carriageways have a recommended upper limit of 130 kph (81 mph) and a minimum speed limit of 40 kph (25 mph).

BY TRAIN

If you do not have an Inter Rail or Eurail pass a considerable variety of tickets and passes are available for travel within Germany. The *Vorzugskarte* is a budget long-distance return ticket offering a reduction of around 20%. The Touristenkarte entitles all travellers over the age of 25 to unlimited second-class travel for 4, 9 or 16 days. There are similar discounts for those under 26 (Juniortouristenkarte or the Tramper-Monats Ticket which is valid for a month) and for families (the Familien-Pass).

BY BICYCLE

Anyone with a railpass or ticket can rent a bicycle at many rail stations throughout the country. Most stations offer this service from April to October only. Generally you can return the bicycle to any station that rents.

CITY TRANSPORT

Large cities have fast city trains (S-Bahn), which railpass holders may ride for free. Other city transport – subway (U-Bahn), streetcars and buses – is not covered by railpasses. Individual rides are expensive so it is probably worth buying a day card (Tagesnetzkarte) or multiple-ride ticket (Mehrfahrkarte). Often you have to get your ticket beforehand at an automat and then validate it in one of the little boxes either in the station or on board the vehicle.

ACCOMMODATION

The gazetteer contains a range of accommodation for less than DM62 per person per night. The prices have been banded as follows:

A DM29–45
B DM45–62

Taking an exchange rate of

DM3.25=£1
DM1.95=US $1

These prices are liable to alter during the currency of this book. Further information can be obtained through the national tourist office or through local tourist bureaus called *Verkehrsamt* or *Verkehrsverein.* Otherwise, look out for *Zimmer frei* (rooms vacant) notices which should offer reasonably priced accommodation.

Abbreviations: pl Platz str Strasse

AACHEN *Nordrhein-Westfalen*

H Frankenberg Bismarckstr 47 ☏ (0241) 508080 bed40 **B**

★Lousberg (n.rest) Saarstr 108 ☏ (0241) 20331 rm25 **B**

◆ Sieberg (n.rest) Rudolfstr 46 ☏ (0241) 503691 rm7 **B**

H Strangenhäuschen Krefelder Str 276 ☏ (0241) 153111 bed18 **A**

◆ Zur Heide Raafstr 76-80 ☏ (02408) 2085 bed57 **A**

ADENAU *Rheinland-Pfalz*

H Berghotel Hohe Acht ☏ (02691) 471 rm11 **A**

H Eifeler Hof Haupstr 26 ☏ (02691) 2112 rm69 **A**

H Historisches Haus Blaue Ecke Markt 4 ☏ (02691) 2005 rm8 **A**

ALPIRSBACH *Baden-Württemberg*

★★Adler ☏ (07444) 2215 bed30 Feb-Jan 10 **A**

◆ Erlenhof Haupstr 51 ☏ (07444) 6246 bed30 **A**

◆ Waldhorn Kreuzstr 4 ☏ (07444) 2411 bed18 **A**

ALSFELD *Hessen*

H Klingelhöffer Hersfelder Str 43-48 ☏ (06631) 2073 bed70 **B**

H Krone Schellengasse 2 ☏ (06631) 4041 bed80 **B**

ALTENAHR *Rheinland-Pfalz*

◆ Burg Sahr ☏ (02643) 7274 bed8 **A**

H Caspari Rossberg 1 ☏ (02643) 2005 bed40 Closed Feb 5-28 **A**

H Central Brückenstr 3-5 ☏ (02643) 1815 rm23 Closed Dec **A**

★★Post Brückenstr 2 ☏ (02643) 2098 rm57 Closed Nov 21-Dec 19 **B**

H Rutland Bruckenstr 6 ☏ (02643) 8318 rm44 **A**

AMBERG *Bayern*

◆ Goldene Krone Waisenhausgasse 2 ☏ (09621) 22994 rm24 **A**

ANDERNACH *Rheinland-Pfalz*

H Andernacher Hof Breite Str 83 ☏ (02632) 43175 bed60 Closed Jan **A**

H Deubacher Hof Cranachstr 1-5 ☏ (02632) 43129 bed37 **A**

H Namedyer-Hof Haupstr 103 ☏ (02632) 491051 bed26 Closed Dec 20-30 **A**

H Zum Stadion Stadionstr 10 ☏ (02632) 43878 bed36 **A**

ARNSBERG *Nordrhein-Westfalen*

H Zur Krone Johannestr 62, Neheim ☏ (02932) 24231 bed50 **A**

AROLSEN *Hessen*

H Luisen-Mühle Luisenmühler Weg 1 ☏ (05691) 3021 bed20 **A**

ASCHAFFENBURG *Bayern*

◆ Weinstube Kahlgrundstr 16 ☏ (06021) 42875 rm5 Closed Jul **A**

H Zum Ochsen Karlstr 16 ☏ (06021) 23132 bed40 **A**

ATTENDORN *Nordrhein-Westfalen*

H Forsthaus Petersburger Weg 4 ☏ (02722) 7317 bed12 May-Sep **A**

◆ Wadhaus-Biggesee Ihnestr 11 ☏ (02722) 7254 rm18 **A**

AUGSBURG *Bayern*

◆ Georgsrast (n.rest) Georgenstr 31 ☏ (0821) 313051 rm24 **A**

◆ Goldener Stern Waldstr 13 ☏ (0821) 92585 bed27 Closed Jul 25-Aug 14 **A**

H Riegele Vikoriastr 4 ☏ (0821) 39039 bed65 **B**

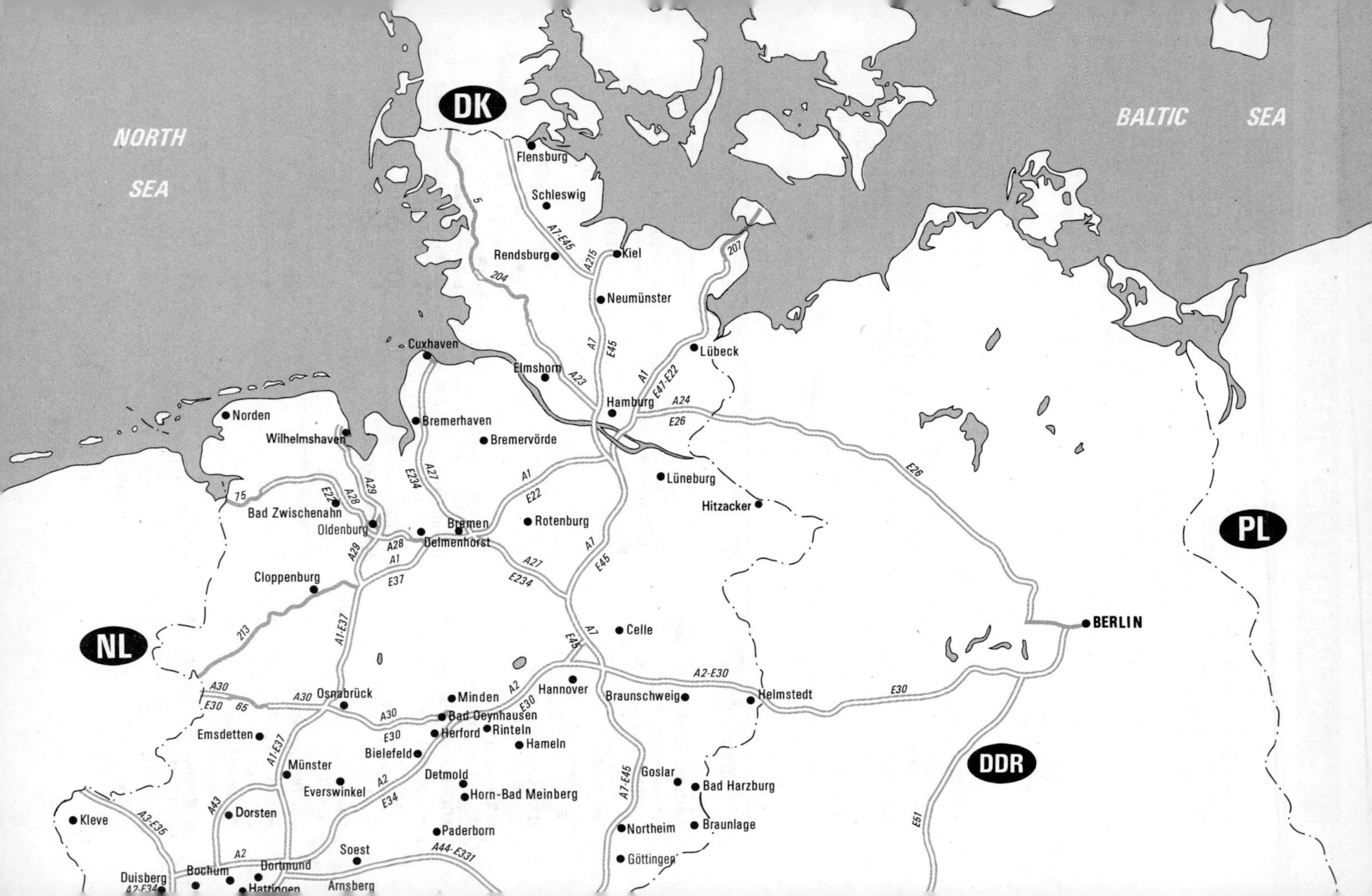
NORTH SEA
BALTIC SEA
DK
PL
NL
DDR
Flensburg
Schleswig
Rendsburg
Kiel
Neumünster
Cuxhaven
Lübeck
Elmshorn
Hamburg
Norden
Wilhelmshaven
Bremerhaven
Bremervörde
Lüneburg
Hitzacker
Bad Zwischenahn
Oldenburg
Bremen
Delmenhorst
Rotenburg
Cloppenburg
BERLIN
Celle
Osnabrück
Minden
Hannover
Braunschweig
Helmstedt
Bad Oeynhausen
Rinteln
Emsdetten
Herford
Hameln
Bielefeld
Münster
Detmold
Goslar
Bad Harzburg
Everswinkel
Horn-Bad Meinberg
Dorsten
Kleve
Northeim
Braunlage
Paderborn
Soest
Göttingen
Duisberg
Bochum
Dortmund
Hattingen
Arnsberg
5
204
A7-E45
A215
207
A7
E45
A1
E47-E22
A23
A24
E26
E234
A27
A29
A28
E22
75
A1
E22
A28
A29
A1
E37
A27
E234
213
A1-E37
A30
E30
65
A30
A2
E30
A2-E30
E30
E51
A1-E37
A2
E34
A43
A3-E35
A2
A44-E331
A7-E45
A2-E34

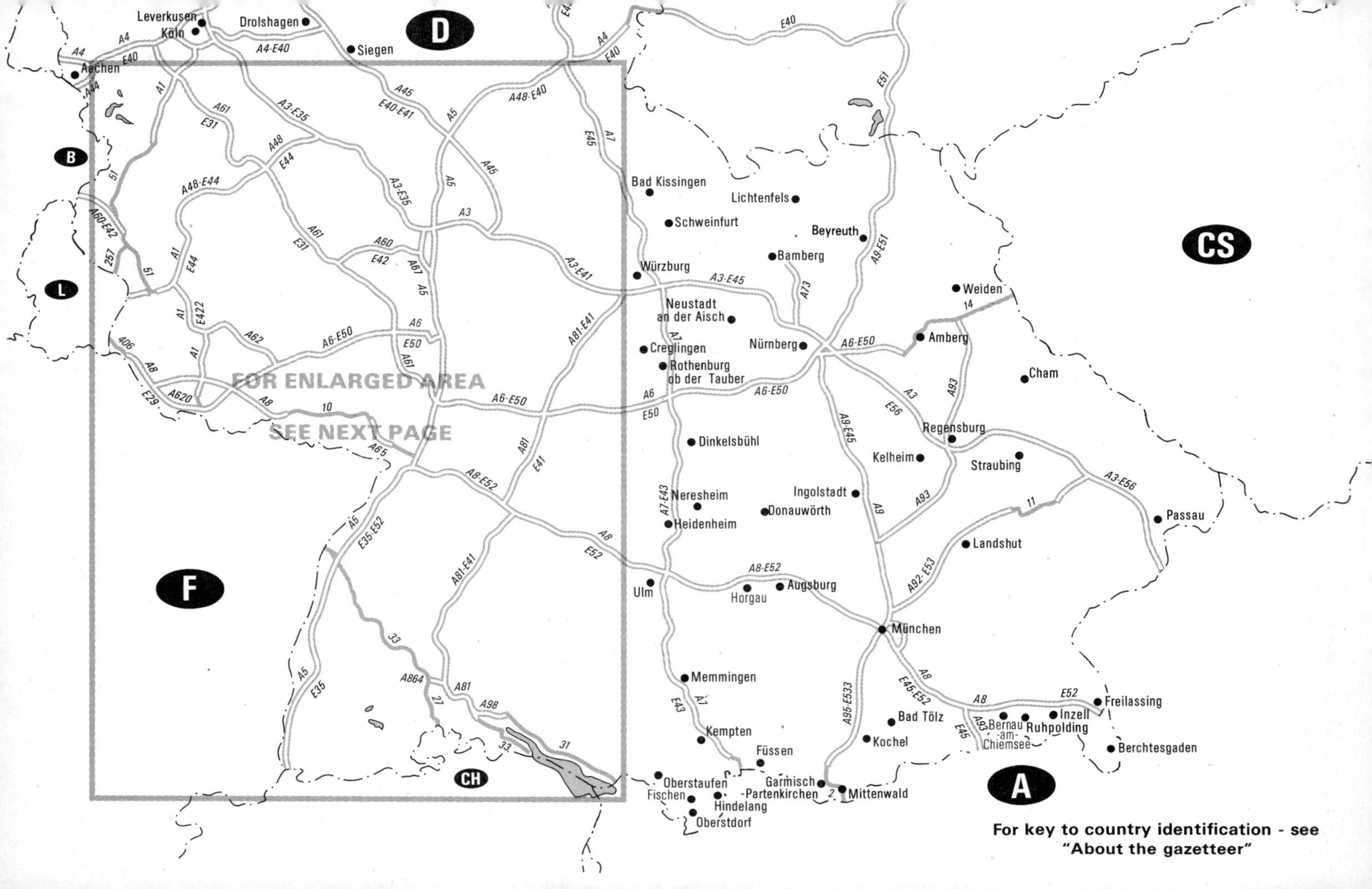

For key to country identification - see "About the gazetteer"

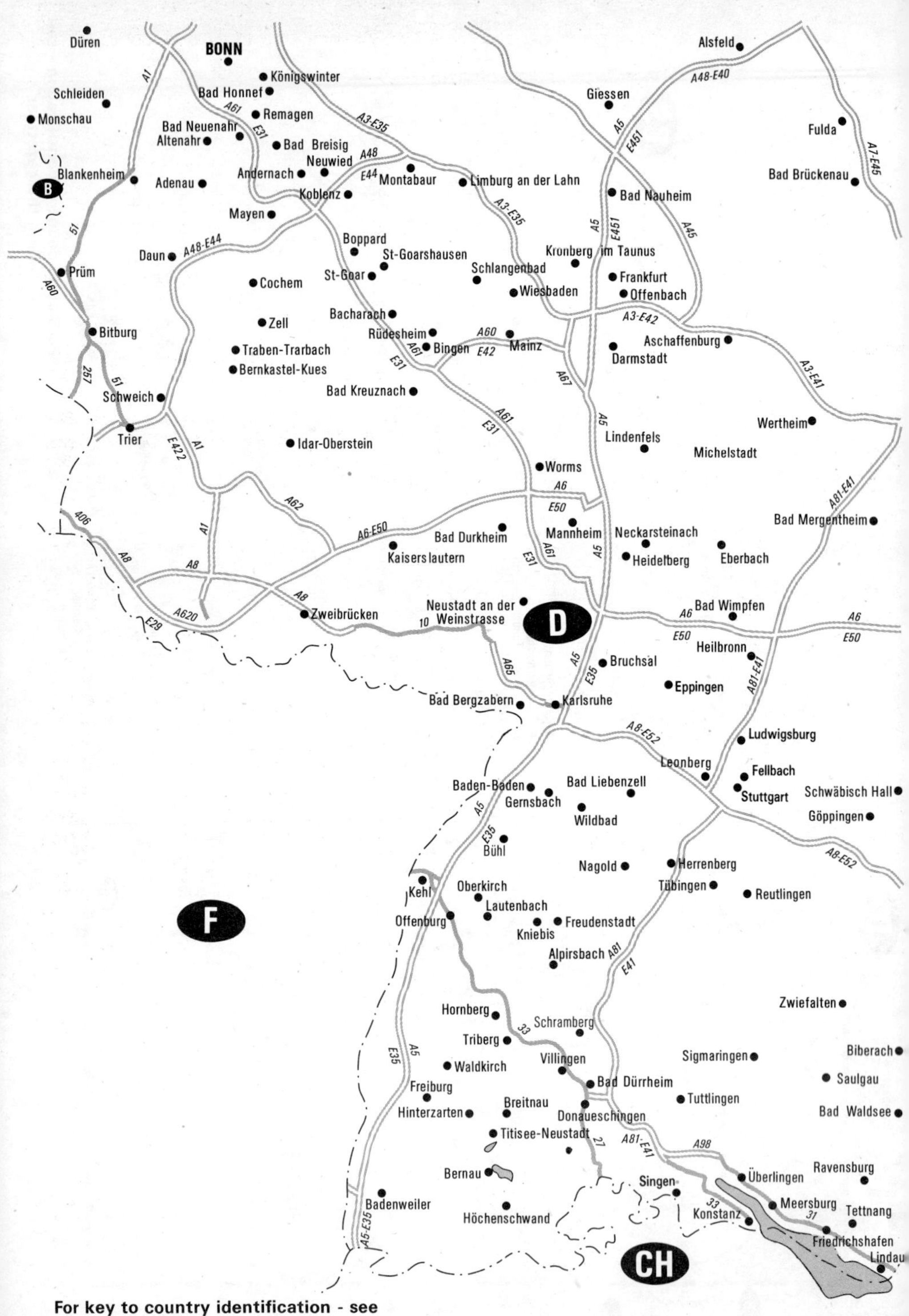

For key to country identification - see "About the gazetteer"

BACHARACH *Rheinland-Pfalz*

◆ **Binz** Koblenzer Str 1 ☎ (06743) 1604 rm4 **A**

◆ **Malerwinkel** (n.rest) Blücherstr 34-41 ☎ (06743) 1239 rm13 **A**

H Park-Café ☎ (06743) 1422 rm24 Mar 16-Nov 14 **A**

H Post Oberstr 38 ☎ (06743) 1277 bed16 **A**

H Rhein Langstr 50 ☎ (06743) 1243 rm15 **A**

◆ **Steeger Tal** Blücherstr 250 ☎ (06743) 1470 rm10 **A**

BADEach place preceded by 'Bad' is listed under the name that follows it.

BADEN-BADEN *Baden-Württemberg*

◆ **Auerhahn** Geroldsauer Str 160 ☎ (07221) 7435 bed40 **A**

★**Bischoff** (n.rest) Römerplatz 2 ☎ (07221) 22378 bed40 Feb-Oct **B**

H Deutscher Kaiser Lichtentaler Haupststr 35 ☎ (07221) 72152 rm20 **A**

H Friedrichsruh Seelachstr 20 ☎ (07221) 72248 bed27 Mar-Dec **A**

H Greiner (n.rest) Lichtentaler Allee 88 ☎ (07221) 71135 rm32 **A**

H Haus Im Mäder Umweger Str 135 ☎ (07223) 52835 rm10 **B**

H Löhr (n.rest) Lichtentaler Str 19 ☎ (07221) 31370 bed30 **A**

H Süss Friesenbergstr 2 ☎ (07221) 22365 bed60 Mar 15-Nov 11 **B**

H Tanneck Werderstr 14 ☎ (07221) 23035 rm17 Mar-Jan 9 **A**

H Zuflucht (n.rest) Auf der Alm 21 ☎ (07223) 6321 rm7 Closed Mar **B**

BADENWEILER *Baden-Württemberg*

◆ **Ebert** (n.rest) Friedrichstr 7 ☎ (07632) 465 bed20 Feb 16-Nov 9 **B**

H Haus Christine (n.rest) Glasbachweg 1 ☎ (07632) 6004 bed21 Closed Jan 7-Feb 15 **B**

◆ **Markgräfler Hof** Ernst-Eisenlohr-Str 7 ☎ (07632) 238 bed38 **A**

◆ **Schwanen** E-Scheffelt Str 5 ☎ (07632) 5228 rm18 Feb 16-Jan 14 **A**

◆ **Zimmermann** Friedrichstr 3 ☎ (07632) 253 rm22 **B**

BAMBERG *Bayern*

◆ **Drei Linden** Memmelsdorfer Str 87 ☎ (0951) 31847 bed14 **B**

★★**Hospiz** Promenade 3 ☎ (0951) 26624 rm35 **A**

BAYREUTH *Bayern*

◆ **Edien Hirschen** R-Wagner Str 77 ☎ (0921) 64141 rm47 **A**

BERCHTESGADEN *Bayern*

H Bavaria Sunklergässchen 11 ☎ (08652) 2620 bed40 Dec 21-Oct 19 **B**

H Grassl (n.rest) Maximillanstr 15 ☎ (08652) 4071 bed53 **B**

◆ **Meisl** Wildmoos 42 ☎ (08652) 3991 bed35 **A**

◆ **Post** Maximilianstr 2 ☎ (08652) 5067 bed80 **A**

◆ **Waldluft** Bergwerkstr 56 ☎ (08652) 2328 bed50 **A**

◆ **Watzmann** Franziskanerplatz 2 ☎ (08652) 2055 rm33 Closed Nov-Dec 22 **A**

BERGZABERN, BAD *Rheinland-Pfalz*

H Pfälzer Wald Kurtalstr 77 ☎ (06343) 1056 bed40 Closed Feb **A**

BERLIN *Berlin* A unique city divided by history, Berlin is one of the most exciting places to visit in Europe. There is a buzz in the air which no one can ignore, a vibrant energy which stems as much from the city as the people themselves. Berlin is a big city of contrasts in every sense of the word. One third of it has peaceful havens of parks, forests and lakes, but the Kurfürstendamm packs no fewer than 1, 000 shops, boutiques, restaurants and galleries into an elegant half mile. Museums and art galleries cater for every interest and taste, and there are palaces and playgrounds, a circus and a world-famous zoo.

Cross the Wall from West to East Berlin and you are literally in another world. For such a dramatic experience it is surprisingly easy to do – just join a sightseeing tour or simply walk through Checkpoint Charlie. Stroll along the Unter den Linden and gain an impression of the 'old' Berlin. You can enjoy a coffee in Alexanderplatz and visit the facinating Pergamon Museum. Back in the West the nightlife stays open as long as you can stay up. Entertainment goes on round the clock and offers opera and theatres, cinemas and cabarets and nightclubs ranging from the cosy to the erotic.

EATING OUT One of West Berlin's most popular mid-priced restaurants is *Hecker's Deele*, close to the lively Kurfürstendamm in Grolmannstrasse. Here you can dine on hearty Westphalian dishes such as knuckle of pork. For vegetarian cuisine the *Thurnagel*, in Gneisenaustrasse, is reliable and fun.

◆ **Castell** Wielandstr 24 ☎ (030) 8827181 rm24 **B**

◆ **Engelberger** Mommsenstr 6 ☎ (030) 8815536 bed12 **A**

◆ **Krebs** Heerstr 2 ☎ (030) 3022660 rm8 **B**

◆ **Pension 22** Schambachweg 22 ☎ (030) 3655230 rm4 **A**

H Reichspost Urbanstr 84 ☎ (030) 6911035 rm37 **B**

◆ **Steinert** Machnower Str 13 ☎ (030) 8156097 rm9 **A**

H Süden (n.rest) Neuköllner Str 217 ☎ (030) 6616093 rm70 **B**

BERNAU *Baden-Württemberg*

H Jägerhof Hinterdorf 29 ☎ (07675) 727 rm18 Closed Nov 5-Dec 18 **A**

◆ **Schwanen** Oberlehen 43 ☎ (07675) 348 rm17 Closed Nov 15-Dec 20 **A**

BERNAU-AM-CHIEMSEE *Bayern*

◆ **Chiemsee** Zellerhornstr 1 ☎ (08051) 7245 bed55 Closed Nov **B**

◆ **Jägerhof** Rottauer Str 15 ☎ (08051) 7377 rm24 Closed Nov 10-Dec 20 **A**

BERNKASTEL-KUES *Rheinland-Pfalz*

H Binz Markt 1 ☎ (06531) 2225 bed20 **A**

◆ **Constance** Auf der Trift 30 ☎ (06531) 8300 rm8 **A**

H Haus Carola (n.rest) Birkenweg 3 ☎ (06531) 4044 bed18 **A**

H Haus Weiskopf (n.rest) Karlstr 14 ☎ (06531) 2351 bed13 **B**

H Panorama (n.rest) Rebschulweg 48 ☎ (06531) 3061 rm15 **B**

★★**Post** Gestade 17 ☎ (06531) 2022 rm40 **B**

H Roders Haupstr 169 ☎ (06531) 2211 rm10 **A**

BIBERACH AN DER RISS *Baden-Württemberg*

H Drei König Markplatz 26 ☎ (07351) 6074 bed18 **A**

BIELEFELD *Nordrhein-Westfalen*

H Büscher Carl-Severing Str 136 ☎ (0521) 450311 bed34 **B**

H Ummelner Mühle Gütersloher Str 299 ☎ (0521) 48907 rm50 **A**

◆ **Welscher** Herforder Str 594 ☎ (0521) 761078 rm17 **A**

H Wiegmann (n.rest) Kronenstr 11 ☎ (0521) 60471 bed17 **A**

BINGEN *Rheinland-Pfalz*

H Engelbert (n.rest) Rheinkai 9 ☎ (06721) 14715 rm25 **A**

H Rochusberg Rochusstr 17 ☎ (06721) 12532 rm19 **A**

H Römerhof Rupertsberg 10 ☎ (06721) 32248 rm34 **A**

H Salztor (n.rest) Salzstr 3 ☎ (06721) 16755 bed20 **A**

★★★**Starkenburger Hof** Rheinkai 1-2 ☎ (06721) 14341 rm30 Feb-Nov **A**

BITBURG *Rheinland-Pfalz*

★**Mosella** Karenweg 11 ☎ (06561) 3147 rm17 **A**

H Zur Wisselbach Bitburger Str 2 ☎ (06561) 3380 rm19 **A**

BLANKENHEIM *Nordrhein-Westfalen*

◆ **St Georg** Ahrstr 3 ☎ (02449) 594 rm6 **A**

★★**Schlossblick** Nonnenbacher Weg 2-6 ☎ (02449) 238 rm34 Closed Nov 15-Dec 20 **A**

BOCHUM *Nordrhein-Westfalen*

H Ostmeier (n.rest) Westring 35 ☎ (0234) 60815 bed50 **B**

H Zum Weilenbrink (n.rest) Massenbergerstr 10 ☎ (0234) 13087 rm12 **A**

BONN *Nordrhein-Westfalen* Bonn, federal capital of West Germany, is situated in North Rhineland-Westphalia, 16 miles south south-east of Cologne on the left bank of the Rhine. The archbishops of Cologne resided here from 1265 to 1794 and the town's beautiful minster (*Münster*), dating from the 11th century, contrasts with extensive modern buildings of the federal parliament and ministries. The University of Bonn was re-established here in 1818 and is housed in the former electoral palace; in 1934 the agricultural college of Bonn-Poppelsdorf was incorporated with it.

Beethoven was born in this city in 1770, at Bonngasse 20, now a museum, and Schumann spent his last years in Sebastianstrasse. Among Bonn's other attractions are the Baroque Jesu Church, the 13th-century Remigius Church, the 18th-century castle *Poppelsdorfer Schloss*, and the Alter Zoll, a bastion overlooking the Rhine.

EATING OUT Bonn has a variety of restaurants serving Chinese, French and German specialities. There are also numerous cafés and wine-bars, notably the *Weinkrüger*, an historic wine-bar in Mauspfad. Located in the heart of Bonn's old town district, the *Schaarschmidt*, in Brüdergasse, serves excellent German cuisine. *Zum Kapellchen*, in the same street, is an atmospheric wine tavern.

H Baden Graurhein-dorfer Str 1 ☎ (0228) 633600 rm23 **B**

★★**Bergischer Hof** Münsterpl 23 ☎ (0228) 633441 rm28 **B**

H Hopfenstübchen Sachsenweg 22 ☎ (0228) 650547 bed10 **A**

H Kluth Rochusstr 221 ☎ (0228) 621531 rm16 **A**

H Weiland (n.rest) Breite Str 98a ☎ (0228) 655057 rm17 **B**

BOPPARD *Rheinland-Pfalz*

★★**Rheinlust** Rheinallee 27-30 ☎ (06742) 30013 rm91 Apr 13-Oct **B**

BRAUNLAGE *Niedersachsen*

H Brauner Hirsch Am Brunnen 1 ☎ (05520) 1064 bed46 **B**

◆ **Brettschneider** Hubertusstr 2 ☎ (05583) 806 bed11 Closed Nov-Dec 20 **A**

◆ **Panorama** Albrecht-str 61 ☎ (05520) 2291 bed18 **A**

H Rust Brande 3a ☎ (05583) 831 bed26 Closed Nov 4-Dec 15 **B**

◆ **Sohnrey** Albrecht Str 39 ☎ (05520) 1061 bed21 **A**

BRAUNSCHWEIG (BRUNSWICK) *Niedersachsen*

H Am Wollmarkt (n.rest) Wollmarkt 9-12 ☎ (0531) 46139 rm31 **B**

H Aquarius ☎ (0531) 79373 bed100 **A**

◆ **Campe** Osterbergstr 67 ☎ (0531) 311510 bed14 **A**

H Garni (n.rest) Altewiekring 68 ☎ (0531) 74620 bed26 **B**

H Lorenz F-Willhelm Str 2 ☎ (0531) 45568 rm46 **B**

H Thüringer Hof (n.rest) Sophienstr 1 ☎ (0531) 81222 rm27 **A**

◆ **Wägener** (n.rest) Schleinitzstr 18 ☎ (0531) 331281 rm10 Closed Jul 15-Aug 15 **A**

◆ **Waldschlösschen** Heidbleekanger 16 ☎ (0531) 62161 bed24 **A**

◆ **Wartburg** (n.rest) Rennelbergstr 12 ☎ (0531) 500011 rm23 **A**

BREISIG, BAD *Rheinland-Pfalz*

H Niederée Zehnerstr 2 ☎ (02633) 9210 rm37 Closed Jan 6-27 **A**

H Quellenhof Albert-Mertes Str 23 ☎ (02633) 9479 rm17 Closed Nov 3-Dec 20 **A**

★**Vater & Sohn** Zehnerstr 78 ☎ (02633) 9148 rm8 **A**

BREITNAU *Baden-Württemberg*

◆ **Löwen** ☎ (07652) 359 bed27 Closed Nov 10-Dec 20 **A**

◆ **Waldvogel** Dorfstr 16 ☎ (07652) 459 bed17 Apr-Nov **A**

BREMEN *Bremen*

H Residence (n.rest) Hoheniohestr 42 ☎ (0421) 341020 rm34 **B**

H Uhlhorn Geeststr 50 ☎ (0421) 611037 rm70 **B**

H Vegesack (n.rest) G-Rohlfs Str 54 ☎ (0421) 669015 bed53 **A**

H Zum Werdersee Holzdamm 104 ☎ (0421) 83504 rm13 **B**

BREMERHAVEN *Bremen*

H Atlantis (n.rest) Hafenstr 144 ☎ (0471) 52937 rm20 **A**

H Börse Lange Str 34-36, Lehe ☎ (0471) 88041 rm34 **B**

H Colombus Lange Str 145 ☎ (0471) 51006 rm40 **B**

H Zum Yachtafen (n.rest) Ulmenstr 23 ☎ (0471) 21510 rm14 **A**

BREMERVÖRDE *Niedersachsen*

H Daub Bahnhofstr 2 ☎ (04761) 3086 rm39 **B**

H Park Stader Str 22 ☎ (04761) 2460 rm15 **B**

BRUCHSAL *Baden-Württemberg*

H Ratskeller Kaiserstr 68 ☎ (07251) 15111 bed45 **A**

BRÜCKENAU, BAD *Bayern*

H Breitenbach E-Gerhard Str 5 ☎ (09741) 2385 rm21 **A**

H Zur Post (n.rest) Ludwigstr 10 ☎ (09741) 5080 bed60 Mar-Dec **B**

BÜHL *Baden-Württemberg*

◆ **Distler** Zienlenweg 8 ☎ (07223) 21742 rm6 **A**

◆ **Zur Blume** Hubstr 85 ☎ (07223) 22104 bed27 **A**

CELLE *Niedersachsen*

H Blühende Schiffahrt Fritzenweise 39 ☎ (05141) 22761 rm14 **A**

H Landgestüt Landgestütstr 1 ☎ (05141) 217219 rm7 **A**

H Sattler am Bahnhof (n.rest) Bahnhofstr 46 ☎ (05141) 1075 rm18 **B**

H Zur Post (n.rest) Grosser Plan 12 ☎ (05141) 22183 bed14 **A**

CHAM *Bayern*

★★**Randsberger Hof** Randsberger-Hof Str 15-17 ☎ (09971) 1266 bed175 **A**

◆ **Sonnenhof** ☎ (09971) 30398 bed20 **A**

CLOPPENBURG *Niedersachsen*

H Deeken Friesoyther Str 2 ☎ (04471) 2585 bed39 **A**

H Jagdhaus Bühren Alte Friesoyther Str 22 ☎ (04471) 83706 bed8 **A**

COCHEM *Rheinland-Pfalz*

H Karl Noss Moselpromenade 17 ☎ (02671) 3612 rm31 Closed Nov 15-Dec 26 **B**

◆ **Regina** ☎ (02671) 7262 rm7 **A**

H Weinhaus Feiden Liniusstr 1 ☎ (02671) 3256 rm10 **B**

COLOGNESee **KÖLN**

CONSTANCESee**KONSTANZ**

CREGLINGEN *Baden-Württemberg*

★★**Krone** Haupstr 12 ☎ (07933) 558 rm24 Closed Dec 20-Jan **A**

CUXHAVEN *Niedersachsen*

H Beckröge Dohrmannstr 9 ☎ (04721) 35519 bed21 **B**

H Frauenpreiss Wernerwaldstr 41 ☎ (04721) 29082 rm20 **B**

H Hohenzollernhof Alter Deichweg 1 ☎ (04721) 35560 rm20 **B**

H Messmer (n.rest) Schmetterlingsweg 6 ☎ (04723) 4169 rm23 **B**

DARMSTADT *Hessen*

H Ernst Ludwig (n.rest) Ernst-Ludwig Str 14 ☎ (06151) 26011 bed32 **A**

◆ **Weinstuben Härting** Heinheimer Str 38 ☎ (06151) 74821 bed13 **A**

DAUN *Rheinland-Pfalz*

H Eifelperle Reiffenbergstr 1 ☎ (06592) 547 rm19 **A**

◆ **Goldenen Fåsschen** Rosenbergstr 5 ☎ (06592) 2248 rm28 **A**

H Gross (n.rest) M-Hilf Str 4 ☎ (06592) 2488 rm14 **A**

DELMENHORST *Niedersachsen*

H Bruggrafen Brauenkamperstr 28 ☎ (04221) 82546 bed17 **A**

H Thomsen Bremer Str 186 ☎ (04221) 70098 rm70 **A**

DETMOLD *Nordrhein-Westfalen*

H Achilles Paderborner Str 87 ☎ (05231) 47204 bed44 **A**

◆ **Forellenhof** Meyer Str 50 ☎ (05232) 87892 bed13 **B**

H Römerhof Maiweg 37 ☎ (05231) 88238 bed35 **B**

DINKELSBÜHL *Bayern*

H Fränkischer Nördlinger Str 10 ☎ (09851) 2371 rm17 Closed Jan 26-Feb 24 **A**

◆ **Küffner** Neustädtlein Nr 9 ☎ (09851) 1247 rm7 **A**

DONAUESCHINGEN *Baden-Württemberg*

H Bahnhofhotel Josefstr 37 ☎ (0771) 2452 rm14 **A**

◆ **Burg** Burgring 6, Aasen ☎ (0771) 3816 rm9 **A**

DONAUWÖRTH *Bayern*

H Drei Kronen Bahnhofstr 25 ☎ (0906) 21077 rm37 **B**

H Goldener Greifen (n.rest) Pflegstr 15 ☎ (0906) 3375 bed17 **A**

★★**Traube** Kapellstr 14 ☎ (0906) 6096 rm43 **B**

DORSTEN *Nordrhein-Westfalen*

◆ **Grewer** Weseler Str 351 ☎ (02369) 4139 bed22 **A**

H Hof Koop Am Markt 13 ☎ (02362) 22629 bed20 **A**

H Humbert Am Burghof 2 ☎ (02369) 4109 rm30 **A**

◆ **Pierick** Lembecker Str 23 ☎ (02866) 227 bed14 **A**

DORTMUND *Nordrhein-Westfalen*

H Drei Kronen (n.rest) Münsterstr 70 ☎ (0231) 818661 rm54 **A**

H Florinblick Wittbräucker Str 465 ☎ (0231) 462449 rm15 **B**

H Fürst (n.rest) Beurhausstr 57 ☎ (0231) 142060 rm18 **B**

H Gildenhof (n.rest) Hohe Str 139 ☎ (0231) 122035 bed71 **B**

H Kaiserbrunnen (n.rest) Arndtstr 56 ☎ (0231) 522280 rm12 **A**

H Ophoff Märkische Str 147 ☎ (0231) 433717 bed48 **B**

H Postkutsche (n.rest) Postkutschenweg 20 ☎ (0231) 441001 rm27 **B**

H Union Arndtstr 66 ☎ (0231) 528243 bed40 **B**

H Weisses Röss 'l (n.rest) Semerteichstr 181 ☎ (0231) 411478 rm8 **A**

DROLSHAGEN *Nordrhein-Westfalen*

◆ **Becker** Am Heliken 6 ☎ (02761) 2831 rm5 **A**

◆ **Hobel** Biggeseestr 4 ☎ (02761) 2582 bed12 **A**

DUISBURG *Nordrhein-Westfalen*

◆ **Hof von Holland** Beriusstr 46 ☎ (0203) 81824 bed10 **A**

H Kolkmann Flutweg 137 ☎ (02135) 61580 bed15 **B**

H Sittardsberg Sittardsberger Allee 10 ☎ (0203) 700001 bed48 **B**

H Werth (n.rest) Siegstr 12 ☎ (0203) 335035 bed30 **A**

H Westfälischer Hof (n.rest) Weseler Str 25 ☎ (0203) 402837 bed22 **A**

DÜREN *Nordrhein-Westfalen*

H Bodes Renkerstr 7-9 ☎ (02421) 51001 bed10 **A**

H Hubertushof (n.rest) Alte Jülicher Str 8 ☎ (02421) 41635 rm7 **A**

★★**Mariaweiler Hof** an gut Nazareth 45 ☎ (02421) 87900 rm17 **A**

★**Zum Nachwächter** Kölner Landstr 12 ☎ (02421) 75081 rm36 Closed Dec 20-Jan 5 **A**

DÜRKHEIM, BAD *Rheinland-Pfalz*

H Leininger Hof Kaiserslauterer str 353 ☎ (06322) 1047 rm6 **A**

DÜRRHEIM, BAD *Baden-Württemberg*

◆ **Gisela** Friedenstr 4 ☎ (07726) 8943 rm19 **A**

DÜSSELDORF *Nordrhein-Westfalen* Düsseldorf is an attractive city on the east bank of the Rhine, its nucleus of a compact semi-circle centres on the original 12th-century settlement.
The city contains many interesting public buildings. Of about 40 churches, the two most imposing are those of St Andrew, completed in 1629, and St Lambert, dating from the 13th and 14th centuries. The *Wilhelm-Marx-Haus* (1924) is Germany's oldest skyscraper. The reconstructed mile-long Königsallee, the main shopping street, has many impressive buildings in modern styles.
Düsseldorf is an important cultural centre; Heine, Brahms, Schumann and Goethe all lived here; Goethe is honored by the *Goethe Museim*. The Museum of Art (*Kunstmuseum*) displays collections of paintings, sculpture, medieval arts and crafts and 200 years of ceramics.
EATING OUT The *Orangerie*, in Bilkerstrasse, offers both atmosphere and good food, and also usually reliable is Robert's Restaurant, in Oberkasseler Strasse. *Frankenheim*, in Wielandstrasse, specialises in hearty local dishes.

H Grober Kurfürst (n.rest) Kurfürstenstr 18 ☎ (0211) 357647 rm22 **B**

H Komet Bismarckstr 93 ☎ (0211) 357917 rm18 **B**

◆ **Sonnen** (n.rest) Bockumer Str 4 ☎ (0211) 402274 rm5 **B**

EBERBACH *Bayern*

H Kettenboot Friedrichstr 1 ☎ (06271) 2470 bed24 Closed Nov 1-15 **A**

H Schiff Lindenstr 27 ☎ (06263) 233 bed70 Closed Nov-Dec 20 **A**

ELMSHORN *Schleswig-Holstein*

◆ **Kubus** Kirchenstr 30 ☎ (04121) 3874 rm9 **A**

H Zur Linde Mühlenstr 23 ☎ (04121) 81430 bed21 **A**

EMSDETTEN *Nordrhein-Westfalen*

H Kloppenborg Frauenstr 15 ☎ (02572) 81077 rm35 **A**

EPPINGEN *Baden-Württemberg*

H Geier Klienbrückentorstr 4 ☎ (07262) 5092 rm26 **A**

◆ **Seeblick** Strandstr 23 ☎ (07262) 7238 rm7 Closed Jan 6-27 **B**

H Villa Waldeck Waldstr 80 ☎ (07262) 1061 rm16 Closed Jan 1-21 **B**

ESLOHE *Nordrhein-Westfalen*

◆ **Reinert** Mescheder Str 31 ☎ (02978) 201 rm10 **A**

◆ **Sauerländer Hof** Südstr 35 ☎ (02973) 777 bed40 **B**

H Vellberg ☎ (02973) 785 rm25 **B**

ESSEN *Nordrhein-Westfalen*

H Altessener Hof Altenessener Str 216 ☎ (0201) 352970 bed24 **B**

H Hasselkuss Bonscheidter Str 63A-65 ☎ (0201) 461559 rm60 **B**

H Nord-Stern Stoppenberger Str 20 ☎ (0201) 31721 rm22 **A**

EVERSWINKEL *Nordrhein-Westfalen*

◆ **Rieping** Vitusstr 22 ☎ (02582) 355 rm5 **A**

FELLBACH *Baden-Württemberg*

H Bürkle Augustenstr 1 ☎ (0711) 513537 rm17 **A**

H City Bruckstr 3 ☎ (0711) 588014 rm26 **B**

◆ **Waldhorn** Burgstr 23 ☎ (0711) 582174 rm16 Closed Jul 5-26 **A**

FISCHEN *Bayern*

◆ **Alpenblick** Maderhalmer Weg 10 ☎ (08326) 337 rm20 Closed Oct 20-Dec 18 **B**

FLENSBURG *Schleswig-Holstein*

H Central Neumarkt 1 ☎ (0461) 24561 rm49 **A**

★★**Europa** Rathausstr 1-5 ☎ (0461) 17522 bed120 **B**

H Stadt Hamburg (n.rest) Grobe Str 59 ☎ (0461) 12611 bed28 **B**

FRANKFURT AM MAIN *Hessen* Electronic room reservation facilities are available at the airport, the main railway station and the ADAC Service Centre, autobahn exit 'Frankfurt West'. These facilities are not operative during Trade Fairs.
Frankfurt represents the largest settlement in a chain of towns and cities stretching over 35 miles along the middle Rhine above and below the Main confluence, and its position in relation to natural routes make it a leading railway hub.
Frankfurt, the birthplace of Goethe, is a cultural centre of considerable significance. It has several theatres (for both operas and plays) and picture galleries – such as the Städel Art Institute (*Städelsches Kunstinstitut*). St Bartholomew's Cathedral dates from the 13th century, as do the *Leonhardskirche* and the *Nikolaikirche*. Other important churches are the 14th century *Liebfrauenkirche* and the *Paulskirche*, where the first German National Assembly met in 1848-9.
EATING OUT Frankfurt residents are closely attached to traditional, regional food, such as sausages – including the famed *frankfurter* – and game, especially venison and boar. One of the city's longest established and most atmospheric cellar restaurants is the up-market *Weinhaus Brückenkeller*, in Schützenstrasse, where specialities include a version of pot roast known as *tafelspitz*. The moderately priced *Bistro 77* in Ziegelhuttenweg serves Alsatian specialities, while those on a budget should seek out *Zum Gemalten Haus*, in Schweizer Strasse, a traditional wine tavern which has a courtyard for summer dining.

H Bristol Ludwigstr 17 ☎ (069) 233235 rm39 **B**

H Diana (n.rest) Westendstr 83 ☎ (069) 747007 rm27 **B**

H Eden (n.rest) Münchenstr 42 ☎ (069) 251914 rm32 **B**

H Hamburger Hof (n.rest) Poststr 10-12 ☎ (069) 235045 rm65 **B**

H Hübner (n.rest) Westendstr 23 ☎ (069) 746044 rm34 **B**

H Post (n.rest) Alt Schwanheim 38 ☎ (069) 357238 rm11 **B**

◆ **Stella** (n.rest) Frauensteinstr 8 ☎ (069) 554026 rm5 **A**

H Tourist (n.rest) Baseler Str 23-25 ☎ (069) 233095 rm54 **B**

H Wiesbaden (n.rest) Baseler Str 52 ☎ (069) 232347 rm40 **B**

FREIBURG IM BREISGAU *Baden-Württemberg*

H City Wasserstr 2 ☎ (0761) 31766 bed100 **B**

H Helene (n.rest) Staufener Str 46 ☎ (0761) 42929 rm37 **B**

H Schiff Basker Landstr 35-37 ☎ (069) 43378 bed80 **B**

◆ **Schützen** Schützenallee 12 ☎ (0761) 72021 bed26 **A**

H Stadt Wien (n.rest) Habsburgerstr 48 ☎ (0761) 36560 bed32 **A**

FREILASSING *Bayern*

H Post (n.rest) Haupstr 30 ☎ (08654) 9768 bed23 **A**

H Zollhäusl Zollhäuslstr 11 ☎ (08654) 62011 rm16 **A**

FREUDENSTADT *Baden-Württemberg*

◆ **Berghof** Hardtsteige 20, , Lauterbad ☎ (07441) 82637 rm32 Closed Nov 17-Dec 13 **A**

★★**Grüner Wald** Kinzigtalstr 23, Lauterbad ☎ (07441) 2427 rm45 **A**

★★**Krone** Marktpl 29 ☎ (07441) 2007 rm27 **A**

◆ **Schauinsland** (n.rest) Hartranftstr 56 ☎ (07441) 2488 rm6 **A**

H Schwanen Forststr 6 ☎ (07441) 2267 bed27 Closed Nov 15-Dec 5 **A**

★**See** Forststr 15-17 ☎ (07441) 2688 rm13 Closed Nov 15-Dec 15 **A**

H Stadt (n.rest) Lossburger Str 19 ☎ (07441) 2719 rm18 **A**

FRIEDRICHSHAFEN *Baden-Württemberg*

◆ **Altes Rathaus** Ittenhauser Str 14-16 ☎ (07541) 51025 bed22 **B**

◆ **Gerbe** Hirschlatter Str 14 ☎ (07541) 51084 bed65 Closed Jan 2-14 **A**

◆ **Goldener Hirsch** Charlottenstr 1 ☎ (07541) 25750 bed27 **B**

H Krager Ailinger Str 52 ☎ (07541) 71011 bed35 Closed Jan 1-12 **B**

H Maier Poststr 1-3 ☎ (07541) 4915 bed84 Closed Jan 24-Feb 13 **B**

◆ **Schwanen** Friedrichstr 32 ☎ (07541) 26018 rm20 **B**

FULDA *Hessen*

H Hessischer Hof Nikolausstr 22 ☎ (0661) 72289 bed52 **A**

H Leipziger Hof Leipziger Str 165 ☎ (0661) 606363 bed21 **B**

★★★**Lenz** Leipziger 122-124 ☎ (0661) 601041 bed73 **B**

◆ **Metzgerei Harth** Frankfurter Str 137 ☎ (0661) 42794 rm14 **A**

FÜSSEN *Bayern*

◆ **Dreimäderlhaus** Oberkirch 19 ☎ (08362) 2936 rm13 Closed Nov 5-Dec 25 **A**

H Geiger Uferstr 18, , Hopfen am See ☎ (08362) 7074 rm25 **A**

◆ **Schwarzenberg** (n.rest) Ziegelwiesstr 15 ☎ (08362) 1690 rm9 **A**

H Schweiger Ländeweg 2 ☎ (08362) 4009 rm16 **B**

GARMISCH-PARTENKIRCHEN *Bayern*

H Flora Hauptstr 85 ☎ (08821) 72039 rm16 **B**

H Roter Hahn (n.rest) Bahnhofstr 44 ☎ (08821) 54065 rm28 **B**

H Zugspitz Klammstr 19 ☎ (08821) 1081 rm38 **B**

GERNSBACH *Baden-Württemberg*

H Forsthaus Staufenberg (n.rest) Hildgrundweg 3 ☎ (07224) 2390 bed21 Closed Nov 1-20 **A**

◆ **Grüner Baum** Süsser Winkel 1, , Reichental ☎ (07224) 3438 bed25 Closed Nov 4-Dec 15 **A**

H Sarbacher Kaltenbronner Str 7 ☎ (07224) 1044 rm14 Closed Mar & Nov **A**

GIESSEN *Hessen*

H Burkart G-Schlosser-Str 13 ☎ (0641) 34591 rm17 **A**

H Köhler Westanlage 35 ☎ (0641) 76086 rm27 **B**

H Ludwigsplatz Ludwigsplatz 8 ☎ (0641) 33082 bed80 **B**

H Möbus (n.rest) Marburger Str 146 ☎ (0641) 51337 rm9 **A**

GÖPPINGEN *Baden-Württemberg*

◆ **Goldener Hasen** (n.rest) Eislinger Str 30 ☎ (07161) 812246 rm9 **A**

◆ **Panorama** Eütenbühl 1 ☎ (07165) 339 bed10 **B**

◆ **Stern** Eislinger Str 15 ☎ (07161) 812213 rm14 Closed Jul 24-Aug 15 **A**

GOSLAR *Niedersachsen*

◆ **Auerhahn** Auerhahn Nr 2 ☎ (05325) 2369 rm7 **A**

H Bellevue (n.rest) Birkenweg 5-7 ☎ (05325) 2084 bed45 **A**

H Harzer Hof Rathausstr 9 ☎ (05325) 2513 rm11 Closed Apr 1-15 **B**

H Kiesow Höhenweg 14 ☎ (05325) 2593 rm21 **B**

◆ **Möller** Schieferweg 6 ☎ (05321) 23098 bed25 **A**

◆ **Warnecke** Claustorwall 19 ☎ (05321) 20946 rm5 **A**

GÖTTINGEN *Niedersachsen*

H Stadt Hannover (n.rest) Goetheallee ☎ (0551) 45957 rm30 **A**

HAMBURG *Hamburg*

Hamburg is a bustling, thriving port city, known for its love of the arts. It also has vast shopping centres, more than 2, 000 restaurants appealing to every kind of taste, and the colourful St Pauli district. Sightseeing possibilities include an exploration of the harbour and attractive Alster Lakes; a visit to the *Planten und Blomen* park, the Botanical Garden built around the city's old ramparts, Hagenbeck's Zoo, the old townhouses on Deichstrasse, and the many museums and art galleries.
Hamburg is also a great place for shopping; prices are reasonable and many historic buildings have been converted into exclusive covered arcades.
Hamburg is renowned for its lively nightlife. There are around 30 theatres, the Ballet Company and the Hamburg State Opera.
EATING OUT One of Hamburg's most popular local delicacies is *aalsuppe*(eel soup), virtually a meal in itself, made from fresh eel with leeks, carrots, dumplings, apricots, prunes and apples, served in a heavily seasoned ham broth. Good traditional German cuisine can be enjoyed at *Peter Lembke*, in Holzdamm, where eel soup can usually be found on the menu together with more conventional dishes such as steaks. *Il Giardino*, in Ulmenstrasse, has an attractive courtyard garden and serves excellent Italian cuisine, while for an inexpensive meal there is the popular *Avocado*, in Kanalstrasse.

◆ **Alpha** Koppel 6 ☎ (040) 245365 rm10 **A**

H Amber Paulinenpl 3 ☎ (040) 313577 bed18 **A**

H Benecke (n.rest) Lange Reihe 54-56 ☎ (040) 243282 rm14 **B**

H Jeanette Schwanenwik 30 ☎ (040) 2205128 rm7 **A**

H Kieler Hof (n.rest) Bremerreihe 15 ☎ (040) 243024 bed45 **A**

H Lilienhof (n.rest) Ernst-Merck-Str 4 ☎ (040) 2802446 bed32 **B**

H Miramar (n.rest) Armgartstr 20 ☎ (040) 2209395 rm14 **B**

◆ **Nord** (n.rest) Bremer Reihe 22 ☎ (040) 244693 rm15 **A**

HAMELN *Niedersachsen*

H Birkenhof (n.rest) Hugenottenstr 1a/1b ☎ (05151) 28752 rm13 Closed Jan 7-Feb 7 **A**

H Hirschmann (n.rest) Deisterallee 16 ☎ (05151) 7591 bed32 **B**

★★**Zur Börse** (n.rest) Osterstr 41a ☎ (05151) 7080 bed47 **B**

HANNOVER *Niedersachsen*

H Elisabetha Hindenburgstr 16 ☎ (0511) 816096 rm28 **B**

H Fösse Fössestr 83 ☎ (0511) 2105883 bed180 **A**

H Gildehof Joachimstr 6 ☎ (0511) 15742 rm41 **B**

H Hospiz am Bahnhof (n.rest) Joachimstr 20 ☎ (0511) 324297 bed50 **B**

H Knuth (n.rest) Marienstr 7 ☎ (0511) 17577 bed16 **B**

H Thielenplatz (n.rest) Am Thielenplatz 2 ☎ (0511) 327691 bed160 Closed Dec 23-31 **B**

H Wülfeler Brauereigaststätten Hildesheimer Str 380 ☎ (0511) 865086 rm39 **B**

HARZBURG, BAD *Niedersachsen*

H Brauner Hirsch Herzog-Julius-Str 52 ☎ (05322) 2260 rm13 **A**

H Fernblick Golfstr 5 ☎ (05322) 4614 rm12 **A**

H Germania (n.rest) Berliner Pfalz 2 ☎ (05322) 2878 rm35 Closed Nov 15-Dec 15 **B**

◆ **Villa Mächen** Am Stadtpark 43 ☎ (05322) 2672 rm12 **A**

◆ **Villa Wihelmshöhe** Sternstr 15 ☎ (05322) 2546 bed17 **A**

HATTINGEN *Nordrhein-Westfalen*

H Berghof Bergstr 11 ☎ (02324) 30630 rm8 **A**

H Raffenberg Am Raffenberg 42 ☎ (02324) 202112 rm9 **A**

H Siebe Am Stuten 29 ☎ (02324) 22022 rm20 **B**

H Westfälischer Hof Bahnhofstr 7 ☎ (02334) 23560 rm21 **B**

HEIDELBERG *Baden-Württemberg*

H Auerstein Dossenheimer Landstr 82 ☎ (06221) 480798 rm12 **A**

H Berger (n.rest) Erwin-Rohde-Str 8 ☎ (06221) 401608 bed17 **A**

★★**Central** (n.rest) Kaiserstr 75 ☎ (06221) 20672 rm52 **B**

H Rose Karlsruher Str 93 ☎ (06221) 314388 rm16 **B**

◆ **Rother** (n.rest) Sitzbuchweg 42 ☎ (06221) 800784 bed12 **A**

HEIDENHEIM AN DER BRENZ *Baden-Württemberg*

◆ **Bäuchle** Friendenstr 14 ☎ (07321) 23091 rm8 **A**

◆ **Hubertus** Giengener Str 82 ☎ (07321) 51800 rm9 **A**

◆ **Schönblick** Sauerbruchstr 4 ☎ (07321) 41000 bed15 **A**

HEILBRONN *Baden-Württemberg*

H Allee-Post (n.rest) Bismarakstr 5 ☎ (07131) 81656 bed15 **A**

★★**Kronprinz** Bahnhofstr 29 ☎ (07131) 83941 bed48 **B**

HELMSTEDT *Niedersachsen*

H Vier Jahreszeiten Holzberg 23 ☎ (05351) 6050 rm15 **A**

◆ **Waldwinkel** Maschweg 46 ☎ (05351) 37161 bed22 May-Dec **A**

HERFORD *Nordrhein-Westfalen*

H Hansa (n.rest) Brüderstr 40 ☎ (05221) 56124 rm20 **A**

◆ **Waldesrand** zum Forst 4 ☎ (05221) 26026 rm17 **B**

HERRENBERG *Baden-Württemberg*

H Botenfischer Nagolder Str 14 ☎ (07032) 3011 bed22 **A**

H Hasen Hasenpl 6 ☎ (07032) 2040 rm80 **A**

HINDELANG *Bayern*

◆ **Alte Schmiede** Schmittenweg 14 ☎ (08324) 2552 rm14 Closed Nov **A**

◆ **Löwen** Pass Str 17 ☎ (08324) 7703 bed44 Closed Nov 2-Dec 19 **A**

HINTERZARTEN *Baden-Württemberg*

◆ **Ketterer** (n.rest) Windeckweg 26 ☎ (07652) 260 rm16 **A**

H Lafette Heiligbrunnenstr 10 ☎ (07652) 360 rm20 Closed Nov 15-Dec 15 **A**

HITZACKER *Niedersachsen*

H Linde Drawehnertorstr 22-24 ☎ (05862) 347 rm11 Closed Jan **A**

H Panorama P-Borchling Str 4 ☎ (05862) 210 bed20 **A**

H Waldfrieden Weinbergsweg 25-26 ☎ (05862) 1011 rm23 Closed Jan **A**

HÖCHENSCHWAND *Baden-Württemberg*

◆ **Alpenblick** St-Georg Str 9 ☎ (07672) 2055 bed47 **A**

H Fernblick im Grün ☎ (07672) 766 rm35 Closed Nov 15-Dec 15 **A**

HONNEF, BAD *Nordrhein-Westfalen*

H Hindenburg Siebengebirgsstr 12 ☎ (02224) 80115 rm8 **A**

HORGAU *Bayern*

H Gaststätte Platzer Haupstr 1 ☎ (08294) 1203 rm13 **A**

HORN-BAD MEINBERG *Nordrhein-Westfalen*

H Mönnich (n.rest) Brunnenstr 55 ☎ (05234) 98845 rm13 Closed Jan 15-Feb 15 **B**

H Post Mittelstr 91 ☎ (05234) 2958 bed16 **A**

H Wilberger Hof Detmolder Str 59 ☎ (05234) 98825 bed13 **A**

HORNBERG *Baden-Württemberg*

H Adler Haupstr 66 ☎ (07833) 367 bed50 **A**

◆ **Rössle** Landstr 5 ☎ (07833) 392 bed12 Closed Oct & Nov **A**

IDAR-OBERSTEIN *Rheinland-Pfalz*

◆ **Beim Ännchem** am Hessenstein 11A ☎ (06784) 6109 rm14 **A**

◆ **Beisszange** Haupstr 584 ☎ (06781) 22041 bed33 **A**

H Idarer-Hof Kobachstr 68 ☎ (06781) 46033 rm12 **A**

H Keller Hauptstr 354 ☎ (06781) 22138 bed15 **A**

H Rieth Weierbacher Str 13 ☎ (06784) 396 rm12 **A**

H Zum Schwan Haupstr 25 ☎ (06781) 43081 rm20 **A**

INGOLSTADT *Bayern*

★★**Rappensberger** Harderstr 3 ☎ (0841) 3140 rm88 Closed Dec 23-Jan 4 **B**

INZELL *Bayern*

H Bergblick (n.rest) Rauschbergstr 38 ☎ (08665) 7101 rm12 **A**

ISERLOHN *Nordrhein-Westfalen*

◆ **Dechenhöhle** Untergrüner Str 8 ☎ (02374) 7334 bed20 **A**

H Horn Seilerwaldstr 10 ☎ (02371) 4871 rm48 **B**

H Zur Mühle Grüner Talstr 400 ☎ (02352) 2963 bed25 **B**

KAISERSLAUTERN *Rheinland-Pfalz*

H Barbarossahof ☎ (0631) 43010 bed96 **A**

◆ **Fröhlich** Dansenberger Str 10 ☎ (0631) 59646 rm22 **A**

H Gelterswoog am Gelterswoog 20 ☎ (0631) 54011 bed80 **A**

H Pommerscher Hof (n.rest) Stahlstr 12 ☎ (0631) 40180 rm16 **A**

H Zepp (n.rest) Pariser Str 4/6 ☎ (0631) 73660 rm55 **A**

KARLSRUHE *Baden-Württemberg*

H Betzler (n.rest) Amalienstr 3 ☎ (0721) 28759 rm28 **B**

H Elite (n.rest) Sachsenstr 17 ☎ (0721) 817363 bed42 Closed Dec 20-Jan 6 **B**

H Fächerstadt (n.rest) Parkstr 27 ☎ (0721) 697816 rm10 **B**

H Goldene Krone Lange Str 1, Rüppurr ☎ (0721) 30219 rm13 **A**

H Kaiser Barbarossa Luisenstr 38 ☎ (0721) 606311 rm48 **B**

H Kübler (n.rest) Bismarckstr 39-43 ☎ (0721) 26849 rm97 **B**

KASSEL *Hessen*

H Kö 78 (n.rest) Kölnische Str 78 ☎ (0561) 17982 rm15 **A**

H Lenz Frankfurter Str 176 ☎ (0561) 43373 bed28 **A**

H Rathaus (n.rest) Wilhelmsstr 29 ☎ (0561) 13768 rm17 **B**

KEHL *Baden-Württemberg*

◆ **Hirsch** Gerbereister 20 ☎ (07851) 3600 rm50 Closed mid Dec-mid Feb **A**

H Rebstock Hauptstr 183 ☎ (07851) 2470 bed58 Closed Dec 27-Jan 12 **A**

◆ **Schwanen Kehl** Haupstr 20 ☎ (07851) 2735 rm13 Closed Jan 1-15 **A**

KELHEIM *Bayern*

◆ **Stockhammer Ratskeller** Am Oberen Zweck 2 ☎ (09441) 3254 rm10 **A**

KEMPTEN (ALLGÄU) *Bayern*

◆ **Berg-Café** Höhenweg 6 ☎ (0831) 73296 rm30 Closed Aug 28-Sep 15 **A**

H Graf (n.rest) Kotterner Str 72 ☎ (0831) 22318 rm25 **A**

KIEL *Schleswig-Holstein*

H Altenholz (n.rest) Kronsberg 18 ☎ (0431) 321073 bed20 **B**

H Alter Waisenhof Muhliusstr 95 ☎ (0431) 91306 bed54 **B**

H Dietrichsdorfer Hof (n.rest) Heikendorfer Weg 54 ☎ (0431) 26108 rm28 **A**

H Ingeborg (n.rest) Goethestr 7 ☎ (0431) 91557 rm8 **B**

H Lucija Schusterkrug 11 ☎ (0431) 391366 rm7 **A**

H Rabe's Ringstr 30 ☎ (0431) 676091 bed50 **B**

KISSINGEN, BAD *Bayern*

H Hanseat (n.rest) Salinenstr 27 ☎ (0971) 4345 rm22 **A**

H Kissinger Hof Bismarckstr 14-16 ☎ (0971) 1044 rm99 Closed Nov-Dec 15 **B**

H Kurhaus-Erika Prinzregentenstr 23 ☎ (0971) 4001 rm20 **B**

KLEVE *Nordrhein-Westfalen*

H Heiligers (n.rest) Turmstr 53 ☎ (02821) 22051 rm10 **B**

H Park ☎ (02821) 807 bed222 **B**

KNIEBIS *Baden-Württemberg*

H Günter Baiersbronner Str 26 ☎ (07442) 2114 rm14 Closed Nov-Dec 15 **A**

KOBLENZ *Rheinland-Pfalz*

H Hähnchen Wolfskaulstr 94 ☎ (0261) 43022 rm56 **B**

H Hamm (n.rest) St-Josef Str 32 ☎ (0261) 34546 bed49 Closed Dec 15-Jan 15 **B**

H Reinhard (n.rest) Bahnhofstr 60 ☎ (0261) 34835 bed34 Closed Jan 15-Feb 15 **B**

H Sporthafen ☎ (0261) 46249 bed26 **B**

H Trierer Hof Clemensstr 1 ☎ (0261) 31060 rm32 **B**

H Zur Weinlaube Haukertsweg 9 ☎ (0261) 72054 bed100 Closed Dec 23-Jan 6 **A**

KOCHEL AM SEE *Bayern*

H Grauer Bär Mittenwalder Str 82-86 ☎ (08851) 861 bed44 **B**

KÖLN (COLOGNE) *Nordrhein-Westfalen*

Köln is one of the largest cities in West Germany and the most important in Rhineland. It stands on the left bank where the Rhine is a quarter of a mile wide, and is 120ft above sea level in a fertile plain. The city's long-standing importance in religious, economic and political affairs is reflected in its buildings. All are dominated by the magnificent cathedral, one of the finest Gothic structures in Europe – 480ft long and with two 511ft-high towers.

Much of Köln, including the fine old churches of St Andrew, St Peter, and St Maria im Kapitol, was destroyed during the Second World War, but many buildings have been reconstructed or restored. The *Wallraf-Richartz Museum* has an important collection of paintings.

EATING OUT Germans have hearty appetites, and restaurateurs in Köln go out of their way to satisfy them. Pork dishes come in a variety of forms, from local ham to spicy *würst* sausages. Other regional specialities include sweet-and-sour red cabbage with apples, raisins and white vinegar; potato pancakes; and potato salad laced with onions and bacon.

H Algarve Venloer Str 196 ☎ (0221) 518331 rm11 **B**

H Drei Könige Marzellenstr 58-60 ☎ (0221) 132088 rm32 Closed Dec 22-Jan 2 **B**

H Güllich Ursulplatz 13-19 ☎ (0221) 120015 rm40 **B**

H Heinzelmännchen (n.rest) Hohe Pforte 5-7 ☎ (0221) 211217 rm17 **B**

◆ **Rheinischer Hof** Schmittgasse 62 ☎ (02203) 82903 rm13 **A**

KÖNIGSWINTER *Nordrhein-Westfalen*

H Immenhof (n.rest) Rheinallee 6 ☎ (02223) 21436 rm7 **A**

H Rheingold Drachenfelsstr 36 ☎ (02223) 23048 bed60 Closed Jan **B**

★**Siebengebirge** Haupstr 342 ☎ (02223) 21359 rm10 Closed Jan **B**

KONSTANZ (CONSTANCE) *Baden-Württemberg*

H Barbarossa Obermarkt 8-12 ☏ (07531) 22021 rm69 **B**

★★Deutsches Haus (n.rest) Markstätte 15 ☏ (07531) 27065 bed56 **B**

H Germania Konradigasse 2 ☏ (07531) 23735 bed28 **A**

◆ Graf Wiesenstr 2 ☏ (07531) 21486 rm14 **A**

H Graf Zeppelin ☏ (07531) 23780 bed60 **B**

◆ Kreuz K-Romer Str 1 ☏ (07533) 5182 bed18 Closed Dec & Jan **A**

H Mainaublick Mainaustr ☏ (07531) 31039 bed30 Closed Dec 27-Jan 6 **B**

H Scheffelhof Zogelmannstr 2 ☏ (07531) 22974 bed30 Closed Dec 15-31 **A**

H St Johann Brückengasse 1 ☏ (07531) 22750 rm51 **A**

H Zur Linde Radolfzeller Str 27 ☏ (07531) 77036 rm11 **A**

KREFELD *Nordrhein-Westfalen*

H Jägerhof (n.rest) Steckendorfer Str 116 ☏ (02151) 64764 rm8 **A**

H Poststuben Dampfmühlenweg 58 ☏ (02151) 800957 bed15 **B**

H Stadt Geldern (n.rest) Südwall 50-52 ☏ (02151) 34363 rm9 **B**

KREUZNACH, BAD *Rheinland-Pfalz*

H Grüner Baum Kreuznacher Str 33 ☏ (0671) 2238 rm35 Closed Jul 16-30 **A**

H Siebe am Kornmarkt 1 ☏ (0671) 31014 rm14 **A**

H Viktoria Kaiser-Wilheim Str 16 ☏ (0671) 2037 rm30 Closed Dec & Jan **B**

KRONBERG IM TAUNUS *Hessen*

H Frankfurter Hof Frankfurter Str 1 ☏ (06173) 79596 rm11 **B**

H Schützenhof F-Ebert-Str 1 ☏ (06173) 4968 bed17 **B**

LANDSHUT *Bayern*

◆ Obermeier Schönbrunn 1 ☏ (0871) 53851 bed58 **A**

H Park Papiererstr 36 ☏ (0871) 69339 rm36 **A**

LAUTENBACH *Baden-Württemberg*

◆ Schwanen Hauptstr 43 ☏ (07802) 4556 bed30 **A**

★Sternen Haupstr 47 ☏ (07802) 3538 bed70 Closed Nov **A**

LEONBERG *Baden-Württemberg*

H Glemseck Glemseck 1 ☏ (07152) 43134 rm16 **B**

H Hirsch Hindenburgstr 1 ☏ (07152) 43071 rm74 **B**

LEVERKUSEN *Nordrhein-Westfalen*

H Haus Janes Bismarakstr 71 ☏ (0214) 64043 bed60 **A**

H Haus Schweigert Moosweg 3 ☏ (0214) 76478 bed20 **B**

LICHTENFELS *Bayern*

H Preussischer Hof Bamberger Str 30 ☏ (09571) 5015 rm26 **A**

LIEBENZELL, BAD *Baden-Württemberg*

◆ Lutz (n.rest) Bergstr 8 ☏ (07052) 2348 bed15 **A**

H Schwarzdrossel (n.rest) Eichendorffstr 4 ☏ (07052) 1442 rm16 **A**

LIMBURG AN DER LAHN *Hessen*

★Huss Bahnhofsplatz 3 ☏ (06431) 25087 rm34 **A**

◆ Reichspost Frankfurter Str 8 ☏ (06431) 6404 rm11 **A**

LINDAU IM BODENSEE *Bayern*

H Goldenes Lamm Schafgasse 3 ☏ (08382) 5732 bed70 **B**

H Peterhof (n.rest) Schafgasse 10 ☏ (08382) 5700 rm28 **B**

◆ Ziegler Bodenseestr 32 ☏ (08382) 5410 rm13 Closed Feb & Nov **A**

LINDENFELS *Hessen*

H Essener Hof Kappstr 9 ☏ (06255) 550 rm21 **A**

◆ Waldschlösschen Nibelungenstr 102 ☏ (06255) 2460 rm13 Closed Nov **B**

◆ Wiesengrund Talstr 3 ☏ (06255) 2877 bed70 Closed Jan 10-21 **A**

LÜBECK *Schleswig-Holstein*

H Absalonshorst Absalonshorster Weg 100 ☏ (04509) 1040 bed12 Closed Jan **B**

H Astoria Fackenburger Allee 68 ☏ (0451) 46763 bed52 **B**

H Grüner Jäger Ivendorfer Landstr 40-42 ☏ (04502) 2667 bed24 **A**

H Retteich (n.rest) Lindenpl 5A ☏ (0451) 82522 rm9 **A**

LUDWIGSBURG *Baden-Württemberg*

H Heim (n.rest) Schillerstr 19 ☏ (07141) 26144 rm45 **B**

H Hoheneck Uferstr ☏ (07141) 51133 rm15 **B**

H Schiller-Hospiz Gartenstr 17 ☏ (07141) 23463 rm52 **B**

LÜNEBURG *Niedersachsen*

H Heiderose Uelzener Str 29 ☏ (04131) 44410 rm21 **B**

MAINZ *Rheinland-Pfalz*

H Königshof Schottstr 1-5 ☏ (06131) 611068 rm59 **A**

H Stadt Coblenz Rheinstr 49 ☏ (06131) 227602 rm12 **B**

MANNHEIM *Baden-Württemberg*

H Basler Hof Tattersallstr 27 ☏ (0621) 28816 rm62 Closed Dec 24-Jan 6 **A**

★★Mack (n.rest) Mozartstr 14 ☏ (0621) 23888 rm57 Closed Dec 24-26 **A**

H Wegener (n.rest) Tattersallstr 16 ☏ (0621) 444071 rm53 Closed Dec 23-31 **B**

◆ Zum Ochsen Hauptstr 70 ☏ (0621) 792065 bed20 **A**

MAYEN *Rheinland-Pfalz*

H Traube (n.rest) Bäckerstr 3-6 ☏ (02651) 3017 rm26 **A**

◆ Wolff am Heckenberg 47 ☏ (02651) 3343 rm12 **A**

◆ Zum Dicken Baum Bürresheimer Str 1 ☏ (02651) 2672 rm16 **A**

MEERSBURG *Baden-Württemberg*

H Schiff Bismarckpl 5 ☏ (07532) 6025 rm35 Seasonal **A**

MEMMINGEN *Bayern*

◆ Lindenbad Lindenbadstr 18 ☏ (08331) 3278 rm16 **A**

MERGENTHEIM, BAD *Baden-Württemberg*

◆ Herrental Löffelstelzerstr 36 ☏ (07931) 7244 rm20 **A**

◆ Wilden Mann Reichengässle 6 ☏ (07931) 7638 rm22 Closed Dec 22-Jan 20 **A**

MESCHEDE *Nordrhein-Westfalen*

◆ Kramer Caller Str 48 ☏ (02903) 6082 rm6 **A**

H Teehaus Auf'm Hahn 2, Freienohl ☏ (02903) 539 rm9 **A**

MICHELSTADT *Hessen*

H Am Kellereiberg (n.rest) Kirchenfeld 12 ☎ (06061) 4880 rm12 **B**

MINDEN *Nordrhein-Westfalen*

◆ **Linde** Mindener Str 1 ☎ (0571) 52585 rm7 **A**

H Victoria (n.rest) Markt 11-13 ☎ (0571) 22240 bed65 Closed Jan 1-15 **B**

◆ **Zur Post** Stemmer Landstr 152 ☎ (0571) 41433 bed20 **A**

MITTENWALD *Bayern*

◆ **Jaghaus Drachenburg** Elmauer Weg 20 ☎ (08823) 1249 bed28 Closed Nov-Dec 15 **A**

H Royal (n.rest) Kresenzerweg 5 ☎ (08823) 1777 rm11 **A**

MÖNCHENGLADBACH *Nordrhein-Westfalen*

H Tannenhof Pfingsgraben 11 ☎ (02161) 54636 bed30 **A**

MONSCHAU *Nordrhein-Westfalen*

★★**Horchem** Rurstr 14 ☎ (02472) 2061 bed26 Closed Feb **B**

H Prümmer Haupstr 88 ☎ (02472) 2298 rm15 **A**

MONTABAUR *Rheinland-Pfalz*

H Kalb Grosser Markt 9 ☎ (02602) 3401 rm15 **A**

★**Schlemmer** Kirchstr 18-20 ☎ (02602) 5022 rm28 Closed Dec 22-Jan 7 **A**

H Stock im Gelbachtal ☎ (02602) 3510 rm18 **A**

MÜNCHEN (MUNICH) *Bayern*

München is the capital of Bavaria and one of the most beautiful cities in Europe; its heritage includes the ornate buildings of the Marienplatz, a fine cathedral, several Baroque churches and a major art collection. Contemporary München features the 1972 Olympic Park, the BMW Automobile Museum where exhibits are displayed in parallel with political and social events, and the celebrated *Hofbräuhaus*, a brewery where you can sample the product at long tables in the courtyard. München has some of Germany's most fashionable shops; tailoring here is among the best in the world, so suits and jackets in the traditional wool Loden cloth are good investments.

EATING OUT Start the day with a hearty breakfast which often includes ham, salami, cheeses and pumpernickel. Veal and pork are popular main dishes, accompanied by excellent potato salads or *sauerkraut* (cabbage cooked with white wine, cloves and caraway seeds). Among the most popular, and tempting desserts, are *apfelstrudel*, plum cake and cherry gâteau. Between meals try a fresh pretzel, and to accompany your meals there is an excellent choice of Mosel and Rhine wines.

One of München's finest restaurants is the *Walterspiel* at the Hotel VierJahreszeiten in Maximilianstrasse, while for those on a budget there is an excellent choice of moderately priced restaurants in Schwabing, the attractive old part of the city.

◆ **Augsburg** Schillerstr 18 ☎ (089) 597673 rm26 **B**

H Brunner (n.rest) U-Mühistr 13 ☎ (089) 8122066 rm7 **B**

◆ **Härti** Verdistr 135 ☎ (089) 8111632 rm10 **A**

H Helvetia Schillerstr 6 ☎ (089) 554745 rm46 Closed Dec 24-26 **B**

H Karlstor Neuhauser Str 34 ☎ (089) 593596 rm28 **B**

H Köberi Bodenseestr 222 ☎ (089) 876339 rm32 **A**

◆ **Maximillian** Reitmorstr 12 ☎ (089) 222433 rm8 **B**

H Schillerhof (n.rest) Schillerstr 21 ☎ (089) 594270 rm22 **B**

◆ **Theresia** Luisenstr 51 ☎ (089) 521250 bed41 **A**

MÜNSTER *Nordrhein-Westfalen*

H Coerclehof (n.rest) Raesfeldstr 2 ☎ (0251) 20757 rm42 **B**

H Hansa-Haus (n.rest) Albersloher Weg 1 ☎ (0251) 64324 rm13 **B**

H Jellentrup Hüfferstr 52 ☎ (0251) 82024 rm18 **B**

H Steinburg Mecklenbecker Str 80 ☎ (0251) 77179 rm17 **B**

H Überwasserhof Überwasserhof 3 ☎ (0251) 40630 rm50 **B**

NAGOLD *Baden-Württemberg*

◆ **Köhlerei** Marktstr 46 ☎ (07452) 2007 rm15 Closed Dec 18-Jan 13 **A**

H Schiff Unterm Wehr 19-21 ☎ (07452) 2605 rm27 **A**

NAUHEIM, BAD *Hessen*

H Gaudes Hauptstr 6 ☎ (06032) 2508 rm8 **A**

H Villa Luise Lindenstr 1 ☎ (06032) 2001 bed15 **A**

NECKARSTEINACH *Hessen*

H Neckarblick (n.rest) Bahnhofstr 27A ☎ (06229) 1224 bed26 **A**

NERESHEIM *Baden-Württemberg*

◆ **Krone** Hauptstr 13 ☎ (07326) 218 rm19 **A**

H Zur Kanne Brühlstr 2 ☎ (07326) 6721 rm40 **A**

NETTETAL *Nordrhein-Westfalen*

H Berghof Panoramaweg 19 ☎ (02153) 3704 rm7 **A**

H Josten Wankumer Str 3 ☎ (02153) 2036 rm10 **B**

H Rütten Hochstr 1 ☎ (02153) 1033 bed23 **A**

H Stadt Lobberich (n.rest) Hochstr 37 ☎ (02153) 5100 rm16 **A**

NEUENAHR, BAD *Rheinland-Pfalz*

H Berg Bonner Str 12 ☎ (02641) 24224 rm12 **A**

H Union Felten Telegrafenstr 10 ☎ (02641) 24153 rm21 **A**

NEUMÜNSTER *Schleswig-Holstein*

H Firzlaffs (n.rest) Rendsburger Str 183 ☎ (04321) 51466 rm18 **B**

H Holsteiner Bürgerhaus Brachenfelder Str 58 ☎ (04321) 23284 rm5 **B**

★★**Lenz** (n.rest) Gasstr 11 ☎ (04321) 45072 rm22 **A**

NEUSTADT AN DER AISCH *Bayern*

H Aischtal Ostendstr 29 ☎ (09161) 2766 rm15 Closed Aug 1-25 **A**

★★**Römerhof** R-Wagner Str 15 ☎ (09161) 3011 rm21 **A**

NEUSTADT AN DER WEINSTRASSE *Rheinland-Pfalz*

H Haardter Herzel Eichkehle 58 ☎ (06321) 6421 rm9 **B**

NEUWIED *Rheinland-Pfalz*

H Schweizer (n.rest) Schlossstr 52 ☎ (02631) 27201 bed25 **A**

H Viktoria Augustastr 37 ☎ (02631) 23766 bed30 **A**

NIESTETAL *Hessen*

H Althans (n.rest) Friedrich-Ebert Str 65 ☎ (0561) 522709 rm21 Closed Dec 20-Jan 7 **A**

◆ **Zum Niestetal** Niestetalstr 16 ☎ (0561) 523068 rm16 **A**

NORDEN *Niedersachsen*

★★**Deutsches Haus** Neuer Weg 26 ☎ (04931) 4271 rm40 **B**

NORTHEIM *Niedersachsen*

H Friesenhof (n.rest) Northeimer Str 19 ☎ (05551) 8147 rm6 **B**

H Leineturm Leineturm 1 ☎ (05551) 3576 rm10 **A**

NÜRNBERG (NUREMBERG) *Bayern*

H Am Ring (n.rest) Am Plarrer 2 ☎ (0911) 265771 rm33 **B**

◆ **Cramer-Klett** Pillenreuther Str 162 ☎ (0911) 449291 bed38 **A**

◆ **Humboldtklause** Humboldstr 41 ☎ (0911) 413801 rm8 **A**

◆ **Kronfleschkuche** Kaiserstr 22 ☎ (0911) 227845 rm20 **A**

◆ **Pfälzer Hof** Am Gräslein 10 ☎ (0911) 221411 rm6 Closed Dec 24-Jan 12 **B**

H Probst Luitpoldstr 9 ☎ (0911) 203433 rm29 **B**

OBERKIRCH *Baden-Württemberg*

◆ **Adler** Gaisbach 7 ☎ (07802) 4519 rm11 Closed Nov 15-Dec 15 **A**

H Pflug Fernacher Pl ☎ (07802) 3255 rm35 **B**

◆ **Renchtalblick** Bellensteinstr 9 ☎ (07802) 3404 rm26 **A**

◆ **Untere Linde** Querstr 9 ☎ (07802) 3312 rm11 Closed Oct 25-Nov 15 **A**

OBERSTAUFEN *Bayern*

H Engel Buflings 3 ☎ (08386) 1647 rm59 Closed Nov 15-Dec 18 **A**

OBERSTDORF *Bayern*

◆ **Evelyn** Sigismundstr 3 ☎ (08322) 4623 rm8 **A**

◆ **Fichtl** Clemens-Wenzeslaus Str 1 ☎ (08322) 3720 rm4 **A**

◆ **Landhaus Schorsch** Schorsch Pape Im Weidach 20 ☎ (08322) 4254 rm11 **B**

OEYNHAUSEN, BAD *Nordrhein-Westfalen*

◆ **Bosse** Herforder Str 40 ☎ (05731) 28061 rm12 **B**

OFFENBACH *Hessen*

H Hansa (n.rest) Bernardstr 101 ☎ (069) 888075 bed30 **B**

OFFENBURG *Baden-Württemberg*

◆ **Blume** Weinstr 160 ☎ (0781) 33666 rm6 Closed Jan 2-14 & Aug 2-16 **B**

H Drei Könige (n.rest) Klosterstr 9 ☎ (0781) 24390 rm24 **A**

H Rheinscher Hof (n.rest) Hauptstr 52 ☎ (0781) 24275 bed20 **A**

★**Sonne** Hauptstr 94 ☎ (0781) 71039 bed59 **B**

At **ORTENBERG**(4km SE)

★**Glattfelder** Kinzigtalstr 20 ☎ (0781) 31219 bed23 **A**

OLDENBURG *Niedersachsen*

H Graf von Oldenburg Heiligengeiststr 10 ☎ (0441) 25077 bed50 **A**

◆ **Harmonie** Dragonerstr 59 ☎ (0441) 27704 rm10 **A**

H Wieting Damm 29 ☎ (0441) 27214 rm68 **A**

ORTENBERG See **OFFENBURG**

OSNABRÜCK *Niedersachsen*

H Neustadt Miquelstr 34 ☎ (0541) 51200 rm26 **A**

H Tebbe (n.rest) Rotenburger Str 20 ☎ (0541) 22695 rm12 **A**

PADERBORN *Nordrhein-Westfalen*

H Alt-Neuhaus Sertürner Str 5 ☎ (05254) 2584 rm7 **A**

H Krawinkel Karlstr 33 ☎ (05251) 23663 rm30 **A**

PASSAU *Bayern*

◆ **Gabriele** A-Stifter Str 12 ☎ (0851) 6446 bed24 **A**

★★**Weisser Hase** Ludwigstr 23 ☎ (0851) 34066 rm117 **A**

PRIEN AM CHIEMSEE *Bayern*

H Reinhart Seestr 117 ☎ (08051) 1045 rm26 **B**

PRUM *Rheinland-Pfalz*

H Kölner Hof ☎ (06551) 2503 rm15 **A**

H Tannenhof Am Kurpark 2 ☎ (06551) 2406 bed40 **A**

H Zum Goldenen Stern Hahnpl 29 ☎ (06551) 3075 bed76 **A**

RATINGEN *Nordrhein-Westfalen*

H Europäisher Hof Mülheimer Str 13 ☎ (02102) 845097 bed27 **B**

RAVENSBURG *Bayern*

◆ **Bräuhaus Obereschach** ☎ (0751) 62063 bed30 **A**

H Lamm Marienpl 47 ☎ (0751) 3914 rm43 Closed Dec 22-Jan 6 **A**

◆ **Landvogtei** Dürnast 1 ☎ (07546) 5239 bed17 **A**

REGENSBURG *Bayern*

◆ **Dechbettener Hof** Dechbetten 11 ☎ (0941) 35283 rm13 **A**

REMAGEN *Rheinland-Pfalz*

H Rhein-Ahr Quellenstr 67-69 ☎ (02642) 44112 rm14 Closed Jan 1-20 **B**

REMSCHEID *Nordrhein-Westfalen*

H Fischer Luttringhauser Str 131 ☎ (02191) 5835 rm24 **A**

◆ **Hoffmann** Rader Str 48 ☎ (02191) 62034 bed18 **A**

H Kromberg Kreuzbergstr 24 ☎ (02191) 590031 rm18 **A**

H Wuppertaler Hof Lüttringhauser Str 34 ☎ (02191) 61737 rm11 **A**

RENDSBURG *Schleswig-Holstein*

H Grüner Kranz Hollesenstr 33 ☎ (04331) 72366 bed14 **A**

H Pelli Hof Materialhofstr 1 ☎ (04331) 22216 rm32 **B**

REUTLINGEN *Baden-Württemberg*

◆ **Germania** Unter den Linden 20 ☎ (07121) 329062 rm25 **B**

H Kurtz (n.rest) Rappenhaldestr 11 ☎ (07121) 37214 rm11 **A**

RINTELN *Niedersachsen*

H Grafensteinerhöh Steinberger Str 42 ☎ (05751) 5277 bed16 Closed end Oct-beg Nov **A**

H Linde Hamelner Str 21 ☎ (05751) 6088 rm19 **A**

ROTENBURG (WÜMME) *Niedersachsen*

H Bürgerhof am Galgenberg 2 ☎ (04261) 5274 bed38 **B**

ROTHENBURG OB DER TAUBER *Bayern*

◆ **Goldener Greifen** Obere Schmiedgasse 5 ☎ (09861) 2281 rm18 **A**

◆ **Steinbachtal** Nr 9 ☎ (09861) 4538 rm34 **A**

H Zur Schranne Schrannenpl 6 ☎ (09861) 2258 bed80 **A**

RÜDESHEIM *Hessen*

H Assmannshausen Rheinuferstr 2a ☎ (06722) 2326 rm16 **A**

H Darmstädter Hof Rheinstr 29 ☎ (06722) 2485 rm46 Closed Nov 15-Mar **B**

H Germinia Rheinstr 10 ☎ (06722) 2584 bed34 **A**

H Zum Bären Schmidstr 24-31 ☎ (06722) 1091 bed46 **A**

RUHPOLDING *Bayern*

H Brigitte (n.rest) Brandstätler Str 38 ☏ (08663) 9488 rm10 **A**

ST-GOAR *Rheinland-Pfalz*

H Germania Heerstr 47 ☏ (06741) 1610 rm11 Closed Jan 15-Feb 15 **A**

★**Hauser** Heerstr 77 ☏ (06741) 333 rm15 **A**

◆ **Mühlenschenke** Grüdelbachtel 73 ☏ (06741) 1698 rm9 **A**

H Schöne Aussicht Heestr 1 ☏ (06741) 7232 rm9 **A**

H Winzerhaus Loreley An der Loreley 49 ☏ (06741) 334 rm21 **A**

ST-GOARHAUSEN *Rheinland-Pfalz*

★★**Erholung** Nasstatterstr 15 ☏ (06771) 2684 rm104 **A**

H Herrmanns Mühle Fortsbachstr 46 ☏ (06771) 7317 bed9 **A**

SAULGAU *Baden-Württemberg*

H Bären Haupstr 93 ☏ (07581) 8778 rm30 **A**

SCHLANGENBAD *Hessen*

H Russicher Hof Rheingauer Str 37 ☏ (06129) 2005 rm23 Closed Jan 10-Feb 10 **A**

SCHLEIDEN *Nordrhein-Westfalen*

H Salzberg Am Lieberg 31 ☏ (02444) 494 rm10 **B**

SCHLESWIG *Schleswig-Holstein*

H Hohrenzollern Moltkestr 41 ☏ (04621) 24919 bed52 **A**

★**Weissen-Schwan** Gottorfstr 1 ☏ (04621) 32712 rm16 **A**

SCHRAMBERG *Baden-Württemberg*

◆ **Burgstüble** Hohenschramberg ☏ (07422) 7773 rm6 Closed Jan **A**

SCHWÄBISCH HALL *Baden-Württemberg*

H Scholl (n.rest) Klosterstr 2-4 ☏ (0791) 71046 rm31 **A**

SCHWEICH *Rheinland-Pfalz*

H Stern Brückenstr 60 ☏ (06502) 8496 rm12 **A**

SCHWEINFURT *Bayern*

◆ **Grafen Zepplin** Cramerstr 7 ☏ (06502) 22173 rm23 **A**

SCHWELM *Nordrhein-Westfalen*

H Frese Schulstr 56 ☏ (02336) 2963 bed24 **B**

SIEGEN *Nordrhein-Westfalen*

H Jakob (n.rest) Tiergatrenstr 61 ☏ (0271) 52375 rm18 **B**

◆ **Meier** St-Johann-Str 3 ☏ (0271) 3335066 rm19 **A**

◆ **Zun Roten Hahn** Freudenberger Str 476 ☏ (0271) 370190 rm6 **A**

SIGMARINGEN *Baden-Württemberg*

◆ **Schmautz** Im Muckentäle 33 ☏ (07571) 51554 rm14 **A**

SINGEN *Baden-Württemberg*

H Lamm Alemannenstr 42 ☏ (07731) 41011 rm79 **B**

◆ **Sternen** Schwarzwaldstr 6 ☏ (07731) 62279 rm24 **A**

H Widerhold Schaffhauser Str 58 ☏ (07731) 62482 rm35 **A**

SOEST *Nordrhein-Westfalen*

H Haus sur Börde Nöttenstr 1 ☏ (02921) 13544 rm11 **A**

H Zum Braustübl Thomästr 53 ☏ (02921) 4166 rm12 **A**

SOLINGEN *Nordrhein-Westfalen*

H Berliner Brücke Kamper Str 5 ☏ (0212) 78064 rm9 **B**

H Diegel (n.rest) Focher Str 10 ☏ (0212) 54405 bed50 **A**

H Landhaus Arnz Burger Landstr 249 ☏ (0212) 44000 rm20 **A**

H Sonneneck Pfaffenberger Weg 112 ☏ (0212) 44233 rm9 **A**

H Stadt Wald Friedrich-Ebert-Str 234 ☏ (0212) 310572 bed18 Closed Jan **A**

STRAUBING *Bayern*

◆ **Lehner** Alburger Hauptstr 26 ☏ (09421) 42360 rm6 **A**

★★**Wittelsbach 25/26** Stadtgraben 25/26 ☏ (09421) 1517 rm37 **A**

STUTTGART *Baden-Württemberg*

H Haus Berg (n.rest) K-Schurz-Str 16 ☏ (0711) 261875 rm15 **A**

◆ **Kramer's Bürgerstauben** Gablenberger Haupstr 4 ☏ (0711) 465481 rm12 **A**

◆ **Sonnenberg** Rembrandstr 190 ☏ (0711) 762576 rm10 **A**

TETTNANG *Baden-Württemberg*

H Bären Bärenpl 1 ☏ (07542) 6945 rm36 Closed Jan 6-28 **A**

◆ **Traube Tettnang** Storchenstr 1 ☏ (07542) 7307 bed10 **A**

TITISEE See **TITISEE-NEUSTADT**

TITISEE-NEUSTADT *Baden-Württemberg*

TITISEESee TITISEE-NEUSTADT

◆ **Lorette** Hochfirstweg 7 ☏ (07651) 8347 bed24 **A**

TÖLZ, BAD *Bayern*

◆ **Bergblick** B-Erdhard-str 6 ☏ (08041) 3622 rm10 Closed Mar **A**

◆ **Marienhof** Bergweg 3 ☏ (08041) 6028 rm21 **B**

◆ **Wald** Austr 39 ☏ (08041) 2788 rm35 Closed Nov 7-Dec 17 **A**

TRABEN-TRARBACH *Rheinland-Pfalz*

H Central Bahnstr 43 ☏ (06541) 6238 rm36 Closed Dec 20-Jan 10 **A**

TRIBERG *Baden-Württemberg*

H Adler Haupstr 52 ☏ (07722) 4574 rm20 **A**

H Bären Haupstr 10 ☏ (07722) 4493 bed60 **A**

H Central (n.rest) Haupstr 64 ☏ (07722) 4360 rm15 Closed 1-20 Dec **B**

H Ketter am Kurgarten Friedrichstr 7 ☏ (07722) 4229 rm10 **B**

H Schwarzwaldhotel Tanne Wallfahrtstr 35 ☏ (07722) 4322 rm22 Closed Nov **A**

TRIER *Rheinland-Pfalz*

H Aulmann (n.rest) Fleischstr 47-48 ☏ (0651) 40033 rm48 **B**

H Estricher Hof Estricher Hof 85 ☏ (0651) 33044 rm16 **B**

H Minnebeck Eurener Str 68 ☏ (0651) 88805 rm14 **A**

H Monopol (n.rest) Bahnhofspl 7 ☏ (06651) 74754 rm35 **B**

H Römerbrücke K-Marx-Str 78 ☏ (0651) 73467 rm5 **A**

H Wienerhof (n.rest) Bahnhofstr 25 ☏ (0651) 25251 rm17 **A**

H Zender Ehranger Str 207 ☏ (0651) 66111 rm18 **A**

TÜBINGEN *Baden-Württemberg*

H Kreuzberg Vor dem Kreuzberg 23 ☏ (07071) 4624 bed18 **A**

◆ **Ritter** am Stadtgraben 25 ☏ (07071) 22502 rm6 **A**

TUTTLINGEN *Baden-Württemberg*

★**Ritter** Königstr 12 ☏ (07461) 8855 rm18 **A**

ÜBERLINGEN *Baden-Württemberg*

H Zähringer Hof Münsterstr 36/38 ☎ (07551) 63655 rm33 May-Nov **A**

ULM *Baden-Württemberg*

★★**Goldenes Rad** (n.rest) Neue Str 65 ☎ (0731) 67048 bed34 **B**

H Lehrertal Lehrer Talweg 3 ☎ (0731) 52099 bed35 **A**

★★**Roter Löwe** Ulmer Gasse 8 ☎ (0731) 62031 rm23 **A**

VILLINGEN *Baden-Württemberg*

◆ **Linde** Strassburger Str 2 ☎ (07721) 22161 rm15 Closed Jul 29-Aug 19 **A**

H Neckarquelle Wannenstr 5 ☎ (07720) 5782 rm22 Closed Jul 29-Aug 19 **A**

◆ **Schlachthof** Schlachthausstr 11 ☎ (07721) 22584 rm10 **B**

WALDECK *Hessen*

H König von Rom Lindenweg 10 ☎ (05623) 2093 rm18 **A**

WALDKIRCH *Baden-Württemberg*

◆ **Löwen** Schwarzwaldstr 34 ☎ (07681) 9868 bed13 Closed Nov 2-Dec 2 **A**

WALDSEE, BAD *Baden-Württemberg*

H Ritter Wurzacher Str 90 ☎ (07524) 8018 rm22 **B**

H Westfalen Badstr 23 ☎ (07524) 5187 rm30 **B**

WEIDEN IN DER OBERPFALZ *Bayern*

H Hölltaler Hof Oberhöll 2 ☎ (0961) 43093 rm27 **A**

WERTHEIM *Baden-Württemberg*

H Hofgarten (n.rest) Untere Heeg 1 ☎ (09342) 6426 rm14 **A**

WIESBADEN *Hessen*

H Aachener Hof (n.rest) Matthias-Claudius Str 16 ☎ (06121) 301203 rm25 **B**

H Karlshof (n.rest) Rheinstr 72 ☎ (06121) 302444 bed30 **B**

H Kliniken (n.rest) Feldstr 6 ☎ (06121) 522202 rm16 **A**

H Krüger Parkstr 24 ☎ (06121) 373300 rm12 **A**

WILDBAD IM SCHWARZWALD *Baden-Württemberg*

◆ **Schmid** (n.rest) Sommerberg ☎ (07081) 2664 rm19 **A**

◆ **Sonnenbring** (n.rest) Olgastor 65 ☎ (07081) 2529 rm27 **A**

◆ **Villa Bätzner** Uhlandpl 6 ☎ (07081) 2609 rm10 **A**

WILHELMSHAVEN *Niedersachsen*

H Kaiser Rheinstr 128 ☎ (04421) 42004 rm84 **B**

H Keil Markstr 23 ☎ (04421) 41414 rm20 **B**

WIMPFEN, BAD *Baden-Württemberg*

★★**Blauer Turm** Burgviertel 5-7 ☎ (07063) 225 rm19 **A**

★★**Weinmann** (n.rest) Marktplatz 3 ☎ (7091) 8582 bed21 Mar 16-Oct **B**

WORMS *Rheinland-Pfalz*

◆ **Baum** Gaugasse 9 ☎ (06241) 51069 bed30 **A**

H Pfeddersheimer Hof Zellertalstr 35-39 ☎ (06247) 811 rm20 **A**

WUPPERTAL *Nordrhein-Westfalen*

★★**Post** Poststr 4 ☎ (0202) 450131 rm55 **B**

WÜRZBURG *Bayern*

H Erholung Petrinistr 19 ☎ (0931) 21977 rm17 **A**

H Fischzucht J-Echter-Str 15 ☎ (0931) 704095 rm45 Closed Aug 15-Sep 6 **A**

★★**Franziskaner** Franziskanerplatz 2 ☎ (0931) 15001 rm47 **B**

H Russ Wolfhartsgasse 1 ☎ (0931) 50016 rm30 **B**

H Urlaub Bronnbacher Gasse 4 ☎ (0931) 54813 rm24 **A**

ZELL AN DER MOSEL *Rheinland-Pfalz*

◆ **Grünewald** Heinzenberg 24 ☎ (06542) 4363 rm5 **A**

★★**Post** Schlossstr 25 ☎ (06542) 4217 rm16 Closed Jan 14-30 **B**

ZWEIBRÜCKEN *Rheinland-Pfalz*

H Erika (n.rest) Rosengartenstr 5, Landstuhler Str 62 ☎ (06332) 2882 rm14 **A**

ZWIEFALTEN *Baden-Württemberg*

◆ **Münsterblick** ☎ (07373) 369 rm17 **A**

◆ **Post** Haupstr 44 ☎ (07373) 302 rm11 Closed Jan 1-23 **A**

ZWISCHENAHN, BAD *Niedersachsen*

H Kämper Georgstr 12 ☎ (04403) 2375 rm10 **A**

GREECE

FACTS & FIGURES

Capital: Athens
Language: Greek, some English, Italian, French
IDD code: 30. To call the UK dial 0044
Currency: Drachma (Dr)
Local time: GMT+2 (summer GMT+3)
Emergency services: Police 100 (large cities), 109 (Athens suburbs); Fire 199 (Athens); Ambulance 166 (Athens).

Business hours – Banks: 0800–1400 Mon–Fri (longer hours in tourist season). National and General Bank, Constitution Square 0900–2000 Mon–Sat (closed Mon–Thur 1400–1530, Fri 1330–1500)
Shops: summer 1330–2030 Mon; 0800–1400 & 1730–2030 Tue, Thur & Fri; 0800–1500 Wed & Sat. Winter 1300–1900 Mon; 0930–1900 Tue, Wed, Thu & Fri; 0900–1500 Sat

Average daily temperatures:
Athens °C

Jan 9	Jul 27
Mar 12	Sep 23
May 20	Nov 15

Tourist Information:
National Tourist Organisation of Greece
UK 4 Conduit Street
London W1R 0DJ
Tel 01-734 5997
USA 645 Fifth Ave
Olympic Tower
New York, NY 10022
Tel (212) 421 5777

Greece is a country of many facets. A land of myths, gods and archaeology, turquoise seas, brilliant blue skies, iridescent light and spectacular landscapes, and where the ancient mingles with the modern to create a unique ambiance.

Every island, every resort, every town and city has its own distinct personality and character. So whether your taste is for hectic nightlife, secluded shores or delving into the past, there will be somewhere in Greece to satisfy you. But as well as the contrasts there are numerous aspects of Greece which are common throughout the country: glorious beaches, beautiful scenery, a wonderful climate, quirky plumbing and, perhaps most notably of all, friendly, hospitable people.

For many, a holiday in Greece is essentially about stretching out on fine, golden sand, soaking up the sun and the relaxed atmosphere, perhaps trying their hand at windsurfing, whiling away the hours in a sea-side taverna or joining the locals over a Greek coffee and a backgammon board.

HOW TO GET THERE

BY CAR

The most direct route for the motorist is through Belgium, Federal Republic of Germany (from Köln/Cologne to München/Munich), through Austria (Salzburg) and Yugoslavia (via Beograd/Belgrade). An alternative road route is through France or Switzerland, Italy (via Milano/Milan and Trieste) and Yugoslavia. You can also reach Greece by driving to southern Italy and using the direct ferry services. The distance to Athinai (Athens) is just under 2,000 miles and would normally require 4 to 5 overnight stops. Car-sleeper services operate during the summer from Brussels and 's-Hertogenbosch to Ljubljana; from Boulogne, Brussels, Paris or 's-Hertogenbosch to Milan; and from Milan to Bari and Brindisi to connect with the ferry services to Greece.

For details of the AA's Overseas Routes Service consult the Contents page.

SPEED LIMITS

Unless signs indicate otherwise, speed restrictions are as follows: in built-up areas 50 kph (31 mph); outside built-up areas 80 kph (49 mph); on motorways 100 kph (62 mph).

PARKING

Parking is prohibited where there is a continuous central white line unless there are 2 lanes running in each direction. In Athinai, it is forbidden to park in the Green Zone except where parking meters have been installed.

BY TRAIN

The Greek train service is slow and infrequent. Moreover, because of the mountainous terrain, many towns are not linked

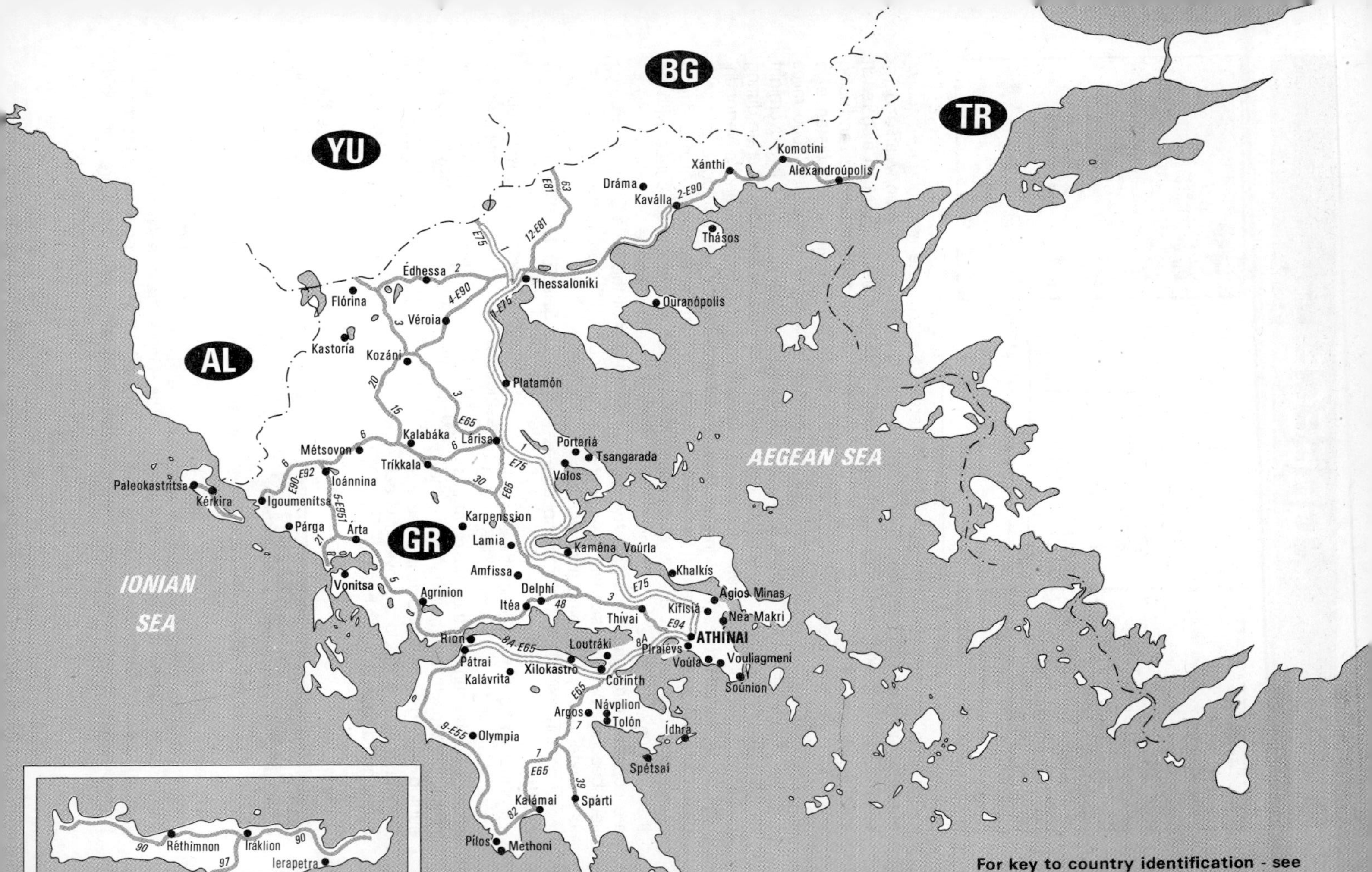

For key to country identification - see "About the gazetteer"

by rail, though connecting buses do operate. If you do not have a Eurail or InterRail Pass, the Greek Tourist Card is available (second class only) for 10, 20 or 30 days unlimited travel.

BY BUS

The bus service is faster and more extensive than rail travel and only slightly more expensive. Large towns have bus stations, but smaller towns often use cafes as bus stations.

BY FERRY

There are frequent direct connections between the major islands and prices are regulated.

ACCOMMODATION

The gazetteer which follows includes a wide range of hotels, pensions and private houses; the majority offer accommodation for under Dr5149 per person per night at some time of the year. The price bands are:

A Dr2439–3794
B Dr3794–5149

taking a rate of exchange at

Dr271=£1
Dr163.25=US $1

It is possible, however, that prices may change during the currency of this book. Other details of accommodation can be obtained through the local Tourist Police Office, through the local Travel Agent or even through the local shopkeeper if you are looking for *dhomatia* (rooms to let) in a rather isolated village or island.

AGIOS MINAS *Central Greece*

H Drossia Beach (n.rest) ☎ (0221) 98248 rm28 **A**

H Saint Minas Beach ☎ (0221) 98411 rm80 Jun-Sep **A**

AGRÍNION *Central Greece*

H Alice 2 Papastratou ☎ (0641) 23056 rm34 **A**

H Esperia 31 H-Trikoupi ☎ (0641) 23033 rm26 **A**

H Galaxy 19 G-Kazatzi ☎ (0641) 23551 rm36 **A**

H Leto Platia Democratias ☎ (0641) 23043 rm36 **A**

★★**Soumelis** 3 Ethniki Odos ☎ (0641) 23473 rm20 **A**

ALEXANDROÚPOLIS *Thrace*

H Alexander Beach ☎ (0551) 29250 rm102 **A**

★★**Astir** 280 Komotinis ☎ (0551) 26448 rm53 **B**

★★**Egnatia** Makris ave ☎ (0551) 28661 rm96 **A**

H Hera 179 Dimokratias Ave ☎ (0551) 25995 rm32 **A**

H Oceanis (n.rest) 20 C. Paleologou ☎ (0551) 28830 rm24 **A**

AMFISSA *Central Greece*

H Amfissaeum 18 Gidoyannou ☎ (0265) 22161 rm40 **A**

ARGOS *Peloponnese*

H Mycenae 12 Platia Aghiou Petrou ☎ (0751) 28569 rm24 **A**

H Telessila 2 Danaou & Vassilissis Olgas ☎ (0751) 28351 rm32 **A**

ÁRTA *Epirus*

H Amvrakia 13 N-Priovolou ☎ (0681) 28311 rm60 **A**

H Cronos Platia Kilkis ☎ (0681) 22211 rm55 **A**

★★**Xenia** Frourion ☎ (0655) 27413 rm22 **A**

ATHÍNAI (ATHENS) *Attica*

Encircled by hills and only four miles from the sea, Athínai is Europe's southernmost capital, and with its modern buildings and bustling streets standing side by side with ancient monuments – reminders of one of the world's oldest civilisations – is a delight to visit. But where to begin? Probably with the Acropolis, Greece's most famous landmark and the great symbol of classical civilisation. It dominates the city by day, the marble pillars of the Parthenon gleaming in the sun, and by night is brilliantly floodlit against a velvety black sky. At the foot of the Acropolis is the oldest part of the city, Plaka, a district formed after Greece's independence, with a mass of narrow streets bursting with life, especially at night when the hundreds of bars, tavernas and clubs offer something to suit practically every taste and pocket. During the day Plaka is a marvellous place to browse among the countless craft shops, while not far away is the famous flea market, Monastiraki, where it is possible to pick up bargains, especially leather goods. But in the midst of the cosmopolitan streets you are just as likely to come across something as typically Greek as a tiny kiosk masquerading as a general store in miniature, or a little man selling pistachio nuts or lottery tickets.
Broadly speaking, the main shopping areas are around Sintagma Square, Kolonaki, Omonia Square, Monastiraki, Patission Street and Kipseli.
If you want to get away from the pace and excitement of the capital, whether for relaxing or sightseeing, a short drive or bus or taxi ride will take you to the Athenian Riviera with its attractive resorts and long beaches.

EATING OUT The Greeks eat out frequently and consequently Athínai has a wide choice of restaurants where Greek food can be enjoyed. In some tavernas it is not unusual to walk straight into the kitchen to choose a speciality such as freshly grilled fish, country salads or more adventurous dishes such as *dolmades* – vine leaves stuffed with lamb, accompanied by the tangy local wine, retsina. For inexpensive Greek and international food the popular and usually crowded *Delphi*, in Nikis, is recommended, as is *O Platanos*, located in the Plaka. At the upper end of the price bracket, *Dionysos*, in Robertou Gali, offers diners a wonderful view of the Acropolis. Right in the centre of town, *Floca's* and *Zonar's*, both in Venizelou Avenue are the leading café restaurants.

H Amaryllis (n.rest) 45 Veranzerou ☎ (01) 5238738 rm57 **A**

H Ami (n.rest) 10 Iras & Sehou Fix ☎ (01) 9220820 rm16 **A**

H Ionis 41 Halkokondyli ☎ (01) 5232311 rm102 **B**

H Plaka 7 Kapnikareas & Mitropoleos ☎ (01) 3222096 rm67 **A**

H Plaza 78 Aharnon & 1 Katrivanou ☎ (01) 8225111 rm126 **A**

H Protea 9 L. Katsoni ☎ (01) 6430736 rm22 **B**

★★★Stanley 1-5 Odisseos ☎ (01) 5241611 rm395 **A**

H Xenophon 340 Acharnon ☎ (01) 2020310 rm186 **B**

CHALKISSee **KHALKÍS**

CORINTH *Peloponnese*

H Acropolis 25 Vassileos Georgiou ☎ (0741) 26568 rm27 **A**

H Ephira 52 Vassileos Konstantinou ☎ (0741) 22434 rm45 **A**

H Korinthos 26 Damaskinou ☎ (0741) 26701 rm34 **A**

CRETESee **KRÍTI**

DELPHÍ *Central Greece*

H Acropole 9 Filelinon ☎ (0265) 82676 rm28 **A**

H Inionhos 27 Vassileos Pavlou &, Friderikis ☎ (0265) 82316 rm15 **A**

H Kasiri 23 Sygrou ☎ (0265) 82322 rm24 **A**

H Leto 25 Apollonos ☎ (0265) 82302 rm22 Mar-Oct **A**

H Pan 53 Vassileos Pavlou, & Friderikis ☎ (0265) 82294 rm14 **A**

DRÁMA *Macedonia*

H Marianna ☎ (0521) 31520 rm45 **A**

ÉDHESSA *Macedonia*

H Alfa 36 Egnatia ☎ (0381) 22221 rm36 **A**

H Helena 4 Dimitriou Rizou ☎ (0381) 23218 rm36 **A**

H Katarraktes 4 Karanou ☎ (0381) 22300 rm44 **A**

H Pella 30 Egnatia ☎ (0381) 23541 rm27 **A**

FLÓRINA *Macedonia*

★★★King Alexander 68 Nikis ave ☎ (0385) 23501 rm38 **A**

H Lyngos 3 Tagmatarchou Naoum ☎ (0385) 28322 rm40 **A**

★★★Tottis ☎ (0385) 22645 rm48 **A**

ÍDHRA (HYDRA) *Island of Hydra*

◆ Greco (n.rest) ☎ (0298) 53200 rm19 Mar-Oct **B**

★★Hydroussa ☎ (0298) 52217 rm36 Apr-Oct **B**

◆ Kamimi (n.rest) ☎ (0298) 52335 rm10 Apr-Oct **A**

H Leto (n.rest) ☎ (0298) 52280 rm39 **A**

◆ Miranda ☎ (0298) 52230 rm28 Apr-Oct **B**

IERAPETRA See **KRÍTI (CRETE)**

IGOUMENÍTSA *Epirus*

H Astoria 147 Aghion Apostolon ☎ (0665) 22704 rm14 **A**

H Jolly (n.rest) 20 Vassileos Pavlou ☎ (0665) 23970 rm27 **A**

H Oscar 149 Aghion Apostolon ☎ (0665) 23338 rm36 **A**

IOÁNNINA (JANINA) *Epirus*

H Alexios 14 Poukevil ☎ (0651) 24003 rm88 **A**

H Dioni 10 Tsirigoti ☎ (0651) 27032 rm44 **A**

H Egnatia (n.rest) 2 Dagli & Aravantinou ☎ (0651) 25667 rm52 **A**

H El Greco (n.rest) 8 Tsirigoti ☎ (0651) 30726 rm36 **A**

H Galaxy (n.rest) Platia Pirou ☎ (0651) 25432 rm38 **A**

H King Pyrros (n.rest) 1 J-Gounari ☎ (0651) 27652 rm23 **A**

H Olympic (n.rest) 2 G-Melanidi ☎ (0651) 25888 rm44 **B**

H Vyzantion Ave Dodonis ☎ (0651) 23898 rm104 **A**

IRÁKLION See **KRÍTI (CRETE)**

ITÉA *Central Greece*

H Kalafati Paralia ☎ (0265) 32294 rm37 **A**

H Nafsika Iroon & Kapodistriou ☎ (0265) 33300 rm77 **B**

H Panorama (n.rest) 153 Akti Possidonos Paralia ☎ (0256) 33161 rm27 **A**

JANINA See**IOÁNNINA**

KALABÁKA *Thessaly*

H Atlantis (n.rest) ☎ (0432) 22476 rm28 **A**

H Galaxias 31 Hatzipetrou ☎ (0432) 23233 rm24 **A**

H Helvetia 45 Kastrakiou ☎ (0432) 23041 rm15 **A**

H Olympia 97 Trikalon ☎ (0432) 22792 rm22 **A**

H Rex (n.rest) 11a Kastrakiou ☎ (0432) 22372 rm32 **A**

KALÁMAI (KALAMATA) *Peloponnese*

H Alexandrion Paralia ☎ (0721) 26821 rm6 **A**

H Filoxenia Navarinou Paralia ☎ (0721) 23166 rm135 **A**

H Flisvos (n.rest) 135 Navarinou Paralia ☎ (0721) 82282 rm41 **A**

H Galaxias (n.rest) 14 Kolokotroni ☎ (0721) 28891 rm27 **A**

H Haicos (n.rest) 115 Navarinou Paralia ☎ (0721) 82886 rm60 **A**

◆ Nedon 153 Navarinou Paralia ☎ (0721) 26811 rm12 **A**

H Plaza (n.rest) 117 Navarinou Paralia ☎ (0721) 82590 rm20 **A**

H Valassis 95 Navarinou Paralia ☎ (0721) 23849 rm37 **A**

KALÁVRYTA *Peloponnese*

H Chelmos (n.rest) Platia Eleftherias ☎ (0692) 22217 rm27 Jun-Oct **A**

H Filoxenia ☎ (0692) 22422 rm26 **A**

H Maria (n.rest) 2 Sygrou ☎ (0692) 22296 rm12 **B**

KAMÉNA VOÚRLA *Central Greece*

H Akti (n.rest) ☎ (0235) 22211 rm19 Apr-Oct **A**

H Alma (n.rest) 141 G-Vassilidi ☎ (0235) 22419 rm28 **A**

H Anastassia (n.rest) 1 Ermou ☎ (0235) 22490 rm14 **A**

H Possidon ☎ (0235) 22721 rm93 **B**

H Radion (n.rest) ☎ (0235) 22325 rm62 Jun-Sep **A**

H Violetta (n.rest) 81 G-Vassiliadi ☎ (0235) 22203 rm37 **A**

KARPENISSION *Central Greece*

H Anessis 44 Zinopoulou ☎ (0237) 22840 rm36 **A**

H Apollonion (n.rest) ☎ (0237) 22025 rm21 **A**

H Helvetia (n.rest) 33 Zinopoulou ☎ (0237) 22465 rm71 **A**

H Lecadin ☎ (0237) 22131 rm104 **A**

H Mont Blanc Vassileos Parlou, & 2 Frederikis ☎ (0237) 22322 rm37 **A**

KASTORÍA *Macedonia*

H Europa ☎ (0467) 23826 rm36 **A**

H Keletron 52 11th Noemvriou ☎ (0467) 22676 rm21 **A**

M Maria ☎ (0467) 74696 rm47 **A**

H Orestion (n.rest) 1 Platia Davaki ☎ (0467) 22257 rm20 **A**

H Tsamis Dispitio 3 Klm Kastoria ☎ (0467) 43334 rm81 **A**

KAVÁLLA *Macedonia*

H Egnatia 139, 7th Merarchias ☎ (051) 835841 rm38 **A**

H Esperia 42 Leoforos Erthrou ☎ (051) 229621 rm105 **A**

H Europa (n.rest) 20 Irinis Athineas ☎ (051) 241227 rm12 **A**

★★**Galaxy** 51 El-Venizelou ☎ (051) 224521 rm149 **A**

H Lucy Kalamitsa ☎ (051) 832600 rm217 **A**

H Nefeli 50 Leoforos Erythrou ☎ (051) 227441 rm94 **A**

H Oceanis 32 L-Erithrou ☎ (051) 221980 rm168 **A**

◆ **Vournelis** ☎ (051) 71353 rm12 **A**

KÉRKIRA See **KÉRKIRA (CORFU)**

KÉRKIRA (CORFU)

KÉRKIRA

◆ **Anthis** (n.rest) Kefalomandouko ☎ (0661) 25804 rm45 Apr-Oct **A**

H Astron 15 Donzelotou ☎ (0661) 39505 rm33 **B**

H Bretagne 27 Georgaki ☎ (0661) 30724 rm44 **A**

H I Calypso (n.rest) 4 Vraila ☎ (0661) 30723 rm19 **A**

H Olympic ☎ (0661) 30532 rm50 **A**

◆ **Phoenix** (n.rest) 2 Hr Smirnis ☎ (0661) 42290 rm18 **A**

PALEOKASTRITSA

H Oceanis ☎ (0663) 41229 rm71 Apr-Oct **A**

H Odysseus ☎ (0663) 41209 rm36 Apr-Oct **A**

H Paleokastritsa ☎ (0663) 41207 rm163 Apr-Oct **A**

KHALKÍS (CHALKIS) *Euboea*

H Hara 21-LKaroni ☎ (0221) 25541 rm51 **A**

H John's 9 Angeli Goviou ☎ (0221) 22496 rm57 **A**

H Manica (n.rest) Panagitsa-Leoforos ☎ (0221) 84400 rm28 **A**

KIFISIÁ *Attica*

H Roses (n.rest) 4 Miltiadou ☎ (01) 8019952 rm37 **A**

H Semiramis 36 Harillaou Tricoupi, & Filadelfeos Kefalari ☎ (01) 8012587 rm42 **B**

H Theoxenia 2 Filadelfeos, & Kolokotroni Kefalari ☎ (01) 8012751 rm65 **A**

KOMOTINI *Thrace*

H Anatolia (n.rest) 53 Anhialou ☎ (0531) 20132 rm56 **A**

◆ **Olympos** (n.rest) 37 Orfeos ☎ (0351) 22895 rm30 **A**

H Orpheus 48 Platia Vassileos, Konstantinou ☎ (0531) 26701 rm79 **A**

KOZÁNI *Macedonia*

H Aliakmon (n.rest) 38 El-Venizelou ☎ (0461) 36015 rm85 **A**

H Helena (n.rest) 27 Vassileos Georgiou ☎ (0461) 26056 rm39 **A**

M Nefeli 2nd Klm., Ethnikis Odou Kozanis, Ptolemaidos ☎ (0461) 36686 rm16 **A**

KRÍTI (CRETE)

IERAPETRA

H Blue Sky (n.rest) Peristera ☎ (0842) 28264 rm24 Apr-Oct **B**

H Camiros (n.rest) 17 M-Kothri ☎ (0842) 28704 rm40 Mar-Oct **A**

H Creta (n.rest) Platia El-Venizelou ☎ (0842) 22316 rm25 **A**

H Kyrva (n.rest) 45 Emm Lambraki ☎ (0842) 22594 rm16 **A**

H Petra-Mare ☎ (0842) 23341 rm219 Apr-Oct **B**

H Zakros (n.rest) ☎ (0842) 24101 rm46 **A**

IRÁKLION

◆ **Ares** 5 Aghissilaou ☎ (081) 280646 rm15 Apr-Oct **A**

H Domenico 14 Almyrou ☎ (081) 228703 rm44 **B**

H Gloria 15 Egeou Poros ☎ (081) 288223 rm52 **A**

H Irene (n.rest) ☎ (081) 226561 rm59 **A**

H Kastro 20 Theotokopoulou ☎ (081) 285020 rm38 **A**

◆ **Kris** (n.rest) 2 Doukos Boulos ☎ (081) 223211 rm10 **A**

H Marin (n.rest) 12 Beaufort ☎ (081) 220737 rm48 **A**

RÉTHIMNON

H Brascos 1ch. Daskalaki & Th-Moatsou ☎ (0831) 23721 rm82 **B**

H Golden Sun (n.rest) Adele ☎ (0831) 71284 rm38 **A**

H Jo-An (n.rest) 6 Dimitrakaki ☎ (0831) 24241 rm50 **A**

H Orion Kambos Adele ☎ (0831) 71471 rm73 Mar-Nov **A**

H Park (n.rest) 7 Igoumenou Gaviil ☎ (0831) 29958 rm10 **A**

H Valari 84 Kountouriotou ☎ (0831) 22236 rm29 **A**

LAMÍA *Central Greece*

★★**Apollonion** (n.rest) 25 Hatzopoulou ☎ (0231) 22666 rm36 **A**

H Helena (n.rest) 6 Thermopylon ☎ (0231) 25025 rm51 **A**

LÁRISA *Thessaly*

H Astoria (n.rest) 4 Protopapadaki ☎ (041) 252941 rm84 **B**

H Dionyssos (n.rest) 30 Vassileos Georgiou ☎ (041) 320101 rm84 **A**

H Grand (n.rest) 16 Papakiriazi ☎ (041) 257711 rm91 **B**

H Metropole 8 Roosevelt ☎ (041) 229911 rm96 **B**

LOUTRÁKI *Attica*

H Akti Loutraki 5 G. Leka ☎ (0741) 42338 rm38 **A**

◆ **Bacos** 4 Ikonomou ☎ (0741) 42518 rm46 Apr-Oct **A**

★★★**Karelion** 23 G. Lekka ☎ (0741) 42347 rm40 **A**

H Paolo 16 Korinthou ☎ (0741) 48742 rm80 **A**

H Pappas Pezoulia-Pefkaki ☎ (0741) 43936 rm84 **A**

H Park 8 G. Lekka ☎ (0741) 42270 rm64 **A**

H Pefkaki ☎ (0741) 42426 rm38 **A**

H Theoxenia (n.rest) 17 G. Leka ☎ (0741) 42257 rm26 Jun-Sep **A**

METHONI *Peloponnese*

H Alex Paralla ☎ (0723) 31219 rm20 **A**

MÉTSOVON *Epirus*

H Bitounis ☎ (0656) 41545 rm24 **A**

H Diasselo Kentriki Platia ☎ (0656) 41719 rm23 **A**

H Egnatia L-Tossitsa ☎ (0656) 41263 rm36 **A**

◆ **Flocas** (n.rest) 12 Tr-Tsoumaka ☎ (0656) 41309 rm6 **A**

H Olympic (n.rest) 3 J-Stanou ☎ (0656) 41337 rm17 **A**

H Victoria ☎ (0656) 41771 rm37 **A**

NÁVPLION (NAUPLIA) *Peloponnese*

H Agamemnon 3 Akti Miaouli ☎ (0752) 28021 rm40 **A**

H Dioscouri 7 Zigomala & Vironos ☎ (0752) 28550 rm51 **A**

H Leto (n.rest) 28 Zigomala ☎ (0752) 28093 rm11 Apr-Oct **A**

H Nafplia (n.rest) 11 Navarinou ☎ (0752) 28167 rm56 **A**

★★**Park** 1 Dervenakion ☎ (0752) 27428 rm70 **A**

H Rex 17 Bouboulinas ☎ (0752) 28094 rm51 May-Oct **A**

H Victoria 3 Spiliadou ☎ (0752) 27420 rm36 **A**

H Xenia Akronafplia ☎ (0752) 28991 rm58 **B**

NEA MAKRI *Attica*

H Marathon Beach ☎ (0294) 91255 rm166 Mar-Oct **A**

H Thomas Beach 3 Leoforos Possidonos ☎ (0294) 92790 rm30 **B**

H Zouberi Leoforos Possidonas Zouberi ☎ (0294) 71920 rm128 May-Oct **A**

OLYMPIA *Peloponnese*

H Antonios ☎ (0624) 22348 rm65 Mar-Oct **A**

H Apollon 13 Douma ☎ (0624) 22522 rm86 Apr-Oct **A**

H Ilis Pr-Kondyli ☎ (0624) 22547 rm57 Apr-Oct **A**

H Kronion 1 Tsoureka ☎ (0624) 22502 rm23 Mar-Oct **A**

H Neon Olympia G-Douma ☎ (0624) 22547 rm31 **B**

★★★**Spap** ☎ (0624) 22514 rm51 **B**

OURANÓPOLIS *Macedonia*

H Pyrgos (n.rest) ☎ (0337) 71281 rm17 May-Oct **A**

PALEOKASTRITSA
See **KÉRKIRA (CORFU)**

PÁRGA *Epirus*

H Acropole (n.rest) 16 Aghias Apostolon ☎ (0684) 31239 rm8 **A**

H Avra 3 Aghiou Athanassiou ☎ (0684) 31205 rm18 Apr-Oct **A**

H Bacoli (n.rest) ☎ (0684) 31200 rm34 **A**

H Olympic (n.rest) 1 Koufa ☎ (0684) 31360 rm16 **A**

H Torini (n.rest) ☎ (0684) 31219 rm11 **A**

H Valtos Beach ☎ (0684) 31610 rm19 May-Nov **B**

PÁTRAI (PATRAS) *Peloponnese*

H Adonis Zaimi & 9 Kapsali ☎ (061) 224213 rm56 **A**

H El Greco 145 Aghiou Andreou ☎ (061) 272931 rm24 **A**

H Galaxy (n.rest) 9 Agiou Nikolaou ☎ (061) 278815 rm53 **A**

◆ **Marie** (n.rest) 6 Gournari ☎ (061) 331302 rm24 **A**

H Moreas Heroon Polythechniou & Kyprou ☎ (061) 425494 rm105 **B**

◆ **Olympic** 46 Aghiou Niclaou ☎ (061) 224103 rm35 **A**

H Rannia (n.rest) 53 Riga Fereou ☎ (061) 220114 rm30 **A**

PÍLOS *Peloponnese*

H Arvanitis (n.rest) ☎ (0723) 22641 rm20 **A**

H Galaxy Platia Trion Navarchon ☎ (0723) 22780 rm34 **A**

H Karalis ☎ (0723) 22960 rm21 **B**

★★**Miremare** 3 Tsamadou ☎ (0723) 22226 rm20 **B**

◆ **Niefs** ☎ (0723) 22518 rm12 Apr-Sep **A**

PIRAIÉVS (PIRAEUS) *Attica*

H Anemoni (n.rest) 65-67 Evripidou ☎ (01) 4111768 rm45 **A**

H Bella Vista (n.rest) 109 Vassileos Paviou ☎ (01) 4121425 rm36 **A**

H Delfini (n.rest) 7 Leocharous ☎ (01) 4123512 rm51 **A**

H Homeridion 32 Harilaou Tripoupi ☎ (01) 4519811 rm59 **A**

H Ideal 142 Notara ☎ (01) 4511727 rm29 **A**

H Kastella (n.rest) 75 Vassileos Paviou ☎ (01) 4114735 rm30 **A**

H Park 103 Kolokotroni ☎ (01) 4524611 rm80 **A**

PLATAMÓN *Macedonia*

H Artemis ☎ (0352) 41406 rm18 **A**

H Maxim ☎ (0352) 41305 rm73 **A**

H Smolicas (n.rest) ☎ (0352) 41010 rm28 Apr-Oct **A**

PORTARIÁ *Thessaly*

◆ **Archontiko** (n.rest) ☎ (0421) 99235 rm9 **A**

H Pelias (n.rest) ☎ (0421) 99290 rm28 **A**

H Theoxenia (n.rest) ☎ (0421) 99527 rm10 **A**

RÉTHIMNON See **KRÍTI (CRETE)**

RION *Peloponnese*

H Porto Rio ☎ (061) 992102 rm267 Apr-Oct **B**

H Rion Beach Akti Possidonos ☎ (061) 991421 rm85 **A**

SALONICASee**THESSALONÍKI**

SOÚNION *Attica*

H Egeon ☎ (0292) 39200 rm44 **B**

H Saron Leoforos Lavriou-Sounion ☎ (0292) 39144 rm28 **A**

H Surf Beach Club Pounta Zeza ☎ (0292) 22363 rm266 May-Sep **B**

H Triton 68th Klm Leoforos, Athinon-Sounion ☎ (0292) 39103 rm41 **A**

SPÁRTI (SPARTA) *Peloponnese*

H Apollo 14 Thermopylon ☎ (0731) 22491 rm44 **A**

★★**Dioscouri** 94 Likourgou ☎ (0731) 28484 rm35 **A**

H Maniatis 60 K-Paleologou & Dion Dafnou ☎ (0731) 22665 rm80 **A**

H Menelaon 65 K-Paleologou ☎ (0731) 22161 rm48 **A**

H Sparta Inn ☎ (0731) 21021 rm79 **A**

SPÉTSAI *Island of Spétsai*

H Faros Kentriki Platia ☎ (0298) 72613 rm47 Apr-Oct **A**

H Myrtoon ☎ (0298) 72555 rm39 **A**

H Roumanis ☎ (0298) 72244 rm34 Mar-Nov **A**

H Star Platia Dapias ☎ (0298) 72214 rm37 Apr-Oct **A**

◆ **Villa Martha** (n.rest) ☎ (0298) 72147 rm23 Apr-Sep **A**

THÁSOS *Island of Thásos*

◆ **Akti** (n.rest) Paralia ☎ (0593) 22326 rm15 Apr-Sep **A**

H Angelika (n.rest) Paralia ☎ (0593) 22387 rm26 **A**

◆ **Diamanto** (n.rest) ☎ (0593) 22622 rm16 **A**

◆ **Dionyssos** (n.rest) ☎ (0593) 22198 rm11 **A**

◆ **Elli-Maria** (n.rest) ☎ (0593) 23133 rm20 May-Oct **A**

H Laios (n.rest) ☎ (0593) 22309 rm27 Apr-Sep **A**

H Lido (n.rest) 12 Megalou Alexandrou ☎ (0593) 22929 rm18 **A**

◆ **Mary** (n.rest) ☎ (0593) 22257 rm9 **A**

H Timoleon (n.rest) ☎ (0593) 22177 rm30 Apr-Oct **A**

THEBES See **THÍVAI**

THESSALONÍKI (SALONICA) *Macedonia*

Greece's second largest city and the birthplace of Aristotle, Thessaloníki, though largely engulfed by modern apartment blocks, is nonetheless well worth exploring. Among the sights are the White Tower, including the Citadel of the Seven Towers, facing the Monastery of Vlatadon; the Rotunda and the Arch of Galerius; the Archaeological Museum, containing impressive gold treasures; and the Museum of Popular Art.

EATING OUT The restaurants *Stratis*, in Nikis, and *Ta Nissia*, in Koromila, are both recommended, the latter for seafood.

H Amalia (n.rest) 33 Ermou ☎ (031) 268321 rm66 **A**

H ABC (n.rest) 41 Angelaki ☎ (031) 265421 rm107 **B**

H Delta 13 Egnatia ☎ (031) 516321 rm113 **A**

H Esperia (n.rest) 58 Olimpou & Venizelou ☎ (031) 269321 rm70 **A**

H Olympia 65 Olimpou ☎ (031) 235421 rm111 **B**

H Park (n.rest) 81 Ionas Dragouni ☎ (031) 524121 rm56 **B**

H Pella (n.rest) 65 Ionos Dragouni ☎ (031) 524221 rm79 **A**

H Rex 39 Monastiriou ☎ (031) 517051 rm59 **A**

★★★**Rotonda** 97 Monastiriou ☎ (031) 517121 rm79 **A**

★★★**Victoria** 13 Langada ☎ (031) 522421 rm68 **B**

THÍVAI (THEBES) *Attica*

H Meletiou (n.rest) 56-58 Epaminonda ☎ (0262) 22111 rm34 **A**

TOLÓN *Peloponnese*

H Aktaeon (n.rest) 60 Aktis ☎ (0752) 59084 rm20 Apr-Oct **A**

H Apollon (n.rest) ☎ (0752) 59015 rm37 Apr-Oct **A**

H Aris 28 Aktis ☎ (0752) 59231 rm30 Mar-Oct **A**

H Barbouna (n.rest) ☎ (0752) 59162 rm12 Apr-Oct **A**

H Dolfin 50 Aktis ☎ (0752) 59192 rm22 **A**

H Elenas 6 Bouboulinas ☎ (0752) 59158 rm19 Apr-Oct **A**

H Flisvos 13 Bouboulinas ☎ (0752) 59223 rm28 Mar-Oct **A**

H Knossos (n.rest) 45a Aktis ☎ (0752) 59174 rm16 Mar-Nov **A**

★★**Minoa** 56 Aktis ☎ (0752) 59207 rm44 Mar-Oct **A**

H Solon ☎ (0752) 59204 rm28 Apr-Oct **A**

TRÍKKALA *Thessaly*

H Dina (n.rest) 38 Asklepiou & Karanassou ☎ (0431) 27267 rm57 **A**

H Divani 13 Dionyssiou ☎ (0431) 27286 rm66 **B**

TSANGARÁDHA *Thessaly*

◆ **Kentavros** (n.rest) ☎ (0423) 49233 rm24 **A**

H San Stefano ☎ (0423) 49213 rm37 Apr-Sep **A**

★★**Xenia** ☎ (0423) 49205 rm46 **A**

VÉROIA *Macedonia*

H Polytimi (n.rest) 35 Megalou Alexandra ☎ (0331) 64902 rm32 **A**

VÓLOS *Thessaly*

H Alexandros 3 Topali-lassonos ☎ (0421) 31221 rm78 **A**

H Electra 16 Topali ☎ (0421) 32671 rm38 **A**

H Filippos (n.rest) 9 Solonas ☎ (0421) 37607 rm39 **A**

H Nefeli (n.rest) 10 Koumoundourou & Dimitriados ☎ (0421) 30211 rm53 **A**

H Park 2 Deligiorgi ☎ (0423) 36511 rm119 **B**

VONITSA *Central Greece*

H Bel Mare (n.rest) ☎ (0643) 22394 rm33 **A**

H Vonitsa (n.rest) ☎ (0643) 22594 rm34 **A**

VOÚLA *Attica*

H Castello Beach 8 Kerkiras& Aktis ☎ (01) 8958985 rm34 **A**

H Noufara 2 Metaxa ☎ (01) 8953450 rm22 **A**

H Parthenis (n.rest) 21 Alkionidon ☎ (01) 8956072 rm16 **A**

H Plaza (n.rest) 17 Alkionidon ☎ (01) 8953575 rm15 **A**

VOULIAGMENI BEACH *Attica*

H Armonia (n.rest) 1 Armonias ☎ (01) 8960105 rm95 **B**

◆ **Hera** 1 Lassonos ☎ (01) 8960321 rm38 Mar-Oct **B**

H Strand 14 Litous ☎ (01) 8960066 rm72 Apr-Oct **B**

XÁNTHI *Thrace*

M Natassa ☎ (0541) 21521 rm70 **A**

H Nestos (n.rest) 1 Kavalas ave ☎ (0541) 27531 rm74 **A**

XILOKASTRO *Peloponnese*

H Apollon (n.rest) 105 J. Ioanou ☎ (0743) 22239 rm27 **A**

H Fadira (n.rest) 2 Agiou Makariou ☎ (0743) 22648 rm48 Mar-Oct **A**

H Rallis 55 J. Ioanou ☎ (0743) 22219 rm74 Apr-Oct **A**

IRELAND

FACTS & FIGURES

Capital: Dublin (Republic of Ireland), Belfast (Northern Ireland)
Language: English, Irish
IDD code: 353. To call the UK dial 03
Currency: Irish pound or punt (IR£ = 100 pence)
Local time: GMT (summer GMT + 1)
Emergency services: Police, Fire and Ambulance 999

Business hours

Banks: 1000–1230 & 1330–1500 Mon–Fri
Shops: 0900–1730 Mon–Sat

Average daily temperatures: Dublin °C

Jan 4	May 11	Sep 13
Mar 6	Jul 15	Nov 7

Tourist Information–Irish Tourist Board:

UK 150 New Bond Street
London W1Y 0AQ
Tel 01–493 3201

USA 757 Third Ave
New York, NY 10017
Tel (212) 418–0800

Northern Ireland Tourist Board

UK 11 Berkeley Street
London W1
Tel 01–493 0601

Ireland is a place to linger, to discover unknown pleasures and to rediscover lost ones. Whether you decide to explore the lush green valleys and cobalt lakes of the Wicklow mountains, the stunning coastlines of the Ring of Kerry, the stone-walled and whitewashed cottage landscape of Connemara or the near-deserted sandy beaches of the west coast, you will find enchantment and a warm welcome.

If you decide to take shelter in a local pub – and there are plenty of them – get yourself a drink, breathe in the delightful aroma of a peat fire, and listen to the rain of conversation. For whichever part of Ireland you choose to visit you will encounter drinking companions with a thousand tales to tell, hosts who will make hospitality a labour of love, and a people of great charm.

A wide variety of sporting activity is available – from angling and sailing to golf and horse-riding. Those who prefer quieter pursuits will find an abundance of history and culture in the form of castles, museums and stately homes and parks.

The north-eastern corner of the island, Northern Ireland, remains a part of the United Kingdom, while the Republic, Eire, has been independent since 1921. Both extend a warm welcome to visitors, and contain much to interest and delight.

Once the home of saints and scholars of early Christian Europe, Ireland is a country rich in prehistoric remains, distinctive Celtic high crosses, Romanesque monasteries, castles, and handsome mansions. It also offers an abundance of lakes, rivers and seas teeming with fish, and some of the most exhilarating walking country to be found anywhere.

Politically, Ireland is divided into two: The Republic which is a sovereign independent state and Northern Ireland which forms part of the United Kingdom.

HOW TO GET THERE

BY CAR

Car ferry services operate from Britain to both the Republic and Northern counties. The services to the Republic operate from Pembroke to Rosslare ($3\frac{3}{4}$ hrs), from Fishguard to Rosslare ($3\frac{1}{2}$ hrs), Holyhead to Dublin ($3\frac{1}{2}$–$4\frac{3}{4}$ hrs) or to Dun Laoghaire ($3\frac{1}{2}$ hrs), Liverpool to Dun Laoghaire $7\frac{1}{2}$ hrs day, $10\frac{3}{4}$ hrs night). The services to Northern Ireland are from Liverpool to Belfast (9 hrs), Stranraer to Larne (2 hrs 20 mins) and Cairnryan to Larne ($2\frac{1}{4}$ hrs). There are also services to and from France.

For details of the AA's Overseas Routes Service consult the Contents page.

SPEED LIMITS

Republic of Ireland – 30 mph (48 kph) in built-up areas; between 40/55 mph (64/88 kph) outside built-up areas as indicated by signs.

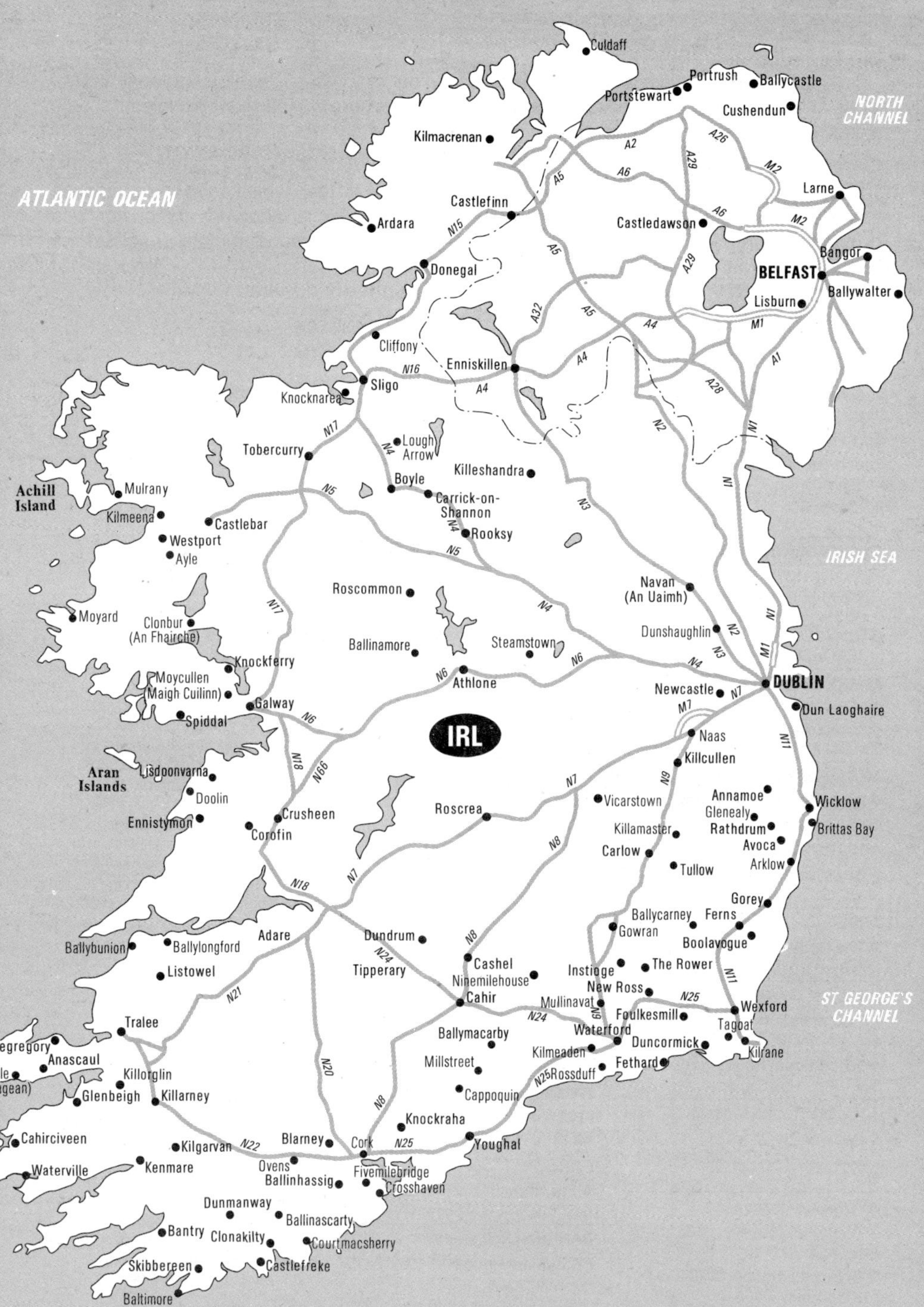

For key to country identification - see "About the gazetteer"

IRELAND

PARKING

Parking meters are in use in the central zones of Dublin. The parking disc system is used in central Cork and Limerick.

BY TRAIN

There are bargain Saver and Family Fares from any British Rail station to any Irish Rail station, if you want to get to Ireland by train. If you do not have a Eurail or Inter Rail pass, you can buy national and regional tickets for inland travel. A Rambler ticket offers either second-class rail or bus travel, or both rail and bus travel for a period of 8 or 15 days in the Republic. The Overlander ticket entitles you to unlimited rail and bus travel in Northern Ireland and the Republic.

BY BICYCLE

Tourist offices have a national list of places where you can rent bicycles.

ACCOMMODATION

The gazetteer which follows includes a wide selection of accommodation for less than £19 per person per night at some time of the year.

The price bands are:

A £9–£14
B £14–£19

Prices may be subject to change during the currency of this book. Other information about accommodation can be obtained from local tourist offices.

Abbreviations: Av Avenue Pk Park Pl Place Rd Road St Street

ACHILL ISLAND *Co Mayo*

◆ **Gray's** Doogort ☏ (098) 43244 rm15 Mar-Sep **B**

ADARE *Co Limerick*

FH Laccabawn Drehidtarsna ☏ (061) 86443 rm5 Mar-Oct **A**

ANNAMOE *Co Wicklow*

◆ **Carmels** ☏ (0404) 5297 rm4 Apr-Oct **A**

ARDARA *Co Donegal*

◆ **Bay View House** Portnoo Rd ☏ (075) 41145 rm7 Mar-Nov **A**

ARDEE *Co Louth*

◆ **The Gables** ☏ (041) 53789 rm5 **B**

ARKLOW *Co Wicklow*

FH Killinskyduff ☏ (0402) 32185 rm3 Jun-Sep **B**

◆ **Woodmount House** ☏ (0402) 32977 rm5 May-Sep **A**

ATHLONE *Co Westmeath*

◆ **Rocwal** The Beeches, , Coosan ☏ (0902) 75640 rm4 Apr-Oct **A**

AVOCA *Co Wicklow*

◆ **Ashdene** ☏ (0402) 5327 rm4 Apr-Oct **B**

◆ **Riverview House** ☏ (0402) 5181 rm5 May-Oct **A**

BALLINHASSIG *Co Cork*

◆ **Blanchfield House** ☏ (021) 885167 rm6 **B**

BALLINSKELLIGS *Co Kerry*

◆ **Sigerson Arms** ☏ (0667) 9104 rm10 May-Oct **B**

BALLYBUNION *Co Kerry*

◆ **Eagle Lodge** ☏ (068) 27224 rm8 Mar-Oct **B**

◆ **The Country House** ☏ (068) 27103 rm4 **A**

BALLYCARNEY *Co Wexford*

◆ **Oakville** Enniscorthy ☏ (054) 88626 rm5 Mar-Sep **A**

BALLYCASTLE *Co Antrim*

◆ **Hilsea** 28 North St ☏ (02657) 62385 rm20 **A**

BALLYMACARBRY *Co Waterford*

FH Clonanav ☏ (052) 36141 rm6 Mar-Oct **A**

BALLYWALTER *Co Down*

FH Abbey Farm 17 Ballywalter Rd ☏ (02477) 207 rm20 **A**

BANGOR *Co Down*

◆ **Ennislare** 9 Princetown Rd ☏ (0247) 472858 rm9 **A**

BANSHA *Co Tipperary*

FH Bansha House ☏ (062) 54194 rm7 Mar-Nov **A**

BANTRY *Co Cork*

◆ **Shangri-La** ☏ (027) 50244 rm6 **B**

BELFAST *City of Belfast*

Belfast, capital of Northern Ireland, straddles the winding River Lagan. To the south it is surrounded by lush green hills, and to the south-west the River Lagan runs along a steep-sided wooded valley. The 18th and 19th-century city is centred around Castle Place and Cornmarket, on the west bank of the river, but many of Belfast's principal visitor attractions are on the outskirts, including the zoo; Belfast Castle, a Scottish Baronial-style pile built in 1870 and standing in the shadow of Cave Hill; the Ulster Folk Museum, a 20-minute drive away near Holywood in County Down; and Stormont Castle. The main shopping streets are centred around Castle Junction and include Donegal Place, Howard Street, Fountain Street, Castle Lane and Cornmarket. Many shops sell craft products – wood carvings, stone and metal artefacts and Irish jewellery. Irish craft work is a rapidly expanding cottage industry. EATING OUT Belfast is not noted for its culinary traditions, but standards have improved enormously in recent years, with more emphasis on the use of fresh ingredients and the avoidance of the old habit of overcooking. The Strand, in Strandmills road, enjoys a good reputation, as does Thompson's in Arthur Sreet. Truffles, in Donegall Square West, is also popular, especially and lunchtime. For traditional oysters and Guinness in an atmospheric pub setting, try Robinson's opposite the Forum Hotel.

◆ **Camera House** 44 Wellington Pk ☏ (0232) 660026 rm11 **B**

BLACKROCK *Co Dublin*

◆ **Priory Lodge** ☏ (01) 888221 rm5 **B**

BLARNEY *Co Cork*

◆ **Casa Della Rosa** Carrigrohane ☏ (021) 385279 rm4 Apr-Oct **A**

◆ **Hill View House** Killard ☏ (021) 385119 rm4 Mar-Oct **A**

BOOLAVOGUE *Co Wexford*

FH Ballyorley House ☏ (054) 66287 rm3 **A**

BOYLE *Co Roscommon*

◆ **Fores Park House** ☏ (079) 62227 rm8 **A**

FH Rushfield Croghan ☏ (079) 62276 rm5 Mar-Nov **A**

BRITTAS BAY *Co Wicklow*

◆ **Parkwood House** ☏ (0404) 7221 rm5 Mar-Nov **B**

BUNCRANA *Co Donegal*

◆ **St Bridget's** ☏ (077) 61319 rm4 **A**

CAHIR *Co Tipperary*

FH Lissava House ☏ (052) 41117 rm4 May-mid Sep **A**

◆ **Wishing Well** Tipperary Rd ☏ (052) 41468 rm6 **A**

CAHIRCIVEEN *Co Kerry*

FH Valentia View ☏ (0667) 2227 rm6 Mar-Nov **A**

CAPPOQUIN *Co Waterford*

◆ **Richmond House** ☏ (058) 54278 rm9 Feb-Oct **B**

CARLOW *Co Carlow*

◆ **Dolmen House** ☏ (0503) 42444 rm5 Jul-Sep **A**

CARRICK-ON-SHANNON *Co Leitrim*

◆ **Scregg House** ☏ (078) 20210 rm4 Mar-Nov **A**

CASHEL *Co Tipperary*

FH Knock Saint Lour House ☏ (062) 61172 rm8 Apr-Oct **A**

CASTLEBAR *Co Mayo*

◆ **Heneghan's** Newtown St ☏ (094) 21883 rm6 Closed Dec 24-31 **A**

CASTLEDAWSON *Co Londonderry*

FH Moyola Lodge ☏ (0648) 68224 rm3 **B**

CASTLEFINN *Co Donegal*

FH Gortfad ☏ (074) 46135 rm5 Apr-Sep **A**

CASTLEFREKE *Co Cork*

FH Kilkern House ☏ (023) 40643 rm6 **A**

CASTLEGREGORY *Co Kerry*

FH Griffins Country ☏ (066) 39147 rm6 Apr-Oct **A**

CLIFFONY *Co Sligo*

◆ **Villa Rosa** Bunduff ☏ (071) 66173 rm6 May-Sep **A**

CLONAKILTY *Co Cork*

FH Desert House ☏ (023) 33331 rm8 **A**

FH Hillside ☏ (023) 33139 rm5 Mar-Sep **A**

FH Liscubba House Lyre ☏ (023) 48679 rm6 **A**

CLONBUR *Co Galway*

◆ **Fairhill** ☏ (092) 46176 rm10 Apr-Oct **A**

CORK *Co Cork*

◆ **Garnish House** ☏ (021) 275111 rm6 **B**

◆ **Killarney House** Western Rd ☏ (021) 270179 rm18 **B**

COROFIN *Co Clare*

FH Fergus View ☏ (065) 27606 rm6 Apr-Oct **A**

FH Inchiquin ☏ (065) 27731 rm5 Mar-Oct **A**

CROSSHAVEN *Co Cork*

◆ **Whispering Pines** ☏ (021) 831448 rm15 Closed Dec 21-31 **B**

CRUSHEEN *Co Clare*

FH Lahardan ☏ (065) 27128 rm8 **A**

CULDAFF *Co Donegal*

◆ **McGory's** ☏ (077) 79104 rm6 Jun-Aug **A**

CUSHENDUN *Co Antrim*

FH Villa 185 Torr Rd ☏ (026674) 252 rm4 Apr-Oct **A**

DINGLE *Co Kerry*

◆ **Alpine** ☏ (066) 51250 rm15 Mar-Oct **A**

◆ **Milltown House** Milltown ☏ (066) 51372 rm7 Apr-1 Oct **B**

DONEGAL *Co Donegal*

◆ **Ardeevin** Lough Eske, Barnesmore ☏ (073) 21790 rm5 Apr-Oct **A**

◆ **White Gables** Tirconnail St ☏ (073) 21106 rm7 Etr-Oct **A**

DOOLIN *Co Clare*

FH Emohrou Cliffs of Moher Rd ☏ (065) 74171 rm4 Mar-Oct **A**

FH Horse Shoe ☏ (065) 74006 rm6 mid Mar-Oct **A**

DOWNPATRICK *Co Down*

FH Havine Farm 51 Bally Donnel Rd ☏ 242 rm4 **B**

DUBLIN *Co Dublin*

Dublin, capital of the Republic of Ireland, is a delightful city of low-profile buildings, many of them outstanding examples of 18th-century architecture. Birthplace and inspiration of many great authors, its contrasts are apparent everywhere: sweeping avenues and intimate side streets, chic shopping and smokey pubs, distinguished museums and colleges and fascinating shops.

History is at your elbow at every turn. Long streets of stately Georgian houses and spacious, peaceful squares and parks take you back into the 19th century.

A good place to begin a tour of this compact city is O'Connell Bridge, which leads to the city's main shopping area, O'Connell Street. The best buys are local products such as Irish linen and lace, homespun tweeds and knitwear. The top fashion houses of Dublin are now world-famous and make special provision for tourists. The quality and design of contemporary jewellery and handicrafts are especially good. Waterford crystal glassware is another popular gift

item, while for old glass and silver Dublin offers fascinating antique shops where bargains can still be found.
City attractions include Parnell Square, one of Dublin's earliest and most attractive squares of handsome, brick-faced Georgian houses; Charlemont House, which contains the Hugh Lane Municipal Gallery of Modern Art; St Mary's Pro-Cathedral; Nassau Street, with its bookstores; Merrion Square, containing a house once occupied by Oscar Wilde's parents; the National Gallery, housing more than 2, 000 works; the National Museum, containing a fascinating collection of Irish treasures; and the Civic Museum.
St Patrick's and Christ Church cathedrals are also worth visiting, while a tourist 'must' is Dublin Castle, guided tours of whose splendid state apartments are offered every half hour. Visitors can also attend a 30-minute film show at the Guinness Brewery, and later sample the famous beverage.
EATING OUT Prime beef, locally raised lamb and pork, free-range poultry and abundant seafood are widely available in Dublin restaurants, together with traditional Irish dishes such as boiled bacon and cabbage and Irish stew. Another speciality is *colcannon* – cooked potatos diced and fried with onions and cabbage or leeks and covered with cream. Other specialities include shellfish such as lobster, Dublin Bay prawns, and oysters. *Le Coq Hardi*, in Pembroke Road, and Ernie's, in Mulberry Gardens, are both excellent, if expensive, restaurants. More moderately priced, Rudyard's in Crown Alley is justly popular. Dublin also has a wide selection of pubs which, with their relaxed atmosphere, have been likened to the cafés of Paris.

◆ **Burtenshaw's "Marian"** 21 Upper Gardiner St ☎ (01) 744129 rm6 **A**

◆ **St-Jude's** 17 Pembroke Pk ☎ (01) 680928 rm8 **B**

DUNCORMICK *Co Wexford*

FH Ingleside ☎ (051) 63154 rm6 Mar-Oct **A**

DUNDRUM *Co Tipperary*

FH Cappamurra House ☎ (062) 71127 rm8 Apr-Oct **A**

DUN LAOGHAIRE *Co Dublin*

◆ **Ferry House** 15 Clarinda Pk ☎ (01) 808301 rm6 **B**

DUNMANWAY *Co Cork*

◆ **Sunville** ☎ (023) 45269 rm4 Apr-Oct **A**

DUNSHAUGHLIN *Co Meath*

◆ **Killeentierna House** Powderlough ☎ (01) 259722 rm4 **A**

ENNISKILLEN *Co Fermanagh*

◆ **Interlaken** 54 Forthill St ☎ (0365) 22274 rm4 Closed Dec **A**

FH Lackaboy Tempo Rd ☎ (0365) 22488 rm8 **A**

FH Lakeview 6m NW on A46 ☎ (036564) 263 rm5 **A**

FERNS *Co Wexford*

FH Clone House ☎ (054) 66113 rm4 Apr-Sep **A**

FIVEMILEBRIDGE *Co Cork*

◆ **Au Soleil** ☎ (021) 888208 rm4 Jun-Oct **A**

FOULKESMILL *Co Wexford*

FH Crosbie's ☎ (051) 63616 rm10 Mar-Oct **A**

FH Horetown House ☎ (051) 63633 rm12 Closed Jan 11-Feb & Xmas **B**

GALWAY *Co Galway*

H Bay View House Gentian Hill ☎ (091) 22116 rm6 Closed Dec & Jan **A**

H Fortaleza Circular Rd ☎ (091) 22845 rm5 Jul-Sep **A**

◆ **Knockrea House** Lower Salthill ☎ (091) 21794 rm9 **A**

◆ **Roncalli House** 24 Whitestrand Av ☎ (091) 64159 rm6 **A**

GLENEALY *Co Wicklow*

FH Ballyknocken House ☎ (0404) 5627 rm8 Jan 5-Dec 22 **A**

GLENEASK *Co Sligo*

FH Lough Talt Inn ☎ (071) 81072 rm3 Apr-Sep **A**

GOREY *Co Wexford*

FH Woodlands Ballynastragh ☎ (0402) 7125 rm5 Apr-Oct **A**

INISTIOGE *Co Kilkenny*

◆ **Ashville** Kilmacshane ☎ (056) 58460 rm5 Closed Xmas **A**

FH Cullintra House The Rower ☎ (051) 23614 rm5 **A**

KENMARE *Co Kerry*

FH Bay View Greenane ☎ (064) 41383 rm6 May-Oct **A**

◆ **Ceann Mara** ☎ (064) 41220 rm6 Apr-Oct **A**

◆ **Commercial** ☎ (064) 41453 rm11 Mar-Sep **A**

FH Sea Shore Tubrid ☎ (064) 41270 rm3 Jun-Sep **A**

FH Templenoe House Greenane ☎ (064) 41538 rm5 May-Sep **B**

KILCULLEN *Co Kildare*

FH Chapel View Gormanstown ☎ (045) 81325 rm9 **B**

KILGARVAN *Co Kerry*

FH Glanlea ☎ (064) 85314 rm8 Feb-Oct **A**

FH Hawthorn ☎ (064) 85326 rm6 Apr-Sep **A**

KILLAMASTER *Co Carlow*

FH Killamaster House ☎ (0503) 63654 rm4 Apr-Oct **A**

KILLARNEY *Co Kerry*

◆ **Avignon** Cork Rd ☎ (064) 31229 rm7 Apr-Nov **A**

◆ **Glendale House** Dromadessert, Tralee Rd ☎ (064) 32152 rm6 Mar-mid Dec **B**

◆ **Green Acres** Fossa ☎ (064) 31454 rm8 **B**

◆ **Killarney Villa** Cork Rd ☎ (064) 31878 Closed mid Dec-mid Jan **A**

◆ **Loch Lein** Fossa ☎ (064) 31260 rm8 Mar-Oct **A**

◆ **Purple Heather** Gap of Dunloe ☎ (064) 44266 rm5 Apr-Sep **A**

◆ **Shraheen House** Ballycasheen ☎ (064) 31286 rm6 Mar-Nov **A**

◆ **St-Rita's Villa** Mill Rd ☎ (064) 31517 rm6 Mar-Dec 15 **A**

◆ **Sunset Villa** Dunrine ☎ (064) 31124 rm5 **A**

KILLESHANDRA *Co Cavan*

FH Derreskit ☎ (049) 34156 rm5 **A**

KILLORGLIN *Co Kerry*

◆ **Hillcrest** Killarney Rd ☎ (066) 61552 rm5 **A**

H Torine House ☎ (066) 61352 rm8 **A**

KILMACRENAN *Co Donegal*

◆ **Angler's Haven** ☎ (074) 39015 rm10 Feb-Oct **A**

KILMEADEN *Co Waterford*

◆ **Hillview Lodge** Adamstown ☎ (051) 84230 rm5 **A**

KILMEENA *Co Mayo*

FH Seapoint House Westport ☎ (098) 41254 rm7 Mar-Oct **A**

KILRANE *Co Wexford*

FH O'Leary's St-Helen's Bay ☎ (053) 33134 rm10 **A**

KILTOOM *Co Roscommon*

H Ballycreggan House ☎ (0902) 88101 rm4 Apr-Oct **A**

KINSALEBEG *Co Waterford*

◆ **Blackwater House** ☎ (024) 92543 rm5 **A**

◆ **The Gables** ☎ (024) 92739 rm5 May-Oct **A**

KNOCKFERRY *Co Galway*

FH Knockferry Lodge ☎ (091) 80122 rm10 May-Sep **B**

KNOCKNAREA *Co Sligo*

FH Primrose Grange ☎ (071) 62005 rm8 Feb-Nov **A**

KNOCKRAHA *Co Cork*

FH Ashton Grove ☎ (021) 821537 rm4 Apr-Oct **A**

LARNE *Co Antrim*

◆ **Derrin** 2 Prince's Gdns ☎ (0574) 73269 rm7 **A**

LISBURN *Co Antrim*

FH Brook Lodge 79 Old Ballynahinch Rd ☎ (084663) 454 rm5 **A**

LISDOONVARNA *Co Clare*

◆ **Ballinalacken Castle** ☎ (065) 74025 rm6 Jun-Sep **B**

◆ **Sunville** ☎ (065) 74065 rm6 **A**

LISTOWEL *Co Kerry*

◆ **North County House** ☎ (068) 21238 rm8 **A**

LOUGH ARROW *Co Sligo*

◆ **Cromleach Lodge** ☎ (071) 65155 rm9 Closed Dec 24-31 **B**

MIDLETON *Co Cork*

FH Wilton House ☎ (021) 667327 rm3 **A**

MILLSTREET *Co Waterford*

FH The Castle Cappagh ☎ (058) 68049 rm5 Apr-Oct **A**

MOYARD *Co Galway*

FH Rose Cottage ☎ (095) 41082 rm6 May-Sep **A**

MULLINAVAT *Co Kilkenny*

◆ **Tory View** ☎ (051) 98124 rm5 **B**

MULRANY *Co Mayo*

◆ **Avondale House** ☎ (098) 36105 rm8 Apr-Oct **A**

NAAS *Co Kildare*

FH Setanta Caragh ☎ (045) 76481 rm6 Apr-Oct **A**

FH Westown Farm Johnstown ☎ (045) 97006 rm5 Mar-mid Dec **A**

NAVAN *Co Meath*

FH Balreask House ☎ (046) 21155 rm4 Apr-Oct 15 **A**

NEWCASTLE *Co Dublin*

FH Ringwood Hazel Hatch ☎ (01) 288220 rm3 Closed Dec 21-31 **B**

NEW ROSS *Co Wexford*

◆ **Inishross House** 96 Mary St ☎ (051) 21335 rm6 **A**

NINE MILE HOUSE *Co Tipperary*

◆ **Grand Inn** ☎ (051) 47035 rm5 **A**

OGONNELLOE *Co Clare*

◆ **Lantern House** ☎ (0619) 23034 rm6 Closed Nov **A**

OVENS *Co Cork*

◆ **Milestone** Carrigane ☎ (021) 872562 rm5 **A**

PORTLAOISE *Co Laois*

◆ **Knockmay Town House** ☎ (0502) 22509 rm6 **A**

◆ **O'Sullivans** ☎ (0502) 22774 rm5 **A**

PORTRUSH *Co Antrim*

FH Loguestown 59 Magheraboy Rd ☎ (0265) 822742 rm7 Closed Dec **B**

◆ **Mount Royal** 2 Mount Royal ☎ (0265) 823342 rm13 **A**

PROSPEROUS *Co Kildare*

FH Silverspring House ☎ (045) 68481 rm4 Apr-Oct **A**

RATHDRUM *Co Wicklow*

◆ **Abhainn Mor House** Corballis ☎ (0404) 46330 rm6 Feb-Nov **A**

◆ **Avonbrae** ☎ (0404) 46198 rm6 Mar-Nov 12 **B**

◆ **St Bridget** ☎ (0404) 46477 rm4 Closed Dec 24-31 **A**

RATHNEW *Co Wicklow*

FH Broadlough House ☎ (0404) 67253 rm5 Apr-Oct **A**

ROSCOMMON *Co Roscommon*

FH Munsboro House Sligo Rd ☎ (0903) 26375 rm4 Mar-Oct **A**

ROSCREA *Co Tipperary*

FH Streamstown House ☎ (0505) 21519 rm6 Apr-Sep 10 **A**

ROSSDUFF *Co Waterford*

FH Elton Lodge ☎ (051) 82117 rm5 Jun-Sep **A**

RYLANE *Co Cork*

FH Flagmount Lodge ☎ (021) 339089 **B**

SKIBBEREEN *Co Cork*

FH Abbeystrewery ☎ (028) 21713 rm5 Jun-Sep **A**

SLIGO *Co Sligo*

◆ **Aisling** Cairns Hill ☎ (071) 60704 rm6 **A**

FH Hillside Glencar Rd ☎ (071) 42808 rm4 Apr-mid Oct **A**

◆ **Tree Tops** Cleveragh Rd ☎ (071) 60160 rm6 **A**

SPIDDAL (SPIDDLE) *Co Galway*

◆ **Ard Aoibhinn** Cnocan Glas ☎ (091) 83179 rm6 **A**

◆ **Ardmor Country House** Greenhill ☎ (091) 83145 rm8 Mar-Nov **A**

STEAMSTOWN *Co Westmeath*

FH Woodlands ☎ (044) 26414 rm6 Mar-Oct **A**

TAGOAT *Co Wexford*

FH Orchard Park ☎ (053) 32182 rm8 **A**

TERMONBARRY *Co Longford*

◆ **Shannon Side** ☎ (043) 26052 rm6 **A**

THE ROWER *Co Kilkenny*

FH Garranavabby House ☎ (051) 23613 rm3 Etr-Sep **A**

◆ **Hillcrest** ☎ (051) 23722 rm5 **A**

TIMOLIN *Co Kildare*

◆ **Woodcourte** ☎ (0507) 24167 rm4 **A**

TIPPERARY *Co Tipperary*

◆ **Ach-na-Sheen House** ☎ (062) 51298 rm10 **B**

FH Barronstown House Emly Rd ☎ (062) 55130 rm6 Mar-Nov **A**

TOBERCURRY *Co Sligo*

◆ **Cruckaun** ☎ (071) 85188 rm5 Closed Xmas **A**

TRALEE *Co Kerry*

◆ **Cnoc Mhuire** Upper Oakpark Rd ☎ (066) 26027 rm5 **A**

TULLAMORE *Co Offaly*

◆ **Moorhill House** ☎ (0506) 21395 rm5 **B**

TULLOW *Co Carlow*

◆ **Laburnum Lodge** Castledermot Rd ☎ (0503) 51718 rm4 **A**

VALLEYMOUNT *Co Wicklow*

H Escombe Cottage ☎ (045) 67157 rm4 Mar-Oct **A**

VICARSTOWN *Co Laois*

◆ **Vicarstown Inn** ☎ (0502) 25189 rm6 Apr-Oct **A**

WATERFORD *Co Waterford*

FH Ashbourne House Slieverue ☎ (051) 32037 rm7 Apr-Oct **A**

◆ **Blenheim House** Blenheim Heights ☎ (051) 74115 rm6 **A**

◆ **Diamond Hill House** Slieverue ☎ (051) 32855 rm10 **B**

◆ **Dunroven** 5 Cluain a Laoi Cork Rd ☎ (051) 74743 rm7 **A**

◆ **Half Way House** ☎ (051) 76055 rm4 Jan-Nov **A**

◆ **Knockboy House** Dunmore Rd ☎ (051) 73484 rm6 Feb-Nov **A**

WATERVILLE *Co Kerry*

◆ **Smuggler's Inn** ☎ (0667) 4330 rm6 Feb 15-Nov 2 **B**

WESTPORT *Co Mayo*

FH Rath-A-Rosa Rosbeg ☎ (098) 25348 rm4 Mar 15-Oct **A**

WEXFORD *Co Wexford*

◆ **Faythe House** ☎ (053) 22249 rm10 **A**

◆ **Rathaspeck Manor** Rathaspeck ☎ (053) 42661 rm7 Jun-Oct **B**

◆ **Whitford House** ☎ (053) 43845 rm25 Closed Dec 21-Jan 5 **B**

WICKLOW *Co Wicklow*

FH Lissadell House Ashtown ☎ (0404) 67458 rm4 Mar-Nov **A**

◆ **Marine** Church Hill ☎ (0404) 68252 rm4 **A**

◆ **Thomond House** St Patricks Rd Upper ☎ (0404) 67940 rm5 Mar-Oct **A**

YOUGHAL *Co Cork*

◆ **Carriglea** ☎ (024) 92520 rm4 Jun-Oct **A**

FH Cherrymount ☎ (024) 97110 rm6 **A**

Devon View Pearse Square **B**

A traditional thatched cottage near Ballinakill, Connemara, Co Galway.

ITALY

FACTS & FIGURES

Capital: Roma (Rome)
Language: Italian
IDD code: 39. To call the UK dial 00 44
Currency: Italian lira (Lit)
Local time: GMR+1 (Summer GMT+2)
Emergency Services: Police, Fire and Ambulance 113

Business hours

Banks:
0830–1330 and 1530–1630 Mon–Fri
Shops:
0830–1300 and 1530–1930 Mon–Sat

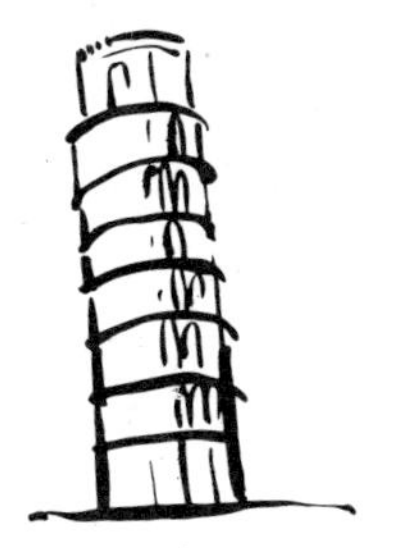

Average daily temperatures:
Roma °C

Jan 8	Jul 25
Mar 11	Sep 21
May 18	Nov 12

Tourist Information:
Italian State Tourist Office (ENIT)
UK 1 Princes Street
London W1R 8AY
Tel 01–408 1254
USA 630 Fifth Ave, Suite 1565
New York, NY 10111
Tel (212) 245–4822

Imagine a land with a superb climate, set in a sparkling sea, almost surrounded by thousands of miles of beaches and spectacular, rugged coastline. Fill it with artistic, architectural and historic treasures; introduce a superb musical tradition; add breathtaking mountains and tranquil lakes, enchanting offshore islands, orange and lemon groves, vineyards, great cities, spas and resorts – plus good hotels, fine cuisine, splendid wines, and a unique atmosphere created by a combination of the country's myriad attractions and the character of its people.

Italy is a land of striking contrasts, hardly surprising, perhaps, since it stretches from snow-peaked mountains in the north to the warm and sunny waters far south in the Mediterranean. It is also a land of dramatic history and great civilisations, of art treasures and of unforgettable historical architectural achievements standing in the midst of the busy, bustling life of cities and towns where the modern style of Italy harmonises happily with its wonderful past.

Italian cities, towns and its very landscape reflect its rich and diverse history, but above all the wonders of Italy and the unparalleled genius of its artistic giants are to be found in almost unbelievable profusion in the art galleries, museums and palaces where the Italians proudly display their artistic heritage.

HOW TO GET THERE

BY CAR

There are several ways of getting to Italy but you will probably travel through France or Switzerland. The major passes, closed in winter, are served by rail or road tunnels. The distance to Milan from the Channel ports is approximately 650–700 miles, requiring one or two overnight stops. Roma is 360 miles further south. Car-sleeper services run during the summer: from Boulogne, Brussels, s'Hertogenbosch or Paris to Milan; from Boulogne to Bologna; Paris to Rimini.

For details of the AA's Overseas Routes Service consult the Contents page.

SPEED LIMITS

In built-up areas 50 kph (31 mph); outside built-up areas 90 kph (56 mph)* and on motorways 130 kph (81 mph)†. Motorcycles under 149 cc are not allowed on motorways.

* One some dual carriageways there is a weekday speed restriction of 110 kph (68 mph).
† This limit applies to weekdays; at weekends, on public holidays and between the dates 14 Jul–2 Sep and 20 Dec–7 Jan the limit is 110 kph (68 mph).

PARKING

There is a blue zone (*zona disco*) in most cities; where parked vehicles must display a disc. Disc park operates 0800–2000 hrs on working days. Discs can be obtained from petrol stations and automobile organisations. There are also green zones (*zona verde*) where parking is absolutely prohibited between 0800–0930 hrs and 1430–1600 hrs.

BY TRAIN

If you do not have a Eurail or InterRail pass, national and regional tickets are

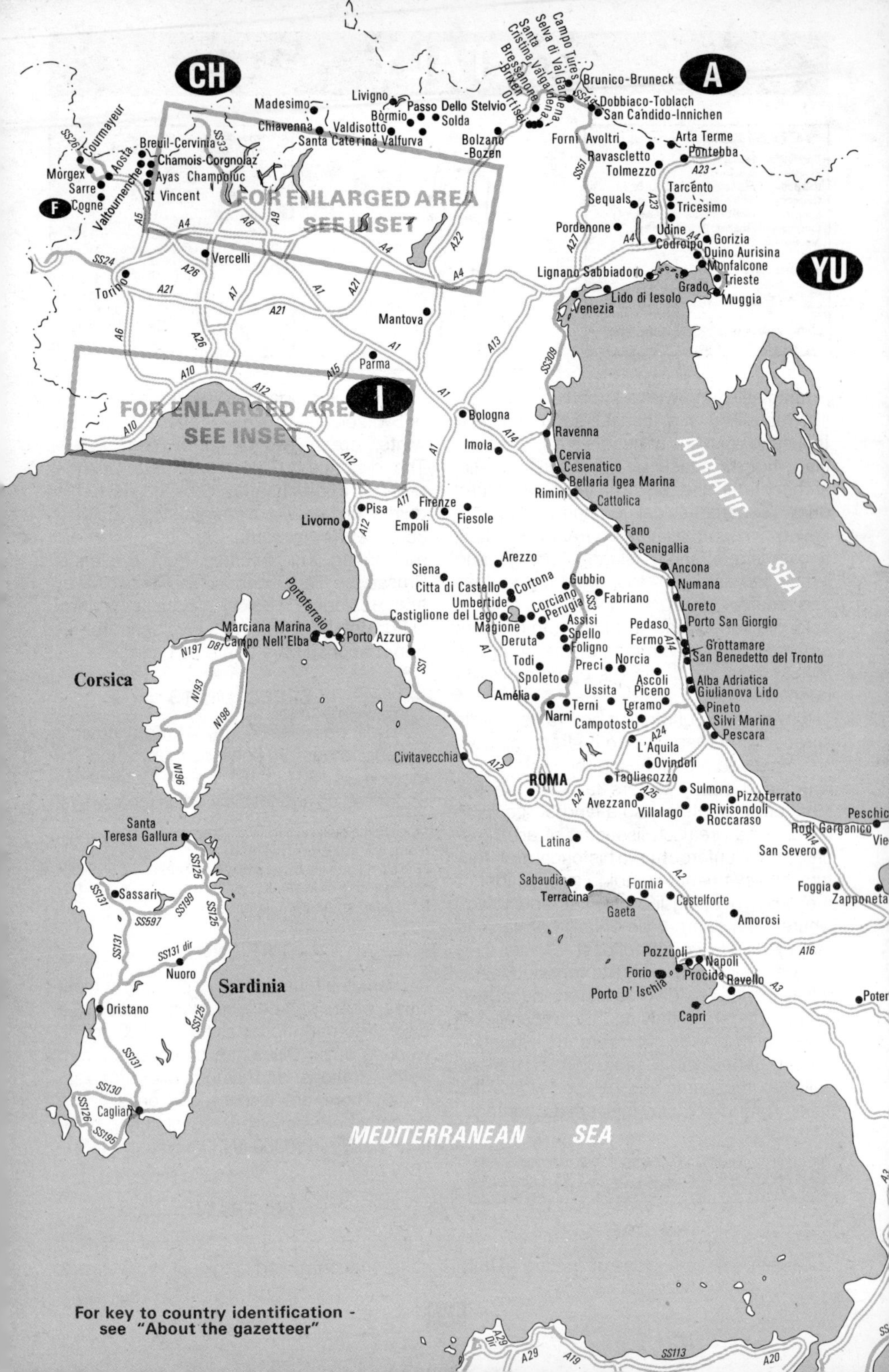

For key to country identification - see "About the gazetteer"

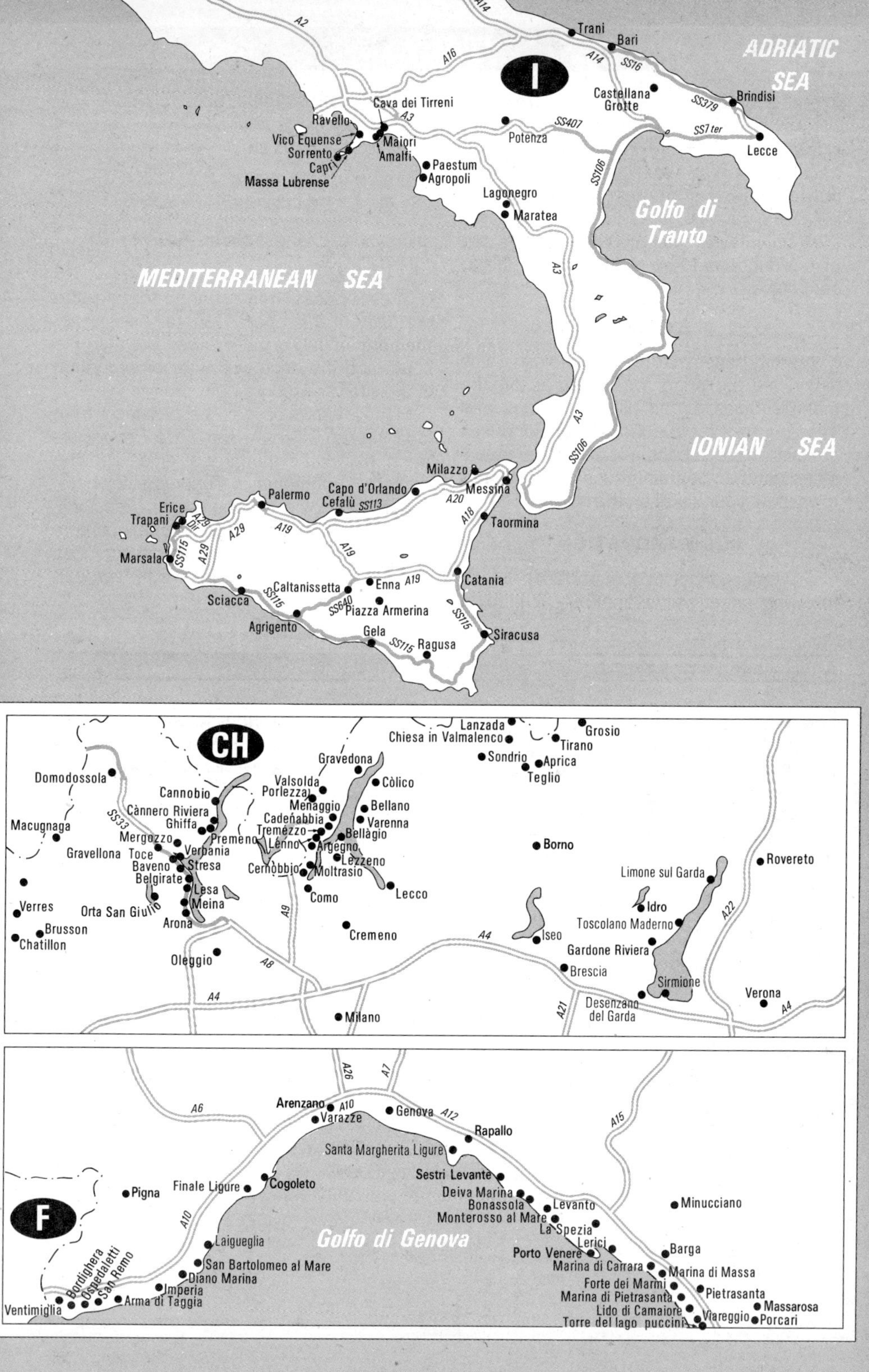

I
ADRIATIC SEA
MEDITERRANEAN SEA
IONIAN SEA
Golfo di Tranto
A14
A2
A16
A3
SS16
SS379
SS407
SS7 ter
SS106
Trani
Bari
Castellana Grotte
Brindisi
Lecce
Potenza
Cava dei Tirreni
Ravello
Vico Equense
Sorrento
Capri
Massa Lubrense
Maiori
Amalfi
Paestum
Agropoli
Lagonegro
Maratea
Milazzo
Messina
Capo d'Orlando
Palermo
Cefalù
SS113
A20
A18
Taormina
Erice
Trapani
A29
A29 Dir
A19
SS115
Marsala
Caltanissetta
Enna
Catania
Sciacca
SS640
Piazza Armerina
Agrigento
Gela
Ragusa
Siracusa
CH
Lanzada
Grosio
Chiesa in Valmalenco
Tirano
Sondrio
Aprica
Teglio
Gravedona
Domodossola
Valsolda
Porlezza
Còlico
Cannobio
Menaggio
Bellano
Cànnero Riviera
Cadenabbia
Varenna
Ghiffa
Tremezzo
Bellàgio
Macugnaga
Mergozzo
Premeno
Lenno
Argegno
Borno
Gravellona Toce
Verbania
Lezzeno
Rovereto
Baveno
Stresa
Cernobbio
Moltrasio
Limone sul Garda
Belgirate
Lesa
Lecco
Como
Idro
Verres
Meina
Orta San Giulio
Toscolano Maderno
Brusson
Arona
Cremeno
Iseo
Chatillon
Gardone Riviera
Oleggio
SS33
A9
A8
A4
A22
A21
Brescia
Sirmione
Verona
Desenzano del Garda
Milano
F
A26
A7
A6
A10
A12
A15
Arenzano
Varazze
Genova
Rapallo
Santa Margherita Ligure
Sestri Levante
Pigna
Finale Ligure
Cogoleto
Deiva Marina
Bonassola
Levanto
Minucciano
Monterosso al Mare
La Spezia
Golfo di Genova
Laigueglia
Lerici
Porto Venere
Barga
San Bartolomeo al Mare
Marina di Carrara
Marina di Massa
Bordighera
Ospedaletti
San Remo
Diano Marina
Forte dei Marmi
Imperia
Pietrasanta
Marina di Pietrasanta
Arma di Taggia
Lido di Camaiore
Massarosa
Ventimiglia
Viareggio
Porcari
Torre del lago puccini

available for rail travel within Italy. 'Travel-at-Will' tickets (Biglietto turistico libera circolazione) allow unlimited travel on any Italian train. They are available at tourist agencies outside Italy or from main railway stations inside the country. There is also a 'Chilometrico' ticket valid for 3,000 km which can give reductions to up to five people at the same time.

BY BUS

Intercity buses may be preferable to trains if you are exploring remote areas off the main rail lines or the hills of Umbria and Tuscany, for example. Tickets for city buses are available in tabacchi stores, most news-stands and on boarding buses – remember to validate your ticket on the bus.

ACCOMMODATION

Our selection of accommodation in the following gazetteer is generally limited to establishments offering accommodation for less than L45,144.

The price bands are:

A L21384–33264
B L33264–45144

taking an exchange rate at L2376 = £1
L1431 = US $1

These prices may change during the currency of this book. Generally speaking, the north of Italy is more expensive than the south and the price of the accommodation is likely to vary accordingly.

More information can be obtained from local tourist offices – the *Ente Provinciale per il Turismo* in the largest cities and the *Azienda Automoma di Turismo* elsewhere. Otherwise, look for the signs *Pensione, Albergo, Locanda, Soggiorno* or *camere libre* (rooms to let in private residences which sometimes cost significantly less than other accommodation).

Abbreviations: pza piazza

AGRIGENTO *Agrigento*
See **SICILIA (SICILY)**

AGROPOLI *Salerno*

H Carola ☎ (0974) 823005 rm34 **A**

H Florida (n.rest) ☎ (0974) 838051 rm45 Jun-Sep **A**

H Mare ☎ (0974) 823666 rm41 **A**

H Serenella ☎ (0974) 823333 rm32 **A**

ALBA ADRIATICA *Teramo*

H Atlas Lungomare Marconi 284 ☎ (0861) 72393 rm35 May-Sep **B**

H Caravel via Toscana 20 ☎ (0861) 72648 rm36 May 19-Sep 22 **A**

H Doge Lungomare Marconi ☎ (0861) 72508 rm44 May-Sep **A**

H Eden Lungomare Marconi 438 ☎ (0861) 77251 rm48 May-Sep **B**

H Excelsior Lungomare Marconi 160 ☎ (0861) 72345 rm56 May 20-Sep 20 **B**

H King Lungomare Marconi 83 ☎ (0861) 72333 rm70 May 10-Sep 25 **B**

H Lido Lungomare Marconi 194 ☎ (0861) 72666 rm55 May-Sep **B**

H Meripol Lungomare Marconi ☎ (0861) 77744 rm44 May 18-Sep 15 **B**

H Petite Fleur Lungomare Marconi ☎ (0861) 72387 rm30 **A**

H President Lungomare Marconi 124 ☎ (0861) 72520 rm76 May 15-Sep 20 **B**

H Sporting Lungomare Marconi 414 ☎ (0861) 72510 rm40 May 15-Sep 15 **B**

H Stefania via Treviso ☎ (0861) 77107 rm12 May-Sep **A**

AMALFI *Salerno*

H Bussola ☎ (089) 871533 rm65 **B**

H Della Principessa (n.rest) ☎ (089) 831333 rm8 **A**

H Fontana (n.rest) ☎ (089) 871530 rm17 Mar 26-Oct 15 **A**

H Garden House (n.rest) ☎ (089) 871344 rm9 Apr-Oct **B**

H Lidomare (n.rest) ☎ (089) 871332 rm13 **A**

★★★**Miramalfi** ☎ (089) 871588 rm44 **A**

At **MINORI**(3km E)

H Bristol ☎ (089) 877013 rm43 **A**

H Settebello ☎ (089) 877619 rm20 **A**

H Villa Romana ☎ (089) 877237 rm53 **A**

AMELIA *Terni*

H Anita via Roma 31 ☎ (05022) 982146 rm23 **A**

AMOROSI *Benevento*

H Ombrellone via Ortale ☎ (0824) 970330 rm17 **B**

H Piana via Telese-Amorosi ☎ (0824) 970510 rm19 **B**

ANCONA *Ancona*

H Adriatica (n.rest) via F-Filzi 2 ☎ (071) 55764 rm18 **A**

H Fortuna pza F-Rosselli 15 ☎ (071) 42662 rm58 **B**

H Garden (n.rest) via della Vittoria 7 ☎ (071) 200374 rm14 **A**

H International ☎ (071) 801001 rm28 **B**

H Roma E Pace via G-Leopardi 1 ☎ (071) 202007 rm74 **B**

H Rosa (n.rest) pza F-Rosselli 3 ☎ (071) 41388 rm36 **A**

H Viale viale della Vittoria 23 ☎ (071) 201861 rm26 **A**

AOSTA *Aosta*

H Cecchin via P-Romano 27 ☎ (0165) 45262 rm10 **B**

H Coin Vert corso Ivrea 112 ☎ (0165) 41485 rm33 **B**

H Excelsior (n.rest) via Chambéry 206 ☎ (0165) 41461 rm14 **B**

H Geraniums ☎ (0165) 552583 rm12 **A**

★★**Gran Paradiso** via Binel 12 ☎ (0165) 40654 rm33 **B**

H Joli via delle Valli Valdostane 11 ☎ (0165) 35747 rm19 **B**

H Milleluci ☎ (0165) 44274 rm16 **B**

H Mont Fleury (n.rest) via P-S-Berbardo 26 ☎ (0165) 551926 rm10 **A**

★★**Turin** via Torino 14 ☎ (0165) 44593 rm51 **B**

APRICA *Sondrio*

H Cristallo ☎ (0342) 746159 rm33 **B**

H Villa Maria ☎ (0342) 746054 rm33 **A**

AQUILA, L' *L'Aquila*

M Amiternum Bivio S-Antonio ☎ (0862) 315757 rm60 **B**

H Castello pza Battaglione Alpini ☎ (0862) 29147 rm44 **B**

H Centrale via Simonetto 3 ☎ (0862) 64211 rm21 **A**

H Gran Panorama ☎ (0862) 315351 rm48 **B**

H Italia corso V-Emanuele 79 ☎ (0862) 20566 rm36 **A**

H Leon d'Oro via Dragonetti 6 ☎ (0862) 26178 rm15 **A**

H Milani via T-Marie 30 ☎ (0862) 27365 rm11 **A**

ARENZANO *Genova*

H Ena via Matteotti 12 ☎ (010) 9112941 rm23 **A**

★★★**Miramare** corso Matteotti 138 ☎ (010) 9127325 rm45 **A**

AREZZO *Arezzo*

H Astoria (n.rest) via G-Monaco 54 ☎ (0575) 24361 rm32 **B**

H Cecco corso Italia 215 ☎ (0575) 20986 rm42 **A**

H Toscana (n.rest) via M-Perennio ☎ (0575) 21692 rm5 **A**

H Truciolini via Pacinotti 6 ☎ (0575) 380219 rm24 **A**

ARGEGNO *Como*

H Argegno ☎ (031) 821455 rm15 **B**

★**Belvedere** ☎ (031) 821116 rm16 **B**

H Griglia ☎ (031) 821147 rm8 **A**

ARMA DI TAGGIA *Imperia*

H Anna via Queirolo 74 ☎ (0184) 43555 rm41 **A**

H Capoverde via Aurelia 207 ☎ (0184) 42942 rm22 Closed Oct 12-Dec 25 **A**

H Eden via N-Pesce 36 ☎ (0184) 43000 rm29 **A**

H Europa via Stazione 137 ☎ (0184) 43797 rm28 Closed Oct & Nov **A**

H Graziella via Lido 3 ☎ (0184) 43140 rm20 **A**

H Miramare via Nazario Sauro 32 ☎ (0184) 43537 rm56 Closed Oct 10-Dec 20 **B**

ARONA *Novara*

H Clipper ☎ (0322) 3364 rm8 **B**

H Cristallo ☎ (0322) 3364 rm8 **B**

H Florida Meublè ☎ (0322) 46212 rm29 **B**

H San Carlo ☎ (0322) 45315 rm9 **A**

H Spagna ☎ (0322) 3052 rm17 **B**

H Splendor dal Bimbo ☎ (0322) 3316 rm15 **A**

ARTA TERME *Udine*

H Alla Fonte Frazione Avosacco ☎ (0433) 92105 rm28 **B**

H Poldo ☎ (0433) 92056 rm33 **B**

H Salon Frazione Piano d'Arta ☎ (0433) 92003 rm26 **A**

H Trieste Fraz Avosacco ☎ (0433) 92061 rm57 **A**

ASCOLI PICENO *Ascoli Piceno*

H Gioli viale A-de-Gasperi 14 ☎ (0736) 52450 rm56 **A**

H Pennile (n.rest) via G-Spalvieri ☎ (0736) 41645 rm28 **B**

H Piceno via Minnuccia 10 ☎ (0736) 52553 rm32 **A**

ASSISI *Perugia*

H Berti pza S-Pietro 24 ☎ (075) 813466 rm10 **A**

H Poppy Inn via Campagna 51 ☎ (075) 8038041 rm9 **B**

H San Francesco via S-Francesco 48 ☎ (075) 812281 rm45 **B**

H San Pietro pza S-Pietro 5 ☎ (075) 812452 rm46 **B**

★★**Umbra** via degli Archi 6 ☎ (075) 812240 rm27 **B**

AVEZZANO *L'Aquila*

M Belvedere ☎ (0863) 59171 rm41 **B**

H Bianchi ☎ (0863) 20388 rm40 **A**

H Velino ☎ (0863) 34263 rm26 **A**

AYAS-CHAMPOLUC *Aosta*

H Alpi Rosa ☎ (0125) 307135 rm27 **A**

H Anna Maria ☎ (0125) 307128 rm20 Seasonal **B**

H Castor ☎ (0125) 307117 rm32 **B**

H Favre ☎ (0125) 307131 rm19 **A**

H Monte Cervino ☎ (0125) 307134 rm33 **A**

BARGA *Lucca*

H Pergola via S-Antonia ☎ (0583) 711239 rm23 **A**

H Villa Libano via del Sasso 6 ☎ (0583) 73059 rm28 **A**

BARI *Bari*

H Adria via L-Zuppetta 10 ☎ (080) 540699 rm38 **A**

H Astoria via G-Bozzi 59 ☎ (080) 216500 rm112 **A**

H Bristol via Calefati 15a ☎ (080) 211503 rm18 **A**

H Costa via Crisanzio 12 ☎ (080) 210006 rm23 **A**

H Euromotel Località Contrada Prete ☎ (080) 441534 rm33 **A**

H Europe via Oberdan 64 ☎ (080) 330857 rm57 **B**

H Moderno via Crisanzio 60 ☎ (080) 213313 rm51 **A**

H Orchidea via G-Petroni 11a ☎ (080) 221937 rm25 **A**

H Residenza Moderno via Carafar 4-12 ☎ (080) 363633 rm13 **B**

BAVENO *Novara*

H Alpi ☎ (0323) 24876 rm37 **B**

H Ankara Touring ☎ (0323) 24471 rm83 **A**

H Azalea ☎ (0323) 24122 rm20 **A**

★★**Beau Rivage** ☎ (0323) 24534 rm74 Apr-Oct **B**

H Eden ☎ (0323) 24560 rm26 **B**

H Florida Frazione Loita ☎ (0323) 24824 rm35 **B**

H Gardenia Meublè ☎ (0323) 24557 rm8 **A**

H Nazionale San Gottardo ☎ (0323) 24529 rm23 **B**

H Posta ☎ (0323) 24509 rm9 **A**

H Rigoli ☎ (0323) 24756 rm28 **B**

H Villa Ruscello ☎ (0323) 23006 rm13 **B**

BELGIRATE *Novara*

H Pellegrino Meublè ☎ (0322) 7491 rm10 **A**

H Terrazza ☎ (0322) 7493 rm16 **A**

BELLÀGIO *Como*

H Europa ☎ (031) 950471 rm10 Apr-Oct **A**

H Fiorini ☎ (031) 950392 rm14 **B**

H Genzianella ☎ (031) 968018 rm11 **A**

H Roma ☎ (031) 950424 rm26 Apr-Oct **A**

H Silvio ☎ (031) 950332 rm19 **A**

BELLANO *Como*

H All'Orrido ☎ (0341) 821203 rm19 **A**

H Cavallo Bianco ☎ (0341) 821101 rm13 Apr-Oct **A**

★★**Meridiana** via C-Alberto 19 ☎ (0341) 821126 rm40 **B**

BELLARIA IGEA MARINA *Forli*

At **BELLARIA**

H Admiral via C-Colombo 52 ☎ (0541) 49334 rm19 **B**

H Bristol via C-Colombo 38 ☎ (0541) 44245 rm68 **B**

H Capanni via Italia 20 ☎ (0541) 46114 rm48 **B**

H Della Motta via Posturnia 20 ☎ (0541) 44339 rm25 **B**

H Elizabeth via Rovereto 11 ☎ (0541) 44119 rm39 **B**

H Ermitage via Ala 11 ☎ (0541) 47634 rm54 **B**

H Miramare via C-Colombo 37 ☎ (0541) 44131 rm64 **B**

H Nautic viale Prosecco 4 ☎ (0541) 47437 rm25 **B**

H Olimpic via Arno 75 ☎ (0541) 49221 rm15 **B**

H President via Vespucci 11 ☎ (0541) 49636 rm58 **B**

At **IGEA MARINA**

H Arizona via Pinzon 216 ☎ (0541) 630043 rm93 **B**

H Elios via Pinzon 116 ☎ (0541) 630453 rm29 **B**

H Internazionale via Pinzon 72 ☎ (0541) 44347 rm43 **B**

H K2 via Pinzon 212 ☎ (0541) 630064 rm53 **B**

H Majestic via Pinzon 209 ☎ (0541) 630242 rm49 **B**

H Metropolitan via Tibullo 60 ☎ (0541) 630094 rm68 **B**

H Savoia via Pinzon 190 ☎ (0541) 630012 rm48 **B**

BELLARIA See **BELLARIA IGEA MARINA**

BOLOGNA *Bologna*

Bologna is the capital of Emilia-Romagna, a region bordered by the River Po, the Adriatic and the Apennine mountains. The old centre is distinctively built in sturdy brick; its leaning towers – two out of several hundred that were built in the city as a type of medieval status symbol by the great ruling famililies – are of special interest. From the top of the Asinelli Tower (320ft) there is a magnificent bird's-eye view over the terracotta rooftops and slender church spires. The old city revolves around the two adjacent squares, Piazza del Nettuno and the Piazza Maggiore. In the first is Giovanni Bologna's splendid bronze statue of Neptune and the opulent *Palazzo di Re Enzo*, in the second the immense Basilica of San Petronio and the Renaissance-style *Palazzo del Podesta*. The university, the oldest in Europe, is a notable seat of learning and the *Pinacoteca Nazionale*, just beyond it, offers a comprehensive view of Bolognese art. Definitely not to be missed is the sanctuary of the Madonna di San Luca, linked to the city gate by a portico of arches, over two miles long and commanding views across Bologna to the Apennines beyond. EATING OUT Bologna is noted for its restaurants, for its pasta sauces, *mortadella* sausages, *tortellini* and the *tagliatelle* reputedly invented for the wedding of Lucrezia Borgia. Regional wines are sparkling Lambrusco, red Sangiovese and the whites, Albana and Trebbiano.

H Accademia via B-Arti 6 ☎ (051) 232318 rm28 **A**

H Eliseo via Testoni 3 ☎ (051) 277738 rm20 **A**

H Maggiore via E-Ponente 62 ☎ (051) 381634 rm62 **B**

H Nettuno ☎ (051) 260964 rm38 **B**

H Orologio via IV Novembre 10 ☎ (051) 231253 rm32 **B**

H Palace via Montegrappa 9 ☎ (051) 278954 rm113 **B**

M Pioppa via M-E-Lepido 217 ☎ (051) 400234 rm46 **B**

H San Felice via Riva Reno 2 ☎ (051) 557457 rm36 **B**

BOLZANO-BOZEN *Bolzano*

H Ariston (n.rest) via Roma 82 ☎ (0471) 916558 rm17 **A**

H Bel Sit (n.rest) via Roma 9 ☎ (0471) 286227 rm10 **A**

H Kampill via Campiglio 11 ☎ (0471) 25993 rm16 **A**

H Post Gries corso della Liberta 117 ☎ (0471) 41130 rm41 **A**

BONASSOLA *la Spezia*

H Belvedere ☎ (0187) 813622 rm24 **A**

H Della Rose ☎ (0187) 813713 rm30 **A**

H Lungomare ☎ (0187) 813632 rm33 May-Sep **A**

BORCA See **MACUGNAGA**

BORDIGHERA *Imperia*

H Aurora via Pelloux 42 ☎ (0184) 261312 rm30 Dec 21-Oct 15 **B**

H Bordighera a Terminus corso Italia 21 ☎ (0184) 261280 rm26 **A**

H Del Capo via al Capo ☎ (0184) 261558 rm14 **A**

H Helios via G-Biamonti 23 ☎ (0184) 261677 rm30 **B**

H Riviera via Trento 12 ☎ (0184) 261323 rm26 **A**

H Rosalia via V-Emanuele 429 ☎ (0184) 261366 rm32 **A**

H Savoia corso Italia 47 ☎ (0184) 261448 rm24 **A**

H Scogliera (n.rest) via Gen-Cantore 17 ☎ (0184) 261412 rm11 Closed Oct-Dec 20 **A**

H Sonia via V-Emanuele 297 ☎ (0184) 262311 rm8 **A**

BÒRMIO *Sondrio*

H Adele ☎ (0342) 901175 rm32 **A**

H Astoria ☎ (0342) 904541 rm44 **B**

H Cervo ☎ (0342) 904744 rm23 **A**

H Cevedale ☎ (0342) 901719 rm20 **A**

H Genzianella ☎ (0342) 904485 rm42 **A**

H Gufo ☎ (0342) 904727 rm29 **A**

H San Lorenzo ☎ (0342) 904604 rm38 Dec-May 15 & Jun 20-Sep **B**

H Stelvio ☎ (0342) 901130 rm39 **B**

H Vallecetta ☎ (0342) 904587 rm39 **A**

BORNO *Brescia*

H Belvedere ☎ (0364) 41052 rm24 **A**

H Tre Pini Croce di Salven ☎ (0364) 41162 rm7 **A**

BRESCIA *Brescia*

H Astron via G-Togni 14 ☎ (030) 48220 rm20 **A**

H Italia via Gramsci 11 ☎ (030) 56273 rm54 **A**

H Milano via Vallecamonica 3 ☎ (030) 311566 rm21 **A**

BRESSANONE-BRIXEN *Bolzano*

H Al Sole via S-Erardo 8 ☎ (0472) 22271 rm18 **B**

H Hofstatt Elvas 26 ☎ (0472) 24420 rm18 **A**

H Millanderhof Millan 58 ☎ (0472) 23348 rm14 **A**

H Vallazza ☎ (0472) 51321 rm21 **A**

BREUIL-CERVINIA *Aosta*

H Derby ☎ (0166) 949067 rm20 **A**

H Edelweiss ☎ (0166) 949078 rm35 **A**

H Fosson ☎ (0166) 949125 rm24 **A**

H Lyskamm ☎ (0166) 949074 rm17 **B**

H Meynet (n.rest) ☎ (0166) 948696 rm7 **A**

H Mignon ☎ (0166) 949344 rm18 **A**

H Rosà ☎ (0166) 949022 rm72 **B**

H Serenella ☎ (0166) 949041 rm14 **B**

H Sporting ☎ (0166) 949112 rm19 **A**

BRINDISI *Brindisi*

H Barsotti via Cavour 5 ☎ (0831) 21997 rm60 **B**

H Bologna (n.rest) via Cavour 41 ☎ (0831) 222883 rm20 **A**

H Regina via Cavour 5 ☎ (0831) 222001 rm42 **B**

BRUNICO-BRUNECK *Bolzano*

H Andreas Hofer via Campo Tures 1 ☎ (0474) 85469 rm54 **B**

H Corso via Bastioni 16 ☎ (0474) 85434 rm27 **A**

H Elisabeth (n.rest) Kaiserwarthe 30 ☎ (0474) 85260 rm9 **A**

BRUSSON *Aosta*

H Beau Site ☎ (0125) 300144 rm17 **A**

H France ☎ (0125) 300175 rm18 **B**

H Laghetto ☎ (0125) 300179 rm17 **A**

H Moderno ☎ (0125) 300118 rm24 **B**

CADENABBIA *Como*

★**Beau Rivage** (n.rest) via Regina 87 ☎ (0344) 40426 rm20 Apr-Oct **B**

H Marianna ☎ (0344) 40451 rm11 **B**

H Riviera ☎ (0344) 40422 rm14 **A**

H Rodrigo ☎ (0344) 40395 rm12 Apr-Oct **B**

CAGLIARI *Cagliari* See **SARDEGNA, ISOLA (SARDINIA)**

CALTANISSETTA *Caltanissetta* See **SICILIA (SICILY)**

CAMAIORE, LIDO DI *Lucca*

H Miami (n.rest) via Roma 47 ☎ (0584) 64417 rm19 **A**

H San Domingo (n.rest) via U-Foscolo ☎ (0584) 64316 rm20 **A**

H Sirio via Italica 6 ☎ (0584) 65047 rm27 May 15-Oct 10 **A**

H Sole E Mare (n.rest) via Pistelli 72 ☎ (0584) 64063 rm24 **A**

H Villa Eden (n.rest) via Don Minzoni 12 ☎ (0584) 64068 rm14 **A**

CAMPO NELL'ELBA See **ELBA, ISOLA D'**

CAMPOTOSTO *L'Aquila*

H Paloma ☎ (0862) 900118 rm18 May-Sep **A**

H St Andrew ☎ (0862) 900148 rm100 **A**

H Valle ☎ (0862) 900119 rm9 May-Sep **A**

CAMPO TURES-SAND IN TAUFERS *Bolzano*

H Feldmuellerhof via Al Castello 9 ☎ (0474) 68127 rm29 **B**

H Post via Nazionale 1 ☎ (0474) 68028 rm26 **A**

CÀNNERO RIVIERA *Novara*

◆ **France** ☎ (0323) 78095 rm11 **A**

H Milano ☎ (0323) 78021 rm28 Mar 30-Oct 15 **B**

H Miralago ☎ (0323) 78282 rm11 Apr-Sep **A**

H Park Italia ☎ (0323) 78488 rm24 **A**

◆ **Piccadilly** ☎ (0323) 78105 rm9 **A**

H Rondinella ☎ (0323) 78098 rm14 **A**

CANNOBIO *Novara*

H Magnolia ☎ (0323) 70393 rm10 **A**

H Vesuvio Piaggio Balmara ☎ (0323) 71483 rm5 **B**

CAPO D'ORLANDO *Messina* See **SICILIA (SICILY)**

CAPRI See **CAPRI, ISOLA DI**

CAPRI, ISOLA DI *Napoli*

CAPRI

◆ **Belsito** via Matermania ☎ (081) 8370969 rm13 **A**

◆ **Da Giorgio** via Roma ☎ (081) 8370898 rm9 **A**

H Villa Krupp via Mattotti ☎ (081) 8370362 rm12 **A**

H Villa Margherita via D-Birago ☎ (081) 8370404 rm24 Apr-Oct **B**

H Villa Sarah via Tiberio ☎ (081) 8377817 rm28 **A**

CARRARA, MARINA DI *Massa Carrara*

◆ **Morgana** via C-Colombo 12 ☎ (0585) 635545 rm17 **A**

H Olga via Garibaldi 27 ☎ (0585) 634090 rm7 **A**

H Paradiso via Colombo 121 ☎ (0585) 633275 rm24 **B**

◆ **Pineta** via C-Colombo 119 ☎ (0585) 633390 rm18 **A**

CASTELFORTE *Latina*

H Terme Sant'Egidio ☎ (0771) 672212 rm55 May-Nov 12 **A**

CASTELLANA GROTTE *Puglia*

H Centro Grotte ☎ (080) 787741 rm24 **B**

CASTIGLIONE DEL LAGO *Umbria*

H Fazzuoli P-Marconi 11 ☎ (075) 951112 rm27 **B**

H Pamela (n.rest) via S-Pellico 8 ☎ (06081) 951313 rm9 **A**

CATANIA *Catania* See **SICILIA (SICILY)**

CATTOLICA *Forli*

★**Bellariva** via Fiume 10 ☎ (0541) 961609 rm26 Apr 5-Sep **A**

★★**Senior** via del Prete ☎ (0541) 963443 rm43 May-Sep **B**

CAVA DE TIRRENI *Salerno*

★★**Victoria** corso Mazzini 4 ☎ (089) 464022 rm61 **A**

CAVALLINO See **VENEZIA (VENICE)**

CAVOLI See **ELBA, ISOLA D'** under **CAMPO NELL'ELBA**

CEFALÙ *Palermo* See **SICILIA (SICILY)**

CERNOBBIO *Como*

★**Asnigo** (n.rest) pza San Stefano ☎ (031) 510062 rm25 Mar 16-Nov **B**

H Centrale ☎ (031) 511212 rm15 **B**

H Della Torre ☎ (031) 511308 rm8 **A**

H Gerardina ☎ (031) 513808 rm6 **A**

H San Giuseppe ☎ (031) 511288 rm12 **B**

H Terzo Grotto ☎ (031) 512304 rm9 **B**

CERVIA *Ravenna*

H Ambasciatori via Grassi 6 ☎ (0544) 992032 rm54 **B**

H Ariella via Mascagni 16 ☎ (0544) 991640 rm19 **A**

H Beau Rivage Lungomare G-Deledda ☎ (0544) 971010 rm32 **B**

H Bologna via 2 Giugno 61 ☎ (0544) 991404 rm26 **B**

H Conchiglia Lungomare G-Deledda 46 ☎ (0544) 71370 rm38 **A**

H Costaverde Anello del Pino 13 ☎ (0544) 992398 rm41 20 May-20 Sep **B**

H Splendid VII Traversa 4 ☎ (0544) 994159 rm27 15 May-Sep **A**

H Stresa XII Traversa 3 ☎ (0544) 994165 rm16 25 May-10 Sep **A**

H Suisse via 2 Giguno 132 ☎ (0544) 991350 rm19 15 May-20 Sep **A**

H Universal Lungomare G-Deledda 118 ☎ (0544) 71418 rm34 Apr-15 Sep **B**

H Zenith via Val Padana 6 ☎ (0544) 987224 rm24 25 May-12 Nov **B**

At **MILANO MARITTIMA**(3km N)

H Condor XII Traversa ☎ (0544) 992210 rm18 May 20-Sep 15 **B**

H Deanna via Matteotti 131 ☎ (0544) 991365 rm63 May-Sep **B**

H Fenice XVII Traversa 6 ☎ (0544) 994325 rm38 May 15-Sep 20 **B**

H Granada IV Traversa 26 ☎ (0544) 992253 rm36 May-Sep **A**

H Lady Mary via E-Toti ☎ (0544) 992007 rm22 May 15-Sep 15 **B**

H Rosen Garden via Anello del Pino 160 ☎ (0544) 994388 rm27 May-Sep 25 **B**

H Torremaura XVII Traversa 8 ☎ (0544) 992217 rm38 May-Sep **B**

CERVINIA-BREUIL See**BREUIL-CERVINIA**

CESENATICO *Forli*

H Bains via dei Mille 52 ☎ (0547) 81119 rm30 **A**

H Eritrea via Carducci 15 ☎ (0547) 80033 rm54 **B**

H Esplanade via Carducci 120 ☎ (0547) 82405 rm56 **B**

H Il Gabbiano via dei Mille 78 ☎ (0547) 80089 rm28 **B**

H Riz via Carducci 182 ☎ (0547) 81333 rm45 **A**

H Roxy via Carducci 193 ☎ (0547) 82004 rm40 **B**

H Sabrina via dei Mille 150 ☎ (0547) 80545 rm48 **B**

H Sporting via Carducci 191 ☎ (0547) 83082 rm40 **B**

★★★**Torino** via Carducci 55 ☎ (0547) 80044 rm45 May 15-Sep **B**

At **VALVERDE**(1km SE)

H Caravelle via Michelangelo 23 ☎ (0547) 86234 rm42 **A**

H Gallia via le Mengoni 19 ☎ (0547) 86312 rm45 **B**

H Rol via Bernini 38 ☎ (0547) 86299 rm80 **B**

H Royal via Carducci 292 ☎ (0547) 86140 rm70 **A**

At **ZADINA PINETA**(3km NW)

H Clipper pza Kennedy 3 ☎ (0547) 82227 rm50 **A**

H Nuovo Renzo via dei Pini 49 ☎ (0547) 82316 rm24 **B**

H Zadina via dei Pini 40 ☎ (0547) 81050 rm45 **A**

CHAMOIS-CORGNOLAZ *Aosta*

H Bellevue ☎ (0166) 47133 rm9 **A**

H Chamois ☎ (0166) 47130 rm16 **A**

H Edelweiss ☎ (0166) 47137 rm13 **A**

CHATILLON *Aosta*

★★**Marisa** via Pellissier 10 ☎ (0166) 61845 rm28 **B**

H Rendez-Vous ☎ (0166) 61662 rm35 **B**

H Rouge et Noir ☎ (0166) 61468 rm12 **A**

CHIAVENNA *Sondrio*

★★★**Conradi** pza Verdi 10 ☎ (0343) 32300 rm34 **B**

H Crimea ☎ (0343) 34343 rm35 **B**

CHIESA IN VALMALENCO *Sondrio*

H Alpen Rose ☎ (0342) 451193 rm30 **A**

H Amilcar ☎ (0342) 451117 rm19 **A**

H Nuovo Mitta ☎ (0342) 451359 rm70 **A**

CITTÀ DI CASTELLO *Umbria*

H Boschetto ☎ (075) 8554728 rm24 **A**

H Europe via V-E-Orlando ☎ (075) 8550551 rm56 **A**

H Mencuccio via Parini 60 ☎ (075) 854409 rm17 **B**

CIVITAVECCHIA *Roma*

H Medusa ☎ (0766) 24327 rm9 **A**

H Traghetto ☎ (0766) 25920 rm33 **B**

CODROIPO *Udine*

H Belvedere Loc Goricizza ☎ (0432) 907586 rm12 **A**

COGNE *Aosta*

H Au Vieux Grenier ☎ (0165) 74002 rm17 **A**

H Bouton d'Or ☎ (0165) 74268 rm10 **B**

H Grand Paradis ☎ (0165) 74070 rm28 **A**

H Notre Maison ☎ (0165) 74104 rm12 **A**

H Petit ☎ (0165) 74010 rm19 **A**

H Sylvenoire (n.rest) ☎ (0165) 74037 rm14 **A**

COGOLETO *Genova*

H Emma (n.rest) via Parasco 11 ☏ (010) 9181685 rm11 **A**

CÒLICO *Como*

H Alpina ☏ (0341) 940389 rm6 **A**

H Aurora ☏ (0341) 940323 rm22 **A**

H Belvedere ☏ (0341) 940330 rm11 **A**

H Continental ☏ (0341) 940217 rm19 **A**

H Dell'Angelo ☏ (0341) 940219 rm9 **A**

H Isolabella ☏ (0341) 940101 rm40 **B**

★★**Risi** Lunge L-Polti 1 rm45 Mar-Oct **B**

COMO *Como*

H Baita Bondella via Bel Paese 9 ☏ (031) 220307 rm14 **A**

H Canova via T-Gallio 5 ☏ (031) 273485 rm13 **A**

H Minerva pza Grimoldi 8 ☏ (031) 266482 rm25 **B**

H Nuovo Mondo via S-Giacomo 52 ☏ (031) 541250 rm17 **A**

H Piemontese via M-Grappa 52 ☏ (031) 265016 rm3 **A**

H Posta via Garibaldi 2 ☏ (031) 266012 rm17 **B**

H Quarcino Salita Quarcino 4 ☏ (031) 263465 rm12 **B**

H Sociale Spendidco via M-Cumacini 8 ☏ (031) 264042 rm7 **A**

H Terminus Lungo Lairo Trieste 14 ☏ (031) 267042 rm27 **B**

H Tre Re pza Boldoni 20 ☏ (031) 265374 rm32 **B**

CORCIANO *Umbria*

H Cosmos via Menotti 72 ☏ (075) 7749218 rm16 **B**

H Ellera via Gramsci 20 ☏ (075) 790243 rm13 **A**

CORTONA *Arezzo*

H Miravalle ☏ (0575) 62232 rm7 **A**

H Oasi Le Contesse ☏ (0575) 603188 rm36 Apr-Oct **B**

H San Michele via Guelfa 15 ☏ (0575) 604348 rm36 **A**

H St Luca pza Garibaldi 2 ☏ (0575) 603787 rm56 **B**

COURMAYEUR *Aosta*

H Berthod ☏ (0165) 842286 rm17 **B**

H Edelweiss ☏ (0165) 841590 rm28 Seasonal **B**

H Laurent ☏ (0165) 841797 rm17 **A**

H Petit Meublè ☏ (0165) 842426 rm9 **A**

H Roma (n.rest) ☏ (0165) 843040 rm8 **A**

H Scoiattolo ☏ (0165) 842300 rm15 Closed Nov **B**

H Svizzero (n.rest) ☏ (0165) 842035 rm30 Seasonal **A**

H Venezia ☏ (0165) 842461 rm15 **A**

H Vittoria (n.rest) ☏ (0165) 842278 rm23 **A**

CREMENO *Como*

H Cacciatori ☏ (0341) 996237 rm24 **A**

H Invernizzi ☏ (0341) 996900 rm12 **A**

H Maggio ☏ (0341) 996440 rm22 **A**

DEIVA MARINA *la Spezia*

H Caravella ☏ (0187) 815833 rm22 **A**

H Clelia ☏ (0187) 815827 rm24 **A**

H La Marina ☏ (0187) 815868 rm17 **A**

DERUTA *Umbria*

H Asso di Coppe ☏ (075) 9710205 rm21 **A**

H Melody ☏ (075) 9711186 rm47 **B**

DESENZANO DEL GARDA *Brescia*

H Flora ☏ (030) 914512 rm13 **A**

H Vela ☏ (030) 9141318 rm15 **A**

DIANO MARINA *Imperia*

H Baia Bianca pza Mazzini 5 ☏ (0183) 495167 rm57 Closed Oct 11-Dec 28 **A**

H Colibri via Kennedy 58 ☏ (0183) 494771 rm33 Apr-Oct 15 **A**

H Delfina via G-Ardoino 107 ☏ (0183) 495564 rm17 **A**

H Divin Maestro (n.rest) via F-Filzi 6 ☏ (0183) 497281 rm84 Closed Oct-Dec 20 **A**

H Eden Park via G-Ardoino 70 ☏ (0183) 403767 rm36 Mar 27-Oct 10 **B**

H Gabriella via dei Gerani 9 ☏ (0183) 403131 rm52 May 15-Oct 10 **A**

H Morchio viale Matteotti 32 ☏ (0183) 494694 rm15 **B**

H Raffy via G-Ardoino 134 ☏ (0183) 496172 rm44 Dec 20-Oct 15 **A**

H Silvano via G-Ardoino 73 ☏ (0183) 495028 rm48 Feb-Oct 15 **A**

H Villa Igea via S.Elmo 1 ☏ (0183) 495100 rm62 **A**

DOBBIACO-TOBLACH *Bolzano*

H Sole viale Rome 19 ☏ (0474) 72225 rm45 **B**

H Toblacherhof via Pusteria 8 ☏ (0474) 72217 rm23 **B**

DOMODOSSOLA *Novara*

H Corona ☏ (0324) 42114 rm27 **B**

H Europa Meublè Frazione Calice (Km4) ☏ (0324) 42116 rm22 **B**

H Piccolo ☏ (0324) 42351 rm30 **B**

H Spinoglio ☏ (0324) 42112 rm27 **B**

DUINO AURISINA *Trieste*

H Pineta loc Sistiana ☏ (040) 299255 rm12 **B**

H Sistiana ☏ (040) 299235 rm17 **A**

H Villa Gruber (n.rest) loc Duino ☏ (040) 208115 rm8 **A**

ELBA, ISOLA D' *Livorno*

CAMPO NELL'ELBA

At **CAVOLI**

◆ **Conchiglia** ☏ (0565) 987010 rm15 **B**

◆ **Lorenza** ☏ (0565) 987054 rm25 Apr-Sep **A**

MARCIANA MARINA

◆ **Andreina** ☏ (0565) 908150 rm8 **A**

H Anselmi viale Amedeo 37 ☏ (0565) 99078 rm29 **A**

H Imperia viale Amedeo 12 ☏ (0565) 99082 rm21 **B**

H Marinella viale Margherita 41 ☏ (0565) 99018 rm57 **B**

H Primula viale Cerboni 2 ☏ (0565) 99010 rm71 **B**

PORTO AZZURRO

H Arrighi via Veneto 18 ☏ (0565) 95315 rm18 **B**

H Plaza Punta Fanaletto ☏ (0565) 95010 rm26 Apr-Oct 15 **A**

H Rocco via Kennedy 36 ☏ (0565) 95129 rm27 **B**

H Villa Italia viale Italia ☏ (0565) 95119 rm13 **A**

PORTOFERRAIO

H Emy via G-Carducci 32 ☎ (0565) 917661 rm12 **A**

H Massimo Calata Italia 23 ☎ (0565) 92766 rm68 **B**

H Nobel via Manganaro 72 ☎ (0565) 915217 rm35 **A**

H Touring via Roma 13 ☎ (0565) 915851 rm31 **A**

H Villa Ombrosa via A-de-Gasperi ☎ (0565) 92363 rm47 **B**

EMPOLI *Firenze*

H Maggino canto Ghibellino 1 ☎ (0571) 74129 rm36 **A**

H Sole pza Don Minzoni 18 ☎ (0571) 73779 rm12 **B**

★★**Tazza d'Oro** via G-del Papa 16 ☎ (0571) 72129 rm51 **B**

H Vittoria (n.rest) via Carrucci 105 ☎ (0571) 73201 rm9 **A**

ENNA *Enna* See **SICILIA (SICILY)**

ERICE *Trapani* See **SICILIA (SICILY)**

FABRIANO *Ancona*

H Europa ☎ (0732) 21906 rm19 **A**

H Janus ☎ (0732) 4191 rm82 **B**

FANO *Pesaro & Urbino*

H Beaurivage viale le Adriatico 124 ☎ (0721) 84682 rm51 Jun-Sep 15 **A**

H Continental viale le Adriatico 148 ☎ (0721) 84670 rm52 May 25-Sep 15 **B**

H Corallo via L-da-Vinci 3 ☎ (0721) 878200 rm22 **B**

H Kings Bay via G-Poggi 51 ☎ (0721) 866238 rm26 **A**

H Plaza ☎ (0721) 866847 rm18 **B**

H Souvenir via Alighieri 104 ☎ (0721) 874151 rm13 **A**

H Umbria via Madonna a Mare 35 ☎ (0721) 804714 rm26 **A**

FASANO DEL GARDA See **GARDONE RIVIERA**

FERMO *Ascoli Piceno*

H Astoria viale Veneto 8 ☎ (0734) 22116 rm64 **A**

H Regina Mundi ☎ (0734) 210101 rm30 **A**

FIESOLE *Firenze*

H Bencistá via Benedetto da Maiano 4 ☎ (055) 59163 rm35 **A**

H Villa Baccano (n.rest) via Bosconi 4 ☎ (055) 59341 rm8 **A**

★★**Villa Bonelli** via F-Poeti 1 ☎ (055) 59513 rm23 **A**

FINALE LIGURE *Savona*

H Internazionale via Concezione 3 ☎ (019) 692054 rm35 **B**

H Orizzonte via Caviglia 67 ☎ (019) 690624 rm44 Apr-Sep **B**

H Park Hotel Castello via Caviglia 26 ☎ (019) 691320 rm19 **B**

H Serenval via Lido 5 ☎ (019) 601231 rm35 **B**

At **VARIGOTTI**(6km SE)

H Plaza ☎ (019) 698078 rm52 **B**

FIRENZE (FLORENCE) *Firenze*

Firenze, spread along both banks of the timeless River Arno, is an exquisite treasure chest of paintings, sculptures and terracotta-domed buildings, a tribute to artists such as Da Vinci, Botticelli and Michelangelo from a glorious golden age with lasted three centuries. Places of interest are all within walking distance of each other, and now that more of the historic centre has been closed to coaches and visiting vehicles, sightseeing is a more leisurely affair.

If any one building could be said to epitomise the entire city, then it must surely be the *Duomo* (Cathedral), created by the architect Brunelleschi, whose marvellous dome is proof of Renaissance ingenuity. In front of the cathedral is Giotto's handsome campanile, and the octagonal baptistry with its glittering mosaics and Ghiberti's famous gilded bronze doors.

Other architectural gems worth exploring include the pretty churches of San Miniato, across the river; Santa Maria Novella, near the station, with its many famous works of art; and Santa Croce, containing the tombs of Michelangelo, Machiavelli and Galileo.

Renowned galleries include the world-famous *Uffizi*; the grand *Palazzo Vecchio*, the *Palazzo Pitti*, with paintings by Titian, Rubens and Raphael; the *Accademia*, housing some of Michelangelo's most powerful stautes, including the impressive *David*, originally on the Piazza della Signoria; and other museums like the *Bargello* and the *San Marco*.

Shoppers will delight in the Via Tornabuoni, one of the most elegant streets in the world, and the Ponte Vecchio, the famous bridge lined with goldsmiths' and jewellers' shops. The biggest market is in the Piazza San Lorenzo (Tuesday to Sunday). The remarkable Straw Market, the *Logge Mercato Nuovo*, near Piazza della Signoria, sells everything from baskets to men's ties made from straw.

EATING OUT *Enoteca Pinchiorri*, in Via Ghibellina, enjoys a reputation as one of the best restaurants in Florence. Much less expensive but with a high reputation for its regional specialities is the atmospheric *Angiolino*, in Via Santo Spirito. Firenze specialities include *bistecca alla fiorentina*, a huge steak usually charcoal-grilled; *fegatelli*, slices of liver rolled in chopped fennel flowers; *bruschetta*, a type of garlic bread with olive oil; or *baccala*, a robust cod stew. For starters, look out for delicious *prosciutto crudo con fichi*, raw ham with fresh figs. Moderately priced restaurants are to be found near Piazza Santa Croce, Borgo San Lorenzo or San Jacopo.

◆ **Burchianti** (n.rest) via del Giglio 6 ☎ (055) 212796 rm10 **A**

◆ **Canada** (n.rest) Borgo San Lorenzo 14 ☎ (055) 210074 rm9 **A**

H Firenze pza Donati 4 ☎ (055) 214203 rm50 **A**

◆ **Kursaal** (n.rest) via Nazionale 24 ☎ (055) 496324 rm9 **A**

◆ **Lombardi** (n.rest) via Fiume 8 ☎ (055) 283151 rm12 **A**

H Madison via Bardazzi 4 ☎ (055) 414740 rm17 **A**

H Orcagna (n.rest) via Orcagna 57 ☎ (055) 670500 rm18 **B**

H Romagna (n.rest) via Panzani 4 ☎ (055) 211005 rm22 **A**

H Satellite (n.rest) via Fiume 14 ☎ (055) 294796 rm7 **A**

H Souvenir via XXVII Aprile 9 ☎ (055) 472194 rm13 **A**

H Stazione via dei Banchi 3 ☎ (055) 283133 rm14 **A**

H Sul Ponte via Senese 315a ☎ (055) 2049056 rm8 **A**

◆ **Toscana** via del Sole 8 ☎ (055) 213156 rm10 **A**

H Varsavia via Panzani 5 ☎ (055) 215615 rm9 **A**

FOGGIA *Puglia*

H Asi via Monfalcone 1 ☏ (0881) 23327 rm94 **A**

H Palace Sarti viale XXIV Maggio 48 ☏ (0881) 23321 rm80 **B**

FOLIGNO *Perugia*

H Bolognese (n.rest) via Istituto Denti 12 ☏ (06034) 52350 rm12 **A**

H Dei Pavoni (n.rest) via Mezzetti 29 ☏ (0742) 56263 rm12 **A**

H Due Coppe via Foligno 2 ☏ (0742) 64113 rm9 **A**

FORIO See **ISCHIA, ISOLA D'**

FORMIA *Latina*

H Ariston via C-Colombo 19 ☏ (0771) 22170 rm56 **B**

H Bajamar loc S-Janni ☏ (0771) 28063 rm27 **B**

H Fagiano Palace via Appia ☏ (0771) 266681 rm57 **A**

FORNI AVOLTRI *Udine*

H Miravalle Chiolos ☏ (0433) 72049 rm20 **A**

H Samassa ☏ (0433) 72020 rm36 **A**

H Sottocorona ☏ (0433) 72023 rm43 **A**

FORTE DEI MARMI *Lucca*

H America via C-Colombo 24 ☏ (0584) 80953 rm32 May-Sep **A**

H Michelangelo via Roma Imp 3 ☏ (0584) 89448 rm24 May 15-Sep **A**

H Mignon via Carducci 58 ☏ (0584) 82583 rm26 May-Sep **B**

H Pueblo via P-Mascagni 45 ☏ (0584) 82700 rm9 Apr-Sep **A**

H Villa Cristina via Mazzini 153 ☏ (0584) 880678 rm54 Jun-Sep 15 **A**

GAETA *Latina*

H Aenea's Landing via Flacca ☏ (0771) 463185 rm22 Apr 15-Oct 15 **B**

H Flamingo corso Italia 109 ☏ (0771) 441284 rm53 **A**

H Mirasole loc Serapo ☏ (0771) 460080 rm136 **A**

H Serapo ☏ (0771) 460067 rm146 **A**

GARDONE RIVIERA *Brescia*

H Nord ☏ (0365) 20707 rm20 **A**

◆ Villa Bellaria ☏ (0365) 20406 rm22 Apr-Sep **A**

At **FASANO DEL GARDA**(2km NE)

H Paradiso ☏ (0365) 20269 rm38 Apr-Sep **B**

GELA *Caltanissetta* See **SICILIA (SICILY)**

GENOVA (GENOA) *Genova*

H Agnello d'Oro Vico Monachette 6 ☏ (010) 262084 rm32 **B**

H Bologna (n.rest) pza Sup del Roso 3 ☏ (010) 208879 rm16 **A**

H Capannina via T-Speri 7 ☏ (010) 363205 rm24 **A**

H Carletto (n.rest) via Colombo 16 ☏ (010) 546412 rm35 **A**

H Crespi via A-Doria 10 ☏ (010) 261723 rm51 **A**

H Della Posta via Balbi 24 ☏ (010) 262005 rm16 **A**

H Helvetia pza della Nunziata 1 ☏ (010) 205839 rm32 **B**

H Nuovo Nord via Balbi ☏ (010) 257363 rm21 **A**

H Principe Pia Acquaverde 2-10 ☏ (010) 262184 rm18 **A**

H Rex via de Gaspaeri 9 ☏ (010) 314197 rm27 **A**

H Sereno Vico della Cittadella 1a ☏ (010) 207919 rm22 **A**

GHIFFA *Novara*

H Park Paradiso rm15 **A**

GIULIANOVA LIDO *Teramo*

H Algeri Lungomare Zara ☏ (085) 862935 rm60 May-Sep **A**

H Atlantic Lungomare Zara 117 ☏ (085) 863229 rm38 May-Sep **A**

H Corallo via Lepanto ☏ (085) 864755 rm23 **A**

H Holiday via Saffi ☏ (085) 867645 rm21 May-Sep **A**

H Promenade Lungomare Zara 119 ☏ (085) 862338 rm54 May 15-Sep **A**

H Ritz Lungomare Zara ☏ (085) 863470 rm40 May-Sep **A**

H Riviera Lungomare Zara 47 ☏ (085) 862020 rm116 May 18-Sep 14 **A**

H Royal Lungomare Zara ☏ (085) 862930 rm45 May-Sep **A**

H Smeraldo Lungomare Zara 119 ☏ (085) 863806 rm80 **A**

GORIZIA *Gorizia*

H Palace corso Italia 63 ☏ (0481) 82166 rm70 **B**

H Sandro (n.rest) via S-Chiara 18 ☏ (0481) 83223 rm8 **A**

GRADO *Gorizia*

H Capri via Vespucci 1 ☏ (0431) 80091 rm27 Apr 25-Oct **A**

H Congress via Marco-Polo 4 ☏ (0431) 80358 rm20 May-Sep **A**

H Helvetia viale Kennedy 15 ☏ (0431) 80598 rm38 May-Sep **A**

GRAVEDONA *Como*

H Crotto Lauro ☏ (0344) 85255 rm17 **A**

H Duemila ☏ (0344) 85478 rm20 **A**

H Italia ☏ (0344) 85294 rm17 **A**

★Turismo ☏ (0344) 85227 rm12 Mar-Nov **B**

GRAVELLONA TOCE *Novara*

★Helios ☏ (0323) 848096 rm19 **B**

H Sant'Antonio ☏ (0323) 848080 rm9 **A**

H Sempione ☏ (0323) 848050 rm15 **A**

GROSIO *Sondrio*

H Dosdè ☏ (0342) 845185 rm17 **A**

H Sassella ☏ (0342) 845140 rm18 **B**

GROTTAMMARE *Ascoli Piceno*

H Concorde via Parini 24 ☏ (0735) 581354 rm29 **A**

H Eden via de Gasperi 37 ☏ (0735) 581407 rm56 May-Oct **B**

H Marconi via Lungomare ☏ (0735) 631165 rm97 Jun-Sep 25 **B**

H Roma via Lungomare 30 ☏ (0735) 631145 rm60 **B**

H Sylvia via Roma 110 ☏ (0735) 631192 rm46 **A**

H Valentino via D-Alighieri 45 ☏ (0735) 581754 rm41 Apr-Sep **A**

GUBBIO *Perugia*

H Della Rocca loc Monte Igino ☏ (075) 9273286 rm15 **A**

H Gattapone via G-Ansidei 6 ☏ (075) 9272489 rm13 **A**

H Oderisi (n.rest) via Mazzatinti 12 ☏ (075) 9273747 rm18 **A**

H San Marco via Perugia 5 ☎ (075) 9272349 rm52 **B**

★★**Tre Ceri** via Benamati 8 ☎ (075) 9273304 rm28 **B**

IDRO *Brescia*

H Da Arrigo Pieve ☎ (0365) 83175 rm8 **A**

H Nabaffa Vantone ☎ (0365) 83202 rm10 **A**

IESOLO See **JESOLO**

IGEA MARINA See **BELLARIA IGEA MARINA**

IMOLA *Bologna*

H Campana ☎ (0542) 23150 rm24 **B**

H Zio ☎ (0542) 35274 rm8 **B**

IMPERIA *Imperia*

H Concordia via G-Berio 41 ☎ (0183) 20315 rm16 **A**

H Corallo corso Garibaldi 29 ☎ (0183) 61980 rm42 **B**

H Italia da Edy viale Matteotti 29 ☎ (0183) 61867 rm17 **A**

H Kristina Splanata Borga Peri 8 ☎ (0183) 23564 rm23 **B**

H Robinia via Pirnoli 14 ☎ (0183) 62720 rm58 **B**

H Stella A.S Novaro 3 ☎ (0183) 24792 rm8 **A**

INTRA See **VERBANIA**

ISCHIA, ISOLA D' *Napoli*

FORIO

H Citara ☎ (081) 907098 rm51 Apr-Oct **B**

H Green Flash via Marina 76 ☎ (081) 997129 rm69 Apr-Oct **B**

H Mediterraneo ☎ (081) 907365 rm39 Mar-Nov **B**

H Park Imperial ☎ (081) 907105 rm45 **A**

H Punta del Sole via R-G-Maltese ☎ (081) 998208 rm34 Apr-Oct **B**

H Punta Imperatore ☎ (081) 907140 rm31 Apr-Oct **A**

H Santa Lucia ☎ (081) 997670 rm50 **B**

H Zaro S. Francesco via Cigliano 85 ☎ (081) 997576 rm32 Apr-Oct **B**

PORTO D'ISCHIA

H Ambasciatori via R-Gianturco ☎ (081) 992933 rm48 Apr-Oct **B**

H Conte ☎ (081) 991003 rm51 **B**

H Flora via A-de-Luca 95 ☎ (081) 991502 rm68 Mar 15-Oct **B**

H Floridiana corso V-Colonna 179 ☎ (081) 991014 rm50 Apr-Oct **B**

H Ischia ☎ (081) 991017 rm29 May-Oct **B**

H Parco Verde via M-Mazzella 29 ☎ (081) 992282 rm50 Mar-Oct **A**

H Royal Terme via Morgione 113 ☎ (081) 992022 rm92 Mar-Oct **B**

H Solemar ☎ (081) 991822 rm56 Apr-Oct **B**

H Terme Parco Edera via Morgione 28 ☎ (081) 991313 rm39 Mar-Nov **B**

ISEO *Brescia*

H Europa Pilzone ☎ (030) 980002 rm30 **A**

H Milano ☎ (030) 980449 rm15 **A**

JESOLO (IESOLO), LIDO DI *Venezia*

H Arizona via Padova 42 ☎ (0421) 971936 rm42 **B**

H Boston via Bafile ☎ (0421) 90204 rm32 **B**

H California via Padova 50 ☎ (0421) 971819 rm24 **B**

H Corallo via Bafile ☎ (0421) 90317 rm45 **B**

H Dainese via Oriente 140 ☎ (0421) 961023 rm28 **B**

H El Paso Pia Torino 4 ☎ (0421) 961150 rm30 **B**

H Embassy via Bafile 113 ☎ (0421) 90606 rm36 **B**

H Florida via Padova 7 ☎ (0421) 971435 rm50 **B**

H Gardenia via Bafile 175 ☎ (0421) 92017 rm40 **B**

H Rosmary via U-Foscolo 90 ☎ (0421) 971022 rm55 **B**

LAGONEGRO *Potenza*

H Montesirino ☎ (0973) 21181 rm6 **A**

H S. Nicola pza della Repubblica ☎ (0973) 21457 rm48 Jul 6-Aug 24 **A**

LAIGUEGLIA *Savona*

★★**Mariolina** via Concezione 15 ☎ (0182) 49024 rm21 **A**

★★**Windsor** pza 25 Aprile 7 ☎ (0182) 49000 rm53 May-Oct **B**

LANZADA *Sondrio*

H Biancospino ☎ (0342) 451692 rm20 **A**

H Moizi ☎ (0342) 451247 rm12 **A**

LATINA *Latina*

H Casale via Appia ☎ (0773) 451087 rm27 **A**

H Europa via E-Filiberto 14 ☎ (0773) 40961 rm68 **B**

H Park via dei Monti Lepini ☎ (0773) 240295 rm48 **B**

LECCE *Lecce*

H Capello via Monte Grappa 4 ☎ (0832) 28881 rm26 **A**

H Patria-Touring pza G-Riccardi 13 ☎ (0832) 29431 rm56 **A**

LECCO *Como*

H Caviate ☎ (0341) 367583 rm7 **B**

H Croce di Malta ☎ (0341) 363134 rm48 **B**

H Moderno ☎ (0341) 362340 rm33 **B**

LENNO *Como*

◆ **Del Grifo** ☎ (0344) 55161 rm3 **A**

◆ **Lavedo** ☎ (0344) 55172 rm13 **A**

H Plinio ☎ (0344) 55158 rm7 **B**

H Roma ☎ (0344) 55137 rm25 (Apr-Oct) **B**

LERICI *la Spezia*

H Florida Loc la Vallata ☎ (0187) 967344 rm32 **A**

H Italia (n.rest) ☎ (0187) 966566 rm14 **B**

H Luisa ☎ (0187) 967400 rm19 **B**

H Panoramic ☎ (0187) 967192 rm19 **A**

H Venere Azzurra ☎ (0187) 965334 rm22 **B**

LESA *Novara*

H Lago Maggiore ☎ (0322) 7259 rm11 **B**

H Manzoni ☎ (0322) 7486 rm10 **A**

H Margherita Meublè ☎ (0322) 7392 rm10 **A**

LEVANTO *la Spezia*

★★**Carla** via M-della-Liberta 28 ☎ (0187) 808275 rm36 **A**

H Dora ☎ (0187) 808168 rm37 **A**

H Nazionale ☎ (0187) 808102 rm36 **A**

H Palace ☎ (0187) 808143 rm43 **A**

H Primavera ☎ (0187) 808314 rm19 **A**

H Stella d'Italia ☏ (0187) 808109 rm38 **B**

LEZZENO *Como*

H Crotto dei Misto ☏ (031) 914541 rm11 **B**

H Crotto dei Pescatori ☏ (031) 914597 rm7 **A**

LIDO DI CAMAIORE See **CAMAIORE, LIDO DI**

LIDO DI JESOLO (IESOLO) See **JESOLO, LIDO DI**

LIGNANO PINETA See **LIGNANO SABBIADORO**

LIGNANO RIVIERA See **LIGNANO SABBIADORO**

LIGNANO SABBIADORO *Udine*

H Athena via Adriatica 52 ☏ (0431) 376834 rm37 May 15-Sep 15 **A**

H Calipso Lungomare Trieste 104 ☏ (0431) 71600 rm28 Apr-Sep **A**

H Cavallino Bianco via dei Platani 88 ☏ (0431) 71509 rm34 **A**

H Italia via Italia 7 ☏ (0431) 71185 rm116 **A**

H Luna Lungomare Trieste 68 ☏ (0431) 71490 rm50 May 15-Sep **A**

H Rio via Friuli 19 ☏ (0431) 71280 rm29 May-Sep **A**

At **LIGNANO PINETA**(5km SW)

H Continental via delle Palme 45 ☏ (0431) 422206 rm40 May-Sep **B**

H Erica Arco del Grecale 21 ☏ (0431) 422123 rm38 May 15-Sep **A**

H Park via delle Palme 41 ☏ (0431) 422380 rm44 May 15-Sep 20 **B**

At **LIGNANO RIVIERA**(7km SW)

H Delle Nazioni C-Nazioni 62 ☏ (0431) 428541 rm48 May 15-Sep 15 **B**

H Meridianus via della Musica 7 ☏ (0431) 428561 rm88 May 15-Sep 20 **B**

LIMONE SUL GARDA *Brescia*

H Berna ☏ (0365) 954047 rm85 **A**

H Ruscello ☏ (0365) rm22 **A**

H Splendid ☏ (0365) 954031 rm62 Mar-Oct **A**

LIVIGNO *Sondrio*

H Alpenrose ☏ (0342) 996038 rm14 **A**

H Alpina via Bondio 3 ☏ (0342) 996007 rm39 **B**

H Bernina ☏ (0342) 996002 rm31 **A**

H Bucaneve via Statale 6 ☏ (0342) 996201 rm38 Dec-Apr & Jun 10-Oct 10 **B**

H Galli ☏ (0342) 996376 rm26 **A**

H Helvetia ☏ (0342) 996018 rm41 **A**

H Lac Salin via S-Rocco ☏ (0342) 996166 rm63 Dec-Apr 15 & Jun 15-Sep 15 **B**

H Paradiso via Freita 17 ☏ (0342) 996633 rm26 **A**

H Parè via Gerus 3 ☏ (0342) 996263 rm40 **B**

H Sport Hotel Livigno-Compagnoni via Palipert 10 ☏ (0342) 996186 rm35 Dec-Apr 25 & Jul-Sep **B**

H Teola ☏ (0342) 996324 rm25 **B**

H Valtellina ☏ (0342) 996781 rm27 **A**

LIVORNO *Livorno*

H Belmare via Italia 109 ☏ (0586) 807040 rm20 **A**

H Etruria (n.rest) via Italia 231 ☏ (0586) 802077 rm8 **A**

LORETO *Ancona*

H Centrale ☏ (071) 970173 rm14 **B**

H Orlando ☏ (071) 978501 rm22 **A**

H Pellegrino e Pace ☏ (071) 977106 rm21 **A**

MACUGNAGA *Novara*

At **BORCA**(3km SW)

H Alpi ☏ (0324) 65135 rm13 **B**

At **PECETTO**(1.5km NW)

H Edelweiss ☏ (0324) 65124 rm24 **A**

◆ **Genzianella** ☏ (0324) 65058 rm10 **A**

H Nuovo Pecetto ☏ (0324) 65025 rm18 **B**

H Signal ☏ (0324) 65142 rm18 **B**

At **STAFFA**(0.5km NW)

H Anza ☏ (0324) 65008 rm43 **A**

H Dufour ☏ (0324) 65116 rm13 **B**

H Girasole ☏ (0324) 65052 rm18 **B**

H Glacier ☏ (0324) 65051 rm16 **A**

H Macugnaga ☏ (0324) 65005 rm12 **A**

H Zumstein ☏ (0324) 65118 rm44 **B**

MADESIMO *Sondrio*

H Andossi ☏ (0343) 53115 rm61 **B**

H Emet ☏ (0343) 53395 rm33 **B**

H Meridiana ☏ (0343) 53160 rm25 **B**

MAEN See **VALTOURNENCHE**

MAGIONE *Umbria*

H Silvana (n.rest) via Martiri di Belfiore 4 ☏ (075) 843617 rm11 **A**

H Villa Carpine via C-Marchesi 2 ☏ (075) 843539 rm9 **A**

MAIORI *Salerno*

H Due Torri ☏ (089) 877377 rm42 Mar 15-Oct **A**

H Garden ☏ (089) 877555 rm76 Mar-Oct **A**

H Miramare ☏ (089) 877225 rm46 Apr 15-Oct **B**

H Sole ☏ (089) 770169 rm25 Apr-Oct **B**

MANTOVA *Mantova*

H Bianchi Stazione (n.rest) pza Don Leoni 24 ☏ (0376) 321504 rm50 **A**

H Mantua via Verona ☏ (0376) 329681 rm15 **A**

H Rinascita (n.rest) via Concezione 4 ☏ (0376) 320607 rm8 **A**

MARATEA *Potenza*

H Marisdea via Castrasella 10 ☏ (0973) 879003 rm40 Jul 6-Aug 24 **B**

H Martino via Citrosello 16 ☏ (0973) 879126 rm19 Jul 6-Aug 24 **A**

MARCIANA MARINA See **ELBA, ISOLA D'**

MARINA DI CARRARA See **CARRARA, MARINA DI**

MARINA DI MASSA See **MASSA, MARINA DI**

MARINA DI PIETRASANTA See **PIETRASANTA, MARINA DI**

MARSALA *Trapani* See **SICILIA (SICILY)**

MASSA, MARINA DI *Massa Carrara*

H Cristallo via P-Rossi 15 ☏ (0585) 240119 rm17 **B**

H Euromar via dei Salici 3 ☏ (0585) 240300 rm40 Apr-Sep **B**

H Giulia via Ascoli 15 ☎ (0585) 240067 rm24 **B**

H Italia via Lungomare Vespucci 4 ☎ (0585) 240026 rm25 Jun-Aug **A**

H Piera (n.rest) via Casamicciola 77 ☎ (0585) 240501 rm16 **A**

H Roma pza Pellerano 16 ☎ (0585) 242748 rm36 **A**

H Scandinavia via Zolezzi 4 ☎ (0585) 240295 rm37 **B**

MASSA LUBRENSE *Napoli*

H Central Park ☎ (081) 8789318 rm33 Apr-Sep **A**

H Delfino Marciano ☎ (081) 8789261 rm49 Apr-Sep **B**

H Montana ☎ (081) 8780126 rm49 Apr-Oct **A**

MASSAROSA *Lucca*

H Sony (n.rest) via della Chiesa ☎ (0584) 92003 rm9 **A**

MAZZARÒ See **SICILIA (SICILY)** under **TAORMINA**

MEINA *Novara*

H Bruna ☎ (0322) 6439 rm8 **A**

H Paradiso ☎ (0322) 6488 rm38 **B**

H Parma ☎ (0322) 6494 rm8 **A**

MENAGGIO *Como*

H Alder ☎ (0344) 32171 rm14 **A**

H Corona ☎ (0344) 32006 rm27 Mar-Oct **A**

H Lario ☎ (0344) 32368 rm10 **A**

H Meneghett ☎ (0344) 32081 rm11 **A**

★★**Miralago** Nobiallo ☎ (0344) 32363 bed28 Apr-Oct **B**

MERGOZZO *Novara*

H Alla Quartina ☎ (0323) 80118 rm11 **A**

H Ancienne Auberge ☎ (0323) 80122 rm9 **A**

MESSINA *Messina* See **SICILIA (SICILY)**

MILANO (MILAN) *Milano*

Rapidly rivalling Paris as Europe's fashion capital, Milano beckons life's connoisseurs. Elegant shops along the Corso Venezia and Corso Vittorio Emanuele rarely fail to inspire a spending spree, while enjoying an aperitif in one of the many cafés of the elaborate Galleria can be just as memorable.

Tourist highlights revolve round the Piazza del Duomo and the white marbled cathedral, third largest in the world, where only the voices of La Scala Opera House rise higher. You can gaze in awe at Leonardo da Vinci's *Last Supper* in Santa Maria della Grazie.

EATING OUT Delicious starters to look out for in Milano's many and varied restaurants include *antipasto misto*, which usually comprises salami, olives, radishes, fennel and pickled mushrooms; and minestrone soup, made from mixed vegetables and tomatoes and served with a sprinkling of grated Parmesan cheese. Other local specialities are lake perch and trout and seafood fried in batter. Milano is famous for its ice creams, which make delicious desserts. Regional cheeses include *gorgonzola*, *mascarpone*, and *Bel Paese*.

The oldest restaurant in Milano is *Boeucc*, in Piazza Belgioso, near *La Scala* opera house, which specialises in traditional Milanese cuisine. In the moderately priced category, *Antica Brasera Meneghina*, in Via Circo, has a lovely garden for *al fresco* dining in summer.

H Ada (n.rest) via Sammartini 15 ☎ (02) 603852 rm10 **A**

H Archimede via Archimede 81 ☎ (02) 718185 rm12 **A**

H Arena (n.rest) via Giulahova 2 ☎ (02) 8692034 rm27 **B**

H Di Porta Romana (n.rest) via Lazzaro Papi 18 ☎ (02) 585890 rm36 **A**

H Garden (n.rest) via Rutilia 6 ☎ (02) 560838 rm23 **A**

H London (n.rest) via Rovello 3 ☎ (02) 872988 rm29 **B**

H Luce via Stambio 20 ☎ (02) 716975 rm11 **A**

H Mistral via Toffetti 4 ☎ (02) 563197 rm26 **A**

H Park (n.rest) via A-Massena 9 ☎ (02) 312525 rm31 **B**

H Susa via Argonne 14 ☎ (02) 7420897 rm21 **A**

H Vignetta via P-Custodi 2 ☎ (02) 8372665 rm15 **A**

MILANO MARITTIMA See **CERVIA**

MILAZZO *Messina* See **SICILIA (SICILY)**

MINORI See **AMALFI**

MINUCCIANO *Lucca*

H Belvedere loc Carpinelli ☎ (0583) 611043 rm28 **A**

H Mini via Primo Tonini 18, Gramolazzo ☎ (0583) 610153 rm13 **A**

MOLTRASIO *Como*

H Posta ☎ (031) 290280 rm13 Mar-Dec **B**

MONFALCONE *Gorizia*

H Carlina via 1 Maggio 29 ☎ (0481) 40130 rm15 **A**

H Excelsior (n.rest) via Arena 4 ☎ (0481) 72893 rm46 **B**

H Italia via Colombo 21 ☎ (0481) 791330 rm20 **B**

MONTEROSSO AL MARE *la Spezia*

H Cinque Terre ☎ (0187) 817543 rm54 **A**

H Degli Amici ☎ (0187) 817544 rm40 **A**

H Jolie ☎ (0187) 817539 rm32 **A**

H Moretto ☎ (0187) 817483 rm13 **B**

MORGEX *Aosta*

H Grivola ☎ (0165) 809550 rm23 **A**

MUGGIA *Trieste*

H Lido via C-Battisti 22 ☎ (040) 273338 rm47 **A**

H Sole Lazzaretto ☎ (040) 271106 rm17 **A**

NAPOLI (NAPLES) *Napoli*

H Bristol pza Garibaldi 63 ☎ (081) 281780 rm35 **A**

H Coral via G-Pica 12 ☎ (081) 260944 rm33 **A**

H Europa corso Meridionale 15 ☎ (081) 267511 rm34 **B**

H Pasadena via Terracina 175 ☎ (081) 616317 rm45 **A**

H Serius via Augusto 74 ☎ (081) 614844 rm69 **B**

H Torino via Depretis 123 ☎ (081) 322410 rm52 **B**

NARNI *Terni*

H Da Carlo via Ortana vecchia ☎ (0744) 742215 rm22 **A**

H Fina via Tuderte 419 ☎ (0744) 733648 rm32 **A**

NORCIA *Umbria*

H Benito via Marconi 5 ☎ (0743) 816670 rm9 **B**

H Hermitage Fraz Savelli ☏ (0743) 875107 rm14 **B**

NUMANA *Ancona*

H Gabbiano ☏ (071) 937114 rm17 May-Sep **A**

H Kon-Tiki ☏ (071) 930192 rm40 May-Sep **A**

H Sandra ☏ (071) 936309 rm20 May-Sep **A**

H Villa Sirena ☏ (071) 936420 rm24 **B**

NUORO *Nuoro* See **SARDEGNA, ISOLA (SARDINIA)**

OLEGGIO *Novara*

H Quattro Ruote ☏ (0321) 91256 rm10 **A**

H Roma ☏ (0321) 91175 rm12 **A**

ORISTANO *Oristano* See **SARDEGNA, ISOLA (SARDINIA)**

ORTA SAN GIULIO *Novara*

H Antico Agnello ☏ (0322) 90259 rm8 **A**

H Leon d'Oro ☏ (0322) 90254 rm29 **B**

H Orta ☏ (0322) 90390 rm33 Mar 15-Sep 15 **B**

ORTISEI-ST ULRICH *Bolzano*

H Cosmea via Setil 1 ☏ (0471) 76464 rm21 **A**

H Lersc (n.rest) via Roma 28 ☏ (0471) 76541 rm26 **A**

H Rainell via Vidalong 19 ☏ (0471) 76145 rm28 **A**

OSPEDALETTI *Imperia*

H Alexandra corso Reg-Margherita 9 ☏ (0184) 59356 rm19 **A**

H Firenze corso Reg-Margherita 97 ☏ (0184) 59221 rm44 **A**

H Italia via Matteotti 11 ☏ (0184) 59045 rm12 **A**

OVINDOLI *L'Aquila*

H Magnola Palace ☏ (0863) 705144 rm78 Closed May, Oct & Nov **A**

H Moretti ☏ (0863) 705174 rm35 **A**

H Park ☏ (0863) 705221 rm58 **A**

PAESTUM *Salerno*

H Esplanade ☏ (0828) 851043 rm30 **A**

H Martini ☏ (0828) 811020 rm13 **A**

H Palme ☏ (0828) 851025 rm50 Mar-Oct **A**

PALERMO *Palermo* See **SICILIA (SICILY)**

PALLANZA See **VERBANIA**

PAQUIER See **VALTOURNENCHE**

PARMA *Parma*

H Lazzaro via XX Marzo ☏ (0521) 208944 rm7 **A**

★★**Milano** via Ponte Bottego 9 ☏ (0521) 773031 rm47 **B**

H Moderno via A-Cerchi 4 ☏ (0521) 77247 rm47 **B**

H Tartaruga via Paganini 2 ☏ (0521) 772437 rm7 **A**

PASSO DELLO STELVIO See **STELVIO**

PECETTO See **MACUGNAGA**

PEDASO *Ascoli Piceno*

H Nuovo Valdaso via Valdaso ☏ (0734) 93349 rm27 **A**

H Verde via Matteotti 24 ☏ (0734) 931426 rm9 **B**

PERGUSA See **SICILIA (SICILY)** under **ENNA**

PERUGIA *Perugia*

H Astor pza V-Veneto 1 ☏ (075) 71843 rm47 **B**

H Iris via Marconi 37 ☏ (075) 20259 rm11 **A**

H Signa (n.rest) via del Grillo 9 ☏ (075) 61080 rm21 **A**

H Umbria via Boncampi 37 ☏ (075) 21203 rm18 **A**

PESCARA *Pescara*

H California via Primo Vere 152 ☏ (085) 60994 rm12 **A**

H Holiday Lungomare C-Colombo 104 ☏ (085) 60913 rm51 **B**

H Marisa via R-Margherita 39 ☏ (085) 27345 rm23 **A**

H Natale via del Circuito 175 ☏ (085) 213479 rm12 **A**

H Primo Vere via Vere 50 ☏ (085) 61733 rm47 **A**

H Residence corso V-Emanuele 301 ☏ (085) 36224 rm16 **A**

PESCHICI *Foggia*

H Bianchi via Podgara 26 ☏ (0884) 94110 rm27 **B**

H Calazzurra (n.rest) via Montebello 26-28 ☏ (0884) 94026 rm20 **B**

H Morcavallo ☏ (0884) 94005 rm41 **A**

H Peschici ☏ (0884) 94195 rm42 **A**

H Pineta via Libetta 77 ☏ (0884) 94126 rm11 **A**

PIAZZA ARMERINA *Enna* See **SICILIA (SICILY)**

PIETRASANTA, MARINA DI *Lucca*

PIETRASANTA *Lucca*

H Cometa via Catalani 52 ☏ (0584) 20376 rm21 May-Sep **A**

H Da Piero via Traversagna 3/5 ☏ (0584) 790031 rm7 **A**

H Italia via Oberdan 9 ☏ (0584) 70175 rm17 **A**

H Oasi via Roma 225 ☏ (0584) 20274 rm24 May-Sep **A**

H Orione via Carducci 29 ☏ (0584) 20434 rm20 **A**

H Palagi pza Carducci 23 ☏ (0584) 70249 rm14 Jul-Aug **A**

H Verdesolemare via Carducci 201 ☏ (0584) 20037 rm21 **A**

PIGNA *Imperia*

H Pigna D'Oro via S Rocco 5 ☏ (0184) 201021 rm5 **A**

PINETO *Teramo*

H Abruzzo via Abruzzo 2 ☏ (085) 939399 rm46 May-Sep **B**

H Columbia S.Sn 16 Sud ☏ (085) 9399105 rm48 **A**

H Corfu via F-P-Michetti ☏ (085) 9399082 rm51 Jun-Sep **B**

H Lunik via C-de-Titra ☏ (085) 939197 rm30 Jun-Sep **A**

H Parisse via Liguria ☏ (085) 9398118 rm24 May-Sep **A**

PISA *Pisa*

H Bologna (n.rest) via Mazzini 57 ☏ (050) 24449 rm56 **A**

H Fenice via Catalani 8 ☏ (050) 25131 rm30 **A**

H Leon Bianco (n.rest) pza del Pozzetto 6 ☏ (050) 45003 rm28 **A**

H Moderno (n.rest) via Corridoni 103 ☏ (050) 25021 rm22 **A**

H Pisa via Manzoni 22 ☏ (050) 44551 rm15 **A**

H Roseti (n.rest) via P-Mascagni 24 ☏ (050) 42596 rm14 **A**

H Touring (n.rest) via G-Puccini 24 ☏ (050) 46374 rm34 **A**

PIZZOFERRATO *Chieti*

H Miramon ☎ (0872) 946115 rm28 Jun 15-Sep 15 & Dec 20-Jan 10 **B**

H Pineto ☎ (0872) 946113 rm13 **A**

PONTEBBA *Udine*

H Spina ☎ (0428) 90919 rm11 **A**

H Wulfenia loc P-Pramollo ☎ (0428) 90506 rm10 **A**

PORCARI *Lucca*

H Bonelli via Fossa Nuova 28 ☎ (0583) 29223 rm16 **A**

H Dell' Angelo Rughi ☎ (0583) 29160 rm12 **A**

PORDENONE *Pordenone*

H Minerva (n.rest) pza XX Settembre 5 ☎ (0434) 26066 rm48 **A**

H Residence Meublè (n.rest) via Montereale 27 ☎ (0434) 35160 rm30 **A**

H Santin via delle Grazie 9 ☎ (0434) 26110 rm97 **A**

PORLEZZA *Como*

H Crotto Caraco ☎ (0344) 61154 rm14 **A**

H Europa ☎ (0344) 61142 rm29 **A**

H Regina ☎ (0344) 61228 rm24 **B**

H Risorgimento ☎ (0344) 61122 rm10 **A**

H Rosen-Garden ☎ (0344) 62228 rm10 **B**

H Stella ☎ (0344) 61108 rm25 **A**

PORTO AZZURRO See **ELBA, ISOLA D'**

PORTO D'ISCHIA See **ISCHIA, ISOLA D'**

PORTOFERRAIO See **ELBA, ISOLA D'**

PORTO SAN GIORGIO *Ascoli Piceno*

H Garden via C-Battisti 6 ☎ (0734) 379414 rm62 **B**

H Nettuno via Vittoria 153 ☎ (0734) 379044 rm23 **A**

★★**Terrazza** via Castelfidaro 2 ☎ (0734) 379005 rm32 **A**

H Tritone via San Martino 26 ☎ (0734) 677104 rm36 **A**

H Victoria via Vittoria 190 ☎ (0734) 49093 rm34 **A**

PORTO VENERE *la Spezia*

H Belvedere ☎ (0187) 900608 rm19 **A**

H Paradiso ☎ (0187) 900612 rm17 **B**

H San Pietro ☎ (0187) 900616 rm31 **B**

POTENZA *Potenza*

H Miramonti via Caserma Lucara ☎ (0971) 22987 rm9 **A**

H Tourist via Vescovado 4 ☎ (0971) 21437 rm87 **B**

POZZUOLI *Napoli*

H American Agnano ☎ (081) 7606529 rm96 **B**

H Hideway Agnano ☎ (081) 7606333 rm50 **A**

PRECI *Umbria*

H Agli Scacchi Quartiere Scacchi 12 ☎ (0743) 99224 rm12 **B**

PREMENO *Novara*

H Moderno ☎ (0323) 47014 rm40 **B**

H Premeno ☎ (0323) 47021 rm60 **B**

PROCIDA *Napoli*

H Arcate ☎ (081) 8967120 rm38 Apr-Oct **A**

H Oasi Ciraccio ☎ (081) 8967499 rm16 **A**

H Riveria Chiaiolella ☎ (081) 8967197 rm23 Apr-Sep **A**

RAGUSA *Ragusa* See **SICILIA (SICILY)**

RAPALLO *Genova*

H Bel Soggiorno via Gramsci 10 ☎ (0185) 50293 rm23 **A**

H Canali via Pietrafaccia 15 ☎ (0185) 50369 rm24 **A**

★★★**Miramare** Lungomare V-Veneto 27 ☎ (0185) 50293 rm28 **A**

H Moderno E Reale via Gramsci 6 ☎ (0185) 50601 rm49 **B**

H Stella via Aurelia Ponente 10 ☎ (0185) 50367 rm31 **A**

H Vesuvio Lungomare V-Veneto 29 ☎ (0185) 50348 rm26 **A**

RAVASCLETTO *Udine*

H Fantinel ☎ (0433) 66046 rm36 **A**

H Harry's Frazione Zovello ☎ (0433) 66050 rm13 **A**

H Peria ☎ (0433) 66039 rm37 **A**

H Valcalda ☎ (0433) 66120 rm32 **A**

RAVELLO *Salerno*

★★**Parsifal** ☎ (0433) 857144 rm19 Mar 20-Oct 20 **A**

RAVENNA *Ravenna*

H Argentario via di Roma 45 ☎ (0544) 22555 rm34 **B**

★★**Centrale Byron** (n.rest) via IV Novembre 14 ☎ (0544) 33479 rm57 **B**

H Diana via G-Rossi 49 ☎ (0544) 39164 rm23 **A**

H Trieste via Trieste 11 ☎ (0544) 421566 rm52 **B**

RIMINI *Forli*

H Admiral via Regina Elena 67 ☎ (0541) 81771 rm90 Mar-Oct **B**

H Atlantico via Trieste ☎ (0541) 24734 rm85 May-Sep **B**

H Biancamano via Cappellini 1 ☎ (0541) 55491 rm72 Mar-Nov **B**

H Gran Sasso via Nuova Circonvallazione 26 ☎ (0541) 770225 rm30 **B**

H Villa Adriatica via Vespucci 3 ☎ (0541) 54599 rm83 **B**

H Villa Verde via Vespucci 38 ☎ (0541) 24742 rm35 **B**

RIVISONDOLI *L'Aquila*

H Botte ☎ (0864) 69129 rm12 Dec-Mar & Jul-Sep **A**

H Calypso ☎ (0864) 699014 rm36 **A**

H Como ☎ (0864) 69127 rm46 Dec 3-Apr 10 & Jun 15-Sep 15 **A**

H Dina's ☎ (0864) 69195 rm27 **A**

H Grand Europa ☎ (0864) 69142 rm57 **B**

ROCCARASO *L'Aquila*

H Excelsior ☎ (0864) 62479 rm35 Dec 20-Apr 10 & Jul-Aug **B**

H Julia ☎ (0864) 62136 rm26 **A**

H Suisse ☎ (0864) 62139 rm48 **A**

H Trieste ☎ (0864) 62128 rm56 **B**

RODI GARGANICO *Puglia*

H Albano via Scalo Marittimo ☎ (0884) 95138 rm12 **A**

H Delle Fave via Trieste ☎ (0884) 95185 rm40 **A**

H Miramare ☎ (0884) 95025 rm29 **B**

◆ **Riveria** ☎ (0884) 95057 rm35 **A**

ROMA (ROME) *Roma*

Roma is one of the world's greatest cultural centres, with evidence of the glory that was ancient Rome to be found everywhere. The Forum contains the ruins of the centre of the Empire's administration and the

heart of its cultural and political life; close by are Trajan's Column, magnificent with its pictoral spiral illustrating the city's earliest history, and the awe-inspiring Coliseum where the people came to be entertained by the feats of the gladiators.
A short drive away is the Vatican City, the smallest sovereign state in the world. This contains not only the residence of the Pope, but also the world's largest church and St Peter's Square, an immense masterpiece designed and completed in less than 12 years, and an incomparable achievement in symmetry. The 1st-century Egyptian obelisk in the centre was once a feature of Nero's Circus. The treasures of St Peter's Basilica include Michelangelo's *Pietà* and a 13th-century bronze statue of St Peter by Arnolfo di Cambio, its foot worn smooth by the kisses of millions of pilgrims. Climb to the top of the Basilica for a magnificent view of Roma and the Vatican City.
In addition to its wide range of museums, art galleries and churches, the city offers delightful city parks and gardens to stroll in, especially the beautiful *Villa Borghese* and the *Giardini degli Aranci*. Markets abound, the best known is the Sunday market at Porta Portese and the daily market at Piazza Vittorio Emanuele, while Roma's best known stores are found close to the Spanish Steps and in Via del Corso, where designer labels include Valentino and Gucci.
EATING OUT You need not spend a fortune to eat in Roma. In traditional areas such as Trastevere you will find small, family-run *trattorie* serving Roman cooking at its best. No visit to Roma would be complete without having tried an appetising pizza or a dish of homemade pasta, such as *spaghetti carbonara*, made with a creamy sauce of beaten egg with bacon. The meat dishes are delicious too, especially the *saltimbocca*, veal with sage and ham in Marsala wine. You will find daily menus *piatti del giorno* in inexpensive *trattorie*, where a carafe of *vino della casa* provides a palatable accompaniment to your meal. For some local flavour try the excellent Frascati and Marino wines which are produced from the vineyards on the hills surrounding the city.
Try cafés in the elegant Via Condotti for *capuccino* coffee and sweet pastries such as *maritozzi*, a kind of brioche roll with sweet custard filling; or, if you feel like splashing out, the stylish *Café de Paris* in Via Veneto, the original *dolce vita* café. Among the city's best restaurants are *Andrea*, in Via Sardegna, and *Alberta Ciarla*, in Piazza San Cosimato, which specialises in seafood.

Abruzzi (n.rest) pza della Rotonda 69 ☎ (06) 6792021 rm25 **A**

H Amalfi (n.rest) via Merulana 278 ☎ (06) 4744313 rm18 **A**

H Esperia (n.rest) via Nazionale 22 ☎ (06) 4744245 rm100 **A**

H Flavio (n.rest) via Frangipane 34 ☎ (06) 6797203 rm23 **A**

H Galeno (n.rest) via del Villini 10 ☎ (06) 862706 rm19 **A**

H Madison (n.rest) via Marsala 60 ☎ (06) 4954344 rm103 **A**

H Medici (n.rest) via Flavia 96 ☎ (06) 4751319 rm68 **B**

H Olympic via Properzio 2a ☎ (06) 6530650 rm48 **B**

H Pavia (n.rest) via Gaeta 83 ☎ (06) 4759090 rm20 **B**

H San Marcoa via Villafranca 1 ☎ (06) 490437 rm66 **B**

ROVERETO *Trento*

H Ancora via delle Scuole 16-18 ☎ (0464) 33707 rm25 **A**

H Quercia via Abetone 68 ☎ (0464) 33650 rm17 **A**

SABAUDIA *Latina*

H Il Gioiello via P-Biancamano ☎ (0773) 55465 rm10 **A**

H La Capricciosa via Folago Morta ☎ (0773) 55205 rm11 **A**

H Mini (n.rest) corso Emanuele III, 120 ☎ (0773) 55987 rm25 **A**

ST VINCENT *Aosta*

H Alba ☎ (0166) 2654 rm10 **A**

H Bijou ☎ (0166) 2770 rm30 **A**

H Corallo ☎ (0166) 2165 rm15 **A**

H Delle Rose ☎ (0166) 2237 rm22 **B**

H Haiti ☎ (0166) 2114 rm25 **A**

H Leon d'Oro ☎ (0166) 2202 rm48 **A**

H Posta ☎ (0166) 2250 rm39 **B**

H Riveria (n.rest) ☎ (0166) 2557 rm14 **A**

SAN BARTOLOMEO AL MARE
Imperia

H Adrimer via Sicilia 36 ☎ (0183) 400869 rm34 Jan 7-Oct 15 **A**

H Bergamo via Aurelia 9 ☎ (0183) 400060 rm46 Mar 20-Sep **A**

★★★**Mayola** Pass ta a mare 140 ☎ (0183) 400739 rm79 Apr 15-Oct 15 **A**

H San Giacomo via Moreno 2 ☎ (0183) 400751 rm43 Mar-Oct **A**

SAN BENEDETTO DEL TRONTO
Ascoli Piceno

H Bolivar via Ovidio 14 ☎ (0735) 81818 rm30 **A**

H Calabresi via Colombo 6 ☎ (0735) 60548 rm68 **B**

H Garden via Buozzi 8 ☎ (0735) 60246 rm54 **B**

H Marconi via Maffei 114 ☎ (0735) 81857 rm42 May 15-Sep 15 **A**

H Royal via Ristori 24 ☎ (0735) 81950 rm30 **B**

H Sporting via Paganini 23 ☎ (0735) 656545 rm53 **B**

SAN CÁNDIDO-INNICHEN
Bolzano

H Capriolo via Pusteria 2 ☎ (0474) 73143 rm28 **A**

H Helm Versciaco 2 ☎ (0474) 76742 rm20 **A**

H Olympia via Drava 2 ☎ (0474) 73105 rm20 **A**

H Posta ☎ (0474) 73355 rm39 **A**

SAN REMO *Imperia*

H Belvedere via Roma 82 ☎ (0184) 80751 rm49 **B**

H Joli Site strada Solaro 61 ☎ (0184) 60797 rm19 **A**

H Marina corso Cavallotti 38 ☎ (0184) 690050 rm13 **A**

H Mogol (n.rest) via Roccasterone 41 ☎ (0184) 83438 rm11 **A**

H Polonia via Matuzia 3 ☎ (0184) 85505 rm23 **A**

H Riviera corso Inglesi 86 ☎ (0184) 85205 rm19 **A**

SAN SEVERO *Foggia*

H Florio ☎ (0881) 82036 rm55 **A**

H Milano via Teano Appulo 10 ☎ (0882) rm61 **B**

SANTA CATERINA VALFURVA *Sondrio*

H Alle Tre Baite ☎ (0342) 935545 rm25 Dec-Apr 15 & Jul-Sep 5 **B**

H Pedranzini ☎ (0342) 935525 rm20 **A**

★★Sobretta ☎ (0342) 935510 rm26 Dec-Apr & Jul-Sep 10 **B**

H Thurwieser ☎ (0342) 935525 rm17 Dec-May 15 & Jun 15-Sep **A**

SANTA CRISTINA IN VALGARDENA *Bolzano*

H Dolomieu (n.rest) via Plesdinaz 54 ☎ (0471) 76764 rm14 **A**

H Kedul (n.rest) via Dursan 26 ☎ (0471) 73308 rm9 **A**

H Marina via Dursan 10A ☎ (0471) 76603 rm12 **A**

H Sasslong Loc Sacun 48 ☎ (0471) 73433 rm12 **A**

H Villa Martha (n.rest) via Plesdinaz 20 ☎ (0471) 76628 rm20 **A**

H Villa Pallua ☎ (0471) 76400 rm30 **A**

SANTA MARGHERITA LIGURE *Genova*

★Europa via Trento S ☎ (0185) 87187 rm16 **B**

★★Villa Anita viale Tigullio 10 ☎ (0185) 86543 rm12 Closed Oct 20-Nov **A**

SANTA TERESA DI GALLURA *Sassari* See **SARDEGNA, ISOLA (SARDINIA)**

SARDEGNA, ISOLA (SARDINIA)

CAGLIARI *Cagliari*

◆ **Alla Vittoria** via Roma 75 ☎ (070) 657970 rm21 **A**

H Quattro Mori (n.rest) via G-M-Angioy 27 ☎ (070) 668535 rm21 **A**

NUORO *Nuoro*

H Grazia Deledda via Lamarmora ☎ (0784) 31257 rm72 **B**

H Grillo via Mons Melas ☎ (0784) 38678 rm46 **B**

H Paradiso via Aosta ☎ (0784) 35585 rm74 **B**

H Sandalia via Einaudi ☎ (0784) 38353 rm49 **B**

ORISTANO *Oristano*

H Ca Ma ☎ (0783) 74374 rm54 **B**

H I.S.A. ☎ (0783) 78040 rm54 **A**

H Piccolo ☎ (0783) 71500 rm16 **A**

SANTA TERESA DI GALLURA *Sassari*

H Esit Miramare pza della Libertà 6 ☎ (0789) 754103 rm14 May-Oct **B**

H Li Nibbari La Testa ☎ (0789) 754453 rm38 **B**

H Moderno via Umberto 39 ☎ (0789) 754233 rm18 **A**

H Riva via Galliano 26 ☎ (0789) 754283 rm8 **A**

SARRE *Aosta*

H Beau Séjour (n.rest) ☎ (0165) 57146 rm12 **A**

H Carla ☎ (0165) 551276 rm21 **A**

H Chuc ☎ (0165) 551555 rm13 **A**

SASSARI *Sassari* See **SARDEGNA, ISOLA (SARDINIA)**

SCIACCA *Agrigento* See **SICILIA (SICILY)**

SELVA DI VAL GARDENA-WOLKENSTEIN IN GRÖDEN *Bolzano*

H Continental via Danterciepies 40 ☎ (0471) 75411 rm30 **A**

H Iris via Danterciepies 86 ☎ (0471) 75233 rm11 **A**

H Savoy via Ciampinei 36 ☎ (0471) 75343 rm26 **A**

H Sun Valley Centro 70 ☎ (0471) 75152 rm21 **A**

H Wolkenstein via Plan da Thiesa 5 ☎ (0471) 76226 rm37 **A**

SENIGALLIA *Ancona*

H Bamby via Rieti 97 ☎ (071) 63466 rm36 May-Sep **B**

H Cristina via Rieti 10 ☎ (071) 64789 rm31 May-Sep **A**

H Europa Lungomare Alighieri ☎ (071) 63800 rm60 May-Sep **B**

H Gabbiano Lungomare L-da-Vinci 91B ☎ (071) 63597 rm45 May-Sep **B**

H Hollywood Lungomare D-Alighieri 62 ☎ (071) 61670 rm32 May-Sep **A**

H Villa Pina via F-Podesti 158 ☎ (071) 62644 rm16 May-Sep **A**

SEQUALS *Pordenone*

H Belvedere ☎ (0427) 93016 rm22 **A**

H Faion Frazione Solimbergo ☎ (0427) 93020 rm12 **A**

SESTRI LEVANTE *Genova*

H Daria via Rimembranza 46 ☎ (0185) 41139 rm23 Apr-Sep **A**

H Elisabetta via P-Novara 7 ☎ (0185) 41128 rm39 Closed Oct-Dec 27 **A**

H Grande Albergo via V-Veneto 2 ☎ (0185) 41017 rm90 May-Sep **A**

H Villa Rosa via C-Raffo 50 ☎ (0185) 42226 rm29 Apr-Sep **A**

SICILIA (SICILY)

AGRIGENTO *Agrigento*

H Bella Napoli pza Lena 6 ☎ (0922) 20435 rm40 **A**

H Belvedere via S. Vito 20 ☎ (0922) 20051 rm35 **A**

H Colleverde via dei Templi ☎ (0922) 29555 rm32 **A**

CALTANISSETTA *Caltanissetta*

H Diprima via Kennedy 16 ☎ (0934) 26088 rm106 **A**

H Europa via B-Gaetani 5 ☎ (0934) 21051 rm26 **A**

CAPO D'ORLANDO *Messina*

H Bristol ☎ (0941) 901390 rm75 **A**

H Tartaruga ☎ (0941) 955013 rm38 **A**

CATANIA *Catania*

H Italia via Etnea 310 ☎ (095) 317833 rm45 **A**

H Moderno via Alessi 9 ☎ (095) 325309 rm47 **A**

H Roma via Libertà 63 ☎ (095) 316167 rm10 **A**

H Torino via P-Toselli 43 ☎ (095) 320909 rm8 **A**

CEFALÙ *Palermo*

H Astro via N-Martoglio 8 ☎ (0921) 21639 rm35 **A**

H Baia del Capitario ☎ (0921) 20005 rm34 **B**

H Terminus via Gramsci 2 ☎ (0921) 21034 rm14 **A**

ENNA

H Belvedere pza F-Crispi 2 ☎ (0935) 21020 rm62 **A**

H Grande Albergo Sicilia pza Colaianni 5 ☎ (0935) 21127 rm60 **A**

At **PERGUSA**(10km S)

H Pergola ☎ (0935) 36017 rm14 **A**

H Serena ☎ (0935) 36113 rm28 **A**

ERICE *Trapani*

H Edelweiss ☎ (0923) 869158 rm15 **A**

H Moderno via V-Emanuele 63 ☎ (0923) 869300 rm26 **B**

GELA *Caltanissetta*

M Gela SS N117 bis Centrale Sicula, Km92 ☎ (0933) 911144 rm91 **B**

H Mediterraneo ☎ (0933) 917583 rm72 **A**

MARSALA *Trapani*

H Stella d'Italia via M-Rapisardi 7 ☎ (0923) 953003 rm51 **A**

MESSINA *Messina*

H Commercio via 1 Settembre 73 ☎ (090) 774404 rm49 **A**

H Europa ☎ (090) 2711601 rm115 **B**

H Excelsior via Maddalena 32 ☎ (090) 2938721 rm44 **B**

H Milano via dei Verdi 65 ☎ (090) 772078 rm28 **A**

H Venezia pza Cairoli 4 ☎ (090) 718076 rm76 **B**

MILAZZO *Messina*

H Diana ☎ (090) 921382 rm24 **A**

H Flora ☎ (090) 921882 rm23 **A**

PALERMO *Palermo*

H Bristol via Maqueda 437 ☎ (091) 589247 rm13 **A**

H Centrale corso V-Emanuele 327 ☎ (091) 588409 rm117 **A**

H Metropol via Turrisi Colonna 4 ☎ (091) 588608 rm44 **A**

H Posta via A-Gagini 77 ☎ (091) 587338 rm21 **A**

H Sausele via V-Errante 12 ☎ (091) 237524 rm40 **A**

H Touring via M-Stabile 136 ☎ (091) 584444 rm24 **A**

PIAZZA ARMERINA *Enna*

H Park Hotel Paradiso ☎ (0935) 81841 rm26 **A**

H Selene ☎ (0935) 82776 rm42 **A**

RAGUSA *Ragusa*

H Jonio via Risorgimento 49 ☎ (0932) 24322 rm47 **A**

H Montreal via San Guiseppe 10 ☎ (0932) 21133 rm63 **B**

SASSARI *Sassari*

H Giusy pza S.Antonio 21 ☎ (079) 233327 rm23 **A**

H Marini Due via Chironi ☎ (07100) 277282 rm54 **B**

SCIACCA *Agrigento*

H Garden via Valverde ☎ (0925) 21203 rm58 **A**

SIRACUSA (SYRACUSE) *Siracusa*

H Bellavista via D-Siculo 4 ☎ (0931) 36912 rm49 **A**

H Grand via Mazzini 12 ☎ (0931) 65101 rm47 **A**

H Panorama via Necropoli Grotticelle 33 ☎ (0931) 32122 rm51 **B**

H Riviera via Eucleida 9 ☎ (0931) 68240 rm15 **A**

TAORMINA

H Continental via Dionisio Primo ☎ (0942) 23805 rm43 **B**

H Garden via C-Patricio 1 ☎ (0942) 25120 rm14 **A**

H Residence Salite Dente 4 ☎ (0942) 23463 rm28 **A**

H Sirius via G-Vecchia ☎ (0942) 23477 rm41 Apr-Oct **B**

H Victoria corso Umberto 81 ☎ (0942) 23372 rm22 **A**

At **MAZZARÒ**(4.5km E)

H Baia Azzurra ☎ (0942) 23249 rm49 **B**

H Isola Bella Isolabella ☎ (0942) 24289 rm42 Apr-Oct **B**

H Raneri ☎ (0942) 23962 rm28 **B**

TRAPANI *Trapani*

H Cavallino Bianco Lungomare D-Alighieri ☎ (0923) 21549 rm64 **A**

H Nuovo Russo via Tintori 4 ☎ (0923) 22166 rm33 **A**

H Vittoria via F-Crispi 4 ☎ (0923) 27244 rm57 **A**

SIENA *Siena*

Siena stands proudly 1, 000ft up in the Tuscan hills at the meeting point of three ridges. One of Italy's great art centres, abounding with buildings of historic and architectural merit, it also ranks among its best preserved medieval towns and is a splendid example of successful early town planning with an abundance of fascinating twisting lanes and alleys that rise and dip as they follow the land's hilly contours.

Siena's main square – the Campo – is a superb vista of marble and red brick paving in the pattern of a gigantic fan dominated by the tower of the Gothic town hall (1297 – 1310). The old Roman forum, surrounded by ancient palaces, shops and restaurants, is very much the focal point of the city. A first glimpse quickly explains how the colour known as burnt sienna obtained its name: the pigment comes from this area, and its hue is imprinted on many of the fine buildings.

EATING OUT *Tullio ai Tre Cristi*, in Vicolo Provenzano, is a long-time favourite of both residents and visitors. *Al Mangia*, in Piazzao del Campo, has outdoor tables on one of the world's most beautiful piazzas.

H Castagneto (n.rest) via del Cappuccini 39 ☎ (0577) 45103 rm11 Mar 15-Dec **A**

H Continentale via Banchi di Sopra 85 ☎ (0577) 41451 rm42 **B**

H Garden via Custoza 2 ☎ (0577) 47056 rm65 **A**

H Italia (n.rest) via Cavour 67 ☎ (0577) 41177 rm73 **B**

H Moderno via B-Peruzzi 19 ☎ (0577) 288453 rm71 **A**

H Vico Alto via delle Regioni 26 ☎ (0577) 48571 rm40 **B**

H Villa Terraia (n.rest) via dell'Ascarello 13 ☎ (0577) 221108 rm27 Apr-Oct **A**

SILVI MARINA *Teramo*

H Astor via B-Croce ☎ (085) 930458 rm30 Jun-Sep **A**

H Candeloro via A-Rossi 12 ☎ (085) 930216 rm15 **A**

H Cirillo via Garibaldi 190 ☎ (085) 930404 rm45 May-Sep **A**

H Maxi via Colombo 74 ☎ (085) 930330 rm47 **B**

H Milano via A-Rossi 6 ☎ (085) 930264 rm34 Jun-Sep **A**

H Silvi via A-Rossi ☎ (085) 930405 rm37 May-Sep 22 **A**

SIRACUSA (SYRACUSE) *Siracusa*
See **SICILIA (SICILY)**

SIRMIONE *Brescia*

H Catullo (n.rest) ☎ (030) 916181 rm28 Mar 20-Oct 15 **B**

H Luna ☎ (030) 916137 rm38 May-Sep **A**

H Marconi ☎ (030) 916007 rm24 Apr-Oct 22 **A**

H Villa Pagoda ☎ (030) 916165 rm7 **A**

SOLDA-SULDEN *Bolzano*

H Cevedale ☎ (0473) 75413 rm22 Jun-Sep & Xmas- Etr **A**

H Cornelia ☎ (0473) 75432 rm20 **A**

H Dangl (n.rest) ☎ (0473) 75416 rm21 **A**

H Eller ☎ (0473) 75421 rm50 **B**

H Marlet ☎ (0473) 75475 rm23 Jun-Sep & Xmas-Etr **B**

H Mignon ☎ (0473) 75445 rm21 Jun-Sep & Xmas-Etr **B**

H Panorama (n.rest) ☎ (0473) 75400 rm16 **A**

SONDRIO *Sondrio*

H Cristello via L-Cadorna 72 ☎ (0342) 213005 rm18 **B**

H Europa via L-Cadorna 15 ☎ (0342) 211444 rm43 **B**

H Schenatti via Bernina ☎ (0342) 213108 rm15 **B**

SORRENTO *Napoli*

H Bellevue Syrene via Marina Grande 1 ☎ (081) 8781024 rm50 **B**

H Carlton International via Correale 15 ☎ (081) 8781681 rm70 Apr-Oct **B**

H Grand Hotel de la Ville via Rota 15 ☎ (081) 8782144 rm120 Apr-Oct **B**

H Regina via Marina Grande ☎ (081) 8782721 rm36 Apr-Oct **B**

H Solara via Capo 118 ☎ (081) 8783030 rm37 Mar-Oct **B**

SPELLO *Umbria*

H Julia via S. Angelo 22 ☎ (0742) 651174 rm22 **B**

H Portonaccio Borge via Centrale Umbra ☎ (0742) 651313 rm29 **B**

SPEZIA, LA *la Spezia*

H Firenze & Continental (n.rest) via Paleocapa 7 ☎ (0187) 31248 rm27 **B**

H Genova via F-Rosselli 84 ☎ (0187) 30372 rm29 **A**

SPOLETO *Perugia*

H Aurora (n.rest) via Apollinare 3 ☎ (0743) 28115 rm14 **B**

H Boni Cerri loc Cortaccione ☎ (0743) 46205 rm7 **A**

H Casaline loc Poreta ☎ (0743) 520811 rm7 **B**

H Paradiso loc Monteluco ☎ (0743) 37182 rm24 **B**

STAFFA See **MACUGNAGA**

STELVIO, PASSO DELLO *Sondrio*

H Folgore ☎ (0342) 903141 rm37 May 15-Oct **B**

STRESA *Novara*

H Ariston ☎ (0323) 31195 rm12 **B**

H Elena Meublè ☎ (0323) 31043 rm14 **B**

H Mon Toc ☎ (0323) 30282 rm15 **A**

H Orsola Meublè ☎ (0323) 31087 rm17 **A**

H Sempione ☎ (0323) 30463 rm17 **B**

SULMONA *L'Aquila*

H Armando's ☎ (0864) 31252 rm18 **A**

H Artu ☎ (0864) 52758 rm23 **A**

H Traffico ☎ (0864) 51221 rm18 **A**

TAGLIACOZZO *L'Aquila*

H Bocconcino ☎ (0863) 6328 rm42 **A**

H Garden ☎ (0863) 6396 rm50 Jul-Aug **B**

H Marina ☎ (0863) 6243 rm31 **A**

H Miramonti ☎ (0863) 6581 rm17 **A**

TAORMINA *Messina* See **SICILIA (SICILY)**

TARCENTO *Udine*

H Centrale ☎ (0432) 79150 rm36 **A**

H Tarcentino ☎ (0432) 785354 rm14 **A**

TEGLIO *Sondrio*

H Combolo ☎ (0342) 780083 rm39 **A**

H Meden ☎ (0342) 780080 rm38 **A**

TERAMO *Teramo*

H Abruzzi via Mazzini 18 ☎ (0861) 53043 rm50 **B**

H Garden via Crucioli ☎ (0861) 3655 rm35 **A**

H Gran Sasso via L-Vinciguerra ☎ (0861) 3897 rm40 **A**

H Michelangelo via Coste S-Agostino ☎ (0861) 53041 rm125 **B**

H Sporting via de Gasperi 41 ☎ (0861) 412661 rm55 **B**

TERNI *Umbria*

H Brenta II (n.rest) via Montegrappa 51 ☎ (0744) 273957 rm21 **B**

H Lido loc Piediluco ☎ (0744) 68354 rm22 **A**

H Velino (n.rest) loc Marmore ☎ (0744) 67425 rm7 **A**

TERRACINA *Latina*

H Bridge via Pontina Km 106 ☎ (0773) 71018 rm14 **A**

H Da Baffone via Appia ☎ (0773) 726007 rm8 **A**

H Il Guscio via Bad Homburg 16 ☎ (0773) 730006 rm38 **A**

H River via Pontina Km 106 ☎ (0773) 730681 rm94 Apr-Sep **A**

H Villa Mirasole via Circe 150 ☎ (0773) 731533 rm10 **A**

TIRANO *Sondrio*

H Bernina ☎ (0342) 701302 rm7 **A**

H Rotonda ☎ (0342) 701966 rm11 **A**

TODI *Perugia*

H Cavour (n.rest) C-Cavour 12 ☎ (075) 882417 rm19 **A**

H Zodiaco via del Crocefisso 23 ☎ (075) 882625 rm29 **A**

TOLMEZZO *Udine*

H Al Benvenuto ☎ (0433) 2990 rm19 **A**

H Cimenti ☎ (0433) 2926 rm21 **A**

H Coop-Ca ☎ (0433) 2572 rm29 **A**

H Roma ☎ (0433) 2081 rm32 **A**

TORINO (TURIN) *Torino*

Torino's grace and charm surprise many visitors. For this delightful city bears a mantle of French influence, characterised by the wide, formal avenues, elegant squares and gardens.

Torino is the capital of the Piemonte region, an important centre for industry and trade and a place of learning and culture. It has many fine art collections, and the world-famous treasure, the Holy Shroud of Turin, is housed in the vast cathedral.

The Via Roma is lined with smart boutiques boasting top names in Italian fashion. For antiques and books, look in the Piazza San Carlo and Via Po. The Balon flea market is held every Saturday morning the the Piazza della Republica.

EATING OUT Local specialities include *agnolotti* – ravioli stuffed with truffles, spinach, lamb or veal; white truffles from Alba; *bolliti con salsa verde* – boiled meats with a green herb sauce; *gianduia* – chocolate pudding; *zabaglione* – whipped egg yolks and Marsala; and *grissini* – thin breadsticks. Regional wines include the red Barolo and the sparkling white Asti Spumante. Vermouth is made in Turin using a blend of wines flavoured with Alpine herbs.

H Adriano via Pollenzo 41 ☎ (011) 380050 rm38 **B**

H Antico Distretto corse Valdecco 10 ☎ (011) 545453 rm30 **B**

H Cairo via la Loggia 2 ☎ (011) 352003 rm52 **B**

H Canelli via San Dalmazzo 7 ☎ (011) 546078 rm29 **B**

H Eden via Donizetti 22 ☎ (011) 659545 rm26 **B**

H Piemontese via Berthollet 21 ☎ (011) 651101 rm29 **B**

H Scoiattolo via 25 Aprile 186 ☎ (011) 670472 rm19 **B**

H Universo corse Peschiera 166 ☎ (011) 336480 rm33 **B**

H Verna & Guarene via B-Galliari 2c ☎ (011) 659358 rm29 **B**

H Villa Regina via Monferrato 2 ☎ (011) 831285 rm19 **B**

TORRE DEL LAGO PUCCINI *Lucca*

H Butterfly via Belvedere Puccini 24 ☎ (0584) 341024 rm10 **A**

H Gio via Aurelia 284 ☎ (0584) 340186 rm16 **A**

H Villa Rosy via Marconi 315 ☎ (0584) 341350 rm16 **A**

TOSCOLANO MADERNO *Brescia*

H Golfo Maderno ☎ (0365) 641240 rm25 Apr-Sep **B**

H Maderno ☎ (0365) 641070 rm30 May-Sep **A**

H San Marco Maderno ☎ (365) 641103 rm19 **A**

TRANI *Puglia*

H Riviera ☎ (0883) 43222 rm28 **A**

H Royal ☎ (0883) 588010 rm50 **B**

H Trani ☎ (0883) 588010 rm51 **B**

TRAPANI *Trapani* See **SICILIA (SICILY)**

TREMEZZO *Como*

H Azalea ☎ (0344) 40424 rm10 **B**

H Villa Marie ☎ (0344) 40427 rm15 Apr 15-Sep **A**

TRICESIMO *Udine*

H Belvedere ☎ (0432) 851385 rm22 **A**

H Stella d'Oro ☎ (0432) 851262 rm20 **A**

TRIESTE *Trieste*

H Impero (n.rest) via Sant'Anastasio 1 ☎ (040) 65933 rm53 **A**

H Istria (n.rest) via Timeus 5 ☎ (040) 795244 rm22 **A**

H Mignon Grignano ☎ (040) 224130 rm10 **B**

H Perù (n.rest) via Ghega 2 ☎ (040) 395911 rm39 **A**

H Roma (n.rest) via Ghega 7 ☎ (040) 61674 rm42 **A**

TURIN See**TORINO**

UDINE *Udine*

H Apollo via Paparotti 9 ☎ (0432) 600061 rm35 **A**

H Casa Bianca via Podgora 16 ☎ (0432) 35612 rm49 **B**

H Plaza (n.rest) pza le Celle 62 ☎ (0432) 530731 rm43 **A**

H Quo Vadis pza le Celle 28 ☎ (0432) 21091 rm14 **A**

H Ramandolo via Forni di Sotto 28 ☎ (0432) 470994 rm37 **A**

UMBERTIDE *Umbria*

H Moderno S-S Tiberina 3 bis ☎ (075) 932159 rm24 **B**

H Rio S-S Tiberina 3 bis ☎ (075) 935033 rm44 **B**

USSITA *Macerata*

H Felycita Frontignano ☎ (0737) 90121 rm26 **A**

H Ussita pza Cavallari ☎ (0737) 99171 rm24 **A**

VALDISOTTO *Sondrio*

◆ **Belvedere** S-Lucia ☎ (0342) 901589 rm20 **A**

H Camoscio ☎ (0342) 950326 rm26 **A**

H Colombano ☎ (0342) 901460 rm23 **A**

VALSOLDA *Como*

H Ombretta ☎ (0344) 68275 rm10 Apr-Oct **A**

H Riviera ☎ (0344) 68156 rm22 **A**

★★Stella d'Italia San Mamete ☎ (0344) 68139 rm35 Apr-Oct **B**

VALTOURNENCHE *Aosta*

At **MAEN**(1.5km SW)

H Sport ☎ (0166) 92066 rm15 **A**

At **PAQUIER**

H Al Caminetto ☎ (0166) 92150 rm15 **A**

H Bijou ☎ (0166) 92109 rm20 **A**

H Ideal ☎ (0166) 92062 rm12 **A**

H Meridiana (n.rest) ☎ (0166) 92218 rm11 **A**

H Meynet ☎ (0166) 92075 rm12 **A**

H Montana ☎ (0166) 92023 rm29 **A**

H Tourist ☎ (0166) 92070 rm35 **B**

VALVERDE See **CESENATICO**

VARAZZE *Savona*

H Cristallo via Cilea 4 ☎ (019) 92764 rm47 Closed Oct **B**

★★Delfino via Colombo 48 ☎ (019) 97073 rm25 **B**

H Eden via Villagrande 1 ☎ (019) 97086 rm49 **B**

H Savoy via Marconi 4 ☎ (019) 97056 rm46 May-Oct **B**

VARENNA *Como*

H Cavallino ☎ (0341) 830223 rm5 **A**

H Milano ☎ (0341) 830298 rm9 **B**

★★Olivedo ☎ (0341) 830115 rm22 Closed Nov 7-Dec 5 **B**

H Sole ☎ (0341) 830206 rm7 **A**

VARIGOTTI See **FINALE LIGURE**

VENEZIA (VENICE) *Venezia*

There are no road communications in city. Vehicles may be left in garages in piazzale Roma at the island end of the causeway or at open parking places on the mainland approaches.Garages will not accept advance bookings. Transport to hotels is by waterbus, etc. for which there are fixed charges for fares and porterage.Hotel rooms overlooking the Grand Canal normally carry a surcharge.

Venezia is built on more than 100 islands with at least as many canals spanned by over 400 bridges. Use the *vaporetto*, the fast cheap waterbus, for travel on the canals; water taxis or gondolas are very expensive.

The imposing *Palazzo Ducale* (Duke's Palace), stands at the heart of the city near St Mark's Square, a superb architectural ensemble dominated by the Basilica of St Mark. Like Venice itself, the Basilica is a magnificent blend of Eastern and Western artistic styles, combining marble, mosaics and glittering gold.

Venezia offers a wealth of great places, churches, museums and galleries to visit, notably the *Accademia*, with its definitive collection of Venetian paintings. You can combine a visit here with a wander round the Zattere, the stone-flagged quay that borders the Giudecca Canal and leads round to the Baroque Church of Santa Maria della Salute.

Among the islands to visit are San Giorgio Maggiore, with its marvellous Palladian church; Murano, famous for glass-making; Burano, noted for its lace; and Torcello, which boasts a magnificent cathedral. The Venice Lido is still one of Europe's most fashionable beach resorts.

Excellent shops are to be found around St Mark's Square, particularly impressive being those in the Mercerie. For budget-priced clothes the best place is around the Rialto where there is also an excellent daily food market with tantalising fruit, vegetables and fish.

EATING OUT Traditional Venetian cooking is largely based on seafood. Lobster, crab, scampi and a tasty white fish locally known as *San Pietro* are popular. Speciality dishes include *Brodetto di pesce* (fish soup); *soppressa* (Venetian sausages) and *fegato alla veneziana* – thinly sliced calves' liver cooked with onions.

For coffee or ice-cream for a treat, patronise *Florian's* or *Quadri's* in St Mark's Square.

Venetian restaurants tend to be expensive even by Italian standards, especially those in the centre, but if cost is not a problem then the terrace restaurants of the Danieli, overlooking the lagoon, and its sister hotel the Gritti Palace, overlooking the Grand Canal, are outstanding. In the moderately priced category, *Fiaschetteria Toscane*, in Campo San Giovanni Cristomo, is deservedly popular with Venetians as well as visitors.

At **CAVALLINO**

H Al Capitello (n.rest) via Fausta 412 ☎ (041) 968696 rm23 **A**

H Fenix via F-Valle Dolce ☎ (041) 968040 rm64 **B**

H International C'a di Valle ☎ (041) 968108 rm52 **B**

H Righetto C'a di Valle ☎ (041) 968083 rm56 **B**

H Rondine (n.rest) via Fausta 60 ☎ (041) 966172 rm26 **B**

H Safari via Batterie 160 ☎ (041) 966101 rm12 **A**

H Sloemare via Fausta 345 ☎ (041) 968023 rm42 **B**

H Valdor C'a Savio 161 ☎ (041) 966108 rm45 **B**

VENTIMIGLIA *Imperia*

★★Posta via Scottoconvento 15 ☎ (0184) 351218 rm18 **A**

H Sole Mare via Marconi 12 ☎ (0184) 351855 rm28 **A**

H Splendid via Roma 33 ☎ (0184) 351503 rm26 **A**

H Torino via Hanbury 9 ☎ (0184) 351173 rm31 **A**

H Vittoria via Hambury 9 ☎ (0184) 351231 rm16 **A**

VERBANIA *Novara*

At **INTRA**(2.5km NE)

H Cavour ☎ (0323) 41132 rm5 **A**

H Da Nando ☎ (0323) 43244 rm4 **A**

H Touring ☎ (0323) 41224 rm24 **A**

H Villa Aurora ☎ (0323) 41482 rm12 **B**

At **PALLANZA**(1km SW)

H Castagnola ☎ (0323) 503414 rm107 Jun-Sep **B**

H Italia Meublè ☎ (0323) 503206 rm14 Mar-Oct **B**

H Novara ☎ (0323) 503527 rm16 **A**

H Sant'Anna ☎ (0323) 503312 rm14 **B**

H Villa Azales Meublè ☎ (0323) 506692 rm12 Apr-Oct **B**

H Villa Lidia Meublè ☎ (0323) 506714 rm10 **A**

H Villa Petronio ☎ (0323) 506015 rm8 **A**

VERCELLI *Vercelli*

H Brusasca corse Magenta 71 ☎ (0161) 66010 rm25 **B**

H Dell'Auto corse Novara 65 ☎ (0161) 53268 rm14 **B**

H Europa via Santorre Santarosa 16 ☎ (0161) 66847 rm22 **B**

H Riz-Vapore via G-Ferraris 90 ☎ (0161) 64742 rm27 **B**

H Sport corse Matteotti 31 ☎ (0161) 2459 rm25 **B**

H Valsesia via G-Ferraris 104 ☎ (0161) 53842 rm11 **B**

VERONA *Verona*

Readers of Shakespeare are familiar with Verona, most obviously through *The Two Gentlemen of Verona*, but also as the setting for *Romeo and Juliet*. A stroll along Via delle Arche Scaligere will reveal the alleged site of *Casa di Romeo* and, at 23 Via Cappello, Juliet's house, complete, of course with balcony. But Verona has much more to offer the visitor than its links with Shakespeare. It became a Roman town in BC49 and contains many reminders of those times. Perhaps the most impressive is the Arena, the 3rd-century amphitheatre seating 22, 000; unlike Rome's Colosseum it is still in use as an opera house and theatre.

Standing on the banks of the River Adige in a setting of cypress-covered hills, Verona has been described as one of the country's most prosperous and elegant cities. The Basilica of San Zeno Maggiore is arguably the noblest Romanesque church in northern Italy, and the *Loggia del Consiglio*, the old town hall, one of the most beautiful of all early Renaissance buildings.

EATING OUT Verona is as well known for its wines as for its food. Some of Italy's best known wines are produced in the area and names such as Soave, Bardolino and Valpolicella have gained international renown. To complement the wines try one of the many local pasta and seafood dishes.

H Aurora via Pellicciai 2 ☎ (045) 594717 rm22 **A**

H Doge via C-Abba 12B ☎ (045) 912491 rm16 **A**

H Mazzanti via Mazzanti 6 ☎ (045) 26813 rm23 **A**

H San Micheli via Valverde 2 ☎ (045) 23749 rm15 **A**

H Scalzi via Scalzi 5 ☏ (045) 32200 rm23 **A**

H Valverde via Valverde 91 ☏ (045) 33611 rm19 **A**

VERRES *Aosta*

H Bon Accueil ☏ (0125) 929015 rm7 **A**

H Da Pierre ☏ (0125) 929376 rm12 **B**

H Evançon ☏ (0125) 929035 rm20 **B**

VIAREGGIO *Lucca*

H Bella Riviera (n.rest) via Manin 34 ☏ (0584) 962182 rm28 **A**

H City (n.rest) via Zara 25 ☏ (0584) 50343 rm13 **A**

H Metropole via Saffi 2 ☏ (0584) 44450 rm17 Jun-Sep **B**

H Midy via F-Gioia 9 ☏ (0584) 962479 rm18 Apr-Sep **A**

H Miramare (n.rest) via Carducci 27 ☏ (0584) 48441 rm31 **B**

H Paolina via Buonarroti 21 ☏ (0584) 962916 rm12 **A**

H Ross (n.rest) via Buonarroti 81 ☏ (0584) 962454 rm15 **A**

VICO EQUENSE *Napoli*

H Aequa ☏ (081) 8798000 rm57 **A**

H Moon Valley ☏ (081) 8798142 rm74 Apr-Oct **A**

★★**Oriente** ☏ (081) 8798143 rm77 **B**

VIESTE *Foggia*

H Due Mari ☏ (0884) 76331 rm36 **B**

H Falcone ☏ (0884) 78251 rm54 **B**

H Lido Carmine ☏ (0884) 76709 rm15 **A**

H Merinum Scialara ☏ (0884) 76721 rm51 **B**

H Riviera ☏ (0884) 78495 rm25 **A**

VILLALAGO *L'Aquila*

H Stella Alphine ☏ (0864) 740132 rm36 **A**

ZADINA PINETA
See **CESENATICO**

ZAPPONETA *Foggia*

◆ **Adriatica** ☏ (0884) 29149 rm16 Jul-Aug **B**

M Italia rm9 **A**

The lovely Torre Guaita is one of the best known sights of San Marino.

LUXEMBOURG

FACTS & FIGURES

Capital: Luxembourg City
Language: French, German
IDD code: 352. To call the UK dial 00 44
Currency: Luxembourg Franc (LFr1 = 100 centimes) The Belgian Franc is also accepted in Luxembourg
Local time: GMT+1 (Summer GMT+2)
Emergency Services: Police 409–401; Emergency 012

Business Hours

Banks: 0900–1200 and 1330–1630 Mon–Fri
Shops: 0900–1800 Mon–Sat

Average daily temperatures:
Luxembourg City °C

Jan 1	Jul 18
Mar 6	Sep 15
May 13	Nov 5

Tourist Information:
Luxembourg National Tourist Office
UK 36–37 Picadilly
London W1V 9PA
Tel 01–434 2800

USA 801 Second Ave
New York, NY 10017
Tel (212) 370–9850

The Grand Duchy of Luxembourg is a small independent state, 998 sq miles in area, situated between France, Germany and Belgium. It comprises parts of the Ardennes uplands and the Lorraine scarplands. Luxembourg, the capital, is an attractive and historic town founded on a natural defensive site. Under successive occupations by the Spaniards, Austrians and French, its fortifications were so elaborated that it came to be considered the strongest inland fortress in Europe – the Gibraltar of the continent. The fortifications, dismantled in accordance with the treaty of London, have been largely replaced by parks and gardens, although many relics, including the Casemates – the network of underground fortifications – remain. Notable buildings include the grand-ducal palace (1572), cathedral (1618) and town hall. The main shopping areas are to be found in the south of the city, around the Place de la Gare.

Apart from Luxembourg, the chief towns are Esch-sur-Alzette, Dudelange, Ettelbrück, Diekirch, Echternach and Wiltz. The Luxembourgeois patois (mainly Germanic) and French are official languages, but side by side with these the German language is freely used.

As a destination for walkers, Luxembourg has few equals, while those interested in history and culture have a choice of no fewer than 130 castles to admire.

HOW TO GET THERE

BY CAR

Luxembourg is easily reached through either Belgium or France. Luxembourg City is just over 200 miles from Oostende (Ostend) or Zeebrugge and about 260 miles from Boulogne, Calais or Dunkerque (Dunkirk), so it is within a day's drive from the Channel coast.

For details of the AA's Overseas Routes Service consult the Contents page.

For location Map, see Belgium.

SPEED LIMITS

In built-up areas speed is limited to 60 kph (37 mph); outside built-up areas 90 kph (56 mph); motorways 120 kph (74 mph).

PARKING

Parking in blue zones is allowed only with a properly displayed parking disc, available from the ACL, petrol stations and principal banks.

BY TRAIN

If you do not have an InterRail or Eurail pass, all train and bus stations sell Network tickets (Billets Reseaux) giving you unlimited second-class train and bus travel (but not valid for buses within the capital) for one day or for 5 days within a period of one month. The Benelux Pass lets you travel for any 5 days in a 17-day period in Belgium, the Netherlands and Luxembourg.

ACCOMMODATION

The gazetteer that follows includes a range of places to stay for less than 1292LFr in most cases.

The price bands are:

A 612 – 952LFr
B 952 – 1292LFr

taking an exchange rate at 68LFr = £1
41LFr = US$1

It is possible, however that prices may change during the currency of this book. Further details can be obtained from local tourist offices.

Abbreviations: av avenue bd boulevard pl place rte route r rue

BEAUFORT

H Binsfeld Montée du Château 1 ☏ 86013 rm20 Mar 20-Nov 15 **A**

◆ **Rustique** r du Château 55 ☏ 86086 rm7 Mar 15-Nov 15 **A**

BECH-KLEINMACHER

◆ **Mosella** rte du Vin 21 ☏ 69124 rm5 Closed Aug 22-Sep 12 & Dec 23-31 **A**

BERDORF

H Herber rte d'Echternach 91 ☏ 79188 rm45 Closed Dec 4-Feb 2 **B**

H Kinnen rte d'Echternach 34 ☏ 79183 rm35 Mar 24-Oct 23 **B**

◆ **Pittoresque** r Um Wues 115A ☏ 79597 rm8 Closed Jan 10-Feb **A**

H Streng rte d'Echternach 62 ☏ 79198 rm18 Mar-Nov 15 **A**

CLERVAUX

★★**Abbaye** Grand r 80 ☏ 91049 rm50 Closed Mar 3-Oct 23 **A**

H Nations r de la Gare 29 ☏ 91018 rm47 **A**

CONSDORF

◆ **Bonne Auberge** Michelshof ☏ 79063 rm8 Dec 15-Jan **A**

H Central rte d'Echternach 6 ☏ 79007 rm16 Closed Jan **A**

H Mersch rte de Luxembourg 1-3 ☏ 79815 rm40 Closed Jan 6-Feb **A**

DIEKIRCH

H Au Bon Accueil (n.rest) av de la Gare 77-79 ☏ 803476 rm11 Closed Dec 26-Jan 4 **A**

★**Beau Séjour** Esplanade 12 ☏ 803403 rm28 Closed Feb 1-15 **A**

H Gare av de la Gare 73 ☏ 803305 rm10 Closed Dec 16-Jan 14 **A**

◆ **Paix** (n.rest) pl Guillaume 7 ☏ 809910 rm4 **A**

ECHTERNACH

H Abbaye r des Merciers 2 ☏ 729184 rm15 **A**

H Aigle Noir r de la Gare 54 ☏ 72383 rm23 Closed Jan & Feb **A**

◆ **Beau Séjour** r Maximillen 18 ☏ 729747 rm9 **A**

H Bon Accueil (n.rest) r des Merciers 3 ☏ 72052 rm11 **A**

★★**Commerce** pl du Marché 16 ☏ 72301 rm50 Feb-Nov 15 & Dec 20-31 **A**

H Étoile d'Or r de la Gare 39 ☏ 72095 rm36 Mar 23-Sep **A**

★★**Parc** (n.rest) r de l'Hôpital 9 ☏ 729481 rm28 Mar 15-Nov 15 **A**

H Petit Poete pl du Marché 13 ☏ 72072 rm17 Mar 15-Sep 25 **A**

H Petite Marquise pl du Marché 18 ☏ 72382 rm33 Feb 10-Nov 11 **A**

H Petite Suisse (n.rest) r A-Duchscher 56 ☏ 72178 rm22 Apr-Sep **A**

◆ **Postillon** r de Luxembourg 7 ☏ 72188 rm16 **A**

H Prince Henri et Terminus r de la Gare 51 ☏ 72131 rm14 May 10-Sep 15 **A**

H Soleil r des Remparts 20 ☏ 72033 rm9 **A**

H Sure r de la Gare 49 ☏ 729414 rm31 May-Sep **B**

ESCH-SUR-ALZETTE

H Acacia r de la Libération 10 ☏ 541061 rm26 **B**

H Carrefour r V-Hugo 1 ☏ 545144 rm20 Closed Aug 16-Sep 5 & Dec 26-Jan 3 **B**

◆ **Mercure** r de l'Alzette 12 ☏ 541133 rm7 **A**

H Paris (n.rest) bd Kennedy 48 ☏ 541188 rm15 **A**

H Poste (n.rest) r de l'Alzette 107 ☏ 53504 rm23 Closed Dec 21-Jan 5 **A**

ESCH-SUR-SÛRE

H Ardennes r de Moulin 1 ☏ 89108 rm26 Apr 20-Sep **A**

H Moulin r du Moulin 6 ☏ 89107 rm25 Mar 9-Dec **A**

H Postillon r de l'Eglise 1 ☏ 899033 rm24 Closed Jan 11-Feb 9 **B**

◆ **Sûre** r du Pont 1 ☏ 89110 rm20 Feb-Nov **A**

ETTELBRUCK

H Herckmans pl de la Résistance 3 ☏ 817428 rm12 **A**

H Lanners r de la Gare 1 ☏ 82127 rm15 Closed Jan 4-28 **B**

H Luxembourg r Prince-Henri 7-9 ☏ 82257 rm20 **A**

GREVENMACHER

H Govers Grand r 15 ☏ 75137 rm14 **A**

◆ **Pigalle** rte de Thionville 30 ☏ 75106 rm5 Closed Oct 10-25 **B**

INSENBORN

H Du Lac (n.rest) Bonnel 1 ☏ 89064 rm10 Closed Sep 16-Oct 14 **A**

◆ **Kler** Maison 41 ☏ 89067 rm10 **A**

H Peiffer Maison 36 ☏ 89897 rm9 **A**

KAUTENBACH

H Huberty Maison 21 ☏ 958551 rm10 **A**

LAROCHETTE

H Château r de Medernach 1 ☏ 87009 rm45 Closed Jan **B**

H Faubourg (n.rest) r de Medernach 34 ☏ 87002 rm3 Closed Aug 29-Sep 19 **A**

LUXEMBOURG

H Atlas (n.rest) r du F-Neipperg ☏ 487255 rm18 **A**

◆ **Bloen Eck** rte de T-Howald 175 ☏ 433956 rm8 **A**

H Carlton (n.rest) r de Strasbourg 9 ☎ 484802 rm45 **A**

H Century (n.rest) r J-Junck 6 ☎ 489437 rm23 **A**

◆ **Chemin de Fer** r J-Junck 4 ☎ 493528 rm25 **A**

H City (n.rest) r de Strasbourg 1 ☎ 484608 rm30 **B**

H Fort Reinsheim rte d'Esch 1-41 ☎ 444136 rm26 **A**

◆ **Parisien** r Zithe 46 ☎ 492397 rm9 **A**

◆ **Pax** rte de Thionville 121 ☎ 482563 rm14 **B**

◆ **Sporting** (n.rest) r de Strasbourg 15 ☎ 484332 rm15 Closed Aug **A**

H Touring r de Strasburg 4 ☎ 484629 rm15 **A**

MONDORF-LES-BAINS

H International av Fr-Clement 58 ☎ 67073 rm44 Closed Dec 25-Feb 4 **B**

H Windsor av des Bains 19 ☎ 67203 rm18 Closed Dec 24-Jan 1 **B**

REMICH

H Moselle pl du Marché 1 ☎ 69127 rm24 Feb 15-Dec 15 **A**

H St-Nicolas Esplanade 31 ☎ 698333 rm46 **B**

H Vignes rte de Mondorf 29 ☎ 69028 rm30 Closed Jan 15-Feb **B**

VIANDEN

H Berg en Dal r de la Gare 3 ☎ 84127 rm48 Jan-Mar 22 & Nov 11-Dec 21 **A**

H Château Grand r 74-78 ☎ 84878 rm30 Closed Nov 27-Jan 11 **B**

◆ **Clees** r de la Gare 8 ☎ 84474 rm10 Mar-Oct 20 **A**

H L'our r de la Gare 35 ☎ 84675 rm9 **A**

⋆**Oranienburg** Grand r 126 ☎ 84153 rm34 Closed Jan-Feb 23 **A**

H Petry r de la Gare 15 ☎ 84122 rm10 Mar 25-Oct 25 **A**

H Réunion Grand r 66 ☎ 84155 rm10 Mar 16-Nov 15 **A**

H Victor Hugo r V-Hugo 1 ☎ 84160 rm22 May-Oct 15 **A**

WILTZ

H Beau Séjour r du X Septembre 21 ☎ 958250 rm70 **B**

◆ **Michel Rodange** r M-Rodange 11 ☎ 958235 rm14 **B**

◆ **Pont** r du Pont 11 ☎ 958103 rm5 **A**

The old city is surrounded by attractive wooded countryside

NETHERLANDS

FACTS & FIGURES

Capital: Amsterdam
Language: Dutch, English
IDD code: 31. To call the UK dial 09 44
Currency: Dutch Guilder or florin (Fls1 = 100 cents)
Local time: GMT+1 (summer GMT+2)
Emergency Services: Refer to local telephone directories

Business hours

Banks:
0900–1600 Mon–Fri
Shops:
0900–1730 Mon–Sat

Average daily temperatures:
Amsterdam °C

Jan 2	Jul 18
Mar 5	Sep 15
May 13	Nov 7

Tourist Information:
Netherlands Board of Tourism (VVV)
UK 25–28 Buckingham Gate
London SW1E 6LD
Tel 01-630 0451
USA 355 Lexington Ave
New York, NY 10017
Tel (212) 370-7367

The Netherlands is a small country, a great advantage for the visitor since there are so many attractions from which to choose within a small area. Amsterdam, for instance, is less than an hour from the sea, while The Hague is almost on the seashore. With so many areas of water, Holland is an ideal country for watersports with countless opportunities to participate.

The country's many and varied attractions include leisure parks, theme parks and wildlife parks, plus a huge selection of museums. There are a staggering 500 of these ranging from great and famous museums such as the Rijksmuseum (National Museum) or the Rijksmuseum Vincent Van Gogh in Amsterdam to the unique open-air museums Nederlands Openluchtmuseum in Arnhem, the Zaanse Schans near Amsterdam, or the Zuiderzee Museum in Enkhuizen. Even a walk through the old part of Amsterdam, Delft, Groningen or Gouda will reveal a fascinating array of artistic wealth, with unbroken rows of 16th, 17th and 18th-century façades adorning the canals and streets.

HOW TO GET THERE

BY CAR

There are direct ferry services to the Netherlands: from Harwich to the Hook of Holland (6¾ hrs day, 8 hrs night); Hull to Rotterdam–Europoort (14 hrs); Sheerness to Vlissingen Flushing (7 hrs day, 8½ hrs night). Alternatively, you could use one of the short channel crossings and drive through France and Belgium. The distance from Calais to Den Haag (The Hague) is just over 200 miles and is within a day's drive.

SPEED LIMITS

Built-up areas (between placename signs) 50 kph (31 mph); outside built-up areas 80 kph (49 mph); and on motorways 120 kph (74 mph). In residential areas, the sign *woonerven* indicates that speed control ramps have been installed across the road.

PARKING

Parking meters and/or parking discs are used in many towns. Discs can be obtained from police stations and many tobacco shops and must be displayed on the windscreen.

BY TRAIN

Eurail and InterRail passes are valid. During the spring and summer there are various Day-excursion trips from all rail stations that entitle users to reduced fares and discounts on tourist attractions.

There are also Rail Ranger tickets for unlimited second-class train travel within the country for a specified number of days. The Benelux-Tourrail card can also be used in Belgium and Luxembourg.

PUBLIC TRANSPORT

The Netherlands is divided into zones for public transportation (bus, tram and metro); fares are calculated according to the number of zones through which you pass. Rides are bought in strip tickets (strippenkaart), available from the vehicle driver but cheaper from transport companies, post offices and some tobacconists.

BY BICYCLE

The country is good for cycling – it is flat and there are usually separate bicycle lanes; most stations hire out bicycles.

ACCOMMODATION

The gazetteer includes a selection of establishments, most of which provide accommodation at less than Fls 70 per person per night at some time during the year.

The price bands are:

A Fls 33–52
B Fls 52–70

taking a rate of exchange at

Fls 3.70=£1
Fls 2.20=US $1

However, these prices may vary depending on the location and the time of year. Once you are in the Netherlands, local tourist offices, identified with a VVV sign, can help you with accommodation.

Abbreviations: pl plein str straat

ALKMAAR *Noord-Holland*

H Ida Margaretha (n.rest) Kanaaldk 186 ☎ (072) 613989 bed18 **A**

AMSTERDAM *Noord-Holland*

Amsterdam is a fascinating city of contradictions. As one of the world's greatest diamond markets, it is undeniably rich, yet the most popular drinking places are 'brown bars', loved for the very sparseness of their décor. The daytime peace and calm of the shady canals belies the vibrant neon-lit nightlife of this cosmopolitan city.

Attractions range from the *Rijksmuseum*, containing some of the finest works of Hals, Rembrandt and Vermeer to the *Rijksmuseum Vincent van Gogh*; the Royal Palace and the Rembrandt House. The Anne Frank House in Prinsengracht, the hiding place of the Frank family during World War II, is now a museum. Lovers of horticulture might care to visit the hothouses of the Botanical Garden, or browse through the famous floating Singel Flower Market.

When it comes to nightlife, Amsterdam has everything from lively discos and sophisticated nightclubs, to a more sedate evening listening to the *Concertgebouw* orchestra or taking in an opera or ballet.

The main shopping streets are Haarlelemmerdijk, Nieuwendijk, Kalverstraat, Damrak, Rokin, Regulierbreestraat, Heilgeweg and Leidsestraat. Popular souveniers include clogs, tea, spices, bottles and candles. Locally made cigars are renowned throughout the world for their aroma. and the city has an international reputation for the cutting and polishing of diamonds.

EATING OUT Dutch food is hearty and uncomplicated. Specialities include pea soup, red kidney bean soup, potato and vegetable hash with Dutch sausage, and fresh sea fish. Dutch apple tart is made with apples, sultanas and cinnamon. Pancakes are also firm favourites with the Dutch, and the *Pannekoekenhuisje*, in Damrak specialises in them. For good value try the *eetcafes* in the Jordaan area. There are numerous international restaurants in the streets around Leidseplein; Indonesian cooking is particularly popular with the Dutch and generaly good value. Bakeries provide tasty and inexpensive snacks, and there are several 'English-style' establishments offering quick meals – Shorts of London, in Rembrandtsplein, is one of them.

At the upper end of the restaurant price range, *Dikkeren Thijs*, in Prinsengracht, has a picturesque canalside setting and specialises in Dutch cuisine. A restaurant which oozes charm and character is *d'Vijff Vlieghen*, located in five converted old houses in Spuistraat. For Indonesian cuisine at its best, *Bali*, in Leidsestraat, is renowned for its wide-ranging menu and generous portions.

H Bema (n.rest) Concertgebouwpln 19b ☎ (020) 701396 bed18 **A**

H Biervliet (n.rest) Nassaukd 368 ☎ (020) 188404 bed18 **A**

H Casa Cara (n.rest) Emmastr 24 ☎ (020) 6623135 bed26 **A**

H De Korenaer Damrack 50 ☎ (020) 220855 bed23 **B**

H De Lantaerne (n.rest) Leidsegr111 ☎ (020) 232221 bed39 **B**

H Holbein (n.rest) Holbeinstr 5 ☎ (020) 6628832 bed15 **B**

H Impala (n.rest) Leidsekd 77 ☎ (020) 234706 bed38 **B**

H Jupiter (n.rest) 2e Helmersstr 14 ☎ (020) 187132 bed39 **B**

H Kabul Warmoesstr 38-42 ☎ (020) 237158 bed265 **B**

H Museumzicht (n.rest) J-Lukkenstr 22 ☎ (020) 712954 bed27 **B**

H Ostade (n.rest) Van Ostadestr 123 ☎ (020) 793452 bed27 **A**

H Vincent Van Gogh (n.rest) Veldestr 5 ☎ (020) 796002 bed34 **B**

APELDOORN *Gelderland*

H Abbekerk (n.rest) Canadain 26 ☎ (055) 222433 bed28 **A**

H Astra (n.rest) B-Backlin 12-14 ☎ (055) 550855 bed53 **A**

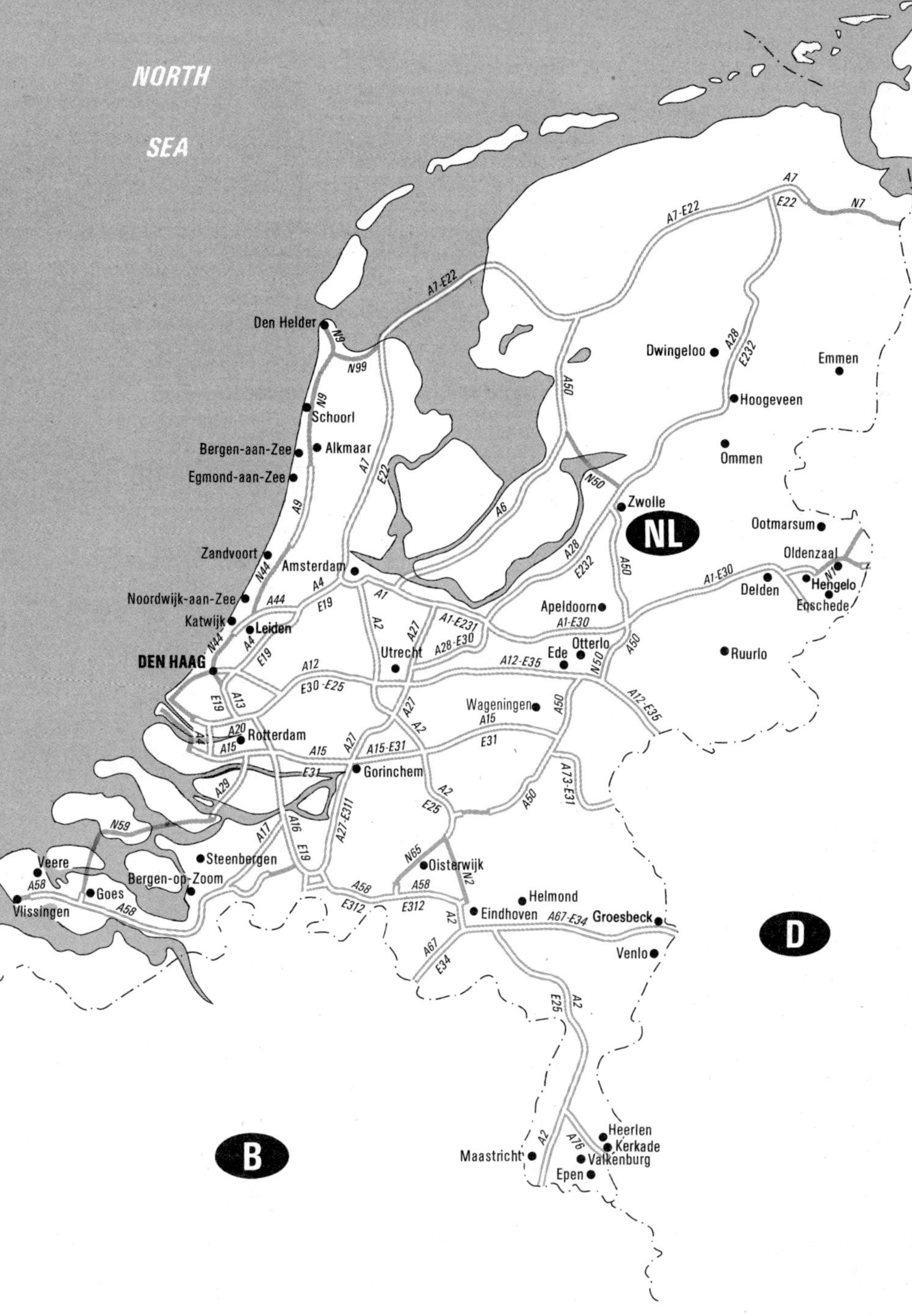

For key to country identification - see "About the gazetteer"

BERGEN AAN ZEE *Noord-Holland*

H Meijer J-Kalffweg 4 ☎ (02208) 12488 bed55 **A**

H Stormvogel (n.rest) J-Kalffweg 12 ☎ (02208) 12734 bed25 **A**

H Victoria Zeeweg 33-35 ☎ (02208) 12358 bed60 **A**

BERGEN-OP-ZOOM *Noord-Brabant*

H Blauwe Vogel Stationsstr 33 ☎ (01640) 55557 bed15 Closed Dec 22-Jan 2 **B**

H Old Dutch Stationsstr 31 ☎ (01640) 35780 bed14 **A**

DELDEN *Overijssel*

H Groene Brug Vossenbrinkwg 78 ☎ (05407) 61385 bed10 **A**

H Het Wapen Van Delden Langestr 242 ☎ (05407) 61355 bed90 **B**

★★**Zwaan** Langestr 2 ☎ (05407) 61206 bed23 **B**

DWINGELOO *Drenthe*

★★**Borken** Lhee 76 ☎ (05219) 7200 bed66 **B**

H Brink Brink 30-31 ☎ (05219) 1319 bed22 **A**

H Drift Drift 3-4 ☎ (05219) 1538 bed35 **A**

EDE *Gelderland*

H Mon Reve Oude Bennekomsewg 2-4 ☎ (08380) 33901 bed18 **A**

EGMOND AAN ZEE *Noord-Holland*

H Cris Voorstr 66 ☎ (02206) 4786 bed32 **A**

H Sonnevanck (n.rest) Wilhelminastr 114-116 ☎ (02206) 1589 bed35 **B**

EINDHOVEN *Noord-Brabant*

H Corso (n.rest) Vestdk 17 ☎ (040) 449131 bed25 **A**

H Eikenburg Aalsterweg 281 ☎ (040) 110957 bed32 **B**

EMMEN *Drenthe*

H Hunebed (n.rest) Ermerwg 90 ☎ (05910) 13364 bed23 **A**

ENSCHEDE *Overijssel*

H Atlanta Markt 12 ☎ (053) 316766 bed36 **A**

H Holterhof (n.rest) Holterhofweg 325 ☎ (053) 611306 bed57 **A**

EPEN *Limburg (Nl)*

H Eureka Kap Houbenstr 4 ☎ (04455) 1654 bed30 **B**

GOES *Zeeland*

H Terminus Stationspln 1 ☎ (01100) 30085 bed60 **B**

GORINCHEM *Zuid-Holland*

H T'Spinnewiel Eind 18 ☎ (01830) 31057 bed15 Closed Dec 16-31 **A**

GROESBEEK *Gelderland*

H De Oude Molen Molenwg 48 ☎ (08891) 71478 bed16 Closed Dec 24-Jan 2 **A**

H De Wolfsberg Mooksebaan ☎ (08891) 71327 bed40 **A**

HAAG, DEN (HAGUE, THE) *Zuid-Holland*

Though not the official capital of the Netherlands, Den Haag is the seat of government, host to more than 60 foreign embassies, home of the International Court of Justice, and home to Queen Beatrix, who chose to live here following her inauguration; wide, tree-lined avenues, spacious boulevards and parks all contribute to a royal grandeur.

Den Haag invites discovery with its charming little oriental shops, pedestrian precincts crowded with boutiques, and the antique market at the Lange Voorhout. This is a vital, cosmopolitan city with some of the most interesting attractions in Holland.

EATING OUT The most luxurious restaurant in Den Haag is the Royal, housed in an elegant, 16th-century mansion in Lange Voorhout. Locally caught seafood is a speciality of the *Auberge de Kieviet*, just outside the city in Wassenaar.

H Bristol Stationsweg 126-130 ☎ (070) 3840073 bed60 **B**

H Cattenburch (n.rest) Laan Copes van Cattenburch 38 ☎ (070) 3522335 bed12 **B**

H Savion (n.rest) Prinsestr 86 ☎ (070) 3462560 bed17 **B**

At **SCHEVENINGEN**

H Albion (n.rest) Gevers Deynoutweg 120 ☎ (070) 3557987 bed35 **A**

H Carmel 'T Witte Huis Bosschestr 2-6 ☎ (070) 3541024 bed37 Closed Dec 24-Jan 4 **B**

H Clavan (n.rest) Badhuiskade 8 ☎ (070) 3552844 bed17 **A**

H Corel Badhuisweg 54-56 ☎ (070) 3559939 bed40 **B**

H Lansink Badhuisweg 7 ☎ (070) 3559967 bed12 Closed Dec 15-Jan 15 **A**

HEERLEN *Limburg*

H 'T Spinnewiel Spoorsngl 10 ☎ (045) 725660 bed40 **B**

HELDER, DEN *Noord-Holland*

M Den Helder Marsdiepstr 2 ☎ (02230) 22333 bed144 **B**

HELMOND *Noord-Brabant*

H Het Beugeltje Beugelspl 8-10 ☎ (04920) 22729 bed15 Closed Dec 20-Jan 1 **A**

HENGELO *Overijssel*

H 'T Tuindorp Tuindorpstr ☎ (074) 912020 bed25 **A**

HOOGEVEEN *Drenthe*

H Toldiek Toldiek 23 ☎ (05280) 70757 bed17 Closed Dec 25-Jan 1 **A**

KATWIJK AAN ZEE *Zuid-Holland*

H Van Der Perk (n.rest) Boulevard 60-62 ☎ (01718) 12369 bed24 **A**

H Witteveen Kon Emmastr 17 ☎ (01718) 15511 bed48 **A**

H Zee en Duin Boulevard 5 ☎ (01718) 13320 bed30 **A**

KERKRADE *Limburg*

H Dutch Inn Heerlenersteenwg 115 ☎ (045) 413831 bed16 Closed Dec 21-31 & Jul 20-Aug 10 **B**

H Herpers (n.rest) Markt 56 ☎ (045) 452632 bed14 **B**

LEIDEN *Zuid-Holland*

H Bik (n.rest) Witte Singel ☎ (071) 122602 bed16 Closed Oct **A**

MAASTRICHT *Limburg*

H Chene (n.rest) Boschstr 104-106 ☎ (043) 213523 bed37 Closed Dec 24-Jan 6 **B**

H Posthoorn Stationstr 47 ☎ (043) 217334 bed24 Closed Dec 18-Jan 3 **B**

NOORDWIJK AAN ZEE *Zuid-Holland*

★**Duinlust** Koepelweg 1 ☎ (01719) 12916 bed40 Apr-Oct **A**

H Golf Quarles van Uffordstr 120 ☎ (01719) 12535 bed36 **A**

H Pirombo (n.rest) O Zeewg 22 ☎ (01719) 12417 bed28 **B**

H Royal Voorstr 76 ☎ (01719) 12988 bed16 **B**

H Waikiki Katenblankweg 2 ☏ (01719) 12434 bed100 **A**

OISTERWIJK *Noord-Brabant*

H Hoeve Belvert Scheibaan 13 ☏ (04242) 82384 bed47 **A**

H Stille Wilde Scheibaan 11 ☏ (04242) 82301 bed28 Closed Nov-Mar **A**

OLDENZAAL *Overijssel*

H Muller Markt 14 ☏ (05410) 12093 bed18 **B**

H Ter Stege Markstr 1 ☏ (05410) 12102 bed17 **B**

OMMEN *Overijssel*

H Euroase Hammerwg 40 ☏ (05291) 1592 bed37 **A**

H Paping Stationswg 29 ☏ (05291) 1945 bed72 Closed Dec 31-Jan 1 **B**

H Stegeman Voorbrug 11 ☏ (05291) 1941 bed23 **B**

OOTMARSUM *Overijssel*

★★Het Wapen Van Ootmarsum Almelosestr 20 ☏ (05419) 1500 bed40 Closed Jan **B**

H Jolanda (n.rest) Westwal 1 ☏ (05419) 1728 bed68 Closed Nov 15-Dec 23 & Jan 2-Mar **A**

H Twents Ethoes Molenstr 22 ☏ (05419) 3085 bed53 **A**

H Vos Almelosestr 1 ☏ (05419) 1277 bed24 **B**

OTTERLO *Gelderland*

H De Wever (n.rest) Onderlangs 35 ☏ (08382) 1220 bed26 Mar 15-Oct **A**

H Jagersrust Dorpsstr 19-21 ☏ (08382) 1231 bed36 **B**

H T'Witte Hoes Dorpsstr 35 ☏ (08382) 1392 bed26 Mar 16-Nov 10 **A**

ROTTERDAM *Zuid-Holland*
Rotterdam rose out of the ashes of World War II like a phoenix, superbly planned and beautifully constructed to cater for every taste – sports, music, shops, theatre, lovely parks covering 10, 000 acres, 12 museums and numerous galleries. A stroll from the centre, however, will bring you to the 17th century preserved or reconstructed in the city's western quarter of Delfshaven. In its old town hall is the Stolk Atlas, one of the best known collections of old maps and sea charts. An interesting visit can also be paid to the *Oude Kerk*, built in 1416, where the Pilgrim Fathers prayed before departing for the New World. By contrast, a boat trip round the port – the largest in the world – is impressive, as is a trip up the Euromast in the revolving space tower which offers a view of 33 miles all round on a clear day.
EATING OUT Rotterdam's restaurants are mostly in the centre of the city, especially in Lijnbaan, Coolsingel, Stadhuisplein, Schouwburgplein and Meent. The Old Dutch, in Rocherssenstraat, is one of the city's best restaurants for atmosphere and Dutch cuisine.

H Bienvenue (n.rest) Spoorsingel 24 ☏ (010) 4669394 bed23 **B**

H Holland (n.rest) Provenierssingel 7 ☏ (010) 4653100 bed53 **B**

H Orion (n.rest) Zwaerdecroonstr 40 ☏ (010) 4763801 bed26 **A**

H Wilgenhof Heemraadsingel 92-94 ☏ (010) 4254892 bed75 **B**

RUURLO *Gelderland*

H Herberg Hengelosewg 1 ☏ (05735) 2147 bed24 **A**

H Lievestro (n.rest) Groenlosewg 42 ☏ (05735) 1439 bed19 **B**

SCHEVENINGEN See **HAAG, DEN (HAGUE, THE)**

SCHOORL *Noord-Holland*

H De Viersprong Laanwg 1 ☏ (02209) 1218 bed10 Closed Dec 25-26 **B**

H Hartland (n.rest) Voorwg 55 ☏ (02209) 1815 bed24 **A**

H Schoorl Laanwg 24 ☏ (02209) 3555 bed45 **B**

H Snow Goose (n.rest) Duinwg 123 ☏ (02209) 1215 bed20 **A**

STEENBERGEN *Noord-Brabant*

H Van Tilburg Burg van Loonstr 87 ☏ (01670) 63550 bed20 **A**

UTRECHT *Utrecht*
Utrecht already existed when the Netherlands was in its infancy, becoming the country's foremost cultural centre by the Middle Ages. Reminders of its long history that have survived include the *Domkerk* with its 367ft-high tower, the former Bishop's Palace, the *Rijksmuseum Het Catharijneconvent*, the *Academiegebouw* of the University, many churches, and picturesque *hofjes* – the courtyards of almshouses.
The city has a wealth of museums, spanning such interests as medieval art, historic trains, musical boxes, barrel organs and an old-fashioned grocer's shop. Visitors can also stroll alongside the canals and perhaps visit one of the terraces which have been built over the old wharves, right on the waterfront, whilst the delightful environs of the city include woods, heaths and the attractive lakeland area around Loosdrecht, Maarseveen and Vinkeveen.
Hoog Catharijne, one of the largest covered shopping complexes in the Netherlands, is located between the Centraal Station and the old central area of the city.
EATING OUT There are many kinds of restaurants offering meals in various price ranges. Most are on the Oude Gracht, often in old buildings or in waterside cellars. Other restaurants can be found in Hoog Catharijne and Vredenburg.

H Ouwi (n.rest) F-C-Dondersstr 12 ☏ (030) 716303 bed44 Closed Dec 20-Jan 4 **B**

VALKENBURG *Limburg*

H All Good Neerhem 10 ☏ (04406) 13380 bed17 Oct 23-Mar 23 **A**

★★Apollo Nieuweweg 7 ☏ (04406) 15341 bed78 Closed Feb **A**

H Bergrust Emmaberg 8 ☏ (04406) 12755 bed45 Closed Dec 28-Jan 7 **A**

H De Postkoets (n.rest) Grotestr 29 ☏ (04406) 12283 bed20 **A**

H Hermens Neerhem 61 ☏ (04406) 13020 bed70 Closed Oct 25-Mar 22 **A**

H Laheije Nieuweweg 76 ☏ (04406) 12852 bed22 Closed Oct-Dec 22 & Jan 1-4 **B**

VEERE *Zeeland*

★Campveerse Toren Kade 2 ☏ (01181) 1291 bed35 **B**

H T'Waepen Van Veere Markt 23-27 ☏ (01181) 231 bed28 Closed Nov 16-Feb **B**

VENLO *Limburg*

H Stationshotel Keulsepoort 16 ☏ (077) 515023 bed45 Closed Dec 21-31 **A**

VLISSINGEN (FLUSHING) *Zeeland*

H Royal Badhuisstr 3-13 ☏ (01184) 12201 bed36 **A**

H Schouten Boulev d Ruyter 416 ☏ (01184) 14646 bed26 **A**

WAGENINGEN *Gelderland*

H Congresgebouw Lawicksee 11 ☏ (08370) 90133 bed176 **B**

ZANDVOORT *Noord-Holland*

H Astoria Dr Gerkestr 155-159 ☏ (02507) 14550 bed27 **A**

ZWOLLE *Overijssel*

H Fidder (n.rest) Wilhelminastr 6 ☏ (038) 218395 bed30 **B**

H Weenink Rode Torenpin ☏ (038) 218182 bed30 **B**

Clothed from head to foot in traditional Dutch costume

NORWAY

FACTS & FIGURES

Capital: Oslo
Language: Norwegian, English
IDD code: 47. To call the UK dial 095 44
Currency: Norwegian Krone (Nok1 = 100 ore)
Local time: GMT+1 (summer GMT+2)
Emergency Services: Oslo, Police 002; Fire 001; Ambulance 003

Business Hours–Banks: 0815–1530 Mon–Wed and Fri; 0815–1700 Thu
Shops: 0900–1700 Mon–Wed and Fri; 0900–1800/1900 Thu; 0900–1400 Sat.

Average daily temperatures:
Oslo °C

Jan 4	Jul 15
Mar 0	Sep 12
May 11	Nov 1

Tourist Information:
Norwegian Tourist Board
UK 5–11 Charles House
Lower Regent St
London SW1Y 4LR
Tel: 01-839 6255 (recorded message in office hours)
USA 655 Third Ave
New York, NY 10017
Tel (212) 949-2333

There is little doubt that if the Scandinavian countries were judged on scenery alone, Norway would come very high up the list. Few can fail to be impressed by the unfolding panorama of mountains, fjords, lakes, waterfalls and rivers – and delightful cities and towns. The west-coast region is particularly attractive. Its three splendid but quite different fjords – Sogne, Hardanger and Nord – embrace a vast region of delightful villages offering much to do and see as well as excellent accommodation. Even the 'gateway' town of Bergen deserves some time.

Norway's coast is steep, fringed with islands, and deeply cut by fjords. The highest mountains are the Jotunheimen in the south. Barren plateaux, lakes and ice-fields separate the mountain ranges.

In addition to Oslo, the capital, and Bergen, the second biggest city, other cities of interest include Trondheim and Tromso, both pleasant places for a visit and located close to glorious countryside.

HOW TO GET THERE

BY CAR

Norway can be reached direct by ferry. Services operate from Newcastle to Bergen and then on to Stavanger and via Hirsthals (Denmark) to Oslo. Crossings vary between 17 and 36 hours. You can also reach Norway by taking one of the short channel crossings to France or Belgium, then driving through the Netherlands and northern Germany to Denmark where you can take a ferry either direct to southern Norway or to Sweden followed by a drive up to Norway. The drive from the Channel ports to Oslo via Sweden is about 1,000 miles and would probably require 3 overnight stops.

For details of the AA's Overseas Routes Service consult the Contents page.

SPEED LIMITS

In built-up areas vehicles are restricted to 50 kph (31 mph) unless there are signs indicating otherwise; outside built-up areas 80 kph (49 mph); and on motorways 90 kph (56 mph). Low speeds are recommended for the narrow roads of western Norway.

Winter conditions. The western fjord district is generally unsuitable for motoring between mid-October and late May, and in places until mid-June. A map showing roads passable in winter can be obtained from the Norwegian Tourist Board.

BY TRAIN

If you do not have a Eurail or InterRail pass, tickets can be bought for travel within Norway but remember that for express trains and other main trains seat reservation is compulsory. The Midtukebillet (midweek ticket) is valid for unlimited travel and stops, towards a specified destination, during a period of 7 days. The Minigruppenbillett (Mini-group ticket) can be used by 2–9 persons travelling together. The Nordturist Ticket, available at any train station allows 21 days of unlimited travel in all Scandinavian countries.

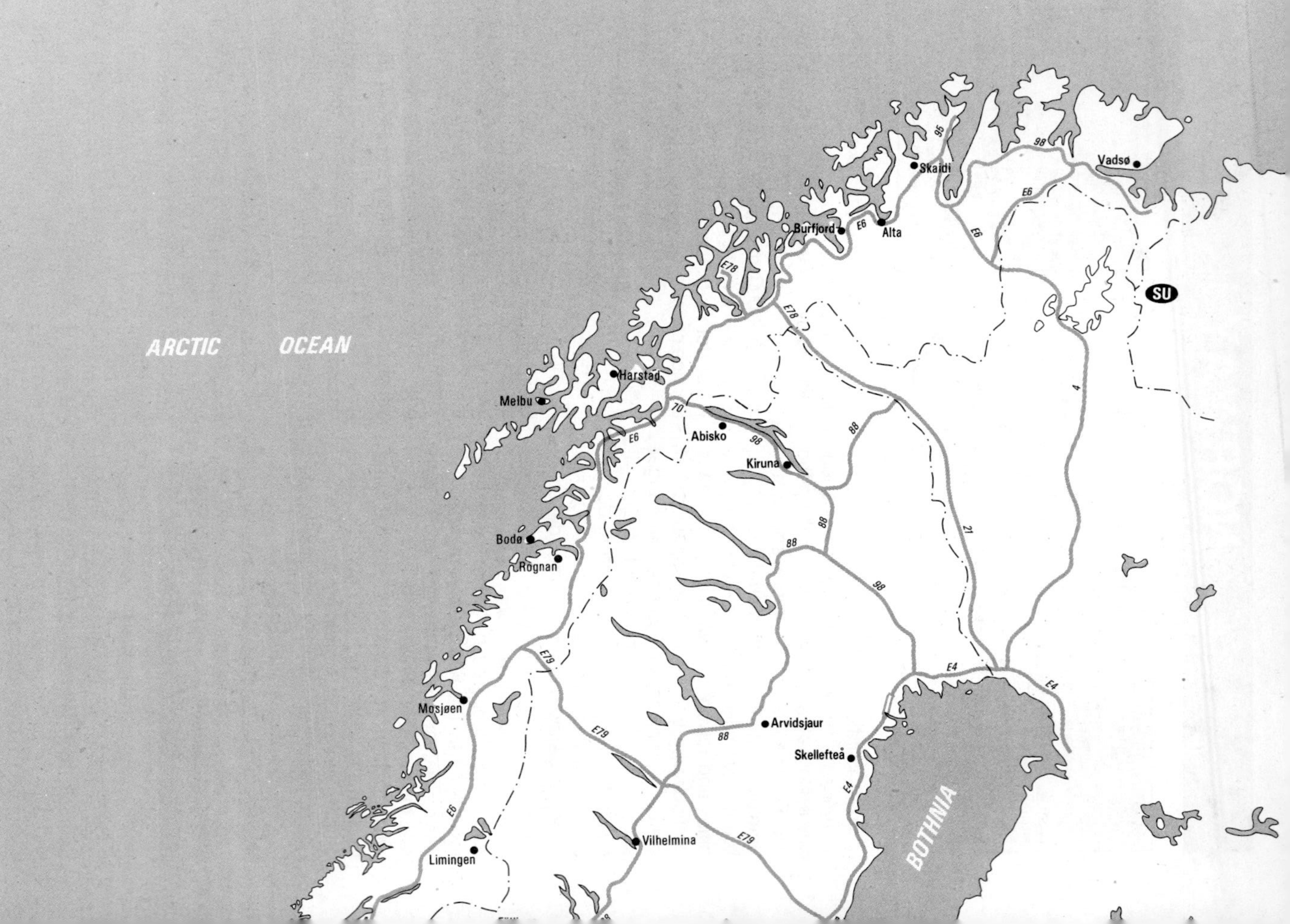

ARCTIC OCEAN
BOTHNIA
SU
Vadsø
Skaidi
Alta
Burfjord
Harstad
Melbu
Abisko
Kiruna
Bodø
Rognan
Mosjøen
Arvidsjaur
Skellefteå
Vilhelmina
Limingen
E6
E78
E79
E4
98
95
70
88
21
4

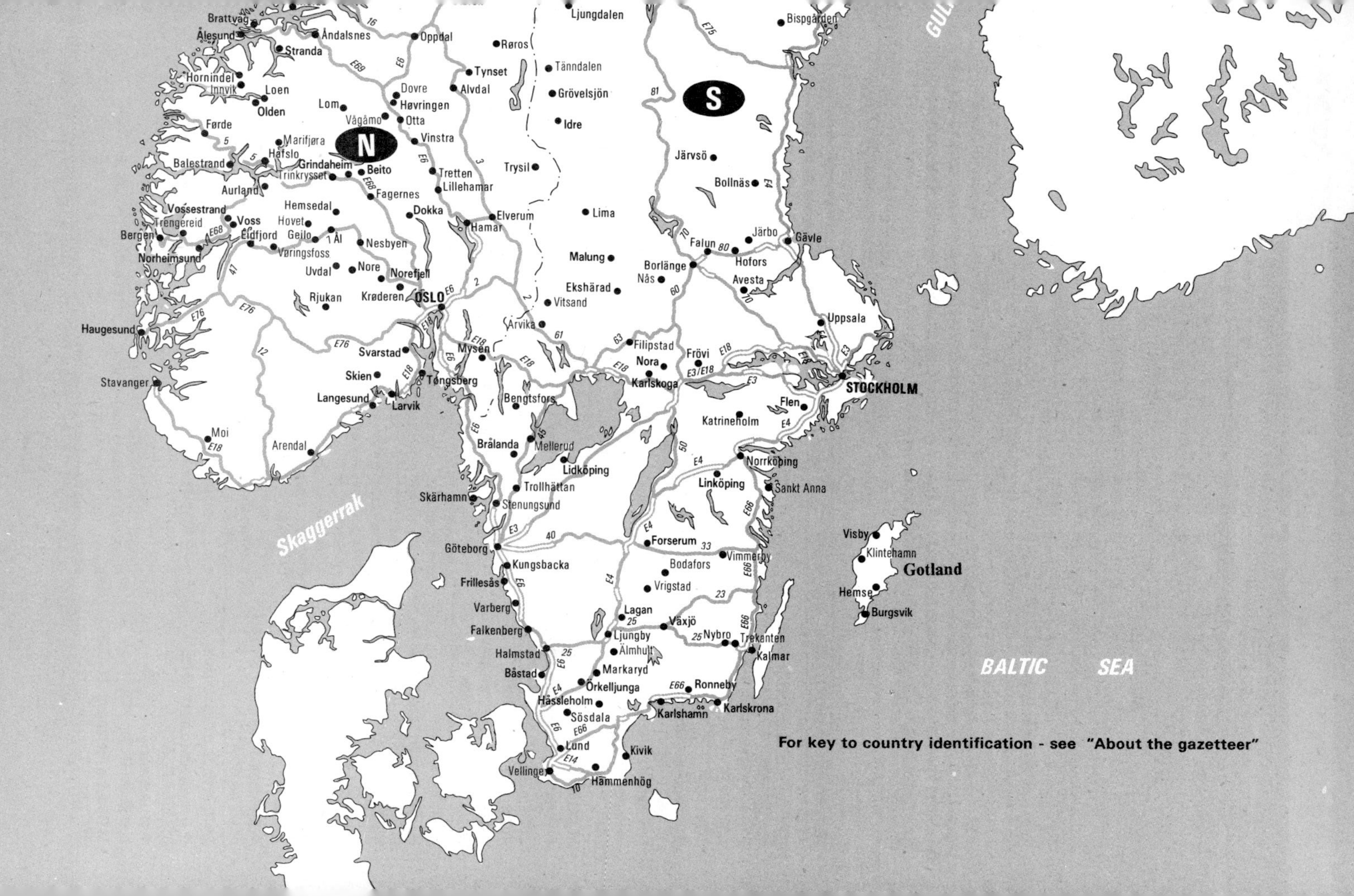

For key to country identification - see "About the gazetteer"

BY BUS

Buses are expensive but they are the only way to get to some areas.

BY PLANE

Flying is often the cheapest and fastest mode of transport in Norway: there are good student discounts and a family discount of 50% if one adult pays full fare.

ACCOMMODATION

Most of the establishments listed in the gazetteer that follows provide accommodation for less than Nok 228 per person per night at some time during the year.

The price bands are:

A NoK 108–168
B Nok 168–228

taking a rate of exchange at

Nok 12=£1
Nok 7.2=US $1

It is possible, however, that these prices will fluctuate during the currency of this book. A local tourist office (turistinformasjon) will provide you with more details and could probably book you a room in a private home at a reasonable price.

Abbreviations: gt gatan vn veien

ÅL *Buskerud*

◆ **Kaslegard Fjellgard** (n.rest) Vats ☎ (067) 84664 bed40 Feb-Apr & Jul-Sep **A**

◆ **Liatoppen Fjellstove** (n.rest) ☎ (067) 83557 bed70 Dec 22-Apr 24 & Jun 24-Sep **A**

★★**Sundre** (n.rest) ☎ (067) 81100 bed50 **B**

ÅLESUND *Møre-og-Romsdal*

◆ **Aarsæthergården** (n.rest) Hellegt 6 ☎ (071) 23203 bed20 **B**

ALTA *Finnmark*

◆ **Øytun** (n.rest) ☎ (084) 35577 bed115 May 16-Aug 14 **B**

ALVDAL *Hedmark*

H Tronsvangen Seter ☎ (064) 87410 bed50 **B**

ÅNDALSNES *Møre-og-Romsdal*

◆ **Gjerset** ☎ (072) 25966 bed13 **A**

◆ **Rauma** (n.rest) Vollan 16 ☎ (072) 21233 bed19 **B**

ARENDAL *Aust-Agder*

◆ **Breidablikk Vertshus** ☎ (041) 85127 bed50 **A**

AURLAND *Sogn-og-Fjordane*

◆ **Aabelheim** (n.rest) ☎ (056) 33449 bed20 **A**

◆ **Østerbø** (n.rest) ☎ (056) 31141 bed60 Jun 16-Sep 14 **A**

M Østerbø Fjellstove ☎ (056) 31177 bed60 Jun 10-Sep 20 **A**

M Wangen (n.rest) ☎ (056) 33580 bed20 **B**

BALESTRAND *Sogn-og-Fjordane*

★**Balestrand** (n.rest) ☎ (056) 91138 bed53 **B**

◆ **Bøyum** (n.rest) ☎ (056) 91114 bed24 **A**

★★**Midtnes** ☎ (056) 91133 bed64 Closed Dec 22-31 **B**

BEITO *Oppland*

◆ **Øyang Feriesenter** ☎ (063) 41121 bed120 Closed May 1-21 **B**

BERGEN *Hordaland*

Norway's second largest city offers everything for an enjoyable and memorable visit. Surrounded by sea and mountains, its location is impressive and a fine panoramic view rewards those taking the funicular up Mount Floyen. Many attractive museums and other places of interest, such as the Aquarium, King Haakon's Hall, Bryggen Wharf and Fantoft Stave Church are well worth exploring, as are the old merchant houses and the imposing 13th-century cathedral. A good programme of excursions, some by fjord steamer, is available, and public transport can also be used for independent sightseeing.
The fish market and the adjoining flower and vegatable market near the city centre are fascinating sights, and so are the 17th-century warehouses and the Bergenhus fortress. Edward Grieg was born in Bergen and his mansion, located 8km from the city, is now a museum.
EATING OUT Of the many noteworthy fish restaurants in this city, *Bryggen Tracteursted*, in Bryggestredet, enjoys a particularly high reputation for the freshness of its fish from the adjacent market.

◆ **Fagerheim** Kalvedalsvn 49a ☎ (05) 310172 bed22 **B**

M Måken Blomvåg ☎ (05) 387105 bed40 **B**

BODØ *Nordland*

◆ **Gunda Johnsens** (n.rest) Prinsensgt 80 ☎ (081) 24250 bed14 **A**

◆ **Opsahl** (n.rest) Prinsensgt 131 ☎ (081) 20704 bed30 **B**

BRATTVÅG *Møre-og-Romsdal*

H Brattvåg Strandgata 48 ☎ (071) 15777 bed29 **B**

BURFJORD *Troms*

◆ **Kaasen Gård** ☎ (083) 68141 bed27 **B**

DOKKA *Oppland*

◆ **Hugulia Fjellstue** ☎ (061) 18514 bed91 **B**

DOVRE *Oppland*

H Toftemo ☎ (062) 40045 bed120 **B**

EIDFJORD *Hordaland*

H Dyranut ☎ (054) 65715 bed35 Jun 2-Sep **A**

ELVERUM *Hedmark*

H Central Storgt 22 ☎ (064) 10155 bed140 **B**

◆ **Glommen** Vestheimg 2 ☎ (064) 11267 bed34 **B**

FAGERNES *Oppland*

◆ **Fagerborg** ☎ (063) 32027 bed40 **A**

H Hovda Fjellstue (n.rest) ☎ (063) 64003 bed60 **B**

◆ **Leira** ☎ (063) 62159 bed35 **A**

H Nythun ☎ (063) 63925 bed42 Closed Jan, May & Oct **A**

FØRDE *Sogn-og-Fjordane*

H Lia Turistheim (n.rest) Halbrendslia 14 ☎ (057) 21164 bed26 **B**

H Skilbrei Ungdomssenter ☎ (057) 17762 bed45 **A**

GEILO *Buskerud*

★★**Alpin** ☎ (067) 85544 bed65 **B**

◆ **Dagali** ☎ (067) 87700 bed80 **B**

◆ **Geilo** ☎ (067) 85036 bed38 Jun 15-Sep 15 & Nov 15-Apr **B**

H Ro ☎ (067) 85150 bed28 **B**

GRINDAHEIM *Oppland*

◆ **Mjøsvang** ☎ (063) 67077 bed70 Closed Dec 22-27 **B**

HAFSLO *Sogn-og-Fjordane*

H Hillestad Turistheim ☎ (056) 84401 bed35 **B**

HAMAR *Hedmark*

◆ **Seiersted** Holsetgt 64 ☎ (065) 21244 bed31 **B**

HARSTAD *Troms*

H Høiland (n.rest) Magnus gt 4 ☎ (082) 64960 bed18 **B**

H Sentrum (n.rest) Magnusgate 5 ☎ (082) 62938 bed15 **B**

HAUGESUND *Rogaland*

★★**IMI** (n.rest) Strandgt 192 ☎ (04) 723699 bed40 **A**

HEMSEDAL *Buskerud*

H Breistølen Fjellstue Hemsedalsfjellet ☎ (067) 68751 bed40 **B**

HORNINDAL *Sogn-og-Fjordane*

H Grodåsheimen ☎ (057) 79602 bed20 **A**

HOVET *Buskerud*

◆ **Raggsteindalen** ☎ (067) 88540 bed70 Feb 18-Apr 16 & Jun 24-Sep **B**

HØVRINGEN *Oppland*

◆ **Haukliseter Fjellstue** ☎ (062) 33717 bed54 Jan-Apr 19 & Jun 24-Sep **B**

★★**Høvringen Høgfjellshotell** ☎ (062) 33722 bed100 Jun 23-Sep & Jan 21-Apr **B**

◆ **Smuksjøseter Fjellstue** ☎ (062) 33719 bed50 Closed May-Jun 5 **B**

INNVIK *Sogn-og-Fjordane*

★★**Misjonsheimen** ☎ (057) 74252 bed45 **A**

KRØDEREN *Buskerud*

◆ **Krøderen Kro** ☎ (067) 47877 bed30 **B**

LANGESUND *Telemark*

◆ **Langesund Bad & Feriested** (n.rest) Badevn 5 ☎ (03) 973529 bed70 **B**

LARVIK *Vestfold*

◆ **Seierstad** (n.rest) ☎ (034) 11092 bed26 **A**

LILLEHAMMER *Oppland*

★**Breiseth** Jerbanegt 5 ☎ (062) 50060 bed80 **B**

★★**Ersgård** (n.rest) Nordsetervn 201 ☎ (062) 50684 bed52 **A**

H Rustad (n.rest) ☎ (065) 63408 bed89 Closed Apr 16-Jun 12 & Oct **B**

LIMINGEN *Nord-Trøndelag*

◆ **Limingen** ☎ (077) 35224 bed45 Closed Jan 1-9 **A**

LOEN *Sogn-og-Fjordane*

◆ **Loen** (n.rest) ☎ (057) 77624 bed48 May 15-Sep 14 **A**

LOM *Oppland*

★★**Fossberg Turiststsajon** ☎ (062) 11073 bed63 Closed Jan-Mar 15 **A**

H Fossheim ☎ (062) 11105 bed120 Mar 16-Dec 14 **B**

◆ **Leirvassbu Fjellstue** ☎ (062) 12932 bed190 Jul-Sep 3 **A**

H Nordal Turistsenter ☎ (062) 11010 bed200 **A**

MARIFJØRA *Sogn-og-Fjordane*

★★**Tørvis Fjord** ☎ (056) 87200 bed76 **B**

MELBU *Nordland*

H Melbuheim P-A-Kvaalsgt 5 ☎ (088) 57106 bed100 **A**

H Rex Gjestgiveri Frederiksensgt 15 ☎ (088) 57077 bed16 **B**

MOI *Rogaland*

◆ **Bondeheimen** ☎ (04) 461141 bed10 **A**

MOLDE *Møre-og-Romsdal*

◆ **Norrøna Kafe** Storgt 27 ☎ (072) 51824 bed18 **B**

◆ **Rimo Hostel** Postboks 394 ☎ (072) 54330 bed78 Jun 20-Aug 15 **A**

MOSJØEN *Nordland*

H Sandvik ☎ (087) 87843 bed70 Closed Jun-Aug 15 **B**

MYSEN *Østfold*

H Villa Hegstad (n.rest) Hegginveien 12 ☎ (02) 891765 bed17 **B**

NESBYEN *Buskerud*

★★**Smedsgården** (n.rest) ☎ (067) 73125 bed70 **B**

H Thoen ☎ (067) 71119 bed48 **B**

NORE *Buskerud*

◆ **Numedal** ☎ (03) 745208 bed25 **B**

NOREFJELL *Buskerud*

★★**Fjellhvil** ☎ (067) 46174 bed98 **A**

NORHEIMSUND *Hordaland*

◆ **Solbakken** (n.rest) ☎ (05) 552106 bed10 **A**

OLDEN *Sogn-og-Fjordane*

◆ **Briksdalsbre Fjellstove** ☎ (057) 73811 bed15 Oct-Apr 19 **A**

OPPDAL *Sør-Trøndelag*

◆ **IMI Stølen** (n.rest) ☎ (074) 21370 bed119 **A**

OSLO *Oslo*

Oslo is justly proud of her Viking ancestry and seafaring heritage, and extends a warm welcome to visitors. The city's history is reflected in her cathedral, parliament buildings and town hall, from where 38 bells peal out every hour – and you can also look inside at the engravings, carvings and artwork recounting Norwegian legends and myths. Lovers of the past should explore the Bergfjerdingen, Oslo's old city, and for a glimpse of the contemporary pay a visit to the Holmenkollen ski-jump, which offers wonderful views. There is a fascinating site at Bygdog, easily reached by ferry, which includes the Viking Ships Museum containing three of these proud vessels, ultimately the graves of their rulers on their final journey to Valhalla; the Kon Tiki – Thor Heyerdahol's balsa raft on which he made his perilous journey from Peru to Polynesia in 1947 – and the Ra II, his reconstruction of an Egyptian papyrus boat in which he crossed the Atlantic; and an open-air site where homes, farms and churches brought from all parts of the country have been rebuilt using the original material.

Frogner Park is the setting for the sculptures of Gustav Vigeland. The collection is unique and controversial, and revolves round the monolith of bodies entitled *The Wheel of Life*. Once a royal fortress, later a political prison, the Akershus castle now contains the Resistance Museum, a reminder of Nazi occupation and a monument to the patriots who fell defending their country.

The Norwegians' legends and their country's striking scenery are reflected in beautiful wood carvings, jewellery and glassware, while their talent for design shows in the furniture and knitwear. Karl Johan'sgate, the main boulevard, provides a wealth of shops, street stalls, cafés, restaurants and department stores.

EATING OUT Breakfast consists not only of rolls and coffee but fish, cold meats and cheeses too – a delicious start to the day. Dinner is the most substantial meal, and as one would expect with Norway's coastline, fish is a great speciality. Trout, salmon, sole and plaice are widely available and always fresh. Norwegian fish and shellfish are specialities of the Grand Hotel's rooftop restaurant, *Etoile*, while Oslo's oldest restaurant is the *Gamle Radhus*, housed in a 17th-century building in Nedre Slottsgate. For inexpensive meals and snacks, the *Café Frohlich*, in Drammensvn, is popular, especially with students and musicians.

H Bella Vista (n.rest) Arundvn 11B ☎ (02) 654588 bed18 **B**

◆ **Katarinahjemmet** (n.rest) Majorstuvn 21B ☎ (02) 601370 bed60 **B**

H Sommerhotell Michelets 55 ☎ (02) 533853 bed70 Jun-Aug 19 **B**

RJUKAN *Telemark*

H Kvitåvatn Fjellstoge ☎ (036) 91174 bed139 **A**

ROGNAN *Nordland*

◆ **Fredheim Folkehøyskole** (n.rest) ☎ (081) 90355 bed130 Jun 16-Aug 14 **A**

RØROS *Sør-Trøndelag*

◆ **Ertzscheider** (n.rest) Spell-Olavn 6 ☎ (074) 11194 bed27 **A**

◆ **Fjellheimen Turiststasjon** (n.rest) ☎ (074) 11468 bed36 **A**

SELBU *Sør-Trøndelag*

H Selbu ☎ (07) 817111 bed70 **B**

SKAIDI *Finnmark*

H Repparfjord Ungdomassenter (n.rest) ☎ (084) 16165 bed28 **A**

SKIEN *Telemark*

◆ **Norrøna** Ligt 3 ☎ (03) 522745 bed30 **B**

STAVANGER *Rogaland*

◆ **Bergeland** (n.rest) Vikedalsgt 1A ☎ (04) 534110 bed100 **B**

H Stavanger Sommer Madlamarkvn 6 ☎ (04) 557000 bed280 **B**

H Strand Axel Lunds 27 ☎ (04) 650222 bed150 **B**

STØREN *Sør-Trøndelag*

◆ **Gyllheimen** (n.rest) ☎ (07) 856342 bed14 **A**

STRANDA *Møre-og-Romsdal*

◆ **Slyngstads overnatting** (n.rest) Dalevegen 92 ☎ (071) 6013 bed8 **B**

SVARSTAD *Hedmark*

H Gavelstad (n.rest) ☎ (034) 28058 bed100 **B**

TØNSBERG *Vestfold*

H Borge (n.rest) ☎ (033) 67425 bed71 **B**

TRENGEREID *Hordaland*

◆ **Gullbotn** ☎ (05) 249030 bed40 **B**

TRETTEN *Oppland*

◆ **Bådstø** (n.rest) Kongsvegen 47 ☎ (062) 76321 bed140 **B**

★**Glomstad Gåid** (n.rest) ☎ (062) 76257 bed54 Dec 21-Sep **B**

◆ **Optun** ☎ (062) 76185 bed30 Closed May & Oct-Dec 21 **A**

TRYSIL *Hedmark*

H Soria Moria ☎ (064) 50850 bed44 **B**

H Trysil (n.rest) Boks 78 ☎ (064) 50833 bed100 **B**

TYINKRYSSET *Oppland*

◆ **Tyinkrysset** ☎ (061) 67727 bed45 **B**

TYNSET *Hedmark*

H Tynset ☎ (064) 80600 bed84 **B**

UVDAL *Buskerud*

◆ **Brøstrud** (n.rest) ☎ (03) 743609 bed45 **A**

◆ **Imingjfell Turistheim** ☎ (03) 743690 bed50 Feb-Sep **A**

H Solheimstulen (n.rest) ☎ (03) 743614 bed43 Jul 7-Mar **A**

VADSØ *Finnmark*

◆ **Lailas** Brugt 2 ☎ (085) 53335 bed54 **B**

VÅGÅMO *Oppland*

◆ **Bessheim Fjellstue** ☎ (062) 38913 bed150 **B**

◆ **Vågå** (n.rest) ☎ (062) 37360 bed11 **B**

VINSTRA *Oppland*

H Sulseter Fjellstugu ☎ (062) 90153 bed45 Jun 16-Sep 9 & Jan-Apr 20 **A**

VØRINGSFOSS *Hordaland*

◆ **Liseth** (n.rest) ☎ (054) 65714 bed72 **B**

VOSS *Hordaland*

★★★**Voss Turistheim** (n.rest) ☎ (05) 511577 bed100 Jun-Aug 14 **B**

PORTUGAL

FACTS & FIGURES

Capital: Lisbon
Language: Portuguese
IDD code: 351. To call the UK dial 00 44
Currency: Escudo (ESc 1 = 100 centavos)
Local time: GMT (summer GMT + 1)
Emergency Services: Police, Fire and Ambulance 115

Business Hours–Banks: 08.30–1145 & 1300–1445 Mon–Fri
Shops: 0900–1300 & 1500–1900 Mon–Fri; 0900–1300 Sat (& 1500–1900 Dec); shopping centres 1000–2400 Mon–Sat

Average daily temperatures:
Lisbon °C

Jan 11	Jul 21
Mar 13	Sep 20
May 17	Nov 14

Tourist Information:
Portuguese National Tourist Office
UK New Bond Street House
1–5 New Bond Street
London W1Y 0NP
Tel 01-493-3873
USA 548 Fifth Ave
New York, NY 10036
Tel (212) 354-4403

Portugal's great charm lies in its infinite variety, with spectacular scenery ranging from tranquil mountainside villages to bustling cities; from forests and vineyards to harsh, rocky landscapes; and from peaceful sandy coves to magnificent, craggy cliffs. The most popular of the holiday areas is undoubtedly the Algarve, whose glorious sandy beaches stretch the length of Portugal's southern coastline. It offers a choice of resorts, and is particularly popular with golfers, having half a dozen or so courses of top international standard.

To the west of Lisbon, the Estoril coast is quieter and more sedate. Bordering the sandy beaches are elegant tree-lined streets with beautiful villas and fine Victorian-style houses.

Madeira, the tiny and enchanting Portuguese island off the north-west coast of Africa, has soil so fertile that almost everything grows, making it a blaze of colour throughout the year. The capital, Funchal, makes an ideal base for exploring the rest of the picturesque island.

Portugal boasts so many attractive and picturesque cities, towns and villages that the visitor is spoilt for choice. There's Lisbon, offering an excellent range of hotels to suit most budgets and tastes, a host of visitor attractions and splendid restaurants. Not far from Lisbon lies Sintra, lauded by poets and writers over the centuries, and noted for both its setting and its wealth of palaces and museums.

On the Costa Verde (Green Coast), the enchanting whitewashed town of Ponte de Lima is attracting an ever-increasing number of visitors; so, too, are Amarante and Viseu in the country's mountainous region, Coimbra, seat of one of the oldest universities in the world, and the museum town of Evora, the latter two in the region known as the Costa de Prata.

HOW TO GET THERE

BY CAR

The usual route to Portugal by road is via France, and getting onto the Biarritz to San Sebastian road at the western end of the Pyrenees, then following it down into Spain to Portugal: the distance from the Channel ports to Lisboa (Lisbon) is about 1,300 miles, a journey that will require 3 or 4 overnight stops. If you do not want to drive all the way, you could use one of the car-sleeper services from Boulogne or Paris to Biarritz or from Paris to Madrid. You can also send your car by freight train from Paris to Lisboa (taking 50 hrs) while you make the same journey on the 'Sud Express'. Another possibility is to take your vehicle on the Plymouth to Santander car ferry and then drive on through Spain to Portugal – Santander to Lisboa is about 550 miles which would need 1 or 2 overnight stops.

For details of the AA's Overseas Route Service consult the Contents page.

For location Map see Spain.

SPEED LIMITS

Unless otherwise signposted, the following restrictions apply: in built-up areas

60 kph (37 mph); outside built-up areas 90 kph (50 mph); and on motorways 120 kph (74 mph), with a minimum speed limit of 40 kph (24 mph).

Visiting motorists who have held a full driving licence for less than 1 year are restricted to a top speed of 90 kph (56 mph); and a disc, available from any vehicle accessory shop in Portugal, must be displayed on the rear of the vehicle.

PARKING

At night, parking is not allowed on roads outside built-up areas. Parking lights must be used in badly-lit areas or when visibility is poor.

BY TRAIN

The Portuguese rail service can be slow and frustrating on all but the most important lines, so you might do better using a bus or an express coach service. If you decide to use the train, there are concessionary offers available if you do not have a Eurail or InterRail pass. Cartão Jovem (student card), Cartão de Familia (family card) or 'Tourist tickets' for 7, 14 or 21 days of travel. To receive these discounts on some direct routes, you must make reservations. You must have a valid ticket before boarding any train.

ACCOMMODATION

Most of the establishments listed in the gazetteer that follows provide accommodation for less than ESc 5054 per person per night at some time during the year.

The price bands are:

A Esc 2394–3724
B ESc 3724–5054

taking an exchange rate of

ESc 266=£1
ESc 160=US $1

It is possible, however, that these prices will change during the currency of this book. You will be able to obtain more information from a local tourist office. Pensions (pensões) are reasonably priced and another cheap option is to find a quarto (room) in a private home either by looking for a sign in a house window or by checking the list at the tourist office.

Abbreviations: av avenida r rua

ABRANTES *Ribatejo*

◆ **Abrantes** r D-Miguel de Almeida ☏ (041) 22119 rm12 **A**

◆ **Alianca** r Cidade Caldas da Rainha 50 ☏ (041) 22348 rm23 **A**

◆ **Central** Praca R-Soares ☏ (9041) 22422 rm14 **A**

AVEIRO *Beira Litoral*

H Afonso r Dr-Manuel das Neves 65 ☏ (034) 25191 rm80 **B**

★★**Arcada** r Viana do Castelo 4 ☏ (034) 23001 rm51 **A**

◆ **Aveirense** r Voluntários G-G Ferandes 14 ☏ (034) 23360 rm26 **A**

BEJA *Baixo Alentejo*

◆ **Coelho** Praca da Republica 15 ☏ (084) 24032 rm26 **B**

◆ **Rocha** Largo D-Nuno A-Pereira 12 ☏ (084) 24271 rm16 **A**

◆ **Tomás** r A-Herculano 7 ☏ (084) 24613 rm9 **A**

BRAGA *Minho*

H João XXI av João XXI-849 ☏ (053) 22146 rm28 **A**

BRAGANCA *Tras-Os-Montes Alto Douro*

◆ **Casa Nova** r Almirante Reis 48 ☏ (073) 22679 rm9 **A**

◆ **Internacional** r Almirante Reis 47 ☏ (073) 22611 rm9 **A**

◆ **Santo Antonio** r E-Navarro rm6 **B**

CASTELO DE VIDE *Alto Alentejo*

◆ **Cantinho Particular** r M-Bombarda 7 ☏ (045) 91151 rm8 **A**

COIMBRA *Beira Litoral*

H Avenida av E-Navarro 37 ☏ (039) 22156 rm25 **A**

◆ **Jardim** av E-Navarro 65 ☏ (039) 25204 rm19 **A**

H Mondego Largo das Ameias 4 ☏ (039) 29087 rm43 **A**

COLARES *Estremadura*

★**Estalagem Do Conde** Quinto do Conde ☏ (01) 2991652 rm11 **B**

CURIA *Beira Litoral*

H Curia ☏ (031) 52444 rm91 **A**

◆ **Portugal** ☏ (031) 52378 rm25 **A**

ELVAS *Alto Alentejo*

◆ **Central** r dos Chilòes 1 ☏ (068) 22310 rm25 **A**

◆ **O Lidador** r de Alcamin 33 ☏ (068) 22601 rm11 **B**

ESTREMOZ *Alto Alentejo*

◆ **Carvalho** Largo de Republica ☏ (068) 22712 rm15 **A**

ÉVORA *Alto Alentejo*
Évora, located in Portugal's vast, rolling plains, is a delightful museum town built on a hill that rises out of the surrounding Alentejo; almost completely surrounded by a perfectly preserved 14th-century wall, it has many monuments testifying to its 1, 000 years of history, enhanced by picturesque white-washed houses and villas.
Here the dissident Roman general Sertorius had a base, while Julius Caesar conferred upon the town the title of Liberalitas Julia, and the granite and marble Temple of Diana – perhaps the most famous of the town's monuments – was built by another Roman Emperor, possibly Hadrian.
Among Évora's many places of interest are the 12th to 13th-century Romanesque-Gothic cathedral, containing religious art treasures, Cadaval Palace – a private museum, a regional museum containing archaeological finds, and Roman art, Calvário convent and church and the palace of Dom Manuel, a 16th-century example of Moorish, Manueline and Renaissance architecture.
EATING OUT Regional specialities are served in the restaurant of the attractive *Pousada dos Loios*, which occupies part of the former monastery of *dos Loios*, built in the 15th century.

◆ **Policarpo** r da Freiria de Baixo 16 ☎ (066) 22424 rm24 **A**

H Santa Clara Travessa da Milheira 19 ☎ (066) 24141 rm21 **A**

FÁTIMA *Beira Litoral*

H Cinquentenário r F-Marto 101 ☎ (049) 97141 rm52 **A**

◆ **Cruz Alta** Cova da Iria ☎ (049) 97481 rm6 **B**

◆ **Davi** Estrada de Leira ☎ (049) 97778 rm11 **B**

H Pax ☎ (049) 97812 rm51 **A**

H Regina r Cónego Dr-M-Formigão ☎ (049) 97303 rm30 **B**

◆ **Zeca** r J-Marto 100 ☎ (049) 97262 rm11 **A**

FIGUEIRA DA FOZ *Beira Litoral*

◆ **Europa** r Candido dos Reis 40 ☎ (033) 22265 rm21 **A**

H Hispania r Dr-A-F-Dinis 61 ☎ (033) 22164 rm34 **A**

◆ **Moderna** Praca 8 de Maio 61 ☎ (033) 22701 rm23 **A**

◆ **Paris** r Dr-A-Lopes Guimarães 23 ☎ (033) 22611 rm28 **A**

GUARDA *Beira Alta*

◆ **Gare** Guarda-Gare ☎ (071) 22488 rm19 **A**

◆ **Santos** r Tenente Valadim 14 ☎ (071) 22931 rm18 **A**

LAMEGO *Tras-Os-Montes Alto Douro*

H Parque Senhora dos Remédios, (1.5 km S on N2) ☎ (054) 62105 rm32 **A**

LEIRIA *Beira Litoral*

◆ **Alcoa** r R-Cordeiro 24 ☎ (044) 22690 rm14 **A**

★★★**Euro Sol** r D-J Alves da Silva ☎ (044) 24101 rm54 **B**

H Lis Largo A-Herculano 10 ☎ (044) 22108 rm42 **A**

LISBOA (LISBON) *Estremadura*
Lisboa, the capital city of Portugal, with 1.5 million inhabitants, lies on seven low hills at the estuary of the river Tagus (Tejo). The attractions of the city lie in the magnificent vistas from its many belvederes, its shady tree-lined avenues and squares with decorated pavements, the freshnness of its public gardens, flower-filled balconies, patterned wall tiles and its wealth of monuments, churches and museums.
The architectural intrigue of the city bears witness to a brilliant historical past. Its origins are shrouded in legend, its mythical founders including Elisha and Ulysses. It was occupied successively by Phoenicians, Greeks, Carthaginians, Romans, Visigoths and Moors and finally conquered in 1147 by Portugal's first king, Afonso Henriques, with the aid of English Crusaders. But it was at the time of the Great Discoveries that Lisboa really came into preeminence as capital of the Portuguese Empire and the world centre for trade in spices, silks, jewels and gold. Relics of this fabulous wealth are to be seen everywhere in the Manueline architecture of Lisboa's churches, monasteries and palaces.
Among the chief places of interest is Alfama, a charming ancient Moorish quarter with narrow winding streets and picturesque white-washed houses, crowned by St George's Castle, which dominates the city. Together with Bairro Alto, Alfama is also the centre of *fado*, the traditional haunting folk song of Portugal.
Other places of interest include Praça do Comércio – a magnificent square with a superb triumphal arch, the city's range of fascinating churches and museums, and Belém, from where the ships of Vasco da Gama and other famous explorers set sail, with its graceful tower and Hyeronimite Monastery – two of the finest examples of the Manueline style of architecture.
EATING OUT As befits a great seafaring nation the Portuguese cook fish to perfection. Meat eaters, on the other hand, can find tasty pork and lamb dishes, while local specialities include *Bacalhau a Gomes de Sa* – dried cod baked with potatoes, onions and olives, and baked kid served with potatoes.
The cafés of Chiado, Alfama and Bairro Alto are worth a visit and a simple but satisfying meal can be enjoyed at a very reasonable price. *Gambrinus*, in Rua Portas S Antão, and *Anarquistas* in Largo da Trindade, are two of Lisboa's longest established restaurants, serving traditional Portuguese dishes. For less expensive local cuisine, the Atinel Bar, in Cais dos Carilheiros, is recommended not only for its satisfying and simple food, but also its setting by the River Tagus.

★★**Borges** r Garrett 108-110 ☎ (01) 846574 rm99 **B**

◆ **Caldense** r T-Ribeiro 49 ☎ (01) 544987 rm6 **A**

◆ **Europa** r do Carmo 35 ☎ (01) 327138 rm10 **A**

◆ **Ibérica** Praca da Figueira 10 ☎ (01) 865781 rm27 **A**

◆ **Italia** av V-Valmor 67 ☎ (01) 777736 rm8 **A**

◆ **Madeira** r J-Antonio de Anguiar 35 ☎ (01) 570305 rm15 **B**

◆ **Rossio** r dos Sapateiros 172 ☎ (01) 327204 rm7 **A**

H VIP r Lopes 25 ☎ (01) 578923 rm54 **A**

OLIVEIRA DO HOSPITAL *Beira Alta*

H São Paulo r Antunes Varela ☏ (038) 52396 rm44 **A**

PORTIMÃO *Algarve*

◆ **Lucio** Largo F-Mauricio 2 ☏ (082) 24292 rm9 **A**

◆ **Santa Isabel** r Dr-J-J Nunes ☏ (082) 24885 rm10 **A**

PORTO (OPORTO) *Douro Litoral*
Capital of northern Portugal and the country's second largest city, Porto is a busy, bustling city with elegant hotels, homely pensions, an abundance of excellent restaurants, rich museums, fine theatres and cinemas, and no shortage of sports opportunities.
One of the most ancient cities of the Iberian peninsula, and birthplace of Henry the Navigator, Porto stands on the banks of the river Douro, which is spanned by three bridges, the most modern of which, *a Ponte de Arrabida*, is an impressive example of Portuguese engineering, having what is claimed to be the largest reinforced concrete arch in Europe.
Many monuments, scattered about the city, provide rich examples of Romanesque, Gothic, Baroque, Roccoco and neo-classical architecture, while the fine Clerigos tower, the city landmark, majestically overlooks the old part of the city.
Being at the centre of the Port wine industry, most visitors take the opportunity to visit one of the ancient Port wine lodges at Vila Nova de Gaia, on the left bank of the Douro.
EATING OUT The best places to eat in Porto are the interesting *tascas*(eating taverns) in the medieval part of the city, among whose specialities is a dish for which the city is famous – tripe. Indeed, the inhabitants of Porto are affectionately known as *tripeiros* (tripe-eaters), a curious epithet gained in 1415 from having given away all the meat they had to the early navigators, keeping only the entrails for themselves. One restaurant specialising in tripe is the appropriately named *Tripeiro*, in Rua Passos Manuel.
Apart from tripe, other regional dishes to look out for include *caldo verde* – finely shredded kale broth, and *cabrito* – roast kid. Desserts include a range of quaintly named egg, almond and sugar cakes such as *Barrigas de Freira* – nuns' tummies.

◆ **Belo Sonho** r P-Manuel 186 ☏ (02) 23389 rm15 **A**

H International r do Almada 131 ☏ (02) 25032 rm35 **A**

◆ **Miradense** r Duque de Saldanha 512-516 ☏ (02) 57727 rm12 **A**

H Paris r da Fabrica 27 ☏ (02) 21095 rm41 **A**

◆ **Portuguesa** Travessa Coronel Pacheco 11 ☏ (02) 24174 rm28 **A**

◆ **Sereia** r C-Neto 6 ☏ (02) 564680 rm7 **A**

◆ **Uniao** r Conde de Vizela 62 ☏ (02) 23078 rm8 **A**

TAVIRA *Algarve*

◆ **Arcada** Praca da Republica 4 ☏ (081) 22226 rm21 **A**

St George's Castle dominates the old quarter of Lisbon

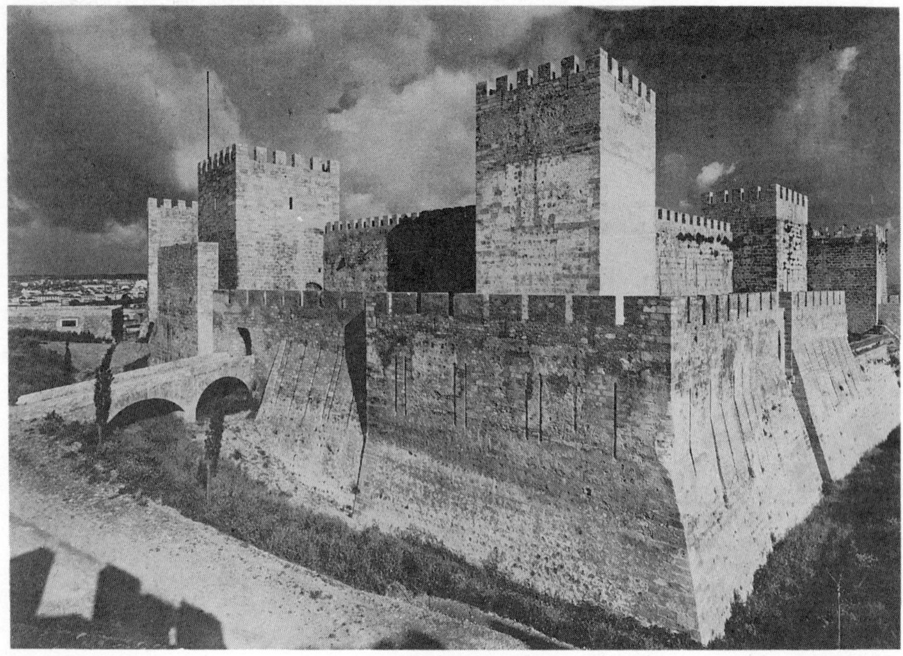

SPAIN AND ANDORRA

FACTS & FIGURES

SPAIN

Capital: Madrid
Language: Spanish (Castilian), Catalan, Galician, Basque
IDD code: 34. To call the UK dial 07 *44 (* wait for second dialling tone)
Currency: Spanish peseta (Ptas 1 = 100 centimos)
Local time: GMT + 1 (summer GMT + 2)
Emergency services: Madrid and Barcelona Police 091; Fire 2323232; Ambulance 092

Business hours–Banks: 0900–1400 Mon–Fri, 0900–1300 Sat
Shops: 0900–1300 & 1630–1930 Mon–Sat

FACTS & FIGURES

ANDORRA

Capital: Andorra la Vella
Language: Catalan, Spanish and French
Currency: French Franc (Fr 1 = 100 centimes), Spanish Peseta (Ptas 1 = 100 centimes)
Local time: GMT + 1 (summer GMT + 2)
Emergency services: Police 10; Fire 18; Ambulance 18.

Business hours

Banks: 0900–1300 Mon–Sat
Shops: 0900–2000 daily

Average daily temperatures:

Madrid °C			Andorra la Vella °C		
Jan 4	May 16	Sep 19	Jan 3	May 11	Sep 16
Mar 9	Jul 24	Nov 8	Mar 7	Jul 19	Nov 6

Tourist Information:

UK Spanish National Tourist Office, Metro House, 57–58 St James' Street, London, SW1A 1LD. Tel 01-499 0901

USA National Tourist Office of Spain, 665 Fifth Ave, New York, NY 10022. Tel (212) 759-8822

An ancient, sundrenched land whose soil has known numerous civilizations, Spain has been dubbed a 'miniature continent', and the contrasts among its various regions and peoples, language and customs certainly support that label. The Iberian Peninsula – Spain and Portugal – takes the form of a pentagon bound by rocky coasts. With a total area of 300,000 square miles it is the third largest country in Europe, ranks seventh in population, and is the most mountainous country in Europe after Switzerland. The distinctive feature of Spanish geography is the vast central plateau with an area of 120,000 square miles and an average altitude of more than 2,000 feet. Flanking this central plateau are great mountain ranges and the lateral depressions formed by the Ebro and Guadalquivir valleys.

Spain is a great museum displaying every facet of artistic endeavour from the prehistoric paintings of the Altamira Caves to Picasso's modern-day abstracts. The world-famous Prado Museum in Madrid contains masterpieces by Velazquez, El Greco, Zurbaran, Ribera and Murillo, and especially Goya, the influence of whose genius is still felt in art today.

The varied landscape of Spain is liberally sprinkled with castles, palaces, monasteries and cathedrals housing precious collections of sculptures, paintings, jewels and tapestries. Toledo is arguably the most complete complex of Spanish art, and boasts one of the finest gothic cathedrals, while Catalonia and the eastern regions imposed a peculiarly personal style on their gothic buildings.

For sun, sea and sand lovers Spain offers a tremendous range of holiday resorts, both on the mainland and the Canary and Balearic islands.

HOW TO GET THERE

BY CAR

From the Channel ports, Spain is approached via France. The two main routes are at either end of the Pyrenean mountains; the Biarritz to San Sebastiàn–Donostia road, or motorway, at the western end for central and southern Spain; or the Perpignan to Barcelona road, or motorway, at the eastern end for the Costa Brava and beyond.

It is about 990 miles from Calais to Madrid, a journey that would probably need 2–3 overnight stops.

If you want to shorten the car journey, you could use a car-sleeper service part of the way: from Boulogne, Calais or Paris to Narbonne; from Boulogne or Paris to Biarritz; or Paris to Madrid. There is also a direct ferry

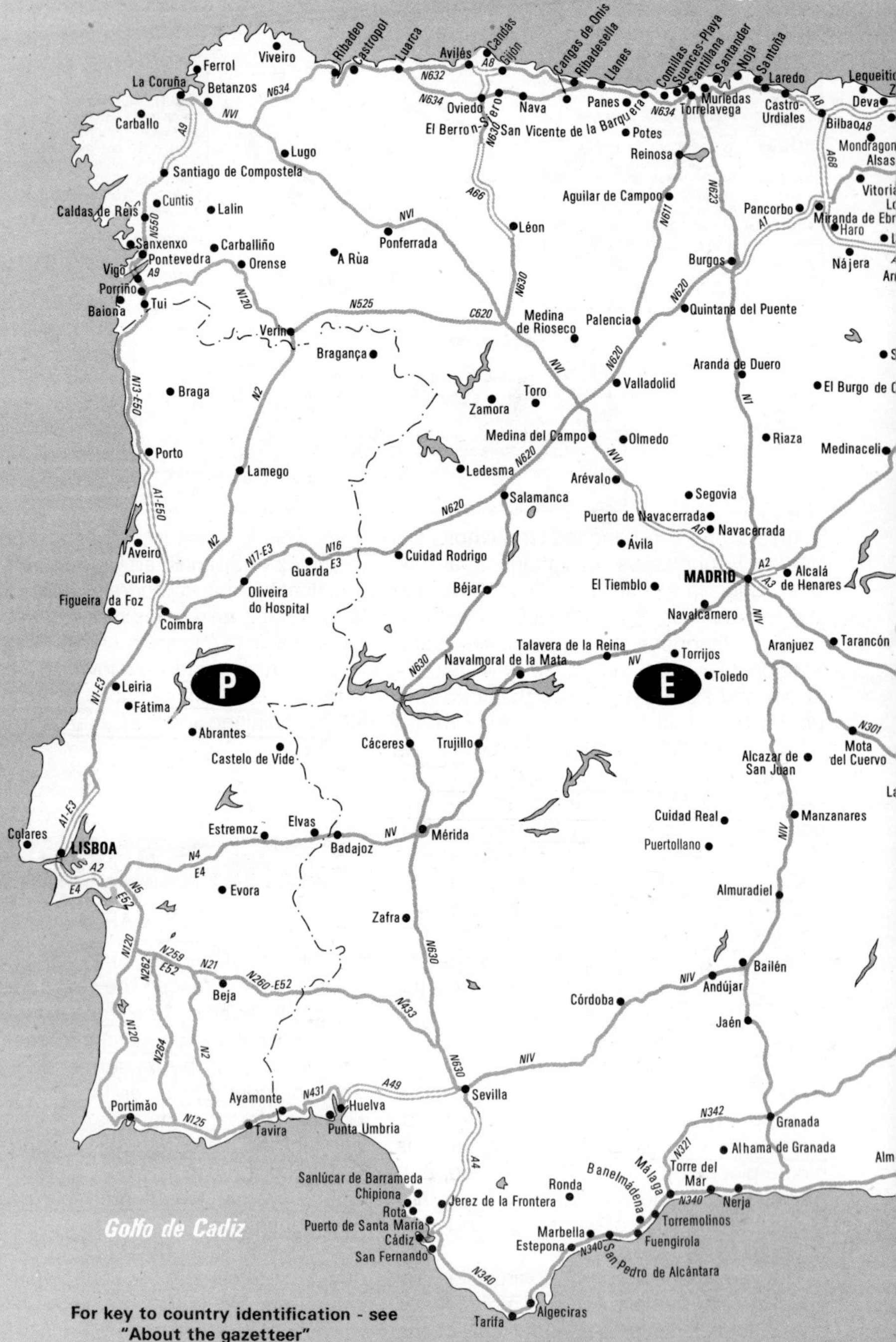

For key to country identification - see "About the gazetteer"

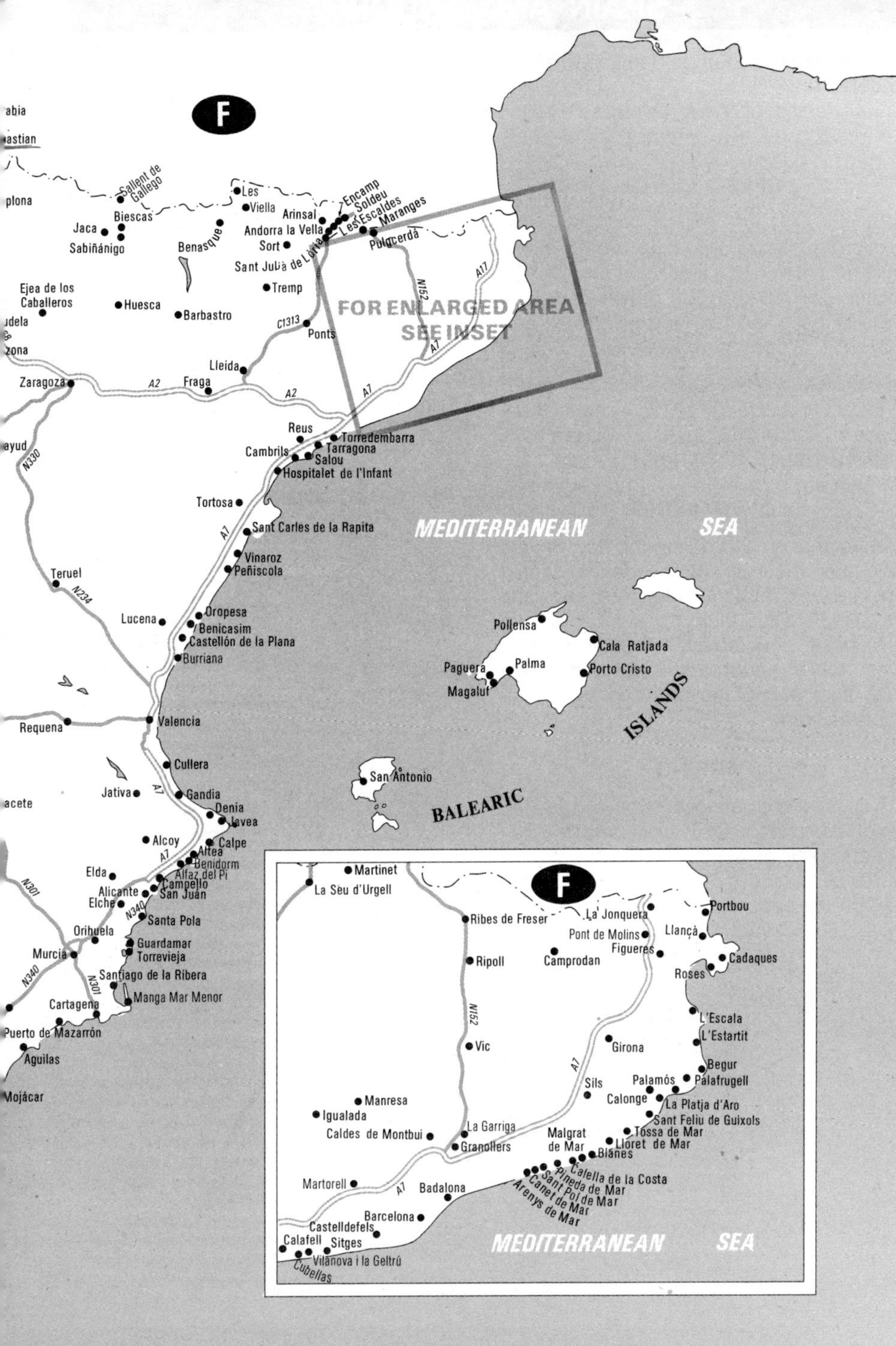
F
abia
astian
plona
Sallent de Gallego
Jaca
Biescas
Sabiñánigo
Benasque
Les
Viella
Arinsal
Andorra la Vella
Encamp
Soldeu
Les Escaldes
Maranges
Sort
Puigcerdá
Sant Julià de Lória
Tremp
Ejea de los Caballeros
Huesca
Barbastro
udela
zona
C1313
Ponts
FOR ENLARGED AREA SEE INSET
N152
A17
A7
Lleida
Zaragoza
A2
Fraga
Reus
Torredembarra
Cambrils
Tarragona
Salou
Hospitalet de l'Infant
ayud
N330
Tortosa
Sant Carles de la Rapita
MEDITERRANEAN SEA
Vinaroz
Peñiscola
Teruel
N234
Lucena
Oropesa
Benicasim
Castellón de la Plana
Burriana
Pollensa
Cala Ratjada
Paguera
Palma
Porto Cristo
Magaluf
Requena
Valencia
ISLANDS
Cullera
San Antonio
Jativa
Gandia
BALEARIC
acete
Denia
Javea
Alcoy
Calpe
Altea
Benidorm
Alfaz del Pi
Elda
Alicante
Campello
San Juan
Elche
N301
N340
Santa Pola
Orihuela
Guardamar
Torrevieja
Murcia
Santiago de la Ribera
Manga Mar Menor
Cartagena
Puerto de Mazarrón
Aguilas
Mojácar
Martinet
La Seu d'Urgell
Ribes de Freser
La Jonquera
Portbou
Pont de Molins
Llançà
Ripoll
Camprodan
Figueres
Cadaques
Roses
L'Escala
L'Estartit
Vic
Girona
Begur
Palamós
Palafrugell
Sils
Calonge
La Platja d'Aro
Manresa
Igualada
Sant Feliu de Guixols
La Garriga
Caldes de Montbui
Malgrat de Mar
Tossa de Mar
Lloret de Mar
Granollers
Blanes
Calella de la Costa
Pineda de Mar
Sant Pol de Mar
Canet de Mar
Arenys de Mar
Martorell
Badalona
Barcelona
Castelldefels
Calafell
Sitges
Vilanova i la Geltrú
Cubellas

service from Plymouth to Santander lasting about 24 hrs.

For details of AA's Overseas Routes Service consult the Contents page.

SPEED LIMITS

SPAIN

In built-up areas 60 kph (37 mph); outside built-up areas cars are limited to 90 kph (56 mph) or 100 kph (62 mph) on roads with wide lanes or on two-lane highways; and 120 kph (74 mph) on motorways.

ANDORRA

In built-up areas 40 kph (25 mph); on other roads 70 kph (43 mph). Some villages have a speed restriction of 20 kph (12 mph).

OVERTAKING

Both at night and during the day, drivers who are about to be overtaken should operate the right-hand indicator to show the driver behind that their intention to overtake has been understood. Outside built-up areas, drivers about to overtake must sound their horn during the day and flash their lights at night.

PARKING

You must not park on a two-way road if it is not wide enough for 3 vehicles. In one-way streets, vehicles are parked on the side of buildings with even numbers on even dates and on the opposite side on odd dates. A special parking zone has been established in central Madrid, parking tickets, available from tobacconists, must be displayed on the windscreen.

BY TRAIN

If you do not have a Eurail or InterRail pass, there are concessionary tickets available for travel within Spain; about 300 days in the year are *dias azules* (blue days) with discounts for everyone; the *Tarjeta Joven* (Youth Card) gives discount of 50%; the *Tarjeta Turistica* (Tourist card) allows unrestricted travel in the country; and there is a half-price family ticket if one adult pays full fare.

ACCOMMODATION

Most of the establishments listed in the gazetteer that follows offer accommodation for less than Ptas 2838 per person per night at some time during the year.

The price bands are:

A Ptas 181–2828
B Ptas 2828–3838

taking a rate of exchange at

Ptas 202 = £1
Ptas 122 = US $1

It is possible, however, that these prices will change during the currency of this book. More detailed information is available from the local tourist offices.

Abbreviations: av avenida c Calle Cdt Commandant ctra carretera Gl Generalisimo pl plaza ps paseo ptda Partida

AGUILAR DE CAMPOO *Palencia*

H Valentin av del Generalisimo 21 ☎ (988) 122125 rm50 **A**

AGUILAS *Murcia*

◆ **Carlos 111** Rey Carlos 111 22 ☎ (968) 411650 rm30 **A**

H Madrid pl de Robles Vives 4 ☎ (968) 410500 rm33 **A**

ALARCON *Cuenca*

H Claridge ctra Madrid-Valencia ☎ (966) 331150 rm36 **A**

ALBACETE *Albacete*

H Albar I-Peral 3 ☎ (967) 216861 rm51 **A**

H Altozano pl del Altozano ☎ (967) 210462 rm42 **A**

ALCALA DE HENARES *Madrid*

◆ **Bari** (n.rest) Nal 11 ☎ (91) 8881450 rm48 **A**

ALCAZAR DE SAN JUAN *Ciudad Real*

H Aldonza A-Guerra 28 ☎ (926) 541554 rm29 **A**

◆ **Don Quijote** av Criptana 5 ☎ (926) 543800 rm44 **A**

ALCOY *Alicante*

H Reconquista Puente San Jorge 1 ☎ (96) 5330900 rm77 **B**

ALFARO *Rioja*

H Palacios ctra de Zaragoza ☎ (941) 180100 rm86 **A**

ALFAZ DEL PI *Alicante*

◆ **El Moli** Gl-Mola 12 ☎ (96) 5888244 rm10 **A**

◆ **Niza** C/herrerias 9 ☎ (96) 5888029 rm24 (Apr-Oct) **A**

ALGECIRAS *Cádiz*

H Al Mar av de la Marina 2-3 ☎ (956) 654661 rm192 **A**

★★★**Alarde** Alfonso X1-4 ☎ (956) 660408 rm68 **A**

H Término av Villanueva, 6 ☎ (956) 650211 rm45 **A**

H Yucas A-Balsamo 2 ☎ (956) 663250 rm33 **B**

ALHAMA DE GRANADA *Granada*

H Balneario Alhama de Granada ☎ (958) 350011 rm116 (Jun 10-Oct 10) **A**

ALICANTE *Alicante*

H Balseta M-Molla 9 ☎ (96) 5206633 rm81 **A**

H Capri Rambla de Méndez Núñez 9 ☎ (96) 5208373 rm34 (Apr-Sep) **A**

◆ **Cervantes** Pascual Prez 19 ☎ (96) 5209910 rm30 **A**

H Covadlonga pl de Los Luceros 17 ☎ (96) 5202844 rm83 **A**

H Cristal López Torregrosa 9 ☎ (96) 5209600 rm54 **A**

◆ **Goya** Maestro Bretón 19 ☎ (96) 5201444 rm95 **A**

H Navas Las Navas 26 ☎ (96) 5204011 rm40 **A**

H Palas Piza Ayuntamiento 6 ☎ (96) 5206690 rm53 **B**

H Reforma Reyes Católicos 7 ☎ (96) 5222147 rm52 **A**

ALMERÍA *Almería*

H Embajador Calzada de Castro 4 ☎ (951) 255511 rm67 **A**

H Fátima San Leonardo 34 ☎ (951) 233111 rm30 **A**

◆ **Guerry** ☎ (951) 231177 rm40 **A**

H Indalico Dolores R-Sopeña 4 ☎ (951) 231512 rm52 **B**

H Torreluz pl Flores 1 ☎ (951) 234799 rm67 **A**

ALMURADIEL *Ciudad Real*

★★★**Podencos** ctra de Andalucia ☎ (926) 339000 rm76 **A**

ALSASUA *Navarra*

★★**Alaska** ctra Madrid-Irún Km 403 ☎ (948) 562802 rm29 **A**

H Hosteria Ulayar ctra Madrid-Irún Km 398 ☎ (948) 562803 rm9 (Apr-Sep) **A**

◆ **Leku Ona** ctra Madrid-Irún Km 398 ☎ (948) 562452 rm7 **A**

ALTEA *Alicante*

H Altaya Generalisimo 113 ☎ (96) 5840800 rm24 **A**

◆ **Trovador** ctr de Valencia Km 132 ☎ (96) 5841275 rm15 **A**

ANDUJAR *Jaén*

◆ **Don Pedro** Capitán Cortés 5 ☎ (953) 501274 rm33 **A**

H Val ctra Madrid-Cádiz Km 321 ☎ (953) 500950 rm79 **A**

ARANDA DE DUERO *Burgos*

◆ **Aranda** pl Dr-Costales ☎ (947) 501600 rm44 **A**

H Juliá San Gregorio 2 ☎ (947) 501200 rm65 **A**

★★**Tres Condes** Pol Res Parcela 4 ☎ (947) 502400 rm35 **A**

ARANJUEZ *Madrid*

H Mercedes ctra Madrid-Cádiz Km 46 ☎ (91) 8910440 rm37 **A**

ARCOS, LOS *Navarra*

◆ **Ezequiel** Gl-Mola ☎ (948) 640296 rm13 **A**

ARENYS DE MAR *Barcelona*

H Carlos 1 Passeig de Catalunya 8 ☎ (93) 7920383 rm100 (May 15-Oct) **A**

H Titus ctra de Francia Km 662 ☎ (93) 7910300 rm44 **A**

ARÉVALO *Ávila*

H Fray Juan Gil av Deportes 2 ☎ (918) 300800 rm30 **A**

ARNEDO *Rioja*

H Victoria ps de la Constitución 97 ☎ (941) 380100 rm48 **A**

H Virrey ps de la Constitución 27 ☎ (941) 380150 rm36 **A**

ÁVILA *Ávila*

★★**Cuatro Postes** ctra Salamanca 23 ☎ (918) 220000 rm36 **A**

H Reina Isabel av de J-Antonio 17 ☎ (918) 220200 rm44 **A**

H Rey Niño pl de J-Tomé 1 ☎ (918) 211404 rm24 **A**

AVILÉS *Asturias*

H Luzana Fruta 9 ☎ (985) 565840 rm73 **B**

H San Felix av de Lugo 48 ☎ (985) 565146 rm18 **A**

AYAMONTE *Huelva*

H Don Diego Ramón y Cajal ☎ (955) 320250 rm45 **A**

H Marqués de Ayamonte Gl-Mola 14 ☎ (955) 320125 rm30 **A**

BADAJOZ *Badajoz*

H Conde Duque Muñoz Torrero 27 ☎ (924) 224641 rm35 **A**

★★★**Gran Zurbaran** ps Castelar ☎ (924) 223741 rm215 **B**

H Lisboa av de Elvas 13 ☎ (924) 238200 rm176 **A**

◆ **Rio** av de Elvas ☎ (924) 237600 rm90 **A**

BADALONA *Barcelona*

◆ **Miramar** Santa Madrona 60 ☎ (93) 3840311 rm42 **A**

BAILÉN *Jaén*

H Zodiaco ctra Madrid-Cádiz Km 294 ☎ (953) 671058 rm52 **A**

BAIONA *Pontevedra*

H Anunciada Elduayén 16 ☎ (986) 355590 rm20 (Jun-Sep) **A**

H Bayona Conde 36 ☎ (986) 355087 rm33 (Jun-Sep) **A**

◆ **Carabela la Pinta** ☎ (986) 355107 rm10 **A**

H Rompeolas L-Calleja ☎ (986) 355130 rm39 (Jun-Sep) **A**

H Tres Carabelas Ventura Misa 72 ☎ (986) 355441 rm10 **A**

BALEARES, ISLAS DE

IBIZA

SAN ANTONIO

H Abrat Es Calo del Moro ☎ (971) 341005 rm110 (Apr-Oct) **A**

H Arenal av de Dr-Fleming ☎ (971) 340112 rm131 (Feb-Nov) **B**

H Helios Playa S-Estanyol ☎ (971) 340500 rm132 (Apr-Oct) **A**

H Pacific ctra de Ibiza Km 15 ☎ (971) 341162 bed156 (Apr-Oct) **A**

H Tagomago Playa Sestanyol ☎ (971) 340962 rm114 (Apr-Oct) **A**

MALLORCA (MAJORCA)

CALA RATJADA

H Aguait av de los Pinos ☎ (971) 563408 rm188 (Apr-Oct) **B**

H Cala Lliteras av Cala Guía ☎ (971) 563816 rm142 (Apr-Oct) **A**

H Lago Playa Playa Son Moll ☎ (971) 563058 rm95 (Apr-Oct) **A**

◆ **Paraiso** av Cala Agulla ☎ (971) 563889 rm7 (Apr-Oct) **A**

H Regana av Cala Agulla ☎ (971) 563862 rm126 (Apr-Oct) **B**

MAGALUF

H Barracuda av Notario Alemany ☎ (971) 681266 rm264 **A**

H Don Paco Terrenova ☎ (971) 681350 rm87 **A**

H Pax av Notario Alemany 12 ☎ (971) 680312 rm161 **B**

H Samos av Solivera 6 ☎ (971) 681700 rm417 (Apr-Oct) **A**

PAGUERA

H Beverly Playa Urb La Romana ☎ (971) 686070 rm443 **A**

H Carabela ctra Andraitx ☎ (971) 686408 rm44 (Apr-Oct) **A**

H Eucalipto Eucaliptus 15 ☎ (971) 686397 rm134 (Apr-Oct) **A**

H Maria Dolores pl Palmira 29 ☎ (971) 686598 rm70 **B**

H Nilo Malgrat 15 ☎ (971) 686500 rm118 **B**

PALMA DE MALLORCA

H Club Náutico Contramuelle 20 ☎ (971) 221405 rm35 **B**

H Madrid Garita 28 ☎ (971) 400111 rm84 **B**

◆ **Nacar** av de Jaime 111 21 ☎ (971) 222641 rm60 **B**

◆ **Regina** San Miguel 77 ☎ (971) 213703 rm10 **A**

H Rex L-Fábregas 4 ☎ (971) 230365 rm81 (Apr-Sep) **A**

H Rimini Carbo Martorell Roca 40 ☎ (971) 400262 rm39 **A**

H Rosamar av J-Miró 74 ☎ (971) 232723 rm44 **A**

At **PLAYA DE PALMA (C'AN PASTILLA)**

H Anfora San Antonio de la Playa 41 ☎ (971) 261662 rm61 **A**

H Java Goletá ☎ (971) 262776 rm249 (Apr-Oct) **B**

H Linda pl Torre Redona ☎ (971) 262982 rm189 **A**

H Miraflores Jabeque 2 ☎ (971) 263100 rm69 (Apr-Oct) **A**

At **PLAYA DE PALMA NOVA**(16km SW)

H Aquarium ps del Mar ☎ (971) 680300 rm109 (Apr-Oct) **B**

H Honolulu Pineda ☎ (971) 680450 rm216 **A**

H Morocco ps del Mar ☎ (971) 681758 rm54 (Apr-Oct) **A**

H Tobago Torrenova ☎ (971) 680500 rm218 **A**

◆ **Villa Nova** ps del Mar 43 ☎ (971) 890497 rm14 (Apr-Oct) **A**

POLLENSA

At **CALA SAN VINCENTE**

H Simar Cpt-Juergens ☎ (971) 530300 rm120 (May-Oct) **A**

◆ **Vistamar** Cala Clara ☎ (971) 530050 rm11 (Apr-Oct) **B**

At **PUERTO DE POLLENSA**(6km NE)

H Marcalma ☎ (971) 531750 rm21 (Apr-Oct) **A**

H Panorama Urb Gomar 5/6 ☎ (971) 531192 rm20 (Apr-Oct) **B**

H Raf ps Saralegui 84 ☎ (971) 531195 rm40 (Apr-Oct) **A**

PORTO CRISTO

◆ **Aguamarina** Sureda 98 ☎ (971) 570248 rm67 **A**

H Castell Dels Hams ctra Manacor-Porto Cristo ☎ (971) 570007 rm131 Closed Apr-Oct **A**

H Estrella Curricán 16 ☎ (971) 570082 rm41 (May-Oct) **A**

H Felip Burdils 67 ☎ (971) 570005 rm87 **A**

BARBASTRO *Huesca*

H Rey Sancho Ramírez ctra Tarragona, - San Sebastian Km 162, 700 ☎ (974) 310050 rm81 **B**

BARCELONA *Barcelona*

Barcelona, capital of Catalonia and of the province of Barcelona, stretches from the Mediterranean to the foot of the mountain of Tibidabo, across a great plain dotted with hills, such as the Taber, on which the magnificent cathedral stands. The city is flanked to the north by the River Besos and to the south by the Llobregat.

Spain's second city rivals Madrid in size, sophistication and sheer entertainment value; the Picasso Museum houses one of Europe's finest collections and no visit would be complete without strolling along the *Ramblas*, where bird and flower markets alternate with restaurants and shops.

EATING OUT Simple, straightforward ingredients fresh from the sea and farm are the basis of Catalan cuisine, with the emphasis very much on fish and shellfish, especially sole, sea bass, red mullet, squid, prawns and lobster. One of the specialities of the region is *zaizuela*, a mixture of seafood in a wine sauce.

Quo Vadis, off the Ramblas, is popular with locals and visitors alike. *Can Culleretes* in Quintana, and *Sete Portes* in Passeig Isabel II, are also long established, while in the budget category, *Agut*, in Gignas, has been popular since the 1920s.

H Cataluña Santa Ana 22 ☎ (93) 3019150 rm40 **A**

◆ **Cortés** Santa Ana 25 ☎ (93) 3179212 rm46 **A**

H Ficus Mallorca 163 ☎ (93) 2533500 rm74 **B**

H Inglés Boquería 17 ☎ (93) 3173770 rm29 **A**

H Lleo Pelayo 24 ☎ (93) 3181312 rm42 **A**

H Lloret Ramblas Canaletas 125 ☎ (93) 3173366 rm53 **A**

H Moderno Hospital 11 ☎ (93) 3014154 rm57 **A**

H Oriente Ramblas 45-47 ☎ (93) 3022558 rm142 **B**

★★**Park** av Marqués de Argentera 11 ☎ (93) 3196000 rm95 **A**

◆ **Prisma** Infanta Carlota 119 ☎ (93) 2394207 rm27 **A**

H San Agustin pl de San Agustin 3 ☎ (93) 3172882 rm71 **A**

H Villa de Madrid pl Villa de Madrid 3 ☎ (93) 3174916 rm28 **A**

BEGUR *Girona*

★★★**Bagur** de Coma y Ros 8 ☎ (972) 622207 rm34 (Apr-Sep) **A**

H Bonaigua pl de Fornells ☎ (972) 622050 rm47 (Apr 4-Oct 15) **B**

H Plaja pl Pella I Forgas ☎ (972) 622197 rm16 **A**

★★**Sa Riera** Playa de Sa Riera ☎ (972) 623000 rm41 (Mar 15-Oct) **A**

BÉJAR *Salamanca*

◆ **Blázquez Sánchez** Travesía de Santa Ana 6 ☎ (923) 402400 rm33 **A**

★★★**Colón** Colón 42 ☎ (923) 400650 rm54 **A**

H Comercio Puerto de Avila 5 ☎ (923) 400304 rm13 **A**

BENALMÁDENA *Málaga*

H Arenas ctra de Cádiz Km 228 ☎ (952) 443644 rm104 **A**

H Bali av Telefónica 7 ☎ (952) 441940 rm372 **A**

H Balmoral ctra de Cádiz-Málaga ☎ (952) 443640 rm210 **A**

H Roca ctra Cádiz-Málaga ☎ (952) 441740 rm53 **B**

H Rubens ctra Nacional 340 Cádiz-Málaga ☎ (952) 442046 rm106 (Apr-Oct) **A**

H San Fermin av San Fermin ☎ (952) 442040 rm316 (Apr-Oct) **B**

H Van Dyck Finca Mena ☎ (952) 442244 rm192 (Apr-Sep) **A**

H Villasol ctra de Cádiz Km 228 ☎ (952) 441996 rm76 **A**

BENASQUE *Huesca*

◆ **Puente** San Pedro ☎ (974) 551279 rm12 **A**

BENICASIM *Castellón*

H Benicasim Bayer 50 ☎ (964) 300558 rm80 **A**

H Miami Gran Avenida ☎ (964) 300050 rm49 (Apr-Sep) **A**

H Orange Gran Avenida ☎ (964) 300600 rm415 (Mar 5-Nov 15) **A**

H Tramontana ps Maritimo ☎ (964) 300300 rm65 (Mar 20-Oct) **A**

H Vista Alegre av de Barcelona 48 ☎ (964) 300400 rm68 (Feb-Oct) **A**

BENIDORM *Alicante*

H Alameda Alameda 36 ☎ (96) 5855650 rm68 **A**

H Brisa Playa de Levante ☎ (96) 5855400 rm70 **A**

H Colón ps Cólon 3 ☎ (96) 5850412 rm37 (Jan 3-Oct) **A**

H Didac via E-Ortuño ☎ (96) 5851549 rm100 (Apr-Oct) **A**

H Fenicia Prolongación del Mercado 9 ☎ (96) 5851146 rm279 (Apr-Oct) **A**

H Haway Viena 2 ☎ (96) 5850400 rm230 (Apr 5-Oct) **A**

★★**Presidente** av Filipinas 10 ☎ (96) 5853950 rm228 **A**

H Riudor av del Mediterráneo ☎ (96) 5852608 rm168 **A**

H Royal via E-Ortuño ☎ (96) 5853500 rm88 **A**

H Tropicana Gardens Sierra Dorada ☎ (96) 5851175 rm251 **A**

H Villa de Benidorm ☎ (96) 5850699 rm120 **A**

BERRON-SIERO, EL *Asturias*

H Samoa ctra Oviedo-Santander ☎ (985) 741150 rm40 **A**

BETANZOS *la Coruña*

H Los Angeles Los Angeles, 11 ☎ (981) 771511 rm36 **A**

BIESCAS *Huesca*

H Giral ctra de Francia ☎ (974) 485005 rm16 **A**

BILBAO (BILBO) *Vizcaya*

◆ **San Mamés** Luis Briñas 15 ☎ (94) 4417900 rm36 **A**

◆ **Zalbalburu** ps M-Artola 8 ☎ (94) 4437100 rm37 **A**

BLANES *Girona*

H Boix Mar av Villa de Madrid ☎ (972) 330276 rm170 (Apr 10-Oct) **A**

◆ **Patacano** Paseig del Mar 12 ☎ (972) 330002 rm6 **A**

H Ruiz Ravel 45 ☎ (972) 330300 rm59 (Jun-Sep) **A**

★★**San Antonio** ps Maritimo 63 ☎ (972) 331150 rm156 (May 15-Oct 10) **A**

★★**San Francisco** ps Maritimo 72 ☎ (972) 330477 rm32 (May-Oct) **A**

H Stella Maris av Villa Madrid 18 ☎ (972) 330092 rm90 (Apr-Aug) **A**

BURGO DE OSMA, EL *Soria*

H Virrey Palafoz Travesía Acosta 1 ☎ (975) 340222 rm20 **A**

BURGOS *Burgos*

H Conde de Miranda Miranda 4 ☎ (947) 265267 rm14 **A**

H Cordon La Puebla 6 ☎ (947) 265000 rm35 **B**

H Corona de Castilla Madrid 15 ☎ (947) 262142 rm52 **A**

H España ps del Espolón 32 ☎ (947) 206340 rm69 **A**

H Norte y Londres pl A-Martinéz 10 ☎ (947) 264125 rm55 **A**

◆ **Rodrigo** av del Cid 42 ☎ (947) 225100 rm64 **A**

H Villa Jimena P-Pisones 47 ☎ (947) 207430 rm23 **A**

BURRIANA *Castellón*

★★★**Aloha** Conde Vallellano ☎ (964) 510104 rm30 (Mar-Sep) **A**

H Plana Area de Servicio Autopista ☎ (964) 512550 rm56 **A**

CÁCERES *Cáceres*

★★★**Alcántara** av Virgen de Guadalupe 14 ☎ (927) 228900 rm67 **B**

★★**Alvarez** Parras 20 ☎ (927) 246400 rm37 **A**

H Extremadura av Virgen de Guadalupe 5 ☏ (927) 221604 rm68 **A**

CADAQUES *Girona*

◆ **S'Aguarda** ctra Port Lligat 28 ☏ (972) 258082 rm27 **A**

◆ **Casa Europa** Paraje Maltret ☏ (972) 258131 rm20 **A**

◆ **Cristina** La Riera ☏ (972) 258138 rm20 **B**

H Port Lligat Port Lligat ☏ (972) 258162 rm30 **A**

CÁDIZ *Cádiz*

H Francia y Paris pl San Francisco 2 ☏ (956) 222348 rm69 **A**

H Regio Ana de Viya 11 ☏ (956) 279331 rm40 **A**

H San Remo ps Maritimo 3 ☏ (956) 252202 rm34 **A**

CALAFELL *Tarragona*

H Alondra Carrer Vilamar 69 ☏ (977) 691100 rm95 (May-Oct) **A**

H Canadá Mosén J-Soler 44 ☏ (977) 691500 rm106 (May 20-Aug) **A**

◆ **Papiol** av San Juan de Dois 56 ☏ (977) 691710 rm15 (May-Oct) **A**

H Salome Monturiol 19 ☏ (977) 690100 rm45 (May 15-Sep) **A**

CALA RATJADA See **BALEARES, ISLAS DE** under **MALLORCA (MAJORCA)**

CALA SAN VINCENTE See **BALEARES, ISLAS DE** under **POLLENSA**

CALATAYUD *Zaragoza*

★★**Calatayud** ctra Madrid-Barcelona Km 237 ☏ (976) 881323 rm63 **A**

CALDAS DE REIS *Pontevedra*

H Balneario Acuña Herreria 2 ☏ (986) 540010 rm21 Closed Oct-Jun **A**

CALDES DE MONTBUI *Barcelona*

◆ **Balearino Termas Victoria** Barcelona 12 ☏ (93) 8650150 rm91 **A**

H Balneario Broquetas pl Font del Lleo 1 ☏ (93) 8650100 rm89 **A**

CALELLA DE LA COSTA *Barcelona*

◆ **Antonia Visa** Esglesia, 309 ☏ (93) 7691853 rm19 (Jun-Sep) **A**

H Oasis Park Montnegre 1 ☏ (93) 7691142 rm237 (Apr 15-Oct) **A**

H Sant Jordi av Turisme 30 ☏ (93) 7692846 rm53 (Apr 15-Oct 10) **A**

H Solimar Costa y Fornaguera 112 ☏ (93) 7690519 rm76 (May 15-Sep) **A**

CALONGE *Girona*

◆ **Mas Pere** La Bisbal 14 ☏ (972) 650101 rm7 **A**

CALPE *Alicante*

H Porte Calpe av Puerto 7 ☏ (96) 5830354 rm60 **A**

◆ **Rocinante** Ptda Estación 10 ☏ (96) 5831200 rm30 **A**

★★**Venta la Chata** ☏ (96) 830308 rm17 Closed Nov & Dec **A**

CAMBRILS *Tarragona*

H Augustus 1 ctra Salou-Cambrils ☏ (977) 381154 rm243 (Apr-Oct) **A**

◆ **Can Llorens** Colón 25 ☏ (977) 360487 rm15 **A**

H Centurión Playa ctra de Salou ☏ (977) 361450 rm233 (May-Oct 15) **B**

H César Augustus ctra Salou-Cambrils ☏ (977) 381808 rm120 (Apr-Oct) **A**

H Mónica G-Marquet 1-3 ☏ (977) 360116 rm56 (Apr-Sep) **A**

◆ **Orly** ctra Nal 340 ☏ (977) 361517 rm14 (Jun-Sep) **A**

CAMPELLO *Alicante*

H Costa Azul av Gobernador Aramburu 103 ☏ (96) 5652250 rm45 (Apr-Oct 15) **A**

◆ **San Juan** Playa Muchavista ☏ (96) 5652308 rm34 (Apr-Sep) **A**

CAMPRODON *Girona*

H Guell pl de España 8 ☏ (972) 740011 rm40 **A**

◆ **Rigat** pl del Dr-Robert 2 ☏ (972) 740013 rm28 (Feb 15-Nov 15) **A**

CANDAS *Asturias*

◆ **Carmen** La Nozaleda ☏ (985) 870314 rm6 **A**

◆ **Piedra** Perlora ☏ (985) 870915 rm12 **A**

CANET DE MAR *Barcelona*

◆ **Miramar** ps de la Maresma 23 ☏ (93) 7940538 rm19 (Apr-Oct) **A**

◆ **Sant Roc** Maresme 15-17 ☏ (93) 7941240 rm61 (May-Sep) **A**

CANGAS DE ONIS *Asturias*

H Favila Calzada de Ponga 16 ☏ (985) 848870 rm33 **A**

H Ventura av de Covadonga ☏ (985) 848200 rm22 **A**

CARBALLIÑO *Orense*

H Arenteiro Alameda 19 ☏ (988) 270558 rm45 **A**

CARBALLO *la Coruña*

H Moncarsol av de Finisterre 9 ☏ (981) 702411 rm32 **A**

CARTAGENA *Murcia*

H Alfonso X111 ps Alfonso X111 30 ☏ (968) 520000 rm239 **A**

★★★**Cartagonova** Marcos Redondo 3 ☏ (968) 504200 rm126 **B**

CASTELLDEFELS *Barcelona*

H Colibri ps Maritimo 138 ☏ (93) 6652450 rm67 **A**

◆ **Eva** Numero 8, 5 ☏ (93) 6651087 rm10 **A**

◆ **Flora Parc** av Constitución ☏ (93) 6651847 rm32 **A**

H Mediterráneo ps Maritimo 294 ☏ (93) 6652100 rm47 **B**

◆ **Miño** av de la Constitución 330 ☏ (93) 6652196 rm34 (Apr-Nov) **A**

★★★**Neptuno** ps Garbi 74 ☏ (93) 6651450 rm38 **B**

H Rialto ps Maritimo 70 ☏ (93) 6652058 rm24 (Apr-Sep) **A**

H Riviera Autovia Castelldefels Km 18 ☏ (93) 6651400 rm35 **A**

◆ **Suiza** ps Maritimo 114 ☏ (93) 6651999 rm12 **A**

CASTELLÓN DE LA PLANA *Castellón*

H Del Real pl del Real 2 ☏ (964) 211944 rm35 **A**

H Myriam Obispo Salinas 1 ☏ (964) 222100 rm25 **A**

H Turcosa av de Buenavista 1 ☏ (964) 222150 rm70 **B**

CASTROPOL *Asturias*

◆ **Casa Vicente** ctra Nacional 634 ☏ (985) 623051 rm14 **A**

H Palacete Peñalba Cotarelo-Figueras ☏ (985) 623150 rm12 **B**

CASTRO-URDIALES *Cantabria*

H Miramar av de la Playa 1 ☏ (942) 860200 rm33 (Mar 15-Oct 15) **A**

◆ **Playa** La Playa s/n ☎ (942) 860200 rm13 (Jul-Sep 15) **A**

H Rocas ctra de la Playa ☎ (942) 860404 rm61 **B**

◆ **Vista Alegre** B-Brazomar ☎ (942) 860150 rm19 **A**

CESTONA *Guipúzcoa*

H Gran Balneario Cestona ps de San Juan ☎ (943) 867140 rm110 **B**

CHIPIONA *Cádiz*

◆ **Brasilia** av del Faro 12 ☎ (956) 371054 rm21 **A**

H Cruz del Mar av Gl-Primo-de-Riveria ☎ (956) 371100 rm85 (Apr-Oct) **A**

H Sur av de Sevilla 2 ☎ (956) 370350 rm54 (Apr-Sep) **A**

CIUDAD REAL *Ciudad Real*

H Almanzor B-Balbuena ☎ (926) 214303 rm66 **B**

H Castillos av del Rey Santo 8 ☎ (926) 213640 rm131 **A**

H Molino ctra Córdoba-Tarragona Km 242 ☎ (926) 223050 rm18 **B**

CIUDAD RODRIGO *Salamanca*

H Conde Rodrigo pl del Salvador 9 ☎ (923) 461408 rm35 **A**

COMILLAS *Cantabria*

H Josein Santa Lucia 27 ☎ (942) 720225 rm23 (Mar 15-Oct 15) **A**

H Paraiso Plaza ☎ (942) 720030 rm36 **A**

CÓRDOBA *Córdoba*

◆ **Colón** Alhaken 11, 4 ☎ (957) 470017 rm40 **A**

★★**Marisa** Cardenal Herrero 6 ☎ (957) 473142 rm28 **A**

◆ **Niza Sur** av de Cádiz 60 ☎ (957) 296511 rm30 **A**

◆ **Riviera** pl de Aladreros 7 ☎ (957) 473000 rm29 **A**

◆ **Selu** E-Dato 7 ☎ (957) 476500 rm118 **A**

◆ **Triunfo** Cardenal Gonzalez 79 ☎ (957) 475500 rm26 **A**

CORUÑA, LA (A CORUÑA) *la Coruña*

◆ **Brisa** ps de Ronda 2 ☎ (981) 269650 rm16 **A**

H España Juana de Vega 7 ☎ (981) 224506 rm84 **A**

◆ **Mara** Galera 49 ☎ (981) 221802 rm19 **A**

◆ **Maycar** San Andrés 159 ☎ (981) 225600 rm56 **A**

◆ **Navarra** pl de Lugo 23 ☎ (981) 225400 rm24 **A**

H Riazor av Barrie de la Maza ☎ (981) 253400 rm176 **A**

H Rivas av F-Latorre 45 ☎ (981) 290111 rm70 **A**

CUBELLAS *Barcelona*

H San Jorge Dr-Fleming 6 ☎ (93) 8950008 rm21 (Mar-Oct) **A**

CUENCA *Cuenca*

H Alfonsa V111 Parque de San Julián 3 ☎ (966) 214325 rm48 **A**

★★★**Cueva del Fraile** ctra Cuenca-Buenache Km 7 ☎ (966) 211571 rm54 **A**

H Francabel División Azul 7 ☎ (966) 226222 rm30 **A**

CULLERA *Valencia*

H Safi Playa Dosel Faro ☎ (96) 1520577 rm30 (Mar-Oct 15) **A**

CUNTIS *Pontevedra*

◆ **Casa Conde** av Circunvalación ☎ (986) 548088 rm13 (Jun-Sep) **A**

DENIA *Alicante*

H Denia ptda Suertes del Mar ☎ (96) 5781212 rm280 (Apr-Oct) **A**

★★**Los Angeles** Playa de las Marinas 649 ☎ (96) 5780458 rm59 (Apr-Oct) **A**

H Rotas ptda Les Rotes 71 ☎ (96) 5780323 rm23 Closed Apr-Sep **A**

DEVA *Guipúzcoa*

H Miramar Arenal 24 ☎ (943) 601144 rm60 **A**

EJEA DE LOS CABALLEROS *Zaragoza*

H Cinco Villas ps del Muro 10 ☎ (976) 660300 rm30 **A**

ELCHE *Alicante*

H Don Jaime av Primo-de-Rivera 5 ☎ (96) 5453840 rm64 **A**

ELDA *Alicante*

H Elda av de Chapi 4 ☎ (96) 5380556 rm37 **A**

ESCALA, L' *Girona*

H Bonaire-Juvines Po Luis-Albert 4 ☎ (972) 770068 rm31 (May-Oct) **A**

H Dels Pins Closa del Llop ☎ (972) 770395 rm40 (Jun-Sep) **A**

◆ **Mediterraneo** Riera 22 ☎ (972) 770028 rm21 (Mar-Sep) **A**

H Nieves Mar ps Maritimo 8 ☎ (972) 770300 rm80 (Feb-Nov) **A**

H Rem av Maria 3 ☎ (972) 770245 rm16 **A**

H Riomar San Marti de Ampuries ☎ (972) 770362 rm26 (May-Sep) **A**

H Voramar ps de L-Albert 2 ☎ (972) 770108 rm40 (Apr-Sep) **A**

ESTARTIT, L' *Girona*

★★**Amer** Del Puerto 41 ☎ (972) 757212 rm57 (May-Oct) **A**

◆ **Bahia** Islas 49 ☎ (972) 758433 rm14 (May-Sep) **A**

H Bell Aire Iglesia 39 ☎ (972) 758162 rm78 (Mar-Oct) **B**

H Club de Campo Torre Grau Descampado ☎ (972) 758160 rm10 Closed Sep **A**

H Club et Catalán (n.rest) Carrerada ☎ (972) 758100 rm112 (May-Sep) **A**

H Flamingo Iglesia ☎ (972) 758327 rm100 (May-Sep) **A**

H Miramar av de Roma 7 ☎ (972) 758628 rm64 (May 15-Oct 15) **A**

★★**Muriscot** ctra Nal II Km 764 ☎ (972) 505151 rm20 **A**

H Pinmar ctra de Torroella 11 ☎ (972) 758217 rm55 (May-Sep) **A**

H Rambla ps del Puerto 2 ☎ (972) 758538 rm15 **A**

◆ **Xumetra** Islas 55 ☎ (972) 758596 rm18 (Jun-Sep) **A**

ESTEPONA *Málaga*

★**Buenavista** ps Maritimo ☎ (952) 800137 rm38 **A**

H Caracas av San Lorenzo 50 ☎ (952) 800800 rm27 **A**

FERROL *la Coruña*

H Almirante Frutos Saavedra 2 ☎ (981) 325311 rm122 **A**

◆ **Almendra** Almendra 4-6 ☎ (981) 318000 rm40 **A**

FIGUERES *Girona*

★★★**Ampurdan** ctra Madrid-Francia ☎ (972) 500562 rm42 **B**

◆ **Bon Retorn** ctra Nal 11 Km 759 ☎ (972) 504623 rm53 **A**

★★★**Durán** c Lasuaca 5 ☎ (972) 501250 rm67 **B**

H Pirineos Ronda Barcelona 1 ☎ (972) 500312 rm53 **A**

H Rallye Ronda Barcelona ☎ (972) 501300 rm15 **B**

H Ronda Ronda Barcelona 104 ☎ (972) 503911 rm43 **A**

H Trave ctra Olot ☎ (972) 500591 rm73 **A**

FRAGA *Huesca*

H Casanova av Generalisimo 78 ☎ (974) 471990 rm56 **B**

FUENGIROLA *Málaga*

H Cendrillon ctra Nal 340 ☎ (952) 475316 rm56 **A**

★★★Florida Playa Florida ☎ (952) 476100 rm116 **A**

H Fuengirola Park ctra Cádiz-Málaga Km123 ☎ (952) 470000 rm391 **A**

H Mas Playa ☎ (952) 475300 rm108 **A**

H Stella Maria ☎ (952) 475450 rm196 **A**

H Stella Polaris ☎ (952) 461040 rm219 **A**

H Torreblanca Torreblanca del Sol ☎ (952) 475850 rm180 **A**

FUENTERRABIA (HONDARRIBIA) *Guipúzcoa*

◆ Alvarez Quintero A-Quintero 7 ☎ (943) 642299 rm14 (Jul-Oct) **A**

★★Guadalupe Ciudad de Pensicola ☎ (943) 641650 rm34 **B**

H Jáuregui San Pedro 31 ☎ (943) 641400 rm53 **A**

GANDIA *Valencia*

H Bayren 11 Mallorca 19 ☎ (96) 2840700 rm125 (Jun-Sep) **A**

◆ Fin de Somana Mare Nostrum 35 ☎ (96) 2840097 rm9 (Jun-Sep) **A**

H Gandia Playa (n.rest) Devesa 17 ☎ (96) 2841300 rm90 (Apr-Sep) **A**

H Porto av M-A-Suarez ☎ (96) 2841723 rm135 **A**

H Riviera ps Neptuno 29 ☎ (96) 2840066 rm72 (Apr-Oct) **A**

H Robles ☎ (96) 2842100 rm240 (Mar-Sep) **A**

H Safari Legazpi 3 ☎ (96) 2840400 rm113 **A**

H San Luis ps Neptuno 6 ☎ (96) 2840800 rm72 (Mar-Dec) **A**

H Tres Anclas Playa ☎ (96) 2840566 rm333 (Apr-Oct) **B**

GARRIGA, LA *Barcelona*

H Blancafort Baños 55 ☎ (93) 8714600 rm52 **A**

GIJÓN *Asturias*

H Aguera H-Felgueroso 28 ☎ (985) 140500 rm32 **B**

H León ctra de la Costa 45 ☎ (985) 370111 rm156 **A**

H Pathos Contracay 5 ☎ (985) 352546 rm56 **A**

GIRONA (GERONA) *Girona*

H Costabella av France 61 ☎ (972) 202524 rm22 **A**

★★Europe J-Garreta 23 ☎ (972) 202750 rm26 **A**

◆ Inmortal Gerona ctra Barcelona 31 ☎ (972) 207900 rm76 **A**

H Nord Gironi Major de Serriá 1-5 ☎ (972) 207404 rm24 **A**

H Peninsular Nou 3 ☎ (972) 203800 rm68 **A**

H Ultonia av Jaime 122 ☎ (972) 203850 rm45 **B**

GRANADA *Granada*

Granada – capital of the Andalusian province of the same name – is situated at the foot of the mighty Sierra Nevada and is dominated by the magnificent pink-gold palace of the *Alhambra*, the most beautiful of Andalusia's Moorish monuments. Also of interest are the *Generalife*, one time summer palace of the emirs, which stands in beautiful gardens, the flamboyant Royal Chapel and the huge cathedral, commisioned in 1521 by Charles V. The Plaza de Bib-Ramblas is a pleasant square animated by outdoor cafés in the summer, while shoppers will find plenty of interest in the streets of the Alcaiceria, including handicrafts inspired by Granada's Moorish heritage.
EATING OUT There are several atmospheric restaurants serving regional and international cuisine in the area of the *Alhambra*, and also in Alcaiceria, where the *Sevilla* has an excellent *tapas* bar as well as an attractive restaurant.

H Alcano ctra Nal 342 ☎ (958) 283050 rm100 **A**

★America Real Alhambra 53 ☎ (958) 227471 rm14 (Mar-Nov 9) **B**

H Ana Maria Camino Rondo 101 ☎ (958) 289215 rm30 **B**

◆ Carlos V pl de los Campos 4 ☎ (958) 221587 rm28 **A**

H Condor av Constitución 6 ☎ (958) 283711 rm101 **B**

H Dauro Acera del Darro 19 ☎ (958) 222156 rm36 **B**

★★Inglaterra Cetti Merien 10 ☎ (958) 221559 rm40 **A**

H Macía pl Nueva 4 ☎ (958) 227536 rm40 **A**

H Manuel de Falla Antequeruela Baja 4 ☎ (958) 227545 rm22 **A**

◆ Montecarlo J-Antonio 44 ☎ (958) 257900 rm74 **A**

H Rallye ps de Ronda 107 ☎ (958) 272800 rm44 **A**

H Sacromonte pl del Lino 1 ☎ (958) 266411 rm33 **A**

H San Gabrièl ctra de Murcia ☎ (958) 201211 rm59 **B**

M Sierra Nevada ctra Madrid 74 ☎ (958) 200061 rm23 (Mar 15-Oct 15) **A**

H Sudán av de J-Antonio 60 ☎ (958) 258400 rm67 **A**

◆ Suecia calle Molinos Huerta, los Angeles ☎ (958) 225044 rm13 (Apr-Oct) **A**

◆ Verona Recogidos 9 ☎ (958) 255507 rm11 **A**

H Victoria Puerto Real 3 ☎ (958) 257700 rm69 **B**

◆ Vistillas ☎ (958) 228172 rm8 (Mar 15-Oct) **A**

H Washington Irving ps del Generalife 2 ☎ (958) 227550 rm68 **B**

GRANOLLERS *Barcelona*

H Europe A-Clavé 1 ☎ (93) 8700312 rm44 **A**

GUARDAMAR DEL SEGURA *Alicante*

H Dunas Playa de Guradamar ☎ (96) 5728110 rm39 (Mar-Sep) **A**

H Europa J-Benavente 1 ☎ (96) 5729055 rm14 **A**

H Meridional Dunas de Guardamar ☎ (96) 5728340 rm37 (Mar 15-Oct) **A**

HARO *Rioja*

◆ Iturrimurri ctra 232 ☎ (941) 311213 rm24 **A**

HOSPITALET DE L'INFANT, L' *Tarragona*

◆ Del Infante ctra del Mar 24 ☎ (977) 823000 rm71 **A**

HUELVA *Huelva*

H Costa de la Luz J-M-Amo 8 ☎ (955) 256422 rm35 **A**

H Santa Ursula ☎ (955) 255242 rm26 **A**

★★★**Tartessos** av M-Alonso Pinzón 13-15 ☎ (955) 245611 rm112 **A**

HUESCA *Huesca*

H Montearagón ctra Tarragona-San Sebastian, Km 208 ☎ (974) 222350 rm27 **A**

◆ **Sancho Abarca** pl de Lizana 15 ☎ (974) 220650 rm50 **A**

IBIZA See **BALEARES, ISLAS DE**

IGUALADA *Barcelona*

★★★**America** ctra Madrid-Francia ☎ (93) 8031000 rm52 **B**

◆ **Canaletas** ctra Madrid-Francia Km 567 ☎ (93) 8032750 rm56 **A**

IRÚN *Guipúzcoa*

★★★**Alcazar** av Iparralde 11 ☎ (943) 620900 rm48 **A**

◆ **Machinventa** ps de Colón 21 ☎ (943) 621384 rm6 **A**

JACA *Huesca*

★★**Conde de Aznar** ps Gl-Franco 3 ☎ (974) 361050 rm23 **A**

H Mur Santa Orosia 1 ☎ (974) 360100 rm68 **A**

H Oroel av Francia 37 ☎ (974) 362411 rm124 **A**

H Paz Mayor 41 ☎ (974) 360700 rm34 **A**

H Pradas Obispo 12 ☎ (974) 361150 rm39 **A**

JAÉN *Jaén*

H Condestable Iranzo ps de la Estación 32 ☎ (953) 222800 rm147 **B**

H Europa pl de Belén 1 ☎ (953) 222700 rm36 **A**

◆ **Reyes Catolicos** av de Granada 1 ☎ (953) 222250 rm28 **A**

H Rey Fernando pl de Coco de la Piñera 7 ☎ (953) 251840 rm36 **A**

◆ **Xauen** pl de D-Mazas 3 ☎ (953) 264011 rm35 **A**

JATIVA *Valencia*

H Murto Del Nuevo de Alineamiento 13 ☎ (96) 2883240 rm21 **A**

◆ **Vernisa** Académico Maravall 1 ☎ (96) 2271011 rm39 **A**

JÁVEA *Alicante*

H Toscamar ctra Cabo la Nao ☎ (96) 5770261 rm140 **A**

H Villa Naranjos ctra Montañar ☎ (96) 5790050 rm145 (Apr-Oct) **A**

JEREZ DE LA FRONTERA *Cádiz*

◆ **Avila** Avila 3 ☎ (956) 334808 rm30 **A**

H Joma Higueras 22 ☎ (956) 349689 rm29 **A**

◆ **Mica** Higueras 7 ☎ (956) 340700 rm38 **B**

H Nova Alvar Nuñez 13 ☎ (956) 341459 rm17 **A**

◆ **Virt** Higueras 20 ☎ (956) 322811 rm20 **A**

JONQUERA, LA *Girona*

H Goya ctra Nacional 11 Km 776 ☎ (972) 540077 rm36 **A**

H Junquera ctra Nacional Km 782 ☎ (972) 540100 rm28 (Apr-Sep) **A**

★★★**Puerta de España** ctra Nacional II Km 22 ☎ (972) 540120 rm26 **A**

LALÍN *Pontevedra*

H Palacio Matemático Rodriguez 10 ☎ (986) 780000 rm32 **A**

LAREDO *Cantabria*

H Cortijo G-Gallego 3 ☎ (942) 605600 rm21 (Jun-Sep 15) **A**

H Montecristo Calvo Sotelo 2 ☎ (942) 605700 rm23 (Apr 15-Sep 15) **A**

◆ **Ramona** Gl-Mola 4 ☎ (942) 605336 rm15 **A**

H Risco La Arenosa 2 ☎ (942) 605030 rm25 **B**

◆ **Rosi** Margués de Valdecilla 3 ☎ (942) 605098 rm24 **A**

LASARTE *Guipúzcoa*

◆ **Ibiltze** arrate 2 Pol Sasoeta ☎ (943) 365644 rm20 **A**

H Txartel ctra General ☎ (943) 362340 rm51 **A**

LEDESMA *Salamanca*

H Balneario de Ledesma Balneario ☎ (923) 570250 rm214 (May-Oct 15) **A**

LÉON *Léon*

H París Generalísimo 20 ☎ (987) 238600 rm77 **A**

★★**Quindos** av J-Antonio 24 ☎ (987) 236200 rm96 **A**

★★★**Riosol** av de Palencia 3 ☎ (987) 223650 rm141 **A**

LEQUEITIO *Vizcaya*

H Beitia P-Abarca 25 ☎ (94) 6840111 rm30 (Apr-Sep) **A**

H Piñupe av P-Abarca 10 ☎ (94) 6842984 rm12 **A**

LES *Lleida*

◆ **Talabart** Baños 1 ☎ (973) 648011 rm24 **A**

LLANÇÀ *Girona*

◆ **Goleta** Pintor Tarruella 12 ☎ (972) 380125 rm45 **A**

H Grifeu Cau del Llod ☎ (972) 380050 rm33 (May-Sep) **A**

H Grimar ctra de Port Bou ☎ (972) 380167 rm38 **A**

At **PUERTO DE LLANÇÀ**(1.5km NE)

★★**Berna** ps Maritimo 13 ☎ (972) 380150 rm38 (May 15-Sep 15) **A**

LLANES *Asturias*

H Don Paco Parque de Posada Herrera ☎ (985) 400150 rm42 (Jun-Sep) **B**

◆ **Europa** San Roque del Acebal ☎ (985) 400945 rm24 **A**

H Montemar J-Riestra ☎ (985) 400100 rm41 **B**

★★**Penablanca** Pidal 1 ☎ (985) 400166 rm31 (Jun 15-Sep 15) **A**

LLEIDA (LÉRIDA) *Lleida*

H Ilerda ☎ (973) 200750 rm106 **A**

H Jamaica ctra Nal Madrid-Francia Km 465 ☎ (973) 265100 rm24 Closed May **A**

H Principal pl Paheria 8 ☎ (973) 240900 rm53 **A**

H Sansi Park Alcalde Porqueres 4 ☎ (973) 244000 rm94 **A**

LLORET DE MAR *Girona*

H Acacias av de las Acacias 19 ☎ (972) 364150 rm43 (May-Oct) **A**

H Alexis La Marina 59 ☎ (972) 364604 rm101 (Apr-Oct) **A**

★★★**Anabel** F-Serra 10 ☎ (972) 364108 rm230 (Mar-Oct) **A**

H Bertrán Park San José 39 ☎ (972) 365901 rm140 (Apr-Oct) **A**

H Carolina cmno de las Cabras 49 ☎ (972) 365058 rm65 (Apr-Oct) **A**

H Copacabana av Mistral 40-48 ☎ (972) 365112 rm162 **A**

H Don Quijote av de América ☎ (972) 365860 rm374 (Apr-Oct) **A**

H Eugenia ctra de Tossa ☎ (972) 364400 rm118 (May-Oct) **A**

★★Fanals ctra de Blanes ☎ (972) 364112 rm80 (Apr-Oct 15) **B**

H Florida Park ☎ (972) 365000 rm99 (May-Sep) **A**

H Garbi-Park Carrer Llauer 1 ☎ (972) 365482 rm255 (Apr-Oct) **A**

H Imperial Park ctra de Blanes 78 ☎ (972) 365512 rm150 (May-Oct) **A**

H Mercedes av Mistral 32 ☎ (972) 364312 rm88 (May-Oct) **A**

H Olimpic-Lloret cami de L'Angel 50 ☎ (972) 365824 rm352 (Apr-Oct) **A**

H Rosamar av P-Casals 8-10 ☎ (972) 364422 rm169 (Apr-Oct) **B**

H Tropic ps Maritimo ☎ (972) 365154 rm40 (May-Oct) **A**

H Xaine Park av F-Agulló 15 ☎ (972) 364250 rm183 (May-Oct) **A**

LOGROÑO *Rioja*

H Gran Gl-Vara de Rey 5 ☎ (941) 252100 rm69 (Jun-Dec) **A**

H Isasa Dr-Castroviejo 13 ☎ (941) 256599 rm30 **A**

H Murrieta Marqués de Murrieta 1 ☎ (941) 224150 rm113 **A**

◆ **Paris** av de la Rioja 8 ☎ (941) 228750 rm36 **A**

LORCA *Murcia*

H Alameda Musso Valiente 8 ☎ (968) 467500 rm43 **A**

H Hoya ctra Nal 340 rm36 **A**

LUARCA *Asturias*

◆ **Casa Consuelo** ctra Nal 634 ☎ (985) 640844 rm26 **B**

★Gayoso ps de Gomez 4 ☎ (985) 640054 rm26 **A**

◆ **Oria** Crucero 7 ☎ (985) 640385 rm14 **A**

LUGO *Lugo*

◆ **Portón do Recanto** ctra Vegaedo ☎ (982) 223455 rm23 **A**

MADRID *Madrid*

This exciting modern capital combines Castilian traditions with a marvellous live-for-today atmosphere, her numerous *tapas* bars seemingly never shut and the art in the Prado including many of the world's great masterpieces. Shopping on and near the Gran Via, particularly for leather goods can produce some real bargains, whilst the most elegant shopping areas are Calle de Serrano and Calle Goya.

Madrid occupies a central position on the Iberian peninsula, and is the highest capital city in Europe at about 2, 170ft; because of its height and exposed position the climate shows great extremes, although sunshine is abundant throughout the year.

Originally growing up on the north bank of the Manzanares river, there are still vestiges of old Madrid in the south-west and around the Plaza Mayor, while the newer areas of the centre and north have wider boulevards, constructed in 1868 on the site of the old city wall. The centre has moved from the Plaza Mayor to the Puerto del Sol.

Buildings of note include the former royal palace with its gardens and famous armoury, the Palace of Justice, parliamentary buildings, national library, opera house, the 18th-century church of San Francisco el Grande and the unfinished cathedral of Nuestra Señora de la Almudena, begun in 1881.

EATING OUT Spanish cooking is hearty and wholesome, with specialities including *Cocido Madrileno*, a tasty hot pot; *sopa Castellana*, a baked garlic soup served with a poached egg; and stewed tripe, known as *Callos a la Madrilena*. Restaurants are officially graded from one to five and meal times are generally much later than in other European countries. Most of the popular establishments are to be found in the old centre of the city, while *tapas* can be found in most cafés and bars.

La Quinta del Sordo, in Sacramento, is noted for its inexpensive cuisine, especially baked chicken and roasts.

H Alexandra San Bernardo 29-31 ☎ (91) 2420400 rm69 **A**

H Anaco Tres Cruces 3 ☎ (91) 2224604 rm37 **B**

H Aramo Po Sta M-Cabeza 73 ☎ (91) 4739111 rm105 **B**

H Claridge pl del conde de Casal 6 ☎ (91) 2519400 rm150 **B**

H Cortezo Dr-Cortezo 3 ☎ (91) 2393800 rm90 **B**

◆ **Medieval** Fuencarral 46 ☎ (91) 2222549 rm7 **A**

◆ **Mendoza** Chinchilla 4 ☎ (91) 5526705 rm12 **A**

★★Mercator ctra de Atocha 123 ☎ (91) 4290500 rm90 **B**

H Mexico Gobernador 24 ☎ (91) 4292500 rm30 **A**

H Nuria Fuencarral 52 ☎ (91) 2319208 rm57 **A**

H Santander Echegaray 1 ☎ (91) 4296644 rm39 **A**

H Trafalgar Trafalgar 35 ☎ (91) 4456200 rm45 **B**

◆ **Triana** Salud 13 ☎ (91) 2326812 rm29 **A**

H Victoria pl del Angel 7 ☎ (91) 2314500 rm110 **B**

MAGALUF See **BALEARES, ISLAS DE** under **MALLORCA (MAJORCA)**

MÁLAGA *Málaga*

H Astoria av del Cdt-Benitez 3 ☎ (952) 224500 rm61 **A**

H Bahía Malága Somera 8 ☎ (952) 224305 rm44 **A**

◆ **Capri** av Pries 8 ☎ (952) 223003 rm10 **A**

◆ **Del Sur** Trinidad Grund 13 ☎ (952) 224803 rm37 **A**

H Don Curro Sancha de Lara 7 ☎ (952) 227200 rm105 **B**

H Lis Córdoba 7 ☎ (952) 227300 rm53 **A**

H Olletas Cuba 1 & 3 ☎ (952) 252000 rm66 **A**

◆ **Venecia** Alameda Pral 9 ☎ (952) 213636 rm40 **A**

MALGRAT DE MAR *Barcelona*

H Sorra D Or Po de Levante 2 ☎ (93) 7610312 rm195 (May-Oct) **A**

H Sorra Daurada ps Marítimo ☎ (93) 7610500 rm252 (May-Oct) **A**

MALLORCA (MAJORCA) See **BALEARES, ISLAS DE**

MANGA MAR MENOR, LA *Murcia*

H Cavanna Gran Via la Manga ☎ (968) 563600 rm407 (Mar 26-Oct) **A**

H Doble Mar Casino Gran Via de la Manga ☎ (968) 563910 rm485 (Apr-Oct) **B**

H Dos Mares pl Bohemia ☎ (968) 563093 rm28 **A**

H Entremares Gran Via de la Manga ☎ (968) 563100 rm245 (May-Oct) **A**

MANRESA *Barcelona*

H Pedro 111 Muralla Sant Francisco 49 ☎ (93) 8724000 rm113 **A**

MANZANARES *Ciudad Real*

★★**Cruce** ☎ (926) 611900 rm37 **A**

MARANGES *Girona*

H Can Borrell Regreso 3 ☎ (972) 880033 rm8 **A**

MARBELLA *Málaga*

H Bellamar ☎ (952) 772300 rm66 **A**

H Club Pinomar ctra Cádiz-Málaga ☎ (952) 831345 rm431 (May-Oct) **A**

H Lima av A-Belón 2 ☎ (952) 770500 rm64 **B**

H Pinomar 11 ctra Cádiz-Málaga Km 196 ☎ (952) 831306 rm101 (May-Oct) **A**

H Rodeo V-de la Serna 2 ☎ (952) 775100 rm100 **B**

H San Cristobal Ramón y Cajal ☎ (952) 771250 rm102 **A**

MARTINET *Lleida*

◆ **Cadi** Segre 50 ☎ (973) 515025 rm20 **A**

MARTORELL *Barcelona*

◆ **Manel** Pedro Puig 74 ☎ (93) 7752387 rm14 **A**

MEDINACELI *Soria*

★★**Nico 70** ctra Nacional 11 Km 151 ☎ (975) 326011 rm22 **A**

MEDINA DEL CAMPO *Valladolid*

◆ **Europa** Padilla 40 ☎ (983) 800200 rm33 **A**

MEDINA DE RIOSECO *Valladolid*

H Almirantes San Francisco 2 ☎ 700125 rm30 **A**

MÉRIDA *Badajoz*

★★★**Emperatriz** pl de España 19 ☎ (924) 313111 rm41 **A**

M Lomas ctra Madrid-Lisboa Km 338 ☎ (924) 311011 rm134 **B**

H Nova Roma Suárez Somonte 42 ☎ (924) 311201 rm28 **A**

★★**Zeus** ctra Madrid Km 341 ☎ (924) 318111 rm44 **A**

MIRANDA DE EBRO *Burgos*

H Tudanca ctra Madrid-Irún 45 ☎ (947) 311843 rm120 **A**

MOJÁCAR *Almeria*

◆ **Continental** Playa el Palmeral ☎ (951) 478225 rm23 **B**

◆ **Flamenco** Playa Mojácar ☎ (951) 478227 rm25 **A**

◆ **Provenzal** Playa del Descargador ☎ (951) 478308 rm26 **A**

MONDRAGON *Guipúzcoa*

◆ **Txirrita** Barrio Guesalibar ☎ (943) 795211 rm16 **A**

MOTA DEL CUERVO *Cuença*

H Mesón de Don Quijote F-Costi 2 ☎ (967) 180200 rm36 **B**

MURCIA *Murcia*

◆ **Churra** Obispo-Davila 2 ☎ (968) 238400 rm95 **A**

H Conde de Floridablanca Corbalán 7 ☎ (968) 214626 rm60 **B**

H Fontoria Madre de Dios 4 ☎ (968) 217789 rm120 **B**

H Majesti San Pedro 5 ☎ (968) rm68 **A**

◆ **Murcia** Vinadel 6 ☎ (968) 219963 rm17 **A**

MURIEDAS *Cantabria*

◆ **Parayas** J-Antonio 6 ☎ (942) 251300 rm22 **A**

H Romano II Santander 4 ☎ (942) 254850 rm18 **A**

NÁJERA *Rioja*

H San Fernando ps A-Martin Gamero 1 ☎ (941) 360700 rm40 **A**

NAVA *Asturias*

H Pangon ☎ (985) 704137 rm19 **B**

NAVACERRADA *Madrid*

H Arcipreste de Hita Praderas de San Sebastian ☎ (91) 8560125 rm39 **A**

◆ **Doña Endrina** av de Madrid ☎ (91) 8560200 rm40 **A**

◆ **Postas** ctra Nacional 601 Km 50 ☎ (91) 8560250 rm20 **A**

NAVALCARNERO *Madrid*

H Vegas ctra de Extremadura Km 25 ☎ (91) 8110400 rm26 **A**

NAVALMORAL DE LA MATA *Cáceres*

H Brasilia ctra Nacional V Km 180 ☎ (927) 530750 rm43 **A**

NERJA *Málaga*

H Balcón de Europe ps Balcón de Europe 1 ☎ (952) 520800 rm105 **B**

◆ **Nerja Club** ctra Almeria ☎ (952) 520100 rm47 **B**

H Portofino Puerta del Mar 2 ☎ (952) 520150 rm12 (Mar-Oct) **A**

◆ **Villa Flamenca** Nueva Nerja ☎ (952) 521869 rm88 **A**

NOJA *Cantabria*

H Arillo Playa de Tregandín ☎ (942) 630080 rm40 **A**

H Hoya Playa de Ris ☎ (942) 630082 rm33 Jun 15-Sep 15 **A**

OLMEDO *Valladolid*

H Piedras Blancas ctra Madrid Km 148 ☎ (983) 600100 rm24 **A**

ORENSE (OURENSE) *Orense*

★★**Barcelona** av de Pontevedra 13 ☎ (988) 220800 rm40 **A**

H Padre Feijoo E-Montes 1 ☎ (988) 223100 rm71 **A**

H Parque Parque de San Lázaro 24 ☎ (988) 233611 rm57 **A**

H San Martin Curros Enriquez 1 ☎ (988) 235611 rm60 **B**

H Sila av de la Habana 61 ☎ (988) 236311 rm64 **A**

ORIHUELA *Alicante*

H Montepiedra Dehesa de Compoamor ☎ (96) 5320300 rm64 **B**

OROPESA *Castellón*

H Ancla Morro Gos 8 ☎ (964) 310238 rm26 (Apr-Sep) **A**

◆ **Central** Alcázar de Toledo 37 ☎ (964) 310104 rm10 (Jun 15-Sep 15) **A**

H Oropesa Sol Auda Madrid 11 ☎ (964) 310150 rm50 (Apr-Sep) **A**

◆ **Palmavera** av Palmavera 20 ☎ (964) 310867 rm10 **A**

H Playa Playa Morro del Gos ☎ (964) 310235 rm40 (Apr-Sep) **A**

H Zapata ctra del Faro 92 ☎ (964) 310425 rm65 (May-Sep) **A**

OVIEDO *Asturias*

H Barbón Covadonga 7 ☎ (985) 225293 rm40 **B**

◆ **Oviedo** Uria 43 rm8 **A**

★★**Principado** San Francisco 6 ☎ (985) 217792 rm66 **B**

H Ramos Corta Puebla 6 ☎ (985) 224000 rm40 **A**

PAGUERA See **BALEARES, ISLAS DE** under **MALLORCA (MAJORCA)**

PALAFRUGELL *Girona*

H Costa Brava San Sebastian 10 ☏ (972) 300558 rm30 **A**

◆ **San Sebastian** Santuario San Sebastian ☏ (972) 300586 rm15 (May-Sep) **A**

PALAMÓS *Girona*

H Ancora Josep pl La Fosca ☏ (972) 315486 rm34 **A**

★★**Marina** av 11 de Septiembre 48 ☏ (972) 314250 rm62 **A**

★★**San Juan** av de la Victoria ☏ (972) 314208 rm31 (Jun-Sep) **A**

H San Luis Once de Septiembre 61 ☏ (972) 314050 rm29 (Jun-Sep) **B**

H Sosiego Rutlla Alta 18 ☏ (972) 317506 rm40 (Apr-Sep) **A**

H Vostra Llar Alba 6 ☏ (972) 314300 rm45 (May 15-Sep) **A**

◆ **Xamary** av P-Macia 70 ☏ (972) 314270 rm36 (Apr-Oct) **A**

PALENCIA *Palencia*

H Colón-27 Colón 27 ☏ (988) 740700 rm22 **A**

H Los Jardinillos E-Dato 2 ☏ (988) 750022 rm39 **A**

H Monclus Menéndez Pelayo 3 ☏ (988) 744300 rm40 **A**

PALMA DE MALLORCA See **BALEARES, ISLAS DE** under **MALLORCA (MAJORCA)**

PAMPLONA *Navarra*

◆ **Ibarra** Estafeta 85 ☏ (948) 220606 rm12 **A**

◆ **Velate** Trav de Velate 2 ☏ (948) 253054 rm10 **B**

PANCORBO *Burgos*

★★★**El Molino** ctra Madrid-Irún Km 306 ☏ (947) 354050 rm48 **A**

PANES *Asturias*

◆ **Covadonga** H-Covadonga Panes Asturias ☏ (985) 414162 rm10 **A**

H Trepalacios Mayor sn ☏ (985) 414032 rm28 **A**

PEÑISCOLA *Castellón*

◆ **Benedicto X111** Las Atalayas ☏ (964) 480801 rm30 **B**

H Cartago ctra Benicarló-Peñiscola Km 2 ☏ (964) 473311 rm26 (Jun-Sep) **A**

H Ciudad de Gaya ctra Benicarló Km 7 ☏ (964) 480024 rm29 (Jun 15-Sep & Jan-Jun 6) **A**

H Felipe 11 ☏ (964) 480200 rm38 **A**

H Porto-Cristo ☏ (964) 480718 rm26 **A**

H Tio Pepe J-Antonio 32 ☏ (964) 480640 rm10 **A**

PINEDA DE MAR *Barcelona*

◆ **Marina** Once de Septiembre 2 ☏ (93) 7690758 rm66 (Jun-Sep) **A**

H Taurus Park ps Maritimo 33 ☏ (93) 7624811 rm440 (May-Oct) **A**

◆ **Tres Banderas** 11 de Septiembre 26 ☏ (93) 7690895 rm45 (Jun-Sep) **A**

H Victoria Playa ps Maritimo ☏ (93) 7623293 rm45 (May-Oct 15) **A**

PLATJA D'ARO, LA *Girona*

H Bellamar av de Madrid 5 ☏ (972) 817550 rm23 (Apr-Sep) **A**

H Claramar Pinar del Mar 10 ☏ (972) 817158 rm36 (Mar 27-Sep) **B**

H Costa Brava Punta d'En Ramis ☏ (972) 817308 rm59 **B**

★★**Japet** ctra de Palamós 18-20 ☏ (972) 817366 rm48 **A**

◆ **Laura** Riera ☏ (972) 817295 rm14 (May-Sep) **A**

H Planamar ☏ (972) 817092 rm85 (Mar 27-Oct) **B**

PLAYA DE PALMA (C'AN PASTILLA) See **BALEARES, ISLAS DE** under **PALMA DE MALLORCA**

PLAYA DE PALMA NOVA See **BALEARES, ISLAS DE** under **PALMA DE MALLORCA**

POLLENSA See **BALEARES, ISLAS DE** under **MALLORCA (MAJORCA)**

PONFERRADA *León*

H Conde Silva av de Astorga 2 ☏ (987) 410407 rm60 **A**

★★**Madrid** av de la Puebla 44 ☏ (987) 411550 rm54 **A**

PONS *Lleida*

H Pedra Negra ctra Lleida Puigcerdá ☏ (973) 460019 rm19 **A**

PONT DE MOLINS *Girona*

H Masía ctra Nal 11 ☏ (972) 503340 rm16 **A**

PONTEVEDRA *Pontevedra*

H Comercio A-González Besada 3 ☏ (986) 851217 rm26 **A**

H México A-Murvais 10 ☏ (986) 859006 rm28 **A**

H Rias Bajas Daniel de la Sota 7 ☏ (986) 855100 rm100 **B**

PORRIÑO *Pontevedra*

H Parque S-Ramilo 6 ☏ (986) 331604 rm32 **B**

PORT-BOU *Girona*

H Comodoro M-Núñez 1 ☏ (972) 390187 rm16 (May-Sep) **A**

PORTO CRISTO See **BALEARES, ISLAS DE** under **MALLORCA (MAJORCA)**

POTES *Cantabria*

H Cabaña La Molina ☏ (942) 730315 rm24 (Jun-Sep) **A**

H Picos de Veldecoro Roscabado ☏ (942) 730025 rm24 **A**

PUERTO DE LLANÇÀ See **LLANÇÀ**

PUERTO DE MAZARRON *Murcia*

H Bahia Playa de la Reya ☏ (968) 594000 rm54 **B**

H Durán Playa de la Isla ☏ (968) 594050 rm29 **A**

PUERTO DE NAVACERRADA *Madrid*

H Corzo ☏ (91) 8520900 rm9 **A**

◆ **Venta Arias** ☏ (91) 8521100 rm15 **A**

PUERTO DE POLLENSA See **BALEARES, ISLAS DE** under **POLLENSA**

PUERTO DE SANTA MARIÁ, EL *Cádiz*

H Cántaros Curva 6 ☏ (956) 864242 rm39 **B**

H Puertobahia av la Paz ☏ (956) 862721 rm330 **B**

PUERTOLLANO *Cuidad Real*

◆ **Cabañas** ctra C.Real-P, Lano 3 ☏ (926) 420650 rm63 **A**

H León A-Prieto 4 ☏ (926) 427300 rm84 **A**

PUIGCERDÁ *Girona*

H Chalet del Golf Devesa del Golf ☏ (972) 880963 rm16 **B**

H Del Prado ctra de Livia ☏ (972) 880400 rm45 **A**

H Lago av del Dr-Piguillen ☏ (972) 881000 rm16 **A**

★★**Maria-Victoria** Florenza 9 ☎ (972) 880300 rm50 **A**

★★**Martinez** ctra de Llivia ☎ (972) 880250 rm15 **A**

H Puigcerdá Park ctra Barcelona ☎ (972) 880750 rm54 **B**

PUNTA UMBRIA *Huelva*

H Ayamontino-Ría pl P-Pastor 25 ☎ (955) 311458 rm20 **A**

H Emilio c Ancha 23 ☎ (955) 311900 rm35 **A**

◆ **Oliver** pl del Cantábrico 4 ☎ (955) 311535 rm8 **A**

H Pato Rojo av Oceano ☎ (955) 311160 rm60 (Jun-Sep) **A**

QUINTANA DEL PUENTE *Palencia*

M Suco ctra Burgos-Portugal Km 54 ☎ (988) 793106 rm10 **A**

REINOSA *Cantabria*

◆ **Vejo** av Cantabria 15 ☎ (942) 751700 rm71 **A**

REQUENA *Valencia*

◆ **Sol 11** ctra Madrid ☎ (96) 2500058 rm13 **A**

REUS *Tarragona*

H Francia Vicaria 8 ☎ (977) 304240 rm39 **A**

★★**Gaudi** A-Robuster 49 ☎ (977) 305545 rm71 **A**

RIAZA *Segovia*

H Trucha av Dr-Tapia ☎ (911) 550061 rm30 **A**

RIBADEO *Lugo*

★★**Eo** av de Asturias 5 ☎ (982) 110750 rm20 (Apr-Sep) **A**

◆ **Ros Mary** San Francisco 3 ☎ (982) 11678 rm23 **A**

RIBADESELLA *Asturias*

◆ **Boston** El Pico 7 rm8 **A**

H Covadonga M-Caseo de la Villa 7 ☎ (985) 860222 rm10 **A**

H Marina Generalisimo 36 ☎ (985) 860050 rm44 **A**

H Playa La Playa 42 ☎ (985) 860100 rm12 (Apr-Sep) **A**

◆ **Rivera** ☎ (985) 860626 rm14 **A**

◆ **Sueve** L-Muñiz ☎ (985) 860369 rm11 **A**

RIBES DE FRESER *Girona*

H Cataluña Park ps S-Mauri 9 ☎ (972) 727198 rm27 (Jul-Sep) **A**

★★**Prats** San Quintin 30 ☎ (972) 727001 rm25 **A**

H San Antonio San Quintin 26 ☎ (972) 727018 rm27 **A**

RIPOLL *Girona*

H Monasterio Placa Gran 4 ☎ (972) 700150 rm40 **A**

RODA, LA *Albacete*

H Juanito Mártires 11 ☎ (967) 440400 rm38 **A**

RONDA *Málaga*

H El Tajo Dr-Cajal 7 ☎ (952) 876236 rm70 **A**

H Polo M-Soubiron 8 ☎ (952) 872447 rm33 **B**

ROQUETAS DE MAR *Almeria*

H Alis av Mediterráneo ☎ (951) 320375 rm254 (Apr-Oct) **A**

H Sabinal ☎ (951) 320600 rm416 Closed Nov 21 & Dec **A**

H Zoraida Park Pez Espada, sn ☎ (951) 320750 rm495 (Apr-Oct) **A**

ROSES *Girona*

H Bahía Po Maritimo 153 ☎ (972) 256354 rm52 (Mar-Oct) **B**

◆ **Cala** Sant Sebastia 61 ☎ (972) 256171 rm22 **A**

H Canyelles Platja ☎ (972) 256500 rm99 (Apr-Sep) **B**

H Goya Park ☎ (972) 257550 rm224 (May-Sep) **B**

H Grecs Parase Grecs ☎ (972) 256162 rm54 (Jun 25-Aug) **B**

H Marian Playa Salata ☎ (972) 256108 rm145 (May-Oct) **B**

H Montecarlo ☎ (972) 256673 rm126 (Apr-Oct) **B**

H Monterrey ☎ (972) 256676 rm138 (Mar-Oct) **B**

H Nautilus Playa Salata ☎ (972) 256262 rm64 (May-Oct) **A**

H Victoria av Commercial ☎ (972) 256201 rm221 (May-Sep) **B**

ROTA *Cádiz*

H Caribe av de la Marina 62 ☎ (956) 810700 rm60 **B**

RÚA, LA *Orense*

H Espada ctra Orense-Ponferrada ☎ (988) 310075 rm35 **A**

SABIÑÁNIGO *Huesca*

◆ **Mi Casa** av del Ejército 32 ☎ (974) 480400 rm72 **A**

★★**Pardina** Str Orosia 36 ☎ (974) 480975 rm64 **B**

SALAMANCA *Salamanca*

H Alfonso X Toro 64 ☎ (923) 214401 rm66 **B**

H Castellano 11 P-Mendoza 36 ☎ (923) 242812 rm29 **A**

H Castellano 111 San Francisco Javier 2-4 ☎ (923) 251611 rm73 **B**

H Ceylán San Teodoro 7 ☎ (923) 212603 rm32 **A**

H Clavero Consuleo 21 ☎ (923) 218108 rm26 **A**

H Condal Santa Eulalia 3-5 ☎ (923) 218400 rm70 **A**

H Gran Via La Rosa 4 ☎ (923) 215401 rm47 **A**

◆ **Los Infantes** Po de la Estación 125 ☎ (923) 252844 rm14 **A**

H Milán pl del Angel 5 ☎ (923) 217779 rm25 **A**

H Pasaje Espoz y Mina 23-25 ☎ (923) 212003 rm62 **A**

H Regio ☎ (923) 200250 rm118 **B**

◆ **Zaguan** Ruiz Aguilera 7-9 ☎ (923) 214705 rm15 **A**

SALLENT DE GALLEGO *Huesca*

H Nievesol Estación de Formigal ☎ (974) 488034 rm162 (Dec-Apr & Jul-Aug) **B**

H Tirol Formigal ☎ (974) 488086 rm10 (Jan-Apr & Jul-Aug) **A**

SALOU *Tarragona*

H Cala Font Cala de la Font ☎ (977) 370454 rm318 (May-Oct) **A**

★★★**Calaviña** ctra Tarragona-Salou Km 10 ☎ (977) 380848 rm70 (May-Oct) **A**

H Calypso pompeu Fabra 52 ☎ (977) 384900 rm252 (May-Oct) **A**

H Carabela Roc P-Casals 108 ☎ (977) 370166 rm98 (Mar 15-Oct) **A**

H Delfin Park Mayor ☎ (977) 380308 rm244 (May-Sep 15) **A**

H Europa Park pl de Europa ☎ (977) 381400 rm325 (Apr-Oct) **A**

H Los Angeles ☎ (977) 381466 rm178 (Mar-Oct) **A**

H Molinos Park ctra El Faro ☎ (977) 371654 rm254 (May-Oct) **A**

H San Francisco ☎ (977) 380666 rm225 (Mar-Oct) **A**

H Sol d'Or Playa del Reco ☎ (977) 371100 rm84 (Apr-Oct) **A**

H Venecia Park Vendrell 13-17 ☏ (977) 381366 rm260 (Apr 15-Oct 15) **A**

SAN ANTONIO See **BALEARES, ISLAS DE** under **IBIZA**

SAN FERNANDO *Cádiz*

H Sal y Mar pl del Ejército 32 ☏ (956) 883440 rm45 **A**

SAN JUÁN DE ALICANTE *Alicante*

M Abril ctra Murcia-Valencia Km 90 ☏ (96) 5653408 rm48 **B**

SANLÚCAR DE BARRAMEDA *Cádiz*

H Guadalquivir Calzada del Ejército ☏ (956) 360742 rm85 **B**

SAN PEDRO DE ALCÁNTARA *Málaga*

H Pueblo Andaluz ctra Cádiz-Málaga Km 172 ☏ (952) 780597 rm179 (Jan-Oct) **A**

SAN SEBASTIAN (DONOSTIA) *Guipúzcoa*

◆ **Alameda** Alameda del Bulevard 23 ☏ (943) 421687 rm30 (Mar 15-Oct 15) **A**

H Avenida Subida a Igueldo ☏ (943) 212022 rm47 (Apr-Oct) **B**

◆ **Bahia** San Martin 54 bis 1 & 2 ☏ (943) 461083 rm57 **A**

◆ **Buena Vista** Barrio de Igueldo ☏ (943) 210600 rm12 **A**

H Codina av Zumalacárregui 21 ☏ (943) 212200 rm77 **B**

◆ **Eder** San Bartolomé 33 ☏ (943) 464696 rm8 **A**

H Estrella pl de Sarriegui 1 ☏ (943) 420997 rm27 **A**

◆ **José Mari** San Bartolomé 3 ☏ (943) 464600 rm30 **A**

◆ **Leku-Eder** Barrio de Igueldo ☏ (943) 210107 rm11 (Jul-Sep) **A**

H Pellizar Bo de Intxaurrondo ☏ (943) 281211 rm33 **B**

◆ **Récord** av Navarra ☏ (943) 285768 rm22 **A**

◆ **Urumea** Guetaria 14 ☏ (943) 424605 rm6 **A**

SANTANDER *Cantabria*

H Alisas N-Salmerón 3 ☏ (942) 222750 rm70 **B**

◆ **Carlos 111** av Reina Victoria 135 ☏ (942) 271616 rm20 (Apr-Oct) **A**

◆ **Corza** H-Cortés 25 ☏ (942) 212950 rm9 **A**

◆ **Ibio** F-Vial 8 ☏ (942) 223071 rm25 **A**

H Maria Isabel av de Garcia Lago ☏ (942) 271850 rm63 **B**

H Mexico M-Nuñez 2 ☏ (942) 212450 rm35 **A**

H Roma av de los Hoteles 5 ☏ (942) 272700 rm52 **B**

SANTA POLA *Alicante*

H Pátilla c de Elche 29 ☏ (96) 5411015 rm72 **A**

H Pola-Mar Playa de Levante 6 ☏ (96) 541320 rm76 **B**

SANT CARLES DE LA RAPITA *Tarragona*

◆ **Casa Ramón** Arsenal 16 ☏ (997) 740361 rm16 **A**

◆ **Juanito** Playa Miami ☏ (997) 740462 rm35 (Apr-Sep) **A**

H Miami Park av Generalisimo 33 ☏ (997) 740351 rm80 **A**

SANT FELIU DE GUIXOLS *Girona*

H Avenida ctra Gerona 10 ☏ (972) 320800 rm28 (Jun 15-Sep 15) **A**

H Curhotel Hipócrates ctra San Pol 229 ☏ (972) 320662 rm87 (Mar 5-Dec) **B**

H Jecsalis ctra de Gerona 9 ☏ (972) 323250 rm64 (May-Oct) **A**

★★**Les Noies** Rambla Portalet 10 ☏ (972) 320400 rm45 (May-Oct 15) **A**

H Montecarlo Abad Sunyer 110 ☏ (972) 320000 rm64 (May-Oct) **A**

◆ **Montserrat** Rambla Portalet 3 ☏ (972) 320604 rm10 (Jul-Sep 15) **A**

H Panorama-Park Travesia del Raig ☏ (972) 320754 rm69 (May-Sep) **B**

H Regente Cruz 25 ☏ (972) 320806 rm36 (Jun-Sep) **A**

H Regina Maragall 1 ☏ (972) 320050 rm53 (Jun-Sep) **A**

◆ **Ronda Barcarola** Paraje San Pol ☏ (972) 321048 rm46 (Mar-Dec) **A**

SANTIAGO DE COMPOSTELA *la Coruña*

H Compostela Gl-Franco 1 ☏ (981) 585700 rm99 **B**

◆ **Garcas** Mourentans-Labacolla rm8 **A**

H Gelmirez Gl-Franco 92 ☏ (981) 561100 rm138 **A**

H Rey Fernando Fernando 111 el Santo 30 ☏ (981) 593550 rm24 **A**

H Santiago Apóstol La Grela 6 ☏ (981) 587138 rm91 **A**

H Universal pl Galicia 2 ☏ (981) 585800 rm54 **A**

◆ **Windsor** República de El Salvador 16 ☏ (981) 592939 rm50 **A**

SANTIAGO DE LA RIBERA *Murcia*

H Lido Conde Campillo 1 ☏ (968) 570700 rm32 **A**

SANTILLANA DEL MAR *Cantabria*

★★**Altamira** Cantón 1 ☏ (942) 818025 rm30 **A**

H Conde-Duque Campo de Revolgo rm14 (Apr-Oct) **A**

H Hidalgos Revlogo ☏ (942) 818101 rm18 (Apr-Oct) **A**

SANTOÑA *Cantabria*

◆ **Berria** Nueva Berria ☏ (942) 660847 rm29 (Jul-Aug) **A**

H Castilla Manzanedo 29 ☏ (942) 662261 rm33 **A**

SANT POL DE MAR *Barcelona*

◆ **Hostalet 111** Santa Clara ☏ (93) 7600251 rm26 (Apr-Oct 25) **A**

SAN VINCENTE DE LA BARQUERA *Cantabria*

H Boga-Boga pl J-Antonio 9 ☏ (942) 710135 rm18 **A**

◆ **Luzon** ctra Santander-Oviedo ☏ (942) 710050 rm30 **A**

SANXENXO *Pontevedra*

H Cervantes Progreso 29-31 ☏ (986) 720701 rm18 (Jun-Sep) **A**

H Lanzada Playa de la Lanzada ☏ (986) 743232 rm26 (Jun-Sep) **A**

H Mar av de Silgar ☏ (986) 720025 rm62 **A**

H Maricielo av del Generalisimo 26 ☏ (986) 720050 rm29 (Jun-Sep) **A**

H Minso Trav Do Porto 1 ☏ (986) 720150 rm21 (Jun-Sep) **A**

H Punta Vicaño av Generalisimo 112 ☏ (986) 720011 rm24 (Jun-Sep) **A**

◆ **Rías Bajas** Progreso 82 ☏ (986) 720247 rm20 (Jun-Sep) **A**

H Rotilio av del Puerto ☏ (986) 720200 rm32 **B**

H Silgar Progreso 78 ☏ (986) 720029 rm29 **A**

◆ **Siroco** av Pontevedra 12 ☏ (986) 720843 rm12 (Jun-Sep) **A**

H Terraza Progreso 67-69 ☏ (986) 720013 rm50 (Jun-Aug) **A**

SEGOVIA *Segovia*

H Acueducto Padre Claret 10 ☏ (911) 424800 rm78 **B**

★★★**Sirenas** J-Bravo 30 ☏ (911) 434011 rm39 **A**

SEU D'URGELL, LA *Lleida*

◆ **Nice** av Pau Claris 4-6 ☏ (973) 352100 rm51 **A**

SEVILLA (SEVILLE) *Sevilla*

Sevilla is the spiritual capital of Andalusia and its most famous city, with a wealth of interesting monuments to explore, and a unique ambience. The cathedral is the largest in Spain, and reputedly the largest Gothic building in the world. It houses the remains of St Ferdinand, Sevilla's liberator, and of Christopher Columbus.

Also worth discovering are Santa Cruz – the Jewish quarter – with its twisting alleys, antique shops and shoe stalls, the Maria Lisa Park – one of the prettiest in Spain, the Plaza de España, with its elaborate tile decorations, and the Fine Arts Museum.

EATING OUT The diner in Sevilla is faced with a huge choice of restaurants and regional cuisine, which includes *ajo blanco*, cold garlic soup with almonds and raisins; *fruituro mixta*, a selection of fried fish; and *huevos a la flamenca*, eggs baked with tomato, onion and ham and garnished with asparagus and spicy sausages.

Egana Oriza, in San Ferdando, offers Basque specialites such as white fish in clam sauce. Also recommended is *Meson Dom Raimundo*, near the cathedral.

◆ **Avienda** Marqués de Parada 28 ☏ (954) 220688 rm6 **A**

◆ **Bonanza** Sales y Ferre 12 ☏ (954) 228614 rm8 **A**

◆ **Cataluña** D-Guiomar 1 ☏ (954) 216840 rm8 **A**

◆ **Don Gonzalo** Jesús del Gran Poder 28 ☏ (954) 381409 rm12 **A**

H Ducal pl de la Encarnación 19 ☏ (954) 215107 rm51 **B**

◆ **Europa** Jimios 5 ☏ (954) 214305 rm11 **B**

◆ **Italica** ☏ (954) 515922 rm27 **B**

◆ **Madrid** San Pedro Mártir 22 ☏ (954) 214306 rm23 **A**

◆ **Manuela Montilla** Archeros 16 ☏ (954) 412325 rm6 **A**

H Montecarlo Gravina 51 ☏ (954) 217503 rm25 **B**

H Murillo Lope de Rueda 7 ☏ (954) 216095 rm61 **B**

H Niza Reyes Católicos 5 ☏ (954) 215401 rm56 **B**

H Rabida Castelar 24 ☏ (954) 220960 rm87 **B**

SILS *Girona*

◆ **Del Rolls** ctra N Km 706 ☏ (972) 853229 rm18 **A**

SITGES *Barcelona*

◆ **Acapulco** ctra Vilanova ☏ (93) 8942449 rm12 **A**

◆ **Alba** av Vinyet ☏ (93) 8943558 rm24 **A**

★★**Arcadia** c Socias 22-24 ☏ (93) 8940900 rm38 (May-Sep) **B**

◆ **Florida** Espalter 16 ☏ (93) 8940221 rm12 (Jun 15-Sep 15) **B**

H Galeon San Francisco 44-46 ☏ (93) 8940612 rm47 (May-Oct) **A**

◆ **Globas** Ntr.Sra de Montserrat ☏ (93) 8943692 rm22 (May-Sep) **B**

◆ **Helvética** ps Maritimo 21 ☏ (93) 8941279 rm11 (Apr-Oct) **B**

◆ **Isi** pl de la Ribera ☏ (93) 8941950 rm13 (Apr-Oct) **A**

◆ **Mayfi** Floreal 6 ☏ (93) 8940194 rm11 (May-Oct) **A**

◆ **Rivamar** ps de Ribera 46 ☏ (93) 8943408 rm14 (Apr-Oct) **A**

★**Romantic** San Isidro 33 ☏ (93) 8940643 rm55 (Apr 15-Oct 15) **A**

◆ **San Pedro** San Pedro 20 ☏ (93) 8940480 rm11 (Jul-Aug & Jun 15-30) **A**

◆ **Sonrisa** ps Villaneua s/n ☏ (93) 8943146 rm49 (Jun 20- Sep 10) **B**

◆ **Veracruz** av Sofia 12 ☏ (93) 8941214 rm26 (Feb-Nov) **A**

SORÍA *Soría*

H Alfonso VIII Alfonso VIII 10 ☏ (975) 226211 rm103 **A**

★★★**Caballero** E-Saavedra 4 ☏ (975) 220100 rm84 **A**

★★★**Meson Leonor** ps del Miron ☏ (975) 220250 rm32 **A**

SORT *Lleida*

H Pessets 11 ctra Seu d'Urgell ☏ (973) 620000 rm80 **A**

SUANCES *Cantabria*

H Castillo de Suances ☏ (942) 810383 rm14 **A**

★**Lumar** ctra de Tagle 3 ☏ (942) 810214 rm30 (Jul-Sep 15) **A**

◆ **Vivero** Palencia ☏ (942) 810071 rm22 (Apr-Sep) **A**

TALAVERA DE LA REINA *Toledo*

H Beatriz av Madrid 1 ☏ (925) 807600 rm161 **A**

H León ctra Extramadura Km 119 ☏ (925) 802900 rm30 **A**

H Perales av Pio X11 3 ☏ (925) 803900 rm65 **A**

H Talavera av G-Ruiz 1 ☏ (925) 800200 rm80 **A**

TARANCÓN *Cuença*

H Sur ctra Madrid-Valencia Km 82 ☏ (966) 110600 rm33 **A**

TARAZONA *Zaragoza*

H Brujas de Bécquer ctra de Zaragoza ☏ (976) 640404 rm60 **A**

TARIFA *Cádiz*

★★**Balcon de España** ctra Cádiz ☏ (956) 684326 rm40 **B**

◆ **Codorniz** ☏ (956) 684744 rm16 **A**

◆ **Hosteria Tarifa** Amador de los Rios 22 ☏ (956) 684076 rm14 (Apr-Oct) **A**

★★★**Meson de Sancho** ctra Cádiz-Málaga ☏ (956) 684900 rm45 **A**

◆ **Millon** Boquete de la Peña rm7 **A**

TARRAGONA *Tarragona*

★★★**Astari** via Augusta 95 ☏ (977) 236911 rm83 **A**

H España Rambla Nueva 49 ☏ (977) 232712 rm42 **A**

★★★**Lauria** Rambla Nova 20 ☏ (977) 236712 rm72 **A**

H Paris Maragall 4 ☏ (977) 236012 rm45 **A**

H Sant Jordi via Augusta ☏ (977) 237212 rm40 **A**

TERUEL *Teruel*

H Civera av Sagunto 37 ☎ (974) 602300 rm73 **A**

H Milagro ctra Sagunto-Burgos Km 123 ☎ (974) 603095 rm27 **A**

H Reina Cristina ps Generalisimo 1 ☎ (974) 606860 rm62 **B**

TIEMBLO, EL *Avila*

H Jaras Embalse del Burguillo ☎ (91) 8625036 rm17 (Jun 6- Sep 8) **A**

◆ **Toros de Guisando** av Madrid 5 ☎ (91) 8625011 rm30 **A**

TOLEDO *Toledo*

H Alfonso V1 Gl-Moscardo 2 ☎ (925) 222600 rm88 **B**

H Almazara ctra Toledo-Arges y Guerva, Km 3, 400 ☎ (925) 223866 rm21 (Mar 15-Nov 3) **A**

H Cardenal ps de Recaredo 24 ☎ (925) 224900 rm27 **B**

H Cigarrales ctra Circunvalación 32 ☎ (925) 220053 rm36 **A**

◆ **Gavilanes** ctra Madrid Km 65 ☎ (925) 224622 rm6 **A**

◆ **Hosteria Madrid** Marques Mendigorria 6 ☎ (925) 221114 rm10 **A**

H Imperio Cadenas 7 ☎ (925) 227650 rm21 **A**

★★**Maravilla** Barrio Rey 7 ☎ (925) 223304 rm18 **A**

H María Cristina Marqués de Mendigorría 1 ☎ (925) 213202 rm43 **A**

H Sol Azacanes 15 ☎ (925) 213650 rm14 **A**

TORO *Zamora*

H Juan 11 pl del Espolón 1 ☎ (988) 690300 rm42 **A**

TORRE DEL MAR *Málaga*

H Myrian av Andalucia 102 ☎ (952) 541300 rm38 (Apr-Sep) **A**

TORREDEMBARRA *Tarragona*

H Costa Fina av de Montserrat ☎ (977) 640075 rm48 (Apr-Oct) **A**

H Morros P-Galdós 15 ☎ (977) 640225 rm81 (Mar 15-Sep) **A**

◆ **Via Augusta** Apartado 82 ☎ (977) 640837 rm43 **A**

TORRELAVEGA *Cantabria*

H Marqués de Santillana Marqués de Santillana 6 ☎ (942) 892934 rm32 **B**

H Saja H-Alcalde del Rio 22 ☎ (942) 892750 rm45 **A**

TORREMOLINOS *Málaga*

H Amaragua Los Nidos ☎ (952) 384700 rm198 **B**

H Bristol av C-Alesandri 286 ☎ (952) 382800 rm58 (Apr-Sep) **A**

H Camino Real av de los Alamos ☎ (952) 383055 rm144 (Apr-Oct) **A**

H Flamingo av Imperial 9 ☎ (952) 383855 rm239 **A**

H Griego av Imperial ☎ (952) 385455 rm238 **A**

H Lago Rojo Miami 1 ☎ (952) 387666 rm144 **A**

H Lloyd av Montemar 74 ☎ (952) 380422 rm90 **A**

H Natali ☎ (952) 385900 rm412 **A**

H Nautilus av Imperial ☎ (952) 385200 rm116 **A**

◆ **Pizarro** Rio Mundo 9 ☎ (952) 387185 rm33 **A**

H Tres Torres av de los Manantiales 9 ☎ (952) 383611 rm47 **A**

TORREVIEJA *Alicante*

H Fontana Rambla de J-Mateo 19 ☎ (96) 5714111 rm156 **B**

TORRIJOS *Toledo*

H Castilla ctra Toledo-Avila Km 27 ☎ (925) 761800 rm30 **A**

H Mesón ctra Toledo-Avila Km 28 ☎ (925) 760856 rm44 **A**

TORTOSA *Tarragona*

H Berenguer IV Cervantes 23 ☎ (977) 440816 rm48 **A**

H Tortosa Park av Conde Baxuelos 1 rm84 **A**

TOSSA DE MAR *Girona*

H Cap d'Or ps de Vila Vella 1 ☎ (972) 340081 rm12 (May-Sep) **A**

★★**Corisco** ps del Mar ☎ (972) 340174 rm28 (May-Sep) **A**

H Delfin av Costa Brava 2 ☎ (972) 340250 rm63 (May-Oct) **A**

H Europark av Costa Brava 25 ☎ (972) 340853 rm59 (Apr-Oct) **B**

★★★**Florida** av de la Palma 21 ☎ (972) 340308 rm45 (Apr-Oct 24) **A**

◆ **Giverola** ctra Giverola 6 ☎ (972) 340158 rm35 (Mar 15-Oct) **B**

◆ **Mas Padro** ps de las Aguas ☎ (972) 340285 rm7 (May-Sep) **A**

H Neptuno La Guardia 52 ☎ (972) 340143 rm49 (May-Sep) **B**

H Ramos av Costa Brava ☎ (972) 340350 rm72 (May-Sep) **B**

H Windsor Carrer Nou 28 ☎ (972) 340186 rm66 (May-Oct) **A**

TREMP *Lleida*

H Siglo XX pl de la Cruz 32 ☎ (973) 650000 rm56 **A**

TRUJILLO *Cáceres*

H Cigueñas ctra Madrid-Lisboa Km 253 ☎ (927) 321250 rm78 **B**

TUDELA *Navarra*

◆ **Nueva Parrilla** pl de Toros ☎ (948) 822400 rm22 **A**

H Santamaria San Marcial 14 ☎ (948) 821200 rm51 **B**

★**Tuledo** ctra de Zaragoza ☎ (948) 820558 rm16 **A**

TÚI *Pontevedra*

H Colón Tuy Colón 11 ☎ (986) 600223 rm45 **A**

VALENCIA *Valencia*

★★**Bristol** av-San Martin 3 ☎ (96) 3521176 rm40 Closed Dec-Jan 14 **A**

H Continental Correos 8 ☎ (96) 3510926 rm43 **A**

H Europa Ribera 4 ☎ (96) 3520000 rm81 **A**

◆ **Florida** Padilla 4 ☎ (96) 3511284 rm45 **B**

H Internacional Bailén 8 ☎ (96) 3519426 rm54 **A**

◆ **Lauria Roma** Roger de Lauria ☎ (96) 3527642 rm90 **A**

H Lehos Gl-Urrutia ☎ (96) 3347800 rm104 **B**

◆ **Mediterráneo** av Barón de Cárcer 45 ☎ (96) 3510142 rm30 **A**

◆ **Miramar** Playa de Levante 32 ☎ (96) 3715142 rm17 (Mar-Sep) **A**

H Patilla Pinares 10 ☎ (96) 3679411 rm28 **A**

H Renasa av Cataluña 5 ☎ (96) 3692450 rm73 **B**

H Sorolla Convento Santa Clara 5 ☎ (96) 3523392 rm50 **B**

VALLADOLID *Valladolid*

H Enara pl de España 5 ☎ (983) 330311 rm26 **A**

H Imperial Peso 4 ☎ (983) 330300 rm81 **A**

★★★**Meliá Parque** Garcia Morato 17 ☎ (983) 470100 rm306 **B**

H Roma Héroes del Alcázar de Toledo 8 ☎ (983) 354666 rm38 **A**

VERIN *Orense*

H Aurora L-Espada 35 ☎ (988) 410025 rm35 **A**

H Dos Naciones L-Espada 38 ☎ (988) 410100 rm25 **A**

VIC *Barcelona*

H Ausa ps del Caudillo 4 ☎ (93) 8855311 rm26 **A**

VIELLA *Lleida*

◆ **Aneto** ps d'Arro ☎ (973) 640013 rm23 **A**

H Arán c J-Antonio 5 ☎ (973) 640050 rm44 **A**

H Baricauba San Nicolás 3 ☎ (973) 640150 rm24 **A**

H Bonaigua Sta Ma del Villar 5 ☎ (973) 640144 rm20 **A**

H Urogallo c J-Antonio 7 ☎ (973) 640000 rm37 **A**

VIGO *Pontevedra*

H Almirante Queipo de Llano 13 ☎ (986) 223907 rm31 **B**

H América Pablo Morillo 6 ☎ (986) 438922 rm56 **A**

◆ **Canaima** Garcia Barbón 42 ☎ (986) 228122 rm18 **A**

H Celta México 22 ☎ (986) 414699 rm45 **A**

H Galicia Colón 11 ☎ (986) 434022 rm53 **A**

H Junguera Uruguay 27 ☎ (986) 434888 rm35 **A**

H Nilo Marqués de Valladares 26 ☎ (986) 432899 rm52 **B**

VILANOVA I LA GELTRÚ *Barcelona*

H Mar Cal Ceferino Passeig de Ribes Roges ☎ (93) 8151719 rm28 (May-Sep) **A**

◆ **Solvi 70** Passeig de Ribes Roges 1 ☎ (93) 8151245 rm30 (Apr-Oct) **A**

VINAROZ *Castellón*

★★**Duc de Vendôme** ctra Nacional 340 Km 144 ☎ (964) 450944 rm11 **A**

◆ **Miramar** ps B-Ibañez 12 ☎ (964) 451400 rm17 **A**

VITORIA (GASTEIZ) *Alava*

H Achuri Rioja 11 ☎ (945) 255800 rm40 **A**

H Bilbaina Prudencio Maria de Veréstegui2 ☎ (945) 254400 rm29 **A**

H Desiderio Colegio San Prudencio 2 ☎ (945) 251700 rm21 Closed Dec 23-Jan 6 **A**

H Páramo Gl-Alava 11 ☎ (945) 230450 rm40 **A**

VIVEIRO *Lugo*

H Ego Playa de Area ☎ (982) 560987 rm22 **A**

H Orfeo Garcia Navia Castrillón 2 ☎ (982) 562104 rm27 **A**

H Tebar N-Cora 70 ☎ (982) 560100 rm27 **A**

ZAFRA *Badajoz*

H Huerta Honda av L-Asme ☎ (924) 550800 rm46 **B**

ZAMORA *Zamora*

★★**Cuatro Naciones** av J-Antonio 11 ☎ (988) 532275 rm40 **A**

H Dos Infantes Cortinas de San Miguel 3 ☎ (988) 512875 rm68 **B**

◆ **Rey Don Sancho** ☎ (988) 523400 rm86 **A**

◆ **Sayagues** pl Puentica 2 ☎ (988) 525522 rm56 **A**

ZARAGOZA *Zaragoza*

H Avenida av C-Augusto 55 ☎ (976) 439300 rm46 **A**

H Cesaraugusta III av Clave 45 ☎ (976) 211030 rm17 **A**

★★**Conde Bianco** Predicadores 84 ☎ (976) 441411 rm83 **A**

H Conquistador H-Cortes 21 ☎ (976) 214988 rm44 **B**

H Estudio Park Vista Alegre 4 ☎ (976) 381715 rm29 **A**

H Europa Alfonso 119 ☎ (976) 224901 rm54 **A**

H Gran Via Gran Via 38 ☎ (976) 229213 rm41 **A**

H Molinos San Miguel 38 ☎ (976) 224980 rm40 **A**

H Oriente Corso 11-13 ☎ (976) 221960 rm87 **B**

H Paris Pedro Maria Ric 14 ☎ (976) 236527 rm62 **A**

H Ramiro 1 Corso 123 ☎ (976) 298200 rm105 **B**

H Sport Moncayo 5 ☎ (976) 311114 rm64 **B**

ZARAUZ (ZARAUTZ) *Guipúzcoa*

★★**Alameda** Seitximenta ☎ (943) 830143 rm26 (Apr-Sep) **A**

◆ **Norte** Narros 1 ☎ (943) 832313 rm4 (May-Oct 10) **A**

★★★**Zarauz** av de Navarra 26 ☎ (943) 830200 rm82 **B**

ANDORRA

(Telephone 16 078 from France, 9738 from Spain) Andorra is a semi-independent principality in a cluster of valleys in the eastern Pyrenées.

ANDORRA LA VELLA

H Bellpi av Santa Coloma 30 ☎ 20651 rm40 Closed Jun **B**

H Cassany (n.rest) av Meritxell 28 ☎ 20636 rm53 **B**

H Consul pl Rebes 5 ☎ 20196 rm27 **A**

ARINSAL

H Comapedrosa ☎ 35123 rm12 **B**

H Solana ☎ 35127 rm40 Closed Oct 16-Nov 14 **A**

ENCAMP

H Paris av C-Princep Episcopal 2 ☎ 31325 rm42 Closed Nov **A**

H Univers r-Boulard 1 ☎ 31005 rm36 Closed Nov **A**

ESCALDES, LES

◆ **Andorra** av Carlemany 34 ☎ 20831 rm35 **A**

H Pubilla av Fiter i Roseli 49 ☎ 20981 rm50 **B**

SANT JULIÀ DE LÒRIA

H Barcelona ctra d'Os de Civis ☎ 41177 rm50 **B**

H Bonavista ctra de la Rabassa ☎ 41231 rm28 **A**

SOLDEU

H Bruxelles ctra General ☎ 51010 rm18 **A**

H Naudi ctra General ☎ 51018 rm53 **A**

SWEDEN

FACTS & FIGURES

Capital: Stockholm
Language: Swedish, English, German
IDD code: 46. To call the UK dial 009 *44 (* wait for second dialling tone)
Currency: Swedish Krona (SKr1 = 100 Öre)
Local time: GMT+1 (summer GMT+2)
Emergency Services: Police, Fire and Ambulance 09 000

Business hours
Banks: 0930–1500 Mon–Fri
Shops: 0900–1800 Mon–Fri; 0900–1600 Sat

Average daily temperatures:
Stockholm °C

Jan −3	Jul 17
Mar 0	Sep 11
May 9	Nov 1

Tourist Information:
UK Swedish National Tourist Office
3 Cork Street
London W1X 1HS
Tel 01-437 5816

USA Swedish Tourist Board
Scandinavian National Tourist Office, 655 Third Ave
New York, NY 10017
Tel (212) 949 2333

The days are long and the nights short during the summer months in Sweden, a popular destination for activity-filled family holidays or tranquil get-away-from-it-all breaks. The scenery is fascinating and wonderfully varied as well as being easy to explore since the roads are good and in many places virtually traffic free. Elk and deer roam the forests, birds and wildflowers abound, for watersports and fishing enthusiasts there are around 96,000 lakes to try, and there's a jagged coastline with countless archipelagoes, as well as forests, mountains and rushing rivers.

Sweden is divided into three geographical regions: Norrland, the northern 60 per cent including Lapland, mountainous but for a narrow coastal plain; Svealand, the central lake plain; and Gotland, the fertile southern plateau and plain including Scania, the chief agricultural district, in the far south.

Each of Sweden's major cities has its own particular atmosphere and character. Stockholm enjoys a wonderful lakeside setting, while Gothenburg is a pleasant and green city noted for its spacious avenues and attractive parks.

HOW TO GET THERE

BY CAR

Direct ferry services operate from Harwich and Newcastle (summer only) to Göteborg (Gothenburg); the crossing takes 22½–27½ hours. It is also possible to reach Sweden via Denmark, using the Harwich or Newcastle (summer only) to Esbjerg car ferry services; sailing time is 19–22 hours. Alternatively take one of the short Channel crossings to France or Belgium then drive through the Netherlands and northern Germany to Sweden using the ferry connections (via Denmark); Puttgarden–Rødbyhavn, and Helsingør–Helsingborg. Crossings from Harwich to Hamburg give a shorter overland journey via Germany or Denmark. The distance from Calais to Stockholm, the capital, is about 1,000 miles and would normally require three overnight stops.

For details of the AA's Overseas Routes Service consult the Contents page.

For location map, see Norway.

SPEED LIMITS

There are maximum speed limits indicated by signs on all roads in Sweden. In built-up areas 50 kph (31 mph); on all minor roads and roads with a high traffic density 70 kph (43 mph); on all other roads 90 kph (56 mph) and 110 kph (68 mph) on motorways.

LIGHTS

Dipped headlights must be used during the day.

PARKING

In Stockholm and most of the larger towns, there are parking restrictions which are connected with road cleaning and are decided locally. A sign (blue disc with red border and red diagonal) is placed under the street name and gives the day and times when parking is prohibited. The restriction applies only to the side of the street on which the sign is displayed.

BY TRAIN

If you do not have an InterRail or Eurail Pass, national and regional tickets can be purchased for rail travel within Sweden. Swedish State railways (SJ) offer a first class 'go-as-you-please' rail card for 7 or 14 days unlimited rail travel between mid-June and mid-August.

The Nordic Railpass entitles you to 21 days unlimited travel in Sweden, Norway, Denmark and Finland.

The scenic Inlandsbanan (Inland Railway) extends 800 miles down the backbone of Sweden, with one stretch involving travel by bus; a special card gives unrestricted travel on the line for 14 and 21 days.

It is essential to reserve a seat on trains marked with an 'R' or 'IC' in the timetable.

BY BICYCLE

Bicycles are available for hire throughout Sweden, details are available from the local Tourist Offices. The hire cost is generally 50 Skr per day or 200 Skr per week.

BY BUS

A network of express buses operates between the larger towns and cities in southern and central Sweden and between Stockholm and the northern coastal towns. There is a postal bus service in the north. GDR Continent bus operates daily express services from Göteborg to many parts of the country.

ACCOMMODATION

Due to the higher cost of living in Sweden the gazetteer is not as extensive as some of the other countries featured in the guide. The majority of hotels, pensions and farmhouses listed offer accommodation for less than Skr 209 per person per night at some time of the year.

The price bands are:

A 99–154
B 154–209

taking a rate of exchange at

Skr 11 = £1
Skr 7 = US $1

Many local tourist offices ('*Turistbyrå*') offer an accommodation booking service.

Abbreviations: gt gatan

ABISKO *Lappland*

★★**Abisko** ☎ (0980) 40000 rm165 Feb 25-Sep **B**

◆ **Gästgarden** ☎ (0980) 40100 rm40 **A**

ALMHULT *Småland*

FH Björkesmåla ☎ (0476) 62025 bed5 **A**

FH Truvedstorp ☎ (0476) 62016 bed8 **A**

ÅRE *Jämtland*

H Angena Gård ☎ (0647) 50066 bed21 Feb 15-Apr 15 **A**

H Lundsgården ☎ (0647) 50100 bed62 **A**

ARVIDSJAUR *Lappland*

H Central (n.rest) Järnvägsgatan 63 ☎ (0960) 10098 rm10 **B**

H Edström (n.rest) Stationsg 9 ☎ (0960) 10708 rm29 **B**

ARVIKA *Värmland*

◆ **Arendsberg** (n.rest) Sulvik ☎ (0570) 22222 bed14 **A**

ÅSELE *Västerbotten*

◆ **Sonios Rum** (n.rest) Centralg 17 ☎ (0941) 10001 bed16 **B**

AVESTA *Dalarna*

H Nya (n.rest) Kungsgt 5 ☎ (0226) 50601 bed12 **B**

BÅSTAD *Skåne*

FH Bjärröd ☎ (0431) 72162 bed5 **A**

★★★**Enehall** Stationsterrassen 10 ☎ (0431) 75015 rm75 Closed Xmas **B**

FH Grevie ☎ (0431) 16309 bed4 **A**

◆ **Nybo** (n.rest) Köpmansg 81 ☎ (0431) 70192 rm16 Jun-Aug **B**

BENGTSFORS *Dalsland*

H Hemgården (n.rest) Brogt 2 ☎ (0531) 10640 bed18 **B**

BISPGÅRDEN *Jämtland*

FH Österrede ☎ (0696) 30325 bed3 **A**

BODAFORS *Jönköping*

FH Säveda ☎ (0380) 30329 bed4 May-Oct **A**

BOLLNÄS *Hälsingland*

◆ **Rehngårdens** Söderhamnsvägen 2 ☎ (0278) 10577 bed29 **B**

BORLÄNGE *Dalarna*

FH Lisgården Gallsbo 143 ☎ (0243) 35209 bed4 **A**

◆ **Värdshuet Älvnäsgården** Repbäcken ☎ (0243) 31010 rm26 **B**

BRÅLANDA *Dalsland*

M Riksrasta Storg 62 ☏ (0521) 30640 rm8 **B**

BURGSVIK *Gotland*

◆ **Holmhällar** ☏ (0497) 98030 rm50 May-Sep 4 **B**

DUVED *Jämtland*

H Duvedsgården ☏ (0647) 20560 rm18 Closed May-Jun 14 & Sep 15-Nov **A**

EKSHÄRAD *Värmland*

◆ **Hedegörds** ☏ (0563) 40024 bed40 **B**

◆ **Wärdshuet Pilgrimen** Klarälvsv 35 ☏ (0563) 40590 rm25 **B**

FALKENBERG *Halland*

H Pallas (n.rest) Åke Tottsg 5 ☏ (0346) 10700 rm6 **B**

M Skrea ☏ (0346) 50170 bed33 **B**

H Steria (n.rest) Arvidstorpv 28 ☏ (0346) 15521 bed21 **B**

FALUN *Dalarna*

H Birgittagården Uddnäs Hosjö ☏ (023) 32147 bed47 **B**

FH Lonnemossa ☏ (023) 34969 bed4 **A**

◆ **Samuelsdals** ☏ (023) 11225 bed50 **B**

◆ **Solliden** Centralv 36 ☏ (023) 32126 rm22 **B**

FILIPSTAD *Värmland*

◆ **Gondolen** Skogsv 4 ☏ (0590) 41909 bed25 Closed Jun 23-24 & Xmas-New Year **B**

FLEN *Södermanland*

◆ **Presenthuset Nygård** (n.rest) Kungsg 11 ☏ (0157) 10116 rm5 **B**

FÖLLINGE *Jämtland*

H Norrgård Backvägen 3 ☏ (0645) 10065 bed21 **A**

FORSERUM *Jönköping*

FH Axlarp ☏ (0380) 20741 bed4 **A**

FH Böke ☏ (0370) 43159 bed4 **A**

FH Broddarp ☏ (0370) 20486 bed6 **A**

FRILLESÅS *Halland*

H Frillesberg Stationsvägen 2 ☏ (0340) 50970 rm14 **B**

◆ **Vallersvik** Vallersvijsvägen ☏ (0340) 53000 rm108 May-Sep **B**

FRÖVI *Västmanland*

H Frövi ☏ (0581) 30013 bed18 **B**

GÄVLE *Gästrikland*

H Hemlingby Friluftsgård ☏ (026) 117015 bed30 **B**

GÖTEBORG (GOTHENBURG) *Bohuslän*

The old city was built by the Dutch with a formal grid of canals and encircling moat; don't miss the Antikhallarna, Scandinavia's largest antiques and collectors' centre, and the 17th-century Queen Kristina's Hunting Lodge where you can stop for coffee and delicious waffles. The 'new' city has wide tree-lined avenues, elegant houses and large parks, the Liseberg Amusement Park – claimed to be the largest leisure complex in Scandinavia – combining the fun of a traditional fair with a stroll through magnificent gardens. Other attractions include the Botanical Garden, the Slottskogen Park and zoo, the bronze statue of Poseidon and the Gotaplatsen cultural centre and art gallery. If you are an early riser, wander down to the fish harbour and watch the weekday auctions. Being Sweden's largest port, Göteborg has many maritime attractions, including the four-masted schooner 'Viking' which you can board and tour.
Swedish design is legendary, and you can find many beautiful products in the city's two miles of car-free streets. EATING OUT One of Göteborg's most popular restaurants is *Rakan*, in Lorensbergsgatan, where the house speciality is shrimps. If expense is not a problem *Johann*, in Sodra Hamngatan, has built up a reputation as one of the best restaurants in Sweden.

◆ **Maria Eriksons** (n.rest) Chalmersg 27 ☏ (031) 207030 rm9 **B**

GRÖVELSJÖN *Dalarna*

◆ **Grövelsjön** ☏ (0253) 23090 bed150 Seasonal **B**

HALMSTAD *Halland*

FH Fotstad (5 km N Halmstad, towards Jön-Köping, then to Sperlingholm) ☏ (035) 39042 bed5 **A**

HAMMENHOG *Skåne*

◆ **Gästivaregården** Ystadsvägen 34 ☏ (0414) 40288 bed12 **B**

HÄSSLEHOLM *Skåne*

◆ **Rumsuthyrning** (n.rest) Magasinsg 8 ☏ (0451) 12219 bed17 **A**

HEMSE *Gotland*

FH Tjängdarve (10 km from Hemse) ☏ (08) 7875590 bed5 May-Sep **A**

HOFORS *Gästrikland*

H Agat (n.rest) Fatbursg 12 ☏ (0290) 20098 bed14 **B**

IDRE *Dalarna*

◆ **Lövåsgården** ☏ (0253) 29029 rm30 Seasonal **B**

H Sport Högstvägen 8 ☏ (0253) 20666 rm20 May-Oct **A**

JÄRBO *Gästrikland*

◆ **Kungsfors Herrgård** ☏ (0290) 62086 bed47 **A**

JÄRVSÖ *Hälsingland*

◆ **Orrabackens** (n.rest) ☏ (0651) 41665 bed18 **A**

KALMAR *Småland*

H Kalmar Lägprishotell (n.rest) Rappegatan 1 ☏ (0480) 25560 bed30 Closed Xmas **B**

H Villa Ängö (n.rest) Baggensgt 20 ☏ (0480) 85415 bed23 **B**

H Villa Lindö (n.rest) Lindölundsgt 18 ☏ (0480) 14280 bed28 **B**

KARLSHAMN *Blekinge*

◆ **Oskar** (n.rest) Saltsjöbadsvägen 25 ☏ (0454) 19141 rm11 Mar-Nov **A**

KARLSKOGA *Värmland*

◆ **Villingsbergsgärden** (n.rest) ☏ (0586) 70140 rm13 **A**

KARLSKRONA *Blekinge*

◆ **Rosenhill** Angerumsv 2 ☏ (0455) 20165 rm12 **B**

KATRINEHOLM *Södermanland*

FH Linds (12 km E Katrineholm, , 3 km from Skolding) ☏ (0150) 50008 bed5 May-Sep **A**

H Merkur (n.rest) Vasav 9 ☏ (0150) 14930 rm9 **B**

KIRUNA *Norrbotten*

◆ **Vassijaure Fjällgård** (n.rest) ☏ (0920) 51913 rm24 Jul-Aug 20 **A**

KIVIK *Skåne*

◆ **Stenshuvud** (n.rest) Svinaberga ☏ (0414) 70215 rm5 May-Sep **B**

◆ **Vitemölle Havsbad** Lejegatan 60 ☎ (0414) 70880 bed16 Closed Jan & Feb **B**

KLINTEHAMN *Gotland*

◆ **Gannarve Gård** ☎ (0498) 44076 bed25 May 15-Aug 20 **B**

◆ **Varvsholm** ☎ (0498) 40010 bed64 May 10-Aug 20 **B**

KUNGSBACKA *Halland*

◆ **Carlsons Rum** (n.rest) Göteborgsvägen 1 ☎ (0300) 11926 bed16 **A**

LAGAN *Småland*

H Lagadalen Storgatan 28 ☎ (0372) 30162 rm11 **B**

LIDKÖPING *Västergötland*

◆ **Hallins** (n.rest) Bäckholmsgat 3 ☎ (0510) 20938 rm6 **B**

LIMA *Dalarna*

◆ **Carlsborg Wärdshus** Rörbäcksnäs ☎ (0280) 80052 bed46 Closed Jun & Oct **A**

LINKÖPING *Östergötland*

M Blåklinten Tallboda ☎ (013) 124181 rm10 **A**

LJUNGBY *Småland*

◆ **Sjöatorpsgården** ☎ (0372) 43010 bed16 Mar-Nov **B**

LJUNGDALEN *Härjedalen*

◆ **Helags** ☎ (0687) 20009 bed24 Closed May 16-Jun 16 **A**

LUND *Skåne*

FH Linebo Odarslov 16 ☎ (046) 98022 bed5 (May-Jun & Sep) **A**

MALUNG *Dalarna*

H Bergli (n.rest) ☎ (0280) 10173 rm4 **B**

◆ **Värdshuset Lugnet** ☎ (0280) 42000 rm13 **B**

MARKARYD *Kronoberg*

FH Amot Skattegård (3 km W Markaryd, road 117, towards Halmstad) bed6 May-Oct **A**

MELLERUD *Dalsland*

◆ **Nya Järnvägshotellet** ☎ (0530) 10026 bed24 **B**

NÅS *Dalarna*

◆ **Skansbackens** ☎ (0281) 30055 bed20 **B**

◆ **Wärdshuset Hjärpholn** (n.rest) Hjärpholn 4552 ☎ (0281) 30100 rm8 Jun-Aug **A**

NORA *Västmanland*

H Lilla (n.rest) Rådstugug 14 ☎ (0587) 10139 rm10 **B**

◆ **Nyhyttan Hälso** ☎ (0587) 60400 rm90 **B**

NORRKÖPING *Östergötland*

H Strand (n.rest) Drottniggt 2 ☎ (011) 169900 bed22 **B**

NYBRO *Småland*

H Turistgården (n.rest) Vassagt 22 ☎ (0481) 10932 bed100 Jun-Aug **A**

ÖRKELLJUNGA *Skåne*

M Åsljunga Värdshus ☎ (0435) 60445 rm10 **A**

ÖSTERSUND *Jämtland*

FH Borgvattnet (50 km from Östersund) ☎ (0695) 50005 bed3 **A**

FH Imnäs In Orrviten 18 km from Östersund ☎ (063) 40252 bed4 **A**

FH Varviken 40 km S of Östersund ☎ (0693) 32142 bed6 Jun 10-Sep 15 **A**

RONNEBY *Blekinge*

H Strandgärden (n.rest) ☎ (0457) 11136 rm7 **B**

SANKT ANNA *Östergötland*

◆ **Båtsholms** ☎ (0121) 51017 bed60 May-Sep **A**

H Sandens Värdshus ☎ (0121) 51012 bed40 May 15-Sep 15 **A**

SKÄRHAMN *Bohuslän*

H Nordevik Hamngatan 60 ☎ (0304) 70311 bed20 Closed Dec 15-Jan 15 **B**

SKELLEFTEÅ *Västerbotten*

◆ **Stiftsgärden** Brännavagen 25 ☎ (0910) 77272 rm30 **A**

SÖSDALA *Kristianstad*

FH Nygärd (5km S Sösdala, Rd23, 20km S, Hässleholm) ☎ (0451) 63091 bed6 May-Sep **A**

STENUNGSUND *Bohuslän*

◆ **Getskärs** ☎ (0303) 77702 bed100 Closed Xmas & New Year **A**

H Reis (n.rest) Göteborgsv 2-4 ☎ (0303) 70011 rm20 **B**

STOCKHOLM *Stockholm*
Stockholm, capital of Sweden, lies on several islands and on the adjacent mainland, in a situation that is widely regarded as one of the most picturesque in Europe. The nucleus of the city is an island in mid-channel called the old town, on which stand the imposing royal palace (1697-1754), the principal church (St Nicholas), the house of the nobles (1648-70) in which they held periodic meetings, and the ministries of the kingdom.
Immediately west of the central island lies the Knight's island, containing the old Franciscan church in which all the later sovereigns of Sweden have been buried.
The districts of Norrmalm and Ostermalm lie to the north of these two islands, separated by a narrow channel in which there's an islet containing the houses of parliament. The largest buildings and institutions in Norrmalm and Ostermalm are the National Museum, with valuable collections of coins, paintings and sculptures; most of the theatres; the Academy of Fine Arts; *Humlegarden*, a magnificent park; and the Academy of Sciences with natural history collections.
East of the old town lies Djurgarden, a beautiful island once a hunting-ground of Gustavus Vasa. Situated there are the Northern Museum, the Biological Museum and a great open-air park and museum (*Skansen*).
Immediately south of the old town island is the extensive district of Sodermalm, the houses of which climb up the steep slopes that rise from the water's edge. An archipelago east of the city forms a large recreational ground popular with residents and visitors alike.
EATING OUT If it is traditional Swedish fare you are after look for *'Husmanskost'* (home cooking), or the special dishes of the day. If it is fish you fancy, go to Ostermalmshaller, a market area where fishmongers' stalls have grown into seafood bars and restaurants. Treat yourself to *gravad lax* (salmon with dill in mustard sauce), or *Jansonns frestele*, a casserole of potatoes, anchovies, onion and cream. Wash down your meal with 'Snaps' – served ice cold in small glasses to be drunk in one gulp.
Food is substantial and nourishing, but eating out is expensive. A good idea is to look for establishments displaying the sign *dagens ratt* (today's special) which usually represents good value.

SWEDEN

One of Stockholm's best known restaurants is *Aurora*, in Munkbron. Housed in a 17th-century building, it offers both Swedish and international specialities. Excellent harbour views can be enjoyed at the *Quarter Deck*, located on the waterfront in the old town, and salmon is a speciality of *Glada Laxen*, centrally located in Regeringsgatan.

H Columbus Tjärhousgat 11 ☏ (08) 441717 bed120 **B**

STORLIEN *Jämtland*

★★Storlien ☏ (0647) 70151 rm14 **B**

TÄNNDALEN *Härjedalen*

H Röstavallen ☏ (0684) 22034 rm11 Closed Jun & Oct **A**

H Siljeströms (n.rest) ☏ (0684) 22013 bed125 Dec 23-May 14 & Jun 3-Oct 14 **B**

TREKANTEN *Småland*

H Lergöken Gamla Vägen 40 ☏ (0480) 50008 bed11 Closed Dec 24-Jan 9 **A**

TROLLHÄTTAN *Västergötland*

H Carliz (n.rest) Garvaregt 18 ☏ (0520) 11139 bed20 **B**

UNDERSÅKER *Jämtland*

◆ **Undersåker** ☏ (0647) 30308 bed25 Dec 10-Apr **B**

UPPSALA *Uppland*

H Elit (n.rest) Bredgränd 10 ☏ (018) 130345 rm17 **B**

◆ **Samariterhemmets** Hamnesplanaden 16 ☏ (018) 177180 bed53 **B**

VARBERG *Halland*

H Bergklinten (n.rest) Västra Vallgt 25 ☏ (0340) 11545 bed22 **A**

H Strandgården (n.rest) ☏ (0340) 16855 bed52 May-Aug **B**

VÄXJÖ *Småland*

FH Kråketorp (20 km S) ☏ (0470) 70088 bed5 May-Sep **A**

FH Väderlanda (25 km S) ☏ (0470) 35193 bed7 **A**

VELLINGE *Skåne*

H Wellingehus Järnvägsgatan 7 ☏ (040) 422861 bed40 **B**

VILHELMINA *Västerbotten*

H Lilla (n.rest) Granvägen 1 ☏ (0940) 10086 bed20 **B**

VIMMERBY *Småland*

FH Långvik ☏ (0492) 72038 bed4 **A**

FH Solnebo (10 km S) ☏ (0492) 32007 bed4 **A**

VISBY *Gotland*

◆ **Fridhem** ☏ (0498) 64010 bed75 May 15-Sep 15 **B**

VITSAND *Värmland*

H Vitsands ☏ (0560) 30191 bed116 **B**

VRIGSTAD *Småland*

◆ **Granbackens** Kristina Nilssonsv 3 ☏ (0382) 30027 bed40 **A**

Riddarholm Church on the island of Riddarholmen is the burial place of Sweden's monarchs.

SWITZERLAND AND LIECHTENSTEIN

FACTS & FIGURES

SWITZERLAND
Capital: Bern (Berne)
Language: German, French, Italian, Romansh
IDD code: 41. To call the UK dial 00 44
Currency: Swiss Franc (SFr1 = 100 centimes)
Local time: GMT+1 (summer gmt+2)
Emergency Services: Police 117; Fire 118; Ambulance 144

Business hours–Banks: 0830–1200 & 1400–1630 Mon–Fri
Shops: 0830–1200 & 1400–1830 Mon–Fri; 0830–1200 & 1400–1600 Sat

Average daily temperatures:
Zurich °C

Jan 0	Jul 19
Mar 5	Sep 15
May 9	Nov 5

Tourist Information:

UK Swiss National Tourist Office
1 New Coventry Street
London W1V 8EE
Tel 01-734 1921

USA Swiss National Tourist Office
608 Fifth Ave
New York, NY 10020
Tel (212) 757 5944

With its breathtaking mountain scenery, some of the world's most luxurious and stylish hotels, winter sports resorts that are without equal, a transportation system that is the envy of the world, and picturesque villages and towns, Switzerland is a magnet for visitors at any time of the year.

Landlocked in the middle of Europe and conditioned by its historic evolution, Switzerland has four natural languages. The German-speaking area north of the Alps is by far the largest, whereas Swiss-German is only a spoken dialect with the added flavour of local versions. In the French-speaking regions of the south-west there is a marked French influence, while south of the Alps the waving palms of the Ticino herald the Italian tongue and way of life. In the Grisons, a small mountainous area of south-east Switzerland, an ancient Latin tongue, Rhaeto-Romanic (Romansh) has survived through the centuries.

LIECHTENSTEIN

The principality of Liechtenstein, although an independent state is represented in diplomatic and other matters by Switzerland. Traffic regulations, insurance laws and the monetary unit are the same as for Switzerland.

HOW TO GET THERE

BY CAR

From Great Britain, Switzerland is usually reached through France. The distance from the Channel ports to Bern, the Swiss capital, is about 530 miles, a distance that would probably require one overnight stop.

For details of the AA's Overseas Routes Service consult the Contents page.

SPEED LIMITS

Driving in Switzerland demands special care and low speeds because of the mountain roads and conditions. Inside built-up areas (between placename signs) there is a limit of 50 kph (31 mph); outside built-up areas the limit is 80 kph (49 mph); on motorways 120 kph (74 mph).

MOTORWAY TAX

A vehicle tax sticker vignette costing SFr 30 must be displayed by vehicles using Swiss motorways. Motorists can purchase the stickers from AA Centres and AA Port Service Centres or at the Swiss frontier.

PARKING

In some large towns there are short-term parking areas known as blue zones, where parked vehicles must display a disc on the windscreen – discs can be obtained from the police, some large shops and tobacconists, in petrol stations and garages. In Lausanne, there is a similar red zone system in operation.

Winter conditions

Some roads may be closed during winter and others will only be open to cars with wheel chains – indicated by the sign showing a tyre with chains on it.

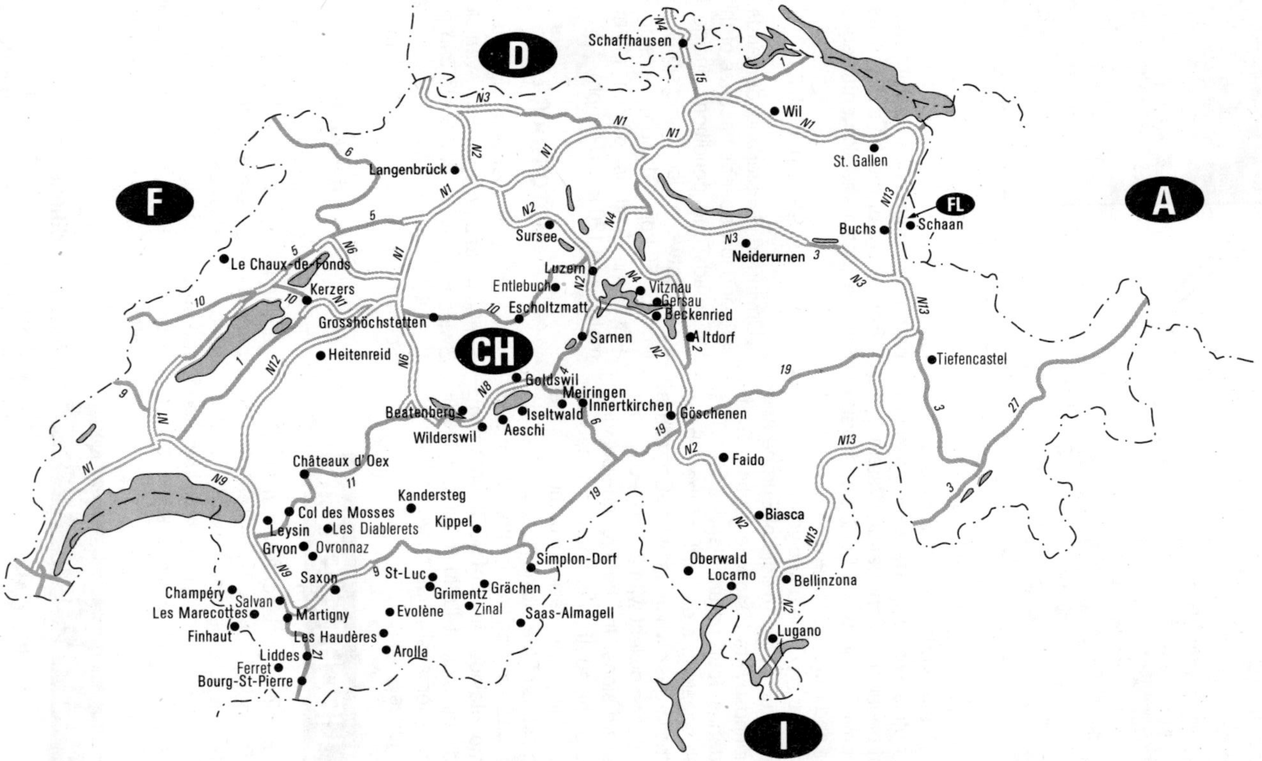

D
A
F
CH
I
FL
Schaffhausen
Wil
St. Gallen
Langenbrück
Buchs
Schaan
Neiderurnen
Sursee
Luzern
Le Chaux-de-Fonds
Kerzers
Entlebuch
Vitznau
Gersau
Beckenried
Escholtzmatt
Grosshöchstetten
Sarnen
Altdorf
Heitenreid
Tiefencastel
Goldswil
Meiringen
Innertkirchen
Göschenen
Beatenberg
Iseltwald
Wilderswil
Aeschi
Faido
Châteaux d'Oex
Kandersteg
Col des Mosses
Leysin
Les Diablerets
Kippel
Biasca
Gryon
Ovronnaz
Simplon-Dorf
Oberwald
Locarno
Saxon
St-Luc
Grimentz
Grächen
Bellinzona
Champéry
Salvan
Les Marecottes
Martigny
Evolène
Zinal
Saas-Almagell
Finhaut
Les Haudères
Lugano
Arolla
Liddes
Ferret
Bourg-St-Pierre

For key to country identification - see "About the gazetteer"

BY TRAIN AND BUS

Federal and private railways, and yellow post buses provide an efficient transport service but fares are very expensive. There are a number of discount deals that are worth considering.

The Swiss pass permits unlimited travel on almost any form of transport (including all lake steamers) for periods ranging from 4 days to 1 month; there are also Regional Holiday Season Tickets. Most of these passes can be purchased through the Swiss National Tourist Office for 5–10% less than in the country itself. A Eurail or InterRail pass is valid only on state-run railways which make up about 60% of the rail network.

The Swiss Card (valid for 1 month) provides free travel from any airport or border railway station to your destination in Switzerland and back, also half price rail, boat and bus tickets and reduced rate travel on the mountain railway.

BY BICYCLE

Bicycles can be hired from all state and most private railway stations, at a cost of SFr 8–SFr 15 per day, and returned to any station.

ACCOMMODATION

Most of the establishments listed in the gazetteer that follows provide accommodation for less than SFr 53 per person per night at some time during the year.

A SFr 25–39
B SFr 39–53

taking a rate of exchange at

SFr 2.80=£1
SFr 1.80=US $1

It is possible, however, that these prices may change during the currency of this book, particularly in the high season and in winter holiday resorts. For more detailed information, go to a local tourist office, usually situated near the rail station. Owing to the high cost of living throughout the country, inexpensive accommodation is rare, but in rural areas you should find guesthouses and rooms in private homes – look for *Zimmer frei* (rooms vacant) signs – offering cheaper accommodation.

Abbreviations: av avenue r rue rte route str strasse

AESCHI *Bern*

★★Baumgarten ☎ (033) 544121 bed40 **B**

H Niesen ☎ (033) 543626 bed60 **A**

ALTDORF *Uri*

H Bahnhof ☎ (044) 21032 bed40 **A**

AROLLA *Valais*

H Lac Bleu ☎ (027) 831166 bed10 **A**

BEATENBERG *Bern*

H Beatus ☎ (036) 411528 bed30 Closed Nov **B**

H Favorita ☎ (036) 411204 bed12 **B**

BECKENRIED *Nidwalden*

★Sonne ☎ (041) 641205 bed50 **A**

BELLINZONA *Ticino*

H San Giovanni ☎ (092) 251919 bed19 **A**

BIASCA *Ticino*

H Al Giardinetto ☎ (092) 721771 bed35 **B**

BOURG-ST-PIERRE *Valais*

H Valsorey ☎ (026) 49176 bed22 **B**

H Vieux Moulin ☎ (026) 49169 bed30 **B**

BUCHS *St-Gallen*

H Bären ☎ (085) 61166 bed18 **A**

CASSARATE See **LUGANO**

CHAMPÉRY *Valais*

H Berra (n.rest) ☎ (025) 791168 bed30 Closed Nov **A**

H Buffet de la Gare ☎ (025) 791329 bed18 **B**

◆ Souvenir (n.rest) ☎ (025) 791340 bed32 **B**

CHÂTEAU-D'OEX *Vaud*

H Florissant ☎ (029) 46060 bed15 Closed Nov **B**

H Le Vanil (n.rest) ☎ (029) 46681 bed20 **B**

H Poste ☎ (029) 46388 bed30 **B**

H Printanière ☎ (029) 46113 bed18 Closed Nov **A**

H Ville ☎ (029) 47477 bed20 **B**

CHAUX-DE-FONDS, LA *Neuchâtel*

◆ France (n.rest) ☎ (039) 231116 bed40 **B**

H Moulin ☎ (039) 264226 bed30 **A**

COL DES MOSSES *Vaud*

◆ Chaussy ☎ (025) 551147 bed40 **B**

DIABLERETS, LES *Vaud*

◆ Isenau ☎ (025) 531293 bed15 Closed Nov & May **A**

H Terminus ☎ (025) 531144 bed8 **B**

ENTLEBUCH *Luzern*

★★Drei Könige ☎ (041) 721227 bed20 **B**

ESCHOLZMATT *Luzern*

◆ **Rössli** ☏ (041) 771241 bed12 **B**

EVOLÈNE *Valais*

H Arzinol (n.rest) ☏ (027) 831665 bed18 **B**

★**Eden** ☏ (027) 831112 bed24 Closed Nov **B**

H Evolène ☏ (027) 831151 bed20 **A**

H Hermitage ☏ (027) 831232 bed40 Jun-Sep & Dec-Apr **B**

FAIDO *Ticino*

H Pedrinis ☏ (094) 381241 bed35 **A**

FERRET *Valais*

H Col-de-Fenêtre ☏ (026) 41188 bed15 Jun-Sep **B**

H Ferret ☏ (026) 41180 bed30 Jun-Sep **B**

FINHAUT *Valais*

H Beau-Séjour ☏ (026) 47101 bed50 May-Oct & Dec-Feb **B**

GERSAU *Schwyz*

★★★**Beau-Rivage** ☏ (041) 841223 bed55 Apr-Oct **B**

H Ilge & Mimosa ☏ (041) 841155 bed70 Closed Nov & Dec **B**

GOLDSWIL *Bern*

★**Park** ☏ (036) 222942 bed50 **B**

GÖSCHENEN *Uri*

★**St-Gotthard** ☏ (044) 65263 bed44 **A**

GRÄCHEN *Valais*

H Alpha ☏ (028) 561301 bed30 **B**

GRIMENTZ *Valais*

H Bouquetin ☏ (027) 651527 bed70 Closed Nov & May **A**

H Mélèze ☏ (027) 651287 bed16 Jun-Oct & Dec-Apr **A**

GROSSHÖCHSTETTEN *Bern*

◆ **Sternen** ☏ (031) 910111 bed16 **A**

GRYON *Vaud*

H Cremaillère ☏ (025) 682155 bed25 Closed Nov **A**

HAUDÈRES, LES *Valais*

◆ **Alpes** ☏ (027) 831677 bed25 **A**

H Gai-Logis ☏ (027) 831413 bed16 Closed Nov **B**

HEITENRIED *Fribourg*

H Sternen ☏ (037) 351116 bed23 **B**

INNERTKIRCHEN *Bern*

H Alpenrose ☏ (036) 711151 bed50 **B**

H Carina (n.rest) ☏ (036) 712515 bed22 **B**

H Hof & Post ☏ (036) 711951 bed40 **B**

H Tännler ☏ (036) 711427 bed18 **B**

ISELTWALD *Bern*

H Bernahof am See ☏ (036) 451107 bed35 Closed Nov-Apr **B**

KANDERSTEG *Bern*

H Alpenblick ☏ (033) 751129 bed20 **A**

H Spycher ☏ (033) 751313 bed20 Closed Nov **B**

KERZERS *Fribourg*

H Hippel Krone ☏ (031) 955122 bed30 **B**

★**Löwen** ☏ (031) 955117 bed25 **A**

KIPPEL *Valais*

H Bietschhorn ☏ (028) 491818 bed12 **A**

H Sporthotel Kippel ☏ (028) 491808 bed30 **B**

LA Each place name preceded by 'La' is listed under the name that follows it.

LANGENBRÜCK *Basel*

◆ **Bären** ☏ (062) 601414 bed36 **B**

LE Each name preceded by 'Le' is listed under the name that follows it.

LES Each name preceded by 'Les' is listed under the name that follows it.

LEYSIN *Vaud*

◆ **Violette** (n.rest) ☏ (025) 341276 bed20 Jun-Sep & Dec-Apr **A**

LIDDES *Valais*

◆ **Auberge des Alpes** ☏ (026) 41380 bed18 **A**

LOCARNO *Ticino*

◆ **Collinetta** ☏ (093) 311979 bed10 Closed Dec-Feb **A**

H Müller (n.rest) ☏ (093) 311971 bed29 Mar-Oct **B**

◆ **Sempione** (n.rest) ☏ (093) 313064 bed34 Mar-Nov **A**

H Stazione (n.rest) ☏ (093) 330222 bed15 Apr-Oct **A**

H Vecchia Locarno ☏ (093) 316502 bed35 **B**

H Villa Daniela (n.rest) ☏ (093) 334158 bed15 Mar-Oct **A**

LUGANO *Ticino*

H Rex (n.rest) via C-Cattaneo 11 ☏ (091) 227608 bed31 Closed Jan **A**

At **CASSARATE**

★**Atlantico** v Concordia 12 ☏ (091) 512921 bed33 Closed Dec & Jan **B**

LUZERN (LUCERNE) *Luzern*

Luzern, for many the most delightful of Switzerland's cities, stands in a magnificent setting bordering the lake of the same name in the foothills of the St Gotthard Pass. Lake excursions are popular with visitors, with a wide selection offered by the Lake Lucerne Navigation Company.

The sights of Luzern, best enjoyed on foot, include the Chapel Bridge, built in 1333, with its numerous gable paintings and sturdy water tower. Nearby are quaint alleys that will intrigue and fascinate, while in the city's arcades you can enjoy the hustle and bustle of the market crowds.

EATING OUT Luzern's favourite soup is *Brotsuppe* (bread soup), and another popular starter is *Bundnerfleisch* , thin slices of dried beef. Pork and veal sausages are widely available, as are *rösti*, grated fried potatoes.

Among the best restaurants in the town are *Chez Marianne*, the *Old Swiss House* and the *Barbatti*, which is located in a fine 19th-century building.

H Linde (n.rest) ☏ (041) 513193 bed9 **A**

MARÉCOTTES, LES *Valais*

H Del l'Avenir ☏ (026) 61461 bed40 Jun-Sep & Dec-Apr **B**

MARTIGNY *Valais*

M Croisée (n.rest) 51 av du Léman ☏ (026) 22359 bed48 **A**

H Du Vieux Stand 41 Av Grand-St-Bernard ☏ (026) 21506 bed58 **B**

◆ **Trois Couronnes** 8 pl du Bourg ☏ (026) 22515 bed27 **B**

MEIRINGEN *Bern*

H Tourist ☏ (036) 711044 bed25 **A**

H Victoria ☏ (036) 71033 bed30 **B**

NEIDERURNEN *Glarus*

★★Mineralbad ☏ (058) 211703 bed11 **A**

OBERWALD *Valais*

H Furka ☏ (028) 731144 bed50 **B**

OVRONNAZ *Valais*

H Beau Séjour ☏ (027) 863434 bed30 Closed Nov **B**

H Grand Muveran ☏ (027) 862621 bed40 **B**

SAAS-ALMAGELL *Valais*

H Christiana (n.rest) ☏ (028) 572863 bed45 Jun-Sep & Dec-Apr **B**

H Edelwiess ☏ (028) 572150 bed12 **A**

H Monte-Moro ☏ (028) 571012 bed40 **B**

H Olympia (n.rest) ☏ (028) 571676 bed45 Closed Nov & May **A**

◆ Pension Central (n.rest) ☏ (028) 572416 bed14 **A**

ST GALLEN *St-Gallen*

H Sporting Straubenzellstr 19 ☏ (071) 271312 bed33 **B**

H Vadian (n.rest) ☏ (071) 236080 bed24 **B**

ST LUC *Valais*

H Favre ☏ (027) 651128 bed32 **B**

H Fougère ☏ (027) 651176 bed18 Jun-Oct & Dec-Apr **B**

SALVAN *Valais*

H Bellevue ☏ (026) 61523 bed20 **A**

SARNEN *Obwalden*

H Hirschen ☏ (041) 661542 bed14 **A**

H Obwaldnerhof ☏ (041) 661817 bed15 Closed May, Oct & Nov **B**

SAXON *Valais*

H Gare ☏ (026) 62878 bed6 **A**

SCHAFFHAUSEN *Schaffhausen*

◆ Kreuz ☏ (053) 61222 bed8 **B**

H Tanne Tanne 3 ☏ (053) 54179 bed20 **A**

SIMPLON-DORF *Valais*

H Fletschhorn ☏ (028) 291138 bed18 **A**

H Grina ☏ (028) 291304 bed30 **B**

SURSEE *Luzern*

H Hirschen ☏ (045) 211048 bed27 **B**

TIEFENCASTEL *Graubünden*

★Albula ☏ (081) 711121 bed80 **B**

★★Posthotel Julier ☏ (081) 711415 bed90 Closed Nov **B**

VITZNAU *Luzern*

H Schiff ☏ (041) 831357 bed12 **A**

WIL *St-Gallen*

◆ Ochsen Grabenstr 7 ☏ (073) 224848 bed30 **B**

WILDERSWIL *Bern*

★Viktoria ☏ (036) 221670 bed20 **A**

YVERDON *Vaud*

H Ange ☏ (024) 212585 bed35 **B**

H Ecusson Vaudois ☏ (024) 214015 bed15 **A**

ZINAL *Valais*

H Poste ☏ (027) 651187 bed18 **B**

LIECHTENSTEIN

Liechtenstein was founded in 1719, when the domain of Schellenberg and the country of Vaduz were welded into an independent principality – a tiny country only 25km long and 6km wide, with just under 30, 000 inhabitants, divided into two political regions and eleven autonomous communities. Together they offer an extensive range of attractions: museums, boutiques, hotels and restaurants, historical sites, vineyards and endless sporting activities, while still retaining Liechtenstein's very own individual charm and appeal.

Vaduz is the capital and also the main tourist centre. Located close to the right shore of the Rhine, it is dominated by Vaduz castle, built around 1300.

The art collection of the *Englanderbrau* is of great interest, with works chiefly from the collection of the Princes of Liechtenstein – one of the oldest and most comprehensive private collections in Europe. Peter Paul Rubens' subtle portraits of his children, as well as his monumental cycle of painting of the Roman Consul Decius Mus are exhibited; also bronzes by Soldani.

Those interested in natural history and the development of civilization will enjoy the Liechtenstein National Museum, also in Vaduz, where exhibits include historical finds from excavations, church carvings and a selection of arms from the private collection of the ruling family.

EATING OUT The cuisine here tends to be Swiss with Austrian overtones. In Vaduz the *Torkel*, owned by the ruling prince, enjoys a good reputation, as does the restaurant of the *Engel Hotel*.

SCHAAN

H Linde ☏ (075) 21704 bed35 **B**

YUGOSLAVIA

FACTS & FIGURES
Capital: Beograd (Belgrade)
Language: Serbo-Croat, Slovene, Macedonian, Italian
IDD code: 38. To call the UK dial 99 44
Currency: Yugoslav dinar (Din1 = 100 paras)
Local time: GMT + 1 (summer GMT + 2)
Emergency services: Police 92; Fire 93; Ambulance 94

Business hours–Banks: 0900–1400 Mon–Fri; 0700–1300 Sat
Shops: 0800–1200 & 1700–20.00 Mon–Fri; 0800–1500 Sat. Many shops and banks are open throughout the day.

Average daily temperatures:
Beograd °C

Jan 0	Jul 22
Mar 6	Sep 19
May 17	Nov 7

Tourist Information:
Yugoslav National Tourist Office
UK 143 Regent Street
London W1R 8AE
Tel 01–734 5243 & 01–439 0399
USA 630 Fifth Ave
New Yorkm NY 10020
Tel (212) 757–2801

For most people, the word Yugoslavia is synonymous with the Adriatic coast, although in fact this is a country of mountains, plains, rivers, lakes, national parks and picturesque towns and villages. Certainly the lovely coast, with its countless coves, bays and islands, sandy and rocky beaches and numerous holiday resorts, is ideal for those who enjoy water sports, cruises, sailing and fishing. And an added bonus is that it has preserved many important monuments which testify to a stormy history: the remains of ancient Greek and Roman towns, medieval fortresses and palaces, churches and monasteries, and hundreds of picturesque fishermen's villages and hamlets.

But if one is in search of historical and cultural monuments it is to the large cities that one must look: Belgrade, Yugoslavia's capital; Zagreb, Ljubljana, Sarajevo, and the other capitals of the six Yugoslav republics and two provinces. Many of the smaller towns are often a treasure-house of historical monuments, too.

Modern roads now give access to even the most remote corners of the country, there are airports near all major cities, and the railway network links up major parts of the country.

HOW TO GET THERE

BY CAR

Yugoslavia is usually approached via Belgium, the Federal Republic of Germany (Köln/Cologne and München/Munich) and Austria (Salzburg), or alternatively via France or Switzerland and Italy (Milan and Trieste). The distance from Calais via Germany to Beograd (Belgrade), the capital, is just over 1,200 miles, a distance normally requiring three or four overnight stops. Car-sleeper services operate during the summer from Brussels and 's–Hertogenbosch to Ljubljana, and from Boulogne, Brussels, 's–Hertogenbosch and Paris to Milan.

For details of the AA's Overseas Routes Service consult the Contents page.

SPEED LIMITS

In built-up areas 60 kph (37 mph); outside built-up areas 80 kph (49 mph) but 100 kph (62 mph) on dual carriageways and 120 kph (74 mph) on motorways.

BY TRAIN

Eurail and InterRail passes are valid in Yugoslavia but supplements are charged for Express and 'fast' trains. Reservations are strongly recommended on the main international expresses.

BY BUS

Coach services connect most towns and are often faster than the trains, although coastal buses can be slow. The main towns have bus services, with tramways and trolleybuses in Belgrade and tramways in Zagreb and Sarajevo. Multi-journey tickets are available from tobacconists, are self-cancelled on board and are half the price of fares paid direct to the driver.

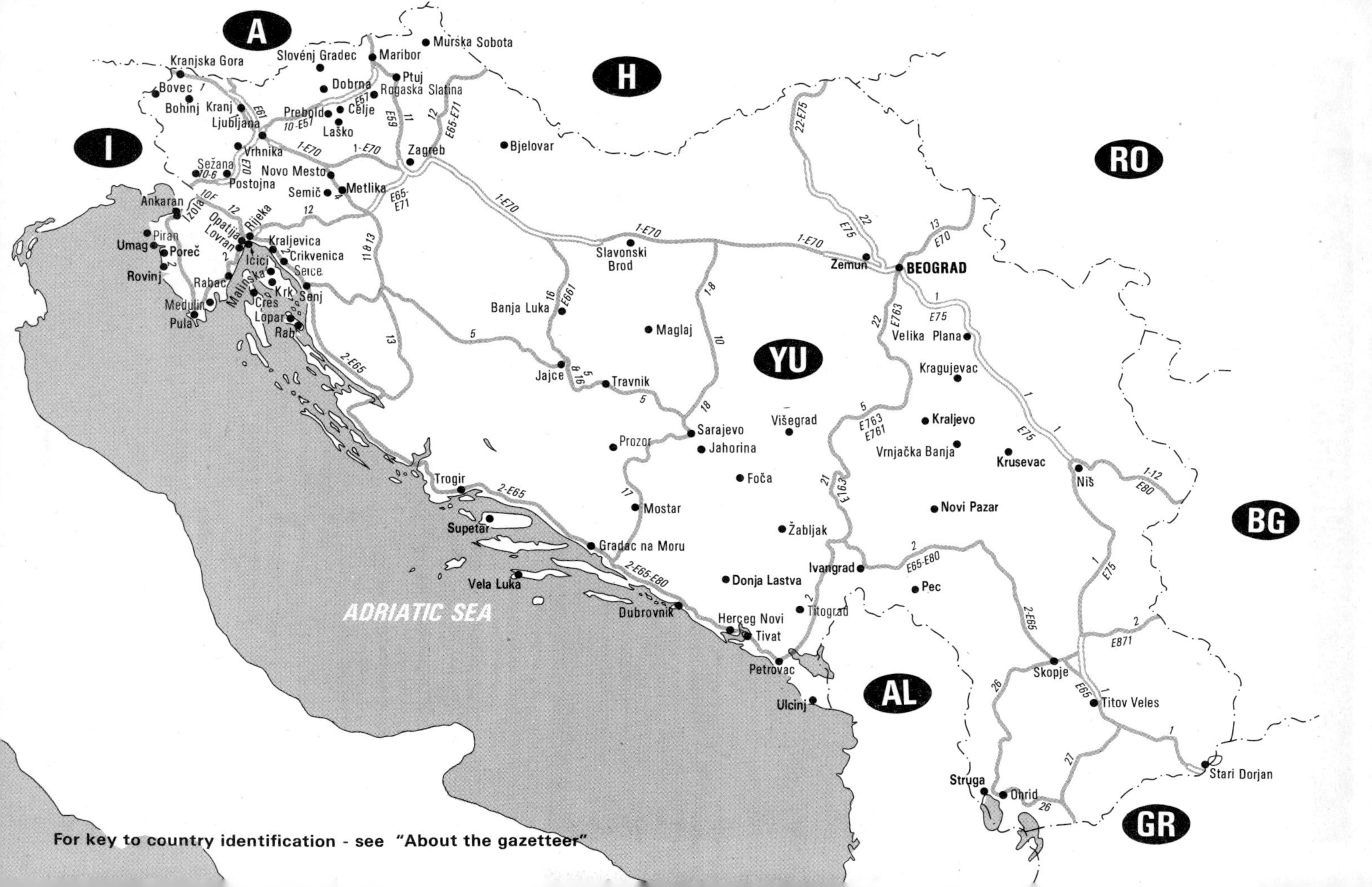

For key to country identification - see "About the gazetteer"

ACCOMMODATION

The gazetteer consists mainly of hotels; the majority provide accommodation in a double room for less than Din 2000925 per person per night at some time of the year.

The price bands are:

A 95175–148050
B 148050–200925

taking a rate of exchange at

Din 10575=£1
Din 6370=US $1

It is possible that prices may change during the currency of this book.

Details of accommodation in private houses can be obtained from national and local tourist offices.

ANKARAN *Slovenija*

H Convent ☏ (066) 518313 bed60 May-Oct **B**

BANJA LUKA *Bosna I Hercegovina*

H Bosna ☏ (078) 41355 bed344 **B**

M International ☏ (078) 32777 bed120 **B**

BEOGRAD (BELGRADE) *Srbija*

Capital of Yugoslavia and of the Socialist Republic of Serbia, Beograd is situated at the confluence of two large rivers, the Sava and the Danube, and occupies a commanding site on a ridge. It is a modern city with an active and varied cultural and sporting life. In addition to being the administrative and legal headquarters of Yugoslavia, it is the residence of the Metropolitan of the Serbian Orthodox church and of the Jewish Grand Rabbi. Its university is the largest in the country and is mainly concerned with legal studies.

Beograd is an important centre of commerce and industry, as befits a town located on one of the finest sites in the Danubian lands. With the construction of road and rail bridges across the Danube and Sava, it was inevitable that Belgrade should become the collecting and distributing centre of the commerce of a rich area. The navigable waterways of the two rivers are of first importance in this connection, and Beograd is easily the chief river port of Yugoslavia. At the same time, the city is the chief railway centre of the country, with several main lines and important roads, including a fast road to Zagreb.

Its many musums, art galleries, cultural institutions and restaurants are a delight, while the atmosphere of the city's old Bohemian quarter can be relived in Skadarska Street whose restaurants and cafés serve local specialities.

Yugoslavia's most famous 'son', Marshal Tito, was buried in Beograd in 1980 and Josip Broz Tito Memorial Centre is today the most visited site in Yugoslavia.

EATING OUT Grilled meats – especially lamb – and fresh fish are among the specialities the visitor will encounter in many of Beograd's restaurants. Specialities include *raznjici* (meat grilled on a skewer) and *cevapcici* (charcoal grilled minced meat). In the upper price bracket *Dva Jelena*, in Skadarska, continues to attract an enthusiastic clientele, while for moderately priced meals the *Klub Knjizevnika*, in Francuska, serves what is often hailed as the best food in Beograd.

H Astorija ☏ (011) 645422 bed152 **B**

H Balkan ☏ (011) 687466 bed145 **B**

H Taš ☏ (011) 343507 bed42 **B**

BJELOVAR *Hrvatska*

H Central ☏ (043) 43133 bed77 **A**

BOHINJ *Slovenija*

H Bellevue ☏ (064) 76331 bed47 **B**

H Kompas ☏ (064) 76471 bed123 **A**

H Rodica (n.rest) ☏ (064) 76461 bed61 **B**

BOVEC *Slovenija*

H Alp ☏ (065) 86040 bed115 **A**

H Kanin ☏ (065) 86021 bed240 **B**

BUNA See **MOSTAR**

CELJE *Slovenija*

H Celeia ☏ (063) 22041 bed120 **B**

H Europa ☏ (063) 21233 bed166 **B**

H Merx ☏ (063) 21917 bed64 **B**

H Turška Macka ☏ (063) 23157 bed43 **B**

CRES, ISLAND OF *Hrvatska*

H Kimen 11-Pavillons ☏ (051) 871161 bed420 **B**

CRIKVENICA *Hrvatska*

M Ad Turres ☏ (051) 781022 bed80 **B**

H Crikvenica ☏ (051) 782022 rm163 **B**

H Mediteran ☏ (051) 782062 bed142 **B**

H Miramare ☏ (051) 781232 bed180 **A**

H Zagreb ☏ (051) 781744 bed125 **B**

DOBRNA *Slovenija*

H Zdraviliška Dom ☏ (063) 778000 bed144 **A**

DONJA LASTVA *Crna Gora*

H Kamelija ☏ (082) 61300 rm212 Apr-Oct **B**

DUBROVNIK *Hrvatska*

Dubrovnik is one of the most important Yugoslav ports and holiday resorts on the Adriatic coast. Of ancient origin, it has changed hands frequently but reached its highest development as an independent small state in the 16th and 17th centuries when it rivalled Venice and gave the name 'argosy' to the English language.

The old walled town is arguably the loveliest and most interesting resort in Yugoslavia, offering a multitude of fascinating monuments, churches, museums, towers and old patrician houses.

By contrast there are modern hotels with beaches and swimming pools, good sports and entertainment facilities, and a casino and congress centre. The nearby island of Lokrum, a national park, is a favourite bathing spot and a cable

car ride from the town will take you to Mount Srdj (413m) which offers a magnificent view of the Adriatic coast.
EATING OUT Fresh fish is usually on the menu at the atmospheric *Amfora*, situated at Gruz Harbour, and *Dubravka*, near Pile Gate, where specialities often include octopus and squid.

H Dubravka ☎ (050) 26293 bed40 **B**

H Gruž ☎ (050) 24777 bed71 **B**

H Petka ☎ (050) 24933 bed200 **B**

H Stadion ☎ (050) 23449 bed160 **B**

FOČA *Bosna I Hercegovina*

H Zelengora ☎ (073) 571102 bed220 **B**

GRADAC NA MORU *Hrvatska*

★★Laguna ☎ (058) 70614 bed260 **B**

HERCEG NOVI *Crna Gora*

H Topla ☎ (082) 43722 bed500 **B**

IČIČI *Hrvatska*

H Ičiči ☎ (051) 712611 bed377 **A**

IVANGRAD *Crna Gora*

H Berane ☎ (084) 61822 bed96 **B**

H Lokve ☎ (084) 62460 bed167 **B**

IZOLA *Slovenija*

H Riviera ☎ (066) 62925 bed270 **A**

JAHORINA *Bosna I Hercegovina*

H Jahorina ☎ (071) 800124 bed256 Dec 15-Apr **B**

JAJCE *Bosna I Hercegovina*

H Jajce ☎ (070) 33285 bed155 **A**

★★Turist ☎ (070) 33268 bed82 **A**

KOSTRENA See **RIJEKA**

KRAGUJEVAC *Srbija*

H Dubrovnik ☎ (034) 60137 bed64 **A**

H Kragujevac ☎ (034) 66510 bed172 **B**

H Šumarice ☎ (034) 68710 bed150 **B**

KRALJEVICA *Hrvatska*

H Almis ☎ (051) 801312 bed48 **A**

H Praha ☎ (051) 801403 bed73 May-Sep **B**

H Uvala Scott ☎ (051) 801226 bed672 **B**

KRALJEVO *Srbija*

H Dobre Vode ☎ (036) 331681 bed110 **A**

H Turist ☎ (036) 22366 bed140 **A**

KRANJ *Slovenija*

H Jelen ☎ (064) 21466 bed102 **A**

KRANJSKA GORA *Slovenija*

H Erika ☎ (064) 88475 bed75 **B**

M Kompas ☎ (064) 88661 bed54 **B**

H Slavec ☎ (064) 88421 bed92 **B**

KRK, ISLAND OF *Hrvatska*

KRK

H Dubrava ☎ (051) 581022 bed66 **B**

MALINSKA

H Malin ☎ (051) 859114 bed305 May-Oct **B**

H Slavija ☎ (051) 859206 bed249 May-Oct **B**

★★★Tamaris ☎ (051) 859111 bed645 May-Oct **B**

H Triglav ☎ (051) 859311 bed66 May-Oct **A**

KRK See **KRK, ISLAND OF**

KRUŠEVAC *Srbija*

H Evropa ☎ (037) 28331 bed76 **B**

H Rubin ☎ (037) 25535 bed200 **B**

LAŠKO *Slovenija*

H Hum ☎ (063) 730908 bed40 **A**

H Zdraviliski Laško ☎ (063) 730010 bed333 **B**

LJUBLJANA *Slovenija*
Ljubljana is the capital of Slovenia, one of the most progressive parts of Yugoslavia. The old town lies in a loop of the Ljubljanica tributary of the Sava where a hill, 600ft above the river level, gives a defensive site near the river crossing. Here the Romans established Emona on the way from Italy to Pannonia.
Immediately around Ljubljana is the basin of the same name which is hemmed in by the Julian and Karawanke Alps to the west and north, and by the Slovene Ksarst to the south-west.
The cultural influence of the town is of particular importance, the Slovenes being proud of their general literacy and literary achievements; in addition to the university there are several publishing houses.
The city is dominated by its castle, at whose feet is the most interesting part of the city, especially near the river, around Mestintrg. Napoleon stayed at the Bishop's Palace, next to the cathedral. Treasures in the National Museum include a magnificent bronze urn.
EATING OUT Home cooking is the speciality of the *Na Brinju*, in Vodovodna, which has a pleasant garden for summer dining *al fresco*.

H Bellevue ☎ (061) 313133 bed46 **B**

M Medno ☎ (061) 611200 bed108 **A**

H Park ☎ (061) 316777 bed180 **A**

H Pri Mraku ☎ (061) 223412 bed72 **A**

H Turist ☎ (061) 322043 bed290 **B**

LOPAR See **RAB, ISLAND OF**

LOVRAN *Hrvatska*

H Belvedere ☎ (051) 731022 bed54 **B**

H Jadran ☎ (051) 731195 bed18 **B**

H Lovran ☎ (051) 781222 bed141 May-Oct 15 **B**

H Miramare ☎ (051) 731066 bed60 **B**

H Park ☎ (051) 731126 bed144 **B**

H Primorka ☎ (051) 731112 bed46 **B**

H Splendid ☎ (051) 731142 bed166 **B**

MAGLAJ *Bosna I Hercegovina*

H Galeb ☎ (074) 812343 bed83 **A**

MALINSKA See **KRK, ISLAND OF**

MARIBOR *Slovenija*

H Habakuk ☎ (062) 631681 rm75 **B**

★★Orel ☎ (062) 26171 bed226 **B**

H Turist ☎ (062) 25971 bed197 **B**

H Zamorec ☎ (062) 28497 bed79 **A**

MEDULIN *Hrvatska*

H Belvedere ☎ (052) 76308 bed898 Apr-Oct **B**

H Medulin ☎ (052) 76646 bed256 **B**

H Mutila ☎ (052) 76004 bed326 Apr-Oct **B**

METLIKA *Slovenija*

H Bela Krajina ☎ (068) 58123 bed50 **A**

MOSTAR *Bosna I Hercegovina*

★★Bristol ☎ (088) 32921 bed110 **B**

★★Mostar ☎ (088) 32941 bed55 **B**

★★Neretva ☎ (088) 32330 bed84 **B**

At **BUNA**

H Buna ☎ (088) 480290 rm80 **A**

MURSKA SOBOTA *Slovenija*

H Diana ☎ (069) 22530 bed156 **B**

H Zvezda ☎ (069) 22510 bed57 **A**

NIŠ *Srbija*

★★Park ☎ (018) 23296 bed161 **A**

NOVI PAZAR *Srbija*

M Ras & Sopocani ☎ (020) 25892 bed60 **B**

H Vrbak ☎ (020) 24844 bed130 **B**

NOVO MESTO *Slovenija*

H Metropol ☎ (068) 22226 bed91 **B**

OHRID *Makedonija*

H Inex Gorica ☎ (096) 22020 bed286 **B**

H Inex Park ☎ (096) 22021 bed184 **B**

H Orce Nikolov ☎ (096) 22036 bed305 **A**

H Palace ☎ (096) 25030 bed480 **B**

H Slavija ☎ (096) 22198 bed107 **A**

OPATIJA *Hrvatska*

H Avala ☎ (051) 712411 bed114 May-Oct 15 **B**

H Bellevue ☎ (051) 711011 bed140 **B**

H Esplanade ☎ (051) 712311 bed86 **B**

H Galeb ☎ (051) 712177 bed74 May-Oct 15 **B**

H Imperial Atlantik ☎ (051) 712133 bed289 **B**

H Jadran ☎ (051) 712333 bed161 May-Oct 15 **B**

★★Palme ☎ (051) 711823 bed187 **A**

PEČ *Srbija*

H Karagač ☎ (039) 21864 bed45 **A**

H Korzo ☎ (039) 22423 bed92 **A**

H Metohija ☎ (039) 22424 bed152 **A**

PETROVAC NA MORU *Crna Gora*

H Castellastva ☎ (086) 61494 bed348 May-Oct **B**

H Oliva Vile ☎ (086) 61297 bed210 May-Oct **B**

H Rivjera ☎ (086) 61314 bed162 May-Sep **B**

PIRAN *Slovenija*

H Sidro ☎ (066) 75292 bed97 **B**

POREČ *Hrvatska*

H Adriatik ☎ (053) 32422 bed31 **A**

H Poreč ☎ (053) 31811 bed117 Apr-Oct **B**

★★Riviera ☎ (053) 32433 bed195 **A**

POSTOJNA *Slovenija*

◆ Erazem ☎ (067) 59185 bed34 **B**

★★Kras ☎ (067) 21071 bed108 **B**

M Proteus ☎ (067) 21250 bed486 **B**

PREBOLD *Slovenija*

H Prebold ☎ (063) 723311 bed59 **B**

PROZOR *Bosna I Hercegovina*

H Gradina ☎ (088) 770060 bed35 **B**

PTUJ *Slovenija*

◆ Beli Križ ☎ (062) 772621 bed25 **A**

◆ Cirkulane ☎ (062) 791001 bed12 Apr 15-Oct 15 **A**

★★Poetovio ☎ (062) 772640 bed56 **A**

PULA *Hrvatska*

◆ Ribarska Koliba ☎ (052) 22966 bed217 Apr-Oct **A**

H Riviera ☎ (052) 23811 bed110 Apr-Oct **B**

H Ts Verudela ☎ (052) 24811 bed594 Apr-Oct **B**

H Zlatne Stijene ☎ (052) 34811 bed688 Apr-Oct **B**

At **RAB**

H Beograd ☎ (051) 771340 bed91 Apr-Oct **A**

H Istra ☎ (051) 771134 bed192 **B**

◆ Jadran bed25 May-Oct **A**

RAB, ISLAND OF *Hrvatska*

LOPAR

H San Marino ☎ (051) 775128 bed1000 May-Oct **B**

RABAC *Hrvatska*

H Fortuna ☎ (052) 872091 bed133 Apr-Oct **B**

H Girandella ☎ (052) 872224 bed1539 Apr-Oct **B**

H Istra ☎ (052) 872243 bed75 Apr-Oct **A**

H St Andrea ☎ (052) 872561 bed120 Apr-Oct **B**

RIJEKA *Hrvatska*

★★★Jadran ☎ (051) 421600 bed152 **A**

H Kontinental ☎ (051) 423495 bed103 **A**

H Neboder ☎ (051) 424255 bed116 **A**

★★Park ☎ (051) 421155 **A**

At **KOSTRENA**(6km E)

H Lucija ☎ (051) 441886 bed152 **A**

ROGAŠKA SLATINA *Slovenija*

H Slovenski Dom ☎ (063) 811330 bed115 **B**

H Soča ☎ (063) 811330 bed81 **B**

H Styria ☎ (063) 811811 bed73 **B**

ROVINJ *Hrvatska*

H Dep II ☎ (052) 811233 bed150 Apr-Oct **B**

H Monte Mulin ☎ (052) 811512 bed341 Apr-Oct **B**

H Ts Monsena ☎ (052) 813044 bed2273 Apr-Oct **B**

H Ts Valalta ☎ (052) 811033 bed1400 May-Nov **B**

SARAJEVO *Bosna I Hercegovina*

Sarajevo, encircled by mountains, is located on both banks of the river Miljacka, tributary of the Bosna. The old city (*Stari Grad*) with its market, Turkish houses and narrow streets stands on the right bank, its core the *Bascsarsija* (old bazaar); this area also contains the 16th-century *Begova Dzamija* (Mosque of the Bey), considered the finest of the city's 73 mosques. The new town is modern, with wide streets and residential areas.

On a street corner by Princip Bridge are two footsteps sunk into the pavement, marking the spot from which a student fired the fatal shots at Archduke Franz Ferdinand of Austria, that precipitated the First World War.

Interesting excursions can be made into the mountains and to the spa of Ilidza, where Archduke Ferdinand spent the evening before his assassination.

EATING OUT Many of Sarajevo's restaurants reflect the centuries of Turkish influence, and you are likely to encounter such Turkish specialities as stuffed vine leaves and grilled meats. *Daire*, in Halaci, is one such establishment. Converted from a 17th-century warehouse, it offers both character and reliable cuisine.

H Bristol ☏ (071) 654811 bed420 **A**

H Central ☏ (071) 215515 bed70 **A**

H Evropa ☏ (071) 532722 bed396 **A**

SELCE *Hrvatska*

H Slaven ☏ (051) 782046 bed440 Apr-Oct **B**

H Tn Jadranka ☏ (051) 781578 bed340 Apr-Oct **B**

SEMIČ *Slovenija*

◆ **Smuk** ☏ (068) 56238 bed16 **A**

SENJ *Hrvatska*

★★**Nehaj** ☏ (051) 881285 bed99 **A**

SEŽANA *Slovenija*

H Tabor ☏ (067) 72551 bed86 **A**

H Triglav ☏ (067) 73361 bed110 **A**

SKOPJE *Makedonija*

H Belvi ☏ (091) 223474 bed88 **A**

H Bristol ☏ (091) 239821 bed74 **A**

H Continental ☏ (091) 220122 bed300 **A**

H Skopje ☏ (091) 239311 bed256 **A**

M Turist ☏ (091) 233275 bed140 **A**

SLAVONSKI BROD *Hrvatska*

H Brod ☏ (055) 231885 bed137 **A**

M Marsonia ☏ (055) 231005 bed138 **A**

H Park ☏ (055) 231901 bed91 **A**

SLOVENJ GRADEC *Slovenija*

H Kompas ☏ (062) 842295 bed115 **B**

H Pohorje ☏ (062) 842291 bed45 **B**

STARI DOJRAN *Makedonija*

H Polin ☏ (093) 83713 bed122 **A**

STRUGA *Makedonija*

H Biser ☏ (096) 72267 bed171 **A**

H Drim ☏ (096) 72511 bed410 **B**

SUPETAR *Hrvatska*

M Kneževravan bed30 May-Oct **A**

H Tamaris ☏ (058) 631155 bed44 May-Oct **B**

H Ts Palma (n.rest) ☏ (058) 631222 bed700 May-Oct **B**

TITOGRAD *Crna Gora*

H Crna Gora ☏ (081) 34211 bed292 **A**

H Ljubovic ☏ (081) 32701 bed206 **A**

H Podgorica ☏ (081) 42050 bed108 **A**

TITOV VELES *Makedonija*

H International ☏ (093) 23255 bed80 **B**

M Mladost ☏ (093) 23111 bed20 **B**

TIVAT *Crna Gora*

H Mimoza ☏ (082) 61344 bed130 **B**

H Pine ☏ (082) 61122 bed66 **B**

TRAVNIK *Bosna I Hercegovina*

H Orijent ☏ (072) 814888 bed122 **A**

TROGIR *Hrvatska*

H Jadran ☏ (058) 73668 bed300 May-Oct **B**

ULCINJ *Crna Gora*

H Bellevue ☏ (085) 81711 bed688 **B**

H Mediteran ☏ (085) 81411 bed370 **B**

UMAG *Hrvatska*

H Istra (n.rest) ☏ (053) 52026 bed943 Apr-Oct **B**

H Punta ☏ (053) 51482 bed512 Apr-Oct **B**

VELA LUKA *Hrvatska*

H Jadran & Dalmacija ☏ (050) 82036 bed180 **A**

H Korkyra ☏ (050) 82024 bed165 **A**

VELIKA PLANA *Srbija*

★**Velika Plana** ☏ (026) 52253 bed60 **B**

VIŠEGRAD *Bosna I Hercegovina*

H Bikavac ☏ (073) 681404 bed120 **B**

H Vilina Vlas ☏ (073) 681704 bed150 **B**

H Višegrad ☏ (073) 681224 bed80 **B**

VRHNIKA *Slovenija*

H Mantova ☏ (061) 751370 bed55 **B**

VRNJAČKA BANJA *Srbija*

H Fontana ☏ (036) 61153 bed410 **A**

H Zvezda ☏ (036) 63770 bed246 **A**

ŽABLJAK *Crna Gora*

H Durmitor ☏ (0872) 88278 **B**

H Žabljak ☏ (0872) 88300 bed70 **A**

ZAGREB *Hrvatska*

Zagreb, the capital of the Socialist Republic of Croatia and the second largest city in Yugoslavia, lies on the banks of the Sava River. Its well-preserved old city quarter, with a fine cathedral and impressive churches, is a special attraction, but the city also boasts lovely Baroque buildings, a rich and varied cultural and entertainment life, good restaurants and excellent hotels. Opera has a long-standing tradition here, and the world-renowned Hlebine school of naive painting is located nearby. In addition to Zagreb's many museums and art galleries there are numerous festivals, one of the most popular of which is the traditional festival of folklore, while the Zagreb Fair is one of the largest in Europe.

The city is well located for excursions: within its vicinity are Marshal Tito's birthplace of Kumrovec, the old Trakoscan and Ptuj castles, many spas, Tuheljske Springs, and the Plitvice national park with its 16 delightful lakes.

Local specialities include *pohovano pile*, a type of breaded chicken. This can usually be obtained at *Gradski Podrum*, in Republic Square, which is one of Zagreb's best known and most fashionable restaurants.

H Park ☏ (041) 233422 bed300 **B**

H Tomislavov Dom ☏ (041) 449821 bed134 **B**

M Zagreb ☏ (041) 533055 bed90 **B**

ZEMUN *Srbija*

H Central ☏ (011) 191712 bed51 **B**

H Grand ☏ (011) 210536 bed65 **B**

Acknowledgements

Thanks are due to the National Tourist Boards of the following countries for permission to reproduce the photographs in this book:

Austria
Belgium
Denmark
France
Ireland
Italy
Luxembourg
Netherlands
Portugal
Sweden

USEFUL WORDS AND PHRASES

English	French	German	Italian	Spanish
Greetings				
Good morning (afternoon), Sir	Bonjour, monsieur	Guten Morgen, (Guten Tag) Herr X	Buon giorno, Signore	Buenos dias señor
Good evening, Madam	Bonsoir, madame	Guten Abend Frau X	Buona sera, Signora	Buenas noches, señora
Good-bye, Miss X	Au revoir, mademoiselle	Auf Wiedersehen, Fräulein X	Arrivederci, Signorina	Hasta la vista, señorita
Excuse me	Excusez-moi	Entschuldigen Sie	Mi scusi	Dispénseme Vd
Please	S'il vous plaît	Bitte	Prego	Por favor
Thank you	Merci	Danke	Grazie	Gracias
Yes. No	Oui. Non	Ja. Nein	Si. No	Si. No
Speaking the language				
Do you speak . . .?	Parlez-vous . . .?	Sprechen Sie . . .?	Parla . . .?	¿Habla Vd . . .?
I speak . . .	Je parle . . .	Ich spreche . . .	Io Parlo . . .	Yo hablo . . .
I do not speak . . .	Je ne parle pas . . .	Ich spreche nicht . . .	Io non parlo . . .	Yo no hablo . . .
French	français	französisch	francese	francés
English	anglais	englisch	inglese	inglés
Spanish	espagnol	spanisch	spagnolo	español
Portuguese	portugais	portugiesisch	portoghese	portugués
German	allemand	deutsch	tedesco	aleman
Italian	italien	italienisch	italiano	italiano
Dutch	hollandais	holländisch	olandese	holandés
Danish	danois	dänisch	danese	danés
Do you understand . . .?	Comprenez-vous . . .?	Vestehen Sie . . .?	Capisce . . .?	¿Comprende Vd . . .?
I do not understand . . .	Je ne comprends pas . . .	Ich verstehe nicht . . .	Non capisco . . .	No comprendo . . .
Speak slowly	Parlez lentement	Sprechen Sie langsam	Parli adagio	Hable Vd despacio
Could you repeat it?	Répétez	Wiederholen Sie	Ripeta	Repita
At the bank				
Where is a Bureau de Change?	Où se trouve le bureau de change?	Wo ist eine Wechselstube?	Dove si trova un ufficio cambi?	¿Dónde hay una oficina de cambio?
Can I change some Pounds Sterling?	Puis-je changer ces livres?	Kann ich diese Pfund Sterling wechseln?	Posso cambiare delle sterline?	¿Puedo cambiar unas Libras?
Can I cash this cheque here?	Puis-je encaisser ce chèque ici?	Kann ich diesen Scheck einlösen?	Posso riscuotere questo cheque?	¿Peudo cobrar este cheque aqui?
I have a Eurocard/ bankcard	J'ai une Euro-carte/une carte bancaire	Ich habe eine Eurokarte/ Scheckkarte	Ho una Eurocard/ cartolina di banca	Tengo Eurocheque/ tarjeta de crédito

English	French	German	Italian	Spanish

At the hotel

English	French	German	Italian	Spanish
Where is the Hotel . . .?	Où se trouve l'Hôtel . . .?	Wo ist das Hotel . . .?	Dov'è l'Albergo . . .?	¿Dónde esta el Hotel . . .?
Where is a telephone?	Où se trouve un téléphone?	Wo ist ein Telephon?	Dov'è c'è un telefono?	¿Dónde hay un teléfono?
Have you a room, two rooms . . .?	Avez-vous une chambre, deux chambres . . .?	Haben sie ein Zimmer, zwei Zimmer . . .?	Aveta una camera, due camere . . .?	¿Tiene una habitación, dos habitaciones . . .?
. . . for one night, for two nights . . .?	. . . pour une nuit, pour deux nuits . . .?	. . . für eine Nacht, für zwei Nächte . . .?	. . . per una notte, per due notti . . .?	. . . para una noche, para dos noches . . .?
. . . for one person, two persons . . .?	. . . pour une personne, pour deux personnes . . .?	. . . für eine Person, für zwei Personen . . .?	. . . per una persona, per due persone . . .?	. . . para una persona, para dos personas . . .?
. . . with a single bed, double bed, two beds . . .?	. . . à un lit, à un grand lit, à deux lits . . .?	. . . mit einem Einzelbett, mit einem Doppelbett, mit zwei Betten . . .?	. . . con un letto per una persona, matrimoniale, due letti . . .?	con cama sencilla, cama doble, dos camas . . .?
. . . with bath, shower, WC?	. . . avec bain, douche, WC?	. . . mit Bad, Dusche, Toilette?	. . . con bagno, doccia, WC?	. . . can baño, ducha, water?
No vacancies	complet	Voll	Completo	No hay habitaciones
May I see the room, please?	Puis-je regarder la chambre, s'il vous plaît?	Kann ich das Zimmer besich-tigen, bitte?	Posso vedere la camera, per favore?	¿Puedo ver las habitaciones, por favor?

At the shops

English	French	German	Italian	Spanish
How much?	Combien?	Wieviel?	Quanto?	¿Cuánto cuesta?
Yes, that's fine (meaning, 'Yes, I'll have it . . .)	Oui, je l'achête	Ja, das möchte ich	Va bene	Si, està bien
Too dear	Trop cher	Zu teuer	Troppo caro	Demasiado caro

Telling the time

English	French	German	Italian	Spanish
Yesterday	Hier	Gestern	Ieri	Ayer
Tonight	Cette nuit	Heute Nacht	Questa notte	Esta noche
This morning	Ce matin	Heute Morgen	Questa mattina	Esta mañana
Today	Aujourd'hui	Heute	Oggi	Hoy
This afternoon	Cet après-midi	Heute Nachmittag	Questo pomeriggio	Esta tarde
At noon	A midi	Um Mittag	A mezzogiorno	A mediodía
At midnight	A minuit	Um Mitternacht	A mezzanotte	A medianoche
This evening	Ce soir	Heute Abend	Questa sera	Esta noche
Tomorrow	Demain	Morgen	Domani	Mañana
The day after tomorrow	Après-demain	Übermorgen	Dopo domani	Pasado mañana
Early, Late	Tôt, Tard	Früh, Spät	Presto, Tardi	Temprano, Tarde
At once	Tout de suite	Sofort	Subito	En seguida
Minute (in time)	Minute	Minute	Minuto	Minuto
Hour	Heure	Stunde	Ora	Hora
What time is it?	Quelle heure est-il?	Wieviel Uhr ist es?	Che ore sono?	¿Qué hora es?

English	French	German	Italian	Spanish

Dining out

English	French	German	Italian	Spanish
Can we eat here?	Peut-on manger ici?	Kann man hier essen?	Possiamo mangiare qui?	¿Se puede comer aqui?
Have you a table for 2 (3, 4, 5, 6)?	Avez-vous une table pour deux (trois, quatre cinq, six)?	Haben sie einen Tisch für zwei (drei, vier, fünf, sechs)?	Avete una tavola per due (tre, quattro, cinque, sei)?	¿Tiene una mesa para dos (tres, cuatro, cinco, seis)?
What time is . . .	A quelle heure est . . .	Um wieviel Uhr servieren Sie (gibt es)?	A che ora é . . .?	¿A qué hora se sirve . . .?
breakfast	le petit déjeuner	das Frühstück	la prima colazione	el desayuno
lunch	le déjeuner	das Mittagessen	la colazione	el almuerzo
dinner	le dîner	das Abendessen	il pranzo	la comida
How much is the meal?	Quel est le prix du repas?	Was kostet die Mahlzeit?	Qual è il prezzo del pasto?	¿Cuánto cuesta el cubierto?
Show me the menu	Montrez-moi le menu	Ziegen Sie mir das Menü	Mi faccia vedere la lista delle vivande	Muéstreme el menú
Give me the wine list	Donnez-moi la carte des vins	Geben Sie mir die Weinkarte	Mi dia la lista dei vini	Déz Vd la lista de vinos

Something to eat

English	French	German	Italian	Spanish
I should like . . .	Je voudrais . . .	Ich Möchte . . .	Vorrei . . .	Yo querría . . .
We would like . . .	Nous voudrions . . .	Wir möchten . . .	Vorremmo . . .	Queremos . . .
some soup	de la soupe	Suppe	della zuppa, della minestra	Sopa
some fish	du poisson	Fisch	del pesce	pescado
some meat	de la viande	Fleisch	della carne	carne
a chop or a cutlet	une côtelette	ein Kotellet	une cotoletta	una chuleta
some veal	du veau	Kalbfleisch	del viteilo	ternera
some beef	du bœuf	Rindfleisch	del manno	vaca
some lamb	du mouton	Hammelfleisch, Schaffleisch	dell'agnello	cordero
some pork	du porc	Schweinefleisch	de maiale	cerdo
some ham	du jambon	Schinken	del prosciutto	jamón
some chicken	du poulet	Huhn	del pollo	pollo
some beefsteak	du bifteck	Beefsteak	una bistecca	bistek . . .
. . . underdone,	. . . saignant	. . . blutig (englisch)	. . . al sangue	. . . poco pasado
. . . well done	. . . bien cuit	. . . durch gebraten, bar	. . . ben cotta	. . . bien pasado
. . . medium done	. . . à point	. . . halbenglisch	. . . cotta a puntino	. . . a punto
some bread	du pain	Brot	del pane	pan
some butter	du beurre	Butter	del burro	mantequilla
Rice	du riz	Reis	del riso	arroz
some eggs	des œufs	Eier	della uova	heuvos
an omelette	une omelette	eine Omelette	una frittata	una tortilla
a salad	une salade	Salat	una insalata	ensalada
some vegetables	des légumes	Gemüse	del legumi	legumbres
some potatoes	des pommes de terre	Kartoffein	della patate	patatas
Cabbage	du chou	Kohl	cavolo	coles
Cauliflower	du chou-fleur	Blumenkohl	cavolfiori	coliflores
Green peas	des petits pois	Grüne Erbsen	dei pisellini	guisantes
Beans	des haricots	Bohnen	dei fagiuoli	habichuelas, judías

English	French	German	Italian	Spanish

Something to eat (contd.)

English	French	German	Italian	Spanish
(with) no garlic, please	(avec) sans ail, s'il vous plaît	(mit) ohne Knoblauch, bitte	senza aglio per favore (con)	sin ajo por favor (con)
Cheeses	Fromages	Käse	Formaggio	Queso
Fruits	Fruits	Früchte	Frutta	Frutas
Biscuits	Biscuits	Biskuits, Kekse	Biscotti	Bizcochos
Tart	Tarte	Torte	Torta	Tarta
Pastries	Pâtisseries	Feines Gebäck	Pasticceria	Pastelería
Jam	De la confiture	Konfitüre	Della marmellata	mermelada
Ice creams	Glaces	Eis	Gelato	Helados

Something to drink

English	French	German	Italian	Spanish
A bottle	Une bouteille	Eine Flasche	Una bottiglia	Una botella
Half a bottle	Une demi-bouteille	Eine halbe Flasche	Una mezza bottiglia	Media botella
Water	De l'eau	Wasser . . .	Dell'acqua	Agua
Iced water	. . . glacée	eisgehühltes Wasser	. . . ghiacciata	. . . helada
Hot water	. . . chaude	warmes Wasser	. . . calda	. . . caliente
White wine	Du vin blanc	Wiesswein	Del vino bianco	Vino blanco
Red wine	Du vin rouge	Rotwein	Del vino rosso	Vino tinto
Rosé wine	Du vin rosé	Wein Rosé	Vino rosato	Vino rosado
Lemonade	De la citronnade	Limonade	Una limonata	Limonada
Beer	De la bière	Bier	Della birra	Cerveza
Mineral water	De l'eau minérale	Mineralwasser	Dell'acqua minerale	Agua mineral
Liqueurs	Des liqueurs	Liköre	Dei liquori	Licores
Coffee	Du café	Kaffee	Del caffè	Café
Tea	Du thé	Tee	Del tè	Té
Milk	De lait	Milch	Del latte	Leche
Sugar	Du sucre	Zucker	Dello zucchero	Azúcar
Chocolate	Du chocolat	Schokolade	Della cioccolata	Chocolate
Cream	De la crême	Sahne	Della panna	Crema

The finale

English	French	German	Italian	Spanish
Waiter! the bill	Garçon! l'addition	Kellner! die Rechnung	Cameriere! Il conto	!Camarero! la cuenta
Are tips included?	Pourboire compris?	Ist das Trinkgeld inbegriffen?	Mancia compresa?	Está incluída la propina?
Service included	Service compris	Bedienung inbegriffen	Servizio compreso	Servicio incluido

At the garage

English	French	German	Italian	Spanish
Fill up the tank, please . . .	Faites le plein s'il vous plaît . . .	Füllen Sie den Tank bitte . . .	Mi faccia il piepo . . .	Sirvase ilenar el depósito . . .
with petrol	d'essence	mit Benzin	di benzina	de gasolina
with oil	d'huile	mit Öl	d'olio	de aceite
Give me five, ten, twenty, thirty litres of petrol	Mettez-moi cinq dix, vingt, trente litres d'essence	Geben Sie mir fünf, zehn, zwanzig, dreissig Liter Benzin	Mi metta cinque, dieci, venti, trenta litri di benzina	Póngame cinco, diez, veinte, trienta litros de gasolina
My car won't start	Ma voiture ne démarre pas	Mein Wagen fährt nicht an	La mia automobile non si mette in moto	Mi coche no arranca
Please check the oil, the water, the tyre pressures	Veuillez vérifier le niveau d'huile, le niveau d'eau, la pression des pneus	Bitte kontrollieren Sie den Ölstand, den Wasserstand, den Reifendruck	Si prega di controllare l'olio, l'acqua, la pressione delle gomme	Por favor, compruebe aceite, agua, presión de las ruedas

English	French	German	Italian	Spanish

At the garage (contd.)

English	French	German	Italian	Spanish
Can you mend	pouvez-vous réparer . . .	Können Sie . . .	Potete riparare . . .	¿Puede reglar . . .
. . . my car?	. . . ma voiture?	. . . meinen Wagen . . .	. . . la mia macchina?	. . . el coche?
. . . my engine?	. . . le moteur?	. . . den Motor . . .	. . . ol mio motore?	. . . el motor?
. . . the clutch?	. . . l'embrayage?	. . . die Kupplung . . .	. . . l'innesto?	. . . el embrague?
. . . the ignition?	. . . l'allumage?	. . . die Zündung . . .	. . . l'accensione?	. . . el encendido?
. . . the radiator (hose)?	. . . le radiateur (durite)?	. . . den Kühler (Schlauch) . . .	. . . il radiatore (manicotto)?	. . . el (tubo de goma del) radiator?
. . . the brakes?	. . . les freins?	. . . die Bremsen . . .	. . . i freni?	. . . los frenos?
. . . the electrical system?	. . . le système éléctrique?	. . . die elektrische Austrüstung . . .	. . . l'impianto elettrico?	. . . el equipo electrico?
. . . this tyre?	. . . ce pneu?	. . . diesen Reifen . . .	. . . questa gomma?	. . . este neumático?
How long will it take?	Pour quand sera-t-elle prête?	Bis wann?	Quanto tempo ci vorrà?	¿Cuando estarà listo?
How much will it cost?	Combien coûtera-t-elle?	Wieviel kostet sie?	Quanto costerà?	¿Cuánto costará?
I wish to hire a car	Je désire louer une automobile . . .	Ich möchte ein Auto . . . mieten	Vorrei noleggiare una automobile	Deseo alquilar un automóvil

ACCOMMODATION REPORT FORM 1990
(CONFIDENTIAL)

To: The Automobile Association, Information Research Unit, Fanum House, Basingstoke, Hants RG21 2EA.

Town

Country

Hotel

Location

Date

Food

Rooms

Service

Sanitary arrangements

Value for money

Name (block letters)

(continued overleaf)

Address (block letters)

Tel. no.

Membership number

(for office use only) acknowledged recorded

General remarks

We welcome comments on any establishments you may have stayed in. If there is insufficient room on this report form please continue on a separate sheet, using this form as a guide.